# Interpretive Consumer Research

Elizabeth C. Hirschman
Editor

1989 Copyright © ASSOCIATION FOR CONSUMER RESEARCH

International Standard Book Number: 0-915552-20-5

International Standard Serial Number: 0098-9258

Elizabeth C. Hirschman, Editor

*Interpretive Consumer Research*

(Provo, UT: Association for Consumer Research, 1989)

With affection, this book is dedicated to

Keith Hunt

....A hedonist at heart

# Reviewers List

David Mick
John Sherry
Grant McCracken
Morton Rothstein
Larry Percy
Peter Wright
David Cheal
Ronald Faber
Jeff Durgee
Laurel Hudson

Eduoardo Camargo
Paul Peter
Melanie Wallendorf
Catherine Axinn
Robert Stinerock
Richard Zakia
Eric Arnould
Harold Kassarjian
Kristine Frederickson
Barbara Stern

Dennis Rook
Tom O'Guinn
Paul Anderson
Paul Speck
Morris Holbrook
Russ Belk
Michael Solomon
Clinton Sanders
Rohit Deshpande
Fuat Firat

# INTERPRETIVE CONSUMER RESEARCH

## Preface

This book began during an ad hoc lunch table discussion during the 1987 AMA Doctoral Consortium at N.Y.U. A group of ten or so faculty interested, one way or another, in interpretive research methods and relativistic philosophies of science were seated together hashing over the morning's events and the state of research, in general. There was a fair amount of agreement that interpretive research was not faring as well as we had hoped: editors were recalcitrant, reviewers hostile, colleagues less than enthusiastic. The moods of the lunch table participants ranged from the mildly ironic to the radically cynical. Various anecdotes of disappointment and distress were recounted.

What to do? Retreat was intellectually unacceptable; once you've crossed over that mental bridge to interpretivism, there's no turning back. Rebellion and secession seemed certainly doomed to failure; internecine warfare is always destructive to all parties and besides, we had no where to go, anyway. Starting our own journal appeared too grandiose and egocentric; holding a conference, too small and redundant with the many "special topic" sessions at ACR that would have preceded it.

Someone, perhaps Paul Anderson or Morris Holbrook, suggested a book. We began discussing the idea and decided it had some distinct advantages compared to the other alternatives (especially those that involved death or dishonor). First, unlike a journal or conference, it did not require much up-front investment of administrative talent or capital (both of which were present in very limited quantities); second, it would provide a permanent vehicle for communicating ideas and ideals. Third, each of us could participate in it equally; except for a nominal editor, we could all present our work on an equal footing - no Chiefs, all Indians. This was important, because although rarely perceived by others, interpretivists do *not* necessarily agree with one another.

Somehow I came to be chosen as editor. (As I look back I realize this was likely due to the fact that I have a widespread reputation as a genuine masochist and also was in possession of the only pen at the table. For those of you who enjoy causal modeling, I believe that the masochistic trait and possession of a writing instrument were roughly equal in contributing to my selection as editor).

As editor it was my task to round-up reviewers (pre-designated by the authors), distribute the manuscripts to them, make sure all authors responded to all reviews, collect the revised manuscripts and floppy discs from the authors, and send this mass of stuff down to Jim Muncy. Although I would like to make all of this seem like a huge, onerous task so I could garner lots of pity and/or appreciation, the truth is, it really wasn't. The reviewers were exceptionally responsible, prompt and diligent; they provided excellent, constructive, insightful reviews. The authors -- a generally rowdy, stubborn and independent lot -- responded to the reviewers' suggestions with remarkable open-mindedness and flexibility. I was amazed and thankful.

And then there was Keith Hunt, undoubtedly the administrative anchor for this project. To our great good fortune, Keith -- a wonderful, warm-hearted pragmatist -- was sitting at the lunch table with our small band of disgruntled malcontents. As we were casting about for possible publishers for our project, Keith suggested that ACR might be interested. It took us about 3 micro-seconds to process the offer and accept it enthusiastically. For in fact it was exactly the ACR constituency that we hoped to reach and perhaps intrigue, intrigue and perhaps convert with our book. Keith is likely the most over-worked and under-applauded person at ACR. So I would like to take the opportunity here to give Keith our heartfelt appreciation for his work on behalf of the book. It was Keith who presented our original prospectus to the ACR Board and won its tentative approval. It was Keith who set-up the original contract and operating plan. So Keith, this book is dedicated to you. Without you our lunch would have been, well, just another lunch....

# INTERPRETIVE CONSUMER RESEARCH
## Elizabeth C. Hirschman, Editor

## TABLE OF CONTENTS

# FOREWORD

The purpose of this Foreword is to welcome the reader to *Interpretive Consumer Research* and to provide an overview of the journey on which you are about to embark. Perhaps the first relevant issue is "What *is* interpretive consumer research?" This issue may be approached in (at least) two constructive ways: via definition and through exemplars. The best definition I have encountered of interpretive consumer research is that presented recently by Holbrook and O'Shaughnessy (1988). They view *interpretation* as "the critical analysis of a text for the purpose of determining its single or multiple meaning(s). . . The meanings of interest might refer to those intended by an author, those inferred by the author's original audience in its historical context, those handed down by tradition, those sanctioned by the contemporary interpretive community, or those extracted by a particular reader, critic or other investigator. . The *text* at hand might consist of a literary artifact of popular culture, or even some type of behavioral action (p. 400)."

The present volume contains exemplars of virtually all the forms of interpretation cited by Holbrook and O'Shaughnessy, and several different types of text. The first section of the book, Philosophies, presents theoretical treatises by Ozanne and Hudson, Anderson, and Peter and Olson advocating relativist, constructionist, and interpretive perspectives of the scientific enterprise. These papers put forward not only their authors' thoughts and ideals, but also serve as texts clarifying the meaning of their earlier texts (cf, Anderson 1983, 1986; Peter and Olson 1983). In this, they serve to exemplify the first type of interpretation named by Holbrook and O'Shaughnessy (1988), i.e., the textual meaning intended by the author. The two papers included in the Commentaries section of this volume (Hunt 1989; Calder and Tybout 1989), which focus much of their attention on these three philosophical papers, may be viewed as the second type of text described by Holbrook and O'Shaughnessy (1988), i.e., those meanings inferred by (at least some) of the authors' original audience in its historical context. As will be discerned by the careful reader of these documents, one of the first "rules" of interpretivism is that authorial intention and audience interpretation do not always result in consistent meanings.

The second section of this volume is titled Methods. The four papers presented in it offer diverse approaches to interpreting textual meaning. The paper by Holbrook, Bell and Grayson provides a historical overview of humanism and the humanities and then provides two examples of method. The first, entitled "Close Encounters" demonstrates the literary technique of irony. In a mock-conciliatory pose, the authors allege to provide the reader with a sophisticated falsificationist test (ala Calder and Tybout 1987) of propositions derived from an earlier interpretive text (Holbrook and Grayson 1986). The second method they present is an adaptation of structural analysis to delineate the bipolar oppositions present in a recent Broadway play, titled `Coastal Disturbances'. Astute readers will no doubt discern not only the wit, but also the impassioned idealism that runs through both these examples.

Barbara Stern, the author of the second methodological paper, which describes and applies literary explication, was trained in literary criticism -- unlike the bulk of the other authors who have academic backgrounds in marketing and/or the social sciences. Her work brings a novel perspective to the interpretive enterprise and provides a view of the text as a work of literature. Her application of a literary critical method to advertisements gives us a new appreciation of this oft-maligned commercial art form.

The paper on historical method by Lavin and Archdeacon draws some constructive parallels between the approaches of interpretive social scientists and historians. They also point out some intriguing analogies between the present philosophical debates in consumer research and on-going methodological schisms in history. It is reassuring to know that our field's current debates and controversies are not unique or idiosyncratic.

The final methodological paper is co-authored by Wallendorf and Belk, the leaders of the Consumer Behavior Odyssey, a cross-country trek via Winnebago during the summer of 1986. Drawing upon their experiences, they put forward a rigorous framework for assessing trustworthiness in ethnographic research. Of particular value in this piece are the authors' personal assessments of which techniques worked well in actual practice and which did not -- invaluable knowledge for those readers who may want to attempt a team approach to ethnography.

The third section of the volume presents six applications of interpretive consumer research, which are instructive for the reader in their convergences and divergences. The first two papers by Mick and Politi and by McQuarrie use advertisements as their textual material (as did Stern's paper), but do so in greatly different ways. The Mick and Politi paper neatly tests a hypothesis gleaned from positivist theory using interpretive protocol analysis. (They said it couldn't be done ---but here it is!). McQuarrie's paper uses a semiological approach to develop a taxonomy of resonance devices (e.g., imagery, verbal puns) used by advertisements to obtain greater consumer recall. Both pieces are "must" reading for information processing researchers, as well as those interested in interpretive inquiry.

The next two papers are also "paired" as they both deal with the meaning of Christmas and consumption. Belk presents an overview of the historical evolution of the Christmas festival (re: the Lavin and Archdeacon paper on historical method) and develops a bipolar (re: the Holbrook, Bell, Grayson paper) opposition between Jesus Christ and Santa Claus. He continues on to semiologically decode several motion pictures, television programs, magazines, short stories, novels, and comic books which have a Christmas theme, finally capping-off his paper with a content analysis of sacred and profane themes in 626 comic book Christmas stories. In contrast, the paper by Hirschman and La Barbera reviews recent social science inquiries into the meaning of Christmas and then develops an interpretive framework using essay excerpts written by consumers on "What Christmas means to me." They, too, utilize a bipolar scheme based on the sacred-secular dialectic to anchor their interpretation and include, additionally, a positive-negative affective dimension.

The last pair of papers is representative of ethnographic inquiry applied to two radically different social texts. The Sherry and McGrath paper continues the Christmas theme by constructing the social meanings of two gift stores. Their creativity and insight in interpreting what these stores represent to their owners, employees, and customers will provide the reader with a new consciousness of shopping rituals from both a buyer's and seller's perspective. McCracken's paper on the social construct of `homeyness' is an instructive account of ethnographic inquiry for several reasons. First, it demonstrates the level of personal time commitment by the researcher conducting this type of inquiry (i.e., 40 interviews X 6 hours per interview = 240 hours of interviews = exhaustion). Second, it represents very well the richness and depth of this form of interpretive research. Taking houses as his texts, McCracken "reads" from them the characteristics that denote homeyness (e.g., diminutiveness, variability, welcomingness) forming as he goes an intricately-textured image in the reader's mind. Third, the image McCracken imparts resonates well with the reader's own intuitive grasp of this social construct -- in other words, it is *believable*, because it recalls commonly-shared cultural knowledge but organizes and crystallizes it in a way not seen before.

Having come this far in the book, the reader is now well-prepared both intellectually and emotionally to deal with the two empiricist critiques which follow. For this reason, I will postpone direct discussion of them 'til the After Word, which follows at the end of the volume.

Elizabeth C. Hirschman
December 29, 1988
Princeton, New Jersey

## REFERENCES

Anderson, Paul F. (1983), "Marketing, Scientific Progress, and Scientific Method", *Journal of Marketing*, 47 (Fall), 18-31.

Anderson, Paul F. (1986), "On Method in Consumer Research: A Critical Relativist Perspective", *Journal of Consumer Research*, 13, (September), 155-173.

Calder, Bobby J. and Alice M. Tybout, (1987). "What Consumer Research Is...". *Journal of Consumer Research*, 14 (June), 136-140.

Holbrook, Morris B. and Mark W. Grayson, (1986), "The Semiology of Cinematic Consumption: Symbolic Consumer Behavior in Out of Africa", *Journal of Consumer Research*, 13 (December), 374-381.

Holbrook, Morris B. and John O'Shaughnessy, (1988), "On the Scientific Status of Consumer Research and the Need for an Interpretive Approach to Studying Consumer Behavior", *Journal of Consumer Research*, Vol. 15, (December), 398-402.

Peter, J. Paul and Jerry C. Olson, (1983), "Is Science Marketing?", *Journal of Marketing*, 47 (Fall), 234-231.

# Exploring Diversity in Consumer Research

Julie L. Ozanne, Virginia Polytechnic Institute and State University
Laurel Anderson Hudson, University of Virginia

## ABSTRACT

Two of the dominant ways of seeking knowledge in the social sciences are positivism and interpretivism. Because these two world views are based on different assumptions and goals, the research process is different. The purpose of this paper is to demonstrate and explore the interdependency of goals, assumptions, theories, and methodologies in positivism and interpretivism. This paper suggests that the knowledge outputs of these two approaches are incommensurable. Nevertheless, consumer research can benefit by exploring and encouraging diversity. First, the philosophical assumptions and goals that underlie positivism and interpretivism are examined. Next, this paper contrasts a specific positivist's and a specific interpretivist's research of the "same" phenomenon in order to demonstrate the powerful link between philosophical assumptions, goals, methods, and theories. That is, these two approaches each form an interdependent system that is self-justifying. Finally, this paper raises and discusses issues that come to light when researchers reflect on their fundamental assumptions and goals: the usefulness of different types of triangulation and ways to examine the conflict between these two systems so that alternative approaches may be envisioned.

## INTRODUCTION

One thing is certain, a man might feel: the building of this bridge will never be completed, but my life will surely have its end. A man might therefore risk a running leap from the unfinished edge to the shore that he thinks he sees ahead. Perhaps he has seen right and has estimated his own powers correctly. In which event, applause. Perhaps he has badly miscalculated on both counts. In which event, a certain dampness sets in. Maybe he can swim back to safety, even if somewhat less than applauded. In any event, he has found out how far he can see and how well he can jump. Even if he is never heard from again, perhaps those who are still dawdling at the edge will learn something useful (Gouldner 1973).

The dominant paradigm within consumer research is positivism (Anderson 1983, 1986; Bagozzi 1980; Hunt 1983; Peter and Olson 1983). Generally, consumer researchers apply the methods of the natural sciences to the study of social beings. If progress is judged in terms of problem solving ability, then consumer research has "added to the bridge" of knowledge. Nevertheless, even our best theories and methods are inadequate. What the social sciences in general and consumer research in particular know about social beings and their world is small when compared to our vast "sea" of ignorance.

While our achievements should be applauded, we must actively strive to improve upon our methods and theories, as well as seek alternative approaches for studying consumers. The field of consumer research can benefit by envisioning different horizons and this monograph represents one such effort. Partly in response to the problems of positivism (Anderson 1983; Peter and Olson 1983; Rubinstein 1981; Suppe 1977), some consumer researchers are exploring interpretivism as an alternative approach to seeking knowledge (Belk, Sherry, and Wallendorf 1988; Hirschman 1985, 1986; Holbrook 1986; Holbrook and Grayson 1986; Hudson and Murray 1986; Hudson and Ozanne 1988; McCracken 1986; Mick 1986; Rook 1985; Sherry and Camargo 1987; Solomon 1983, 1986; Tucker 1967; Wallendorf 1987; Wallendorf and Arnould 1988). Interpretive researchers reject the idea that consumers can be studied like the physical world and, instead, generally hold that researchers must consider the meaning of the phenomena from the perspective of the consumers involved.

Interpretivism offers great potential problem solving ability that will attract many researchers. Yet, dangers exist. Blind conversion to interpretivism is just as dangerous as blind adherence to positivism. Each action is dangerous because each action limits our horizon. Instead, diversity offers merit by expanding our horizons.

This paper suggests that positivism and interpretivism represent two different approaches to understanding social beings and their world. However, researchers need not take an advocacy position and argue for the supremacy of one approach over the other approach (Hudson and Ozanne 1988). Rather, the fundamental conflicts between positivism and interpretivism can be harnessed to better understand each approach and to produce alternative approaches to consumer research. While the social bases of knowledge may act as barriers to the creation of alternative approaches, the basic premise of this paper is that the field of consumer research will benefit most from the acceptance and pursuit of a plurality of approaches to seeking knowledge (Belk 1986; Holbrook 1987; Lutz 1987).

This paper (1) lays out the underlying philosophical differences between positivism and interpretivism and suggests that these two approaches each form interdependent systems that are self-justifying, (2) contrasts an actual example of a positivist's and an interpretivist's approach to emotion in order to demonstrate how the assumptions and goals justify the research conceptualization and methodology, and (3) discusses two issues that arise when philosophical assumptions and goals are considered: the usefulness of different types of triangulation and the exploration of alternative approaches to seeking knowledge. The first issue, triangulation, involves the use of either different data, investigators, theories, or methodologies to study the same problem. The feasibility of each type of triangulation becomes clearer upon examination of each approach's philosophical underpinnings. The second issue, the exploration of

*Interpretive Consumer Research,* © *1989*
*Association for Consumer Research*

alternative approaches, is tackled by employing dialectic analysis to explore the conflicts between positivism and interpretivism. Dialectics is particularly well suited here because it seeks to understand contradictions and generate knowledge based on contradiction. As will become evident in the next section, many contradictions exist between positivism and interpretivism.

## POSITIVISM AND INTERPRETIVISM

This next section lays out the two opposing views--positivism and interpretivism--and tries to make explicit the underlying, taken-for-granted assumptions. Because the underlying assumptions and goals of positivism and interpretivism are discussed at length elsewhere (Bogdan and Taylor 1975; Bredo and Feinberg 1982; Bruyn 1966; Burrell and Morgan 1979; Hirschman 1986; Hudson and Ozanne 1988; Keat and Urry 1975; Lincoln and Guba 1985; Morgan and Smircich 1980; Rubinstein 1981), we only present an overview of positivism's and interpretivism's axiology, ontology, and epistemology.

### Axiology

Each approach subscribes to different goals or axiologies (see Table 1). The positivist's central goal is explanation via subsumption under universal law. (It should be noted that positivists are unable to achieve this goal because of the problem of induction--see Anderson 1983). As well, they seek prediction. A phenomenon is explained and understood if one can demonstrate an underlying systematic association of variables. Of course, if one can demonstrate a systematic association then one can also predict the phenomenon.

While some interpretivists do try to identify patterns of behavior, their central goal is understanding. Understanding involves grasping the individual and shared meanings. Interpretivist researchers may state interpretations--their present understanding--however, they view understanding as a never-ending hermeneutical circle. Past interpretations influence current interpretations and current interpretations will influence future interpretations. Thus, understanding is never finished or complete. For example, in Coombs and Goodman's (1976) study of emotional detachment within intensive care units, they found that the nursing staff used terminology differently than the researchers' use of the words. Death was often referred to as the "incident" and "the situation." Knowing this shared meaning was a prerequisite to further understanding. Through active participation in the culture, the researcher strives for an insider's view or being knowledgeable of the shared meanings.

### Ontology

Positivists hold a realist stance regarding the nature of reality; that is, they believe that a single, unchanging reality exists, which is divisible and fragmentable. Thus, a phenomenon can be removed from its natural setting and studied in a controlled environment. Interpretivists, however, believe that reality is mental and perceptual, and many realities exist because of different individual and group perceptions. The context in which a behavior or event arises

influences the meaning of the phenomenon; thus, reality must be viewed holistically and parts of this reality cannot be separated from their natural setting and studied in isolation.

In addition to holding different views about reality, both approaches make different assumptions about the nature of social beings. On the one hand, many versions of positivism hold that human behavior is determined by outside influences--external factors and/or internal states, which act as objects that cause behavior. On the other hand, interpretivism generally holds a voluntaristic model of humans. Humans actively create and shape their environment, rather than merely reacting to their environment and internal states.

### Epistemology

Finally, based on their separate assumptions and goals, each world view strives toward different types of knowledge. Despite the problems of induction, positivists seek to generate nomothetic statements: that is, they seek general laws that can be applied to many different people, places, and times (Kerlinger 1973). As well, the positivist believe that real causes temporally precede behavior. To achieve this type of knowledge, the positivist emphasizes adherence to the proper scientific protocol (Campbell and Stanley 1963). Adherence to this protocol allows one to produce accurate, repeatable results. At all times, care is taken to keep the researcher and the subject separate so the researcher will not influence the results. Central elements of this research protocol involve the *a priori* identification of a conceptual framework and the use of a controlled environment where extraneous sources of variance are minimized so "true" relationships among variables may be identified. Through applying this protocol, the positivist seeks to reveal relationships that can be generalized and predicted to other contexts.

Interpretivists believe that phenomena are time- and context-bound and, thus, they seek idiographic descriptive knowledge. Geertz (1973) refers to this type of knowledge as "thick description." While interpretivists may identify patterns of behavior, they believe that the world is so complex and dynamic that causal relationships cannot be identified. The interpretivists' belief in mutual, simultaneous shaping between entities is consistent with their belief that reality should be viewed holistically (Lincoln and Guba 1985). Thus, interpretivists do not specify *a priori* relationships that are then tested in a fixed design. While researchers may enter the field with some general ideas and questions, they do not know enough to specify a fixed design and must rely on the assistance of informants. Meaning is cooperatively developed. The research design evolves as researchers immerse themselves in the natural and changing environment.

In summary, positivists seek the goal of explanation and prediction. A single, immutable social reality exists, which is fragmentable. Furthermore, the behavior of social beings is generally viewed as being determined by internal states and/or external forces. Finally, positivists generally seek nomothetic knowledge, assume real causes exist, and adopt a stance of separation between researcher and subject. Conversely, interpretivists seek the goal of

**TABLE 1**

**A SUMMARY OF THE POSITIVIST AND INTERPRETIVIST APPROACHES**

| BASIC ASSUMPTIONS | POSITIVIST | INTERPRETIVIST |
|---|---|---|
| AXIOLOGICAL: | | |
| Overriding Goal | -"explanation" via subsumption under general laws, prediction | -"understanding" |
| ONTOLOGICAL: | | |
| Nature of Reality | -objective, tangible<br>-single<br>-fragmentable<br>-divisible | -socially-constructed<br>-multiple<br>-holistic<br>-contextual |
| Nature of Social Beings | -deterministic<br>-reactive | -voluntaristic<br>-proactive |
| EPISTEMOLOGICAL: | | |
| Knowledge Generated | -nomothetic<br>-time-free<br>-context-independent | -idiographic<br>-time-bound<br>-context dependent |
| View of Casuality | -real causes exist | -multiple, simultaneous shaping |
| Research Relationship | -dualism, separation<br>-privilged point of observation | -interactive, cooperative<br>-no privileged point of observation |

understanding. Reality is socially constructed, thus many realities exist. Behavior cannot be removed from the context in which it occurs because meaning is context-dependent. As well, social beings are voluntaristic. Finally, the interpretivists generally seek idiographic knowledge, assume real causes cannot be identified, and view the research-informant relationship as interactive and cooperative.

## TWO APPROACHES TO EMOTION

The previous section delineates positivism and interpretivism as being based on different philosophical foundations. Nevertheless, the pervasive impact of these underlying assumptions and goals on the research conceptualization and methodology is still not evident. In this section, the strong link between fundamental assumptions and goals and the research process is highlighted. To illustrate this link, two different approaches to emotions research are discussed: Gordon Bower's positivist approach and Norman K. Denzin's interpretive approach. We look at the integrated research process, but most importantly, demonstrate the interdependencies of guiding assumptions, goals, methodology, and theory; that is, these two approaches form interdependent systems that are self-justifying and self-perpetuating. Thus, the meaning of a phenomenon changes as it is explored within different world views.

While these two approaches are incommensurable, we can examine the differences in assumptions between the two approaches. These differences in assumptions and goals may provide the basis for new approaches, which will be discussed in the section that follows.

### Bower's Positivist Approach

Although Bower does not offer a comprehensive theory of emotion, his approach to emotion is grounded in cognitive psychology (Bower 1981; Bower, Gilligan and Monteiro 1981; Bower, Monteiro and Gilligan 1978). Nevertheless, he develops a theory of memory and emotion, which is based on the associative network model of the human memory. Briefly, memory is analogous to an electrical network in which terminals are linked by wires, just as events and concepts form linking nodes in memory. If an event is activated in memory then other associated events are also activated, like electrical power going through a network of terminals. Bower assumes that emotions are also stored in memory in an associative network. For example, an emotion, such as joy, could be linked in memory to expressive behaviors, autonomic patterns, verbal labels, past events, and so on. The emotional nodes can be activated by a variety of stimuli, which would also activate the other associated events and physical responses. For instance, the activation of the grief node might also activate memories about specific events such as the death of a friend, as well as physical responses such as crying. Therefore, consistent with positivism, humans are viewed as reactive and deterministic.

Bower conceptualizes emotion primarily as a physiological, internal state that is not dependent on the surrounding context. Thus, emotion is assumed to be an objective phenomenon. This conceptualization is consistent with Bower's methodological approach. Emotional states are context-independent so they can be removed from their naturally occurring context and studied in a controlled laboratory setting. Also, emotional states can be produced and manipulated in the laboratory by such techniques as emotional statements and hypnosis. This method is compatible with the assumption that the nature of reality is fragmentable and divisible. In fact, in many of his studies Bower manipulates mood by hypnotizing subjects in lab settings and then asking them to recall very happy or sad events in their lives. Bower confirmed that the emotional state was achieved by measuring physical indicators such as the way the subjects looked and spoke, and their autonomic nervous responses (measured by galvanic skinresponse). Thus, the physical response is the emotion. Emotion is assumed to be a tangible, real state.

Bower is interested in the relationship between emotional states and memory; specifically, he hypothesizes that recall of information is better when one recalls the information while in the same emotional state as when the information was learned. Bower poses a specific question: does emotion influence recall? Consistent with the epistemological assumption of causality, he then develops a controlled, temporal sequence of events to establish this relationship. For example, in one experiment (Bower et al. 1978), a 2 x 2 factorial design was used: subjects were either in a happy or sad mood during learning and in a happy or sad mood during recall. First, subjects were hypnotized and then told to put themselves in a happy or sad mood by imagining a scene when they had felt happy or sad. Subjects were then given a word list to learn while still under hypnosis and in the emotional state. The next day while under hypnosis, the subjects were asked to create a happy or sad mood, as before, and then they were asked to recall the list of words. At all times care was taken to standardize the procedure so that the subjects were treated in the same manner. Here, the separation of researcher and subject is evident, as well as the positivist's desire to follow research protocol.

With their research output, Bower et al. (1978) attempt to establish the hypothesized relationship between emotion and memory. For example, they report a series of three experiments. In the first two experiments, they are unable to establish the hypothesized relationship. In the third attempt they "finally produced the mood-dependent retention effect for which we had been searching" (1978, p. 582). This statement implies that the nature of reality is objective, real, and immutable.

Bower's research process is strongly influenced by positivists' assumptions, but it is also consistent with their goals. For instance, Bower (1981) speculates on extensions of his research to such areas as mood perpetuation, dream recall, and drug dissociation. Like positivists, he explicitly states that the goal of all basic science is to create theories that are generalizable. Furthermore, he stresses parsimony in his attempt to generalize cognitive theories to the area of emotion.

In summary, Bower's theory and methods are grounded on the same underlying assumptions and goals. These underpinnings provide the support and justification for the research process that he employs (Laudan 1984).

## Denzin's Interpretivist Approach

Although Denzin (1978, 1983, 1984) offers a comprehensive theory of emotion, we present only the core theoretical and methodological elements of his approach. Emotions are defined as self-feelings; they are feelings of and for oneself. These feelings may include bodily sensations, but they may also include moral and value feelings, etc. While emotions are lived experiences that define the person, they occur in a social context. Emotions, such as embarrassment or shame, can only arise in an environment with the actual or imagined presence of other people and then they are experienced by the self. Finally, the meaning of emotion is based on the individual's interpretation of it; "one person's joy may be another's sorrow" (1984, p. 5). The individual's interpretations of an emotion are always shifting, so an emotion is never experienced in exactly the same way. In summary, an emotional experience is reflective--it consists of self-feelings; it is situational-- it is a lived experience that is temporal and situated; and it is relational--it involves interactions with others. Denzin's conceptualization of emotion is consistent with interpretivists' ontological assumptions. Emotion is perceptual, socially-constructed, and context-dependent.

For example, in Denzin's study of emotion in family violence, violence is "the attempt to regain, through the use of emotional or physical force, something that has been lost" (1984, p. 169). An enacted violent emotion embodies the reflective, the situational, and the relational components. The "loss" refers back to the self and the violent act is an attempt to regain what the self has lost. The violent emotion is tied to a specific, temporal situation. And this act defines the relationship between the self and other for the emotion has meaning for both. As well, people choose their actions, which is consistent with the interpretivist's voluntaristic assumption.

This basic conceptual framework leads Denzin to some methodological prescriptions. Because emotions are self-feelings, they should be studied as a lived phenomenon from the point of view of the emotional person. In addition, these feelings are found in the world and arise interactively with the world. "There is no division between people, their emotion, and the world" (1984, p. 7). Therefore, agreeing with the interpretivist's view of reality, Denzin believes that the phenomenon of emotion should be studied holistically in the natural world of lived experience. Emotional experiences cannot be separated from the context in which they occur. Any instance of emotion in a natural setting may be studied.

The process of interpretation involves a number of steps. First, through a variety of sources--

observations, interviews, filmings, and so on--the basis of the interpretation, or what is called the text, is gathered. Next, the text is divided into parts, such as phrases or acts, that are examined to reveal the inner meanings of the text. Working hypotheses and interpretations develop for each subtext and these are checked against other subtexts. The creation of a total interpretation arises as the subtextual interpretations are fit together. However, multiple interpretations often arise. In the research output, the researcher's own interpretation is presented along with alternative interpretations. Here, it is evident that the research act is an interactive, cooperative enterprise. Also, the view of multiple realities is consistent with the expectation of many alternative interpretations.

In Denzin's study of emotion in family violence, we find an example of this interpretive process. Denzin placed no restrictions on the type of data gathering techniques employed. For instance, Denzin relied on field observations, case studies, fictional literature, plays, legal cases, and in-depth interviews. And consistent with his assumptions, violent emotion was studied as a lived experience from the perspective of the violent person.

The end product is an in-depth, complex interpretation and Denzin concludes that "emotionality and the self are at the core of violence" and "that self stands in bad faith with itself" (1984, p. 167). Denzin uses the interpretation to make suggestions for breaking the violent network existing in the family. For example, the family must create new patterns of nonviolent behavior to change the meanings of the home and family interactions. These suggestions, however, are not predictions; they are prescriptions that assume that people freely choose their actions, but "the meanings of this new choice cannot be estimated, for freedom's possibilities cannot be charted" (1984, p. 200). The purpose of offering the interpretation is to help people *understand* their lives, not to predict them.

What emerges from this analysis of Denzin's approach is an intimate relationship among his philosophical assumptions, theory, and methodology. The same philosophical assumptions underlie both the theory and the methodology. The methodology is consistent with the theory, while the theory supports the methodology (Laudan 1984). The same parallel holds for the relationship among Bower's assumptions, theory, and methodology. Within each researcher's approach these three components combine to form an interdependent system that is both self-justifying and self-perpetuating. Thus, what is perceived as emotion is radically different between the two approaches. Moreover, the outputs of the two approaches are different. The end product of Denzin's research is a detailed and descriptive interpretation, which can be used to make prescriptions, but its primary purpose is to help ordinary people understand their individual lives. The end product of Bower's research is an explanation of an association between emotion and memory, which can be generalized to a number of other domains.

We question whether these two researchers are even studying the same phenomenon. However, we do not question the value of both research enterprises. In fact, the field of consumer research is large enough to incorporate both research traditions as separate intellectual activities.

## RELEVANT ISSUES FOR CONSUMER RESEARCH

The previous section laid out, in a concrete example, the pervasive impact of philosophical assumptions and goals on the research process. A number of issues become salient when we consider the underpinnings of our approaches. For example, how should the review process deal with potential incommensurability between reviewers and authors? Can knowledge outputs from different world views be merged into a single analysis? What problems arise when theories or methods are borrowed from incommensurable paradigms? How are other approaches, such as critical theory, philosophically related to positivism and interpretivism? If we reevaluate and alter our assumption base, can alternative approaches be constructed? These examples represent just a few of the issues that arise when we reflect upon our assumption base.

This paper will tackle two specific issues: triangulation and exploring alternative approaches. The former issue is discussed because of its prevalence within consumer research, while the latter issue is discussed because of its potential long-run implications.

### Triangulation

The definitions and aims of the concept of triangulation vary. Denzin (1978) identified four different types of triangulation: 1) data triangulation-- which uses a variety of data sources, such as times, situations, and individuals; 2) investigator triangulation--where more than one researcher is used; 3) theory triangulation--where a situation is examined from the standpoint of competing theories; and 4) methodological triangulation--where many methods are used to study the same problem. Neither positivism nor interpretivism explicitly addresses the issue of triangulation across paradigms. Most of the discussion of triangulation within these two approaches assumes that the same philosophical assumptions underlie the data, theories, and methods. Therefore, the discussion that follows is relevant *within* positivism and interpretivism, respectively.

Within positivism, data, investigator, and methodological triangulation are generally consistent with positivist assumptions and aims for generalization, researcher objectivity, and the discovery of "truth." Convergent results are expected from these types of triangulation. It is the convergence of data, investigators, and methods that is of interest to the positivist. For example, Hunt (1983) states that scientific knowledge "must be objective in the sense that its truth content must be intersubjectively certifiable (p. 243)." Thus, different investigators can empirically test the same theory and get the same results. Any individual differences should converge on a single reality in the aggregate. Theory triangulation, however, is generally aimed at pitting one theory against another to discover the "true" theory. Or, an attempt is made to subsume two or more theories within a single, comprehensive theoretical framework.

Within interpretivism, these types of triangulation are also acceptable, but for different reasons. Data, investigator, theory, and methodological triangulation allow for the emergence of patterns, along with the recognition of many differing descriptions of reality. The interpretivist's expectation is that some patterns might emerge but there would also be divergent results, reflecting the many social constructions of reality. Moreover, these divergent results are of interest to the interpretivist. Here, theory triangulation is different from the positivist's approach. Theories are interpretations of phenomena and--consistent with their view of reality--interpretivists accept the existence of multiple interpretations.

However, all forms of inter-paradigm triangulation may present problems. A researcher who is unreflective of the assumptions underlying data, theories, and methods from different paradigms might try to combine the outputs of different world views. But making the results of research from different world views based on different assumptions fit together is to change them (Hudson and Ozanne 1988).

In the previous section, it was clear that what was perceived to be the phenomenon of emotion changed when investigated by different researchers using different methodologies and theories. Different approaches address different questions and will not come together to form a single, well-integrated picture of the phenomenon. Regarding methodology, Shapiro (1973) describes her difficulty in integrating the data of a more interpretive methodology and the data of a more positivist methodology. She concluded that the conflicts were the result of her measuring different things; that is, the phenomenon became different when studied through the use of different methodologies. In fact, due to the different world views, what results is what Wallendorf (1985) calls divergent validity. That is, different results would be expected because the phenomenon studied changes due to the research methodologies, which are based on different assumptions and goals. If the aim of triangulation is to find the "truth" or reduce error, triangulation across incommensurable paradigms will not accomplish this goal. As Fielding and Fielding (1986) point out, if the assumptions of certain theories and methodologies are more consistent with certain research questions, it is unlikely that the inadequacies of one approach will complement the adequacies of another. The researcher who reflects on underlying assumptions would not expect triangulation across paradigms to reduce uncertainty.

## Exploring Alternative Approaches Using Dialectic Analysis

The second issue is how these two views might generate insights from which new systems could be constructed. We have suggested elsewhere that dialectic analysis would be helpful in dealing with diversity (Hudson and Ozanne 1988).

While many meanings of dialectics exist, here, dialectics is used to refer to a method for juxtaposing opposing points of view (Churchman 1971; Hudson and Ozanne 1988; Mason and Mitroff 1981; Mitroff and Mason 1983; Morgan 1983). Consistent with an

Hegelian interpretation (Churchman 1971), the researcher explores one viewpoint (thesis) and builds the best possible support for this position based on any available data. Next, the researcher constructs an opposing viewpoint (antithesis) and constructs a different view of reality from the available data. This antithesis is the viewpoint that is in greatest conflict or competition with the thesis. Finally, the opposition between the thesis and antithesis is studied. Through debate and juxtaposition of conflicting parts, different alternative approaches may be realized (see Mitroff and Mason 1983 for applications to a number of different domains). Here, the researcher is struggling with the conflict in order to arrive at a new thesis, which may or may not resolve the conflict. Nevertheless, somehow the researcher gets beyond the conflict by moving to a higher plane, giving a different perspective, or resolving the conflict. This new thesis is called the *synthesis*. Thus, the goal is to achieve fuller and richer forms through the careful examination of the contradiction (Churchman 1971; Mitroff and Mason 1983). It is important to note that the existence of a contradiction does not insure that a fuller form will be realized. Instead, a third approach, which may be different from the thesis and antithesis, may evolve.

Because of the relationship between positivism and interpretivism, dialectics is a particularly appropriate method for dealing with these two approaches. First, these world views represent two diametrically opposed ways of seeking knowledge (Hirschman 1986; Hudson and Ozanne 1988; Lincoln and Guba 1985). A method that attempts to deal with conflict across polar positions would be a useful approach for dealing with diverse ways of seeking knowledge. In addition to offering a method that may resolve contradictions or encourage change, dialectics as a method tries to make explicit what is often implicit. Dialectics specifically focuses on differences in fundamental underlying assumptions (Mitroff and Mason 1983). The questioning and rethinking of these implicit assumptions is an important source of change. (Dialectics does not offer a neutral point from which to view positivism and interpretivism. We believe that no such point of neutrality exists. Instead, dialectics challenges one approach by comparing its underlying assumptions to another approach's assumptions.)

Whether assumptions are made explicit or remain implicit, it is clear that they provide the foundation and justification for the research process. In this section, two underlying differences between the positivist research of Bower and the interpretivist research of Denzin are explored: the nature of social beings and the nature of reality. Examination of these conflicts sometimes results in insights and a synthesis of the conflict that may offer ideas for creating new alternative approaches to research.

*The Nature of Social Beings.* The positivist's and interpretivist's assumption about the nature of social beings is contradictory. Positivist approaches view social beings as passive subjects who can be manipulated. The researcher directs the study and the subject follows. This view was demonstrated by Bower in his information processing approach to his subjects. Here, man is a thing or an :hp2.object:ehp2., whose moods are manipulated. The researchers role is to identify the laws that underlie behavior. On the other hand, interpretive approaches stress humans as agents who are completely volitional. The meanings of phenomena are sought from the perspective of those people involved. This view was exemplified by Denzin in his examination of emotion as a lived phenomenon from the point of view of the informant. Informants were assumed to choose their actions freely.

Neither of these positions seems tenable. Some actions of consumers do not appear to be chosen freely. For instance, it is unclear the extent to which our language and conceptual categories influence the way in which we view the world or to what extent we can break away from these influences. Furthermore, societal influences, in the form of socialization, may direct consumers' behavior to some extent. Social norms and consequences often make it difficult to perform, or, in some cases, not perform certain behaviors. However, a choice still exists. People do deviate from social norms, form new words and conceptual categories, and create new ideas. Perhaps some middle ground position is more reasonable: that is, humans seem to indicate some evidence of choosing freely and some evidence of being influenced by internal/external forces. In other words, humans are neither entirely voluntaristic nor entirely deterministic.

A resolution of this contradiction by taking a middle ground position would influence the way that research is done. For example, a problem that would become relevant is when do people behave more voluntaristically and when do they behave more deterministically. In fact, Mark Snyder (1979) has worked on this issue in his research on self-monitoring. Upon studying a phenomenon, it would be important to examine the phenomenon for indications of volition. For example, in the United States, a consumer might take for granted that he/she is going to use some form of money in exchange for a good in the marketplace. In another culture, there may be a more conscious choice because the form of payment is not taken for granted. When consumers are not aware of the taken for granted assumptions, it might be more appropriate for the researcher to structure and guide the study. However, in the case where the consumer makes a conscious choice, it might be more appropriate for the informant to be relied upon to direct the study. A middle ground, as is outlined here, may make viable different research approaches. Thus, syntheses may open up our choice of research process as opposed to constraining choice.

*The Nature of Reality*. Some conflicts do not easily lead to a synthesis. For example, the positivists hold a realist view and assume that a single, immutable reality exists. As well, a phenomenon can be removed from the context in which it arises. This stance was reflected in Bower's view of emotion primarily as a physiological, internal state that is not dependent on the surrounding context. Denzin's approach, which is consistent with interpretivism, holds that reality is perceptual and, thus, many realities exist. In addition, the meaning of a phenomenon arises and gets part of its meaning from the surrounding environment. It seems clear that the issue of one or many realities is not resolvable by taking a middle ground position (i.e., a

few realites exist). Here, it seems like researchers must take their own stand.

## SUMMARY AND CONCLUSIONS

In summary, the philosophical assumptions and goals that underlie positivism and interpretivism were examined. In a concrete example of two different approaches to emotions, it was demonstrated how each approaches' assumptions and goals justify and are consistent with their chosen theories and methods. In many ways, these two world views are incommensurate and generate very different outputs (Anderson 1986). These two positions represent two different ways of knowing. But benefit may be realized by understanding the philosophical foundations of these approaches. In fact, many problems that face consumer research must be resolved at a philosophical level. Two issues were explored from an analysis of the underlying philosophical assumptions: triangulation and the existence of alternative approaches. It was suggested that the usefulness of four different forms of triangulation depends on whether or not the data, investigator, theory, or method are based on different assumptions. In addition, a method for exploring new approaches, dialectic analysis, was discussed. Dialectic analysis explores the conflict between opposing views in order to find a synthesis. The goal here was not to find the best synthesis or integration of positivism and interpretivism--an ideal union of these two world views probably is impossible. Nevertheless, alternative positions do exist. As we question our assumption base and explore alternative assumptions (Laudan 1984), we inject the potential for flexibility and change in our approaches for studying consumers.

New approaches to consumer research were not created in this paper, however, potential starting points exist: goals, the nature of social beings, the nature of reality, and so on. To construct a new research paradigm from a new assumption base represents a tremendous challenge. This challenge may result in a better understanding of one's current approach, a broadening of one's own approach, or--perhaps for a few researchers--a leap off the safety of the bridge to swim in unfamiliar waters toward unknown shores.

## REFERENCES
Anderson, Paul F. (1983), "Marketing, Scientific Progress, and Scientific Method," *Journal of Marketing*, 47 (Fall), 18-31.

_____ (1986), "On Method in Consumer Research: A Critical Relativist Perspective," *Journal of Consumer Research*, 13 (September), 155-173.

Bagozzi, Richard P. (1980), *Causal Models in Marketing*, New York: John Wiley & Sons.

Belk, Russell W. (1986), "What Should ACR Want to be When It Grows Up?," in *Advances in Consumer Research*, Vol. 13, ed. Richard J. Lutz, Provo, UT: Association for Consumer Research, 423-424.

_____, John F. Sherry, and Melanie Wallendorf (1988), "A Naturalistic Inquiry into Buyer and Seller Behavior at a Swap Meet," *Journal of Consumer Research*, 14 (March), 449-470.

Bogdan, Robert and Steve Taylor (1975), *Introduction to Qualitative Research Methods: A Phenomenological Approach to the Social Sciences*, New York: John Wiley and Sons.

Bower, Gordon (1981), "Mood and Memory," *American Psychologist*, 36 (February), 129-143.

_____, Stephen Gilligan, and Kenneth Monteiro (1981), "Selectivity of Learning Caused by Affective States," *Journal of Experimental Psychology: General*, 110 (December), 451-473.

_____, Kenneth Monteiro, and Stephen Gilligan (1978), "Emotional Mood as a Context for Learning and Recall," *Journal of Verbal Learning and Verbal Behavior*, 17, 573-585.

Bredo, Eric and Walter Feinberg (1982), *Knowledge and Values in Social and Educational Research*, Philadelphia: Temple University Press.

Bruyn, Severyn T. (1966), *The Human Perspective in Sociology: The Methodology of Participant Observation*, Englewood Cliffs, N.J.: Prentice-Hall.

Burrell, Gibson and Gareth Morgan (1979), *Sociological Paradigms and Organizational Analysis*, London: Heinemann.

Campbell, Donald T. and Julian C. Stanley (1963), *Experimental and Quasi-Experimental Designs for Research*, Chicago: Rand McNally College Publishing Company.

Churchman, C. West (1971), *The Design of Inquiring Systems*, New York: Basic Books, Inc.

Coombs, Robert H. and Lawrence J. Goldman (1976), "Maintenance and Discontinuity of Coping Mechanisms in an Intensive Care Unit," in *Doing Social Life*, ed. John Lofland, New York: John Wiley & Sons, 223-248.

Denzin, Norman K. (1978), *The Research Act: A Theoretical Introduction to Sociological Methods*, Chicago: Aldine Publishing Co.

_____ (1983), "Interpretive Interactionism," in *Beyond Method: Strategies for Social Research*, ed. Gareth Morgan, Beverly Hills: Sage Publications, 129-146.

_____ (1984), *On Understanding Emotion*, San Francisco: Jossey-Bass Publishers.

Geertz, Clifford (1973), "Thick Description," in *The Interpretation of Cultures*, New York: Basic Books, 3-30.

_____ (1979), "From the Native's Point of View: On the Nature of Anthropological Understanding," in *Interpretive Social Science*, eds. Paul Rabinow and William Sullivan, Berkeley, CA: University of California Press.

Fielding, Nigel G. and June L. Fielding (1986), *Linking Data*, Beverly Hills: Sage Publications.

Gouldner, Alvin (1970), *The Coming Crisis of Western Sociology*, New York: Basic Books.

_____ (1973), *For Sociology: Renewal and Critique in Sociology Today*, New York: Basic Books.

Hirschman, Elizabeth C. (1985), "Primitive Aspects of Consumption in Modern American Society," *Journal of Consumer Research*, 12 (September), 142-154.

_____ (1986), "Humanistic Inquiry in Marketing Research: Philosophy, Method, and Criteria," *Journal of Marketing Research*, 23 (August), 237-249.

Holbrook, Morris B. (1986), "I'm Hip: An Autobiographical Account of Some Musical Consumption Experiences," in *Advances in Consumer Research*, Vo. 13, ed. Richard Lutz, Ann Arbor, MI: Association for Consumer Research, 614-618.

_____ (1987), "What is Consumer Research?," *Journal of Consumer Research*, 14 (June), 128-132.

_____ and Mark W. Grayson (1986), "The Semiology of Cinematic Consumption: Symbolic Consumer Behavior in *Out of Africa*," *Journal of Consumer Research*, 13 (December), 374-381.

Hudson, Laurel Anderson and Julie L. Ozanne (1988), "Alternative Ways of Seeking Knowledge in Consumer Research," *Journal of Consumer Research*, 14 (March), 508-521.

_____ and Jeff B. Murray (1986), "Methodological Limitations of the Hedonic Consumption Paradigm and a Possible Alternative: A Subjectivist Approach," in *Advances in Consumer Research*, Vol. 13, ed. Richard J. Lutz, Provo, UT: Association for Consumer Research, 343-348.

Hunt, Shelby D. (1983), *Marketing Theory*, Homewood, IL: Irwin.

Keat, Russell and John Urry (1975), *Social Theory as Science*, London: Routledge & Kegan Paul.

Kerlinger, Fred N. (1973), *The Foundation of Behavioral Research*, New York: Holt, Rinehart, and Winston.

Laudan, Larry (1984), *Science and Values*, Berkely: University of California Press.

Lincoln, Yvonna S. and Egon G. Guba (1985), *Naturalistic Inquiry*, Beverly Hills, Calif.: Sage Publications.

Lutz, Richard J. (1987), "Statement of Review Philosophy," for *Journal of Consumer Research*.

Mason, Richard O. and Ian I. Mitroff (1981), *Challenging Strategic Planning Assumptions*, New York: John Wiley & Sons.

McCracken, Grant (1986), "Culture and Consumption: A Theoretical Account of the Structure and Movement of the Cultural Meaning of Consumer Goods," *Journal of Consumer Research*, 13 (June), 71-84.

Mick, David Glen (1986), "Consumer Research and Semiotics: Exploring the Morphology of Signs, Symbols, and Signifigance," *Journal of Consumer Research*, 13 (September), 196-213.

Mitroff, Ian I. and Richard O. Mason (1983), *Creating A Dialectical Social Science*, London, England: D. Reidel Publishing Company.

Morgan, Gareth (1983), "Toward a More Reflective Social Science," in *Beyond Method*, ed. Gareth Morgan, Beverly Hills, Calif.: Sage Publications, 368-376.

_____ and Linda Smircich (1980), "The Case for Qualitative Research," *Academy of Management Review*, 5 (4), 491-500.

Peter, J. Paul and Jerry C. Olson (1983), "Is Science Marketing?," *Journal of Marketing*, 47 (Fall), 111-125.

Rook, Dennis W. (1985), "The Ritual Dimension of Consumer Behavior," *Journal of Consumer Research*, 12 (December), 251-264.

Rubinstein, David (1981), *Marx and Wittgenstein*, London: Routledge & Kegan Paul.

Sherry, John F. and Eduardo G. Camargo (1987), "May Your Life Be Marvelous: English Language Labelling and the Semiotics of Japanese Promotion," *Journal of Consumer Research*, 14 (September), 174-188.

Shapiro, Edna (1973). "Educational Evaluation: Rethinking the Criteria of Competence," *School Review*, November, 523-549.

Solomon, Michael R. (1986), "Deep-Seated Materialism: The Case of Levi's 501 Jeans," *Advances in Consumer Research*, ed. Richard J. Lutz, Vol. 13, Ann Arbor, MI: Association for Consumer Research, 619-622.

_____(1983), "The Role of Products as Social Stimuli: A Symbolic Interactionism Perspective," *Journal of Consumer Research*, 10 (December), 319-329.

Suppe, Frederick (1974), *The Structure of Scientific Theories*, Urbana, IL: University of Illinois Press.

Snyder, Mark (1979), "Self-Monitoring Processes," in *Advances in Experimental Social Psychology*, vol. 12, ed. L Berkowitz, New York: Academic Press.

Tucker, William T. (1967), *Foundations for a Theory of Consumer Behavior*, New York: Rinehart and Winston.

Wallendorf, Melanie (1985), Presentation at the American Marketing Association Theory Workshop, Blacksburg, Va.

_____(1987), "On Intimacy," Presentation at the American Marketing Association Winter Educator's Conference, San Antonio, Texas.

_____ and Eric J. Arnould (1988), "My Favorite Things: A Cross-Cultural Inquiry Into Object Attachment, Possessiveness, and Social Linkage," *Journal of Consumer Research*, 14 (March), 531-547.

# On Relativism and Interpretivism--With A Prolegomenon to the "Why" Question
## Paul F. Anderson, Pennsylvania State University[1]

## INTRODUCTION

The relationship between relativism (especially critical relativism) and methodologies that fall under the rubric of interpretivism has always been somewhat opaque in our discipline. Unfortunately, the waters have recently been muddied further by Calder and Tybout (1987). One objective of this paper is to clarify some of the misunderstandings created by Calder and Tybout's view of critical relativism. A second objective is to begin the process of explicating the reasons why some researchers in social science and consumer research have abandoned "positivistic" approaches in favor of interpretivism. It is not, however, a general defense of interpretivism.

## ON SPECIOUS CLASSIFICATIONS

Calder and Tybout begin their article by creating a classification system that divides the knowledge produced by consumer research into three categories: 1.) the everyday, 2.) the scientific, and 3.) the interpretive. Here they have dredged up a philosophical controversy with a history reaching back more than two millennia: the so-called demarcation problem. As I have noted elsewhere (Anderson 1983), the inability of science studies researchers to agree on the existence of a unique scientific method suggests that we currently have *no* universally applicable criterion by which we can demarcate scientific knowledge from any other kind of knowledge (Laudan 1983a). As Laudan has stated, "The fact that 2,400 years of searching for a demarcation criterion has left us empty-handed raises a presumption that the object of the quest is non-existent" (1980, p. 275).[2]
Unfortunately this is often thought to imply that all knowledge claims are on an equal epistemic footing (Hunt 1984). Of course, nothing could be further from

the truth. Indeed, very little follows from the fact that philosophers have been unable to come up with a *universal* demarcation criterion. The fact that all of the proffered alternatives have crumbled under the weight of criticism is nothing more than an empirical statement whose epistemological import is of minimal consequence. This can be seen in the diversity of philosophers who disagree on almost everything else-but are as one in their opposition to demarcationism. Thus Laudan (a rationalist, anti-relativist and anti-realist), Rosenberg (a naturalist, anti-relativist, and realist), and Feyerabend (an *epistemological* anarchist, relativist, and "flippant Dadaist") all agree that no one has yet to produce a defensible criterion of demarcation. Moreover, as I tried to show in Anderson (1986), the lack of such a criterion is no hindrance in critically evaluating the knowledge claims of alternative research programs. Thus, the search for unique characteristics that mark off the scientific from the non-scientific is a chimerical quest that (like the medieval crusades) is very likely to lead to failure.

Regrettably, Calder and Tybout have associated themselves with one of the least defensible of the demarcation criteria: Popperian falsificationism (Popper 1959). On this view, a discipline is scientific if it is willing to make predictions that can be refuted by empirical data. To quote Laudan (1983b) again, this view

> Has the untoward consequence of countenancing as "scientific" every crank claim which makes ascertainably false assertions. Thus, if I subscribe to some aberrant theology which says the world will end on January 4th in the year 2000, I can establish my Popperian scientific *bona fides* by saying that if the world endures beyond that date, then I was mistaken! (p. 23).

The problem with Popper's demarcation criterion is that it can be construed in such a way that it excludes disciplines taught as science in our major universities while at the same time it includes fields that have yet to attain the status of what I have elsewhere called science$_2$-the definition of science by societal consensus (Anderson 1983). Thus, Popper's (1957) notorious claim that evolutionary theory is not testable must call into question the scientific status of most, if not all, of modern biology. Similarly, if "The key features of scientific knowledge are that there have been empirical attempts to refute a theory and that the theory has performed better than any available competitors" (Calder and Tybout 1987, p. 137), we are left with the problematic case of parapsychology. The practitioners of this field will claim that they have met and even exceeded Calder and Tybout's criteria. Indeed, as two outside observers have noted, "It seems likely

[1]The author would like to thank Elizabeth Hirschman, Jerry Olson, J. Paul Peter, John Sherry, Harish Sujan and Melanie Wallendorf for their very helpful comments on various portions of earlier drafts of this paper.

[2]As suggested by the philosopher Richard Rorty (1979), this does not mean that epistemology [or the broader field of science studies] is the ultimate "foundational" discipline that "legitimizes or grounds the others" (p. 6). Nor does it mean that scientists in a substantive field (like Pierre Duhem) cannot make contributions to epistemology. I am simply suggesting that when philosophy of science issues are at stake, it seems reasonable to consult the work of professionals who have devoted their careers to such matters. Whether we accept or reject their (often conflicting) positions is another matter entirely.

that the best of modern parapsychology comprises some of the most rigorously controlled and methodologically sophisticated work in the sciences" (Collins and Pinch 1979, pp. 243-44).[3] (In fact the field tries to maintain such standards because of society's unwillingness to grant it epistemic authority!)[4] They go on to state that,

> Although a group of scientists have dedicated a considerable portion of their lives to the attempt to discredit psi [e.g., telepathy, clairvoyance, precognition, etc.] ..., they have not succeeded in revealing any universally acceptable criteria to distinguish parapsychology from science (Collins and Pinch, 1979, p. 250).

Thus, if Calder and Tybout wish to maintain the integrity of their classification system, they must do what has eluded philosophers since the time of Parmenides: develop a demarcation criterion that divides knowledge into mutually exclusive categories.

## ON SOME HONEST MISUNDERSTANDINGS

Calder and Tybout argue that sophisticated falsificationism *should be* the methodology for generating "scientific" knowledge in consumer behavior. In so doing, they are asking us to adopt a philosophy of science that has long since been abandoned by the broader science studies community. Of course, rejection by scholars in this field does not, by itself, constitute sufficient grounds for its dismissal in consumer research. If falsificationism is to be repudiated, it must be because "good" reasons have been offered for its inadequacy. (Indeed, some of these reasons have already appeared in the marketing and consumer behavior literature.) However, it would appear that Calder and Tybout do not find these arguments compelling. They apparently believe that the only arrow in the relativist's quiver is the charge that all scientific data are fallible (Calder and Tybout 1987, p. 138). This is indeed a point made by relativists, but if it were our only concern with falsificationism, our position would reduce to an empty skepticism. Unfortunately, the problems with falsificationism run far deeper than this.

---

[3]Collins and Pinch are sociologists of science who have done extensive empirical research on parapsychology. They have no vested interest in its scientific legitimacy; and have, in fact, observed and publicly reported cases of fraud in so-called "paranormal metal bending" (Collins and Pinch 1982).

[4]Of course, this does not suggest that society *should* recognize parapsychology as science. My point is that Calder and Tybout's criteria are not strong enough to rule parapsychology out of court on *their own* conception of scientific knowledge.

First, it should be clear that falsificationism rests on the very same inductivism that Calder and Tybout find so objectionable (Calder, Phillips and Tybout 1981; Calder and Tybout 1987). In the Popperian system, a theory is said to be "corroborated" (tentatively accepted) if it has survived repeated and determined efforts at falsification. However, it should be clear that Popper has simply substituted accumulated "failed falsifications" for accumulated verifications. He is thus making an inductive leap from a finite number of experiments to the "corroboration" of a theory with alleged universal applicability. As I have noted elsewhere, this mode of inference runs headlong into the "problem of induction" (Anderson 1983, p. 19); and, as Calder and Tybout have noted, induction is not a deductively valid form of inference.

Second, falsificationism also falls victim to the Duhem (1906, 1954) thesis. Since all theory tests depend on other theories concerning initial conditions, measuring devices and auxiliary assumptions--any alleged falsification can always be "deflected by assuming that something else in the maze of assumptions and premises caused the result" (Anderson 1983, p. 21). Moreover, since all experiments are inherently "open systems" (Pickering 1981, 1984), it is rarely possible to determine if a study is actually a rigorous test of a hypothesis (in the sense that we can determine that the theory actually had a genuine chance at failing).

Third, Calder and Tybout claim that they are proposing "a methodology of sophisticated falsificationism" (p. 138) derived from the works of Popper (1959) and Lakatos (1970). However, in Popper's 1959 book [actually published in 1934] he expounds a view that Lakatos (1978) criticizes as "naive methodological falsificationism" (p. 108n). Moreover, Calder and Tybout do not take note of the fact that Lakatos's "sophisticated falsificationism" *was never intended to give normative guidance to practicing scientists.* Lakatos's "methodology of scientific research programs" was devised to give historians of science a means of creating "rational reconstructions" of actual historical episodes (Lakatos 1970, 1978). A rational reconstruction is a historical narrative that "recreates" the actual events so as to produce "some characteristic pattern of rational growth of scientific knowledge" (Lakatos 1978, p. 118). As Lakatos (1971) himself put it:

> I, of course, do not prescribe to the individual scientist what to try to do in a situation characterized by two rival progressive research programs ... Whatever they *have* done, I can judge: I can say whether they have made progress or not. But I cannot advise them--and do not wish to advise them--about exactly what to worry and about in which direction they should seek progress (p. 178, emphasis in original).

Thus, Lakatos counsels that in any reconstruction of the work of Niels Bohr "the historian, describing with hindsight the Bohrian program, should include electron spin in it [even if Bohr may never have thought of electron spin], since electron spin fits naturally in the original outline of the program" (1978, p. 119). Lakatos took this rather idiosyncratic approach to philosophy of science because he realized that it is only "*with long hindsight*" that we can judge one program to be superior to another (Lakatos 1970, p. 173, emphasis in original). This is also why his sophisticated falsificationism can provide no rules for the contemporary scientist. The history of science is replete with examples of "degenerating research programs" that have staged spectacularly successful comebacks (Lakatos 1978; Chalmers 1982). Thus he can say that, "One may rationally stick to a degenerating program until it is overtaken by a rival *and even after*" (Lakatos 1978, p. 117n, emphasis in original). However, since "one can be "wise" only after the event" (Lakatos 1978, p. 113), one never knows when it is time to jump ship.[5]

Finally, falsificationism is suspect because it fails to accord with either the history of scientific advance or the empirical study of contemporary science. As I have noted elsewhere, heliocentrism, oxygen theory, natural selection, relativity theory, continental drift, etc., are all examples of "successful" theories that were at one time or another "falsified" (Anderson 1983). More importantly, *empirical* study of the practice of contemporary science also shows that falsificationism does not accurately describe scientific method *in the supposedly "advanced" natural sciences* (see, for example, Collins 1975, 1981; Gilbert and Mulkay 1984; Knorr-Cetina 1981; Latour 1987; Latour and Woolgar 1979; Law and Williams 1982; Pickering 1981, 1984; Pinch 1980, 1982, 1986).

Of course, the "falsification" of theories that are now considered to be successful could be patched up with the argument that "Researchers may make some effort to protect a new theory or to reserve judgment because of the possibility of erroneous interpretation of data" (Calder and Tybout 1987, p. 138). Unfortunately, this view of Lakatos's argument runs into the same difficulty mentioned above. There are no guidelines available to determine how long we should protect a theory, or when anomalies or "falsifications" imply that it is time for a change of research programs.

Indeed, it is ironic that Calder and Tybout (1987) charge relativists with attempting to "escape from data" (p. 138), when much of the evidence for relativism is *based* on empirical data. In this paper and in two others (Anderson 1983, 1986), I have cited numerous empirical studies that support a relativistic construal of scientific practice. Moreover in Anderson

(1986) I demonstrated that four *empirically-based* approaches to consumer behavior are unable to resolve their differences despite their alleged commitment to adjudication by data.

Calder and Tybout go on to suggest that relativists see scientific knowledge arising, not out of consensus about data, but out of consensus per se. On their view, if scientists do not attempt to persuade each other on the basis of data, there is nothing left to use as a tool of persuasion. There are at least three problems here. As noted above, it is patently false to suggest that relativists retreat from data. I attempted to make this as clear as possible when I stated that "critical relativists do not eschew empirical testing" (Anderson 1986, p. 156). (This includes both quantitative and qualitative tests.) Second, I did my best in Anderson (1986) to demonstrate that commitment to an encapsulated research program in consumer behavior involves more than a reliance on empirical evidence. Indeed, the whole point of my Exhibit was to show that data are not always sufficient to adjudicate among competing theories or research programs.

Third, numerous sociological studies of ongoing controversies in natural science have shown that scientific debates are not readily "closed down" by simple appeals to empirical evidence. If Calder and Tybout wish to maintain their "data *über alles*" position, they must show that these studies are all somehow tragically flawed. For example, they must explain why Dr. Joseph Weber felt that he was "out marketed"[6] in his attempts to persuade the physics community that he had detected gravitational radiation in the late 1960's (Collins 1975, 1981). Similarly, they must explain why in 20 years no one has attempted to replicate Professor Raymond Davis's "anomalous" finding that the sun produces less than a third of the neutrinos predicted by theory (Pinch 1980, 1986; Bahcall 1987).[7] Finally, they would have to deconstruct Pickering's (1981) study of the search for free quarks in which he concludes that "scientific communities tend to reject data that conflicts with group commitments and, obversely, to *adjust their experimental techniques and methods* to "tune in" on phenomena consistent with those commitments" (p. 236, emphasis added). Numerous other studies could be (and have been) cited (Anderson 1983, 1986); however, the main point has been made. One of the fundamental underpinnings of critical epistemic relativism is *empirical*, and any critique of its tenets

---

[5]Here I am not claiming veridical exegetical powers when it comes to the work of Popper and Lakatos. I prefer to simply present their own words (or criticisms that are well documented in the literature), and allow the reader to draw his or her own conclusions.

---

[6]Personal communication from Harry M. Collins, October 30, 1982.

[7]The recent fortuitous explosion of Supernova 1987a *may* provide evidence that will be sufficient to bring closure to the solar neutrino debate (Bahcall, Dar and Piran 1987). However, the leading expert in the sociology of this controversy has expressed serious reservations about this eventuality (Pinch 1987).

must show that this empirical base is in some way suspect.

Unfortunately, Calder and Tybout's failure to acknowledge the empirical basis of critical relativism is not their only misunderstanding of my work. On page 138 they declare that "Interpretive knowledge implies critical relativistic methodology" (Calder and Tybout 1987). There are two very serious problems with this view. The first is that I took great pains in Anderson (1986) to deny any necessary linkage between critical relativism and interpretivism. Indeed, in 1986 a leading proponent of "interpretive" or humanistic methodology put it thusly:

> Though relativism *per se* does not constitute an ontology or a methodology, the issues it raises about the socially constructed and context-bound nature of human knowledge have generated consideration of various philosophical traditions and methodological avenues that earlier would have been viewed as unacceptable within the boundaries of marketing science (Hirschman 1986, p. 237).

Hirschman's insightful recognition that critical relativism is not a scientific methodology brings us to the second major problem with Calder and Tybout's exegesis of my position on the relationship between relativism and method. As I noted in my article, "critical relativism is first and foremost a descriptive enterprise" (Anderson 1986, p. 157), and descriptions clearly do not constitute a set of normative guidelines. Since statements of "ought" cannot be deductively derived from statements of what "is", critical relativism underdetermines methodology (Anderson 1986). That is to say, two committed relativists can (and frequently do) disagree on the normative implications of their preferred philosophy of science.

Critical relativism is a descriptive philosophy of science with *potential* implications "for 'workbench'-level issues in consumer research" (Anderson 1986, p. 169). In my article I tried to suggest a number of specific methodological topics and areas where critical relativism might be salutary. Currently work is under way that will attempt to deliver on this promissory note. Ironically, Calder and Tybout recognize that I have yet to cash out the methodological implications of my position. They state that, "Although Anderson (1986) provides a conceptual framework for critical relativism, specific criteria for critical relativism as a methodology are yet to be presented" (p. 139). If this, then, is the case, how can they know that interpretivism implies a critical relativistic methodology?

## ON APPEAL TO A SOCIALLY SANCTIONED INSTITUTION

Calder and Tybout state that "scientific knowledge implies sophisticated falsificationist methodology" (p. 137) and suggest that alternative ways of knowing (while legitimate) do not measure up to "scientific" standards. Of course, in western societies we are all enculturated with the belief that science occupies the highest rung on the ladder leading to wisdom and insight (e.g., Gieryn 1987). By relegating "everyday"[8] and "interpretive" knowledge to a "legitimate", but non-competing status with science, they are making an appeal to a shared cultural belief that is itself nothing more than a subset of everyday ("unscientific") knowledge.

This becomes clear in their characterization of "interpretivism". Among other things we are told that, "The hallmark [of interpretive research] is the application of a given conceptualization, or way of viewing, to consumer behavior (p. 138). We are also warned that, "because [interpretive data] may be used selectively and multiple interpretations of them may coexist, there is no intention of comparing interpretations in order to *choose* among them (p. 139, emphasis in original). Moreover, interpretive researchers make "no pretense of searching for refuting evidence or competing explanations for the same data" (p. 139). Worse yet, interpretive "insight is subjective and relative to a particular time, setting, and group of researchers... [where] empirical data do not play a self-correcting role" (p. 139). Finally, "The consensus of [interpretive] researchers may result more from dogmatic acceptance than critical debate and agreement... [thus] such conceptualizations should not be equated with scientific knowledge" (p. 139).

Since it is not my intention to argue for or to defend the many approaches that fall under the rubric of "interpretivism", I shall leave a detailed critique of these points to others more qualified than myself. Suffice it to say that, when applied to the majority of work done under the banner of interpretivism, all of Calder and Tybout's claims are patently false.[9] Moreover, a perusal of the science studies literature would reveal that each of these very same points have been made in connection with what Calder and Tybout would count as empirical science.

## ON THE "WHY" QUESTION

Perhaps the most important question that defenders of interpretivism in consumer behavior must answer is: why interpretivism? While many in consumer research have engaged in such studies, with few exceptions (e.g., Sherry 1987b; Hudson and Ozanne 1988), these writers have not been keen to cash out the reasons why interpretive methods evolved as an alternative to the application of the alleged methods of the natural sciences to the study of human behavior. This is puzzling in light of the fact that the so-called *Geisteswissenschaften* debate has been

---

[8]While Calder and Tybout (1987) note that "anthropology ... includes research aimed at everyday knowledge and research seeking scientific knowledge" (p. 138n), they do not mention ethnomethodology--a field whose sole purpose is the "scientific" and empirical study of everyday knowledge (Garfinkel 1967).

[9]In this regard, some useful citations would include Sherry (1983, 1987a, 1987b).

going on in social science for more than a hundred years.

The fact of the matter is that there are *reasons* why some social scientists have found "positivism" (in all of its various incarnations) inappropriate for human studies. While one could (and some authors have) devoted entire volumes to this issue, I will use only a single illustration from consumer research to give but the slightest hint of what some have found objectionable in certain types of experimental consumer behavior.

The study in question was conducted by Tybout, Sternthal and Calder (1983) and provides a quintessential example of what (for lack of a better name) I shall call "psychological instrumentalism." Instrumentalism is the view that the "unobservable" theoretical constructs mentioned in a theory have no "real world" referents. (Ironically, Calder and Tybout's (1987) hero, Karl Popper, is a strident *anti-instrumentalist*! (Popper 1962)). That is to say, "they "exist" only at an abstract level" (Sternthal et al. 1987, p. 115). Or as Sternthal (1987) recently put it, they are to be found in the "head of the researcher". This entails that, "Theories are best viewed as heuristics that are useful in explaining a phenomenon" (Sternthal et al. 1987, p. 120). Thus, "Instrumentalism views theories merely as calculating devices that generate useful predictions. . . " (Anderson 1982, p. 20). On this view, theory testing is a comparative process in which the superior theory is the one that explains (predicts) more findings with the same number of constructs as its rivals or requires fewer constructs to explain (predict) those findings.

The best known example of instrumentalism in the social sciences is mainstream neoclassical economics (Anderson 1982, 1986). The extremes of economic instrumentalism in consumer behavior can be found in the work of Becker (1965, 1976, 1981). The problem with instrumentalism is that it places no constraints on the "explanatory" concepts that may be postulated in a theory, and it (allegedly) admits of no other evaluative criteria than "prediction". As long as the theory "out-predicts" its rivals, the ontological status of the theory's concepts cannot be questioned. Indeed, in his seminal work on the topic, Friedman (1953) argues that no other criteria are relevant to a theory's veridicality just so long as it produces "confirmed" predictions. Thus, theorists such as Becker (1976) can assert that households attempt to maximize a "utility function" subject to the constraints of a "production function" and "full income" by solving a "Lagrangian equation". If these axioms produce accurate "predictions", the theory can be judged superior to competitor theories, because said competitors must invoke the "unnecessary" concept of "tastes" to explain the same phenomena. (It should be noted that "realism", often viewed as instrumentalism's polar opposite, is equally bankrupt (Laudan 1981, 1984a; Hardin and Rosenberg 1982; van Fraassen 1980; Fine 1986). As such, a position of "ontological agnosticism" is strongly recommended.)

While at an abstract level, the parallels between the instrumentalism of Sternthal et al. and Becker are striking, it may be objected that psychological instrumentalism does not engage in the kind of ontological excesses that one finds in economic theories of consumer behavior. However, on closer examination we may find that, as Wittgenstein (1953) would put it, we are "tricked" by the residuum of our own socialization. That is, we are all raised in a culture in which attitudes, values, beliefs, comprehension, memory, etc., are regularly attributed to ourselves and to others and are frequently invoked as causal determinants of behavior. These terms constitute the ontology of what has been called "folk psychology" (Stich 1983), and it should be clear that contemporary cognitive psychology has been built on the foundation of this ontology. Thus, when we are told by an instrumentalist that a household buys a product because its members "believe" that it will satisfy their needs, we are less likely to recognize the instrumental usage of this term because it is rooted in our everyday discourse. In fact, psychological instrumentalists trade on this tendency in order to give their theories a certain "plausibility". Indeed, in addition to the explicit criterion of "prediction", psychological instrumentalists often use the "shadow" criterion of intuitive plausibility to gain acceptance for their theories. Unfortunately, this plausibility can quickly evaporate under closer scrutiny.

An example may be found in the work of Tybout, Sternthal and Calder (1983) on multiple request effectiveness. While a full critique of this study is beyond the scope of the present paper, the essential points can be made with reference to their experiment III (pp. 286-87). The major objective of the article is to demonstrate that their "version" or "extension" of Tversky and Kahneman's (1973) availability theory is superior to the extant self-perception and bargaining-concession explanations (Tybout et al. 1983, p. 282).

It is important to note that the original "availability hypothesis" stated that, "A person is said to employ the availability heuristic whenever he estimates frequency or probability by the *ease* with which instances or associations could be brought to mind" (Tversky and Kahneman 1982, p. 164, emphasis added). However, Tybout et al. assert that, "Our version of the availability notion states that individual's decisions depend on the *favorableness* of the issue-relevant information *available in memory*" (1983, p. 282, emphasis added). Thus, Tybout et al. not only use a very different "availability" theory, but their approach seems to be a more rigorous conceptualization of availability. Tversky and Kahneman assert that judgements depend only on the ease with which instances can be generated, and they suggest that this may occur "without explicitly retrieving or constructing any instances at all" (1982, p. 166). As they note, Hart (1967) has shown that subjects can accurately assess their *ability* to remember items even when they cannot *recall* those items. However, Tybout et al. apparently require *information* to actually be accessed from memory, and they also require people to *make judgements on the valence of this information*. Moreover, all ten of Tversky and Kahneman's empirical studies supporting the availability heuristic required subjects to *consciously* access their "memories" (1973). The issue of "conscious access" becomes important because Hastie and Park (1986) [working firmly within the positivist paradigm] have recently argued that most judgment situations may actually be characterized by what Schatzki (1983) would call "unreflective action" (p. 132).

Based on their own empirical work and a review of more than 50 published studies on the memory-judgment relationship, Hastie and Park have proposed a distinction between "on-line" and "memory-based" judgment tasks. In their view, the Tversky/Kahneman availability model is the paradigmatic case of memory-based judgments. Here the subject's decision is assumed to result from the functioning of a mental "judgment operator" with input to the operator coming from long-term memory rather than directly from the external environment. However, they argue that the far more common judgment situation (both in laboratory and natural settings) may be characterized by their on-line model. Here "information for the operator follows a path from the stimulus environment external to the subject into working memory and directly to the judgment operator" (1986, p. 261). They argue further that "true memory-based judgments [i.e., judgments based on recall of issue-relevant information] may be rare because so many judgments are made on-line (spontaneously) and because when a new judgment must be made in the absence of perceptually available evidence, subjects rely on previous judgments rather than *remembered evidence*" (1986, p. 263), emphasis added).

Of course, it may be argued here that a subject's use of previous judgments is a memory-based process because on-line decisions require the individual to access judgment conclusions "stored in working memory" (Hastie and Park 1986, p. 260). However, if this is "in fact" the process model being employed it is clearly at odds with Tybout et al.'s (1983) "availability hypothesis" in which "critical request compliance is a *judgment* that depends on the favorableness of available *information*" in memory (p. 289, emphasis added).

The significance of the distinction between the on-line and memory-based models for memory-judgment correlations is that, in memory-based decision settings, a direct relationship among evidence, memorability and judgment is predicted on the basis of the availability hypothesis. However, if the judgment is made on-line, Hastie and Park (1986) suggest that any one of four process models may be instantiated: 1.) the two-memory independence hypothesis, 2.) retrieval bias, 3.) encoding bias, and 4.) incongruity-biased encoding.[10] The problem is, depending upon which process model is assumed to be operating, the prediction for the memory-judgment

relationship "can be either direct, indirect or null" (Hastie and Park 1986, p. 262). Thus, even if judgments are "actually" made on-line, the data from an experiment may well support a memory-based availability hypothesis. As Lynch and Srull (1982) have noted:

> For any set of data, it is possible to draw different inferences about the nature of the mental representation by changing one's assumptions about the processes operating on the stored knowledge base to produce the observed responses... Anderson (1978) maintained that the indeterminancy is so great that one can *never* draw inferences about memory representations from behavioral (i.e., nonphysiological) data, because *any* hypothesized representation can be reconciled with an observed response by making appropriate assumptions about the processes that operated... to produce the observed behavior. A less radical view... that we would endorse is that to draw inferences about memory structure from behavioral data, one must simultaneously consider both the memory representation and the processes that act upon it (p. 24, emphasis in original).

The implications of all this for the Tybout et al. (1983) "availability" studies should be clear. Not only have they altered the original theory so that it is no longer clear what version of the Tversky/Kahneman model they are testing; it is similarly unclear if the subjects in their various experiments are making on-line or memory-based judgments. Perhaps this is easiest to see in experiment III. Here subjects in two of the conditions were asked to participate in a 5 minute phone survey (the small request), and were then asked if they would participate in a 15 minute phone survey (the large request).[11] The results of the study supported the Tybout et al. version of availability theory. However, given the nature of the research setting (phone requests to participate in surveys) it is not obvious that subjects had any *information* in "memory" on which to base the second judgement. As Hastie and Park (1986) suggest, they may have been relying solely on their prior judgements "stored" in working memory. Thus, the Tybout et al. design raises the question of whether they were, in fact, testing an "availability" (memory-based) hypothesis. In other words, the lack of any process data concerning the correlation between "memory" and "judgment" makes it impossible to even begin to cull the list of competing models.

It must be quickly noted that I am in total agreement with Sternthal, Tybout and Calder's (1987) view that the use of manipulation checks, process

---

[10]For ease of exposition, I have purposely remained within the cognitive "paradigm" here. However, a case will also be developed for a Wittgensteinian explanation as well (Wittgenstein 1953).

---

[11]Subjects in the first condition did not perform the small request, whereas compliant subjects in the second condition did perform the small request.

measures, and repeated operationalizations is a contingent decision that depends upon the circumstances of each particular study. However, in light of their desire to rule out alternative hypotheses, it seems that their "availability" studies have come up short. Moreover, it is not clear whether the problem stems primarily from their failure to employ a particular set of methods, or from a failure to carefully specify the nature of the process and ontology entailed by their version of availability theory.

Indeed, this approach to theory testing tends to be characteristic of the instrumentalist world view. That is, instrumentalism often encourages a "hands-off" attitude towards research. As long as the theory predicts accurately, one need not be bothered greatly be the "details" of process. As we have seen, however, this lack of attention to process can raise serious questions about the validity of a study. Moreover, instrumentalism also plays fast and loose with a theory's ontology. The reluctance of Tybout et al. to clearly specify the meaning of their version of "availability" leaves them open to the sort of criticism emanating from the work of Hastie and Park (1986).

The bottom line here is that it is Sternthal, Tybout and Calder's (1987) version of psychological instrumentalism that may lead consumer research to the dire consequences that Calder and Tybout (1987) attribute to critical relativism. Ironically, the foregoing criticism of their availability research follows directly from critical relativism's chief demand:

> To know a theory's mode of production, the criteria by which it is judged, the ideological and value commitments that inform its construction,. . . the metaphysical beliefs that underwrite its research program, [and] most importantly, . . . [its] realizable cognitive and practical aims (Anderson 1986, p. 156).

This is why I have argued that critical relativists are actually more "hard-headed" in their evaluation of theory than their positivistic counterparts (Anderson 1986, p. 167). Indeed, it is through this example that we may find a hint of the methodological implications that will follow from critical relativism.

The relativist is not afraid to roll up his or her sleeves in order to dig into a study, theory, or research program in order to reveal the soft underbelly that may lie within. Moreover, the relativist realizes that theories have always been evaluated on multiple criteria (Laudan 1977, 1984b). To adopt comparative "predictive" power as the sole arbiter of theoretical disputes is to open the door to the kind of ontological flights of fancy that one observes in neoclassical economics. Finally, psychological instrumentalists will find little support in Laudan's (1977) comparative model of theory evaluation. On Laudan's view, when one is faced with the decision to accept or reject competitive theories that are all flawed along various dimensions, agnosticism is the appropriate position to adopt (1987). Indeed, I would argue that this is exactly the situation in which we find ourselves with

respect to the explanation of multiple request effectiveness. We must realize that in science it is no great sin to admit that, at the present time, we lack an adequate explanation for a phenomenon.

Thus, we can see in the Tybout et al. study and in the Sternthal et al. approach to theory testing some of the reasons why their "hyperbolic" form of positivism has been rejected by many researchers in social science. The instrumentalists' lack of concern for the details of process, their excessive emphasis on prediction, and their casual attitude toward the *meaning* of the key concepts mentioned in their theories has led "positivists" and interpretivists alike to turn away from this approach.

Of course, there are innumerable reasons for the existence of "interpretivism", but space limitations prevent a detailed explication of this enormously complicated issue. Instead, I should like to focus on a particular perspective that undergirds both realist and instrumentalist applications of cognitive psychology in consumer research. As Wittgenstein put it, this is the notion that psychology can treat constructs "in the psychical sphere, as does physics in the physical" (1953, p. 151).

## A WITTGENSTEINIAN APPROACH TO "MEMORY"

On the traditional view, psychological predicates (interpreted instrumentally or realistically) can be "operationalized" and can, in turn, be related causally to other mental constructs or behaviors. This so-called "billiard ball" model of social science is one of the main concerns that many interpretivists have with positivism. Under the influence of the later Wittgenstein, many reject this "picture" of the human sciences because it fails at the outset to understand the nature and meaning of mental constructs.

In his later work, Wittgenstein argued that we fail to treat psychological phenomena correctly because we tend to assimilate them all under the rubric of "mental processes". In contrast, Wittgenstein differentiated between two very different types of mental concepts: 1.) states of consciousness (or mental processes) and 2.) dispositions and abilities. The key distinction between them has to do with the "kind" of duration they display. The former have duration *that can be continuously monitored and reported upon.* Examples would include the sensations of pain or hearing. It is possible (i.e., it makes sense to say) that one's pain is growing more or less and that one has heard a sound for a certain period of time. In contrast, dispositions and abilities display a different type of duration. For one thing, they generally do not cease as the result of a good night's sleep or a redirection of one's attention. Examples include understanding, believing, intending, remembering, etc. Moreover, we typically do not constantly monitor dispositions or abilities. It makes no sense to ask someone: "Since you booked your flights has your intention to go abroad been continuous or has it been interrupted? Obviously, an "interruption" of one's intention would mean that one no longer intended.

Another critical concept in Wittgenstein's later philosophy is the notion of "criteria". A criterion for ascribing a mental predicate to an individual *is not empirical*. Rather "a criterion... defines or partially defines that for which it is a criterion" (Hacker 1986, p. 308). On this view, the criterion for ascribing "understanding" to someone is a public demonstration of said understanding. With purposeful "exaggeration for emphasis" (McGinn 1984), Wittgenstein warns us not to think of understanding as a mental construct that an individual holds privately in his or her mind. Instead, it is an *ability* that can only be shown by some type of action (e.g., speaking French, differentiating an equation, programming a computer etc.). Moreover, the criterion for understanding is the same for the individual as it is for others. Since one can be mistaken about one's ability to understand, say, spoken French, proper public demonstration is necessary even for oneself. This is because *part of the meaning* of "understanding spoken French" is the ability to do so.

## Memory

As with "understanding" Wittgenstein argues that it is also potentially misleading to think that "remembering" gets its meaning from a private mental process that takes place in our minds. On this view, remembering is also an ability that requires appropriate public demonstration. What Wittgenstein is trying to do is to get us to recognize that (like "understanding") no *one* thing counts as remembering and that the referent of "memory" is not a private mental experience.

This can be seen by carrying out a logico-grammatical analysis of the words "memory" and "remember". (Or, as he would put it, we must describe the "language games" played with these words.) This involves a "perspicuous description" of all the ways in which these words are used in ordinary language. (For Wittgenstein, the meaning of a word is given by its actual use.) His objective in all this is to show that, "Remembering has no experiential content" (Wittgenstein 1953, p. 231). Of course, he is not denying that we cannot call up images before the "mind's eye". Rather, he is denying that this "process" teaches us the correct *meaning* of the verb "to remember". This is something we learn only by socialization in a particular culture.

Consider, for example, the following possible uses of "remember" and "memory": 1.) You are asked for your name by a maitre d' and you give it to him/her straight off. What subjective experience accompanied your remembering your name? 2.) At lunch you are asked what you have been doing for the last three hours and you give the questioner a veridical report. Do detailed "pictures" of your activities "flash before your mind" as you recount your comings and goings during the morning? 3.) Upon request, you give a small electric shock to someone who has never experienced one so he can feel what it is like. Can you do the same thing in the case of memory experience?-- so the person can now say: "Yes, now I know what it is like to remember something" (Wittgenstein 1980, p. 24). As Wittgenstein has noted, we can certainly

teach the person the *use* of the words remember and memory, but if he then says:

> "Yes, now I have experienced what that is!"... If he were to say so, we should be astonished, and think "What can he have experienced?" For we experience nothing special (1980, p. 24).

What Wittgenstein is trying to do here is to disabuse us of the notion that we come to learn the *meaning* of remember and memory via private "inner" experiences. However, in the *Philosophical Investigations* his interlocutor protests that, "You surely cannot deny that, for example, in remembering an inner process takes place" (Wittgenstein 1953, p. 102). To this Wittgenstein replies:

> What gives the impression we want to deny anything? When one says "Still, an inner process does take place here"--one wants to go on: "After all, you *see* it". And it is this inner process that one means by the word "remembering" (1953, p. 102, emphasis in original).

He goes on to state that the belief that he wishes to deny a "fact" of everyday life arises because he is attacking a "truism" of folk psychology--that remembering is an inner mental process. Instead, what Wittgenstein actually wishes to deny "is that the picture of the inner gives us the correct idea of the *use* of the word to 'remember'" (1953, p. 102).

Of course, neurophysiology shows us that "memory" is "inner" in at least one sense. We know, for example, that if the hippocampus and temporal stem on each side of the brain is damaged, the ability to register memories will be lost. However, this is not the kind of inner process that Wittgenstein is concerned to deconstruct. The fact that the ability to remember depends on physiological processes has no bearing on the "misuse" of the term in psychological explanations. Wittgenstein is simply trying to point out that the "psychological" ascription criterion for memory is not an inner "experience" or "feeling" and that we do not learn the *use* of the word memory via inner ostensive definition.

## Implications for Positivism and Interpretivism

The Wittgensteinian perspective on memory is a two-sided coin. On the one hand, it is highly critical of cognitive psychology's conceptualization of the act of remembering and the functioning of memory. On the other hand, it offers a new perspective on these concepts that undergirds a number of interpretivist research programs. Perhaps the most damaging implication for positivistic psychology is Wittgenstein's acausalism. Note that for Wittgenstein the "criterion" for ascribing memory to an individual is proper public demonstration. Recall also that a criterion is not empirical in the sense that it can be cited as "evidence" for some unseen construct called memory. Instead, criteria are definitional. When a person engages in certain actions and activities (within a particular context), it may be said that he or she "remembered". Remembering is neither a unique phenomenological "experience" nor the actions I undertake when I have "remembered". Perhaps the easiest way to comprehend its criteriological status is to see it as a fusion of both (within the context of a person's *Lebensform*--translated as "form of life" and very roughly equivalent to one's culture and "natural history"). Of course, by this point many readers may assume that Wittgenstein is just a behaviorist. However, Wittgenstein explicitly denied this on numerous occasions (see, for example, Wittgenstein 1953, pp. 102-103), and most knowledgeable scholars of ordinary language philosophy agree that his program is radically distinct from behaviorism (especially the behaviorism of B.F. Skinner).

The implications of all this for the treatment of memory in cognitive psychology are straightforward. On a Wittgensteinian construal, there can be no question of invoking memory as a *cause* of behavior. (Except perhaps in the special sense of Malcolm's (1977) mnemic causation which instantiates no universal laws.) This is because a person's behavior supplies part of the meaning of the verb "to remember". Their relationship is criteriological (definitional) rather than causal. One's "remembering" cannot be thought of as a mental process temporally prior to behavior, since part of what it means to remember *is* "remembering behavior". (Note that even if "remembering" were solely an "inner mental process" (whatever that would mean), we would still be unable to say that a person remembered without behavioral criteria!) Hence, there is a codefinitional relationship between the two constructs. As Wittgenstein put it (in a slightly different context), "If this upsets our concepts of causality then it is high time they were upset" (1980, p. 160).

If, on Wittgenstein's view, we cannot treat the relationship between memory and behavior as causal, then *a fortiori* we are unable to link memory and other "mental constructs" in a causal fashion. Again, this is because we would lack any criterion to assert that something called "memory" was instantiated in the alleged causal train. For example, returning to the Tybout et al. (1983) experiment discussed earlier, differential behavioral effects are attributed to the fact that different types of information are "available" in the memories of the subjects in the different conditions. On this view, participants in the "request own behavior available" treatment would access the contents of their memories and find that "favorable information about their own behavior was no more available than unfavorable information about the request behavior" (Tybout et al. 1983, p. 287). In contrast, subjects in the "own behavior available" condition would find that "favorable information about their own behavior" was more available (Tybout et al. 1983, p. 287). Given these assumptions, differential behavioral responses were predicted and confirmed.

As noted above, the problem here is that we have no criterion by which to assert that "memory" was even involved in the observed effects. Treatments were applied and differential behaviors were

manifested, but there is nothing to show us that "memory" played a role in the outcomes. Indeed, even if we were to conceptualize memory purely as an "inner process"; given the short time that elapsed between the telephone request and the response--it is hard to believe that Tybout et al. envisioned their subjects engaging in a *conscious* "memory look-up". However, even a casual logico-grammatical analysis of the meaning of the verb "to remember" would reveal that what we call "remembering" is a conscious process. It simply makes no sense to say that I remembered something "unconsciously". (For Wittgenstein "grammar" defined the limits of what it makes sense to say.) Again, the ordinary-language meaning of memory instantiates a conscious process in which a person can display his or her ability to remember.

The Wittgensteinian perspective also raises problems for Hastie and Park's on-line model. Their approach assumes that information from the environment enters "working memory" and proceeds to a "judgement operator" which presumably issues a conclusion that results in some type of verbal or motor behavior. Moreover, "biased retrieval" can occur (when some time has passed since the original judgement) because previous judgements can act to "edit" any "traces" from the original information input stored in "long-term memory". On this view, judgement biases "access" to traces in long-term memory "such that traces that "fit" the judgement are likelier to be found in the memory search or to be reported at the memory decision stage" (Hastie and Park 1986, p. 260). While Hastie and Park's "computerese" model of judgement and memory can be found to be in accord with empirical data, we must recall Lynch and Srull's (1982) insightful recognition of the fact that a large number of process models will also be consistent with the body of literature in this field.

Of course, from a Wittgensteinian perspective, talk of "traces", "working memory", "judgement operators", "long-term memory", or "access" makes no sense since we lack *criteria* for these entities and processes. Moreover, from an ethnomethodological perspective (a branch of "interpretive" sociology that shares much with Wittgensteinian philosophy), such a model makes human beings out to be what Garfinkel, the founder of ethnomethodology, has called "judgemental dopes". In other words, both the Tybout et al. and Hastie and Park models portray human decision making as the inexorable consequence of computational processes that appear to be under minimal human control. In contrast, while both Wittgenstein and Garfinkel place great stress upon the "unreflective" nature of human behavior, both resist the extreme psychologizing found in Tybout et al. and Hastie and Park.

## THE ETHNOMETHODOLOGICAL PERSPECTIVE

While space limitations make it impossible to cash out a full-blown ethnomethodological approach to the multiple request phenomenon, it should be clear that ethnomethodology would display the same kind of incommensurability with cognitive psychology that Anderson (1986) demonstrated within positivistic approaches to consumer behavior, and Hudson and Ozanne (1988) illustrated between positivistic and interpretivist perspectives on emotion. While psychological approaches would stress prediction, operationalization of constructs, causal relationships, and an ontology consisting of complex yet unobservable mental processes; ethnomethodology would emphasize an understanding of how social actors maintain a "life-as-usual" stance by making reflective or unreflective choices in social interactions. Here, we can catch a fleeting glimpse of the different axiologies and ontologies of the two approaches. These in turn are reflections of the radically different philosophical world views of the two programs. Indeed, the important point to recognize here is that *both* perspectives rest on *some* foundation. While in each case practitioners (due perhaps to training and socialization in their respective programs) may not be fully aware of the philosophical undergirding of their research, the fact remains that there *are* reasons for alternative approaches to the study of human behavior that go beyond mere whim or personal preference. Moreover, it is on these grounds that the battle for the legitimacy of alternative research programs must be fought.

For example, while I am not a trained ethnomethodologist, we can, perhaps, speculate briefly on how ethnomethodology might approach the social process known as "multiple request effectiveness". One of the questions that ethnomethodology is concerned to investigate is: how do social actors sustain the "nothing-unusual-is-happening" and "life-as-usual" stance in social interaction? Thus, in a typical "greeting interaction", if the recipient of the initial greeting does not return or acknowledge the greeting, the life-as-usual social setting will have been "breached" (Heritage 1984). In other words, the

> initial greeter may accountably infer that "normal circumstances" do not obtain and that "something is up" which needs looking into. Where, for whatever reasons, actors wish to avoid [this outcome], they will engage in the "perceivedly normal"/ normatively provided for conduct (Heritage 1984, pp. 116-117).

We may speculate that one reason that an actor may wish to avoid the "something-is-up" interpretation is that s/he will generally find that his/her interests are served by "appropriate" behavior. Again, as Heritage (1984) has put it:

> It is the very reflexivity of the actors, *their awareness of the options* together with their anticipation of some of the interpretations to which their exercise of the options will give rise, which may ultimately keep them "on the rails" of perceivedly normal/normatively provided for conduct (p. 119, emphasis added).

On Heritage's (1984) view, three conditions must be met for "normal" social interaction to occur in this setting: 1.) social actors know the "greeting" norm, 2.) they are (at least on some occasions) capable of reflexive anticipation of the consequences of breaching the norm, and 3.) they attribute (1.) and (2.) to each other.

Garfinkel's ethnomethodology is purposely set in contraposition to the Parsonian notion that everyday social order is maintained by "internalized" norms that emerge from an actor's history of rewards and punishments. On this view, action is "caused" by these internalized rules or norms. While Garfinkel's approach does not deny "normative internalization... as an *empirical phenomena*" (Heritage 1984, p. 120), it does deny that such rules can determine the *specifics* of an individual's actions (see, also, Wittgenstein 1953).

More importantly, Garfinkel (1967) wishes to deny the model of the social actor as a rule-governed, psychological "judgmental dope" (p. 67). This means that, on Garfinkel's view, human beings are not automatons constantly under the control of a central nervous system (CNS) that has been either "programmed" or "hardwired" to function in a specific manner in all possible situations. Ethnomethodologists argue that (while much, if not most, of our behavior is "unreflective"), we are nevertheless, free to make choices in social settings (Emerson 1970). Thus, in the greeting example the recipient is free to purposefully ignore the greeting-- knowing full well that s/he will be held "normatively accountable" for his or her behavior by the other. However, as noted earlier, social actors "will routinely find that their interests are well served by normatively appropriate conduct" (Heritage 1984, p. 117). Thus, while both Parsons and Garfinkel are interested in explicating the manner in which everyday, routine, institutionalized expectations are carried out, it can be seen that they approach the problem with radically different research programs.

**Ethnomethodology and Multiple Requests**

Returning to the multiple request phenomenon, we might speculate, for illustrative purposes, on ethnomethodology's approach to this process. For simplicity of exposition, we will continue with Tybout et al.'s (1983) experiment number three. It will be recalled that this is a "foot-in the-door" study in which respondents were contacted by phone and asked to participate in surveys. Based on the results, it is clear that it is something about *actually performing* the small request that leads subjects in this "treatment" to be more compliant than "subjects" in the other two groups. We have already reviewed Tybout et al.'s "availability hypothesis" explanation for this result. It can now be seen that this is a species of what I have called a "hardwiring" explanation in that a subject's mind is expected to retrieve information from memory and make judgements on its valence. Moreover, this *appears* to require a *conscious* "memory look-up" on the part of the individual. However, as noted previously, given the nature of the social interaction in this experiment, it is not clear that subjects had the time to consciously carry out *this* complex cognitive process. Thus, it appears that Tybout et al.'s proposed process may actually be some version of a "non-conscious" on-line model (Hastie and Park 1986).

If this is the case (as it appears to be for Hastie and Park), then we are working with a model of human beings who are hardwired psychological "judgmental dopes". That is, when faced with a judgement to comply with a large request, the subject's CNS automatically "kicks in" and assesses the relative favorability of information in "memory" and issues a command to produce one type of verbal response or another.

However, from an ethnomethodologist's perspective, any type of psychological on-line model line model ignores the fact that social interaction *is social*. Thus, it fails to comprehend that social norms are "doubly constitutive" (Heritage 1984, p. 108). That is, norms serve to maintain the normality of the situation, but they also provide the standard by which breaches are recognized, interpreted, and sanctioned *as breaches* (Garfinkel 1967). Moreover, while norms are usually "seen but unnoticed... [they are] nevertheless constitutive" in that their observance or their breach will determine the very nature of the actors' perceptions of the social situation (Heritage 1984, p. 110).

### Seen But Unnoticed

The "seen but unnoticed" (Garfinkel 1967, p. 36) quality of norms is a crucial aspect of ethnomethodology's *Weltanschauung*. While the view that norms are constitutive of social settings seems to vitiate their traditional role in sociology as regulative principles, the "constraining" function of such norms is recaptured precisely because ethnomethodology recognizes that actors have a *choice* in the matter. Thus, most social interaction proceeds smoothly because actors *unreflectively* follow the "appropriate" norms. However, this is not done because actors have "internalized" the norm in a psychological sense, nor does it result from the functioning of an "atonomous" central nervous system. On ethnomethodology's view, actors always have the choice of breaching the norms and facing the consequences of being normatively accountable to others. While this latter factor probably creates the excruciating normality of everyday life, the cause of this mundane normalcy often goes unnoticed except in the breach.

### Waiting for Godot

This can be seen in Garfinkel's (1967) famous breaching experiments. In one study Garfinkel (1963) had an experimenter and a subject play a game of ticktacktoe. The experimenter allowed the subject to go first, whereupon the experimenter erased the S's mark, moved it to another box and made his own mark without giving any hint that what he was doing was out of the ordinary. In 253 trials 75% of the Ss objected to the move or demanded some type of explanation. Many of these Ss were visibly disturbed by the incident. In contrast, subjects who either assumed that a new game was in progress or that the experimenter was playing a practical joke showed little disturbance.

A number of implications follow from this (and other) breaching experiments. First, it shows that mundane social "reality" can fall to pieces when "seen but unnoticed" norms are not followed. As a corollary it may also be observed that the maintenance of social interaction requires what ethnomethodologists often refer to as interpretive "work" in order to sustain social interaction. That is to say, actors must adhere to "perceivedly normal/normatively provided for conduct" (Heritage 1984, p. 119) so that they can get on with their everyday mundane affairs. Second, breaching studies also demonstrate that everyday actors are largely unaware that they are structuring "social reality" through their adherence to "seen but unnoticed" norms. Third, the experiments illustrate the fact that breaches tend to motivate actors to resolve (or normalize) the resultant social anomaly. Finally, it is clear that actors who tried to "normalize" the situation while attempting to maintain the notion that a "standard" game of ticktacktoe was still in process showed the greatest amount of disturbance. In contrast, subjects who gave up ticktacktoe as an interpretive "grid" for understanding the social setting found the experiment far less disturbing.

Other examples can be found in the study of humor, since much of what we find humorous involves normative breaches. This can be seen, for example, in the dialogue and stage directions that close Act I of Beckett's *Waiting for Godot*:

> Vladimir: We can still part, if you think it would be better.
> Estragon: It's not worth while now.
> *Silence*
> Vladimir: No, it's not worth while now.
> *Silence*
> Estragon: Well, shall we go?
> Vladimir: Yes, let's go.
> *They do not move*
>
> *Curtain*

Clearly, the humor here derives from the fact that Gogo and Didi agree on a normative course of action which they leave unfulfilled. Collins (1985) has noted a similar example from a somewhat less literary source:

> A few years ago a sketch on television's *Monty Python's Flying Circus* featured a misleading Hungarian phrasebook. "Can I have a box of matches?" was mistranslated into English along the lines of "I would like to feel your beautiful thighs." The appropriate rebuff in English was mistranslated into Hungarian as "Your eyes are like liquid pools." The phrasebook turned what should have been a routine exchange between a large Hungarian and a meek tobacconist into a violent brawl. The phrasebook introduced disorder into what the participants expected to be a routine orderly interaction (p. 5).

## And Now for Something Completely Different

The foregoing should make it clear that social "reality" is maintained and sustained by a largely "seen but unnoticed" adherence to certain norms and practices; however, the question remains: can ethnomethodology be used as an alternative grid to interpret the multiple request phenomenon? While it is likely that different ethnomethodologists would approach this "problem" in different ways, perhaps some informed speculation can give us a hint of how a radically different (interpretivist) program might deal with this issue.

Let us assume, for the sake of argument, that the following "norm" (N1) is loosely and contingently observed by social actors: "in order to be perceived as "helpful", try not to disappoint other actors by refusing "reasonable" requests." How might this be played out in the context of multiple request interaction? In the case of the foot-in-the-door phenomenon, N1 obviously sustains compliance with "reasonable" requests made by strangers. Moreover, having invested some effort that demonstrates to the other that one is helpful, the "subject" would be aware that a refusal to comply with the large request would disappoint the other, and could give the impression that one is not, in fact, helpful. Indeed, this may be made more salient because the subject has already demonstrated his/her helpfulness in a "publicly observable" fashion.

Turning now to the door-in-the-face interaction, N1 implies non-compliance with "unreasonable" requests made by strangers in that non-compliance does not violate the norm. However, N1 *does* sustain compliance with the small request in that it avoids disappointing the other actor and, at the same time, demonstrates that one is indeed helpful.

It must be quickly added that this is not meant to be a full-blown alternative theory of multiple request effectiveness. (Indeed, it is not clear that ethnomethodologists would even wish to "explain" any *particular* social phenomenon like multiple requests. As Garfinkel (1967) has noted, their interests tend to lie elsewhere.) Thus, the purpose of an ethnomethodological approach to this issue is, at this stage, purely expository. A full fledged theoretical assault on the question would require careful explication, extensive pretesting, and *empirical* testing.

In this regard, it might be noted, almost parenthetically, that one of the advantages of the "ethnomethodological" approach is that it would be much easier to obtain process data via verbal protocols. Unfortunately, the same can not be said of "non-conscious on-line models" in which the CNS is assumed to function in an autonomous or semi-autonomous fashion. Of course, as noted earlier, the ethnomethodological perspective does not assume that individuals consciously follow norms as if they were strict rules of conduct. In this post-Wittgensteinian age it is no longer possible to assert that human behavior is "rule following behavior" (Wittgenstein 1953). However, the ethnomethodological approach at least holds out the hope that depth interviews, debriefings, projective techniques, etc. can be used to test the assumed "process model". Unfortunately, not only are these techniques discouraged by "psychological instrumentalists", but they would be useless if the posited process is that of autonomous CNS functioning.

Of course, it could always be argued that the instantiation of N1 amounts to nothing more than ex post theorizing. However, on this basis, it is no different than the postulation of an "availability" explanation. Moreover, the ethnomethodological perspective does not emerge *ex nihilo*. It is built upon the conceptual foundations laid down by Schutz's "phenomenological sociology" and Garfinkel's successful attempts at empirically validating the phenomenological program.

Finally, following Anderson (1986) and Hudson and Ozanne (1988), it is important to point out that the "psychological" and ethnomethodological approaches to this phenomenon are largely incommensurable. The axiological, methodological, conceptual, metaphysical, ontological, and ideological/value commitments of the two programs are so different as to render them noncomparable. While it can be seen that both perspectives "cover" or "save" multiple requests, it should also be clear that they do so by completely redefining the subject matter of the problem. Thus, the *"interpretive"* ethnomethodological approach is no more (and no less) "the application of a given conceptualization, or way of viewing" (Calder and Tybout 1987, p. 138) the problem than is psychological instrumentalism. Moreover, given the empirical and experimental foundation of ethnomethodology (Garfinkel 1967), it cannot be said that the field attempts to "escape from data" or fails to compare interpretations "in order to *choose* among them" (Calder and Tybout 1987, p. 139).

In the final analysis, however, it is the different (metaphysical) conceptions of man that lay at the heart of the distinctions between ethnomethodology and psychological instrumentalism. For the latter, man is often a judgmental dope whose verbal and motor behavior result from the operation of an autonomous central nervous system. On the other hand, while ethnomethodologists see man performing his mundane everyday activities in a largely unreflective fashion, there is always the possibility of choice. On this view, man can always breach the norms of a particular scene with the full knowledge of the interpretive consequences. When we do consumer research, choosing between these two models of "others" is often a matter of training and analytical convenience. But perhaps the question we should be asking is: which model would we like to have applied to ourselves?

## REFERENCES

Anderson, Paul F. (1982), "Marketing, Strategic Planning and the Theory of the Firm," *Journal of Marketing*, 46 (Spring), 15-26.

_____ (1983), "Marketing, Scientific Progress and Scientific Method," *Journal of Marketing*, 47 (Fall), 18-31.

_____ (1986), "On Method in Consumer Research: A Critical Relativist Perspective," *Journal of Consumer Research*, 13 (September), 155-173.

Bahcall, John N. (1987), "Solar Neutrinos," presentation at the Massachusetts Institute of Technology, March 10, 1987.

_____, A. Dar and T. Piran (1987), "Neutrinos From the recent LMC Supernova," *Nature*, 326 (March 12, 1987), 135-136.

Becker, Gary S. (1965), "A Theory of the Allocation of Time," *The Economic Journal*, 75, 493-517.

_____ (1976), *The Economic Approach to Human Behavior*, Chicago: University of Chicago Press.

_____ (1981), *A Treatise on the Family*, Cambridge, MA: Harvard University Press.

Calder, Bobby J., Lynn W. Phillips and Alice M. Tybout (1981), "Designing Research for Applications," *Journal of Consumer Research*, 8 (September), 197-207.

_____ and Alice M. Tybout (1987), "What Consumer Research Is ... ," *Journal of Consumer Research*, 14 (June), 136-140.

Chalmers, Alan F. (1982), *What Is This Thing Called Science?* 2nd ed., St. Lucia, Australia: University of Queensland Press.

Collins, H. M. (1975), "The Seven Sexes: A Study in the Sociology of a Phenomenon, or the Replication of Experiments in Physics," *Sociology*, 9, 205-224.

_____ (1981), "Son of Seven Sexes: The Social Destruction of a Physical Phenomenon," *Social Studies of Science*, 11, 33-62.

_____ (1985), *Changing Order*, London: Sage.

_____ and T. J. Pinch (1979), "The Construction of the Paranormal: Nothing Unscientific is Happening," in Roy Wallis ed., *On The Margins of Science: The Social Construction of Rejected Knowledge*, Keele, U.K.: University of Keele.

_____ and T. J. Pinch (1982), *Frames of Meaning*, London: Routledge & Kegan Paul.

Duhem, Pierre (1906), *La Théorie Physique, Son Object et sa Structure*, Paris: Chevalier et Riviere.

_____ (1954), *The Aim and Structure of Physical Theory*, New York: Atheneum.

Emerson, J. P. (1970), "Nothing Unusual is Happening", in *Human Nature and Collective Behavior*, ed. T. Shibutani, Englewood Cliffs, NJ: Prentice-Hall, 208-222.

Fine, Arthur (1986), *The Shaky Game*, Chicago: University of Chicago Press.

Friedman, Milton (1953), "The Methodology of Positive Economics," in *Essays in Positive Economics*, Chicago: University of Chicago Press.

Garfinkel, Harold (1963), "A Conception of, and Experiments with "Trust" as a Condition of Stable Concerted Actions", in *Motivation and Social Interaction*, ed. O.J. Harvey, New York: Ronald Press, 187-238.

_____ (1967), *Studies in Ethnomethodology*, Englewood Cliffs, NJ: Prentice-Hall.

Gier, Nicholas F. (1981), *Wittgenstein and Phenomenology*, Albany, NY: SUNY Press.

Gieryn, Thomas F. (1987), "Science and Coca-Cola," *Science and Technology Studies*, 5 (Spring), 12-21.

Gilbert, Nigel and Michael Mulkay (1984), *Opening Pandora's Box*, Cambridge, U.K.: Cambridge University Press.

Hacker, P.M.S. (1986), *Insight and Illusion*, Oxford, UK: Clarendon Press.

Hardin, Clyde and Alexander Rosenberg (1982), "In Defense of Convergent Realism," *Philosophy of Science*, 49 (December), 604-615.

Hart, J. T. (1967), "Memory and the Memory-Monitoring Process," *Journal of Verbal Learning and Verbal Behavior*, 6, 685-691.

Hastie, Reid and Bernadette Park (1986), "The Relationship Between Memory and Judgement Depends on Whether the Judgement Task is Memory-Based or On-Line," *Psychological Review*, 93, 258-268.

Heritage, John (1984), *Garfinkel and Ethnomethodology*, Cambridge, MA: Polity Press.

Hirschman, Elizabeth C. (1986), "Humanistic Inquiry in Marketing Research: Philosophy, Method and Criteria," *Journal of Marketing Research*, (August), 237-249.

Hudson, Laurel Anderson and Julie L. Ozanne (1988), "Alternative Ways of Seeking Knowledge in Consumer Research," *Journal of Consumer Research*, 14 (March), 508-521.

Hunt, Shelby D. (1984), "Should Marketing Adopt Relativism?" in *Scientific Method in Marketing*, eds. Paul F. Anderson and Michael J. Ryan, Chicago: American Marketing Association, 30-34.

Knorr-Cetina, Karin D. (1981), *The Manufacture of Knowledge*, Oxford, U.K.: Pergamon.

Lakatos, Imre (1970), "Falsification and the Methodology of Scientific Research Programs," in *Criticism and The Growth of Knowledge*, eds. Imre Lakatos and Alan Musgrave, Cambridge, U.K.: Cambridge University Press, 91-195.

_____ (1971), "Replies to Critics," in Roger C. Buck and Robert S. Cohen eds., *Boston Studies in the Philosophy of Science*, Dordrecht: D. Reidel, 1974-182.

_____ (1978), "History of Science and its Rational Reconstructions," in John Worral and Gregory Currie eds., *The Methodology of Scientific Research Programs*, Cambridge, U.K.: Cambridge University Press, 102-138.

Latour, Bruno (1987), *Science in Action*, Cambridge, MA: Harvard University Press.

_____ and Steve Woolgar (1979), *Laboratory Life*, Beverly Hills, CA: Sage.

Laudan, Larry (1977), *Progress and Its Problems*, Berkeley, CA: University of California Press.
_____ (1980), "Views of Progress: Separating the Pilgrims from the Rakes," *Philosophy of the Social Sciences*, 10, 273-286.
_____ (1981), "A Confutation of Convergent Realism," *Philosophy of Science*, 48 (March), 19-49.
_____ (1983a), "The Demise of the Demarcation Problem," in R. S. Cohen and L. Laudan eds., *Physics, Philosophy and Psychoanalysis*, Boston: D. Reidel, 111-127.
_____ (1983b), "The Demise of the Demarcation Problem," in *The Demarcation Between Science and Pseudo-Science*, Vol. 2, ed. Rachael Laudan, Blacksburg, VA: Center for the Study of Science in Society, Virginia Polytechnic Institute.
_____ (1984a), "Realism Without the Real," *Philosophy of Science*, 51 (March), 156-162.
_____ (1984b), *Science and Values*, Berkeley, CA: University of California Press.
_____ (1987), Personal communication September 3, 1987.
Law, John and R. J. Williams (1982), "Putting Facts Together: A Study of Scientific Persuasion," *Social Studies of Science*, 12, 535-558.
Lynch, John G., Jr. and Thomas K. Srull (1982), "Memory and Attentional Factors in Consumer Choice: Concepts and Research Methods," *Journal of Consumer Research*, 9 (June), 18-37.
Malcolm, Norman (1977), *Memory and Mind*, Ithaca, NY: Cornell University Press.
McGinn, Colin (1984), *Wittgenstein on Meaning*, Oxford, UK: Basil Blackwell.
Pinch, T. J. (1980), "Theoreticians and the Production of Experimental Anomaly: The Case of Solar Neutrinos," in *The Social Process of Scientific Investigation*, eds. Karin D. Knorr, Roger Krohn and Richard Whitley, Dordrecht: D. Reidel, 77-106.
_____ (1982), *The Development of Solar-Neutrino Astronomy*, unpublished Ph.D. dissertation, Bath, U.K.: University of Bath.
_____ (1986), *Confronting Nature*, Boston: Dordrecht.
_____ (1987), Personal communication March 11, 1987.
Pickering, Andrew (1981), "The Hunting of the Quark," *Isis*, 72 (June), 216-236.
_____ (1984), *Constructing Quarks*, Chicago: University of Chicago Press.
Popper, Karl (1957), *The Poverty of Historicism*, New York: Harper Torchbooks.
_____ (1959), *The Logic of Scientific Discovery*, New York: Harper Torchbooks.
_____ (1962), *Conjectures and Refutations*, New York: Harper & Row.
Rorty, Richard (1979), *Philosophy and the Mirror of Nature*, Princeton, NJ: Princeton University Press.

Schatzki, Theodore R. (1983), "The Prescription is Description: Wittgenstein's View of the Human Sciences," in Sollace Mitchell and Michael Rosen eds., *The Need for Interpretation*, London: Athlone Press, 118-177.
Sherry, John F. Jr. (1983), "Gift Giving in Anthropological Perspective," *Journal of Consumer Research*, 10 (September), 157-168.
_____ (1987a), "Keeping the Monkeys Away From the Typewriters: An Anthropologist's" View of the Consumer Behavior Odyssey," in Melanie Wallendorf and Paul Anderson eds., *Advances in Consumer Research*, 14, Provo, UT: Association for Consumer Research, 370-373.
_____ (1987b), "Heresy and the Useful Miracle: Rethinking Anthropology's Contributions to Marketing," in Jagdish Sheth ed., *Research in Marketing*, 9 Greenwich, CT: JAI Press, 285-306.
Sternthal, Brian (1987), "Analytical Science," presentation at the 1987 American Marketing Association Doctoral Consortium, New York University, August 1, 1987.
_____, Alice M. Tybout and Bobby J. Calder (1987), "Confirmatory Versus Comparative Approaches to Judging Theory Tests," *Journal of Consumer Research*, 14 (June), 114-125.
Stich, Stephen P. (1983), *From Folk Psychology to Cognitive Science*, Cambridge, MA: MIT Press.
Tversky, Amos and Daniel Kahneman (1973), "Availability: A Heuristic for Judging Frequency and Probability," *Cognitive Psychology*, 5, 207-232.
_____ (1982), "Availability: A Heuristic for Judging Frequency and Probability," in Daniel Kahneman, Paul Slovic and Amos Tversky eds., *Judgement Under Uncertainty: Heuristics and Biases*, Cambridge, U.K.: Cambridge University Press, 163-178.
Tybout, Alice M., Brian Sternthal and Bobby J. Calder (1983), "Information Availability as a Determinant of Multiple Request Effectiveness," *Journal of Marketing Research*, 20 (August), 280-290.
van Fraassen, Bas C. (1980), *The Scientific Image*, Oxford, U.K.: Claredon.
Wittgenstein, Ludwig (1953), *Philosophical Investigations*, Oxford, U.K.: Basil Blackwell.
_____ (1980), *Remarks of the Philosophy of Psychology*, Chicago: University of Chicago Press.

# The Relativistic/Constructionist Perspective on Scientific Knowledge and Consumer Research

J. Paul Peter, University of Wisconsin
Jerry C. Olson, Penn State University

In a recent article Calder and Tybout (1987) promoted their conceptions of scientific method, philosophy of science, and the nature of scientific knowledge. According to them, there are three types of knowledge, each with its own methodology or philosophy of science. Everyday knowledge implies qualitative methodology; scientific knowledge implies sophisticated methodological falsificationist methodology; interpretive knowledge implies critical relativistic methodology.

Any attempt to label some research as "science" or "scientific knowledge" and to withhold this label from other research needs careful scrutiny. This is because in Western cultures such labels have special meaning and are highly honorific; approaches to knowledge that are not scientific are commonly denigrated in our culture.

The purpose of this paper is to critique the Calder and Tybout position. First, we review arguments that led to the demise of falsification as a viable philosophy of science as well as our own reasons for eschewing that approach. We do not exclude falsification studies from science, however, we reject falsification as a general philosophy of science and as the only approach that produces scientific knowledge. Second, we demonstrate that Calder and Tybout have misconstrued our relativistic/constructionist approach leading to improper inferences about what it has to say about the nature of science. In the final section, we discuss several implication of our R/C perspective for consumer research.

## WHAT'S WRONG WITH CALDER AND TYBOUT'S PERSPECTIVE?

Calder and Tybout offer two criteria that are designed to distinguish scientific knowledge from other types. Their criteria are (1) there are empirical attempts to refute the theory, and (2) the theory has performed better than available competitors. They argue that the tenets of sophisticated methodological falsification (Lakatos 1970; Leong 1985) provides the only methodology for scientific knowledge. Other forms of knowledge have different objectives, require their own methodologies, and do not produce scientific knowledge.

There are at least two major reasons why the conception of science sketched by them is unacceptable. We discuss them below in terms of the demarcation problem and problems with falsification. While they have been discussed previously in the consumer research literature, they bear repeating since they apparently have been ignored.

### The Demarcation Problem

Professional philosophers of science have been unable to construct criteria by which science could be demarcated from non-science. A review of the history of debates over demarcation criteria reveal that they are typically used in polemical battles between rival camps, such as Popper's attempts to discredit Marx and Freud (see Laudan 1983).

It seems clear that Calder and Tybout are using a ploy similar to that of Popper. As practitioners and advocates for laboratory experimentation in the social psychology tradition, they have singled out their preferred approach as scientific and categorized qualitative and interpretive research as something less than science. However, the Calder and Tybout criteria fail to demarcate scientific knowledge from other forms on several grounds.

First, by excluding from science any theory that has not been empirically tested by researchers with falsification motivations, Calder and Tybout have eliminated almost all of what philosophers of science and practicing researchers would consider science. For example, in physics, the work of Newton and Einstein would be classified as non-science since they were not concerned with falsifying their own theories but instead, championed them strongly. Most people recognize them as two of the greatest scientists in history.

In consumer research there are also many other types of work that would be eliminated from science if Calder and Tybout's criteria were accepted. For example, attempts to construct general models of consumer behavior, such as the work of Howard and Sheth, would be considered non-scientific activity. In fact, all attempts to create theories that do not involve empirical falsification activities would be considered non-scientific. Similarly, attempts to construct mathematical models to fit data would be eliminated under the Calder and Tybout constraints.

Second, few social science researchers seriously attempt to falsify theories. Rather, in most cases, they attempt to falsify the null hypothesis in order to support their favored hypothesis or they attempt to falsify someone else's theory in order to support their own or one that they champion. Greenwald et. al.(1986) have discussed at length the strong confirmation bias in social science and have pointed out that publication practices overwhelmingly favor supportive results. In fact, Greenwald et. al. argue that researchers who do not obtain supportive results are unlikely to even try to publish the work. In many cases, then, there is little chance that a "falsifying" result will be widely disseminated in a field and become part of scientific knowledge.

Third, we note that the Calder and Tybout criteria are not specified precisely enough to be applied. How many attempts to refute a theory must be made to conclude that a theory is falsified? In comparative "tests" of alternative theories, how much better must the empirical results be before the winner is identified? Who decides what constitutes a valid falsification test? What is to be concluded when some comparative results support one theory and some support the other?

In sum, we concur with Laudan (1983) that "For these and a host of other reasons familiar in the philosophical literature, neither verificationism nor falsificationism offers much promise of drawing useful distinctions between the scientific and the non-scientific" (p. 26). Without this demarcation, Calder and Tybout's judgement of their own approach as scientific and the other approaches as non-scientific is fully discredited. We now turn to the second problem with their perspective, the technical inadequacies of sophisticated methodological falsification.

## Problems with Falsification

It should be clear that falsification in all of its forms has been rejected as an adequate philosophy of science. Although there are a variety of problems with the approach, there is one of central importance to this discussion. Namely, that while Calder and Tybout recognize the error of asserting that theories can be shown to be true, they apparently accept the idea that theories can be falsified empirically. However, Duhem (1953), Laudan (1983) and others have explained why it is impossible to do so. In addition, falsification does not give a good account of the history of science.

## What Theory Do Data "Test"?

A central problem with the concept of falsification is that much more is involved in an empirical study than simply the substantive hypotheses under investigation. There are a whole set of assumptions about initial conditions, auxillary hypotheses, and the validity of measuring instruments, sampling, and data analysis procedures. No study can totally unravel these and "test" only the substantive hypothesis of interest. Thus, any attempt to conclude that a theory has been refuted can easily be deflected by suggesting that something else in the maze of assumptions and premises caused the "falsifying" result (Laudan 1977; Anderson 1983).

In addition, imaginative researchers can make ad hoc modifications to a theory to dispute inconsistent results or argue that any unsupportive results demonstrate certain boundary conditions to the theory's applicability, but do not refute the theory. Finally, they may produce another set of empirical results that again supports their favored theory and attempt to persuade the research community that their theory remains valid.

In sum, theories can not be falsified by empirical data alone. Thus, it is not surprising that we know of no instances in our field (or others) where advocates for a theory simply gave up and accepted that their theory was totally incorrect because someone produced empirical results inconsistent with the theory. In fact, Mitroff (1973) found in his research on the NASA moon scientists that the most

respected scientists believed strongly in their theories and ignored data that did not support them.

## What Does History Show About Falsification?

Falsification has long been rejected as providing an adequate account of the history of science. This is because there are many examples of well-accepted theories for which there is abundant empirical evidence that they are incorrect (see Anderson 1983).

In consumer research, it is clear that many theories survive and prosper despite a lack of empirical support. Familiar examples include need theory, personality theory, and theories of the attitude-behavior relationship. In addition, given the weak statistical criteria used to judge the adequacy of empirical results and the failure to reject theories with little supporting empirical evidence, it appears that falsification does not provide an adequate account of consumer research.

In sum, the only reasonable conclusion is that falsification does not provide a good description of how science is performed. Apparently, it is also not a good normative model since the greatest scientists in history did not follow falsification tenets.

# WHAT IS THE RELATIVISTIC/CONSTRUCTIONIST PERSPECTIVE?

Calder and Tybout have misconstrued our R/C perspective leading to inappropriate conclusions and implications about what relativism has to say about science. We will discuss Calder and Tybout's misconceptions in terms of the fallability, concensus, and methodology arguments.

## The Fallability Argument

Calder and Tybout assert that

Both Anderson (1983; 1986) and Peter and Olson (1983) have argued that what is called scientific knowledge is the product of relativistic methodology. Basically they contend that because falsification depends on data and concensus about data, which may be fallible, this methodology is untenable (p. 138).

This statement in no way represents our view, and we are puzzled that anyone could interpret our writings in this way. There are at least two problems with the Calder and Tybout reconstruction of our position.

First, our major concerns with falsification are described earlier in this paper; the issue of the "fallibility of data" is not part of these arguments. Strictly speaking, in fact, to assert that data "may be fallible" suggests the possibility of perfect data that is not fallible. Such a view is inconsistent with relativism.

Second, we note that Calder and Tybout's concern with "fallibility" suggests their positivistic assumptions about the possibility of ultimate criteria and objective standards for judging the truth or falsity of data and/or consensus about data. However, from our R/C perspective, consensus involves subjective decisions by a group of scientists to accept a theory and its support or not to do so; whether the concensus is true or not is a non-question from our perspective.

### The Consensus Argument

Calder and Tybout assert that

> We believe that relativism retreats unnecessarily to the position that scientific knowledge is based not on empirical testing but on social agreement. The observation that concensus about data *may* be erroneous does not imply that it is preferable to avoid the use of data and instead rely on consensus per se. We need not give up the primacy of empirical data in confronting theory and relegate scientists to theory peddlers (p. 138).

Calder and Tybout are in error in arguing that relativists eschew empirical data and empirical research. Relativists do not believe that data are worthless and should not be constructed. However, researchers with an R/C perspective do view empirical data differently than do positivistic falsificationists. For example, in line with modern philosophical positions, relativists recognize that data are theory-laden. In other words, data are created and interpreted by scientists in terms of a variety of theories and theoretical perspectives. It is impossible to collect data that are "theory neutral", since at least some implicit theory is needed to create measures and attach a meaning to them.

Relativists accept empirical data as an important part of science and recognize that empirical results can play an important role in generating social consensus about theories. However, it should be clear that relativistic researchers are much less impressed with empirical data and its role in science than are Calder and Tybout. Part of this skepticism occurs because we know that well-trained researchers can construct empirical data and results to support or refute almost any theory without violating "accepted standards" of research in a field. In fact, we have pointed out that the creation of empirical data and empirical results is a process that is controlled by the researcher (Olson, 1987; Peter, 1984). For example, if an initial laboratory experiment does not produce desired effects, a researcher can continue to do "pilot" studies (in the name of "pretesting" or "calibrating measures") modifying the manipulations and methods until the desired results are created. Given this view of data, it should be no wonder that we are more conservative in our evaluations of empirical results than are researchers who purport to be falsificationists.

### The Methodology Argument

A final error made by Calder and Tybout was to categorize relativism as a research methodology. The relativistic/constructionist perspective is not a methodology. Rather, it is a set of metatheoretical presuppositions about the nature of reality and human capabilities for creating knowledge which, taken collectively, constitute a general philosophy of science. We believe that our perspective has a number of important implications for scientific practice, but it is not a methodology.

We suspect that Calder and Tybout characterize relativism as a methodology to avoid having to deal with the serious philosophical criticisms it levels at their preferred approach. The point of their paper is that relativism may be OK for non-scientific interpretivists, but has no relevance or value for scientists whose only valid approach is sophisticated methodological falsification. By characterizing relativism as a second-class methodology that does not produce scientific knowledge, Calder and Tybout try to dismiss it and the criticisms it has of their preferred approach.

### Implications of the R/C Perspective for Consumer Research

To this point we have demonstrated that the Calder and Tybout conception of science is untenable and that they have misconstrued our R/C perspective. In this final section we offer several implications of our perspective for practicing consumer researchers. These include methodological pluralism, evaluative pluralism, and cognitive and behavioral changes in research practices.

### Methodological Pluralism

From an R/C perspective, no single approach (such as sophisticated methodological falsification) can be universally applied to guarantee scientific knowledge. Rather, the relativist recognizes many approaches to creating scientific knowledge, including qualitative, quantitative, and interpretive approaches and that no single method is always better than the others for constructing scientific knowledge. Every method can be useful, can provide convincing evidence, and can create meaningful scientific knowledge in particular situations and contexts. Every method, including falsification, entails construction and interpretation by scientists. Restricting consumer research to a single method like falsification is likely to stifle the creativity of researchers in the field since it encourages them to discard any ideas they have for which they cannot readily design a "falsification experiment." For example, we find no reason to view Holbrook and Grayson's (1986) work as something less than science nor do we believe that a falsification experiment would have been appropriate for their purposes. Thus, we believe consumer researchers should welcome and respect research of many types, including qualitative and interpretive work, and not prejudge these as less scientific than traditional empirical studies.

### Evaluative Pluralism

From our R/C perspective, no single criterion or set of criteria can be universally applied to judge theories, research results, or scientific knowledge. However, this position does not mean that R/C researchers have no standards for judging scientific knowledge.

In previous work we have subsumed a number of criteria under the general category of "usefulness." Usefulness is a relative concept. It involves many types of subjective evaluations by scientists that are contingent on or relative to a host of factors. Scientists may judge a theory to be useful for many reasons including (1) it describes the workings of a phenomenon in a way consistent with prior beliefs and/or behaviors; (2) it makes them feel that they better understand a phenomena; (3) it makes predictions, novel or otherwise, that are supported by empirical data; (4) it offers a parsimonious account of a complicated phenomenon; (5) it is aesthetically appealing or mathematically elegant; (6) it offers a potential solution to a problem deemed important by the research community or society; (7) it identifies a variety of new, interesting questions that can be researched; (8) it appears to helps people get along in the world; (9) it appears to increase the quantity and/or quality of human life; (10) it appears to lead to technological changes deemed good for society or an organization.

We believe that these and many other forms of usefulness are currently used to evaluate scientific theories and research. Which criteria are or should be applied depends on the particular context and the relevant goals and values of individual researchers and research communities. In consumer research, for example, we believe that different individuals and groups vary in the emphasis they place on criteria such as managerial relevance, mathematical sophistication, theoretical significance, and simply, whether the theory and research tell an interesting story.

In sum, from an R/C perspective, theories, research results and scientific knowledge can be and should be judged on a variety of context-dependent criteria. Contrary to Calder and Tybout, we do not believe that adopting a relativistic approach to evaluating theories has or will have a negative impact on the field nor will it lead to anarchy in the sense that research reports will be accepted uncritically.

**Cognitive and Behavioral Changes**

Finally, we think it is important for consumer researchers to make a number of changes in the way they think about, conduct, and report their research. For one thing, it is quite clear that much more consideration should be given to constructing interesting theories and creating insightful questions rather than "testing" theories.

We also believe that it would be useful for consumer researchers to develop a less pretentious language for reporting research results than the outdated one used by positivists and falsificationists. For example, empirical data and research do not and cannot "test" hypotheses or theories. Rather, they typically provide demonstrations of the researcher's predilections or skill at post hoc rationalization. In fact, we agree with McGuire (1973) who referred to laboratory experimenters as "stage managers." Words such as "confirm," "disconfirm," "prove," and

"disprove" should have no place in modern consumer research. Stripped of such pretentious language, traditional empirical studies could be seen more clearly to have no magical powers which make them universally or scientifically superior to qualitative and interpretive efforts.

## SUMMARY AND CONCLUSIONS

This paper investigated Calder and Tybout's conception of scientific knowledge and their misinterpretation of our relativistic/constructionist perspective. Their conception of scientific knowledge was found to be untenable and long rejected by philosophers and historians of science. Their interpretation of our perspective and its implications for science were demonstrated to be in error.

We continue to believe that relativism is currently the best available philosophy of science for consumer researchers. We also continue to believe that our analysis of science as marketing is a useful conception. We view successful scientists as skilled manufacturers and marketers of knowledge rather than "theory peddlers," as suggested by Calder and Tybout. Finally, we consider the diversity of interests and research approaches currently accepted in consumer research to be a welcome sign of growing maturity for the field.

## REFERENCES
Anderson, Paul F. (1983), "Marketing, Scientific Progress, and Scientific Method,: *Journal of Marketing*, 47 (Fall), pp. 18-31.
_____ (1986), "On Method in Consumer Research: A Critical Relativist Perspective," *Journal of Consumer Research*, 13 (September), pp. 155-173.
Calder, Bobby J. and Alice M. Tybout (1987), "What Consumer Research Is..." *Journal of Consumer Research*, 14 (June), pp. 136-140.
Duhem, Pierre (1953), "Physical Theory and Experiment," in *Readings in Philosophy of Science*, Herbert Feigl and May Brodbeck, eds., New York: Appleton-Century-Crofts, pp. 235-252.
Greenwald, Anthony G., Anthony R. Pratkanis, Michael R. Leippe, and Michael H. Baumgardner (1986), "Under What Conditions Does Theory Obstruct Research Progress?" *Psychological Review*, 93, No. 2, pp. 216-229.
Holbrook, Morris B. and Mark W. Grayson (1986), "The Semiology of Cinematic Consumption: Symbolic Consumer Behavior in Out of Africa," *Journal of Consumer Research*, 13 (December), 374-381.
Lakatos, Imre (1970), "Falsification and the Methodology of Science Research Programs," in *Criticisms and the Growth of Knowledge*, Imre Lakatos and Alan Musgrave, eds., London: Cambridge University Press, pp. 91-196.
Lauden, Larry (1977), *Progress and Its Problems*, Berkely CA: University of California Press.

_____ (1983), "The Demise of the Demarcation Problem," in *The Demarcation Between Science and Pseudo-Science*, Vol. 2, Rachael Lauden, ed., Blacksburg, VA: Center for the Study of Science in Society, Virginia Polytechnic Institute.

Leong, Siew Meng (1985), "Metatheory and Metamethodology in Marketing: A Lakatosian Reconstruction," *Journal of Marketing*, 49 (Fall), pp. 23-40.

McGuire, William J. (1973), "The Yin and Yang of Progress in Social Psychology: Seven Koan," *Journal of Personality and Social Psychology*, 26 (June), 446-456.

Mitroff, Ian I. (1974), "Norms and Counter-Norms in a Select Group of Apollo Moon Scientists: A Case Study of the Ambivalence of Scientists," *American Sociological Review*, 39 (August), 579-595.

Olson, Jerry C. (1987), "Constructing Scientific Meanings," in *Marketing Theory*, Russell W. Belk, et al., eds., Chicago: American Marketing Association, pp. 384-388.

Peter, J. Paul (1984), "On Ignoring a Research Education," in *Distinguished Essays in Marketing Theory*, S. Brown and R. Fiske, eds., New York: Wiley, pp. 324-327.

_____ and Jerry C. Olson (1983), "Is Science Marketing," *Journal of Marketing*, 47 (Fall), pp. 111-125.

# The Role of the Humanities in Consumer Research: Close Encounters and Coastal Disturbances

Morris B. Holbrook, Columbia University
Stephen Bell, Columbia University
Mark W. Grayson, Columbia University[1]

The inner history of the last thousand years is the history of mankind achieving self-expression: this is what philology, a historicist discipline, treats. This history contains the records of man's mighty, adventurous advance to a consciousness of his human condition and to the realization of his given potential (Auerbach 1969, p. 5).

The ultimate comparison...measures literature against life itself, authenticating the one while enhancing the other (Levin 1972, p.75).

## ABSTRACT

This paper describes a broadened view of humanistic inquiry and emphasizes the relevance of the humanities in general and the arts in particular to consumer research. It offers a counterexample of the scientific approach to interpretive hypothesis testing, with self-critical attention to its potential shortcomings. Finally, it illustrates a potentially more insightful interpretive approach that draws on the humanities to analyze the meaning of consumption symbolism in a work of art.

## INTRODUCTION

Recent developments in consumer research indicate that, at last, humanistic approaches have begun to creep into our field of inquiry. These indications include general review articles on semiotics (Holbrook 1987b; Mick 1986), hermeneutics (Hudson and Ozanne 1988), and humanistic inquiry (Hirschman 1986); conferences (Umiker-Sebeok 1987), conference sessions (Biocca 1987; Camargo 1987; Holbrook 1988c), and conference papers (Holbrook 1987a, 1988b) on various aspects of the interpretive approach; and occasional interpretive applications that have begun to appear in the literature (Hirschman 1987a, 1987b; Holbrook 1988a; Holbrook and Grayson 1986). Yet, already, this flurry of activity involving the movement by consumer researchers toward embracing the humanities has begun to encounter barriers, resistance, and other limitations.

First, one often confronts lingering reactions of reviewers, editors, and various self-appointed critics to the effect that this kind of approach is inappropriate for studies in marketing and consumer research (Holbrook 1987a, 1987b, 1988b). Second, one faces overt attacks on interpretivism as inherently nonscientific, as merely entertaining, or as only a source of hypotheses to be tested by more rigorous approaches ( Calder and Tybout 1987). Third, one suspects that even the most supportive efforts may fail to move all the way toward defining humanism with sufficient breadth and may stop short of fully acknowledging the potential role of the humanities in consumer research (Hirschman 1986).

In response to these three concerns, we shall begin by providing a general description of our broadened view of humanistic inquiry and our emphasis on the relevance of the humanities in general and the arts in particular to consumer research. We shall then offer a counterexample of the scientistic approach to interpretive hypothesis testing, with self-critical attention to its potential shortcomings. Finally, we shall illustrate what we regard as a more insightful interpretive approach that draws on the humanities to analyze the meaning of consumption symbolism in a work of art.

These three stages account for the title and subtitle of our paper. Specifically, the first stage explains "The Role of the Humanities in Consumer Research." The second stage illustrates the partial breakdown of the scientistic approach via a positivistic study of the effects of consumption symbolism in a short story (here entitled "Close Encounters"). The third stage illustrates what we consider the fruitful application of a semiotic/hermeneutic approach to the analysis of consumption symbolism in a recent highly acclaimed play by Tina Howe ("Coastal Disturbances").

However, the subtitle also carries some significance beyond its relevance to particular works of art. Specifically, we wish to argue that the time has come for "close encounters" between consumer research and what has thus far seemed an alien viewpoint. For many, enmeshed in the positivistic approach to research in our field, the humanities appear as an invasion from outer space. Yet, increasingly, some consumer researchers (including many of those represented by this volume of collected papers) have begun to call for welcoming such alien influences into our midst. This project is bound to cause "coastal disturbances" in the form of debates and disputes at our boundaries. The questions posed by attacks on interpretivism concern the issue of whether the boundaries of science in consumer research will turn out to be permeable or whether, as interpretivists, we must simply expand our horizon past the coastlines

[1]The authors thank Laurie Hudson, David Mick, and Barbara Stern for their helpful comments on an earlier draft. The paper also benefitted from the criticisms of Paul Surgi Speck, though it appears clear the latter reviewer disagrees with several aspects of the analyis. Finally, the first author gratefully acknowledges the support of the Columbia Business School's Faculty Research Fund.

of scientism to encompass a broader world of human meaning that lies beyond.

## THE ROLE OF THE HUMANITIES

### Beyond Humanistic Inquiry

In a recent article entitled "Humanistic Inquiry in Marketing Research" Hirschman (1986) provided an excellent description of a post-positivistic approach to research that has been treated at greater length in works by, among others, Geertz (1973), Morgan (1983), and Lincoln and Guba (1985). In Hirschman's (1986) view, humanism "advocates *in-dwelling* of the researcher with the phenomena under investigation" (p. 238). Yet she never really defines humanism, but rather focuses on a series of parallel comparisons between humanistic and positivistic methods of inquiry. In a sense, her treatment delineates humanism by contrasting it against what it is *not* -- namely, positivism -- extrapolating this distinction into a discussion of one type of method from among a variety of approaches more generally known by such names as "naturalistic inquiry" (Lincoln and Guba 1985).

We applaud Hirschman's (1986) attempt to highlight viable alternative modes of consumer research and admire the careful organization and provocative viewpoint of her article. Yet we fear that she may have unintentionally and unnecessarily worked toward narrowing our conception of humanism by implicitly restricting the scope of its potential contribution to that associated with naturalistic inquiry. This paper counteracts that unintended consequence of Hirshman's article by arguing for a broader view of humanistic inquiry in consumer research.

Toward this end, we adopt the first dictionary definition of humanism as "devotion to the humanities" (Holbrook 1987a). This specification, of course, immediately raises the cognate question of how we would define the humanities. Here, the dictionary proves somewhat less helpful, describing this vague concept as "the branches of learning...that investigate human constructs and concerns as opposed to natural processes" (Holbrook 1987a). Apparently, our notion of the humanities has evolved with changes in the course of human constructs and concerns. All this, therefore, requires some preliminary discussion.

### Humanism and the Humanities

Briefly, from this perspective, humanism traces its roots back to Fourteenth Century Florence.[2] Although some historians simply argue that humanism originated in the social and political influences broadly operating in this Italian city-state, Pfeiffer (1976) claims quite convincingly that the movement ultimately derived from the ideas of a single

man -- namely, Petrarch, whose study of ancient texts was motivated by "a longing for true wisdom": "He did not long, however, for the logic of metaphysics or natural sciences offered by the Aristotelian revival of the later Scholastic philosophy, but for knowledge of the human soul and human values" (p. 11). Petrarch's study of texts from the ancient world (Rome and the early Church) led to his belief that "the litterae he cultivated paved the way to moral values and true wisdom" (p. 15). This link "between litterae and humanitas" (p. 15) entails what Pfeiffer describes as a compassionate attitude to one's fellow man. The term "humanitas," however, was also used more specifically to refer to the critical scholarship that Petrarch recreated. Indeed, it has remained closely associated with the study of the letters, philosophy, politics, and ethics of the ancient world. Academies were formed to educate the Florentian elite in the humanities. Thence, the study of classical texts spread throughout the rest of Europe.

A crucial moment in the development of humanism and the emergence of the humanities occurred in the anti-Enlightenment revolt during the Eighteenth Century. For example, though he influenced few of his contemporaries, Vico (ed. 1976) argued, against the Baconian and Cartesian emphasis on science and rationality, that humans can best understand the social products that they themselves have created (Burke 1985, p. 78) so that the historical cycles of the social world (versus the causal phenomena of nature) are most intelligible to human thought. As explained by Cassirer (1961):

> According to Vico, the true goal of our knowledge is not knowledge of nature but human self-knowledge.... For Vico, the highest law of knowledge is the statement that any being truly conceives and fathoms only that which it itself has *produced*.... Nature is the work of God and accordingly is completely intelligible only to that divine understanding which brought it forth. What man can truly conceive is...the structure and specificity of his own works.... And it is above all to these that Vico turns his gaze in constructing...the logic of the humanities -- as the logic of language, poetry, and history (pp. 52-54).

The humanities build their basic rationale upon this fundamental insight. As Spitzer (1967) puts it, "The Humanist believes in the power bestowed on the human mind of investigating the human mind" (p. 24).

This central premise informed the distinction drawn by Dilthey (ed. 1972) between the *Naturwissenschaften* (the natural sciences) and the *Geisteswissenschaften* (the human studies). Dilthey's view of the human studies harks back to Vico's point that "the one who examines history also makes history" (quoted by Makkreel 1975, p. 25) and places its emphasis on types of knowledge that can be known *from within* (Kermode 1966). Thus, Dilthey (ed. 1972) sees "the theory of interpretation," driven toward an understanding or *Verstehen* of this "inner reality," as "an essential component in...the human

---

[2]Here, we refer to the growth of humanism rather than to broader aspects of interpretivism such as that found in the development of hermeneutics (beginning with very early examples of Biblical exegesis and classical scholarship).

studies" (p. 244). Toward this end, he pursues the hermeneutic approach developed by Schleiermacher (ed. 1978). Like Schleiermacher, he shows a deep concern for the validity of interpretation and raises questions about the objectivity of the Hermeneutic Circle that have only begun to reach resolution in more recent hermeneutic approaches (e.g., Gadamer 1975; Ricoeur 1976, 1981). In short, Dilthey's split between Naturwissenschaften and Geisteswissenschaften ratified a distinction that has, in one way or another, confronted us ever since. Thus, even while denying any simplistic division between the sciences and the humanities, Frye (1966) manages to retain the essential spirit of Dilthey's central dichotomy when he characterizes science as exhibiting "a method and a mental attitude...of a stabilized subject and an impartial and detached treatment of evidence" and the humanities as expressing "the nature of the human involvement with the human world, which is essential to any serious man's attitude to life" (p. 54).

In a sense, "humanism" simply refers to everything on the "Geistes" side of Dilthey's split between the natural sciences and human studies. Yet, as noted by Bird (1976), the term "humanistic" simply "has too many connotations that are wrong and misleading." Put differently, "humanism" lacks specificity (Abbagnano 1967), referring to a wide range of disciplinary perspectives that deserve to be distinguished. Toward that end, we propose the schematic breakdown between the natural sciences and human studies shown in Figure 1.

Several aspects of this scheme require brief comment. First, it preserves the basic distinction between natural sciences and human studies (Dilthey ed. 1972; Makkreel 1975). In our usage, "humanism" would refer to everything vertically aligned with the human studies column (where the upper portion refers primarily to "doing" and the lower to "knowing"). Second, the top part of the scheme distinguishes vertically between "humanitarianism" and "ethical or religious humanism" (Lamont 1962). The former places its emphasis on working toward the welfare and happiness of mankind (Bahn 1962) and may well use the tools of science for that purpose. Also in partial sympathy with the aims of science, the latter has been defined by Lamont (1982) as "rejecting supernaturalism and seeking man's fulfillment in the here and now of this world" (p. xi) via "joyous service for the greater good of all humanity" based on "the methods of reason, science, and democracy" (p. 12). Third, we follow Hulme (ed. 1987) in drawing a contrast between ethical or religious humanism (as just defined) and the realm of "pure" ethics or "pure" religion as directed toward producing objective, absolute, abstract knowledge and, therefore, as outside the bounds of any subjective, relativistic, action-oriented humanism. Fourth, like many recent commentators, we retain the familiar breakdown between the natural sciences, the social sciences, and the humanities (Adelson 1985; Kaufmann 1977; Matthews 1968). In this connection, vertically, we place the social sciences at an intermediate position between the natural sciences and the humanities.

Fifth, we follow a number of authorities in regarding the humanities as uniquely concerned with the historical and cultural products of mankind (Abbagnano 1967; Lamont 1962). Several commentators list literature, the arts, history, and philosophy as providing the primary exemplars of such historical cultural products (Beardsley 1966; Frye 1966; Kaufmann 1977).

As a passionate spokesman for the humanities, Cassirer (1961) defines their contribution as that of providing unique insights into life and the world of lived experience so as "to understand the universal and basic cultural orientation" (p. 36). This focus on the interpretive aims of literary or artistic studies, history, and philosophy extends throughout Olafson's (1979) account of history as "the dialectic of action":

The humanities...are interested in man primarily as the possesor of certain powers.... These powers have traditionally been held to comprise those of thought and articulate speech, of purposive action and will, as well as of feeling that is informed by thought and purpose... history, as well as literature and philosophy, is concerned with human beings and with human beings as possessed of and exercising these distinctive powers (p. 6).

Not incidentally, one area in which humans exercise their powers of thinking, feeling, and acting - in ways that give structure to their lived experience - occurs in their everyday consumption activities. Thus, Cassirer (1961) quotes with approval [3] the following comment, of clear relevance to the pervasive role of consumer behavior, from Taine's *History of English Literature*:

True history first emerges for us when the historian succeeds in taking us across the barrier of time and face to face with living human beings -- human beings...with the same completeness and clarity belonging to those human beings who walk our own streets.... The genuinely real...is what can be handled, the bodily and visible human being, who eats, works, and fights...the human being at work, in his office, in his field, with his sunshine, his soil, his shelter, his clothes, and his mealtime (pp. 27-28).

## The Two Cultures and, Perhaps, a Third

The venerable distinction between the natural sciences and human studies -- or, more loosely, between Science and Humanism -- reached its modern apotheosis in the controversy surrounding Snow's (ed.

---

[3]Today, as noted by one reviewer, Cassirer's approval would not be shared by such anti-historicists as the Yale School, the post-structuralists, the deconstructionists, and the "New" New Critics. By contrast with these latter perspectives, we focus here on somewhat more venerable viewpoints.

**FIGURE 1**

A SCHEMATIC PORTRAYAL OF THE NATURAL SCIENCES
AND HUMAN STUDIES

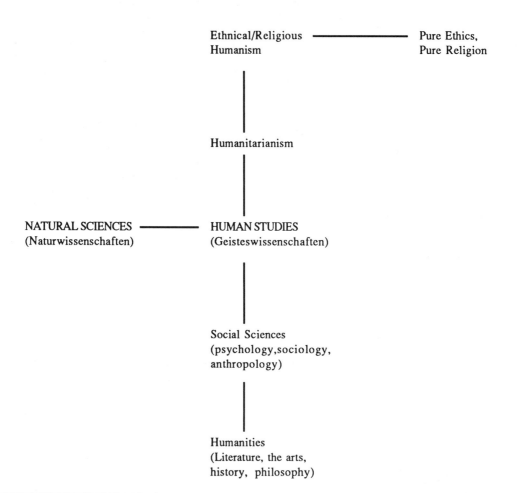

1964) famous reflections in his 1959 Rede Lecture on "The Two Cultures and the Scientific Revolution." Snow (ed. 1964) argued that "the intellectual life of the whole of western society is increasingly being split into two polar groups" (p. 3) and that "at one pole we have the literary intellectuals...at the other scientists, and as the most representative, the physical scientists" (p. 4). Snow predicted that this split would produce dire consequences and sought relief in the form of a revised educational system oriented toward "closing the gap between our cultures" (p. 50). Critics gleefully leaped to the challenge of repudiating Snow's implicit elevation of the scientific above the literary culture. For example, Leavis (ed. 1972) caustically referred to Snow as "portentously ignorant" (p. 41) and "intellectually as undistinguished as it is possible to be" (p. 42); condemned Snow's essay as exhibiting "an utter lack of intellectual distinction and an embarrassing

vulgarity of style" (p. 44); charged that Snow was a bad novelist and an incompetent scientist; and concluded, contra Snow, that "what we need...is something with the livingness of the deepest vital instinct; as intelligence, a power -- rooted, strong in experience, and supremely human -- of creative response to the new challenges of time; something that is alien to either of Snow's cultures" (pp. 60-61). Others responded to Snow's critique in more moderate tones. Thus, Polanyi (1959) questioned the scientific "ideal of impersonal objectivity" (p. 32) and called for "a humanistic revisionism" (p. 32) that would counteract "the disregard of truth in favour of hard-boiled scientific ideals" (pp. 27-28). Meanwhile, Bantock (1960) questioned whether a rapprochement between science and the humanities is even possible given that, in his view, science focuses on descriptive regularities "in the grip of the facts" whereas a writer pursuing the humanities expresses "a unique vision" whose "coherence...is...emotional" (p. 39).

Perhaps the most constructive critical response to the issues raised by Snow (ed. 1964) appeared in a book by Davy (1978) entitled *Towards a Third Culture*. In this work, Davy blames the rational scientific consciousness for leading mankind into a predicament in which "we are able to study the processes of nature in fine analytical detail and thus to gain control over them, but we are strangers in a universe which has lost human meaning" (p. 51). In Davy's view, the restoration of "human meaning" requires a humanizing counter-current in the form of a "third culture":

> the third culture...will retain the particular virtues of the scientific outlook -- disciplined thinking, respect for facts, testing by experiment -- but it will use them differently.... it will be...also a religious and an artistic culture (p. 93).

Thus, echoing Leavis (1952) in *The Common Pursuit*, Davy hopes that the third culture will assert "a humanizing influence which would correct the tendencies of science...to lose sight of the whole human being" (p. 104).

## The Humanities and the Social Sciences

All this -- the gap between the natural sciences and human studies, the coexistence of the social sciences and the humanities as subspecies of humanism, and the need for a humanizing focus on the meaning of the world -- suggests the possibility of a role for the humanities in the social sciences in general and consumer research in particular. Not surprisingly, numerous thinkers have articulated views compatible with this position from a number of different perspectives. We shall briefly review three such perspectives, the third of which corresponds most closely to our own viewpoint.

(1) First, some commentators have attempted to abolish the cleavage between the humanities and the natural sciences by arguing for a positivistic view of the humanities. For example, Northrop (1947) suggests that the natural sciences, social sciences, and humanities are subject to the same philosophy of science -- namely, one based on "experimentally verified theory" (p. 361). One application of this viewpoint appears in the approach to literary analysis taken by Lane (1961). Following the "practical criticism" of Richards (1935), Lane (1961) calls for the greatest possible denotative precision in the critic's use of language (p. 100). Ultimately, in this pursuit, he tends to dissolve the difference between the natural sciences and the humanities:

> There is not, in particular, any formal difference between the humanities and the sciences in the appropriate method of theory formation, conceptualization, classification, verification, and evaluation.... there are not, in any event, *two* sets of methods.... there is only one logic (with different notations) that

gives each of these schemes its rationale (p. 123).

(2) The construal adopted by Northrop (1947) and Lane (1961) neglects what we regard as the venerable distinction between Naturwissenschaften and Geisteswissenschaften. A second, more tenable position emphasizes the contrast between the contexts of discovery and justification, regarding the humanities as suitable aids to the development of theory or generation of hypotheses to be tested by more scientific means. For example, Nisbet (1976) emphasizes the role for artistic creativity in the process of discovery:

> What is vital is the underlying act of discovery or illumination or invention that is the clue to all genuine creative work. The greater scientists have long been aware of the basic unity of the creative act as found in the arts and in the sciences. A large and growing literature attests to the awareness. Only in the social sciences....has awareness of the real nature of discovery tended to lag. Countless works in the social sciences reveal the inability of their authors to bear in mind the crucial difference between what may properly be called the *logic of discovery* and the *logic of demonstration*. The second is properly subject to rules and prescriptions; the first isn't (p. 5).

Bird (1976) calls attention to this same parallel between art and science in the act of discovery wherein a scientific theory is "a work of creative imagination" so that "science, as a creative achievement," is no different from any of the most creative works of the humanities and the arts" (p. 168). From this perspective, it follows that literature (or the other humanities) may suggest an "hypothesis" to be tested by "further observations that confirm its truth" via more rigorous approaches (Beardsley 1966, p. 27). In essence, this argument borrows from Popper's (1959) falsificationist criterion. Indeed, numerous commentators (e.g., Hirsch 1967; Ricoeur 1976, 1981), including Popper (1976) himself, have noted the fundamental consistency between falsificationism and the interpretive task of checking hypotheses concerning the humanities against the evidence provided by a close reading of their text. Here, for example, Bruner (1986) views the humanities as a potential source of hypotheses suitable for a sort of falsificationist testing. In his perspective, "the humanities have as their implicit agenda the cultivation of hypotheses, the art of hypothesis generating" (Bruner 1986, p. 52). But, for him, the tests imposed on humanistic hypotheses differ from those imposed on science in that they emphasize the more human perspective of "verisimilitude" in the sense of "true to conceivable experience" (p. 52):

> With science, we ask finally for some verification (or some proof against falsification). In the domain of narrative and explication of human action, we ask instead

that, upon reflection, the account correspond to some perspective we can imagine or "feel" as right. The one, science, is oriented outward to an external world; the other, inward toward a perspective and a point of view toward the world. They are, in effect, two forms of an illusion of reality -- very different forms. But their respective "falsifiability" in Popper's sense does not fully distinguish them (pp. 51-52).

One must emphasize that, from this viewpoint, the distinctive hypothesis-generating contribution of the humanities stems from their unique ability to put us in touch with the human condition: "My interest in theater and literature...has joined me to the possible worlds that provide the landscape for thinking about the human condition, the human condition as it exists in the culture which I live" (Bruner 1986, p. 128). In this, Bruner echoes the arguments offered by Huxley (1963) in his treatment of *Literature and Science*. Huxley (1963) lavished considerable attention on the contrasts between science and literature (cf. Richards ed. 1970) in terms of content (public/private), stance (objective/subjective), manner (abstract/concrete), approach (general/particular), level (quantitative/qualitative), language (technical jargon/rich allusions), and goals (to simplify reality into a rational order/to communicate multiple meanings). However, Huxley (1963) continued to insist on the humanistic premise that "the proper study...of mankind is man" (p. 80) and steadfastly regarded literature as a window on the nature and meaning of life through which "our own immediate experiences come to us, so to say, through the refracting medium of the art we like" (p. 71).

(3) From here, it requires only a short advance to arrive at a third perspective favored by the current authors -- namely, that works of art (literature and the other humanities) can themselves provide evidence against which to test the hypotheses concerning the nature of the human condition that they themselves suggest. In this, we move close to the position adopted by Berger (1963) contra all "humorless scientism" (p. 165) and in support of his view of "sociology as a humanistic discipline" (p. 176):

> Sociology...has...traits that assign it to the immediate vicinity of the humanities.... sociology is vitally concerned with what is, after all, the principal subject matter of the humanities -- the human condition itself.... sociology comes time and again on the fundamental question of what it means to be a man.... Openness to the humanistic scope of sociology further implies an ongoing communication with other disciplines that are vitally concerned with explaining the human condition. The most important of these are history and philosophy (pp. 167-168).

On this same note of humanistic concern, Berger and Luckmann (1966) conclude their "treatise in the sociology of knowledge" with a "conception of sociology in general" (p. 189) that they might almost have torn from the pages of Vico (ed. 1976) in which:

> Sociology takes its place in the company of the sciences that deal with man *as* man.... it is, in that specific sense, a humanistic discipline.... sociology must be carried on in a continuous conversation with both history and philosophy or lose its proper object of inquiry. This object is society as part of a human world, made be men, inhabited by men, and, in turn, making men, an an ongoing historical process (p. 189)

The implications of this view for the role of the humanities in the social sciences receive their fullest elaboration in the work by Brown (1977) entitled *A Poetic for Sociology*. Herein, Brown (1977) contrasts what he calls the "positivistic" (rational, scientific, empirical) and "romantic" (intuitive, metaphysical, evaluative) views, but refuses to be trapped by this stultifying split and instead adopts a self-consciously interpretive approach:

> our project -- a poetic for sociology -- is an attempt to provide an epistemic self-consciousness for sociological thought.... we no longer are forced to choose between two sociologies: one positivist, which tells us everything about society and nothing about ourselves; the other romantic, which expresses insight into moral agency but lacks empirical rigor. We can begin instead to cast such sterile dichotomies aside -- scientific sociology can be seen as interpretive, while insight or interpretation can be made a disciplined, rule-bound procedure (p. 234)

An even more poetically interpretivistic view of the social sciences informs the recent work by Geertz (1988) subtitled "The Anthropologist as Author." Geertz argues that ethnographers use their writing persuasively "to convince us that what they say is a result of their having actually penetrated...another form of life" (p. 4) so that the criteria for judging works of cultural anthropology come to resemble those applied in the humanities:

> as the criticism of fiction and poetry grows best out of an imaginative engagement with fiction and poetry themselves, not out of imported notions about what they should be, the criticism of anthropological writing...ought to grow out of a similar engagement with *it*, not out of preconceptions of what it must look like to qualify as science (p. 6).

From this perspective, in an echo of Brown, Geertz concludes that "ethnographies tend to look at least as much like romances as they do like lab reports" (p. 8) so that ethnographical writing occupies an intermediate position "between author-saturated texts like *David Copperfield* and author-evacuated ones like

'On the Electrodynamics of Moving Bodies'" (p. 141).
Thus, for Geertz, the natural sciences and humanities
merge in the realm of social science:

> the burden of authorship cannot be evaded....
> ethnography..., like quantum mechanics or the
> Italian opera,...is a work of the imagination,
> less extravagant than the first, less methodical
> than the second....   writing of ethnography
> involves telling stories, making pictures,
> concocting symbolisms, and deploying tropes
> (p. 140)

In his review, Schweder (1988) summarizes Geertz as
suggesting that "a great ethnography is not simply a
compilation of facts; it is an imaginative way of
seeing through experience" (p. 13).  Clearly, in this
view, the line between social scientist and novelist
grows very thin indeed:

> According to Mr. Geertz, ethnographic reality
> does not exist apart from our literary versions
> of it....  the appreciation of Mr. Geertz's
> brilliant writing is much like the appreciation
> of a brilliant metaphor.  Both suffer from
> explication; something inevitably gets lost in
> translation....  to disentangle substance from
> style destroys the object of enhancement (p.
> 13).

## The Humanities in Consumer Research

In studying customer behavior, consumer
research has traditionally employed methodology
borrowed from the social sciences, which have
themselves tended to emulate the natural sciences.
Hirschman's (1986) article raises the issue whether
other methods might be relevant as well and suggests
that a humanistic approach might provide useful
insights.  While we agree with her proposition, the
mode of research that she describes is based on a rather
narrow conception of humanism.

A fully humanistic approach would embrace
the humanities and thus would include research based
on the direct involvement of a critical interpreter in a
literary text or artistic work.  In addition, as noted
earlier, the humanities would encompass various
aspects of history, philosophy, and other related areas
of inquiry.  However, here, we shall focus primarily on
those humanistic contributions associated with
literature and the arts.  In this connection, Holbrook
(1987a, 1987b, 1988b) has argued that the humanities
in general and the arts in particular are relevant to
marketing and consumer research precisely because
consumer products function symbolically in art as
they do in everyday life.  They communicate as part of
a complex network of symbolic meanings.  For
example, the third author recently reviewed ten films
directed by John Huston, tracking the use of imagery
associated with guns, alcohol, and tobacco and
arriving at the tentative conclusion that consumption
of these products differentiates Huston's male
characters in the degree to which they possess
strength, power, aggressiveness, cunning, and sexual
potency.  This conclusion depends on the interpreter's

own subjective judgment and on the critical experience
he brings to the analysis of these movies.  While
these conclusions seem intuitively plausible, they
only suggest ways in which products might be read in
consumers' minds within the context of these
particular films.  They remain idiographic with no
intended claims to nomothetic generalizability.

Such interpretive readings may do much to
suggest the meaning of marketing and consumer
behavior.  However, inextricably anchored in
subjective responses, they inevitably elicit criticisms
from adherents to the positivistic view of marketing
research.  Yet, as Hirschman's article and many others
have already conveyed, the "received view" of logical
empiricism no longer remains tenable without
qualification (Anderson 1987; Deshpande 1983; Peter
and Olson 1983).  Once we have turned to other
approaches, a key remaining issue concerns the
substantive areas of their application.  This latter
issue poses a question that the humanities seem well-
suited to answer.

## Art, Life, and Consumption

A well-known tenet underlying much literary
and esthetic criticism claims that art imitates life by
providing a representation of reality (Auerbach 1953).
Assumptions about the character of this mimetic
function do, of course, change through time and
therefore vary radically from one historical moment to
another.  Thus, the classicists believed that art holds a
mirror up to nature and copies various external
properties of the world around us (Abrams 1981).  By
contrast, the romantics felt that art illuminates various
human emotions and thereby expresses something
from the universe within (Abrams 1953).  More
contemporary criticism tends to regard art as a
conceptual embodiment of ideas that raise questions
about the artwork's own ontology (Danto 1981).
Nevertheless, whatever their contrasting viewpoints,
all these perspectives interpret art as a microcosm of
larger meanings that, together, say something
important about life by commenting significantly on
the human condition.

This point aligns closely with the view of
those who would apply insights from the arts and
humanities to the advancement of knowledge in the
social sciences.  For example, drawing on Goffman's
(1959) dramaturgical model, Elam (1980) suggests
that "the way in which we make sense of our lives and
their component acts is very considerably influenced
by our experience of dramatic worlds, where actions
are seen in their intentional and teleological purity"
and that "in this sense, the elements of a general
theory of human action...are not only directly
applicable to but directly derivative from the drama"
(p. 134).  Similar arguments have appeared in work on
the role of narrative in the social sciences (Burke
1945; Fisher 1985; Olafson 1979).  Indeed, Bruner
(1986) regards narrative as the key to social
understanding:

> Insofar as we account for our own actions and
> for the human events that occur around us
> principally in terms of narrative, story, drama,

it is conceivable that our sensitivity to narrative provides the major link between our own sense of self and our sense of others in the social world around us. The common coin may be provided by the focus of narrative that the culture offers us. Again, life could be said to imitate art (p. 69).

This view suggests that interpretive strategies useful for understanding the meaning of an artistic text or other artwork can fruitfully be applied to the problems of an artistic text or other artwork can fruitfully be applied to the problems of understanding life in the abstract or lived events in particular. One such analytic approach involves the use of consumption symbolism or marketing imagery in a work of art to suggest or to bolster an interpretation of its meaning (Holbrook 1987a, 1988b; Holbrook and Grayson 1986). Here, we intend "consumption symbolism" to refer to all suggestive aspects of the acquiring, usage, and disposition of products (goods, services, events, or ideas) that produce valued experiences. Similarly, we intend "marketing imagery" to refer to any concretization that conjures up a visual or other sensory mental representation of consumer activities or related business practices via either pictorial or verbal signs (e.g., a photograph or a use of figurative language). (For further discussion of symbolism and imagery, see Abrams 1981.) In short, this viewpoint regards consumption in an artistic text as an imaginative microcosm that tells us something about the artwork's significance. Similarly, that artistic interpretation may radiate outward so that, by extension, the microcosm of consumption within an artwork may bear on life's larger meanings.

## CLOSE ENCOUNTERS

As one recent illustration of the humanistic viewpoint just described, Holbrook and Grayson (1986) have analyzed the manner in which consumption symbolism contributes to the development of plot and character in an artwork -- namely, the movie *Out of Africa*. This interpretive approach in general and the Holbrook-Grayson article in particular have prompted a thoughtful critique by Calder and Tybout (1987). These authors acknowledge that a semiological approach may help to establish what they call "interpretive knowledge" in which "the conceptual argument is used to give an account of the data" (p. 138) and admit that such an analysis can make "provocative and entertaining reading" (p. 139). But they explictly deny the scientific status of interpretive studies when they assert that "such conceptualizations should not be equated with scientific knowledge" (p. 139) so that "interpretive knowledge must stand apart...from science" (p. 140). Science, they suggest, requires a methodology of falsificationism (Lakatos 1970; Popper 1959) in which "the goal of research is to expose a theory to possible refutation" (p. 138) in a process wherein "scientific knowledge comes from the confrontation of theory with data" (p. 138). It follows, in this view (echoing Nisbet 1976, Bird 1976, and Beardsley

1966, discussed earlier), that the interpretive approach can contribute to the progress of science only when it aids the development of hypotheses that a falsificationist approach can then subject to empirical testing:

> There is no reason that the conceptualizations of interpretive knowledge cannot be submitted to sophisticated falsificationist methodology; they may, in fact, be a good source of scientifically testable hypotheses (p. 139).

We have commented elsewhere (Holbrook and O'Shaughnessy 1988) on what we regard as the profound *conceptual* problems that pervade Calder and Tybout's (1987) scientist attack on interpretivism. (For further critical replies from the viewpoint of the philosophy of science, see Anderson 1987.) We shall not repeat these arguments in the present paper. Here, by contrast, we propose to focus on the *practical* consequences of heeding Calder and Tybout's advice. Toward this end, in a conscientious attempt to follow that advice as closely as possible, we apply the Calder-Tybout perspective by using a falsificationist approach to test an interpretive hypothesis. Specifically, we employ an experimental design to collect data that confront Holbrook and Grayson's (1986) conceptual argument that consumption symbolism contributes to the development of character in a work of art. Here, to facilitate testing, the artwork we use is a very short story entitled "Close Encounters," while the symbolic consumption of interest involves different brands or types of automobiles, drinks, cats, books, and shirts.

### Method

*Projective Technique.* As our basic method, we used a structured projective technique in which subjects inferred a consumer's personality characteristics from a short story that, among other topics, described his consumption behavior. This procedure draws on the early shopping-list study by Haire (1950), except that we substituted an artwork for the grocery list, used a more complex factorial design, and collected a more structured set of response ratings as suggested by, among others, Westfall, Boyd, and Campbell (1957). We believe that our structured projective task represents an advance in methodological sophistication over comparable techniques used in previous research (e.g., Holbrook and Hughes 1978).

*Stimuli.* The basis for constructing our set of stimuli was a very short story describing a "close encounter" between a man (George) and a woman (Julia). Written by the authors for purposes of this experiment and therefore not claimed as an exemplar of literary excellence, this story served as a carefully controlled vehicle for the manipulation of consumption symbolism. Specifically, as indicated in the following quotation, it mentioned five consumer products shown here in brackets [AUTOMOBILE, DRINK, CAT, BOOK, and SHIRT] that served as factors for our factorial design (based on two different versions for each bracketed factor):

*Close Encounters*

Julia rang the doorbell again.  This time she held the buzzer for a few seconds.  Where could he be? The [AUTOMOBILE] was parked outside, so he could not have gone far.  Besides, they had agreed that she would meet him at his apartment, since she would be in the neighborhood.  She turned the doorknob.  To her surprise it was unlocked.

Tiger, George's big, orange [CAT], tried to slip through the crack in the door.  Julia let herself in quickly.  The apartment was quiet, though it revealed that George had been there only minutes before.  A [DRINK] stood next to an open book, [BOOK].  Julia smiled.  It was so like George.  She picked up the book and started flipping through the pages.  Within minutes, she was lost in another world.  His world.

An opening door broke her concentration.  She looked to the front of the apartment.  No sign of George.  Then she heard a cough from behind her.

"Don't turn around," a familiar baritone voice intoned.

"And why not?"

"I'd be embarrassed and so would you."

"Why?" Julia spotted his yellow [SHIRT], jeans, and boxers on the bed.  "Oh," she coyly added, "Do you need your clothes? Here, let me get them for you."

George hid behind the hall door.

"What do you want me to do, leave the room?"  She laughed at his discomfort.  "C'mon, George, be a sport.  So many other women have seen you in the raw.  Why not me?"

"Why not? Because your my sister."

Using this short story as a frame, the factorial design replaced each bracketed product name with one of two contrasting versions so as to create 32 different stimuli from the $2^5$ possibilities shown in Table 1.

*Instrument.*  Each subject read one version of the story and then rated the male protagonist (George) on ten bipolar adjectival scales.  These ten scales were chosen on the basis of a pilot study with 60 respondents drawn from the same pool of MBA students that were later used in the main test.  In the pilot interviews, each subject read a version of the

story and then gave free responses as to the adjectives that might describe its hero George.  Among these responses, ten adjectives were mentioned by at least four respondents.  We selected these ten for further use, created bipolar adjectival scales in the seven-position check-mark format, and then randomized these scales in terms of both order and direction.  The final form of the instrument appeared as shown in Figure 2.

*Subjects.*  Our subjects were 109 MBA candidates at a major Eastern university who completed the reading-and-rating task as a requirement in a beginning marketing class (after which they were debriefed as to the nature and purpose of the study).  Subjects were assigned randomly to the 32 different factorially designed stimuli.  Generally, in the debriefing session, they showed no awareness that different subjects had received different stimuli (thereby suggesting that we had succeeded in guarding against this potential source of demand effects).

*Procedure.*  The subjects began by completing an exercise intended to give them practice with the instrument.  Specifically, they first read a sample story (different from the test story but the same for all subjects) and rated its female protagonist on the ten adjectival scales.  After this practice task, each subject read one of the 32 versions of the test story (assigned at random) and completed the structured rating scales to assess the character of George.

*Data Analysis.*  We began by using principal components analysis with varimax rotation to reduce the original ten adjectival scales to a smaller number of uncorrelated dimensions.  Taking these rotated principal components as dependent variables, we then regressed the component scores on independent variables constructed to represent the various product categories (coded as -1/+1 dummy variables).  (Recall that the principal components were, by definition, uncorrelated and therefore permitted the use of single dependent variables rather than some sort of MANOVA procedure.)  We performed these regressions both with and without the inclusion of 2-, 3-, and 4-way multiplicative interaction terms.  Overall, however, the interaction effects turned out to be generally without statistical significance.  Hence, we shall not discuss these interactions further, but shall focus instead on the main effects due to the contrasting versions of the product factors.

*Hypothesis.*  To repeat, our main interpretive hypothesis (derived from Holbrook and Grayson's

## TABLE 1

| **Product Factor** | **Contrasting Versions** | |
|---|---|---|
| AUTOMOBILE | BMW | Toyota |
| DRINK | Chivas Regal | Can of Budweiser |
| CAT | Persian cat | Alley cat |
| BOOK | *Dress for Success* | *Small is Beautiful* |
| SHIRT | Alligator Shirt | "Ban the Nukes" T-Shirt |

**FIGURE 2**

| | | |
|---:|:---:|:---|
| upscale | _:_:_:_:_:_:_ | downscale |
| ambitious | _:_:_:_:_:_:_ | unambitious |
| thoughtful | _:_:_:_:_:_:_ | thoughtless |
| shy | _:_:_:_:_:_:_ | bold |
| not conscious of image | _:_:_:_:_:_:_ | conscious of image |
| intelligent | _:_:_:_:_:_:_ | unintelligent |
| liberal | _:_:_:_:_:_:_ | conservative |
| rich | _:_:_:_:_:_:_ | poor |
| secure | _:_:_:_:_:_:_ | insecure |
| young | _:_:_:_:_:_:_ | old |

semiotic analysis) is that consumption symbolism (as represented by the two different versions of each product factor) contributes to the development of character (as assessed by principal components based on the subjects' adjectival ratings of the male protagonist).

## Results

*Principal Components Analysis.* Three varimax-rotated principal components, accounting for 56.7 percent of the variance, had eigenvalues greater than 1.0. Because the inclusion of fewer or more dimensions failed to improve the interpretability of the principal components solution, we retained these three components for further analysis. Based on the following set of loadings (with scales reordered to provide clarity), we named the components "Down-And-Out," "Out-Of-It," and "Outrageous," respectively Table 2).

*Regression Analyses.* In the regression analyses, we adopted a level of $p < .05$ as our criterion for establishing a statistically significant effect of a product version on a character dimension. Using this criterion, we found significant tendencies for the interpretation of George's character to depend on the product versions contained in the story (Table 3). Specifically, George appeared more "down-and-out" (i.e., unambitious, etc.) when he drove a Toyota, drank Budweiser, and read *Small Is Beautiful*. He seemed more "out-of-it" (i.e., conservative, etc.) when he wore an Alligator shirt. And he conveyed more of an "outrageous" (i.e., thoughtless, etc.) character when he read *Dress For Success*.

## Falsificationist Conclusion

Like any single set of findings in consumer research, our experimental results are limited by the fact that they might vary with different stimuli (e.g., poetry versus prose), different contexts (e.g., listening versus reading), or different subjects (e.g., members of the Book-of-the-Month Club versus students). Thus, future laboratory research along similar lines should explore the replicability, robustness, and boundary conditions for the present set of findings.

Subject to these limitations, our results do appear to support the Holbrook-Grayson hypothesis that consumption symbolism contributes to the development of character in a work of art. We found

no significant effects of the difference between a Persian and an alley cat (suggesting that, perhaps, we should have included more extreme types of pets such as a Persian and a German Shepherd). However, readers' interpretations of George's character as down-and-out, out-of-it, and outrageous did depend significantly on the consumption symbolism conveyed by his choice of car, libation, clothing, and reading material. From the perspective of a falsificationist, this finding corroborates (by failing to refute) the interpretive hypothesis of a link between consumption symbolism and character development in works of art.[4]

## The Literal and Ironic Meanings of the Conclusion

The experimental study reported here permits at least two sorts of readings, both valid in their own terms and both tending toward the support of the Holbrook-Grayson analysis. For purposes of this discussion, we shall call the first *positivistic* and the second *interpretivistic*, though other terms (such as "scientist" and "humanistic") might apply equally well.

*The Positivistic Reading.* The positivistic reading would accord, we hope, with the dictates laid down by Calder and Tybout (1987). It would accept those authors' contention that the only proper scientific use for an interpretation lies in its ability to suggest hypotheses suitable for a confrontation with data. From this viewpoint, it would regard Holbrook and Grayson's (1986) interpretation concerning the role of consumption symbolism in shaping the development of character in an artwork as, at best, an hypothesis to be tested by subjection to possible empirical falsification. On this logic, it would take the test provided by the present study literally. Specifically, it would see the fictional variations in consumer products as experimental treatments designed to manipulate consumption symbolism in a short story and would accept the semantic differential scales as measures of the readers' responses to these

---

[4]One reviewer suggested, apparently as a criticism, that Calder and Tybout would agree with this conclusion. Indeed, we hope that they would, though we do not dare to take any such acquiescence for granted.

**TABLE 2**

**SCALE LOADINGS ON THE ROTATED PRINCIPAL COMPONENTS**

|  | Down-And-Out | Out-of It | Outrageous |
|---|---|---|---|
| Unambitious | .81 | .03 | -.04 |
| Downscale | .81 | -.01 | .09 |
| Poor | .71 | .22 | .17 |
| Not Conscious of Image | .57 | -.35 | .06 |
| Conservative | -.34 | .65 | -.14 |
| Insecure | .17 | .63 | -.09 |
| Old | -.00 | .56 | .28 |
| Thoughtless | .08 | .13 | .83 |
| Bold | .04 | -.42 | .72 |
| Unintelligent | .20 | .48 | .52 |

differences in the hero's character-revealing consumption habits. Indeed, countless other positivistic studies have used comparable experimental manipulations and comparable response measures to reach comparable conclusions concerning other questions of interest. Such applications provide the bread and butter of the positivist's approach. Simple logical consistency compels the positivist to accept them, here, as one more example of the hypothetico-deductive method that the falsificationist holds as the standard for scientific verification and that therefore, in the present case, supports the validity of the Holbrook-Grayson thesis rather convincingly. Needless to say, such a positivistic reading would correspond to the *literal* statement of the authors' intentions in performing and reporting the study.

*The Interpretivistic Reading.* In vivid contrast to what we might regard as the relatively straightforward positivistic reading that logical consistency and operational precedent would compel someone of the falsificationist faith to follow, one might entertain various interpretive approaches to understanding the the text of the authors' research report. One such interpretive strategy might regard the meaning of the report as at least partly *ironic*. Here, we emphatically do *not* intend the term "irony" to refer to parody, sarcasm, or invective; rather, we refer to what Abrams (1981) calls "the root sense of...a difference between what is asserted and what is actually the case" (p. 89). In other words, one might interpret the authors' real (latent) intent as something rather different from their literal (manifest) content and might infer that the study claims overtly to use falsificationist procedures to show something about responses to an artwork which the authors covertly believe that the standard positivistic hypothetico-deductive method is in fact ill-equipped to demonstrate. One might bolster this self-critical interpretation by pointing to the difficulty of capturing the organic unity of an artistic gestalt via anything so clumsy as a set of factorially designed experimental manipulations. One might further note

the departure from reality involved in assessing the most delicate nonverbal esthetic responses by means of verbal paper-and-pencil semantic differential scales. The credibility of this ironic interpretation would gain some contextual support (of the type sometimes referred to as "auctorial intent") from the fact that one of the authors of the study has himself raised exactly these (and other) arguments on behalf of interpretivism at the expense of narrow or scientistic positivism on several previous occasions (Holbrook 1987a, 1987b, 1988b, 1988c). This self-critical move toward interpretivism would discredit the positivistic reading of the study, would reject its falsificationist premises, and would argue for its sustained ironic implications as an embodiment of the inadequacies inherent in using the hypothetico-deductive approach to understand a work of art. However, precisely because this ironic reading would rely on an interpretation of the authors' text, it would serve to support Holbrook and Grayson's original claims on behalf of interpretivism by virtue of its very existence. In other words, however valid its arguments, the ironic interpretation would actually instantiate the value of the kind of reading initially proposed by Holbrook and Grayson.

*The Meaning.* Either way, by either route, the literal or the ironic, we arrive at essentially the same meaning for the "Close Encounters" study. The positivistic reading simply regards it literally, in the spirit of the Calder-Tybout suggestion, as providing support for the Holbrook-Grayson interpretation viewed as a falsifiable hypothesis. The interpretivistic reading regards it, somewhat more subtly, as a piece of sustained irony that casts self-critical doubt on the usefulness of the falsificationist procedures to clarify the meanings of artworks and that thereby reaffirms the potential validity of interpretivism. In sympathy with the latter perspective, Abrams (1981) regards irony as "an ultimate test of skill in reading between the lines" and suggests that "recourse to irony by an author carries an implicit compliment to the intelligence of the reader"

**TABLE 3**

**REGRESSION RESULTS SIGNIFICANT AT THE .05 LEVEL**

| Dependent Variable | Independent Variable | t-Value | p-Level |
|---|---|---|---|
| Down-And-Out | Toyota/BMW | 3.56 | .0006 |
| | Budweiser/Chivas Regal | 2.19 | .03 |
| | *Small / Dress* | 2.53 | .01 |
| Out-of-It | T-Shirt/Alligator | -2.28 | .02 |
| Outrageous | *Small / Dress* | -3.16 | .002 |

(p. 90).[5] Similarly, Brown (1977) has commented at length on the use of irony, drawn from the humanities, as a mode of discovery and way of knowing in the social sciences -- though, unfortunately, irony loses much of its force if, as here, it needs to be explained (p. 219). Even so, irony can serve to make its point in a manner more gentle than could be accomplished via righteous invective. Thus, Brown (1977) translates and quotes Anatole France as follows:

The irony I invoke is not cruel. It mocks neither love nor beauty. It is mild and benevolent. Its laughter calms anger, and it is this irony that teaches us to make fun of the fools and villians whom otherwise we might have been weak enough to hate (p. 213).

In short, then, someone wishing to criticize the present study, cannot have it both ways. *Either* the study supports the Holbrook-Grayson hypothesis in a fairly straightforward way (thereby lending credit to their interpretive approach), *or* it invites an ironic interpretation based on the apparent shortcomings of the falsificationist approach (thereby assuming the validity of interpretivism that we set out to demonstrate in the first place).

*Apologia.* One might wonder with which of these two readings -- the positivistic or the interpretivistic -- we happen to agree. The answer is that we lean toward the second reading. We did try conscientiously to reflect the spirit of the Calder-Tybout suggestion by designing a test to collect some evidence with which to confront the Holbrook-Grayson interpretation. However, we freely acknowledge the inevitable limitations and weaknesses inherent in this empirical enterprise.

[5]One reviewer, who refused to acknowledge the essentially pro-interprevistist implications of the ironic viewpoint, apparently did not wish to accept this intended compliment. The moral seems to be that those who prefer literal interpretations tend to resist irony.

Apparently, the humanities in general and artworks in particular contain truths that escape procedures of the hypothetico-deductive method. These limitations ultimately force us to turn toward interpretivism. An immediate benefit of our move toward interpretivism comes from our potential understanding of the present study as a piece of irony. A more dramatic and long-lasting benefit comes from recognizing the way in which this ironic reading implicitly assumes the validity of the interpretive approach.

**COASTAL DISTURBANCES**

Although the preceding apologia for interpretivism and its relevance to a role for the humanities in consumer research strikes us as plausible at the general level, it would be considerably more convincing if we could show that a specific artwork can insightfully be interpreted in a manner that supports our critical stance. In other words, our abstract argument would gain force if we could provide a concrete example of an artistic text that uses consumption symbolism to comment on the meaning of life and the nature of humanity. Toward that end, we shall critically examine the thematic and imaginative structure of a recent play by Tina Howe entitled *Coastal Disturbances*

**An Extended Illustration**

As a critically acclaimed dramatic production that enjoyed successful runs both off and on Broadway, *Coastal Disturbances* exhibits the repeated use of consumer behavior to build consumption microcosms that attain larger metaphorical significance by providing links between art and life. By thus tying together consumption, art, and life, Tina Howe's play uses consumer behavior as a source for symbolic imagery that illuminates the human condition.

In exploring these theatrical devices, we do not mean to suggest that all plays function in this way nor that our own critical analysis is the only acceptable interpretation of this particular artwork. We do suggest, however, that the consumption-in-art-in-life theme provides one valid viewpoint on the meaning of Howe's play and that its validity can be supported by evidence drawn from a close reading of the text -- or, in this case, a careful (re)viewing of the theatrical production. Specifically, the authors have attended several performances of *Coastal Disturbances*, have examined a pre-publication copy of the script (generously supplied by the playwright's associates), and have converged on the interpretation that follows.[6] Our consensus provides some degree of triangulation or intersubjective agreement, but in no way rules out the possibility that others might reach alternative conclusions. Such is the relativity inherent in the critical enterprise that confronts the multiple meanings or "plurivocality" immanent in any artistic or literary text (Ricoeur 1976, 1981).

### Synopsis

*Coastal Disturbances* portrays six adults and two children who spend the last two weeks of August at a private beach on Massachusetts' North Shore. In a rather striking set design, the stage is covered ankle-deep in sand. Its major piece of scenery consists of a tall seat occupied by Leo Hart, the lifeguard who oversees the activities of Faith Bigelow and Ariel Took, two young mothers and former roommates at Wellesley who visit the beach each day with their respective children, Miranda and Winston. The only other regular visitors are M.J. and Hammy Adams, an older couple who appear to be entrenched Bostonians (accustomed to such amenities as playing touch football with the Kennedy family). The action begins with the arrival of Holly Dancer (a beautiful young photographer), who has come from New York to stay with her aunt, fleeing an unhappy love affair with Andre Sor (the owner of a photo gallery) in the City. Holly gradually falls in love with the lifeguard Leo, only to be jolted back to reality when Andre arrives and announces his determination that she return to New York (where she feels trapped and unhappy but alive).

### The Theme

A central theme of the play emerges in a monologue spoken by Andre (his dramatic *raison* d'etre)as he pleads with Holly to come back to New York with him. We shall take this speech as our point of departure, our *Ansatzpunkt*, from which radiate the play's peripheral constellation of meanings (cf. Auerbach 1953, 1969). In this monologue, Andre tells the story of childhood experiences with his father, a Jewish immigrant who left his trade as a jeweler in Antwerp and fled the Nazis to settle in Brooklyn. Having lost access to his artistic materials, Andre's father brought with him only his talent. Every Sunday, Mr. Sor would take his children

---

[6]At the time of writing this paper, *Coastal Disturbances* had not yet reached the stage of publication. However, since Tina Howe's other plays have regularly appeared in print, we trust that this one will also be available, in due course, for any readers who wish to examine its text more closely for purposes of verifying or questioning the validity of our interpretation.

down to a pier by the East River to gaze at Manhattan and to learn the names of its tall buildings. As a former professional diamond cutter and amateur watch maker, now forced to support his family by means of odd jobs and menial labor, Mr. Sor retained the gift of finding the possibilites in the world's minutiae and then turning these possibilities into wonderful creations, much as a jeweler crafts a beautiful gem from a rough stone: "It was his *eye*! He could see the jewel where none existed." In his fallen stature as a handyman and an inveterate collector of discarded odds and ends, Andre's father would bring home huge quantities of other people's cast-off junk ("clock springs, sewing machine parts, glass door knobs, old eyeglasses"). Then, three or four times a year, he would suddenly announce that he had made a new creation, and his delighted children would discover that he had used his apparently worthless assortment of trash to fashion something wonderful. The most marvelous of such creations was a glass sphere containing a miniature clock-like replica of their beloved view of lower Manhattan. Thus, in Andre's story, does consumption inform art via the transformation of otherwise trivial trash into a wondrous invention; thus does art reflect life via a crystal ball that captures a family's most cherished moments; and thus does life imitate artistry via Mr. Sor's visionary ability to delight his children by creating something magical from what to others would seem like the meaningless dross of an otherwise depressing existence: "My father's fancy had not only animated our secret world, it also made it tangible -- something we could hold in our hands."

This compact and crystalline image itself serves as a reflexive embodiment of what it purports to represent -- namely, the creative power of the artist. It stands as a central symbol producing what Spitzer (1967) calls a "click" of awareness through which we can view the rest of the play. In this literary use of marketing imagery, Howe has condensed all phases of the process wherein consumption provides the material from which to construct an artwork that itself presents a microcosm of life. Andre (the businessman) sees his father's ability to turn junk into inventive creations as "a testament to the transforming eye of the artist." He laments to Holly (the photographer) that he himself lacks this gift, "but you and my father - you walk with the angels."

This view of consumption as art, and art as life, and all three as the creative process of finding immanent possibilities and helping them take shape permeates and integrates Tina Howe's play. Andre's tragedy -- the wedge that ultimately estranges him from Holly -- is that he can appreciate the gift but does not himself possess its power. He can admire it, but he cannot do it. Indeed, paradoxically, the more mundane characters in the play come closest to art when they are least concerned with artistic creativity and most concerned with living their lives as ordinary consumers by finding ways to develop their hidden possibilities, much as Andre's father discovered the facets of the stones with which he once worked. Cutting diamonds provides the central metaphor for Mr. Sor's creative vision. Thus, in a telling self-description for the play's program notes, Tina Howe speaks of herself (the playwright) as "pounding her typewriter into jewelry." By implication, she sees her play as a cut diamond whose facets reflect the artistic lesson conveyed by the story in which Andre's father walks with the angels.

## The Structure

This central theme in *Coastal Disturbances* is organized around the setting of the beach (the titular "coast") as the locus for three pairwise matchings, each of which contains a basic contrast, conflict, or contradiction (the titular "disturbances"). These tensions and their associated consumption symbolism provide the play's chief dynamics. Yet, crucial to the play's development, each "coastal disturbance" holds out the possibility of resolution via a type of creative achievement. In Howe's worldview, reconciliation, reconstitution, or rescue remains possible via the enactment of life as a work of art.

The following sections will describe these tensions and potential resolutions. Toward this end, we shall pursue the schematic outline shown in Table 4.

Like the mode of analysis associated with structuralism (e.g., in linguistics, Saussure ed. 1966; in anthropology, Levi-Strauss 1963; in literary criticism, Culler 1975 and Scholes 1974; in consumer research, Levy 1981), our schematic outline is constructed via a series of parallel binary oppositions (tensions associated with various consumption symbolism) that reveal certain homologies (resolutions associated with various creative consumption experiences). However, we intend the validity of our scheme to depend on the internal evidence of the play rather than its tenuous links with structuralism. Let us, therefore, turn to a detailed discussion of that internal evidence.

## Faith Bigelow and Ariel Took

Faith exudes a feeling of fecundity and an overflowing of motherly impulses. Formerly childless, she adopted Miranda, but now has managed to get pregnant and conspicuously displays about six months of fetal progress. She finds herself obsessed by the reproductive process and regards it as endlessly fascinating that baby girls have all their eggs when they are first born and that they therefore possess their childbearing potential from the very beginning. She compares them to nesting Russian dolls that contain dolls inside dolls, layer after layer, until finally one arrives at what seems as if it must surely be the last doll, only to find that it holds lots of tiny seeds with faces painted on them. Cleary, Faith sees children as full of multi-layered potentialities, full of endless seedlike possibilities that need (like Mr. Sor's jewels) to be discovered, shaped, and developed. Unfortunately, however, her parental instincts are lax and overindulgent. She lets Miranda run around the beach with Winston, making a general nuisance of herself and irritating everybody, especially Leo the lifeguard.

By contrast, Ariel sees herself as one of "the true lunatics, the certifiables" and seems to regard her

parental relationship to Winston as a contest of wills - one that she approaches with gratingly shriek-like threats and warnings and one that she appears to be losing in the face of Winston's fractious intractability. Unlike Faith, who has recently found fecundity, Ariel has separated from her husband, has entered menopause prematurely, and now dwells on her perception of herself as infertile and desiccated. Feeling "dried up" and "filled with dust" like a "walking sand bag,": she fantasizes about giving birth, after hard labor, to a small gray ring-tailed moth that flies into the air where the docctor tries to catch it.[7] Ariel's gaze moves upward and encounters Winston, who has climbed onto the railing of the lifeguard chair, where he perches precariously with his arms outstretched like wings and shouts insistently, "Hey everybody, look at me!"

The resolution of the implicit tension between Faith and Ariel lies in the potential fulfillment of their creative roles as mothers of what M.J. calls "those dreadful children." Both Miranda and Winston are obnoxious and ill-behaved; both are disruptive and interruptive. Indeed, other characters must frequently pause in their lines while the mothers yell at their kids in desperate but futile efforts to persuade them to behave and while the children yell back and emit ear-shattering vulgarities. Yet, even in this unruly behavior, there resides the possibility for a creative shaping of these misbegotten children's hidden capacities. In one dramatic scene, Miranda (out of control as usual) steps on some glass, hurts her foot, and requires Leo's expert first-aid assistance. Via the magical restorative powers of some spray disinfectant and via Leo's tender concern for her injury, she is healed -- literally and figuratively. In a parallel movement within the same scene, Leo chides Ariel for yelling at Winston. At first, Ariel is furious; but, during Leo's ministrations to Miranda, Ariel and Winston grow calmer. Ultimately, mother and son appear to have reached some kind of reconciliation. Ariel says that she is "OK...more or less." "More," Winston replies sympathetically. They embrace. Then, together, they carry their collection of umbrellas, tote bags, and picnic baskets from the beach, arm-in-arm in relative tranquility. Ultimately, Winston too is healed -- or, at least, accepted -- when Ariel recognizes his potential: "You're going to be a great man some day.... You've got a lot of spirit. Spirit counts for everything in this world."

---

[7]As implied by one reviewer, regarding this moth imagery as an example of consumption symbolism requires some stretch of the imagination. Those who feel similarly reluctant to tax their imaginative powers may take some comfort in the clear parallelism with the aforementioned Russian doll metaphor. In any event, all will presumably agree that motherhood -- the conceiving, bearing, and raising of children -- is inextricably embedded within the context of daily consumption activities (as in the ritual healing via spray disinfectant discussed in the next paragraph).

**TABLE 4**

| Character Pair | Consumption Symbolism | Tension | Creative Resolution |
|---|---|---|---|
| Faith Bigelow | Russian dolls | Fecundity | Motherhood |
| Ariel Took | Ring-tailed moth | Infertility | (ritual healing) |
| | | | |
| Hammy Adams | Brain coral | Capacity for wonder | Marriage |
| M.J. Adams | Failed sketches | Jaded cynicism | (ceremonial feast) |
| | | | |
| Leo Hart | Lifeguard tower | Stability, vision, and creativity | Relatioship (living |
| Holly Dancer | Camera and tripod | Lost bearings | sculpture) |

## Hammy and M.J. Adams

A parallel tension between the constructive and destructive forces of playfulness and seriousness pervades the actions of an elderly couple, Hammy (an apparently prosperous and probably retired eye surgeon) and his wife M.J. (a rather dour and cynical amateur painter). Hammy shows a capacity for wonder and endless fascination over such otherwise mundane objects as a piece of brain coral and other "treasures from the deep" that he finds washed up onto the shore. In this, paradoxically, he evinces more of the artistic temperament than does his less imaginative wife (who regards his fantastic treasures as "perfectly obscene"). Thus, when he extravagantly admires a sketch that M.J. has just drawn of the beach, she rudely acknowledges his esthetic sensitivity by crumpling it into a wad of paper and storming off. As an eye surgeon, Hammy possesses the power to heal sight, a faculty in which his wife shows some weakness. Indeed, M.J.'s sketches and water colors only serve as ironic manifestations of her own lack of artistic vision. She cranks them out in great numbers, but they mean nothing. She regards them only as pathetic "scribblings" that merely serve to distract her from her loneliness. Herein, she reveals a highly developed capacity for jaded cynicism, commenting importunately to anyone who will listen about Hammy's past marital indiscretions. One senses that these complaints convey more about the relative balance of their creative powers than they do about any tendency toward real infidelity on his part.

Yet, together, in an almost mystical moment of joint creativity, Hammy and M.J. construct the play's most moving artistic symbol. In the last scene, they arrive at the beach carrying a picnic supper, champagne, a table, chairs, a lantern, china, and a billowing tent made from gauzelike white cheesecloth. With Leo's help, they erect this tent and begin a ritual feast performed each year as a celebration of their wedding anniversary. As they sit at twilight, pouring wine and reminiscing over past celebrations, they suddenly reveal the depth of feeling that sustains their long marital bond. We realize that, for all its flaws, their marriage stands (like their bright tent) as their ultimate artistic creation (cut like a shining diamond from the material in their lives). The tent looms as a sculpturesque embodiment of their sustaining love. This effect is heightened by the deeply ironic spectacle of Leo, watching their happiness from the vantage point of his seat on the lifeguard tower, where he contemplates the state of his own precarious relationship with Holly.

## Leo Hart and Holly Dancer

Leo the lifeguard, king and guardian of the sandy beach, is a reformed drifter who has moved through a series of jobs (auto mechanic, double-A ballplayer, contractor, and possibly skydiver or stockcar racer), whose most recent relationship with a woman has failed after three years, and who now longs for the feeling of permanence that would come from settling down and building a solid relationship. His urge toward stability is figuratively embodied by the throne-like lion-hearted majesty of his enormous lifeguard tower -- the tallest, sturdiest, and most overtly phallic object to be found amidst the shifting sands of the beach. From it, he commands a godlike view of all he surveys. His godlike powers appear in his role as guardian (protecting people from drowning), his responsibilities as rule enforcer (preserving the decorum of the beach), his flair for magic (performing parlor tricks to the delight of the audience below), and his capabilities as medicine man (healing Miranda's injured sole). But, most of all, his godlike powers appear in his elevated and expanded vision. His lofty perch instantiates an ability to see comparable to that which Andre ascribes to the artist. Indeed, Andre himself remarks that, on Leo's tower, you "feel like a king.... You can see for miles!" Early in the play, Holly looks across the ocean and jokes that she cannot quite make out the coast of Europe; Leo replies that he can see the Pyramids. More importantly, like an artist, he views life in terms of its creative possibilities. This artistic vision finds its symbolic expression in Leo's sculpturesque reshaping of Holly who, in one vividly evocative scene, lies immobile on the beach while he piles sand on top of her and molds it until she literally cannot move. Having created a sort of living supine statue, he passionately declares to her a love that she reciprocates. Figuratively, their relationship has become his masterpiece.

The relationship between Leo and Holly parallels that of Hammy and M.J. in that, imaginatively as sand sculptor, Leo is the true artist though, as a professional photographer, Holly is the one who makes ostensible claims to artistic stature. Leo tells Holly that she has "incredible eyes," and Andre describes her imagination in similar terms: "No one sees the world like you." Yet, as both an artist and a person, Holly has lost her bearings. She longs to escape from the tormented, unfulfilling relationship with Andre that makes her feel alive but that also sends her into the streets of New York to yell at the traffic. As a person, she balances precariously on the edge of hysteria (constantly on the verge of uncontrollable tears and incessantly complaining that she is "crazy" or "falling apart"). As a photographer, she snaps her camera haphazardly at what appear to be unpromising subjects (the water or Miranda and Winston in candid but essentially uninteresting poses). Indeed, in one crucial scene, Holly struggles in vain to set up her tripod. She swears and curses at it, but cannot make it open. Thus, despite her vilest vituperation, she finds that she cannot get it to work: "I can't handle my equipment, I can't set up a decent shot.... I can't even hold the camera steady." Symbolically, Holly has lost her support and her triangulation on reality. The three-legged foundation for her camera work has failed her. Lately, her art has consisted of taking nude self-portraits of herself. Now the basis for even this mechanistic and narcissistic gesture towards creativity has collapsed. Without Leo's protective, magical, and visionary assistance, her own artistry fails. Her tripod, a symbol for her photographic imagination, will not function without his help.

Later, Holly foresakes this crucial support when she tears herself away from Leo and prepares to return to New York with Andre. Leo feels mortally wounded and draws a clear parallel between himself and a dead whale that has washed up on the beach, its side torn open by sharks: "Did you ever stop to think about how it feels to be going along thinking 'what a nice day' and then you're blindsided?" When Holly arrives at the beach to say goodbye, she wears a chic blue jumpsuit with a black leather belt and high heels. While Holly's feet wobble precariously, Leo steps on Winston's shovel, hurts his own foot, and falls down. Meanwhile, Holly lurches around until he wrestles her to the ground, removes her shoes, and makes her tell him her address and phone number. He scribbles these on an invitation to a showing at Andre's gallery that he snatches from her purse. Significantly, Holly still cannot walk properly -- even without her high-heeled shoes -- but, literally overcome with emotion, she crawls from the beach and leaves Leo to contemplate the ceremonial festivities of Hammy and M.J. from his solitary perch. At first, Leo stares at Holly's empty shoes (which he still holds in his hands as an emblem of his encroaching loneliness). But, while Hammy and M.J. reminisce with growing warmth and affection about their past anniversaries in the glowing white tent, Leo's attention suddenly shifts to the phone number and address scrawled on what we ultimately realize is the invitation to an artistic event. Metaphorically, he clutches his potential access to a creative life with Holly, his living sculpture. As the play ends, Leo begins to smile.

## CONCLUSION

Based on an illustrative interpretation of *Coastal Disturbances*, we may conclude that the humanities in general and the arts in particular bear directly on at least some of the problems of consumer research. If consumption fills life, if art mirrors life, and if both life and art embrace microcosms of consumption behavior that, in turn, capture and reflect the totalities in which they participate (like Mr. Sor's crystal ball), then it follows that consumption and art are interwoven inextricably in our lives. First, as numerous counsumer researchers have pointed out, we consume artistic creations in a manner that deserves study for its implications concerning esthetic value (Holbrook and Zirlin 1985). Second, art represents activities that include the ways in which we consume and that may therefore serve as a source of information about consumer behavior (Belk 1986). Third, art and entertainment may help indoctrinate us into culture of consumption via processes of socialization (O'Guinn, Lee, and Faber 1986). Fourth, art may reflect latent myths and symbols buried in a collective unconscious that underlies our orientation toward pop culture (Hirschman 1987b). Fifth, art may achieve some of its most powerful effects via the manipulation of consumption symbolism and marketing imagery (Holbrook 1987a, 1988a; Holbrook and Grayson 1986). Sixth, as we have tried to show in our interpretation of Tina Howe's play, art may reach beyond the meaning of a specific work to weave symbolic consumer behavior into a pattern that says something about life itself and that thereby comments on the human condition.

All six of these points deserve careful study by consumer researchers, and all six areas of study may benefit from the use of interpretive methods borrowed from the humanities. In this paper, we have played variations primarily on the themes associated with the fifth and sixth points. Here, with respect to the fifth point, our positivistic study of "Close Encounters" should suggest both that the methods of conventional positivism *can* be adapted to investigate topics of interest to the humanities *but* that such applications may well sacrifice the richness of insight and depth of understanding available to more interpretive approaches. As an illustration of the latter, our interpretation of *Coastal Disturbances* attempts to push our understanding of consumption symbolism toward a deeper appreciation of its significance for the human condition. The latter theme, linked to our sixth point, appears to engage areas of lived experience into which conventional positivistic methods can seldom if ever penetrate.

In essence, a work of art such as *Coastal Disturbances* shows consumers going about their daily routines, engaged in processes of consumption. They bring their towels and blankets and umbrellas and chairs to the beach. They eat their picnics and drink their iced tea with fresh orange juice squeezed into it. They wear their swimsuits and show off their chic wardrobes. They put on and take off their sweat shirts.

They work fitfully on their sun tans. In short, they allocate their leisure time to a variety of consumption experiences. But, at a much deeper level, they transform their consumption behavior into the core of their beings. Their consumption experiences provide metaphors for the central concerns in their lives. Their lives become artistic expressions, and those artistic expressions revolve around their experiences as consumers. Those lived consumption experiences - like the play, like the creations of Andre's father, like motherhood, like the festive tent, like Holly's photography, like the jewelry into which the playwright creatively pounds her typewriter -- are works of art. In this, consumer behavior becomes a microcosm of the human condition. In this, consumer research and the humanities comprise one vision in which consumption is a window. In this, like Holly's camera, beneath the watchful eye of a more clairvoyant Lifeguard, our vision rests precariously amidst the shifting sands of time atop a wobbly tripod on the beach, awaiting close encounters along a disturbed but fascinating coastal frontier.

## REFERENCES

Abbagnano, Nicola (1967), "Humanism," in *The Encyclopedia of Philosophy*, Vol. 4, ed. Paul Edwards, New York: Macmillan Publishing Co., 69-72.

Abrams, M. H. (1953), *The Mirror and the Lamp: Romantic Theory and the Critical Tradition*, New York: Oxford University Press.

Abrams, M. H. (1981), *A Glossary of Literary Terms*, Fourth Edition, New York: Holt, Rhinehart and Winston.

Adelson, Joseph (1985), "The Social Sciences and the Humanities," in *Challenges to the Humanities*, ed. Chester E. Finn, Jr., Diane Ravitch, and P. Holley Roberts, New York: Holmes and Meier, 96-107.

Anderson, Paul F. (1987), "On Rhetoric and Research in Consumer Behavior -- A Reply to Certain Psychological Instrumentalists," Working Paper, Pennsylvania State University.

Auerbach, Erich (1953), *Mimesis: The Representation of Reality in Western Literature*, trans. Willard R. Trask, Princeton: Princeton University Press.

Auerbach, Erich (1969), "Philology and *Weltliterature*," *The Centennial Review*, 13 (Winter), 1-17.

Bahn, Archie J. (1962), "Humanitarianism," in *Dictionary of Philosophy* , ed. Dagobert D. Runes, Totowa, NJ: Littlefield, Adams & Co., 132.

Bantock, G. H. (1960), "A Scream of Horror," in *Two Cultures: A Discussion*, pub. Prabhakar Padhye, New Delhi: Congress for Cultural Freedom, 36-43.

Beardsley, Monroe C. (1966), *"The Humanities and Human Understanding,"* in *The Humanities and the Understanding of Reality*, ed. Thomas B. Stroup, Lexington: University of Kentucky Press, 1-31.

Belk, Russell W. (1986), "Art Versus Science As Ways of Generating Knowledge About Materialism," in *Perspectives on Methodology in Consumer Research*, ed. David Brinberg and Richard J. Lutz, Berlin: Springer-Verlag.

Berger, Peter L. (1963), *Invitation to Sociology: A Humanistic Perspective*, New York: Anchor Books.

Berger, Peter L. and Thomas Luckmann (1966), *The Social Construction of Reality: A Treatise in the Sociology of Knowledge*, New York: Anchor Books.

Biocca, Frank, chairman (1987), Special Session on Semiotics, 42nd Annual Conference, American Association for Public Opinion Research, Hershey, PA.

Bird, Otto A. (1976), *Cultures in Conflict: An Essay in the Philosophy of the Humanities*, Notre Dame: University of Notre Dame Press.

Brown, Richard H. (1977), *A Poetic for Sociology: Toward a Logic of Discovery for the Social Sciences*, Cambridge: Cambridge University Press.

Bruner, Jerome (1986), *Actual Minds, Possible Worlds*, Cambridge, MA: Harvard University Press.

Burke, Kenneth (1945), *A Grammar of Motives*, Berkeley: University of California Press.

Burke, Peter (1985), *Vico*, New York: Oxford University Press.

Calder, Bobby J. and Alice M. Tybout (1987), "What Consumer Research Is....," *Journal of Consumer Research*, 14 (June), 136-140.

Camargo, Eduardo G., chairman (1987), Special Session on "Marketplace Semiotics," Summer Marketing Educators' Conference, American Marketing Association, Toronto, Canada.

Cassirer, Ernst (1961), *The Logic of the Humanities*, trans. Clarence Smith Howe, New Haven: Yale University Press.

Culler, Jonathan (1975), *Structuralist Poetics: Structuralism, Linguistics and the Study of Literature*, Ithaca, NY: Cornell University Press.

Danto, Arthur (1981), *The Transfiguration of the Commonplace*, Cambridge: Harvard University Press.

Davy, Charles (1978), *Towards a Third Culture*, Edinburgh, England: Floris Books.

Deshpande, Rohit (1983), ""Paradigms Lost": On Theory and Method in Research in Marketing," *Journal of Marketing*, 47 (Fall), 101-110.

Dilthey, Wilhelm (ed. 1972), "The Rise of Hermeneutics," *New Literary History*, trans. Frederic Jameson, 3 (Winter), 229-244.

Elam, Keir (1980), *The Semiotics of Theatre and Drama*, New York: Methuen.

Fisher, Walter R. (1985), "The Narrative Paradigm: In the Beginning," *Journal of Communication*, 35 (Autumn), 74-89.

Frye, Northrop (1966), "Speculation and Concern," in *The Humanities and the Understanding of Reality*, ed. Thomas B. Stroup, Lexington: University of Kentucky Press, 32-54.

Gadamer, Hans-Georg (1975), *Truth and Method*, ed. Barrett Barden and John Cumming, New York: Crossroad.

Geertz, Clifford (1973), "Thick Description: Toward an Interpretive Theory of Culture," in *The Interpretation of Culture*, ed. Clifford Geertz, New York: Basic Books, 3-32.

Geertz, Clifford (1988), *Works and Lives*, Stanford, CA: Stanford University Press.

Goffman, Erving (1959), *The Presentation of Self in Everyday Life*, New York: Doubleday.

Haire, Mason (1950), "Projective Techniques in Marketing Research," *Journal of Marketing*, 14, 649-656.

Hirsch, E. D., Jr. (1967), *Validity in Interpretation*, New Haven: Yale University Press.

Hirschman, Elizabeth C. (1986), "Humanistic Inquiry in Marketing Research: Philosophy, Method, and Criteria," *Journal of Marketing Research*, 23 (August), 237-249.

Hirschman, Elizabeth C. (1987a), "'Beverly Hills Cop' and Consumer Behavior," in *Proceedings*, Winter Educators' Conference, Chicago: American Marketing Association, 136-141.

Hirschman, Elizabeth C. (1987b), "Movies as Myths: An Interpretation of Motion Picture Mythology," in *Marketing and Semiotics: New Directions in the Study of Signs for Sale*, ed. Jean Umiker-Sebeok, Berlin: Mouton de Gruyter, 335-374.

Holbrook, Morris B. (1987a), "The Dramatic Side of Consumer Research: The Semiology of Consumption Symbolism in the Arts," in *Advances in Consumer Research*, Vol. 14, ed. Paul F. Anderson and Melanie R. Wallendorf, Provo: Association for Consumer Research.

Holbrook, Morris B. (1987b), "The Study of Signs in Consumer Esthetics: An Egocentric Review," in *Marketing and Semiotics: New Directions in the Study of Signs for Sale*, ed. Jean Umiker-Sebeok, Berlin: Mouton de Gruyter, 73-122.

Holbrook, Morris B. (1987c), "Progress and Problems in Research on Consumer Esthetics," in *Artists and Cultural Consumers*, ed. Douglas V. Shaw, William S. Hendon, and C. Richard Waits, Akron, Ohio: Association for Cultural Economics, 133-146.

Holbrook, Morris B. (1988a), "An Interpretation: *Gremlins* as Metaphors for Materialism," *Journal of Macromarketing*, forthcoming.

Holbrook, Morris B. (1988b), "The Positivistic and Interpretive Sides of Semiotic Research on Artistic Consumption," *Proceedings*, Winter Marketing Educators' Conference, Chicago: American Marketing Association, forthcoming.

Holbrook, Morris B., chairman (1988c), "Societal Effects of Market Related Symbols: Hermeneutics and Semiotics," Winter Educators' Conference, American Marketing Association, San Diego, CA.

Holbrook, Morris B. and Mark W, Grayson (1986), "Cinematic Consumption: Symbolic Consumer Behavior in *Out of Africa*," *Journal of Consumer Research*, 13 (December), 374-381.

Holbrook, Morris B. and Neville C. Hughes (1978), "Product Images: How Structured Rating Scales Facilitate Using a Projective Technique in Hypothesis Testing," *The Journal of Psychology*, 100, 323-328.

Holbrook, Morris B. and John O'Shaughnessy (1988), "On the Scientific Status of Consumer Research and the Need for an Interpretive Approach to Studying Consumption Behavior," working paper, Columbia University.

Holbrook, Morris B. and Robert B. Zirlin (1985), "Artistic Creation, Artworks, and Esthetic Appreciation: Some Philosophical Contributions to Nonprofit Marketing," in *Advances in Nonprofit Marketing*, Vol. 1, ed. Russell W. Belk, Greenwich, CT: JAI Press, i-54.

Hudson, Laurel Anderson and Julie L. Ozanne (1988), "Alternative Ways of Seeking Knowledge in Consumer Research," *Journal of Consumer Research*, 14 (March), 508-521.

Hulme, T. E. (ed. 1987), *Speculations: Essays on Humanism and the Philosophy of Art*, ed. Herbert Read, London: Routledge & Kegan Paul.

Huxley, Aldous (1963), *Literature and Science*, New Haven: Leete's Island Books.

Kaufmann, Walter (1977), *The Future of the Humanities*, New York: Reader's Digest Press.

Kermode, Frank (1966), "The University and the Literary Public," in *The Humanities and the Understanding of Reality*, ed. Thomas B. Stroup, Lexington: University of Kentucky Press, 55-74.

Lakatos, Imre (1970), "Falsification and the Methodology of Science Research Programs," in *Criticism and the Growth of Knowledge*, ed. Imre Lakatos and Alan Musgrave, London: Cambridge University Press.

Lamont, Corliss (1962), "Humanism," in *Dictionary of Philosophy*, ed. Dagobert D, Runes, Totowa, NJ: Littlefield, Adams & Co., 131-132.

Lamont, Corliss (1982), *The Philosophy of Humanism*, Sixth Edition, New York: Frederick Ungar Publishing Co.

Lane, Robert, E. (1961), *The Liberties of Wit: Humanism, Criticism, and the Civic Mind*, New Haven: Yale University Press.

Leavis, F. R. (1952), *The Common Pursuit*, London: The Hogarth Press.

Leavis, F. R. (ed. 1972), "Two Cultures? The Significance of Lord Snow," in *Nor Shall My Sword*, London: Chatto & Windus, 41-74.

Levin, Harry (1972), *Grounds for Comparison*, Cambridge: Harvard University Press.

Le'vi-Strauss, Claude (1963), *Structural Anthropology*, trans. Claire Jacobson and Brooke Grundfest Schoepf, New York: Basic Books, Inc.

Levy, Sidney J. (1981), "Interpreting Consumer Mythology: A Structural Approach to Consumer Behavior," *Journal of Marketing*, 45 (Summer), 49-61.

Lincoln, Yvonna S. and Edward G. Guba (1985), *Naturalistic Inquiry*, Beverly Hills: Sage Publications.

Makkreel, Rudolf A. (1975), *Dilthey: Philosopher of the Human Studies*, Princeton, NJ: Princeton University Press.

Matthews, George (1968), *The Domains of Knowledge, The Humanities: The Other Side of the River?*, Cranbrook: The Cranbrook Press.

Mick, David Glen (1986), "Consumer Research and Semiotics: Exploring the Morphology of Signs, Symbols, and Significance," *Journal of Consumer Research*, 13 (September), 196-213.

Morgan, Gareth (1983), *Beyond Method: Strategies for Social Research*, Beverly Hills: Sage Publications.

Nisbet, Robert (1976), *Sociology as an Art Form*, New York: Oxford University Press.

Northrop, F. S. C. (1947), *The Logic of the Sciences and the Humanities*, Woodbridge, CT: Ox Bow Press.

O'Guinn, Thomas C., Wei-Na Lee, and Ronald J. Faber (1986), "Acculturation: The Impact of Divergent Paths on Buyer Behavior," in *Advances in Consumer Research*, Vol. 13, ed. Richard J. Lutz, Provo: Association for Consumer Research, 579-583.

Olafson, Frederick A. (1979), *The Dialectic of Action: A Philosophical Interpretation of History and the Humanities*, Chicago: The University of Chicago Press.

Peter, J. Paul and Jerry C. Olson (1983), "Is Science Marketing?" *Journal of Marketing*, 47 (Fall), 111-125.

Pfeiffer, Rudolf (1976), *History of Classical Scholarship from 1300 to 1850*, New York: Oxford University Press.

Polanyi, Michael (1959), "A Different Perspective," in *Two Cultures: A Discussion*, pub. Prabhakar Padhye, New Delhi: Congress for Cultural Freedom, 22-32.

Popper, Karl (1959), *The Logic of Scientific Discovery*, New York: Harper Torchbooks.

Popper, Karl (1976), *Unended Quest: An Intellectual Autobiography*, La Salle, IL: Open Court.

Richards, I. A. (1935), *Practical Criticism, A Study of Literary Judgment*, New York: Harcourt, Brace & World.

Richards, I. A. (ed. 1970), *Poetries and Sciences*, New York: W. W. Norton & Company.

Ricoeur, Paul (1976), *Interpretation Theory: Discourse and the Surplus of Meaning*, Fort Worth TX: The Texas Christian University Press.

Ricoeur, Paul (1981), *Hermeneutics and the Human Sciences: Essays on Language, Action and Interpretation*, ed. and trans. John B. Thompson, Cambridge: Cambridge University Press.

Saussure, Ferdinand de (ed. 1966), *Course in General Linguistics*, trans. Wade Baskin, New York: McGraw-Hill.

Schleiermacher, Fr. D. E. (ed. 1978), "*The Hermeneutics*: Outline of the 1819 Lectures," trans. Jan Wojik and Roland Haas, *New Literary History*, 10 (1), 1-16.

Scholes, Robert (1974), *Structuralism in Literature*, New Haven: Yale University Press.

Schweder, Richard A. (1988), "The How of the World," *The New York Times Book Review*, (February 28), 13.

Snow, C. P. (ed. 1964), *The Two Cultures: And a Second Look*, Cambridge: Cambridge University Press.

Spitzer, Leo (1967), *Linguistics and Literary History: Essays in Stylistics*, Princeton: Princeton University Press.

Umiker-Sebeok, Jean, ed. (1987), *Marketing and Semiotics: New Directions in the Study of Signs for Sale*, Berlin: Mouton de Gruyter.

Vico, Giambattista (ed. 1976), *The New Science*, trans. Thomas Goddard Bergin and Max Harold Fisch, Ithaca: Cornell University Press.

Westfall, Ralph L., Harper W. Boyd, Jr., and Donald T. Campbell (1957), "The Use of Structured Techniques in Motivation Research," *Journal of Marketing*, 21, 134-139.

# Literary Explication:  A Methodology for Consumer Research

Barbara B. Stern, Rutgers University

## ABSTRACT

This paper examines advertising in a literary context, and demonstrates the use of poetic explication as a methodology to analyze the language of ads. The paper presents the method step by step, illustrates it by analyzing sample ads, and suggests research questions for the future. The paper discusses the following five elements: grammar - the form and structure of individual words; syntax - the arrangement of words in units up to and including the full sentence; diction - the definitional denotation and connotation of words; figures of speech - the language of imagery, especially simile, metaphor, and symbol; and prosody - meter, rhythm, and sound patterns within a text. Questions for research are framed as suggestions for the use of explication to analyze advertising effects on consumers.

> That the one and only goal of all critical endeavors, of all intepretation, appreciation, exhortation, praise or abuse, is improvement in communication may seem an exaggeration. But in practice it is so. The whole apparatus of critical rules and principles is a means to the attainment of finer, more precise, more discriminating communication (Richards 1929, p. 10).

Advertising as a form of communication can be compared to literature: both are "imaginative creations or artful representations of possible worlds [which] strive mightily to redescribe reality" (Leiss, Kline and Jhally 1986, p. 241). The verbal techniques used in ad copy ultimately derive from literature, particularly the metaphorical process that is often considered the source of a text's power to shape perceived reality (Ricouer 1977). When advertising is viewed within a literary context, its imaginative mission bears resemblance to that of poetry: both are encompassed by the Aristotelian concept "imitation of action." Mimesis - poetic imitation - in this sense is defined not as superficial copying, but as "the representation of the countless forms which the life of the human spirit may take, in the media of the arts" (Fergusson 1961, p. 4). When advertising is viewed as one of the newer "arts media," it can be studied in relation to other traditional aesthetic forms: not only poetry, but also music, dance, drama, novels, and song.

The literary relationship can be adapted for advertising research by means of a methodology often found in poetic criticism: explication of a text. Explication is a traditional method for the exhaustive analytical treatment of a small unit of composition: "a line-by-line or episode-by-episode commentary on what is going on in a text...literally, unfolding or spreading out" of the lines (Barnet 1979, p. 9). It entered twentieth-century English poesy by way of the classical French *explication du texte*: a pedagogical method requiring students to explain fully all the language elements in a selected passage. The method's authority in poetic criticism is traceable to Aristotle's *Poetics*; in modern use, it became the "determining principle for the close attention to the text'" practiced by the "New" Critics (Handy and Westbrook 1974, p. 304). Detailed examination of text as document is based on the critical conviction that "the *differentia* of literary art is precisely its formal use of language designed to create a presentational symbol" (Handy and Westbrook 1974, 304). Textual meaning is made accessible through analysis of what Ciardi and Williams call "the poetic structure as a poetic structure" (1975, p. 362). The New Critics usually limit their analyses to the text as an autonomous unit, and do not examine authorial intention, historical context, or biographical data (see Lentricchia 1980). Their explicative methodology may prove useful for advertising researchers bent on understanding the effects of language on consumers, for it provides a systematic and orderly set of guidelines for laying bare the workings of words.

Figurative language in advertising has often been considered in a variety of other word-oriented contexts: semiotic (Cleveland 1986; Durgee 1986; Leiss, Kline and Jhally 1986); psycholinguistic (Harris et al. 1986; Percy 1982; 1987); communication (Berman 1981); mythological (Levy 1986; Olson 1986); symbolic consumption (see e.g. Holbrook and Grayson 1986; Holbrook and Hirschman 1982); and rhetorical (Deighton 1985). Additionally, copy as semiotic text has been discussed in reference to Japanese meanings (see Sherry and Camargo 1987), and copy as a visual (graphic) entity has been examined as well (see Bellizzi and Hite 1985). Headlines have been discussed in reference to alpha-numeric word composition (Boyd 1985), and content categories (Beltramini and Blasko 1986). Only recently has some research attention been focused on copy as literary text (Denny 1986; Stern 1988a,b,c).

This researcher suggests that the Aristotelian criticism of the New Critics represents a "good source of scientifically testable hypotheses" (Calder and Tybout 1987, p. 139) for consumer research. Further examination of advertising within a traditional literary context requires a methodology, and the paper suggests explication as one which can be adapted. Explicative critical readings, while interpretive, appear less subjective once the common vocabulary, theoretical underpinnings, and systemic rules are made clear. Because explication is an organized and rule-laden analytical system, reasonably well-defined poetic dimensions can be adapted to positivist uses. The technical analyses can be used to derive independent variables whose effects on consumer responses to advertising can then be measured. The philosophical stance in this paper is one of rapprochement. A way of bridging the gap between humanistic and scientific research (Hirschman 1986) is suggested in the selection of more rather than less scientific literary criticism (see Lentricchia 1980) and its practical use to illuminate hitherto neglected areas of advertising language. This paper will first set forth the abridged system, next illustrate the points on sample ads, and then suggest research questions for the future.

*Interpretive Consumer Research,* © *1989*
*Association for Consumer Research*

Full and detailed examination of advertising's verbal text is especially worth investigating at present, for a somewhat ironic reason. The trend towards less and less language in advertising implies that less may be more in terms of perceiver effects. Historical analysis of the number of words in ads indicates that "the text has been declining in importance....Textual information has been condensed, its actual content or emphasis changed, and the qualities and function of language transformed" (Leiss, Kline and Jhally 1986, p. 180). While this shift away from words points to the importance of continued research on the increasing pictorial content of ads (Percy 1980), we feel that it also indicates a need to study the words more closely from vantage points other than psycholinguistic. Since ads are likely to contain fewer words, each one may have to convey more to the consumer.

Explication seems an appropriate method because of the structural analogy between ads and poems: both are short and consciously shaped works which use evocative language to affect perceivers (see Cleveland 1986; Durgee 1986; Stern 1988a,b). The goal of this system for textual commentary is to "separate the different parts; the reason for this is the crudely practical one that, although we can perceive several things at once, we cannot describe the several things that we perceive at once, all at the same time; we cannot think two complete sentences simultaneously" (Boulton 1982, p. 6). Explication consciously sets out to untangle the strands in the text, separating them into small manageable units in order to consider each individually. Ultimately, the various strands are recombined into a global whole, for the point is increased understanding of the *gestalt*, the entire work whose meaning resides in numerous and interconnected small parts which synergistically recombine as a totality (Barnet 1979).

The conventions of explication are based on agreed-upon notational rules: the texts are usually quoted in full because they are short, and centered on the page. Each line is numbered: the rule of thumb is that if the passage is longer than one or two lines, each line should be numbered at the right to permit easy reference. Organization of the commentary is generally chronological, beginning with analysis of the first line and continuing in consecutive order to the last (Barnet 1979). However, the relationship between textual chronology and reader processing is not yet known. While there is no set order for considering the various language elements discussed below, we suggest beginning with the more familiar (grammar and figures of speech), and then considering the less familiar: the technical element of prosody (rhythm and sound) which requires a special vocabulary.

The rationale for learning this technically rigorous apparatus lies in its applicability to advertising language (Stern 1988b). Ciardi and Williams's description of language creation is thought-provoking, especially if we replace their "poet" by our "adman": "One sees a wizard of a poet tossing his words in the air and catching them and tossing them again -- what a grand stunt!" (1975, p. 6) The explicative goal of careful examination of "word-wizardry" may facilitate an increased ability to understand verbal effects on consumer/perceivers.

# GRAMMAR

Grammar refers to the form and structure of individual words (Jespersen 1938), and is mostly concerned with case endings: declensions (verbs) and inflections (nouns, adjectives, adverbs). Modern English, however, lacks a full-fledged case ending system: as Jespersen says, "there is a complete disappearance of a great many of those details of inflexion which made every Old English paradigm much more complicated than its modern successor" (1938, p.189). The individual word has become the discrete building block of sentence sense, taking its meaning from position ("John hit Mary" vs. "Mary hit John"), rather than functional endings. Most case endings have disappeared over time, as the language changed away from its heavily inflected ancestors to its modern form. However, analysis of the form of an individual word often requires an assessment of its historical development to understand why it now appears the way it does, and what the form/meaning relationship signifies.

In advertising, where a lone word may be the entire copy, its grammatical form demands particularly careful scrutiny. The minimalist ad is likely to be a brand name: for example, fashion advertising commonly uses proper nouns as the only text - such as "Mimmina" and "Laura Biagotti." Further elaboration involves adding a place name: "Krizia de Milan," or "Chloe´ Paris." Additional nouns, such as stores where products can be purchased or noun descriptors of the product line, can also be included: "Calvin Klein Footwear," and "Geoffrey Beene Knitwear." These lists can be extended by adding complete geographical directories of distributors, enumeration of multi-product lines, listing of telephone numbers, and so forth.

Simple grammatical matters such as the use of case endings become important when advertisers must make purposeful structural choices in an environment of rapid linguistic transition, characteristic of modern English (see e.g. Sapir 1949). The rules for the modern genitive (possessive), for example, are in flux: older forms are being modified, away from "correctness" and towards ease of elocution. "Pears' soap" as Jespersen points out, avoids the juxtaposition of three *s*'s (the full formal usage would be Pears's soap) by adopting an apostrophe. He notes that the guiding principle here is economical "haplology (prouncing the same sound once instead of twice)" which is acceptable -- in fact, found in Shakespeare's plays and poems -- probably because it sounds better than several *s*'s in a row. Jespersen adds, "the genitive of the plural is now always haplologized," and the omission of the genitive sign before a word beginning with *s* is commonplace ("for fashion sake") (1938, p. 197). Likewise, the "s" can migrate (as in "for heaven sakes"), to make pronunciation easier.

Differences in meaning, however, characterize variant forms of genitive use: the presence or absence of an "'s" affects content as well as form. A current ad for Molson beer says, "Molson's [italics mine] is Canada," using the full older genitive. This connects the company, the beer, and the country of origin: the full meaning is "The beer *of* Molson is Canada," since "s" is understood as the contraction of the possessive "of." If the ad were to omit the "s" altogether, ("Molson is

Canada"), the meaning would differ. This invented variant means "Molson [the company itself, rather than its product] is Canada," which makes a different claim: it is a quasi-symbolic identification seen in an Alitalia ad ("Alitalia is Italy"). Whether the copywriter consciously intended this distinction is not known, but the company's implicit approval of the message as it stands is assumed.

Another interesting genitive example is "Lands' End": in the February, 1987 catalogue, a letter writer questions the editor: "I must ask you about your improper use of the apostrophe in your name" (p.55). The "correct" form is Land's End (singular), for Lands' End implies all lands in the plural, surely not what the letter writer thinks the company meant. In a reply, the president writes (Comer 1987, p.55):

> It was a typo in our first printed piece, and we couldn't afford to reprint and correct it. Then we found there were other companies named Land's End (with the apostrophe in the right place). A lot of them. And since we wanted to register copyrights and trademarks, we decided to remain forever Lands' End.

While few readers left to their own devices would notice the incorrect use, the company emphasizes it in a recent ad (May 9, 1988):

> Now that our stock is listed on the New York Stock Exchange (Symbol LE), it seems a good time to make sure you understand we're still the same Lands' End you've always known - right down to the misplaced apostrophe in our name.

Thus, the company positions its misplaced apostrophe as a distinguishing legal and promotional feature in advertising: a tacit acknowledgment of the differentiating potential of even small linguistic elements.

The need to examine each linguistic bit carefully is suggested by a question framed in advertising research: "Why risk losing a successful encoding through a cumbersome grammatical construction?" (Percy 1982, p. 107). Percy further notes that evidence points to "the semantic and grammatical structure of verbal communications as significant mediators of effective communication" (1982, p. 107). This seems especially evident in reference to brand names (see Boyd 1985), an issue requiring additional study to ascertain "whether the initial meaning or lack of it has any bearing upon the speed with which consumers come to learn that name as having `secondary meaning,' that is, as being associated with a product/service from a particular source" (Ross 1982, p. 480). Research on the effects of "plosive" sounds ("c," "k," and "p," for example) in brand names suggests that memorability is enhanced by these sounds (see Schloss 1981; Vanden Bergh 1982/3; Vanden Bergh, Adler, and Oliver 1987). Other effects relating to the form of individual words suggest several questions: What is the effectiveness of one-word ads, presenting a brand or manufacturer's name only? How do they compare to multi-word ads, providing additional information? What is the effect of lists of words (stores, products) on consumers? What results occur when alternative word forms, such as genitives with or without the "'s" are used? To what extent do these rather subtle effects, probably not consciously apprehended by most readers, influence verbal processing? What are the implications of spelling out an entire product name ("Clinique glossy nail enamel") versus the manufacturer's name alone (simply "Clinique" on the product illustrated)? Study of the differences in grammatical form may reveal a wider range of consumer effects than has been suspected.

## SYNTAX

Syntax refers to the arrangement of words in units up to and including the full sentence (Baugh 1957): words, phrases, and clauses, commonly called the building blocks of sentence structure (Hodges and Whitten 1972, p. 489). Because there are so few vestigial case endings in modern English, syntax tends to be regular: "Words in English do not play at hide-and-seek, as they often do in Latin, for instance, or in German, where ideas that by right belong together are widely sundered in obedience to caprice, or more often to a rigorous grammatical rule" (Jespersen 1938, p.11). Yet English is not as rigid as, for example, Chinese, where the same word order occurs virtually 100% of the time. This is an interesting syntactical situation, implying that translation of ads into languages entirely different from our own may require more literary skill than mere transference of meaning. Studies indicate that English word order has become more regular as the language changed from Anglo-Saxon's strong Teutonic syntax to its current shape, characterized by "order and consistency" in the modern stage (Jespersen 1938, p.13). The tradeoff, of course, is that as the language loses its inflectional endings, the word order becomes less flexible.

Because predictable word order is the English norm, any variation disrupts the flow, and merits close attention. Explication often deals with variations, for a legitimate question is: Why has a departure from the norm occurred? Ads with irregular word order are not uncommon, and sentence parsing -- describing and labeling the parts of speech -- is a useful adjunct for identifying irregularities. For example, a Foltene ad - "This is Europe's answer to thinning hair in its attack phase" -- seems a peculiar construction. The adjectival "in its attack phase" by dint of sentence position appears to modify the nearest noun object "hair," yet construing the attack to modify the noun subject "Foltene" itself ("Europe's answer") is also possible. The next sentence seems to support the latter reading: "Foltene. The remarkable European system that actually revitalizes thinning hair." But the placement of the modifying phrase is odd, for it disrupts the accustomed English pattern of adjectivals directly before or after the nouns they modify. The syntax is at least ambiguous, since we do not know whether to interpret the message as the product's attack on thinning hair, thinning hair's attack on the consumer, or -- perhaps -- both. If we assume that the ambiguity is intentional, the syntactical fragmentation moves from the realm of form to that of content. The reader can assume that the ambiguous usage was intended to elicit both readings, to cover - as it were

- all possible bases for conveying the product's "attack" benefit.

Another ad which has aroused considerable comment is "Winston tastes good like a cigarette should," judged "bad" syntactically because "like" is used instead of "as." Formal rules define "like" as a preposition and "as" as a conjuction; grammarians point out that "although widely used in conversation and in public speaking, like as a conjunction is still controversial in a formal context" (Hodges and Whitten 1972, p.218). While this view may express linguistic correctness, it seems more useful to interpret advertising as a genre of communication governed by poetic license rather than by formal prose rules. Jespersen notes that "modern poets do not take their grammar from any one old author or book, but are apt to use any deviation from the ordinary grammar they can lay hold of anywhere....in English a wide gulf separates the grammar of poetry from that of ordinary life" (1938, p.245).

Study of advertising within the canon of poetic grammar can help isolate and classify effects of word constructions on consumers. Poesy studies the aesthetic effects of grammatical constructions, and thus may be a valuable adjunct to linguistic research on better constructions for communication (see Percy 1988). The syntactical matters of sentence length and voice (active vs. passive) have received some research attention (see e.g. Percy 1982), as has headline content (see e.g. Beltramini and Blasko 1986), but many questions remain. Two inter-related ones of some importance are: What effects do syntactical novelty produce on the consumer? And, the corollary: What effects would perfectly correct grammar have? How do consumers react to unexpected word order or apparent violations of a pattern? Does the word patterning encourage the consumer to understand the ad in the way the advertiser intended? Attention can be shifted away from what is "proper" to what elicits the best results and why. Poetry, in fact, is assumed to be most memorable precisely when it breaks free from the expected and surprises the reader. As Percy notes in reference to an experiment with advertising text, "learning, recall, and comprehension all varied, and often significantly, as a function of the grammatical construction of the message" (1988, p. 158). Further study of syntax seems necessary to determine what is going on in advertising language, how, and with what results.

## DICTION

Diction refers to definitional denotation and connotation of a word (Barnet 1979): denotative meaning is what a word actually signifies, while connotative meaning is what is suggested or implied, including the surrounding "emotions or associations" (Hodges and Whitten 1972, p. 230). Virtually all words have connotative associations in addition to their literal dictionary definitions, and convey factual as well as emotional meaning (see Holbrook 1978). Ciardi and Williams emphasize that connotative meaning is a basic quality of words not simply in poetry, but in any context: "a word is a feeling [and] we commonly select language for its feeling (connotation) rather than for purposes of identification (denotation)" (1975, pp. 101-2). In addition, they point out that every word embodies a personal and idiosyncratic history, and "tends to keep its history...as an immediate and intrinsic force" (p. 104). As Brooks and Warren point out, both advertising and poetry are prime users of connotative diction, precisely because the power of verbal association is a desired goal (1960, p.7):

Any writer of advertising copy is perfectly aware of the fact that he is trying to persuade his readers to adopt a certain attitude. Writers of advertising copy, anxious to sell a product, are not content to rest on a statement of fact, whether such a statement is verifiable or not. They will attempt to associate the attitude toward a certain product with an attitude toward beautiful women, little children, or gray-haired mothers; they will appeal to snobbishness, vanity, patriotism religion, and morality...Even the man who is quite certain that he cares nothing for "literature" will find that he constantly has to deal with literary appeals and methods while living in the hardheaded, scientific, and practical twentieth century.

These associations invoke connotations to create a resonance of meanings beyond the literal definition. Advertising creatives assume that the "language of experience is not the language of classification" (Brooks and Warren 1960, p. 2), and thus take liberties with "proper" -- formally correct -- word choice as needed. A language with as rich and varied a word stock as English offers many non-standard usage categories -- archaic, dialectical, rare, regional, vulgar, slang, and so forth -- which make choice of the "right" word extremely complex. Further, "since language is constantly changing, the classification of words is often difficult. There are no clear-cut boundaries between the various classes, and even the best dictionaries do not always agree" (Hodges and Whitten 1972, p.197), often because they are outdated by the time of publication. Because the creative writer habitually reshapes formal rules, the concept of correct usage in ad language is more realistically viewed as `rightness in context': that is, appropriateness to the speaker, the message, and the situation.

The context, of course, changes over time: both denotative and connotative word choices differ as a result of a constantly evolving language. One example of denotative change is an ad for flour: the mid-nineteenth century descriptor "sure-raising" (Strasser 1982, p. 200) has been replaced by "self-rising" (Pillsbury), for consumers would no longer understand the older form. Examples of connotative change in diction can also be found. A 1930's ad for Lux soap powder says, "Avoid undie odor...use new Quick Lux" (Leiss, Kline and Jhally 1986, p. 188); a new ad for a product positioned as an odor and stain remover (Surf detergent) asks, "Does your son's college jersey smell like he's a student at P.U.?" Similarly, an 1891 ad for Kirkman's Borax refers to "Happy Laundry Girls" (Strasser 1982, p. 119); the modern Borax ad avoids mention of any laundry-doers, and instead says: "20 mule-team. Since 1889. 99 1/2% pure." Mule teams, now obsolete, are probably judged an appealingly traditional bit of Americana; "girls," on the other hand, would be read as old-fashioned and sexist. An example of denotative change because of unwelcome connotation is seen in a 1900's ad for underwear: "Root's underwear is made for all sizes of people ---From Babies up to the Largest Men and Women." Nowadays, reference to outsize men and women is more circumspect: large men are called "he men" or "king size," and women "special," "exceptional," or "forgotten." Directing attention to these consumers by labeling them "the largest" is likely to be considered offensive, rather than merely descriptive.

Advertising, like poetry, seems to allow wide scope for non-standard and non-formal usage. However, the word-choice parameters within which ads are most effective are not yet well-understood. Several dictional questions relate to the concept of synonymity: words imputed to have the same meaning. Synonymity of meaning is generally considered theoretically impossible but practically operative. As Hirsch says, "if language is sufficiently flexible to allow the same words different meanings, it is sufficiently flexible to allow different words the same meaning" (1976, p. 63). Percy makes a similar point in reference to advertising: "While it is true that no two words actually have exactly the same meaning, synonyms are those words that are perceived to generally have the same meaning" (1982, p. 108). The practical issue seems to center on whether a word's meaning is studied as a discrete entity or within a particular context, but neither the exact nature nor precise effects of synonymity is fully clear. Although Hirsch suggests that we could test all poetry to determine the extent of synonymity, he quickly adds that it would be a "waste of effort" (1976, p. 59). However, the effort may be worthwhile in advertising research. Questions of synonymity are: What effects result from use of different words connoting similar attributes (such as "quick"/"speedy"/"fast")? Do consumers understand synonyms and homonyms (words with more than one meaning) as intended? Do consumers understand combinative effects of similar word groups as additive synonymy, or does each separate word mean something slightly different? This is especially important when multiple words are used - such as describing a new food product as "quick, easy, and convenient" (Percy 1987, p. 565), for varying connotations may make grouped words "semantically incompatible" (Percy 1982; 1987) in ways the advertiser does not intend.

Another area of concern is the level of dictional difficulty, thought to influence consumer responses.. While "keep it simple" is commonly received wisdom, this may be an oversimplification (Macklin, Bruvold and Shea 1985). Some studies have found that technical wording can have a positive influence, especially on educated audiences (Anderson and Jolson 1980). Less well-educated audiences have been found to perceive number-oriented ads as "more informative, readable, and aceptable" (Bush, Bush and Ortinau 1987, p. R82), despite a decrease in ease of reading. However, the value of number-based copy or technical jargon may be limited or counterproductive in emotional rather than rational appeals. Some questions are: Are there dictional levels appropriate to all advertising, a base-line generic "good usage" similar to that deemed acceptable in formal writing or speech? Or is the appropriate level determined by product type and/or consumer segment? How can the demands of various linguistic publics - copywriters, account supervisors, clients, consumers, writers, professors of English - be balanced to arrive at codes of usage both acceptable and effective? What do consumers perceive as effective word choice? Diction, along with grammar and syntax, merits further study, the better to analyze the meaning of advertising language from the inside out.

## FIGURATIVE LANGUAGE: FIGURES OF SPEECH

The language of imagery, also called figures of speech, is familiar territory, but the terminology as used in literary criticism requires some comment. The literary use is restricted to words alone (not visuals), and the analysis of word combinations in various "figures of speech," -- especially simile, metaphor, and symbol. Imagery is ordinarily defined as "the total sensory suggestion of poetry" (Brooks and Warren 1960, p. 243) -- the sense appeal conveyed by aesthetically appropriate words. Verbal imagery is also essential in advertising, a kindred art inviting "the reader to become an actual participant" in the text. Imagery is what is thought to spark the imagination of the reader, so that "he is taken out of the role of the passively entertained" (p. 242) spectator, and motivated to experience the reality of the text.

Often -- and somewhat confusingly -- the terms "metaphor and metaphoric serve for all figurative comparisons in poetry" (Ciardi and Williams 1975, p. 243). Their importance cannot be overstated: many critics feel that "with a few exceptions, every word traced back far enough is...a metaphor" (p. 105). Even when the metaphorical origins are distant or forgotten, the "pictures locked up in words" affect readers. Ciardi and Williams cite "Billingsgate" (name of the old London fishmarket) as a "dead" metaphor whose original referent is dimly recalled, but whose current usage "conceals within it a picture of the whole wrangling, competitive, and coarse squabbling of a pennygrafting street market" (1975, p. 105). Obviously, "metaphor abounds in advertising," whether the source be rhetoric (Deighton 1985, p. 433) or poetry (Stern 1988a,b).

Metaphors, however, are not the only figures of speech, and differences among the various forms are important. These differences hinge less on what each does than on the process by which it is done. All figures of speech convey comparisons among dissimilar entities, but do not present them in precisely the same way. The definitions adapted here are based on ones given in many poetry handbooks and texts (see e.g. Barnet 1979; Brooks and Warren 1960; Korg 1962), in which the figures are differentiated by overtness of comparative expression. Similes are the most open, metaphors next, and symbols most allusive.

*Similes* signify a direct comparison, in which the reader is told exactly what is like what. A simile "controls the comparison narrowly" (Korg 1962, p. 10) by using "like" or "as" to state the comparison openly: the Citizen Noblia watch is "as sleek as a seal." In contrast, the Winston ad -- "Winston tastes good like a cigarette should" -- is not a simile, because Winston is a cigarette: a statement of fact, rather than a comparison between two things which are dissimilar.

*Metaphors* express comparisons more indirectly, but still in overt fashion: "metaphor differs from simile...in omitting the comparative word" (Korg 1962, p. 9), but still using some form of the verb "to be" (or any other linking verb). For example, "Poison is my potion" compares the Dior perfume to a magical brew, perhaps a love potion, in a fully expressed metaphor. Estee Lauder's new perfume uses the metaphor "Knowing is all" to equate the product with all good things. The fully spelled out equation in a metaphorical format -- A:B::C:D -- is, "Knowing: all other perfumes:: all: nothing." Metaphors are likely to be specific and sensory, for the reader is told that one entity is connotatively equivalent to another which it cannot literally be.

*Symbols* are more allusive and conceptual structures in which the comparative term ("as" or a linking verb) is omitted: one thing (X) is presented as an analogical equivalent to another (Y) which it literally cannot be. However, the transference of qualities is not made overt, for the X term is discussed as if it simply *were* the Y term. A symbol proceeds without open statement of the comparison, and the reader is forced to do the perceptual work necessary to understand what is going on. Symbolism is thought to express "a mysterious connection between two ideas....a very profound function of the mind" (Huizinga 1924, p. 205). In the poetically acceptable language of layered meanings, even though the symbol's X term is never clearly stated, by implication it takes on all the salient characteristics of the Y.

In an advertising example, La Prairie's skincare treatment is symbolically called "skin caviar," a reference to the rarity, costliness, and luxury status of fish roe. The skin cream is discussed as if it were caviar, with no mention of the equivalence ("this cream is caviar"); the reader must deduce the symbolic transference. Since symbols are rarely "pat equivalents, but [instead] areas of meaning" (Ciardi and Williams 1975, p. 18), they may be familiar and clear to the consumer. In this ad, readers can be expected to understand the connotations of "caviar," for the meaning of a symbolic ad is not necessarily obscure.

On the other hand, neither is it automatically clear. Confused ad executions can occur when symbols or metaphors are used without precision or accuracy, in violation of what Ciardi and Williams call the "metaphoric contract" between writer and reader. A "mixed metaphor [is] the situation in which the writer does not abandon metaphor, but slides unwittingly from one metaphor to another" (1975, p. 242) through accident or lack of skill. For example, Charles Jourdan shoes are advertised as worn by "My Angel/ My Devil," a complex symbol later clarified as "a pure woman with a dark side." But the central idea becomes rather convoluted. While most of the copy refers to the woman as devil/angel ("her ambiguity was an art form"), the statement that she was "singing like an angel while dancing *with* [italics mine] the devil" casts some doubt on who the devil really is. Further, Charles Jourdan is said to be "her accomplice, standing by and high, always ready to deter any would-be wooers," which makes the role of the shoe designer and/or company even less clear. How are we to understand shoes "standing by and high"

as deterrents to suitors of a she-devil? Is the woman a devil, attainable sexually only by another devil? If so, what about her angelic purity? Is the point of the ad to show that she can be corrupted? Or that she can NOT be won by the devil? In both poetry and prose, this kind of confusion is often considered careless usage, and odd verbal mixtures critically condemned as inept or grotesque.

Some investigation of concrete imagery has found it superior to abstract or non-imagistic usage in influencing consumer attitudes towards new product innovations (see Debevec et al. 1985). The relative effects of standard vs. novel-pallid metaphors vs. abstract statements have been found associated with product evaluation and persuasion (Kehret-Ward 1987). But researchers have not yet distinguished between kinds of verbal imagery, and we do not know whether similes and metaphors are more or less effective than the admittedly more subtle and allusive symbols. Advertising researchers might want to investigate these issues, since the power of figurative language is commonly tapped, but rarely measured. These effects should be easier to isolate than others, since images ordinarily represent the unifying matter in ads as well as poems. Some questions are: Do metaphors work better for certain product classes? Do consumers understand symbols in the way the advertisers intended? Can different classes of imagery change attitude towards brands and/or ads by making comparisons in overt versus covert ways?

Relevant questions also need to be raised in reference to deceptive advertising. It has been suggested that advertisers might purposely aim at miscomprehension of literal statements, "because it would enable them in apparent innocence to convey messages deliberately that they otherwise could not get into the consumer's head" (Preston and Richards 1986, p. 140.) Can symbolism be used to mislead or deceive consumers by implying, though not stating outright, claims which are unrealistic or even false? While regulatory effort monitors the literal denotative statements in ads, more attention needs to be paid to the symbolic understructure. Here almost anything goes, since the advertiser does not state openly that a brand IS one thing or another; merely that it resembles something else, all of whose desirable qualities are then transferred by implication to the sponsor's product. Ads, like poems, "are mixtures of metaphor and statement," in which metaphor is "the language of double meaning" and statement that of single (Ciardi and Williams 1975, p. 265). But we do not yet fully understand the persuasive strength of one type of figurative comparison versus another, or versus a non-figurative (literal) statement. In order to differentiate legitimate from illegitimate use of imagery, as well as other poetic and rhetorical tropes (Deighton 1985), we must find out whether the consumer attends most to a "single" factual statement, or to the "double" meanings inherent in most figures of speech.

## PROSODY: METER, RHYTHM, RHYME

Perhaps the most under-researched element in advertising is prosodic structure: meter and rhythm, inherent in all language, and rhyme, the singular characteristic of poetry (see MacLachlan 1984). These are technical elements considered in explication, requiring a specialized vocabulary and set of critical conventions for analysis and discussion. In general, the distinctions among the terms are as follows (Ciardi and Williams 1975, p.137, italics mine):

> The movement of language through a pattern of sound variation produces *rhyme* and *rhythm*: *rhyme* is produced by the movement of language through a pattern of variation in *sound quality*; *rhythm* is produced by movement through a pattern of variation in *sound intensity*.

*Rhythm*, the variation in sound intensity, is produced by a pattern of stressed (accented) syllables and unstressed syllables occurring at regular intervals throughout a poem as a whole. English poetry is characterized by emphasis on syllabic stress because of the nature of the language (see Sapir 1949). Rhythm includes *Meter*, the pattern of stressed sounds which occur at regular intervals within the poetic foot, the basic unit of measurement (see also Barnet 1979; Brooks and Warren 1960). Meter thus deals with small poetic units, and rhythm with total pattern. Meter is often considered to include rhyme as well as other sound effects, but we are treating each separately for purposes of clarity. Rhyme, in fact, is but one variation in sound quality, more characteristic of poetry than prose; rhythm is present in both. Brooks and Warren emphasize that "all language has the quality of rhythm," but point out that many degrees of formalization exist between the extremes of ordinary prose and strict rhymed verse (Brooks and Warren 1960, p.562).

## RHYTHM AND METER

Metrical explication seeks to uncover "the systematization of rhythm in so far as this systematization is determined by the relationships between accented or stressed and unaccented or unstresed syllables" in the various kinds of poetic feet found in English verse. Metrical description treats "the kind of foot and the number of feet" (Brooks and Warren 1960, pp. 562-5). Common lengths of line range from monometer (one foot) to alexandrine (six feet); lines of over six feet tend to break up into smaller units. Common types of feet, along with the notation used for description (see also Ciardi and Williams 1975), are as follows in Table 1.

Iambs and anapests are considered "rising meter," trochee and dactyl "falling metre," and spondee neither, but instead, a substitute for an iamb or trochee. An example of metrical analysis of a short ad text -- for Napier Jewelry Company -- is as follows:

$$\text{Napier} \mid \text{is} \mid \text{Twinklier}$$

Two dactyls plus an extra unaccented syllable emphasize the brand name and the benefit. The internal suffix-rhyme sets up an interesting tension between sound and sense, for the name of the company is a real brand, but the stated benefit ("twinklier") an invented word. Nevertheless, the benefit itself is intended to be

---

### TABLE 1

´  accented (stressed) syllable

~  unaccented (unstressed) syllable

| |  pause

| FOOT | DEFINITION | EXAMPLE |
|------|-----------|---------|
| iamb | unaccented and accented syllable | avoid |
| anapest | two unaccented, one accented | intervene |
| trochee | one accented, one unaccented | only |
| dactyl | one accented, two unaccented | happily |
| spondee | two accented | I say |

interpreted as real. The light-verse beat carries the reader along, but the forced rhyme slows him down, demonstrating what Ciardi and Williams call the elements of balance and countermotion that give poetry its emotional force as "countermotion across a silence" (1975, p. 362). Rhythm is expected to function as an element in meaning, for "all metric effect must result from the interplay of the mechanical and the meaningful beat" (Ciardi and Williams 1976, p. 309).

Even more interesting is an ad which seems to show either no discernible rhythm or possibly a discordant one. Estee Lauder's ad for skin perfecting cream reads:

~ ´ ´ ~ ~
At last, perfect skin.

´ ~ ´ ~ ´
Skin perfecting creme

´ ~ ´ ~ ~
Firming nourisher

There does not seem to be a clear metrical pattern: each line has five syllables, but the first line is mixed (an iamb and a trochee), the second trochaic, and the third also mixed, though unlike line 1 (one trochee, one dactyl). Because so much variation exists in fifteen syllables, the lines are judged unscannable. Both because of the constant change, and the large number of stressed syllables (7 out of 15), the reader is forced to proceed very slowly (see below, section on "Cacaphony"). It is a fundamental concept in metrics that "the more caesuras and the more stressed syllables that occur in a given passage, the slower its pace will tend to be" (Ciardi and Williams 1975, p. 307). But this is not necessarily a negative comment, since the writer may want the reader to go slowly, and attend to every word. Speck's analysis (1988, p. 7), in fact, suggests that the pattern is one of "rhythmic diminution," a "calming pattern ... also reflected in the text's use of sound" (see below).

However, we know very little about consumer reactions to different kinds of meter and rhythm. Poetry, at first spoken aloud, is thought to "retain enough of the influence of its origin to make use of sound as one of its major resources. If the reader does not read the poem aloud, he is expected to imagine how it would sound if it were actually read" (Korg 1962, p. 20). The general critical precept is that "verbal music," for the most part read silently now, has universal appeal to the "inner" ear. Pattern in language, present in all recorded tongues, is fundamental to poetry, thought to be rooted in the human desire for orderly and harmonious experience (Ciardi and Williams 1975, p. 137):

Man has always been taken with the patterns through which the things of this world move....Pattern is not the poet's invention: language moves through patterns for anyone who says "willy-nilly," or "See ya later, alligator," or who joins in most any football yell, or who repeats any of a number of good political slogans.

And, we would add, "advertising slogans." Nevertheless, the kind of appeals different metrical patterns possess are mysterious. Some questions about rhythmic effects are: Do certain meters/rhythms work better than others to reinforce textual sense? What situations or conditions determine effectiveness of structured vs. "open" rhythm? What do consumers read as the smallest unit of advertising text (the analogue to a poetic foot)? Scansion of advertising samples can help researchers frame questions about relationships between types of meter/rhythm and product messages which may better illuminate ways of reaching consumers through appeals to their inner ear's sensitivity to tempo.

## SOUND EFFECTS AND RHYME

In addition to rhythm, sound effects characterize poetic language. These are thought to be innately appealing to readers, who enjoy responding not only to the movement, but also to the sound of words (Ciardi and Williams 1975, p.137). While numerous sound effects occur in poetry, the following ones seem especially relevant to advertising text: pauses, euphony and cacaphony, alliteration and assonance, and rhyme. These patterns are often not evident from simple consideration of one or another of the above, and are only revealed when the fullness of sound effects are assessed.

### Pauses

The internal line pause (caesura) is an important sound device, both as a long full-stop and a shorter secondary semi-stop often called a "hovering effect" (Brooks and Warren 1960, p. 563). Writers use pauses to create variations within a pattern, and thus avoid monotonously regular lines. While the location of pauses is ordinarily determined by units of sense, sense and line units need not coincide. That is, not every line ends where the syntactical division -- phrase, clause, or sentence -- ends. Sense divisions can end within a line or spill over beyond the end of one or more lines. Forced pauses, those which interrupt syntax in some way, are especially important, for they are usually associated with emphatic meaning. For example, a Windsor Sail Cruises ad uses pauses as follows:

The first cruise that feels more like a yacht

That sails | | than a hotel that floats.

The line break after line 1 forces a pause before the subordinate clause is ended ("a yacht that sails"), and emphasizes the last word: "yacht." The pause within line 2 emphasizes the word "sails." Both reinforce the message that the Sail Cruise combines the elegance of luxury yacht travel with the romance of sailing ships. The ad goes on to say that these cruises deliver the twin benefits without the drawbacks of "traditional approaches to cruising" which consign passengers to "such stimulating activities as bingo or shuffleboard." Two pauses within one clause appear to be a means by which syntax is deliberately disrupted to focus attention on meaning.

## Euphony and Cacaphony

Certain groups of consonants are considered cacaphonous when they "cause a sense of strain in pronunciation and a slowing of rhythmical tempo" (Brooks and Warren 1960, p. 564). Euphony, the opposite, occurs when "consonant combinations easily pronounced give a sense of ease and tend to speed up the rhythmical tempo." Euphony results from agreeable relationships among vowel sounds, and is present when "a line dominated by closely related vowels gives -- provided other factors support this effect -- a sense of ... fluency" (p. 565). It is important to note that poetic euphony itself is never a primary objective; neither is cacaphony, the difficult pronunciation of certain consonants sequentially, intrinsically unpleasant (Brooks and Warren 1960, p. 149). Both, rather, are useful to produce different poetic effects -- euphony an accelerated "tripping" line, and cacaphony, an impeded "labored" one.

Estee Lauder's ad, previously cited as unscannable, also shows cacaphony:

At last, perfect skin.

Skin Perfecting Creme

Firming nourisher.

The consonantal effects both within and between words (line 1 - "st-p" "rf" "ct-sk"; line 2 - "sk" "p" "rf" "ct" "ng-cr"; line 3 - "f" "rm" "ng-n" "sh") are tongue-twisters, laborious combinations which force the reader to readjust mouth shape and tongue/teeth alignment from word to word. Speck, however, (1988, p. 7) finds that the "cacaphony of lines 1-2 yeilds to euphony in line 3," and suggests that "Perhaps the creators of the ad are trying to imitate the calming, healing, soothing effect of the skin cream that they are describing." His alternate reading, however, is problematical because synonymity of meaning of "firming" and "nourisher" does not seem present.

In contrast, and considerably simpler, the first line of a Mexico Tourism Board ad is euphonious:

When Miguel played it made me feel like a million miles away.

The number of long vowel sounds ("uel" "ay" "made" "feel" "like" "miles" "ay") plus the liquid "l's" (six in one line) create a rolling tempo. The line trips easily off the tongue, and seems to be used to create an experience of pleasant sounds for the reader, perhaps in order to link sound with a delightful product: a beach vacation. Thus, cacaphonous/euphonious sounds can be used to create a sense of tension or a sense of ease, respectively, and the same sounds can be used to force the reader to slow down (and scrutinize each individual unit of meaning) or glide along (and perhaps pay less attention to each word).

## Alliteration and Assonance

In addition to cacaphony and euphony, alliteration and assonance describe important relationships among vowel and consonant sounds: they "involve the element of repetition of identical or of related sounds" (Barnet 1979, p.176). Assonance is defined as "an identity of vowel sounds"; alliteration as "the repetition of consonants, particularly initial consonants" (Brooks and Warren 1960, p.565). In practice, both are used in unaccented and accented syllables.

Advertising alliteration is found in the Motel Six radio ad: "Microprocessor, Megabyte, and Motel-Six....We'll leave the light on for you" ("m" and "l" sounds). The slogan "Introducing Chrysler's Crystal Key Program" ("c/k" sounds) uses alliteration of the same beginning sounds with different spellings, common in English where variable spelling is the norm. Assonance is used in a Kuo Feng tours ad: "Our China tours will have you climbing the wall," ("China-Climb" "Tours-You" "have"-"wall" [inexact]). Pairs of similarly pronounced vowels determine the rhythm here. Both effects are used in a short Regency Hotel ad -- "As preferred as Park Avenue": assonance in "as"/"Park"/"Av," and "-ferred," and "--venue"; alliteration in the "p" sounds, and secondarily, the near-identity of the "f"/"v" pronunciation of "preferred" and "avenue."

## Rhyme

Rhyme, the "regular echoes in the quality of sounds" (Ciardi and Williams 1975, p. 138), functions powerfully in emphasizing key words and highlighting contrasts among words. A fixed pattern -- the rhyme scheme -- demarcates a group of lines as a unit, although irregular rhyme can also appear as a device of emphasis where desired. While much technical analysis of prosody deals with end rhyme (masculine and feminine), traditional patterns (couplets, quatrains), and verse forms (sonnets, lyrics), these do not seem relevant to modern advertising. Most ads resemble "free" (or "open") verse, in which rhyme -- if used at all -- is scattered throughout the text without any fixed pattern or scheme.

Some common types of advertising rhyme are internal (occurring within a line unit), approximate or slant (close rather than full sound correspondence), and weak (unstressed or lightly stressed rhymed syllables). All can be used for special effects. An advertising example of internal rhyme appears in the Hertz ad: "Street smarts....You don't just rent a car. You rent a company." The first phrase is an unusual form of rhyme, resembling a palindrome ("Able was I ere I saw Elba"): here, the opening and closing sounds are identical but reversed - "str-rts." The last sentences show "perfect" internal sound and sight rhyme: the same words -- "you," "rent," and "a" -- are repeated. Internal sight rhyme which is not identical but still near-perfect occurs in the two-word headline for a restaurant, "Le Paris Bistro": "Nouvelle, Schmouvelle," where only the first consonant sound differs, and the second word (made-up) is spelled to correspond exactly with the first.

Slant, internal, and weak end-rhymes are used with free verse randomness throughout the following ad for *Redbook* magazine, titled "A Juggler's Life":

1    She's 34 and a real estate broker.
2    Seven days a week she makes New
3        Englanders feel right at home.
4    Makes her home in Brattleboro, Vermont.

5    Married to Scott.
6    Mother to Jordan, 4 (preschool
7        valedictorian).
8    Loves to lift her spirits with a daring
9        downhill run.
10   Has been known to quote:
11       "Cleaning your house while the kids
12       are still growing is like shoveling the
13       walk before it stops snowing."
13A      (Phyllis Diller)
14   This baby boomer relies on Redbook
15       and her tenacious drive to open
16       new doors.

Slant rhymes occur in 1 and 15 ("broker"-"open") and 4 and 5 ("Vermont"- "Scott"), where the same vowel precedes different consonants; 14 and 16 ("book"-"doors") where sight rhyme occurs in the repetition of "oo"; 7,9, and 15 ("valedictorian," "run," "open"), where "n" consonants are repeated as endings; and perhaps 12 and 13 ("shoveling"-"snowing"), although line 12 ends with "the," a weakly accented extra syllable. Alliteration is found within lines 1, 2, 4, 5, and 6; it unifies lines 8 and 9 ("l" and "d" sounds). Assonance is present in lines 2 ("days"-"makes," "week"-"new"), 4 ("home," "- boro," "-mont"), 6 ("mother"-"Jordan"), and 10 ("known"-"quote").

The quote attributed to Phyllis Diller is characterized by both assonance (ll 11-15 "h<u>ou</u>se/gr<u>ow</u>/sh<u>ov</u>eling/ sn<u>ow</u>ing") and perfect end rhyme ("clean<u>ing</u>/grow<u>ing</u>/ shovel<u>ing</u>/snow<u>ing</u>"). Interestingly, if the quote were rearranged on the page, it would be a recognizable quatrain:

1    Cleaning your house while the kids
2    Are still growing
3    Is like shoveling the walk
4    Before it stops snowing

As Speck points out, "this is a simile ("is like") that uses parallel syntax ("cleaning...while...growing" ‖ "shoveling...while...snowing"), internal rhyme (words ending in "-ing"), and a combination of alliteration and end rhyme ("still growing, stops snowing") to strengthen the comparison." He adds a cogent analysis of the lines (1988, p. 8):

The syntactical parallel is so strong (antithesis) and the contrast so stark (hyperbole) that the passage seems "ironic" and the author's intent "humorous." Thus, sound qualities (alliteration and rhyme) serve to enhance a syntactical parallelism that strengthens a figurative comparison [simile] that creates irony which in turn leads to humor....this attributed quote provides a humanizing and ironic counterstatement...[which] allows the reader to think "she's not perfect, she has felt overwhelmed, she's like me."

The subtle rhythmic pattern thus may reinforce *Redbook's* decision to downplay the superwoman message, the "too, too perfect...image they were trying to avoid" (Speck 1988, p. 8).

Many questions related to rhythm and sound effects arise in advertising. In reference to pauses, we do not know what effects natural and/or forced pauses have on readers. Do consumers understand advertising text where syntactical sense is interrupted by artificial pauses? When euphony and cacaphony are used, do certain consonants/vowels strike consumers as pleasant/unpleasant? Are there generic precepts in advertising governing sound combinations, or, like poetry, do pleasing/displeasing effects relate to product/message context rather than sounds *per se*? What are the uses of euphony and cacaphony in different product areas? In what situations might incongruous messages - pleasing product, cacaphonous verbals or vice versa - be effective?

Prior research has indicated that alliteration and other prosodic elements function in brand name selection strategy (Schloss 1981; Vanden Bergh 1982/3; Vanden Bergh, Adler, and Oliver 1987). But extended uses of alliteration and assonance in the full ad text raise further questions. To what extent do consumers find them memorable? Most of us recall the alliterative "Four P's," but we do not know the effects of interactive combinations of alliteration and/or assonance in multiple word groups. Do consumers "see" either effect when it is inexact visually ("c/k") but exact in pronunciation? As for rhyme, what are the effects of strong (end) versus less strong internal or approximate rhyme schemes? Do certain kinds of rhyme suit certain product classes? Indeed, do consumers perceive the subtler forms of rhyme (slant, internal, inexact) at all, given the limited time and attention devoted to advertising messages? Until the uses of advertising rhyme are catalogued and tested, it seems fair to say that advertising may not be paying close enough attention to a traditionally powerful tool for affecting perceivers.

## CONCLUSION

Thus, explication permits investigation of advertising in new ways as a result of a methodology of close textual analysis long used in poetics. The study of effects of ad language on consumers can be refined by this methodology, for it aims at breaking down the components of copy into separate testable bits. As information is garnered about the pieces, patterns for discerning effects of the whole can be expected to emerge.

Methods drawn from literature's sister arts - music, painting, dance, cinematography - may also have much to contribute to advertising research, since visual, lyrical, and kinetic effects often accompany verbal messages. Both rhetorical and dramatic effects inherent in a speaker's delivery, not normally considered in explications, require further research efforts. Advertising as communication can profitably be viewed from the vantage point of art as well as science, for the element of creativity -- what Brooks calls the great poetic power of "awakening the mind" (1947) -- sparks greatness wherever it alights. Analyzing the components of creativity in a variety of humanistic disciplines can foster positive interaction between art and science, giving rise to a relationship in which each illuminates the other as intertwined facets of human experience. T.S. Eliot's homage to words has deep meaning for advertisers as well as other communicators in our society (1962, p.144):

....And every phrase
And sentence that is right (where every word is at
    home,
Taking its place to support the others,
The word neither diffident nor ostentatious,
An easy commerce of the old and the new,
The common word exact without vulgarity,
The formal word precise but not pedantic,
The complete consort dancing together)
Every phrase and every sentence is an end and a
    beginning.

## REFERENCES

Anderson, Ralph E. and Marvin A. Jolson (1980), "Technical Wording in Advertising: Implications for Market Segmentation," *Journal of Marketing*, 44 (Winter), 57-66.

Barnet, Sylvan (1979), *A Short Guide to Writing About Literature*, Fourth Edition. Boston, MA: Little, Brown, & Co.

Baugh, Albert C. (1957), *A History of the English Language*, Second Edition. New York, NY: Appleton-Century-Crofts, Inc.

Bellizzi, Joseph A. and Robert E. Hite (1985), "The Effects of Sale Headline Size and Position on Perceived Discount Levels and Other Perceptual Measures," in *1985 AMA Educators' Proceedings*, Robert F. Lusch et al.(eds.), Chicago, IL: American Marketing Association, 245.

Beltramini, Richard F. and Vincent J. Blasko (1986), "An Analysis of Award-Winning Advertising Headlines," *Journal of Advertising Research* 26 (April/May), 48-52.

Berman, Ronald (1981), *Advertising and Social Change*, Beverly Hills, CA: Sage Publications.

Boulton, Marjorie (1982), *The Anatomy of Poetry*, Revised Edition. London, England: Routledge & Kegan Paul.

Boyd, Colin W. (1985), "Point of View: Alpha-Numeric Brand Names," *Journal of Advertising Research*, 25 (October/November), 48-52.

Brooks, Cleanth (1947), *The Well Wrought Urn: Studies in the Structure of Poetry*, New York, NY: Harcourt, Brace and Company.

Brooks, Cleanth and Robert Penn Warren (1960), *Understanding Poetry: Third Edition*, New York, NY: Holt, Rinehart, and Winston.

Bush, Robert P., Alan J. Bush, and David J. Ortinau (1987), "The Effect of Number-Based Copy on Readers' Perceptions of Print Advertising: An Exploratory Study," in *Proceedings of the 1987 Conference of The AmericanAcademy of Advertising*, Florence G. Feasley (ed.), Columbia, SC: The American Academy of Advertising, R79-82.

Calder, Bobby J. and Alice M. Tybout (1987), "What Consumer Research is...," *Journal of Consumer Research*, 14 (June), 136-140.

Ciardi, John and Miller Williams (1975), *How Does a Poem Mean? Second Edition*. Boston, MA: Houghton Mifflin Co.

Cleveland, Charles E. (1986), "Semiotics: Determining What the Advertising Message Means to the Audience," in Jerry Olson and Keith Sentis (eds.),*Advertising and Consumer Psychology*, *Volume 3*, New York, NY: Praeger Publishers, 227-241.

Comer, Gary (1987), "Lands'(sic) End," in "Letters to Lands' End," *Lands'End Catalogue*, (February), 55.

Debevec, Kathleen, Patricia W. Meyers, and Kenny K. Chan (1985), "The Effects of Knowledge and Imagery on Advertising Responses to an Innovation," in *Advances in Consumer Research, Vol. XII*, Elizabeth C. Hirschman and Morris B. Holbrook (eds.), Provo, UT: Association for Consumer Research, 273-278.

Deighton, John (1985), "Rhetorical Strategies in Advertising," in *Advances in Consumer Research, Vol. XII*, Elizabeth C. Hirschman and Morris B. Holbrook (eds.), Provo, UT: Association for Consumer Research, 432-436.

Denny, Rita (1986), "Can Metaphors Be Harnessed for Advertising?" Discussion Paper for Special Session, "The Effects of Metaphor in Advertising," Association for Consumer Research Annual Conference, Toronto: Unpublished.

Domzal, Teresa J. and Lynette S. Unger (1985), "Judgments of Verbal versus Pictorial Presentations of a Product with Functional and Aesthetic Features," in *Advances in Consumer Research, Vol. XII*, Elizabeth C.Hirschman and Morris B. Holbrook (eds.), Provo, UT: Association for Consumer Research, 268-272.

Durgee, Jeffrey F. (1986), "Richer Finds in Qualitative Research," *Journal of Advertising Research* (August/September 1986), 36-44.

Eliot, T.S. (1962), "Little Gidding," in *The Complete Poems and Plays 1909-1950*, New York, NY: Harcourt, Brace & World, Inc.

Fergusson, Francis (1961), *Aristotle's Poetics*, S.H. Butcher (trans.), New York, NY: Hill and Wang.

Handy, William J. and Max Westbrook, eds. (1974), *Twentieth Century Criticism: The Major Statements*, New York NY: The Free Press.

Harris, Richard J., Ruth E. Sturn, Michael L. Klassen, and John I. Bechtold (1986), "Language in Advertising: A Psycholinguistic Approach," in *Current Issues and Research in Advertising, Volume 9, Nos. 1 and 2*,James H. Leigh and Claude R. Martin, Jr. (eds.), Ann Arbor, MI: University of Michigan, 1-26.

Hirsch, Jr. E.D. (1976), *The Aims of Interpretation*, Chicago, IL: The University of Chicago Press.

Hirschman, Elizabeth C. (1986), "Humanistic Inquiry in Marketing Research: Philosophy, Method, and Criteria," *Journal of Marketing Research*, 23 (August), 237-249.

Hodges, John C. and Mary E. Whitten (1972), *Harbrace College Handbook, Seventh Edition*. New York, NY: Harcourt Brace Jovanovich, Inc.

Holbrook, Morris B. (1978), "Beyond Attitude Structure: Toward the Informational Determinants of Attitude," *Journal of Marketing Research*, 15 (November), 545-556.

_____ and Mark W. Grayson (1986), "The Semiology of Cinematic Consumption: Symbolic Consumer Behavior in *Out of Africa*," *Journal of Consumer Research*, 13(December), 374-381.

_____ and Elizabeth C. Hirschman (1982), "The Experiential Aspects of Consumption: Consumer Fantasies, Feelings, and Fun," *Journal of Consumer Research*, 9(September), 132-140.

_____ and William L. Moore (1981), "Feature Interactions in Consumer Judgments of Verbal Versus Pictorial Presentations," *Journal of Consumer Research*, 8 (June), 103-113.

Jespersen, Otto (1938), *Growth and Structure of the English Language, Ninth Edition*, Garden City, NY: Doubleday & Company, Inc.

Kehret-Ward, Trudy (1987), "Explaining the Effects of SENSING IS EVALUATING Metaphors: The Mediation of Vividness and Novelty," in *Advances in Consumer Research, Vol. 15*, Melanie Wallendorf and Paul Anderson (eds.),Provo, UT: Association for Consumer Research, 403.

Leiss, William, Stephen Kline, and Sut Jhally (1986), *Social Communication in Advertising: Persons, Products, & Images of Well-Being*, Toronto, Canada: Methuen, Inc.

Lentricchia, Frank (1980), *After the New Criticism*, Chicago, IL: The University of Chicago Press.

Levy, Sidney J. (1986),"Meanings in Advertising Stimuli," in Jerry Olson and Keith Sentis (eds.), *Advertising and Consumer Psychology, Volume 3*. New York, NY: Praeger Publishers, 214-226.

Olson, Jerry (1986), "Meaning Analysis in Advertising Research," in Jerry Olson and Keith Sentis (eds.), *Advertising and Consumer Psychology, Volume 3* New York, NY: Praeger Publishers, 275-283.

MacLachlan, James (1984), "Making a Message Memorable and Persuasive," *Journal of Advertising Research*, 23 (December/January), 51-59.

Macklin, M. Carole, Norman T. Bruvold, and Carol Lynn Shea (1985), "Is It Always as Simple as `Keep It Simple'?" *Journal of Advertising*, 14, 28-35.

Percy, Larry (1982), "Psycholinguistic Guidelines for Advertising Copy," in *Advances in Consumer Research, Vol 9*, Andrew Mitchell (ed.), Provo,UT: Association for Consumer Research, 107-111.

_____ (1987), "Understanding Semantic Compatibility in Communication," in *Advances in Consumer Research, Vol. 15*, Melanie Wallendorf and Paul Anderson (eds.), Provo, UT: Association for Consumer Research, 565.

_____ (1988), "Exploring Grammatical Structure and Nonverbal Communication," in *Nonverbal Communication in Advertising*, Sidney Hecker and David W. Stewart (eds.), Lexington, MA: D.C. Heath and Company, 147-158.

Preston, Ivan L. and Jef I. Richards (1986), "The Relationship of Miscomprehension to Deceptiveness in FTC Cases," in *Advances in Consumer Research, Vol. 13*, Richard J. Lutz (ed.), Provo, UT: Association for ConsumerResearch, 138-142.

Richards, Ivor A. (1929), *Practical Criticism: A Study of Literary Judgment*, New York, NY: Harcourt Brace and Company.

Ricoeur, Paul (1977), *The Rule of Metaphor*, Toronto, Canada: University ofToronto Press.

Ross, Ivan (1982), "The Effect of Brand Names, " in *Advances in Consumer Research, Vol 9*, Andrew Mitchell (ed.), Provo, UT: Association for Consumer Research, 478-480.

Sapir, Edward (1949), *Language: An Introduction to the Study of Speech*, New York, NY: Harcourt, Brace & World, Inc.

Schloss, Ira (1981), "Chickens and Pickles: Choosing a Brand Name," *Journal of Advertising Research*, 21 (December), 47-49.

Sherry, John F. Jr, and Eduardo G. Camargo (1987), "`May Your Life Be Marvelous': English Language Labellling and the Semiotics of Japanese Promotion," *Journal of Consumer Research*, 14 (September), 174-188.

Smith, Lawrence D. (1986), *Behaviorism & Logical Positivism: A Reassessment of the Alliance*, Stanford, CA: Stanford University Press.

Speck, Paul S. (1988), "Letter to the Author," Knoxville, TN: Unpublished.

Stern, Barbara B. (1988a), "Figurative Language in Services Advertising: The Nature and Uses of Imagery," in *Advances in Consumer Research, XV*, Michael J. Houston (ed.), Provo, UT: Association for Consumer Research, 185-190.

_____ (1988b), "How Does an Ad Mean? Language in Services Advertising," *Journal of Advertising*, 17 (Summer), 3-14.

_____ (1988c), "Medieval Allegory: Roots of Advertising Strategy for the Mass Market," *Journal of Marketing*, 52 (July), 84-94.

Strasser, Susan (1982), *Never Done: A History of American Housework*, New York, NY: Pantheon Books.

Vanden Bergh, Bruce G. (1982/3), "Feedback: More Chickens and Pickles," *Journal of Advertising Research*, 22 (December/January), 44.

_____ , Keith Adler, and Lauren Oliver (1987), "Linguistic Distinction Among Top Brand Names," *Journal of Advertising Research*, 27 (August/September), 39-44.

# The Relevance of Historical Method for Marketing Research

Marilyn Lavin, Northeastern University
Thomas J. Archdeacon, University of Wisconsin-Madison

## INTRODUCTION

For several decades a small group of researchers has recognized that history can make important contributions to the understanding of marketing and consumer activities. Preeminent among this band has been Stanley Hollander. In the past 30 years Hollander produced numerous works that examine such diverse topics as the evolution of retail organizations (1960; 1966; 1977; 1980), repression of traveling salesmen in the United States during the 19th century (1964), the history of consumerism and retailing (1973), the historical dimensions of the service encounter (1985), and historians' views of consumption (1986). Hollander's work has been well-received, but until recently it inspired few other marketing and consumer behavior academicians to incorporate an historical perspective in their studies.

The reasons for the lack of enthusiasm shown to history have been outlined by Ronald Savitt (1980). While urging marketers to give greater consideration to the role of history in their discipline, he recognized that most marketers favor research based on the operationalization of constructs and on the testing of explicit hypotheses. As a consequence, he argued, they are naturally ill at ease with the majority of historians, who write within the framework of a narrative structure and construct their theses inductively rather than deductively.

In recent years some academicians in marketing and consumer behavior have begun to question their disciplines' absolute reliance on positivist/empiricist methodology and have become interested in humanistic/interpretive approaches. This intellectual shift has been contemporaneous with and has perhaps facilitated the consideration of the possible contributions of history. Several conferences held at Michigan State University have brought researchers together to consider the relevance of history for marketing (Hollander and Savitt, 1983; Hollander and Nevett, 1985). Other scholars have participated in sessions devoted to the topic at the annual conferences of the Association of Consumer Research (Firat, 1985; 1987).

Marketing and consumer researchers who have turned to history have readily accepted the importance of understanding the development over time of marketing institutions and consumer behaviors. Many of the papers offered at the Michigan State and ACR conferences have presented brief studies of marketers or marketing practices from earlier eras. Others have sought to acquaint researchers with unfamiliar data sources that might prove useful in reconstructing the histories of certain contemporary marketing practices. And following an investigation using traditional historical methodology, Fullerton (1988) has raised serious questions about the widely-accepted scheme of periodization that divides the business history of the last 100 years into the Production, Sales, and Marketing Eras.

The recent outpouring of historically-oriented research has enriched the literature of marketing and consumer behavior. At the same time, however, those works have often at least implicitly misrepresented the methods of historical research. More important, they seem sometimes to have reduced the "historical method" to a willingness to gather enough information to reach a definitive understanding of the past, which, in turn, can be used to illuminate the present.

Historical method involves more than a consideration of temporal context and more than a reliance on non-quantitative analytical techniques. Modern historical research operates from the assumption that the concerns of the present will inevitably color the scholar's insights into the past. Historians do not necessarily believe that truth is relative, but they do recognize that the search for it inescapably uses current values in understanding the "facts." Historical research on any topic involves not only an accumulation of knowledge but also a dialectical assessment of how particular personal or cultural biases have influenced previous historians' interpretations. For those reasons, the historical method demands a special consciousness of the role of interpretative paradigms. Insensitivity to that aspect of any historical argumentation can be very dangerous.

In pursuing its points, this paper first considers how historians align themselves in the positivist-interpretive debate and discusses changes within the discipline of history that are bringing its practical techniques for analyzing data closer to those of the other social sciences. It next calls attention to the continuing importance for history of internal critical methods born of the dialectical nature of the discipline and necessary to the role it plays in shaping social discourse. Finally, the paper attempts to give substance to its abstract arguments by examining the course of historical argumentation on a specific issue with serious implications for contemporary marketing and consumer behavior researchers.

## METHOD IN HISTORY AND MARKETING

### a. Quantitative and Qualitative Approaches

Marketers and other researchers interested in consumer activities who have acknowledged the importance of history have insisted on the significance of historical context, that is the placing of an event within its broader temporal framework. Although such an appreciation of temporal background initially appears benign, closer examination reveals that the advocacy of "context" has in many cases been equated with historicism, a philosophically dubious viewpoint that emphasizes the uniqueness of all temporal phenomena (Fullerton, 1987; 1988; Kumcu, 1987).

More important, such a limited construal of "context" may unnecessarily confound the acceptance of historical method with a debate, which is currently being carried on in both marketing and consumer behavior, on the utility of empiricist/positivist methodologies versus interpretive/humanistic approaches (Hirschman, 1986; Hudson and Ozane, 1988).

The majority of historians view reality as socially constructed, recognize individual freedom, and acknowledge multiple causation. Their intellectual inclinations appear consistent with humanistic/interpretive paradigms. A substantial minority of historians, however, would argue that the "interpretive" paradigm slights the importance of theory in research and, because of its inductive approach, cannot be considered scientific.

Those historians who criticize the interpretive paradigm do not form a united front. Some are primarily students of the philosophy of history, interested in definitions of cause and effect and in concepts of progress and change. Others have sought to develop grand theories of history. Perhaps the most notable of those are Marxists, whose ideas about economic determinism and class struggle afford them a critical framework for analyzing much of the modern age. Although both of the preceding groups incorporate elements of the positivist approach, a final group of historians is much more directly indebted to it. Those scholars may lack a grand theory of history, and many will deny that creating one is even a reasonable goal. They make the more limited argument that theories -- usually of the mid-range kind -- inevitably shape the formulation of research; that historians must strive to make explicit those theories they implicitly use; and that a properly stated theory is one that, in keeping with the canons of modern science, permits the development of testable hypotheses.

For the most part, interpretive and scientific historians have largely ignored one another and peacefully coexisted within the discipline. Their divergent approaches, however, have become enmeshed with an on-going controversy among historians over the utility of quantitative research techniques. The debate should be of interest to marketing and consumer researchers. For more than a decade numbers of political, economic, and social historians have argued that at least a subdivision of their discipline must operate as a quantitative social science. Marketers who skim through journals like *Historical Methods Newsletter*, the *Journal of Interdisciplinary History*, or *Social Science History* will find themselves in friendly territory of research models and statistical analyses.

In some sense, the work of quantitative historians may be seen as an effort to move their discipline toward the positivist-empiricist tradition. Those scholars seek to place their work within carefully defined theoretical frameworks. Moreover, they argue strongly for the operationalization of constructs, and they utilize sophisticated statistical techniques to test their hypotheses.

Quantitative social scientists are a minority among historians, but they have made progress against resistance to their approach. They have convinced a number of their "mathematically anxious" colleagues that quantitative evidence is sometimes useful and that some historians should be able to work with it. They have argued against fears that an increased "technicalism" will cut historians off from their potential mass audience. Noting that professional historians have only rarely been popular historians, they argue that academics tend to write for each other and to trust that what is lasting in their work will eventually reach the general public.

Supporters of the scientific approach have more trouble with the arguments of such renowned scholars like Carl Bridenbaugh (1963) and Jacques Barzun (1974) that quantification cannot answer the really important questions. The social scientists can reasonably claim that, in the past two decades, historians who rely on quantitative evidence have reshaped the profession's understanding of voter behavior, the institution of slavery, patterns of economic and social mobility, and other vital topics. Nevertheless, they admit that the critics are not simply cranks, and are sensitive to allegations that the quantitative approach can exalt the trivial. They know that the sharp focusing of questions prized in their approach can yield insights with broad implications. But they are also aware that a set of good data - good in the sense of available and manageable - can tempt some to undertake research that is long on technical virtuosity and short on substance.

Whatever their orientation, most historians agree that the significance of the questions asked is more important than the access to data that can answer them. The issues of interest to the vast majority of historians involve eternal conflicts in human values. Moreover, historians are sensitive to individual peculiarities and to special circumstances, and wary of supposed "rules" of human behavior. And while social scientist historians think that their discipline must seek higher levels of generalization than many of their peers believe possible, the difference between the two camps is one of degree rather than one of kind. Even as they espouse their version of the scientific approach, quantitative historians also recognize that they can never totally escape their own temporal context or their own personal value systems.

The obstacles to the acceptance of quantitative methods among historians should be of interest to marketers and consumer researchers, who have enthusiastically accepted this methodology and have eagerly sought new statistical techniques. Overall, marketers' openness has led to impressive advances in research, but the direct ties of their techniques to the logical positivist tradition and to theory verification may also have narrowed the scope of their studies. Some marketers, including Jagdish Sheth (1981) and Rohit Deshpande (1983), have argued that qualitative methods may be more appropriate for the early, exploratory stages of research. Their suggestions that non-quantitative methods can play a role in discovery is important, but even that recognition may radically underestimate the significance of qualitative approaches.

Marketing exchanges and other consumer activities occur in dynamic environments, often involve large groups rather than individual buyers or sellers, and may be influenced by diverse cultural, social, and political forces. Although quantitative methods easily gained ascendancy in the discipline, few studies have examined the impact of such broad factors on marketing. Indeed, the constraints and assumptions of the dominant methodology may be partly responsible for the major research gaps. Have the kinds of data necessary to apply quantitative techniques to essentially qualitative macro questions been too costly to obtain, or, in some cases, even impossible to generate, given the current level of knowledge about identifying and measuring the pertinent phenomena? More to the point, has a commitment to measuring of regularities in human behavior caused marketers to underestimate the impact of unique circumstances or of temporal discontinuities? If the answer to either or both of those questions is "yes," marketers must ask themselves whether methodological convenience or the imperatives of immediate problems determine the course and content of marketing and consumer behavior investigations.

Elizabeth Hirschman (1986) has recently pointed out the relevance of the participant-observer method for marketing studies. Her insightful argument, however, does not exhaust the potential contributions of humanist inquiry to the broadening of marketing method. Historians have benefited from partly subjective interpretations of such diverse sources as archival records, artifacts, diaries, and government documents. Their methods of critical, albeit non-quantitative, analysis of those data have led to better understanding of major phenomena, including the development of democratic institutions, the effects of industrialization, and changes in family structure.

## b. Historiographic Method

The second point of the paper touches on the social purpose of the historian's endeavor and the nature of the critical methods associated with it. The historian's role is to make the past intelligible in terms that will allow people of the present to understand better what has shaped their world and their lives. For example, as concerns about issues of gender have gained increasing attention in recent years, historians have re-examined the history of women and reconsidered their importance in shaping the social order. It is this interaction between the present and the past that prevents the content of history from becoming stagnant.

At the same time, however, historians are conscious that bringing the concerns of the present to the study of the past can put at risk two of their central imperatives: that they respect the integrity of the past and that they call attention to what was unique about it. Most of them, therefore, will be appalled when a researcher reduces such a Puritan religious dissident as Anne Hutchinson to a prototype of modern feminism (Koehler, 1974). They recognize, however, that such interpretative excesses inevitably crop up in research that is informed by contemporary relevance, and they are confident that the discipline's internal defenses will quickly weed out clear distortions.

History is a dynamic, not a definitive discipline. An important part of the historical method is its continuing internal dialectic. Historical understanding grows by a process in which historians subject to

criticism the ways in which the present-mindedness of their predecessors caused them to distort the past. Historians not only correct outmoded concepts through this endeavor; they also maintain an awareness of their own susceptibility to time-bound biases. Historiography, the analysis of the writing of history is, therefore, integral to the discipline. The introspection it provides is an essential element of the historical method and is a source of strength as well as an admission of imperfection.

No discipline is immune from the kinds of time-bound intellectual biases against which historians openly struggle. Not even those disciplines that pride themselves on being scientific and on demanding numerical verification of evidence are as objective as they like to believe. The best quantitative analyses are no stronger than the hypotheses that they test. As Thomas Kuhn's (1962) dissection of the cultural clashes in scientific revolutions and Stephen Jay Gould's (1981) critical history of the rise of psychometric testing have demonstrated, the fundamental theories in any era may be based as much on its subjective assumptions as on available objective evidence.

Marketing and consumer behavior research may presently have special needs for introspection. During the past several decades, marketing theorists have given considerable attention to demarcating the scope of their field and to asserting its status as a science (Kotler, 1972; Hunt, 1976). Over the same period consumer research has undergone parallel development (Sheth and Gross, 1988). Together they have produced a body of literature capable of supporting an intellectual history that would explain why different topics came to the fore or received special emphasis at various times.

Several scholars have attempted to describe chronologically the evolution of marketing thought and to connect it with broader intellectual and academic trends. Bartels (1965) sketched an account of marketing's formative periods, and Sheth and Gardner (1982) briefly considered the development of the six dominant schools in contemporary marketing. But, if marketers are to use historical studies to help define an identity for their discipline, as recommended by Savitt (1980), they must move beyond general descriptive approaches to more fundamental questions. They might consider, for example, the extent to which the immediate needs of practitioners have or have not shaped marketing and consumer studies. They might also ask whether the distinct schools within marketing simply reflect different facets of common theory or whether they signify a more unifying intellectual structure has not yet emerged.

Researchers in the history of marketing and consumer behavior might also survey the fields from which their colleagues heavily borrow their theories and techniques to discover whether they have been adopted for substantive or idiosyncratic reasons. For example, using a typology of scientific styles proposed by Mitroff and Kilman, Hirschman (1985) has demonstrated how world views, academic training, intellectual interests, and methodological commitments influenced the approaches of four central researchers in consumer behavior. Rajiv Dant (1985) has examined the influence that several theoretical frameworks borrowed from social psychology have had on the character of marketers' research on channel behavior. Additional work of this kind, especially of a more inclusive scope, might explain why some marketing topics have received considerable, if not excessive attention, while others have remained largely neglected. It might also raise issues about the appropriateness of taking theoretical paradigms from other disciplines.

## HISTORICAL METHOD IN MARKETING: AN APPLICATION

The importance of understanding both history and historical method is apparent by examining, from an historian's perspective, a problem of growing concern to marketing and consumer behavior researchers. It involves the description and explanation of the marketplace activities of the several million residents of the United States who are aliens or the offspring of immigrants and who spend their lives within ethnic - and particularly Hispanic or Asian - subcommunities. The argument presented is that marketing and consumer researchers, because they have not been historically sensitive, have not sufficiently considered the policy aspects of this problem. Instead, in their present attempts to understand and reach these sets of consumers they have adopted a theoretical framework in danger of becoming outmoded; they have slighted potentially important distinctions between the groups being targeted; and they have perhaps even risked creating a backlash against their efforts.

### a. The Problem

When marketers contemplate strategies aimed at appealing to the cultural affinities of ethnic and linguistic minorities, they step into a long-standing political and social controversy in our society. Tensions between the successive waves of immigrant nationalities coming to the New World and those peoples who preceded them have been constant. During the 17th and 18th centuries, English settlers established cultural dominance in the 13 North American colonies, but by the mid-19th century Irish Catholic and non-English speaking Germans represented a sizable proportion of the United States population and challenged extant Anglo-Protestant norms. In the late 19th and in the 20th centuries, the cultural unity of the nation endured further shocks: at the turn of this century, sources of migration shifted to southern and eastern Europe and large numbers of Italians and Russian Jews came to American shores. In more recent decades, adverse political and economic conditions in their homelands have brought a new influx of culturally different peoples, in the form of Hispanic and Asian immigration to this country. Across the centuries newcomers have tried to preserve and to pass on their cultures, and natives have expected them to adapt to the mores of the majority. What has varied, however, have been the society's confidence in its ability to absorb and acculturate alien peoples and the intensity of its effort to force immigrants and their offspring to conform.

Each encounter between aliens and Americans has led to a re-examination of the processes of immigration and assimilation. But theories about that process, such as the "melting pot," the "triple melting pot," and "cultural pluralism" have been essentially historical generalizations intended mainly to explain past events. They have not been designed for predictive purposes, and they lack the level of specification about the actions and interactions of variables that one would expect from true models. Moreover, the theories that have been proposed often seem to support "social myths" used to restore communal stability and to rationalize the accommodations that have been reached with each succeeding wave of newcomers. As such, those theories are time-bound. Like the interpretative paradigms of the historian, they fuse insights into the past with present concerns.

Marketing and consumer researchers do not seem especially aware of the historical contexts that have shaped immigration and assimilation in America and the society's understanding of those phenomena. Practitioners and academics, therefore, have based their applications and their research on current assumptions about those processes, without critically examining the reasons for those notions. As a result, they may misjudge the limits of the theories that they implicitly apply, and they may miss future shifts in social attitudes.

Modern ethnic marketing campaigns probably took off during the racial crisis of the 1960s, when black Americans complained about the discriminatory message implicit in commercials that treated them as invisible. Once it became socially responsible for firms to acknowledge one minority, they had to include others to avoid alienating them. Eventually, marketing went beyond this passive policy of inclusiveness to an active identification of minority and ethnic groups as potential market segments. Marketers conducted research to uncover distinctive consumer behaviors in non-English speaking markets, and they developed extensive advertising campaigns based on direct appeals to specific ethnic groups.

Despite the proliferation of ethnic marketing, it has not generated much academic interest. An examination of the leading journals over the past five years reveals no articles on the topic in the *Journal of Marketing Research*, two each in the *Journal of Marketing* (Schaninger et al., 1985; Wilkes and Valencia, 1985) and the *Journal of Advertising Research* (O'Guinn and Meyer, 1984; Valencia, 1983-184), and four in the *Journal of Consumer Research* (Wallendorf and Reilly, 1983; Saegert et al., 1985; Deshpande et al., 1986; Reilly and Wallendorf, 1987). More important, publications on ethnic marketing are concerned mostly with documenting the existence in various groups of cultural traits related to consumer behavior.

An historian is struck by the dearth of scholarship on the social policy issues involved in ethnic marketing, because, at least within the context of American history, such a strategy is potentially controversial. The lack of adequate work implies that marketing and consumer academicians either exclude such analytical dimensions or lack expertise in disciplines that would naturally pursue questions involving history and policy. Whatever the reason, it is doubtful that either marketing practice or the understanding of consumption activities is well served by this intellectual blind spot.

## b. The Model of Cultural Pluralism

In documenting the existence and persistence of separate identities and cultural differences among ethnic groups, marketers are contributing to a research stream fed also by historians, political scientists, sociologists, economists, anthropologists, and psychologists. Over the past quarter century, a consensus has developed among them that, contrary to previous expectations, ethnic identities have proved surprisingly resilient. Holding together much of their work, however, has been the assumption that ethnic differences are non-threatening and that cultural diversity may even be beneficial to the society. Working within this context, neither marketing nor consumer researchers have needed to ask whether individual groups or the whole society pays a price when ethnic differences are exploited for the purpose of selling goods.

The interpretative theme of benign "cultural pluralism," however, is of recent vintage. In particular, its emergence has been tied to the study, by their descendants in the 1960s and 1970s, of the southern and eastern European ethnic groups that made their first sizable appearances in the United States between 1890 and 1920 (Archdeacon, 1985). That research is an example of a phenomenon described a half century ago by the historian Marcus Lee Hansen (1937). He argued that by the time an ethnic group was in the United States three generations, its members would have achieved enough social and economic security to be able to express feelings of pride in their heritage that the immigrants had been unable to articulate and that their children often rejected.

The theory of "third-generation interest" may apply to all ethnic groups, but the interpretations vary from generation to generation. Thus, works done on those "Old Immigrant" groups from northern and western Europe whose members arrived in large numbers during the mid-nineteenth century analyzed the immigrants' adaptation to America in ways very different from studies on the "New Immigrant" groups arriving at the turn of the twentieth century. In particular, the former de-emphasized the extent to which the immigrants and their children retained old values and ways. They stressed, instead, the Americanization of those peoples.

Several factors underlay the change in the interpretation of assimilation from the "melting pot" model applied to the "Old Immigrant" nationalities to the "cultural pluralist" one applied to the "New Immigrant" arrivals of the early twentieth century. Within the discipline of history, a shift of scholarly concerns from chronicling the activities of the affluent, educated, and powerful to studying the everyday lives of ordinary people drew attention to elements of the society less likely to have achieved complete integration. In addition, the groups of the New Immigration were more distant from the Anglo-1American culture that was the norm of the host society than were those of the Old Immigration. It was logical, therefore, that investigators would find signs of cultural differences persisting longer among the former than among the latter.

Societal forces also played a role in the rise of cultural pluralism. The constructive reinterpretation of an ethnic group's history in America is one of the later elements in the process of its assimilation, and the research has tended to present the people being studied in a light that will advance their acceptability in the body politic. The coming of age of the New Immigrant nationalities coincided with the emergence of the civil rights movement, which emphasized the separate status of American Blacks and the presence of seemingly permanent cultural divisions in the United States. The nation's rejection of racism and its acceptance of the reassertion of Black pride legitimated the existence of cultural pluralism and led to policy decisions that distributed social benefits not to the completely assimilated but to those whose minority status was documented. Unlike the super-patriotism of the post World War I era, which demanded that the Old Immigrants prove how completely they had been assimilated, the developments of the 1960s encouraged, and perhaps made necessary, emphasis on the retention of ethnic differences in the New Immigrant experience (Archdeacon, 1983).

Acceptance of an interpretative framework that accepts the existence of ethnic differences as desirable and of indefinite duration, however, may have passed its apex. Indeed, it experienced problems from the beginning. As early as the mid-1960s Milton M. Gordon, whose *Assimilation in American Life* (1964) was one of the seminal works on the importance of ethnoreligious differences, warned that cultural pluralism does not exist in the United States. He argued that American society has instead experienced "structural pluralism," in which different groups operate within separate economic and social networks while conforming to general expectations that they share in the nation's version of Anglo-Saxon culture, including use of the English language.

During the 1980s, in a natural and even predictable example of the historiographic revision of an interpretative scheme in vogue for nearly a quarter century, scholars of immigration and ethnicity have begun a re-evaluation of the cultural pluralist interpretation. In an important essay, John Higham (1982), who is perhaps the dean of American historians working in the field and who once protested the tendency of Americans to "homogenize" their history (1959), has criticized the cultural pluralist paradigm for underestimating the power of the forces working to integrate those who have come to the United States into a single people. Stanley Lieberson (1985), another longtime student of the subject, has called attention to the fact that the fastest growing group in surveys of ethnic identifications are those Americans who feel no European ties at all. Likewise, after extensive research on Italian Americans, supposedly one of the most culturally retentive nationalities, Richard D. Alba (1985) has presented the thesis that the ethnicity of the descendants of the European immigrants is now in its "twilight" phase.

The preceding summary of the waxing and possible waning of the cultural pluralist outlook should make marketing and consumer behavior academicians more sensitive to concerns that are prominent in historical studies. It should warn them of the on-1going need to attempt to separate the understanding of fundamental historical processes - such as the assimilation of immigrants and their descendants - from the time-bound normative interpretations made about them. And it should make marketing and consumer researchers appreciative of the importance of particular circumstances on general processes. The discussion presented, for example, would appear to lead to the conclusion that the strength and the content of ethnic identity as well as the willingness to express or tolerate it depends not only on a underlying tension between new and old experiences and mores. It also reflects personal factors in the possessor's life, including generational status and specific ethnic background, and societal circumstances, most notably the contemporary political climate of the host society.

## c. Applications to Hispanic and Asian Markets

In regard to the issue of marketing to ethnics, the preceding discussion suggests some immediate considerations for understanding consumption behaviors and developing marketing strategies. Of course, as presented here, those ideas are tentative and often lacking the quantitative support that most marketing and consumer researchers would like to see. The suggestions, however, could easily be re-expressed as hypotheses suited to a marketing/consumer behavior context and evaluated with data collected specifically for the purposes of testing them.

The preceding discussion indicates that researchers studying the relationship between ethnicity and market/consumption behavior must consider the number of generations that have passed since the era of an ethnic group's main period of immigration to the United States. For example, one recent article examined ethnic origin as a possible explanation for differing patterns of food consumption detected among Poles, Blacks, and Hispanics (Reilly and Wallendorf, 1987). The researchers found the ethnic variable had a very weak effect. They did not, however, take into account the facts that Poles have been in this country for several generations; that Blacks are a racially distinct group; and that many Hispanics are first generation immigrants.

Researchers should not assume ethnic identification to be equivalent across various groups. The revival of interest in ethnic origin shown by European groups, and especially by those from the southeastern quadrant of the continent, in the third generation after their arrival was a key to the rise of the cultural pluralist theory. Archdeacon (forthcoming), however, has warned against confusing the third generation's increased interest in heritage with a serious "return to ethnicity" that some cultural pluralists believe occurs.

Current research treats the ethnicity of peoples long established in the United States as a "symbolic" rather than a primordial phenomenon. As Gans (1979) has noted, for such people ethnicity involves "less of an ascriptive than a voluntary role" that they can express "in ways that do not conflict with other ways of life" (pp. 7-8). The evidence suggests that, with the passage

of time, ethnic feelings become less a nostalgia for remembered peasant folkways and more an identification with abstract or refined elements of the ancestral culture with which the immigrant forebears had little contact. Tricarico (1984) has indicated that Italian-Americans seeking to express pride in their roots are likely to link quality with fashionable items produced in the old country. In a similar vein, Shannon has noted that large numbers of socially mobile Irish-Americans are unconcerned about Northern Ireland but "like to give their child a very Irish name and drink Bailey's Irish Cream and buy Waterford crystal" (*New York Times*, August 1, 1986).

Appeals of the kind that may sell the accouterments of continental sophistication to affluent Americans of remote European ancestries may prove premature when directed at ethnic groups composed heavily of recent arrivals. Despite the fact that some Hispanics and Asians have been in North America for generations, the most rapidly growing portion of those markets is composed of recent arrivals; moreover, almost all the Hispanics and many of the Asians are of low socioeconomic status. A conflict between the merchandise offered and the socioeconomic status of the targeted consumers may at least partly underlie the economic difficulties that the *New York Times* recounted as plaguing Houston's El Mercado del Sol mall, which had been touted as "a showplace of Hispanic culture and commerce." More appropriate may be marketing efforts that cater to the immediate needs of such newcomers and help them function within the larger society. The *Wall Street Journal* has pointed, for example, to the growing number of banks operated by Hispanics that are providing the same service for Spanish-speaking residents as the Bank of America offered an earlier generation of immigrants in its days as the Bank of Italy (November 24, 1986).

Designing a marketing strategy to reach the American offspring of the immigrants who have been entering this country legally or illegally in increasing numbers since the mid-1960s is more problematic. The objective evidence, from all historical periods, is that members of the second generation are caught between the culture of their families and that of the nation. Historians, however, have imposed conflicting subjective values on that generalization. Cultural pluralists have chided the host society for demanding conformity; as marketers, they might see efforts to reach second-generation Americans in terms of their ethnic heritage not only as potentially effective but also as humane. Another, older interpretation, however, has argued that the second-generation wants to be "American" and, as part of a reasonable commitment to the future, consciously resents the overtones of foreignness that it cannot escape. As marketers, those "assimilationists" might argue that appeals to second-generation ethnics as anything but complete Americans can backfire.

History, therefore, may not give a clear answer to the problem of understanding the consumer behaviors and formulating appropriate marketing strategies for the second generation. It does, however, indicate what issues researchers should consider. They must first determine the feelings that their potential target markets have regarding their position as ethnic minorities. In that regard, they must second recognize that the responses of different groups - for example, of Hispanics and Asians - may not be the same. And, finally, they must take into account the prevailing attitude among most members of the host population toward the presence of visible cultural divisions in their society, because that outlook will determine the political climate in which ethnic groups must operate.

Compared with immigrants of previous generations, those coming in recent years may be more desirous of preserving their heritages and better able to accomplish that goal. On the one hand, some Asian newcomers to the United States have levels of education high enough to make them good carriers and transmitters of culture. On the other, while Hispanics have tended to be poor and unschooled like past immigrants, they have not moved far and are able to maintain close and constant ties with their native cultures.

Nevertheless, it would be imprudent to assume, without empirically verifiable evidence, that Asians and Hispanics will not suffer the sharp decline of native culture that other ethnic groups have voluntarily or involuntarily experienced in the second generation. Like other immigrant peoples before them, Asians may hold tight to their religions in America and seek to marry within their specific ethnic groups. But, as educated and aspiring men and women, whose families have already made one fundamental decision to opt for the West, they are likely also to see a road to acceptance and accomplishment in rapid Americanization. Likewise, assimilative pressures seem to be at work among the Hispanic population. Deshpande, Hoyer, and Donthu (1986), for example, have found that Mexican-Americans display varying degrees of ethnic affiliation that, in turn, are associated with differing patterns of consumption behavior. It would be interesting to know what else the authors might have discovered had they included a generational variable in their study.

Of all the issues involved with devising an ethnic marketing strategy, those relating to general public opinion are the most ethically and practically troublesome. Marketers should be deeply bothered that current academic criticism of cultural pluralism may be a signal of even more volatile shifts in popular attitudes. The scholars mentioned and others making similar arguments are uniformly people of generous spirit who deeply identify with newcomers to these shores and believe in America's destiny as a "nation of immigrants." But the rhythms of historiographic change suggest that their findings may now indicate that Americans, in general, may be moving toward an era of declining sympathy with diversity. Such a development would not be unprecedented; indeed, it would be more typical than the liberalism of recent years in regard to traditional American attitudes.

Cultural pluralism was the intellectual product of a society that had learned to manage the ethnic divisions left over from an earlier age of immigration. As a philosophy of survivors, its credibility depended in part on the assumption that American culture would endure no further challenges from newcomers. Now, however, immigration is once again a major phenomenon, seen by many to be out of control and to be at the root of all the nation's ills. Popular willingness to tolerate alien cultures may be withering. When "Sixty Minutes" (October 5, 1986) telecast a segment on the economic revival created in Miami by Cubans and other Hispanics, irate native Floridians wrote to the show to express their anger at living in an increasingly bilingual society. Likewise, Justice Department officials have identified violence against Asians as the fastest growing form of discrimination in the United States (*Wall Street Journal*, November 28, 1986).

Ominous portents of the future may be emerging in California, which has anticipated the nation in so many other social trends. In November, 1986, 73 percent of those who went to the polls in California voted in favor of Proposition 63, which gives any resident or person doing business there the right to sue if the legislature or state officials act in ways that "diminish or ignore the role of English as the state's common language" (*Los Angeles Times*, November 6, 1986). Likewise, Californians who support the movement to make English the sole official language of the United States, have been vigorously protesting advertisements present in various Asian languages (*New York Times*, July 21, 1986).

As a final consideration, therefore, marketers must realize that ethnic appeals may lead to a backlash in even larger markets. They must not be afraid to exercise their right to free speech, and they should also be willing to stand up against prejudice and bigotry. But marketers must also recognize that the difference between offering legitimate services to minorities and unnecessarily inflaming among the members of the broader community fears of an impending ethnic Balkanization of their society.

## CONCLUSION

Accepting contemporary theory structures as givens is a risky business for marketing and consumer researchers. By overlooking the evolution of those operating assumptions and the social conditions that have nurtured them, those scholars may base their analyses on what may prove to be unstable and transient foundations. They might be wise to examine more closely the larger issues behind the problems for which they are asked to provide understanding and strategies. In that endeavor, history can be a valuable ally.

## REFERENCES

Alba, Richard D. (1985), "The Twilight of Ethnicity among Americans of European Ancestry: The Case of the Italians," *Ethnic and Racial Studies*, 8, 134-57.

Archdeacon, Thomas J. (1983), *Becoming American: An Ethnic History*, New York: Free Press.

———— (1985), "Problems and Possibilities in the Study of American Ethnic History," *International Migration Review*, 19, 112-34.

———— (forthcoming), "Hansen's Hypothesis as a Model of Immigrant Assimilation," in Dag Blanck and Peter Kivisto, eds., *The Third Generation Immigrant Revisited*, Urbana: University of Illinois Press.

Bartels, Robert (1965), "Development of Marketing Thought: A Brief History," in *Science in Marketing*, edited by George Schwartz, New York: Wiley, 47-169.

Barzun, Jacques (1974), *Clio and the Doctors: Psycho-lHistory, Quanto-lHistory, and History*, Chicago: University of Chicago Press.

Bridenbaugh, Carl (1963), "The Great Mutation," *American Historical Review*, 68, 313-131.

Dant, Rajiv (1985), "Behavioral Channel Conflict Research: Slave of Paradigms" in Proceedings of the Second Workshop on Historical Research in Marketing, Stanley Hollander et al., eds., East Lansing: Department of Marketing and Transportation, 441-155.

Deshpande, Rohit (1983), "'Paradigms Lost': On Theory and Method in Research in Marketing," *Journal of Marketing*, 47, 101-110.

Deshpande, Rohit, Wayne D.Hoyer, Naveen Donthu (1986), "The Intensity of Ethnic Affiliation: A Study of the Sociology of Hispanic Consumption," *Journal of Consumer Research*, 13, 214-120.

Firat, A. Fuat (1985), "A Critique of the Orientations in Theory Development in Consumer Behavior: Suggestions for the Future," in *Advances in ConsumerResearch*, 12, E.C. Hirschman and M.B. Holbrook, eds., Provo: Association for Consumer Research.

_____ (1987), "Historiography, Scientific Method, and Exceptional Historical Events," in *Advances in Consumer Research*, 14, M. Wallendorf and P.F. Anderson, eds., Provo: Association for Consumer Research.

Fullerton, Ronald A. (1987), "The Poverty of Ahistorical Analysis: Present Weakness and Future Cure in U.S. Marketing Thought", in *Philosophicaland Radical Thought in Marketing*, A.F. Firat, N. Dholakia and R.P. Bagozzi, eds., Lexington: Lexington Books.

_____ (1988), "How Modern is Modern Marketing? Marketing's Evolution and the Myth of the 'Production Era,'" *Journal of Marketing*, 57, 108-125.

_____ (1988), "Modern Western Marketing as a Historical Phenomenon:Theory and Illustration", in *Historical Perspectives in Marketing*, T. Nevett and R.A. Fullerton, eds., Lexington: Lexington Books.

Gans, Herbert (1979), "Symbolic Ethnicity: The Future of Ethnic Groups and Cultures in America", *Ethnic and Racial Studies*, 2, 1-120.

Gordon, Milton M. (1964), *Assimilation in American Life: The Role of Race, Religion and National Origins*, New York: Oxford University Press.

Gould, Stephen Jay (1981), *The Mismeasure of Man*, New York: Norton.

Hansen, Marcus Lee (1937), "The Problem of the Third Generation Immigrant," republication with introductions by Peter Kivisto and Oscar Handlin, Rock Island, Illinois: Swenson Swedish Immigration Research Center and the Augustana College Library.

Higham, John (1959), "The Cult of 'American Consensus': Homogenizing Our History," Commentary, 27, 93-1100.

_____ (1982), "Current Trends in the Study of Ethnicity in the United States," *Journal of American Ethnic History*, 2, 5-115.

Hirschman, Elizabeth C. (1985), "Scientific Style and the Conduct of Consumer Research," *Journal of Consumer Research*, 12, 225-139.

_____ (1986), "Humanistic Inquiry in Marketing Research: Philosophy, Method, and Criteria," *Journal of Marketing Research*, 22, 237-149.

Hollander, Stanley C. (1960), "The Wheel of Retailing", *Journal of Marketing*, 24, 37-147.

_____ (1964), "Anti-1Salesmen Ordinances of the Mid-1Nineteenth Century". In S.A. Greyser, ed., *Toward Scientific Marketing*, Chicago: American Marketing Association. 334-151.

_____ (1966), "Notes on the Retail Accordion", *Journal of Retailing*, 42, 29-140.

_____ (1973), "Consumerism and Retailing: A Historical Perspective", *Journal of Retailing*, 48, 6-122.

_____ (1977), "Comments of the Retail Life Cycle", *Journal of Retailing*, 52, 83-186.

_____ (1980), "Oddities, Nostalgia, Wheels and Other Patterns in Retail Evolution". In R.W. Stampfl and E. Hirschman, eds., *Competitive Structure in Retail Marketing: The Department Store Perspective*, Chicago: American Marketing Association.

_____ (1985), "A Historical Perspective on the Service Encounter". In J. Czepiel, M. Solomon, and C. Surprenant, eds., *The Service Encounter*, Lexington: Lexington Books.

_____ and Terence Nevett, eds. (1985), Marketing in the Long Run: Proceedings of the Second Workshop on Historical Research in Marketing, East Lansing: Department of Marketing and Transportation, Michigan State University.

_____ and Kathleen Rassuli (1986), "Desire -1-1 Induced, Innate Insatiable?", *Journal of Macromarketing*, 6, 4-124.

_____ and Ronald Savitt, eds. (1983), Proceedings of the First North American Workshop on Historical Research in Marketing, East Lansing: Department of Marketing and Transportation Administration, Michigan State University.

Hudson, Laurel and Julie Ozane (1988), "Alternative Ways of Seeking Knowledge, in Consumer Research", *Journal of Consumer Research*, 14, 508-121.

Hunt, Shelby D. (1976), "The Nature and Scope of Marketing," *Journal of Marketing*, 40, 17-128.

Koehler, Lyle (1974), "The Case of the American Jezebels: Anne Hutchinson and Female Agitation during the Years of Antinomian Turmoil, 1636-11660," *William and Mary Quarterly*, 31, 55-178.

Kotler, Philip (1972), "A Generic Concept of Marketing," *Journal of Marketing*, 36, 46-154.

Kuhn, Thomas (1962), *The Structure of Scientific Revolutions*, Chicago: University of Chicago Press.

Kumcu, Erdogan (1987), "Historical Method: Toward a Relevant Analysis of Marketing Systems", in *Philosophical and Radical Thought in Marketing*, A.F. Firat, N. Dholakia and R.P. Bagozzi, eds., Lexington: Lexington Books.

Lieberson, Stanley (1985), "Unhyphenated Whites in the United States," *Ethnic and Racial Studies*, 8, 158-180.

*Los Angeles Times*, November 6, 1986, pp. 3 & 6.

*New York Times*, July 21, 1986; August 1, 1986, p. A1; October 26, 1986, p. C1.

O'Guinn, Thomas and Timothy P. Meyer (1983/84), "Segmenting the Hispanic Market: The Use of Spanish Language Radio," *Journal of Advertising Research*, 23, 9-116.

Reilly, Michael D. and Melanie Wallendorf (1987), "A Comparison of Group Differences in Food Consumption Using Household Refuse", *Journal of Consumer Research*, 14, 289-194.

Saegert, Joel, Robert J. Hoover, and Marye Tharp Hilger (1985), "Characteristics of Mexican American Consumers", *Journal of Consumer Research*, 12, 104-1109.

Savitt, Ronald (1980), "Historical Research in Marketing," *Journal of Marketing*, 44, 52-158.

Schaninger, Charles M., Jacques C. Bourgeois, and W. Christian Buss (1985), "French-1English Canadian Subcultural Consumption Differences," *Journal of Marketing*, 49, 82-192.

Sheth, Jagdish N. (1981), "Discussion" comments in *Advances in Consumer Research*, vol. 8, Kent Monroe, ed., Ann Arbor: Association for Consumer Research, 355-156.

_____ and David M. Gardner (1982), "History of Marketing Thought: An Update", in *Marketing Theory: Philosophy of Science Perspectives*, R. Bush and S. Hunt, eds., Chicago: American Marketing Association, 52-158.

_____ and Barbara L. Gross (1988), "Parallel Development of Marketing and Consumer Behavior: A Historical Perspective", in *Historical Perspectives in Marketing*, T. Nevett and R.A. Fullerton, eds., Lexington: Lexington Books.

*Sixty Minutes*, "Letters," October 5, 1986.

Tricarico, D. (1984), "The 'New' Italian-1American Ethnicity," *Journal of Ethnic Studies*, 12, 75-193.

Valencia, Humberto (1983/84), "Point of View: Avoiding Hispanic Market Blunders," *Journal of Advertising Research*, 23, 19-122.

*Wall Street Journal*, November 24, 1986; November 28, 1986.

Wallendorf, Melanie and Michael D. Reilly (1984), "Ethnic Migration, Assimilation, and Consumption," *Journal of Consumer Research*, 10, 292-1305.

Wilkes, Robert and Humberto Valencia (1985), "A Note on Generic Purchaser Generalizations and Subcultural Variations," *Journal of Marketing*, 49, 114-120.

# Assessing Trustworthiness in Naturalistic Consumer Research

Melanie Wallendorf, University of Arizona
Russell W. Belk, University of Utah[1]

Any research approach, regardless of the philosophy of science from which it emanates, requires ways to assess the trustworthiness of the research. The particular way that trustworthiness is evaluated will vary considerably depending on the research program and philosophy within which the research operates (Anderson 1986), but its importance is postulated to be a scientific universal. The purposes of this chapter are (1) to discuss some proposed criteria for evaluating trustworthiness in research based on participant-observation or ethnographic field work, particularly when done by a team, and (2) to discuss and evaluate the use of several techniques for establishing trustworthiness in data collection, in the formation of interpretations based on the data, and in presenting the interpretation to readers. We will concentrate on method-as-technique rather than more fundamentally on methodology as logic of justification as the term is used in the philosophy of science literature (Smith and Heshusius 1986). That is, this chapter is intended as a contribution to our understanding of the use of certain research techniques, rather than primarily as a discussion of philosophy of science. We will be concerned primarily with the workbench level (Anderson 1986).

Before proceeding with this task, we must note that the present discussion focuses on evaluating trustworthiness as distinct from determining the overall quality of research based on participant-observation or ethnographic field work. We present procedures for establishing trustworthiness, but not procedures for insuring high quality, insightful research. The latter goal is not one that can be achieved merely by following a set of prescriptive guidelines. Most noticeably missing from our discussion is any consideration of whether the research is in some sense interesting. [For a discussion of this criterion as it relates to overall quality, see Zaltman, LeMasters, and Heffring (1982), and Davis (1971).] Also missing is discussion of whether the research provides novel, deep insights. Certainly missing are guidelines for developing interesting ideas or deep insights. In fact, to provide such a list of "how-to" steps is likely to negate the essential spontaneity and serendipity that guide good research. It is our personal experience that such ideas are much more likely to emerge from playfulness and openness than from mechanistic procedures (see Belk 1984). In spite of the absence of a discussion of interestingness and insightfulness, we regard these as

very important considerations in evaluating research, but find them to be beyond the scope of this work.

Our purpose here is to discuss those research procedures that establish the trustworthiness of the research enterprise, even though they in no way insure that the output is "good" in an overall sense. Trustworthiness is one component of good research, but is certainly not enough by itself. In fact, it is our sense that merely following the procedures we outline here would likely produce a rather boring output.

With these cautions in mind, we will proceed to discuss how researchers, reviewers, and readers of participant-observation, ethnographic studies might come to trust the conclusions reached in such research.

In their frequently-cited (1985) book entitled *Naturalistic Inquiry*, Lincoln and Guba indicate that there are four questions concerning trustworthiness that are important for any kind of inquiry. The questions that they raise are:

1. How do we know whether to have confidence in the findings?

2. How do we know the degree to which the findings apply in other contexts?

3. How do we know the findings would be repeated if the study could be replicated in essentially the same way?

4. How do we know the degree to which the findings emerge from the context and the respondents and not solely from the researcher?

While we do not fully agree with the answers that Lincoln and Guba (1985) provide for these questions, we agree that the questions are generally appropriate to raise in evaluating naturalistic research. We would add a fifth question that is an extension of the fourth one:

5. How do we know whether the findings are based on false information from the informants?

Each research program and philosophy of science develops its own criteria and procedures for answering these questions. This definition of the goals of a science is foundational to the conduct of a self-critical practice of science. However, it is essential that we do not assume that the epistemology underlying these questions is the same for positivist and non-positivist inquiry (see Smith and Heshusius 1986, Hudson and Ozanne 1988).

Lincoln and Guba (1986) note that positivist inquiry has developed a set of criteria for answering the first four questions that fit with its ontological and epistemological assumptions. These criteria are:

[1]We would like to thank Laurel Hudson, Grant McCracken, Tommy O'Guinn, J. Paul Peter, and Clint Sanders for their helpful comments on an earlier draft of this paper. However, the positions taken here reflect our own attempts to grapple with these issues and are not necessarily reflective of the positions of these colleagues.

*Interpretive Consumer Research,* © *1989*
*Association for Consumer Research*

internal validity, external validity, reliability, and objectivity. These criteria are based on assumptions that link positivist philosophy and positivist approaches to methodology.

But these criteria are not appropriate when the research is based on a post-positivist philosophy and employs participant-observation, ethnographic methods. As Lauden (1984) and Anderson (1986) note, philosophic aims and empirical methods are inextricably linked. Lincoln and Guba assert that these four positivist criteria for evaluating positivist research methods are inconsistent with a post-positivist philosophy of science in the following ways:

1. Internal validity assumes a mirroring of research with a single external reality which is not assumed to exist by post-positivists.

2. External validity conflicts with post-positivist notions that question the goal of generalizeability.

3. Reliability assumes stability and replicability that do not fit with the use of emergent design to respond to the human as an instrument attempting to understand a dynamic and subjectively shaped phenomenon.

4. Objectivity assumes an independence between knower and known which naturalistic inquiry takes as impossible.

Therefore, instead of employing positivist answers to the four questions concerning trustworthiness, Lincoln and Guba suggest as substitute criteria:

1. **Credibility** (adequate and believable representations of the constructions of reality studied)

2. **Transferability** (extent to which working hypotheses can also be employed in other contexts, based on an assessment of similarity between the two contexts)

3. **Dependability** (extent to which interpretation was constructed in a way which avoids instability other than the inherent instability of a social phenomenon)

4. **Confirmability** (ability to trace a researcher's construction of an interpretation by following the data and other records kept)

These are meant to answer the same underlying questions as the criteria employed in positivist research, but to address them within the tenets of post-positivist philosophy of science. [Also see Hirschman (1986) for elaboration of these four criteria.] We suggest a fifth criterion that corresponds to the additional question raised about findings based on false information from informants:

5. **Integrity** (extent to which the interpretation was unimpaired by lies, evasions, misinformation, or misrepresentations by informants).

In this chapter we will outine specific techniques which can be used by researchers for assessing the extent to which their research meets each of these five criteria. Lincoln and Guba suggest several research techniques for assessing fit with their criteria (and, we suggest, integrity as well) in naturalistic research which include:

a. prolonged engagement/persistent observation
b. triangulation of sources, methods, and researchers
c. regular on-site team interaction
d. negative case analysis
e. debriefings by peers
f. member checks
g. seeking limiting exceptions
h. purposive sampling
i. reflexive journals
j. independent audit

The use of these techniques enables researchers who are conducting as well as those who are reading the output of naturalistic inquiry to evaluate the completeness (or, alternatively, what Lincoln and Guba call "sloppiness") of the research procedures used and the human instrument employed.

In the remainder of this chapter, we will describe the techniques appropriate for assessing trustworthiness on each of these five criteria and the logic that motivates their use. However, beyond this description, we will evaluate these techniques based on our use of them in research stemming from the Consumer Behavior Odyssey, a field research project on consumption conducted in the summer of 1986 by a rotating team of two dozen academic researchers travelling across the U.S. in a recreational vehicle (Wallendorf and Belk, 1987). We will employ examples from our research primarily because it is the work which we know best and therefore, we are best able to provide details concerning its conduct which are not usually available in written (realist) presentations of research results (Van Maanen 1988).

It is not the intention of this chapter to present a "new orthodoxy" which suppresses variety and responsiveness in the design and implementation of interpretive research. Above all, we support the idea that research design should be responsive to the nature of the research focus, and the techniques employed should address the questions presented above within the varieties of context participant-observation, ethnographic researchers choose to explore.

## CREDIBILITY ASSESSMENT

In assessing the credibility of a research project, we must consider what was done during data collection, in the formation of an interpretation, and in the presentation of the final interpretation to readers. Techniques for enhancing credibility during data collection include prolonged engagement, persistent observation, and triangulation across sources and methods. Since the construction of an interpretation in ethnographic fieldwork begins during data collection (Glaser and Strauss 1967), the techniques for enhancing credibility in interpretation formation also begin in the field. These techniques include regular on-site team interaction, negative case analysis, triangulation across researchers, and debriefings by peers. Techniques for enhancing credibility that pertain most appropriately to the stage of preparing a presentation of the interpretation for readers include member checks and audits. With the exception of audits which will be discussed in a later section, each of these will be discussed and evaluated in this section.

## Prolonged Engagement and Persistent Observation

Conducting ethnographic research requires spending sufficient time in a context to develop an understanding of the phenomenon, group, or culture in broad perspective before focusing on a particular aspect or theme imbedded in that context. Lincoln and Guba point to Freeman's (1983) objection to Mead's (1928) early focus on aspects of adolescence (arising from the a priori theories that her advisor Franz Boas advocated) without first attempting to understand the context of Samoan culture in which this behavior was embedded. The problem was not the existence of a priori theory, either explicit or implicit, but rather the lack of attention to the key feature of naturalistic inquiry--namely, that it takes place *in situ* and is therefore subject to a much broader set of influences than apply in the laboratory. That is, despite her lengthy stay in Samoa (roughly one year in the initial fieldwork), Mead did not really conform to the spirit of prolonged engagement as a means to emergent interpretation.

But how prolonged is prolonged? Clearly the amount of time required varies. Cultural anthropologists conducting fieldwork for an initial project in an exotic culture with which they are unfamiliar often spend at least a year enmeshed in the culture. Werner and Schoepfle (1987) suggest that even after this time period, language skills are likely to be woefully inadequate to obtain a deep understanding of the concepts of the culture. Urban sociologists conducting fieldwork in their home culture may begin to focus on one aspect of social action more quickly since the context is already a part of their experiential portfolio. Typically, rather than living at a research site (Manning 1987), they maintain frequent contact with social actors in the social world they are studying, and conduct their fieldwork through these interactions (see for example, Snow and Anderson 1987). Similarly, researchers conducting fieldwork in a context with which they have previously become intimately familiar may more readily be able to conduct diagnostic research in a new, but similar setting. However, in familiar contexts there is the danger of being *too* familiar with phenomena so that an appreciation of that which is taken-for-granted (Wirth 1964) is more difficult to

acquire. Here the researcher must work to intentionally cultivate a more distanced and critical naivete, which also requires prolonged engagement and an ability to perceive things with "new eyes" and "new ears".

Of course, more is needed than just spending a long time in a setting or social world. Prolonged engagement is recommended partly in order to acquire sufficient observations to be able to assess the distortion which may exist in the data. Through persistent observation, the researcher acquires sufficient depth of understanding to assess the quality of the data. This is a topic to which we will return in the section on integrity.

The length of time appropriate to spend in a particular context is thus a function of the purpose of the research and the prior experience of the researchers. Prototypical single site ethnographies in consumer research have been completed in the United States by Heisley, McGrath and Sherry (1988) at a farmers' market and by McGrath (1988) at a gift store. (See also Sherry and McGrath--this volume.) The goal in each of these projects was constructing a description and interpretation of social action at a single site that was initially unfamiliar to the researchers. In each case, participant-observation research was actively conducted over a time span of at least two complete cycles of the phenomenon of interest (agricultural seasons for the farmers' market project and the yearly occurrences of the gift occasions of Christmas and Hanukkah for the gift store project).

The shorter length of time spent at a swap meet for the Consumer Behavior Odyssey pilot project (Belk, Sherry and Wallendorf 1988) completed one microcycle (the four days of one week's trading cycle) embedded in several longer cycles governing seasonal changes and facility location. Because the data were gathered primarily during one microcycle, we could only employ **perspectives of action** (informant explanations of their actions to the researcher) in referring to patterns pertinent to longer cycles; however, we could employ both perspectives of action as well as **perspectives in action** (observations of actual behaviors) in interpreting patterns within this microcycle (see Snow and Anderson, 1987; Gould, Walker, Crane, and Lidz 1974). In summary, one consideration in determining how prolonged the engagement must be is the length of the cycle over which the phenomenon of interest manifests itself.

Because the broader Consumer Behavior Odyssey sought to explore phenomena and themes in American consumption that were not site- or region-specific, movement across sites was employed. Neither the swap meet project nor the Consumer Behavior Odyssey project followed the approach taken by a lone anthropologist studying an exotic culture, because neither project utilized a single researcher or focused on largely unfamiliar phenomena. Instead, the time spent in fieldwork at a particular site emerged from a consideration of the overall goals of the project and the information obtained. In all cases, reporting the amount of time spent at a site, the number of researchers, and the roles taken by the researchers

(Adler and Adler 1987) is important in establishing trustworthiness in the presentation of the interpretation.

In advocating persistent observation, we are not referring to disguised observation, which Punch (1986, p. 72) notes may amount to "ripping and running." By being open with informants about purposes and researcher identities, we have often been allowed access to a wider range of behaviors than would otherwise have been the case. Overt conduct of research allows the researcher to ask questions and probe issues which would seem inappropriate for a supposed non-researcher participant (see Prus 1985). Disguised observation inhibits the participant-observer's ability to remain in the context for a prolonged period of time without calling his or her role into question. This persistent observation may be needed to overcome potential impression management on the part of informants. Open recruitment and involvement of informants as informants allows researchers from the culture to more quickly ascertain the nature of the context and to go on to focus on specific themes of interest.

## Triangulation across Sources and Methods

A second means by which trustworthiness is enhanced during data collection is through triangulation across sources and methods. Triangulation across sources requires the researcher to develop evidence for an interpretation from interaction with several informants, particularly several types of informants as the purposive sampling plan unfolds. Triangulation across methods requires the researcher to test an interpretation in data gathered using several different methods. The ability to employ multiple methods may depend upon other aspects of fieldwork, including the presence of a team of researchers (see Denzin 1970).

For example, in the study of a farmers' market by Heisley, McGrath, and Sherry (1988), the researchers found certain sellers who were not on friendly terms with other sellers. The use of a research team for data collection enabled different researchers to speak with sellers on different sides of this competition without harming rapport by appearing to these sellers to have multiple allegiances (see also Douglas 1976 for a discussion of the use of teams to study multiperspectival realities in conflictful societies).

We have found that members of a research team have differential access to various types of informants and each researcher may obtain different types of information from the informant. Douglas (1976) refers to this as the role specialization and complementarity of team members. For example, the type of information and relation we develop with an informant is based at least partially on the gender combination of the researcher and the informant. [See the collection of chapters edited by Whitehead and Conaway (1986), and the monograph written by Warren (1988).] In addition, we have found that access to children may be differentially available to male and female researchers, particularly in communities with a strong (need for) concern with protection of children

from strangers (see Fine 1980 and Fine and Glasner 1979). Since no one researcher has ideal access to all types of informants, team research enhances the ability to triangulate across sources.

This is not to imply that triangulation across sources is limited to informant sources. Material from art and literature can serve as a valuable additional source in constructing an interpretation (e.g., Belk, Wallendorf, Sherry, Holbrook, and Roberts, 1988; Belk 1986; Wallendorf 1988). Such sources can provide a narrative and historical perspective that informants may be unable to provide.

Except for secondary sources, triangulation across sources requires careful attention to recording contact with informants in fieldnotes that provide as much detail as possible. This is especially important in a team context given the possibility that something that one team member does not consider important may in fact be important when triangulating on something that another team member discovers to be important to an interpretation. Detailed fieldnotes allow the researcher to check for lack of agreement in a systematic and non-defensive manner at a later point in time when details of informant interactions may not be accessible to memory (Wyer and Srull 1980).

Like triangulation across sources, triangulation across methods might incorporate secondary data, but it normally requires multiple types of primary data collection. Videorecording and still photography are two very useful methods in this regard (see Belk, Sherry, and Wallendorf 1988). They provide the researcher with the "new eyes" mentioned in the earlier discussion of prolonged engagement. The use of videorecording and still photography for triangulation across data collection methods is one reason we disagree with Hirschman's (1986) objection to the use of audio and video recordings in humanistic research in marketing. Although certainly not providing the unbiased perspective on human interaction (Sontag 1973) that positivist science believes exists, still and video photography do provide a perspective on field interactions that is meaningfully different from that provided in fieldnotes (Collier and Collier 1986; Becker 1986). As such, video and still photography serve as separate methods for assessing an interpretation and thereby enhancing its trustworthiness. In our experience there is generally much more to gain in obtrusively, openly, and honestly videorecording and talking to consumers than in completely foregoing this opportunity and relying only on unobtrusive observation. In the absence of videorecording, the same can be said of audiorecording, as Douglas (1985, p. 83) notes:

> The recorder is both a reassurance of the seriousness of your pursuit and a brutal technological reminder of human separateness that undermines the intimate communion you are trying to create. The recorder is a double-edged sword and is thus quite problematic. But it is such a powerful weapon in the fight for truth that it must be used in all situations where it is allowed by the goddesses.

Although we would not make such a universal proclamation concerning the use of audiorecorders, we do support their use where the researcher deems them an appropriate technology for developing trustworthy interpretations.

Finally, triangulation across methods sometimes means supplementing other data with that gained through personal reflection (e.g. Holbrook 1986a), particularly when systematic data searches have gone as far as they are able and additional needed data can only be provided by introspection. Implicitly all research employs introspection as a source of hypotheses, empathy, and testing of whether an explanation seems to "play" in the experience of the researcher. Intentionally and systematically reflexive journal entries in field research provide formal access to these reflections that can be shared across researchers.

Some examples of the usefulness of journals in our own research come to our minds here. We serendipitously discovered, through the use of systematic computerized data searches (Belk 1988) that our own data collection activities mirrored those of interest in a project on collectors and collections (Belk, Wallendorf, Sherry, Holbrook, Roberts 1988). Similarly, some of our concerns about privacy and time to be alone while our team traveled across the country in a recreational vehicle mirrored those of informants who discussed their day-to-day concerns about privacy in their homes (Wallendorf 1988). In both cases, reflexive material from journals became primary data about the phenomenon of interest, adding to the ability to triangulate across methods.

However, at this point a concern about the dysfunctional consequences of employing multiple methods and sources must be raised. Each of them lengthens the amount of time a research project will take before data collection, data analysis, and report preparation are completed and the project is ready to be submitted for review. Yet, as is the case with any type of research, speed to print must be traded against trustworthiness of the effort. The tradeoff can most fully be seen by the researcher, but hopefully careful editors and reviewers in consumer research will assess trustworthiness as well as interestingness and timeliness of a manuscript.

## Regular On-Site Team Interaction

Credibility is also facilitated by regular on-site team interaction. This allows each team member to contribute to the collective sense of what is appropriate to the emergent design. In particular, on-site team interaction can focus on plans for purposeful sampling. It also can serve to re-energize the team in the tiring process of fieldwork.

In our own fieldwork, we frequently meet at a site to discuss such issues. In addition, during the conduct of fieldwork, the Consumer Behavior Odyssey project routinized such meetings each evening in what has come to be called a DOA, or Daily Odyssey Audit (see Belk, Sherry, and Wallendorf 1988). However, such interactions take on a peculiar character because of a set of informal rules that we have found helpful to invoke. Until fieldnotes are completed by each team member for that day's fieldwork, we confine our discussions to methodological details such as sampling plans, or to operational details such as directions or meal plans; we deliberately do not discuss any statements made by an informant (e.g., "Could you believe he said, ...?") or any interpretations of informants' comments (e.g., "That's the most compulsive collector we've talked to yet.") until we have each completed recording fieldnotes for the day's interactions. This makes for a strange form of social interaction in the interim, but makes triangulation across sets of notes more legitimate by not altering each other's recall or understanding of what was said or done before we record it. Therefore, although we routinely engage in regular on-site team interaction, we would stress the importance of being acutely sensitive to the need to conduct such meetings in a way that, if it doesn't avoid the potential for groupthink entirely, avoids shaping a specific interpretation too soon in response to the group processes which emerge in team research.

## Negative Case Analysis

In constructing a credible interpretation of ethnographic data materials, Lincoln and Guba also suggest the use of negative case analysis, in which the researchers construct an interpretation and then successively modify it as they encounter instances that provide negative support for the original hypothesis. This is somewhat akin to the analytic approach suggested by Glaser and Strauss (1967) in what they call the constant comparative method (see also Miles and Huberman 1984; McCall and Simmons 1969). Both discussions are based on the presumption that purposive sampling has attempted to insure that negative instances have been sought during fieldwork. That is, as an interpretation emerges from fieldwork, it is the researcher's obligation to seek data which would be most likely to not confirm the emerging hypothesis. For elaboration of different perspectives on the advantages and disadvantages of this procedure, see Huber (1973, 1974), Schmitt (1974), and Stone, et al. (1974).

In doing negative case analysis after fieldwork has been suspended, it is necessary to rely on a detailed set of fieldnotes that contain all aspects of interactions with informants. Although we recognize that they are holding out an ideal, we find it difficult if not impossible to actualize the strong form of negative case analysis described by Lincoln and Guba (1985, p. 309):

> The object...is continuously to refine a hypothesis until it *accounts for all known cases without exception* (italics in original).

As will be discussed in the section on assessing research integrity, we recognize that data are never perfect reflections of the phenomena being studied. Thus we reject the absolute form of negative case analysis in which no exceptions are allowed. However, Lincoln and Guba (1985, p. 312) also have some reservations in this regard and seem to suggest a weak form of negative case analysis that we find more acceptable:

> But perhaps the insistence on *zero* exceptions may be too rigid a criterion. Indeed, on its face it seems almost impossible to satisfy in actual studies....In situations where one might expect lies, fronts, and other deliberate or unconscious deceptions (as in the case of self-delusions), some of the cases ought to *appear* to be exceptions even when the hypothesis is valid simply because the false elements cannot always be fully penetrated. Yet, if a hypothesis could be formulated that fit some reasonable number of cases--even as low, say, as 60 percent--there would seem to be substantial evidence of its acceptability. After all, has anyone ever produced a perfect statistical finding, significant at the .000 level?

In presenting an interpretation to readers, the ways in which negative case analysis has been employed should be explicitly detailed to enable readers to judge the credibility of the procedures for themselves. Readers should be provided with the researcher's sense of the range and nature of exceptions as well as the strength of support for an interpretation. This presentation style also allows the researcher to build the argument for the interpretation, rather than just presenting the interpretation. It allows the reader to judge the research and come to conclusions concerning credibility for himself or herself. In these ways, negative case analysis serves to temper the natural enthusiasm of the researcher.

## Triangulation across Researchers

Triangulation across researchers is another technique used for enhancing the credibility of an interpretation. Obviously, it is only available to team research. Triangulation across researchers adds to the credibility of a project in two ways: (1) by permitting a check on the reporting completeness and accuracy of each researcher through comparisons of multiple sets of fieldnotes covering the same interaction, and (2) by enabling the consideration of an interpretation from the vantage of several different researchers. This latter feature of triangulation does not always mean that only one interpretation will emerge. Instead, we have often found that multiple interpretations emerge, which may differ based on other differences in background between researchers (e.g., field of training, age, gender, class origin, religion). Given the post-positivist rejection of the assumption of a single causal reality, this is entirely appropriate if the data have been sufficiently mined for depth of insight. However, we would assert that the multiple interpretations developed by a team should be able to co-exist if the interpretation is to be regarded as trustworthy; they should not negate each other. If there are multiple interpretations that emerge from a team, each interpretation can be presented to the reader for consideration.

For example, Belk, Wallendorf, and Sherry (1989) distinguish among cultural, social, and psychological interpretations of the functions of sacred consumption. While the co-authors embrace the various interpretations to different degrees, the interpretations do not contradict each other. The key point is that the interpretations developed by a team should appear plausible and firmly grounded to each member of the team and should not be mutually exclusive. This is what is meant by this feature of triangulation across researchers.

## Debriefings by Peers

Lincoln and Guba (1985) also suggest debriefings by peers as a technique for enhancing credibility of interpretation. By this they mean that researchers should periodically meet with peers who are not researchers on the project but who will serve to critique and question the emerging interpretation before the researchers become fully committed to it.

In two ways we employed this technique on the Consumer Behavior Odyssey project. Most formally, a debriefing session was held approximately midway through the data collection phase. Included in this meeting were several researchers who had been involved continuously in the data collection on the project, one researcher who had been initially involved in the data collection but had not been traveling for the most recent few weeks, several researchers who had been gathering data at one site throughout the previous months, and two individuals who were interested in the project, but had not been involved in data collection. The mixture of persons represented served to permit the group to draw from the data gathered so far, but without all present having full knowledge of the data. This challenged the researchers who had been involved in all of the sites visited thus far to begin to explain what they were finding to the others present. In doing so, commonalities across sites and interactions emerged that led to the development of a list of themes. Smaller debriefing meetings of this sort were held at several sites along the way where colleagues in other universities and in sponsoring organizations hosted or met with us. In all cases, the goal was to sensitize researchers to concepts which might be applicable in interpreting the data in a way which facilitated later data collection. Premature formulation of one complete explanation or interpretation was deliberately avoided by concluding at the point of identifying themes to be explored in later fieldwork.

A second, less formal way in which debriefings by peers became a part of the Odyssey project was in what were ostensibly briefings held for those who were just joining the project's data collection efforts as we moved across the country. While the prior establishment of group culture made these somewhat difficult and sometimes ineffective rites of transition, they also served to introduce the researchers to new colleagues who wanted to know what we were finding. Such explanations served to sharpen our interpretations as well as to see whether they "played" to a new audience. In response to such interactions, researchers who had already begun to develop personal ways of understanding the data were challenged to formalize this understanding for others through memos and discussions during DOAs.

In general, we found debriefings by peers to be enjoyable, but not always as productive as other techniques suggested. However, this evaluation may stem from the somewhat unusual rotating character of the team formed for this project. Debriefings by peers may be more useful in a project where the team formed is more constant and enduring in character, a feature we would prefer in the future.

## Member Checks

A final technique for establishing credibility is a member check, in which the interpretation and report (or a portion of it, perhaps rewritten for the lay reader) is given to members of the sample (informants) for comment. Their comments serve as a check on the viability of the interpretation. However, contrary to the procedure reported by Hirschman (1986), comments provided through member checks need not serve as the basis for revising the interpretation. Informant disagreement with elements of a report that claim to be emic description would require revision. However, since actors do not always have access to the range of information about a phenomenon that researchers do, informants may disagree with some etic interpretation based on the uniqueness of their position relative to that of the researchers. For example, in a project on a swap meet, we found different reactions to the report in separate member checks with a buyer and with some sellers (Belk, Sherry, and Wallendorf 1988). In such cases, it is appropriate to note the informants' disagreement in the report and attempt to explain it based on differences in sources of information available to the informant and to the researchers. This position acknowledges the idea that some informants (and all informants some of the time) are systematically and necessarily wrong in what they suppose or report is going on. We will return to this issue in our discussion of integrity.

Thus, the several possible negative outcomes to a member check should be treated differently depending on whether the point of disagreement concerns descriptive emic material or interpretive etic material. For example, in our research on swap meets, we did not expect to have the informants who participated in the member checks respond by saying, "Why, of course, I have often noted the importance of the sacred/profane concept in explaining what happens here." Even when some of the informants are capable of assessing abstract interpretations, it is not expected that all informants will be equally insightful. When both etic interpretation and emic description is the goal, it is possible (and desirable) that the informant not disagree with the interpretation, but instead essentially say, "I never quite thought of it that way." Generally the more abstract the interpretation, the greater the potential for deferring to the researcher's interpretation of the entire corpus of data and the lesser the usefulness or appropriateness of a member check. Similarly, if informants disagree with abstract etic interpretations (e.g., as some might with the conclusion that collections legitimize acquisitiveness--Belk, Wallendorf, Sherry, Holbrook, and Roberts 1988), this may not be considered grounds for rejecting the interpretation.

Some etic interpretations may be rejected by informants for reasons of self-presentation and social desirability. We found this to be the case when swap meet informants used in a member check suggested that we overestimated the incidence of illegal activity at the meet, for example (Belk, Sherry, and Wallendorf 1988). The most troublesome outcome for establishing credibility is a member check in which an informant disagrees with items in the report that comprise emic description. Unless such disagreements can clearly be attributed to the particular informant's access to the phenomenon being different from that of most informants or to the desire to present oneself in a socially desirable way, such outcomes imply that the report should be revised and that perhaps the fieldwork is incomplete.

Here, we should point out several other, more logistical, problems with member checks based on the varying success we have enjoyed in attempting to use them in several projects. Not all informants are willing to read through an academic report merely to do the researchers a favor. Another related problem is that a member check may often represent an upscale bias. It favors those who are more insightful and articulate, but Werner and Schoepfle (1987) suggest that this may not be a problem. We are not troubled by using articulate and insightful persons for member checks since finding an informant who is willing and interested in providing such feedback is not always easy. In general, we have found member checks to serve a useful function in our research, especially when we had questions about the adequacy of our understanding based on limited time of exposure to the site (Belk, Sherry, and Wallendorf, 1988). Thus, a member check can serve to counterbalance concerns about whether engagement was sufficiently prolonged.

In an informal sense, member checks are carried out verbally throughout the conduct of fieldwork as the researcher constantly checks his or her understanding of the phenomenon with informants. (E.g., "Some collectors have told us that.... Does that seem accurate to you?" "So what you're saying is that...?" "Is it true that...?") The ability to conduct this constant check on interpretation as it emerges is yet another advantage to undisguised observation and fully informed consent from informants. Because engaging in such checking would seem out of character for a disguised participant who is really a researcher, it is less likely to be employed in covert research (e.g., Hirschman 1986). For further discussion of the moral dilemmas of covert observation, see Erikson (1967) and Bulmer (1982).

In summary, member checks conducted informally throughout fieldwork and more formally after drafting a report serve to enhance the credibility of the constructed interpretation. Together with prolonged engagement, various types of triangulation, team interaction, and possibly negative case analysis and debriefings by peers, such procedures can help create credibility for a naturalistic research project. However, other criteria for trustworthiness must also be considered.

## TRANSFERABILITY ASSESSMENT

Lincoln and Guba (1985, p. 290) present the issue underlying applicability as: "How can one determine the extent to which the findings of a particular inquiry have applicability in other contexts or with other subjects (respondents)?" This issue is parallel to the issue of external validity in experimental and survey research (Campbell and Stanley 1966). Lincoln and Guba (1985) along with Schmitt (1974) suggest an easy, but perhaps too facile answer to this question in post-positivist research; namely, that if other researchers are concerned with the applicability of the findings in another context, they should do research using similar methods in another time or place and then compare. This may be the best answer when the study is an in-depth descriptive ethnography of a single site, organization, or group; however, in other broader or more explanatory research, including those addressed by the Consumer Behavior Odyssey, applicability is a concern.

For many of the phenomena investigated by the Odyssey, the data were collected across a variety of sites using what Whyte (1984) calls "hunt and peck ethnography." In such fieldwork, rather than seeking to understand a single site, organization, or group, we sought to understand consumption phenomena *across* a variety of sites, organizations, and groups. Sometimes the phenomenon was a type of behavior, such as selling used merchandise. In other cases, such as the conversion of artifacts from profane commodities to sacred icons, the phenomenon could occur through a variety of behaviors. The procedures for establishing transferability in these two cases are somewhat different as explained in the next two sections.

### Triangulation across Sites through Purposive Sampling

In constructing an understanding of a type of behavior that takes place fairly predictably in particular contexts, we sought to establish transferability by going to multiple venues of these types to study the phenomenon. For example, selling used merchandise takes place predictably at swap meets, garage sales, pawn shops, antique auctions, and other such second order market institutions. Therefore, our research on the selling of used merchandise involved doing fieldwork at swap meets in different locales because they are similar second order market institutions. We began by considering the initial swap meet examined (Red Mesa Swap Meet) on different days of the week and at different times of day (see Belk, Sherry, and Wallendorf 1988 and Belk, Kassarjian, Sherry, and Wallendorf 1987). We revisited this same swap meet during three different months to provide some temporal comparisons over a longer period of time. We next moved to other locales. Once we had some evidence that similar behaviors and motivations were in evidence in swap meets in several cities and states, we sought to

investigate other types of swap meets such as Hispanic meets and ones specializing in specific merchandise such as antiques. We also began to investigate other second order markets, including auctions, antique stores, and garage sales. Such purposive sampling examines the question: will the same behaviors be found here too? This procedure focuses the research on explanatory concepts rather than merely on producing thick description of particular sites.

### Seeking Limiting Exceptions

To establish the transferability of a phenomenon represented by a set of behaviors that can occur in a number of sites or groups, we progressively expanded the types of sites and contexts in which the phenomena of interest were investigated. We sought to gather sufficient understanding of consumption phenomena that we could understand the transferability and limits of our findings. Limiting exceptions not only define the boundaries or limits of transferability, they also offer the opportunity for understanding *why* the theory doesn't work in some instances. Such insights then require other testing at additional purposively sampled sites, chosen to see if the predictions from a tentative understanding of the boundaries of the explanation are borne out.

For instance, we had begun to think that once items entered an individual's collection, they would not leave. But we found instances where items from a collection *were* disposed of. Initially, it seemed that the explanation was that this was acceptable to collectors when the item was replaced by a better one, thus upgrading the collection. We then obtained support for this expectation, but also found that such upgrading was most likely when the collection was limited by space and funds, as is often the case with automobiles. This led to the development of the concept of "serial collections" in which the set of things in the collection could exist across the collector's lifetime involving ownership of only one item at a time, but still viewed by the owner as being a collection. Besides automobiles, this was found to hold for collections of places some people had visited (see Belk, Wallendorf, Sherry, Holbrook, and Roberts 1988).

### Emergent Design

Assessing the transferability of an understanding of phenomena found in a variety of behaviors is a bit more difficult. Perhaps the discussion is best begun through example. We found profane to sacred conversions in a variety of contexts that eventually led to a typology of profane to sacred conversions. Among the types of conversion processes identified (see Belk, Wallendorf, and Sherry 1989) were gift-giving, bequeathing, and acquisition during pilgrimage (e.g., souvenirs). With such a diverse set of phenomena, the people and venues in which this theoretical phenomenon can be investigated are obviously quite broad. Such a situation makes purposive sampling more of a challenge, but it also makes finding potential test cases much easier. In some instances we found that the same people could be interviewed concerning multiple types of profane to sacred conversions. We created one such opportunity by going to a particular community and interviewing people in their homes about the possessions contained in these homes. Certain possessions showed some hint of sacredness in their manner of display and therefore were selected as objects of focus in the depth interviews conducted with the owners. Because the possessions on display may have been acquired through any of the three sacralizing processes identified (and may also be planned to be bequeathed in the future), this allowed us to investigate the transferability of the theorized phenomenon and taxonomy across, as well as within households. We also sought multiple perspectives on heirlooms and gifts by interviewing pairs of donors and recipients separately. Our theory of sacred to profane conversions turned out to be quite robust, making it more difficult to gain closure in the quest for boundaries and exceptions.

This diverse array of data collection and sampling approaches resulted from an emergent research design constructed in the field in our attempts to build a theory which was robust in its transferability. Such broad transferability suggests greater explanatory power for the theory being tested.

It is important to realize that within the emergent nature of post-positivist qualitative research, transferability is not simply a matter of stating a hypothesis and formally testing it. The very notion of emergent design implies continual refinement. Exceptions may suggest placing boundaries on ideas about the transferability of one's theory, but they may also suggest modifications of the theory (Glaser and Strauss 1967). In the preceding example, the taxonomy of sacralizing processes emerged while testing an initially more restricted notion of sacralization within the realm of gift-giving. We expanded initial boundaries while also detecting different types of and rationales for sacralization (e.g., associations with persons in gift-giving versus associations with experiences in souvenirs).

## ESTABLISHING DEPENDABILITY

The issue of dependability in post-positivist research is similar to the issue of test-retest reliability in positivist research and is translated by Lincoln and Guba (1985, p. 290) as: "How can one determine whether the findings of an inquiry would be repeated if the inquiry were replicated with the same (or similar) subjects (respondents) in the same (or similar) context?" As Lincoln and Guba (1985) point out, this question makes more sense within a philosophy of science in which one assumes that there is a single objective reality (in this case, unchanging persons and contexts) "out there" to be discovered. If one does not adopt this positivist philosophy, as is the case in post-positivist inquiry, then the question makes much less sense. [However, for a differing perspective, see Kirk and Miller, 1986.] Just as one cannot cross the same stream twice, one may not interview the same informant twice or go back to the same context twice.

People and contexts both continually change. However, this is an inadequate argument for totally dismissing the concern with producing dependable findings. If the argument were to be totally embraced, we would be saying that all is idiosyncracy and findings can therefore never be challenged. This is not the position we wish to take.

Instead, we believe it is important to ascertain the extent to which the explanation advanced previously is enduring, and the extent to which it derives from the peculiar convergence of a particular time and place. Dependability then, as a criterion, is linked to time and to change processes, rather than to stability and similarity as reliability issues are in positivist inquiry. Thus, for assessing dependability, we suggest observation over time and explanation of change. Before turning to these suggestions, we will briefly mention another technique which we have found less useful, namely a dependability audit.

### Dependability Audit

Lincoln and Guba's primary suggestion concerning the dependability or consistency issue is to conduct a dependability audit by giving raw materials as well as resulting inferences to an external auditor. However, we find this suggestion to be inadequate. Although an audit can be useful in establishing confirmability (discussed in the next section), we find audits less useful in establishing dependability because they do not directly address the issue of change over time.

### Observation over Time and Explanation of Change

Rather we would suggest that a certain sort of replication can help the researchers assess the boundaries of the dependability of findings. Rather than returning to informants a week or two after previous contact and expecting everything to be the same aside from random variation, we suggest returning to informants or sites months or even years later when things *should* have changed in various ways (see for example the series of reports from the Middletown studies; e.g., Lynd and Lynd 1929; Lynd and Lynd 1937; Caplow 1984). Such revisits can help correct the extant cross-sectional bias in social science research. By learning what has changed and whether these changes have affected the phenomenon previously detected, a deeper understanding of the phenomenon of interest and its boundaries is attained. The revisit provides a more dynamic opportunity to see whether the changes which have occurred are still consonant with the original theory. If they are not, the theory must either be modified to accommodate the unexpected findings or else discarded. It can be seen that the emergent nature of such research does not end when one initially leaves the field or publishes the findings of one wave of data collection.

At this writing, researchers on the Consumer Behavior Odyssey project have returned to people and sites in at least five locales. We have returned several times to talk with a man who accumulated several garages full of possessions to give to others (see Wallendorf and Belk 1987). We have returned several times (and in several different locales across the country) to talk to some swap meet sellers who have served as informants and as participants in a member check (see Belk, Sherry, and Wallendorf 1988). We have recontacted one informant to autodrive him (as suggested by Heisley and Levy 1988) using photographs of his possessions taken previously. We have returned to re-interview several women in a suburban community whose homes and possessions are a continuing focus of our research. And we have returned to re-interview several men in a small town whose cars and trucks were the focus of our previous interviews. In each case at least several months (and up to a year) separated the visits. In other cases, we have kept in contact with informants, and with changes in their lives and consumption patterns, through continuing contact and letters, often at their initiation. In the revisits, informants and circumstances were anticipated to have changed in various ways. We plan to continue returning to these informants as their lives, families, careers, and ages change even more. Such research procedures certainly lock the researcher into a long-term commitment to a project, but the focus explored in reinterviews may shift slightly over time in response to changes in the person and situation as well as in response to changes which become apparent in the researcher.

In the cases of the men and their automobiles for example, our initial interviews led us to infer that for these (then young single) men, the automobile was sometimes viewed as a rival by their girlfriends. If and when these men and their girlfriends marry, we would expect the car to be seen as less of a rival (since marriage implies a commitment), but we would also expect the males to divert some of the time previously spent on their cars to home and family activities instead. We have thus far had only a limited opportunity to test these expectations, because only one marriage has thus far taken place among these men. Nonetheless, we look forward to further testing with future follow-up visits.

In summary, rather than establishing dependability through an audit as recommended by Lincoln and Guba, we recommend the use of revisits over time in a longitudinal approach. This approach is not meant to preclude periodically writing interpretations of the data, but is meant to temper the cross-sectional bias inherent in social science research.

## ESTABLISHING CONFIRMABILITY

The issues of confirmability is raised by Lincoln and Guba (1985, p. 290) in their question: "How can one establish the degree to which the findings of an inquiry are determined by the subjects (respondents) and conditions of the inquiry and not by the biases, motivations, interests, or perspectives of the inquirer?" The term neutrality is an inappropriate term for this concern because post-positivist research recognizes that there can be no absolute objectivity; at best the researcher can become conscious of and hopefully reduce his or her ethnocentrism, semantic accents, and biases. In light of this constructive recognition of the impossibility of objectivity, there are three recommended techniques to address this concern: triangulation across researchers and methods, reflexive journals, and auditing. We are more in agreement with Lincoln and Guba (1985) on the techniques for assessing confirmability than we were for dependability, although we feel that these authors place too much emphasis on auditing as the best approach to establishing confirmability.

### Triangulation

Triangulation is meant here primarily in the sense of collecting data by multiple members of a research team. Especially when investigating a site where partially independent work is possible (as with a swap meet as contrasted with a small private home), team members can work separately and later compare data. Even when two or more researchers are present in a single interview however, triangulation is very useful. As discussed with reference to assessing credibility, in all cases, it is essential that each researcher write up fieldnotes and journals separately before discussing anything about the interview with the other researchers. Without this safeguard there is very likely a mixing of ideas and the possibility of groupthink increases. Because it is unlikely that multiple researchers will have identical biases, the comparison of *independent* fieldnotes then provides an opportunity both to strive for independent confirmation of observations, findings, and interpretations, and also to learn more about the nature of one's biases as differences are detected. As mentioned earlier, it may well be that male and female members of a research team will learn different things from the same informant, even when that informant is jointly interviewed by the research team. For this reason, having a research team composed of researchers of both genders is very valuable. We have also tried to represent different disciplinary training and backgrounds among researchers participating in the Consumer Behavior Odyssey project. What is being compared in such triangulation is the intersubjective certifiability of findings.

Triangulation over data collection methods is also sometimes useful in establishing confirmability. For example, photographs provide additional information that can be compared to fieldnotes for at least some descriptive details about persons, places, and things observed. Video and audio recordings also provide a check on what actions took place and what was said. We have also found transcriptions of these records to be of use in adjudicating differences in researcher fieldnotes. Another good example of triangulation over data collection methods is the work of O'Guinn and Faber (1987) in which their qualitative findings from observations and depth and group interviews with compulsive shoppers were supplemented with quantitative measurement of compulsiveness among consumers from the same groups and among other consumers as well. The comparisons of qualitative and quantitative results in this case provides an excellent model that others might follow.

## Reflexive Journals

Journals also aid in establishing confirmability of findings. Journals are reflexive documents kept by researchers in order to reflect on, tentatively interpret, and plan data collection. The intent in this personal diary is both to reflect on what one is learning and on what is going on with the individual keeping the diary. Werner and Schoepfle (1987) refer to trying to learn about oneself and how one may be affecting the information being gathered as trying to learn about one's "personal equation." Ideally, the journal allows a day-by-day or even hour-by-hour gauge on the fieldnotes of the researcher. In this respect, the journal is useful in detecting the influences of the researcher's personal frame of mind, biases, and tentative interpretations on the data being gathered. Because of this shift in frame of reference and purpose, we find it useful for ourselves to separate the journal from fieldnotes, recognizing that the physical separation is dichotomous, while the processes have more permeable boundaries. [For an argument favoring the combination of the two in one log, see Holbrook 1986b]. The constructive recognition of personal biases in the journal is an important learning experience for the researcher. Some even suggest that fieldworkers undergo psychoanalysis to become more insightful regarding their personal equation, although few fieldworkers follow this advice.

## Confirmability Audit

The final recommended method for addressing the issue of confirmability is an audit. Like a financial auditor, the qualitative research auditor examines the correspondence between the data and the report. In the case of qualitative research, the data consist of fieldnotes, journals, photographs, audio tapes, videotapes, artifacts, and records of the analytical process. Together, such materials comprise the audit trail that shows how the data were collected, recorded, and analyzed (see Lincoln and Guba 1985). The auditor is asked to comment not so much on the "truth" of the report and inferences drawn by the researchers as on the plausibility of their interpretations and the adequacy of the data. In other words, auditors are asked to examine whether the researchers have either played fast and free with the data or have perhaps deluded themselves by making inferences that cannot be fully supported by or adequately grounded in the data. Auditors who are familiar with the use of the methods employed but who are not a part of the project team are selected.

We have used auditing in Odyssey and post-Odyssey work; we have been involved in being audited by several others (Belk, Sherry, and Wallendorf 1988 was audited by three colleagues) as well as in auditing the work of others (Wallendorf has audited some work done by O'Guinn and Belk). To our knowledge, these have been the only applications of auditing in consumer research. Auditing involves supplying an auditor with all raw data materials, as well as the interpretation derived from them; it goes beyond merely asking colleagues to read an interpretation and comment on it. Based on our experience, we see the

audit as a useful procedure, although it does not provide an absolute guarantee that the inferences drawn are confirmable or confirmed.

Because data interpretation is an on-going process that begins in the field, triangulation among researchers can also be seen as a form of "internal audit" use in team research, just as is true of negotiating interpretations between researchers on the team once they are out of the field. In some ways, due to the close proximity of researchers on a team to the phenomena of interest in a particular research project, this internal audit is more useful than the external audit where even with excellent data records, the auditor remains something of an outsider.

Auditing, like the other procedures discussed here, has its limits and problems. We would be remiss if we did not mention the political and personal difficulties of carrying out the role of auditor as well as that of researcher being audited. The auditing process is one in which the researchers must bare their souls in a much more personal and direct way than occurs in review processes. As a result, the auditing process can become fraught with hostilities and misunderstandings which do not serve to improve the research and may negatively shape the character of the relationship between the parties, either directly or indirectly.

An additional limitation on external auditing is that it becomes cumbersome or impossible as the project becomes very large. In the case of the sacred and profane work for the Odyssey (Belk, Wallendorf, and Sherry 1989), an auditor would have to read approximately 1000 pages of raw fieldnotes and journals, read again this many pages of annotated fieldnotes used in analysis, view approximately 130 videotapes, and peruse 4000 photographs and slides. These would then have to be assessed in light of a 140+ page report of sacred and profane interpretations. To say that this would place a substantial burden on the would-be auditors is a gross understatement. Auditing in this case is simply not feasible. However, the issue of confirmability remains, nonetheless.

Therefore, instead, in such cases, the authors must provide sufficient verbatim material from fieldnotes that a reader is able to assess confirmability without resorting to testimony from an auditor. We have found auditing to be much more useful for smaller scale projects, especially those in which one would reasonably question whether sufficiently prolonged engagement and persistent observation was attained. Even then it is important to keep in mind that this time-consuming procedure adds another subjective assessment of the project and thus does not guarantee its correctness. Because of the impossibility of auditing large-scale projects from the Consumer Behavior Odyssey, we have chosen to address the confirmability issue by placing the data, after appropriately disguising names to protect informant anonymity, in an archive at the Marketing Science Institute in Cambridge, Massachusetts. This allows others to use the data to develop alternate interpretations of phenomena and to challenge our interpretations.

## INTEGRITY ASSESSMENT

The problem of lack of integrity in naturalistic (and other) research arises from the possibility of conflict between the researcher and informants, rather than from the temptations that may present themselves to the researcher. For example, given the complexity of producing qualitative fieldnotes, videotapes, and photographs, it is likely that it is more difficult for ethnographic researchers to fabricate data.

However, problems with integrity may arise when informants fear the researcher (especially where the subject of investigation is socially undesirable or illegal), dislike the researcher, or simply try to present themselves in more attractive ways (see Nachman 1984 for more discussion of the ways these may affect the data). Jack Douglas (1976) has suggested four resulting problems: misinformation, evasions, lies, and fronts, each of which represents a successively more elaborate deception. However, he points out that:

> Sure, people tell the truth most of the time in their everyday lives, at least as they see it. How often do people bother to lie about the weather or where the salt is? But the outsider trying to find out what the truth is about the things that count most to people, such as money and sex, must look upon all their accounts about those things as suspicious until proven otherwise (Douglas 1976, 55-56).

Besides the general strategy of skepticism (e.g., Dean and Whyte 1958), there are several other means of assessing and increasing the integrity of naturalistic research. These methods include:

1. Prolonged engagement and the construction of rapport and trust
2. Triangulation (across sources, methods, and researchers)
3. Good interviewing technique
4. Safeguarding informant identity
5. Researcher self-analysis and introspection

### Prolonged Engagement and Construction of Rapport and Trust

What the strategy of constructing rapport and trust attempts to do is to change from a conflict paradigm between researcher and informant to a cooperation paradigm. Suspicious informants often learn to trust a researcher who shows sustained interest and cultivates familiarity and intimacy with them and with others (Wallendorf 1987). Because establishing trust with some informants in a setting may cause distrust in others, the use of a research team in which different members can cultivate different informants is especially useful.

Prolonged engagement gives the researchers time to learn the nuances and language of a setting or phenomenon through participant observation. The subtlety of this appreciation is shown in the gradual development of an ability to know when something "feels right" or "feels wrong" (see also the discussion

below on self-analysis and introspection). The researcher also learns more about the character of informants, their potentially marginal status or ax-to-grind motivations within the group, and what others think of them. Thus, while prolonged engagement allows the researcher to develop rapport and trust with informants, it also provides a better basis for assessing clues to the potential deceptiveness of the information these informants may provide.

### Triangulation Across Sources, Methods, and Researchers

Another means of assessing potential distortions in naturalistic research is by comparing the information gathered using different informants, data collection methods, and members of the research team. Subsequent informants are routinely asked many of the same questions asked of earlier informants in an effort to check the accuracy of this information and the extent to which it is shared. Often key informants are assumed to provide better information, but because they may be marginal members of a group, it is well advised to check their information with others. When contradictions are found, ulterior motives, character traits, and other incentives to deceive must be considered in weighing the information. Becker (1970) suggests that the context in which comments are elicited should also be taken into consideration. Statements made spontaneously by informants should be valued more than responses to direct researcher questions; statements made in the presence of the researcher only are to be valued over statements made in a group setting. Such guidelines, of course, can only be followed if detailed fieldnotes or tapings of each interaction and its circumstances have been kept. And as Werner and Schoepfle (1987) note, statements made later in fieldwork with a given informant (after rapport and trust have presumably been built) should be trusted over statements made early in the interviewing process.

Triangulation over methods is especially helpful in comparing interview-based perspectives on action to observation-based perspectives in action (Snow and Anderson 1987). For example, an informant who presents a personal front of lack of involvement with household pets may be contradicted by observations of the informant petting and tenderly talking to the pet (Wallendorf 1987). The use of photo or video records of such behavior in autodriving the informant may be a way to preclude or correct such misstatements (Heisley and Levy 1988).

Triangulation over researchers helps to assess and improve data integrity by taking advantage of the ability of researchers of different genders, ages, appearances, and personalities to obtain different information from an informant. In multiple researcher observations, personal observer biases can also be detected. We have occasionally also employed a mild form of "good cop/bad cop" joint interviewing technique in which two (or sometimes even three) researchers simultaneously interview the same informant. If one of these interviewers takes a more direct and bold approach to asking questions and the other takes a more indirect and milder approach, the informant is able to open up to one of the researchers (most often the latter) who is perceived more favorably.

## Good Interviewing Technique

Obviously employing skillful and creative interviewing can also help to preclude misinformation and aid in its detection. Interviews should begin with broad non-threatening questions that cover a broad agenda in relatively little detail. Subsequently in the same or later interviews with an informant more detailed and sensitive questions can be employed, often going back to ideas only covered superficially during initial questioning. Probing, reframing, and trying alternative approaches are additional parts of good interviewing technique (see Douglas 1985). But perhaps most important is sensitivity and adaptability. A team setting allows the possibility of employing the interviewer who is working best with a given informant to take over more of the interview once this pattern is detected.

Another useful interviewing technique is self-revelation. Contrary to the distanced approach advocated by positivist researchers, naturalistic inquirers often make it a point to offer details from their personal lives to the informant. One intent in doing so is to defuse concerns about embarrassing revelations by offering some personal information to the informant. However, such revelations need not, and often should not, be directly parallel to those being investigated. Instead, the fact that the researcher is willing to talk a bit about himself or herself makes the interview more natural and less threatening to informants. It also permits the researcher and informant to temporarily connect as fellow humans, laying aside the research roles in which they are engaged (Wallendorf 1987). Sometimes disguised descriptions of the behavior of other informants can have the same effect.

Becker (1970) suggests an interviewing technique of planned naivete in which the researcher plays ignorant in order to get the informant to explain things concretely and explicitly. While we believe that this technique is sometimes useful in penetrating some evasions, it need not be carried to the extremes of Davis' (1973) "Martian" interviewer. If the researcher, like a recently-landed Martian, brings *no* knowledge that can be implicitly assumed to be shared with the informant, the interview would have to obtain explanations of why people are breathing and why adults are larger than children. Clearly, the researcher brings an open mind concerning appropriate interpretation into the field; however, this does not mean that the researcher has a blank mind and is unequipped with concepts and theories which may be usefully employed in interpreting the action observed (Blumer 1969; Schmitt 1974).

The question thus is what should be assumed and what should be explicated. One technique we have found useful in team research is to have one researcher who is less familiar with an informant, culture, or group setting conduct the interview. Such a researcher can legitimately ask the informant questions that might otherwise fall in the region of taken-for-granted

assumptions (Wirth 1964) that should be examined by the researchers. Because informants may hide information by making it seem that some things are simply "known by all" or "not to be talked about," these techniques may help penetrate such evasions.

Finally, the best interview is one which is supplemented by and embedded in observations of behavior in a naturalistic setting. In other words, over-reliance on interview material without supplementary contextualizing observations and participation in the culture of the informant opens the door to the impatient researcher being duped.

## Safeguarding Informant Identity

In conducting interviews care should also be taken to explain how the information provided will be used, what will be done to assure informant anonymity, and the fact that the informant can at any time rescind permissions previously given. The use of pseudonyms and disguises should be explained and practiced in fieldnotes, journals, and reports. Where the researcher seeks information considered sensitive by the informant, attempts to mechanically record the conversation are not generally well advised. However, what researchers and informants may consider sensitive often differs. For example, recently one of the authors interviewed an informant who did not mind openly discussing illegal drug use on videocamera, but requested that the camera and an audio recorder be turned off while she discussed her opinions about her two brothers' occupational choices. What is most sensitive to an informant can not always be anticipated ahead of time. However, prolonged engagement using multiple methods (sometimes employing videorecording and sometimes not) provides an opportunity to penetrate such problems.

Explicitly and repeatedly assuring the anonymity of an informant's identity removes one potential reason why informants may misrepresent or distort information reported to a researcher. As this behavior necessitates explicit research conduct, it precludes the possibility of conducting covert research. Oddly, this undermines the argument that covert research will somehow produce data which gives a "truer" picture of the social world investigated. Rather, it appears from our own research experience that covert research builds in problems which prevent this possibility.

## Researcher Self-Analysis and Introspection

Introspection is the basis for empathy and is the first test by which the integrity of research findings are assessed. Introspection is important to acknowledge since naturalistic research findings may also lack integrity because of biases directly brought about by the researcher. Greater research integrity can be brought about by researchers more completely and openly understanding themselves. To this end, Werner and Schoepfle (1987) advise that researchers undergo psychoanalysis, although they recognize that the number of qualitative researchers who have done so is quite small.

One example of qualitative research that benefitted greatly from such analysis is Holbrook

(1988). In this piece the author begins with an interpretation by other members of the Consumer Behavior Odyssey that his decor reflects an unintentional "great white hunter" motif. Drawing on five years of psychoanalysis, he is able to trace the likely origin of this decor to the resolution of childhood fears that would be unlikely to have been detected with the most intensive naturalistic inquiry.

Douglas (1985) advocates "researcher know thyself" in order that we might assess not only our biases, but also our strengths. He too cites Freeman's (1983) criticisms of Margaret Mead's Samoan research as a cautionary example:

> Mead's idyllic picture of sexual liberation on this supposed faraway utopia was probably a projection of her own lonely cravings (Douglas 1985, 40).

Not only does self-knowledge potentially aid in assessing effects on informants and data interpretation, it also aids in appreciating biases in problem and informant selection. This is an important reason for keeping researcher journals and for keeping this material in addition to fieldnotes (see Bogdan and Taylor 1975). Doing so allows others to potentially assess such biases in research as well.

## CONCLUSIONS

In this chapter we have critically discussed the use of a number of techniques for assessing the trustworthiness of participant-observation, ethnographic research in consumer behavior. Issues concerning credibility, transferability, dependability, confirmability, and integrity as components of trustworthiness have been discussed. Techniques for establishing and assessing these components have been explained and evaluated based on our use of them. The techniques discussed and evaluated include: prolonged engagement combined with persistent observation; triangulation across sources, methods, researchers, and sites; regular on-site team interaction; negative case analysis; debriefings by peers; member checks; purposive sampling; seeking limiting exceptions; emergent design; observation over time and the explanation of changes; reflexive journals; dependability and confirmability audits; interviewing techniques; safeguarding informant identity; and researcher self-analysis and introspection. Particularly given the lack of a research tradition in consumer behavior utilizing this approach, we endorse careful attention to issues concerning trustworthiness as this field develops such a tradition.

## REFERENCES

Adler, Patricia A. and Peter Adler (1987), *Membership Roles in Field Research*, Qualitative Research Methods, vol. 6, Beverly Hills: Sage.

Anderson, Paul F. (1986), "On Method in Consumer Research: A Critical Relativist Perspective," *Journal of Consumer Research* 13 (September), 155-173.

Becker, Howard S. (1970), *Sociological Work: Method and Substance*, Chicago: Aldine.

Becker, Howard S. (1986), *Doing Things Together*, Evanston, IL: Northwestern University Press.

Belk, Russell W. (1984), "Against Thinking," *1984 Winter Educators' Conference: Scientific Method in Marketing*, eds. Paul F. Anderson and Michael J. Ryan, Chicago: American Marketing Association, 57-59.

Belk, Russell W. (1986), "Art Versus Science as Ways of Generating Knowledge About Materialism," *Methodological Perspectives in Consumer Research*, Richard Lutz and David Brinberg, eds., New York: Springer Verlag.

Belk, Russell W. (1988), "Qualitative Analysis of Data from the Consumer Behavior Odyssey: The Role of the Computer and the Role of the Researcher," *Proceedings of the Division of Consumer Psychology*, Linda F. Alwitt ed., Washington, D. C.: American Psychology Association, 7-11.

Belk, Russell W., Harold Kassarjian, John Sherry, and Melanie Wallendorf (1987), "Red Mesa Swap Meet: A Pilot Study for the Consumer Behavior Odyssey," unpublished report, Boston: Marketing Science Institute.

Belk, Russell W., John F. Sherry, Jr., and Melanie Wallendorf (1988), "A Naturalistic Inquiry into Buyer and Seller Behavior at a Swap Meet," *Journal of Consumer Research*, 14 (March), 449-470.

Belk, Russell W., Melanie Wallendorf, and John Sherry (1989), "The Sacred and the Profane in Consumer Behavior: Theodicy on the Odyssey," *Journal of Consumer Research*, 16 (June), forthcoming.

Belk, Russell W., Melanie Wallendorf, John F. Sherry, Jr., Morris Holbrook, and Scott Roberts (1988), "Collectors and Collecting," *Advances in Consumer Research*, vol. 15, Michael Houston, ed., Provo: Association for Consumer Research.

Blumer, Herbert (1969), *Symbolic Interactionism: Perspective and Method*, Englewood Cliffs, N.J.: Prentice-Hall.

Bogdan, Robert and Steven J. Taylor (1975), *Introduction to Qualitative Research Methods*, New York: Wiley-Interscience.

Bulmer, Martin, ed. (1982), *Social Research Ethics*, London: Macmillan Press, Ltd..

Campbell, Donald T. and Julian C. Stanley (1966), *Experimental and Quasi-Experimental Designs for Research*, Chicago: Rand-McNally.

Caplow, Theodore (1984), "Rule Enforcement without Visible Means: Christmas Gift-Giving in Middletown," *American Journal of Sociology*, 89 (May), 1306-1323.

Collier, John, Jr., and Malcolm Collier (1986), *Visual Anthropology: Photography as a Research Method*, Albuquerque, University of New Mexico Press.

Davis, Fred (1973), "The Martian and the Convert: Ontological Polarities in Social Research," *Urban Life*, 3 (October), 333-343.

Davis, Murray S. (1971), "That's Interesting! Towards a Phenomenology of Sociology and a Sociology of Phenomenology," *Philosophy of the Social Sciences*, 4, 309.

Dean, John P. and William F. Whyte, (1958), "How Do You Know If the Informant is Telling the Truth?" *Human Organization*, 17, 34-38.

Denzin, Norman K. (1970), *The Research Act: A Theoretical Introduction to Sociological Methods*, Chicago: Aldine.

Douglas, Jack D. (1976), *Investigative Social Research: Individual and Team Field Research*, Beverly Hills: Sage.

Douglas, Jack D. (1985), *Creative Interviewing*, Beverly Hills: Sage.

Erikson, Kai T. (1967), "A Comment on Disguised Observation in Sociology," *Social Problems*, 14, 366-373.

Fine, Gary (1980), "Cracking Diamonds: Observer Role in Little League Baseball Setting and the Acquisition of Social Competence," *Fieldwork Experience: Qualitative Approaches to Social Research*, William B. Shaffir, Robert A. Stebbins, and Allan Turowetz, eds., New York: St. Martin's Press, 117-132.

Fine, Gary and Barry Glassner (1979), "Participant Observation with Children," *Urban Life*, 8 (July), 153-174.

Freeman, Derek (1983), *Margaret Mead and Samoa: The Making and Unmaking of an Anthropological Myth*, Cambridge: Harvard University Press.

Glaser, Barney G. and Anselm L. Strauss (1967), *The Discovery of Grounded Theory: Strategies for Qualitative Research*, Chicago: Aldine Publishing Co.

Gould, Leroy C., Andrew L. Walker, Lansing E. Crane, and Charles W. Lidz (1974), *Connections: Notes from the Heroin World*, New Haven: Yale University Press.

Heisley, Deborah, Mary Ann McGrath, and John Sherry, Jr. (1988), "A Day in the Life of a Farmers' Market," Northwestern University working paper.

Heisley, Deborah and Sidney J. Levy (1988), "Familiar Interlude: Autodriving in Consumer Analysis," Northwestern University working paper.

Hirschman, Elizabeth C. (1986), "Humanistic Inquiry in Marketing Research: Philosophy, Method, and Criteria," *Journal of Marketing Research*, 23 (August), 237-249.

Holbrook, Morris (1986a), "An Audiovisual Inventory of Some Fanatic Consumer Behavior: The 25-Cent Tour of a Jazz Collector's House," *Advances in Consumer Research*, eds. Melanie Wallendorf and Paul Anderson, vol. 14, Provo: Association for Consumer Research, 144-149.

Holbrook, Morris (1986b), "From the Log of a Consumer Researcher: Reflections on the Odyssey," *Advances in Consumer Research*, eds. Melanie Wallendorf and Paul Anderson, vol. 14, Provo: Association for Consumer Research, 365-369.

Holbrook, Morris (1988), "Steps Toward a Psychoanalytic Semiology of Artistic Consumption: Toward a Meta-Meta-Meta-Analysis of Some Issues Raised by the Consumer Behavior Odyssey," *Advances in Consumer Research*, Vol. 15, Michael J. Houston, ed., Provo: Association for Consumer Research, 537-542.

Huber, Joan (1973), "Symbolic Interaction as a Pragmatic Perspective: The Bias of Emergent Theory," *American Sociological Review*, 38 (April), 274-284.

Huber, Joan (1974), "The Emergency of Emergent Theory," *American Sociological Review*, 39 (June), 463-467.

Hudson, Laurel A. and Julie L. Ozanne (1988), "Alternative Ways of Seeking Knowledge in Consumer Research," *Journal of Consumer Research*, 14 (March), 508-521.

Kirk, Jerome and Marc L. Miller (1986), *Reliability and Validity in Qualitative Research*, Beverly Hills: Sage.

Lauden, Larry (1984), *Science and Values*, Berkeley: University of California Press.

Lincoln, Yvonna S. and Egon Guba (1985), *Naturalistic Inquiry*, Beverly Hills: Sage Publications.

Lynd, Robert S. and Helen Merrell Lynd (1956/orig. 1929), *Middletown: A Study in Modern American Culture*, New York: Harcourt, Brace, and World.

Lynd, Robert S. and Helen Merrell Lynd (1937), *Middletown in Transition: A Study in Cultural Conflicts*, New York: Harcourt, Brace, and Company.

Manning, Peter K. (1987), *Semiotics and Fieldwork*, Newbury Park, CA: Sage.

McCall, George J., and J. L. Simmons (1969), *Issues in Participant Observation: A Text and Reader*, Reading, Mass.: Addison-Wesley.

McGrath, Mary Ann (1988), "An Ethnography of a Gift-Store," unpublished Ph.D. dissertation, Northwestern University, Department of Marketing.

Mead, Margaret (1928), *Coming of Age in Samoa*, New York: Morrow.

Miles, Matthew B. and A. Michael Huberman (1984), *Qualitative Data Analysis*, Beverly Hills: Sage.

Nachman, Steven R. (1984), "Lies my Informants Told Me," *Journal of Anthropological Research*, 40 (Winter), 536-555.

O'Guinn, Thomas C. and Ronald J. Faber (1987), "An Exploration of the World of Compulsive Consumption: Correlates, Aetiology and Consequences," working paper, University of Illinois College of Communications.

Punch, Maurice (1986), *The Politics and Ethics of Fieldwork*, Qualitative Research Methods, vol. 3, Beverly Hills: Sage.

Prus, Robert (1985), "Sociologist as Hustler: The Dynamics of Acquiring Information," *Fieldwork Experience*, William D. Shaffir, Robert Stebbins, and Allan Turowetz, eds., New York: St. Martins Press, 132-135.

Schmitt, Raymond L. (1974), "SI and Emergent Theory: A Reexamination," *American Sociological Review*, 39 (3), 453-456.

Sherry, John R., Sr. and Mary Ann McGrath "A Comparative Ethnography of the Gift Store," this volume

Smith, John K. and Lous Heshusius (1986), "Closing Down the Conversation: The End of the Quantitative-Qualitative Debate Among Educational Inquirers," *Educational Researcher*, 15 (January), 4-12.

Snow, David A. and Leon Anderson (1987), "Identity Work Among the Homeless: The Verbal Construction and Avowal of Personal Identities," *American Journal of Sociology*, 92 (May), 1336-1371.

Sontag, Susan (1973), *On Photography*, New York: Farrar, Straus and Giroux.

Stone, Gregory P., David R. Maines, Harvey A. Farberman, Gladys I. Stone, and Norman K. Denzin (1974), "On Methodology and Craftsmanship in the Criticism of Sociological Perspectives," *American Sociological Review*, 29 (June), 456-463.

Van Maanen, John (1988), *Tales of the Field: On Writing Ethnography*, Chicago: University of Chicago Press.

Wallendorf, Melanie (1987), "On Intimacy," paper presented at the American Marketing Association Winter Educators' Conference, San Antonio, TX, February.

Wallendorf, Melanie (1988), "Consumption Symbolism in Women's Private Spaces: Findings from Fiction, Photos and Fact," presentation made at Popular Culture Association meetings, New Orleans, March.

Wallendorf, Melanie and Russell W. Belk (1987), "Deep Meaning in Possessions: Qualitative Research Findings from The Consumer Behavior Odyssey," Cambridge, MA: Marketing Science Institute.

Warren, Carol A. B. (1988), *Gender Issues in Field Research*, Qualitative Research Methods Series, vol. 9, Beverly Hills: Sage.

Werner, Oswald and G. Mark Schoepfle (1987), *Systematic Fieldwork: Ethnographic Analysis and Data Management*, Vol. 1, Beverly Hills: Sage.

Whitehead, Tony Larry and Mary Ellen Conaway, eds. (1986), *Self, Sex, and Gender in Cross-Cultural Fieldwork*, Urbana: University of Illinois Press.

Whyte, William F. (1984), *Learning From the Field: A Guide from Experience*, Beverly Hills: Sage.

Wirth, Louis (1964), *On Cities and Social Life*, Chicago: University of Chicago Press.

Wyer, R. S. and T. K. Srull (1980), "The Processing of Social Stimulus Information: A Conceptual Integration," in R. Hastie, T. M. Ostron, E. B. Ebbesen, R. S. Wyer, D. Hamilton, and D. E. Carlston, eds., *Person Memory: The Cognitive Basis of Social Perception*, Hillsdale, N. J.: Erlbaum.

Zaltman, Gerald, Karen LeMasters, and Michael Heffring (1982), "Being Interesting," in *Theory Construction in Marketing: Some Thoughts on Thinking*, New York: John Wiley and Sons, 25-44.

# Consumers' Interpretations of Advertising Imagery: A Visit to the Hell of Connotation

David Glen Mick, University of Florida
Laura G. Politi, University of Florida[1]

## ABSTRACT

The semanticity of advertising imagery is investigated through the use of a protocol interpretive method. It is shown that, beyond contributions to theory building, interpretive methods are also valuable for testing propositions. In addition, a close inspection of the protocols reveals several dimensions of advertising comprehension formerly ignored. We conclude that the concept of denotation in advertising illustrations is misguided and that an alternative meaning model of advertising consumption is needed to more fully appreciate the complexities and nuances of consumers' interpretations of advertising imagery.

## INTRODUCTION

Consumers' interpretations of advertising messages have long been an important and controversial topic in advertising research (Jacoby and Hoyer 1982a, 1982b, 1987; Mick 1988b; Russo, Metcalf, and Stephens 1981; Shimp and Preston 1981).[2] Historically, most empirical work has centered on consumers' processing of *linguistic* information; recently, researchers have payed increased attention to *nonlinguistic* features (e.g., Childers and Houston 1984; Edell and Staelin 1983; Johnson, Zimmer, and Golden 1987; Richards and Zakia 1981; Rossiter and Percy 1980; Zakia 1986). Lengthy theoretical writings on visual communication in advertising have also appeared (Rossiter and Percy 1983). Despite this trend, few have actually studied the semiotic substance of consumers' interpretations of advertising illustrations. For instance, Thematic Apperception Tests remain widespread in the advertising industry for pretesting visual content. Yet, advertising scholars have exerted little effort to employ such semantic-unveiling methods to inform theory and assess propositions about consumers' interpretations of nonverbal ad information.

In several linguistic domains, there has been a surge of interest in protocol (think-out-loud) techniques: textlinguistics (Ballstaedt and Mandl 1984); reading research (Graesser and Clark 1985); and literary analysis (Kintgen 1983). These researchers eschew the traditional, circumscribed, *post hoc* measures of comprehension, e.g., recall and recognition tests. Instead, they favor concurrent protocols for the fertile insights provided about the dynamic, iterative nature of meaning processes, including spontaneous inferences, tentative hypotheses, and reconstructed meanings. According to Olson, Duffy, and Mack (1984), p. 257), protocol data can reveal processing strategies used, knowledge structures employed, and types of representations (meanings) constructed. Only a handful of advertising researchers have utilized open-ended, on-line measures of interpretive processes, and they have concentrated strictly on verbal information (e.g., Levy 1986; Mick 1987). In a recent expose' on psychological meaning in advertising, Friedmann and Zimmer (1988) called for wider usage of these methods.[3] Data produced by unstructured techniques can be analyzed both quantitatively and qualitatively, the latter emphasis being closer in spirit to the interpretive methods and *raison d'etre* of this volume (see also Belk, Sherry, and Wallendorf 1988; Hirschman 1987; Holbrook and Grayson 1986; Hudson and Ozanne 1988; Mick 1988a). Most researchers, regardless of their methodological predilictions, are willing to accept that interpretive methods can serve as a logic of discovery, i.e., to develop theory and empirically testable propositions (see Hunt 1983). However, there is far less agreement on whether interpretive methods can and should be used as a logic of justification, i.e., to support or falsify theory, including the testing of propositions as commonly

---

[1] The authors are indebted to the following individuals who provided valuable comments on an earlier draft of this article: Joseph Alba, Morris Holbrook, Richard Lutz, Dean McCannell, Grant McCracken, Winfried Nöth, Srinivasan Rathneshwer, and Richard Zakia.

[2] The terms *comprehension* and *interpretation* are used interchangeably here. Readers who question the synonymy of those terms are also likely to believe that denotation and connotation are separate constructs--likely because they associate comprehension with denotation and interpretation with connotation. This article seeks to defy the denotation/connotation distinction with respect to advertising illustrations. Comprehension itself is conceptualized generally in this article from a levels of processing perspective, specifically as a cue-induced spread of activation of semantic concepts (knowledge structures). Inferencing is the basic mechanism of this activation and also accounts for the meanings constructed as a function of bridging two already-activated concepts.

[3] Although there is a long tradition of collecting cognitive responses in advertising studies, the coding schemes have remained wedded to attitude theory in social psychology (support arguments, counterarguments, etc.). The semantic content of the responses are treated superficially, at least in terms of what they can reveal about comprehension. Two recent exceptions to this trend include Chattopadhyay and Alba (1988) and Mick (1987).

done with positivist techniques such as surveys and experimentation (see Calder and Tybout 1987; Hudson and Ozanne 1988).[4]

The purpose of our study is twofold. First, we adopt a protocol technique to capture consumers' interpretations of a pictorial print ad. Through *our* interpretation of the protocol data, we seek to contribute to both theory and method aimed at understanding *consumers'* interpretations of visual advertising messages. Second, as a preliminary demonstration work, we show how these interpretive data can be used to test certain propositions about advertising.

## ADVERTISING ILLUSTRATIONS: OPEN OR CLOSED TEXTS?

The classic model of communication employed by advertisers involves a sender who encodes a message which is then transmitted through a specific medium to a receiver who, in turn, decodes the message. Ideally, the receiver is a member of a targeted market segment whose linguistic and nonlinguistic codes have been sufficiently researched, the result being a code-sharing between sender and receiver that maximizes efficient, effective communication. A major goal is to have targeted consumers interpret brand messages as the advertiser intends (denotates). When this occurs, comprehension of the message is said to have taken place. According to a number of longstanding advertising theories (e.g., McGuire 1969), comprehension is a necessary step on the route to a positive brand attitude and purchase behavior.

In the terminology of semiotics, it seems clear that advertisers construct their messages to be "open" texts, i.e., understandable as intended by a select group of individuals. According to Eco (1979, p.3),

> An 'open' text cannot be described as a communicative strategy if the role of its addressee (the reader, in the case of verbal texts) has not been envisaged at the moment of its generation *qua* text. An open text is a paramount instance of a syntactic-semantico-pragmatic device whose foreseen interpretation is a part of its generative process.

In other words, as open texts, ads are aimed at sets of "model consumers" for whom the advertiser has endeavored to structure the appropriate signs to form a meaningful message.

Related specifically to advertising illustrations, the proposition that ad messages are open texts in turn reflects Bryson's (1983) notion of the essentialness of denotation in painting, i.e., interpretation of visual content is guided by iconographic codes which lead the presupposed

---

[4]It must be noted that some researchers who are sympathetic to interpretive methods reject altogether the distinction between a logic of discovery and a logic of justification.

observer to its intended, fixed meaning. Hence, a carefully crafted advertising photograph should communicate the same message to individuals from a relevant market segment.

In his incisive semiotic article, however, Baker (1985) charges that the concept of denotation is worthless in the analysis of visual imagery, because it is impossible. He argues that there is rarely a shared, descriminable code but rather "a sloppy, blurry thing, firmest at the center where its stereotypes are most stupid and its prejudices most entrenched, but always slipping into abjection at its edges" (Baker 1985, p. 173; see also Holbrook 1983, pp.68-69). According to Baker's position, then, advertising pictorials are more likely to be "closed" texts, as semioticians would call them. As Eco (1979, p.8) explains,

> Those texts that obsessively aim at arousing a precise response on the part of more or less precise empirical readers....are in fact open to any possible 'aberrant' decoding. A text which is so immoderately 'open' to every possible interpretation [is] a *closed* one.

Thus, a closed text attempts to overdetermine receiver response and always fails.

It must be stressed that the open/closed text distinction represents poles on a continuum, not an all-or-none dichotomy. Nevertheless, Baker's (1985) discussion suggests that, irrespective of apparent success or effectiveness, an advertising illustration is inherently more like a closed text than advertising theory and practice assumes. From that proposition Baker goes on to pose some troubling thoughts for advertisers, quoting the French semiologists Baudrillard (1981, p. 196) and Barthes (1964, p. 43):

> If the possibility of denoting is removed, what is left? Is it, as Jean Baudrillard suggests the Bauhaus designers feared, that beyond the desperate illusion of a nucleus of intended meanings or functions, 'all the rest is coating, the hell of *connotation*: residue, superfluity, excrescence, eccentricity, ornamentation, uselessness'?....What Barthes called 'the terror of uncertain signs' is far more likely to be felt in cases where direct and unambiguous communication is attempted, where it is thought necessary to get a specific message from sender to receiver.

In a recent empirical work, Zakia (1986) partly addressed the advertising implications surrounding Baker's (1985) claims. Zakia had a small sample of consumers respond rapidly with a single word upon exposure to a highly visual liquor ad. The reactions were multifarious, including "absorbing," "cold," "embraceable," "evil," "primitive," "seductive," and "vulnerable." Zakia (1986) concluded that without multiple potential meanings, an extensive and diverse audience could not be attracted to the product. In other words, from a managerial perspective, a closed text in pictorial advertising may be superior to an open text. Like Zakia, the textlinguist Nöth (1987, 1988) has noted that advertisements are usually unambiguous with respect to their purpose, but vary so dramatically in surface structure that the range of possible semantic interpretations is virtually limitless.

In essence then, the standard theories and models of advertising communication are diametrically opposite to the Baker-Zakia-Nöth viewpoint, i.e., whether advertising visuals are generally open or closed texts for their destined market segments. If the prevailing perspective is wrong, then the notions of comprehension and denotative meaning will require serious reconsideration with respect to advertising pictorials and advertising theory.

Although revealing, Zakia's work requires extension beyond single word responses in order to more thoroughly investigate the semanticity of advertising illustrations. Such an effort would also permit a more detailed examination of the open/closed text issue. We reasoned that by having consumers from a given market segment describe a segment-appropriate pictorial ad and indicate what they think the advertiser intended with the visual content, we could determine the extent of interpretive agreement (disagreement) as an assessment of ad-text openness (closedness).

## DOES SEX SELL?

As a message strategy, sexuality is replete across advertising illustrations. Given the premise that the primary goal of an advertisement is to produce consumer desire for the brand, MacCannell (1987, p.528) contends that sexual innuendo is effective in advertising pictorials precisely because it *models* desire. This hypothesis derives from MacCannell's scanning of contemporary advertising, based on sociocultural insights about myths and a semiotic appreciation for the role of kinesics and proxemics in nonverbal communication. According to MacCannell (1987, p.528),

> a close reading reveals that it is not actual bio-reproductive sex that is used for selling. Rather, it is a kind of sexual suggestion which covers over the censure of actual sex.... Specifically, what is represented is not sex but the blockage, censure, or inhibition of the sex act which is simultaneously suppressed from the image and is also the only possible motive for it.

By MacCannell's account, a person desires only what he or she does not have already; uninterrupted desire is maximally maintained when the object of desire is nearby, but just beyond reach. Hence, pervasive sexual suggestion in mass advertising serves as a model for culturally-engrained product desire, coalescing the desire for commodification with the commodification of desire. MacCannell notes that most sexual imagery is masculine oriented and, as such, "anything that simultaneously suggests and denies, or seems to invite while barring male sexual involvement, reproduces the essential structure of the

cultural production of desire under a male sign" (p. 530).

In saying that sex in advertising models desire, we take MacCannell to mean--at the least--that there is an implicit association between depicted sexual desire and brand desire. Whether this means that the two desires are in some sense parallel but separate, or perhaps parallel and superimposed, is not wholly clear from MacCannell's comments, though that distinction does not appear critical to his thesis. It is the association which is tantamount. The association could be instrumentalist (the picture displays brand desire in which product acquisition may serve to fulfill sexual desire); the association could be metaphorical (the picture suggests that brand desire has intrinsic similarities to sexual desire); or the association could be metonymic (the picture simply co-presents brand desire and sexual desire contiguously). Additional associations may be possible and certainly more than one type could be involved in a given illustration.[5]

The feasibility and the power of MacCannell's proposition depend on consumers interpretively associating brand desire with depicted sexual desire. Those who interpret such an association must represent more than an inconsequential percentage of sample consumers, otherwise the proposition bears no import.

## METHOD

Consumers for this study consisted of a convenience sample of junior and senior undergraduate students from a major southeastern university. Twenty subjects were scheduled; two failed to keep their appointments and one was subsequently dropped from the study because English was not her native language. This left 17 subjects, nine females and eight males. Subjects were compensated with monetary payment ($3) or course credit, whichever they preferred.

Subjects were processed individually and their spoken responses were taped with a small, unobstrusive recorder. Introductory instructions informed subjects that the study focused on people's interpretations of magazine advertisements. They were told that we were interested in their natural thoughts and feelings in answering some questions about each ad they were about to be shown. Subjects were then exposed to four consecutive full-page magazine advertisements (not facsimiles), each matted inside a separate manilla folder. After opening each folder, subjects were given 15 seconds to view the ad and then, with the ad still available, subjects were

---

[5]The mechanisms by which this proposed correlation has developed between product/brand desire and sexual desire are likely to be complicated and subtle on both biological and cultural levels. One explanation derived from classical conditioning would suggest that a positive brand attitude might emerge through the association of the brand with other message stimuli (sexuality) that are reacted to positively (see Gorn 1982).

handed four consecutive 3x5 cards on which a different response request was typed. Subjects read the cards silently and then verbalized. At the end of each initial response, the researcher probed once more with "Anything else?" Then the next card was handed to them. After the fourth card for the fourth ad, subjects completed a one-page information sheet about their prior use of the products and brands shown in the ads. They were then debriefed, paid, and dismissed.

The four cards for each of the four ads were identical in terms of content and order of presentation. The questions were:

1) In your own words, please *describe* what's going on in the picture.

2) Ignore for now what the advertiser may have intended and tell us *your opinions and feelings* about what's going on in this picture.

3) What do you think the *advertiser was trying to communicate* with the picture in this particular ad?

4) What kinds of *evidence* can you identify in the picture to support your ideas *about what the advertiser tried to communicate*?

The four ads in this study were taken from general circulation magazines which college students occasionally view. Each ad was predominantly nonlinguistic, with minimal verbal information. It is worth emphasizing that ads which have no verbal content are practically nonexistent and, for this initial study, we chose not to alter the actual ads. The advertised brands represented product classes for which 20-22 year old adults demonstrate strong interest: sunglasses, cigarettes, liquor, and perfume. The ads themselves each included young adult models.

The target ad for this study was a Gordon's gin ad (see the Figure) and it was always the third ad shown to the subjects. This particular ad has been used by the firm for several years; obviously, company executives have judged the ad to be an effective communication about their brand to young adults.

The ad portrays a man and a woman on a beach. She is painting, seated on a stool in front of an easel; he is sitting on the sand close behind her, pulling on her dresscoat. He is looking up at her, whereas she is looking downward at her painter's palette. The brand is placed in the lower-right corner, accompanied in the middle-bottom with the quote "I could go for something Gordon's" and the slogan "The possibilities are endless." The picture itself is black and white, while the colors yellow, orange, and green appear on the bottle or in the lime inside the glass.

As already noted, this ad was selected because young adults can easily relate to both the product and the situational content of the ad. In addition, for assessing the propositions previously discussed, the picture is vivid and plainly harbors sexual innuendo. The standard open-text proposition would be called into question if more than one interpretation theme was produced by the subjects. MacCannell's

proposition would be undermined if few subjects associated the sexual desire with desire for the brand.

## ANALYSIS AND RESULTS

After the protocols were transcribed, the first author reviewed them and discerned three themes specifically related to subjects' thoughts on what the advertiser was trying to communicate with the picture. A theme represented the central, dominating idea expressed by the subject. A fourth category was used for those subjects who were unable to associate the picture and the brand. The four categories were:

1) A *peacefulness* theme expressed through associations between the physical setting (beach context) and the brand (e.g., its relaxing effects);

2) A *desire* theme expressed through associations between the sexual innuendo and desire for the brand;

3) A *status* theme expressed through associations between the type of people shown in the ad (e.g., young, healthy, stylish, etc.) and the brand (its ability to transform the viewer into a similar sort of individual); and

4) No association apparent between the picture and the brand.

The two authors then independently classified each subject's protocol according to the four categories above, with extra attention given to subjects' comments about the intended message and related evidence in the illustration (i.e., the third and fourth response tasks). Agreement between the two authors was 15 out of 17 classifications; the remaining two were resolved through review and discussion of the subjects' protocols.

The results indicated that six subjects generated the *peacefulness* theme, five subjects produced the *desire* theme (three males, two females), one subject derived the *status* theme, and five subjects perceived no relationship between the ad illustration and the brand. No subject expressed more than one theme. Examples of six subjects' partial protocols appear in the Table, along with their respective classifications.

## DISCUSSION

### Propositions Tested

The proposition that ad pictorials typically represent open texts to their respective market segments is not supported by our data. If the gin ad was an open text, then more agreement and certainty across the total seventeen subjects should have emerged with respect to their picture-brand interpretations. Consequently, while many pictorial ads are meticulously designed for a target audience, intended to be relatively constrained to key denotative meanings, it may be that the majority of pictorial ads are semantically closed. Denotatively they are sterile;

connotatively they border on anarchy. Myers'(1983, p. 214-16) warning is prophetic for ad comprehension researchers:

> There is a danger in the analysis of advertising of assuming that it is in the interests of advertisers to create one "preferred" reading of the advertisement's message. Intentionality suggests conscious manipulation and organization of texts and images, and implies that the visual, technical and linguistic strategies work together to secure one preferred reading of an advertisement to the exclusion of others....The openness of connotative codes may mean that we have to replace the notion of "preferred reading" with another which admits a range of possible alternatives open to the audience. [6]

It seems that pictorial ads for highly symbolic products such as liquor, jewelry, automobiles, cologne and perfume, fashion clothing and accessories, and home furnishings would be most likely to spur elaborate inferential interpretations. Whether these same findings would hold for less symbolic products (e.g., kitchen appliances, house and garden tools) remains to be shown.

MacCannell's proposition appears marginally supported by our data. Five out of the seventeen total subjects (29%) produced interpretations congruent with the proposition that sexual desire in advertising imagery can serve as a model for product desire. However, in looking only at the twelve subjects who constructed interpretations associating the picture and the brand, 42% produced the "desire" theme (5/12). Several of our subjects definitely linked the ad's sexual innuendo with brand desire.

## Limitations

Some limitations of this study must be acknowledged before moving to further discussion topics. Foremost is the fact that in this study we utilized only one ad, for a single product class (liquor).[7] Therefore, our results are strictly suggestive, not definitive. They should only be taken as a springboard to further theory and research on the substantive and methodological issues addressed here.

Secondly, a set of limitations revolves around our use of a protocol technique to address the semantic content of consumers' interpretations during visual processing. By requesting verbalized reports, we may have encouraged some subjects to construct meanings which would not have emerged under normal

---

[6]Readers should note that Myers uses the term "openness" in its everyday sense, which is more similar to Eco's notion of closed text rather than open text.

[7]Data from the other ads are being analyzed as part of a larger study.

processing conditions. Moreover, Lutz and Lutz (1977) and Rossiter (1982) have pointed out that pictures are quite effective in eliciting *mental* imagery, some of which probably formed the semantic substance of our subjects' interpretations. According to MacInnis and Price (1987, p.485), verbal reports of mental imagery require translations between imagery and discursive (verbal) processing modes, potentially confounding them. Since we were not focused on separating the modes per se, this is only a serious problem in our study to the degree that the translations altered the semantic contents of subjects' *basic thematic interpretations*. Though our data do not permit us to deflect this concern completely, we have no evidence to suggest that it happened. Prior research has shown that adults spontaneously assign verbal labels to most pictorial stimuli (Pezdek and Evans 1979) and, as a whole, the subjects who generated picture-brand associations in our study responded effortlessly.

Another limitation concerns articulate individuals who may have performed the imagery-to-discursive translation easier than less verbose individuals. If so, the less verbose subjects may have been more inclined to say there was no association between the illustration and the brand when, in fact, they may have mentally imaged an association.

Other limitations (and criticisms) surrounding the general use of protocol methods to uncover mental processes are well known and will not be repeated here (Ericsson and Simon 1984; Russo, Johnson, and Stephens 1986). We make no claims as to capturing the whole or the majority of meanings our subjects abscribed to the Gordon's gin ad. Our intent was to glimpse the pictorial interpretation process sufficiently enough through verbalization in order to identify significant semantic concepts and to characterize overall themes. The protocol method used in this study was partly retrospective and partly concurrent, given that our subjects were allowed 15 seconds to view the ad before verbalizing. Future studies may seek to reduce retrospectiveness by requesting verbalizations from the moment of stimulus presentation.

## Further Insights and Future Directions

Baker's (1985) provocative article sensitizes us to the ambiguous and arguable division between denotation and connotation in graphic art. As he points out, for years semioticians and other communication theorists have recognized the arbitrariness of the relation between linguistic signs (words) and their referents (concepts)--a condition which makes the meaning of words anything but intransigent. As a result, the boundary line between denotation and connotation quickly fades, blurring those comfortable and seemingly self-evident distinctions between intended versus unintended meaning, primary versus secondary meaning, and literal versus inferential meaning. This is especially true when viewed from the message receiver's perspective.

Nonetheless, arbitrariness between sign and referent has not been seriously considered in graphic

**FIGURE 1**

---

## TABLE
## SIX PARTIAL PROTOCOLS AND THEIR CLASSIFICATIONS

*Peacefulness Theme*

S#5: A drink with Gordan's will make you feel good, relaxed, easy-going, nothing too heavy, light and airy. You can almost see a breeze on the ocean.

S#14: They're out in this carefree atmosphere enjoying themselves. Very beautiful scenery, a wonderful place. By drinking this brand, this can also bring about or help you feel even more in that type of atmosphere that they're in.

*Desire Theme*

S#2: Evidently the guy is trying to get this girl. Oh, I guess the gin is going to be part of it. I guess they're trying to give advice to guys who are trying to pick up sophisticated women....He's trying to convince her to go somewhere. He's trying to lure her with the gin.

S#10: If they had a couple of drinks with Gordan's in it, maybe he's thinking that's a possibility, if I give her a couple of drinks that sex is a possibility.

*Status Theme*

S#8: The advertiser is trying to associate his product, this liquor, with attractive people who are having a good time....If you buy this liquor, you'll be more like those people in some way.

*No Association*

S#13: The picture pretty much has not too much to do with the advertisement. I can't really tell what the advertiser was trying to communicate.

---

art. The received view, which Baker strives to dislodge, is that graphics--compared to verbal language--more readily incorporate a demarcation between denotative and connotative meaning. In marketing and consumer research this belief is variously propagated (e.g., Rossiter and Percy 1983). Also, in their thorough review on mental imagery processing, MacInnis and Price (1987, p. 475) state that "Compared with symbolic or language-like processing, imagery processing bears a non-arbitrary correspondence to the thing being represented." In fact, there is broad support in psychology for the contention that an object and its mental image are structurally isomorphic (see Shepard 1978). However, it would be erroneous to conclude that that structural isomorphism is related to denoted meaning when consumers have mental images elicited by advertising illustrations. If this were true, the denotative meaning of Gordon's pictorial ad should have been straightforward and widely shared across our subjects. It was not.

The immediate implications of this argument form a momentous hurdle to advertisers who seek lucid communication through pictures and to researchers who strive to understand the nature of pictorial interpretation. Perhaps the only path from the horror of connotative anarchy is to return to the marketing nucleus: like the proverbial customer, the interpreter is always right. For, as Baker (1985, p.173) reminds us, "it is really of very little consequence to the viewers if their reading is not the intended one." A possible reaction to this viewpoint is to say that if the reading is not the intended one, then perhaps it is false, in the sense of advertising miscomprehension (see Jacoby and Hoyer 1987). We are skeptical of that rationale and find ourselves in broad agreement with Freundlieb (1984, p.82):

Interpretive statements, although undoubtedly the result of complex cognitive processes, are not empirically true or false of some independently existing object in the external world....For empirical statements to be true or false, there must be external objects or states of affairs of which those statements are true or false. In the case of interpretations concerning higher level meanings, no such independent truth conditions exist.

Borrowing from Schmidt's (1984) philosophical argument, we submit that the interpretation of advertising is a subject-dependent, internal monologue through which consumers generate, change, and maintain their individual reality.

McCracken (1987, p.122) has also articulated a meaning model of advertising consumption, characterized by consumers "looking [at ads] for symbolic resources, new ideas, and better concrete versions of old ideas with which to advance their project," i.e., the construction of a unified life system of self, family, community, nation, and world. This is not an altogether novel idea, since a small band of researchers has long argued that consumers interpret advertising for the cultural and psychological meanings it symbolizes (Friedman and Zimmer 1988; Levitt 1970; Levy 1959; McCracken 1986; Sherry 1987; White 1959). However, the systematic application of this meaning model in advertising theory and research has been thwarted by the combined forces of the techno-rational information processing model and a reluctance to adopt open-ended, interpretive methodologies. On the other hand, our data substantiate the value of this revisionist perspective on advertising consumption, including the barrenness of denotation in traditional models of advertising communication. Beyond our study, future research must look at a wider array of product categories and different market segments. In addition, selecting or manipulating ads with varying degrees of pictorial clarity and verbal-visual message interactions should also prove insightful.

Other than attempting to show the efficacy of an interpretive protocol in assessing propositions about advertising, a number of other issues naturally arose which are quite germane to a meaning model of advertising consumption. We turn now to some of those related insights.

*Same Ad? Different Worldviews.* Research has shown that sex and gender are strong determinants of visual processes (Johnson, Zimmer, and Golden 1987). In our study, males and females provided some conspicuously dissimilar descriptions of the ad illustration (first response task). Male subjects commented that the ad-male was attracted to the ad-female:

S#2: "He seems to be very attracted to her and is trying to seduce her."

S#4: "The way he's looking at her, you'd assume that he cares for her, that they might even be lovers."

S#6: "Guy is lying on the ground, tugging on her, seems to be only thinking of her."

Female subjects expressed a more profound interpretation:

S#5: "She's very artistic. He looks like he adores her."

S#10: "He is admiring her because she's really pretty and her work on the canvas."

S#17: "The guy is kind of in awe."

For female subjects, the picture suggests both romance and the ad-female's artistic talents. Females acknowledge the ad-female as something more than a here-and-now sexual target; she is lovable and has skills and value that transcend the ad setting. At least, that is what the female subjects want the ad-male to recognize. If the diffused feminist's disposition of the 1980s is truly operative, our female subjects' interpretations may well reflect what they want the men in their own lives to recognize about them.

For male subjects, the picture reads quite differently: sexual gameship (though not all the males thematically associated the sexual desire with brand desire). For them, the image is erotic and hints at behaviors prefatory to consummation. As one male subject put it, "He's in an enviable position, beside her and alone."

While these interpretational discrepancies between males and females are hardly surprising, they do underscore that the meaning of the ad image, *even on a surface descriptive level*, is not literal or inherent to the ad, i.e., it is not denotational. The ad we used in this study depicts an asymmetry of gender quite different from those in Goffman's (1979) earlier work. Unlike his ads, ours reveals a woman in a comparatively more powerful, less dependent, and less attentive posture. While several of our female subjects interpreted the ad-female to be in control of the pictorial scene, most of our male subjects were oblivious to such a possibility.

Our data also reveal that pictorial advertising which evokes human sexuality invites readings commensurate with acculturated sexual orientations. Whether such ads are equally capable of garnering positive brand attitudes, ad attitudes, and brand recall across the sexes remains unknown. Apparently, the pictorial interpretation routes taken by males and females can be quite different, and deserve more detailed research.

*Idiosyncracies in the Mindspace.* Although our study used neither a Thematic Apperception Test nor any similar request for fabricated elaborations, several of our subjects automatically constructed mini-stories around the ad illustration, including unique inferences. One female subject hypothesized that the ad-male "might have come up from out of nowhere...and he just decided to sit down next to her and watch her and admire her." One male subject conjured up the unseen private destination the ad-male had in mind, i.e., trying to "get her inside the beach house." Another male subject speculated that "they might have some alcohol in them, they might be a little tipsy." Instantly and unabashed, one female had a positive hedonic response to the beach setting. This subject went on to say,

S#5: The way she's painting the picture, it's like a changing thing, and being on the beach, the beach is a changing thing itself, the waves and the sand shift....She could paint anything, you know her colors, different mixtures would create a whole different mood with the painting....the possibilities are endless and also with their relationship.

Personalized meanings have been highlighted by some advertising researchers (e.g., Leavitt, Waddell, and Wells 1970; Shavitt and Brock 1986), though neither idiosyncratic nor personalized meanings have been accorded any status in advertising comprehension theory or research. Recently, however, in a study by Morris et al. (1985), recall results suggested that illogical conclusions drawn from an OTC drug ad were precipitated by consumers' inclinations to elaborate idiosyncratically while processing the message. Our data also suggest that idiosyncratic inferences can play an important part in the interpretation of pictorial advertising.

These may be "small meanings," as McCracken (1987, p.121) calls them, perhaps--as above--revealing the emotional rush of meeting someone new, beliefs about alcohol's power to induce a desired mood, or a life philosophy symbolized in a physical setting. Yet, by calling these meanings "small," neither we nor McCracken believe they are immaterial. They provide a looking glass on the role of personal history, self-esteem, fantasies, aspirations, doubts, fears, and other individual factors which contribute to ad-imagery interpretation.

*Interpretive Knots.* Subjects' interpretations also varied along a continuum of complexity not commonly considered or uncovered in ad comprehension studies. With the gin ad, intricate interpretation was often dependent on a keen eye for the proxemic and kinesic cues of flirtation. Laing (1970, p.48) has poignantly noted the spiral of courtship cognition in this way:

She wants him to want her

He wants her to want him

To get him to want her

she pretends she wants him

To get her to want him

he pretends he wants her

Jack wants              Jill wants

Jill's want of Jack     Jack's want of Jill

so                      so

Jack tells Jill         Jill tells Jack

Jack wants Jill         Jill wants Jack

a perfect contract

Some of our subjects echoed Laing in interpreting the ad image:

S#12: She looks like she's totally ignoring him and he thinks it's kind of funny too, that

she's ignoring him, like maybe he knows that she's purposefully ignoring him.

S#17: She seems to be in her own little world maybe like, not even ignoring him, but strategically ignoring him, kind of playing hard to get because he's tugging on her shirt and she has like a little smile on her face, so she's kind of like teasing or something. ...Ignoring him, but not really ignoring him, kind of also acknowledging at the same time.

However, other subjects were insensitive to these subtle nonverbal signs. They developed comparatively simple interpretations:

S#4: They're out on a beach somewhere. She's painting a seascape, intimate, there's nobody around. Just a time with the two of them. Not dressed for swimming. They're dressed, just in their regular street clothes, casual, comfortable. Obviously she came down there to paint. She's got everything she needs.

Overall, female subjects tended to be more attuned to the range of body language signs in the illustration, especially those produced by the ad-female.

Besides the complexity dimension, a different interpretive knot of paradox and contradiction also appeared. In particular, some subjects casually constructed inconsistent meanings:

S#1: His expression, it looks like he's almost pleading with her to go. Her expression, she's almost ignoring him. It seems like there could be *a conflict of interest here.* And again, the sand, the water, the ocean, it looks like they're out in the open and not really into anything serious. It looks like they're both *in peace of mind,* just by where they are and what they're doing. [our italics]

Consistent, deductive cognition is no more commonplace in advertising interpretation than it is in consumer choice behavior. Yet, past studies have focused on ad comprehension using measures that penalize the creative interpreter. This is shortsighted because, at a metaphorical level, life is a struggle between opposing forces which consumers arbitrate or admix in the daily marketplace: indulgence versus discipline, the profane versus the sacred, commonality versus uniqueness, etc. Hence, paradoxical interpretations of advertising pictorials are not necessarily degenerate. Their nature and role in advertising consumption is completely undetermined.

*Envisionment.* Meaning is molded through a formative interpretation process. Language researchers such as Miyake (1986) refer to this aspect of interpretation as iteration, Rumelhart (1984) likens it to hypothesis testing, and Langer (1986) calls it envisionment. As Langer (1986) puts it,

Meaning derived from any given portion of the text is shaped by how earlier segments were interpreted and continues to develop and change in light of later segments. These changing "envisionments" are records of the "text internal" world that is constructed by the reader while processing the text. These envisionments are the primary "dynamics" through which the reader experiences the "message."

Several of our subjects demonstrated that envisionment is quite relevant to pictorial interpretation as well:

S#11: She's trying to paint and he's bothering her and she doesn't want him to bother her. She may be a bit, well, she doesn't look like she's irritated. No, she has a slight smile on her face.

S#15: He's having a decent time, just watching, although maybe not, he's pulling on her, maybe looking for attention for himself.

Focusing on the tentative, groping, and even playful character of interpretation should provide insights about other significant dimensions of ad-picture comprehension which have gone unresearched. These include foci of attention (Chafe 1979, 1980), the activation of schemas (Langer 1986), and metacomprehension strategies (Flavel 1976; Raphael et al. 1981).

## CONCLUSION

Though it is often remarked that ads are intricate, multidimensional stimuli and that consumers perceive them through a cocktail of contexts and epistemic structures (individual, social, and cultural), most advertising researchers cling to the belief that meaning can be affixed denotatively to advertising messages. Moreover, this denotated meaning is considered both primary and necessary to the derivation of secondary, connotative meanings. This article has challenged those premises.

Research in advertising comprehension requires a fundamental reprioritization of its goals, most dramatically in the case of pictorial advertising. The central question is not "How much of advertising illustrations do consumers understand or misunderstand?" (see Watkins 1984) Instead, the question should be "What characterizes the process of advertising interpretation, such that consumers pass through these consumption experiences reinforced or changed with respect to the meaning of their lives?" Lannon and Cooper (1986), Levy (1986), McCracken (1987), Mick (1986), and Sherry (1987) have each argued for a cultural, subjective-meaning model of advertising consumption. Empirical research within this framework is greatly needed.

This study was conducted as a demonstration work, illustrating that open-ended, interpretive methods are not strictly for theory development; they can also be utilized to assess propositions in much the same manner experiments and surveys are employed. In addition, when coupled with an imagistic ad, the interpretive protocol method revealed a number of advertising consumption issues which have been undervalued or overlooked in past comprehension research. Adopting a cultural, subjective-meaning model, interpretive protocol methods appear especially useful for examining the semanticity of advertising illustrations, notably their connotations.

The mind is its own place, and in itself
Can make a heav'n of hell, a hell of heav'n.

Milton, *Paradise Lost*, Book 1, line 253

## REFERENCES

Baker, Steve (1985), "The Hell of Connotation," *Word and Image*, 1 (2), 164-175.

Ballstaedt, Steffen-Peter and Heinz Mandl (1984), "Elaborations: Assessment and Analysis," in *Learning and Comprehending of Text*, eds. Heinz Mandl, Nancy Stein, and Tom Trabasso, Hillsdale, NJ: Erlbaum, 331-352.

Barthes, Roland (1964), "Rhetoric of the Image," in *Working Papers in Cultural History*, (Spring 1971), translated by Brian Trench, 37-50.

Baudrillard, Jean (1981), *For a Critique of the Political Economy of the Sign*, translated by Charles Levin, St. Louis, MO: Telos Press.

Belk, Russell W., John F. Sherry, Jr., and Melanie Waldorf (1986), "A Naturalistic Inquiry into Buyer and Seller Behavior at a Swap Meet," *Journal of Consumer Research*, 14 (4), 449-470.

Bryson, Norman (1983), *Vision and Painting: The Logic of Gaze*, London: MacMillan.

Calder, Bobby J. and Alice M. Tybout (1987), "What Consumer Research Is..." *Journal of Consumer Research*, 14 (1), 136-140.

Chafe, Wallace L. (1980), "The Development of Consciousness in the Production of a Narrative," in *The Pear Stories: Cognitive, Cultural, and Linguistic Aspects of Narrative Production*, ed. Wallace L. Chafe, (Volume III, in Roy O. Freedle, ed., *Advances in Discourse Processing*), Norwood, NJ: Ablex.

_____ (1979), "The Flow of Thought and the Flow of Language," in *Syntax and Semantics*, ed. T. Givon, New York: Academic Press.

Chattopadhyay, Amitava and Joseph W. Alba (1988), "The Situational Importance of Recall and Inference in Consumer Decision Making," *Journal of Consumer Research*, 15 (1), 1-12.

Childers, Terry L. and Michael Houston (1984), "Conditions for a Picture Superiority Effect on Consumer Memory," *Journal of Consumer Research*, 11 (2), 643-655.

Eco, Umberto (1979), *The Role of the Reader: Explorations in the Semiotics of Texts*, Bloomington, IN: Indiana University Press.

Edell, Julie A. and Richard Staelin (1983), "The Information Processing of Pictures in Print Advertising, *Journal of Consumer Research*, 10 (1), 45-61.

Ericsson, Anders K. and Herbert A. Simon (1984), *Protocol Analysis: Verbal Reports as Data*, Cambridge, MA: MIT Press.

Flavell, J. H. (1976), "Metacognitive Aspects of Problem Solving," in *The Nature of Intelligence*, ed. B. Resnick, Hillsdale, NJ: Erlbaum.

Freundlieb, Dieter (1984), "Explaining Interpretation: The Case of Henry James's *The Turn of the Screw*," *Poetics Today*, 5 (1), 79- 95.

Friedmann, Roberto and Mary R. Zimmer (1988), "The Role of Psychological Meaning in Advertising," *Journal of Advertising*, 17 (1), 41-48.

Goffman, Erving (1979), *Gender Advertisements*, New York: Harper and Row.

Gorn, Gerald J. (1982), "The Effects of Music in Advertising on Choice Behavior: A Classical Conditioning Approach," *Journal of Marketing*, Vol. 46 (Winter), 94-101.

Graesser, Arthur C. and Leslie F. Clark (1985), "The Generation of Knowledge-based Inferences during Narrative Comprehension," in *Inferences in Text Processing*, eds. G. Rickheit and H. Strohner, Amsterdam: North Holland Publishing, 53-90.

Hirschman, Elizabeth C. (1987), "Movies as Myths: An Interpretation of Motion Picture Mythology," in *Marketing Signs: New Directions in the Study of Signs for Sale*, ed. Jean Umiker-Sebeok, Berlin: Mouton de Gruyter, 335-373.

Holbrook, Morris B. (1983), "Product Imagery and the Illusion of Reality: Some Insights from Consumer Esthetics," in *Advances in Consumer Research*, Vol. 10, eds. Richard P. Bagozzi and Alice M. Tybout, Provo, UT: Association for Consumer Research, 65-71.

_____ and Mark W. Grayson (1986), "The Semiology of Cinematic Consumption: Symbolic Consumer Behavior in *Out of Africa*," *Journal of Consumer Research*, 13 (3), 374-381.

Hunt, Shelby D. (1983), *Marketing Theory: The Philosophy of Marketing Science*, Homewood, IL: Richard D, Irwin.

Hudson, Laurel Anderson and Julie L. Ozanne (1988), "Alternative Ways of Seeking Knowledge," *Journal of Consumer Research*, 14 (4), 508-521.

Jacoby, Jacob and Wayne D. Hoyer (1982a), "Viewer Miscomprehension of Televised Communication: Selected Findings," *Journal of Marketing*, 46 (Fall), 12-26.

_____ and _____ (1982b), "On Miscomprehending Televised Communication: A Rejoinder, " *Journal of Marketing*, 46 (Fall), 35- 43.

_____ and _____ (1987), *The Comprehension and Miscomprehension of Print Communications: An Investigation of Mass Media Magazines*, New York: Advertising Educational Foundation.

Johnson, Keren A., Mary R. Zimmer, and Linda L. Golden (1987), "Object Relations Theory: Male and Female Differences in Visual Information Processing," in *Advances in Consumer Research*, Volume 14, eds. Melanie Wallendorf and Paul Anderson, Provo, UT: Association for Consumer Research, 83-87.

Kintgen, Eugene R. (1983), *The Perception of Poetry*, Bloomington, IN: Indiana University Press.

Laing, R. D. (1970), *Knots*, New York: Vintage Books.

Langer, Judith A. (1986), "The Construction of Meaning and the Assessment of Comprehension: An Analysis of Reader Performance on Standardized Test Items," in *Cognitive and Linguistic Analyses of Test Performance*, ed. Roy O. Freddle, New York: Ablex.

Lannon, Judie and Peter Cooper (1983), "Humanistic Advertising: A Holistic Cultural Perspective," *International Journal of Advertising*, 2, 195-213.

Leavitt, Clark, C. Waddell, and William Wells (1970), "Improving Day-After Recall Techniques," *Journal of Advertising Research*, 10, 13-17.

Levitt, Theodore (1970), "The Morality(?) of Advertising," *Harvard Business Review*, 48 (July-August), 84-92.

Levy, Sydney (1986), "Meanings in Advertising Stimuli," in *Advertising and Consumer Psychology*, eds. Jerry C. Olson and Keith Sentis, New York: Praeger, 214-226.

_____ (1959), "Symbols for Sale," *Harvard Business Review*, (July-August), 117-124.

Lutz, Kathy A. and Richard J. Lutz (1978), "Imagery-Eliciting Strategies: Review and Implications of Research," in *Advances in Consumer Research*, Vol. 5, ed. H. Keith Hunt, Ann Arbor, MI: Association for Consumer Research, 611-620.

MacCannell, Dean (1987), "'Sex Sells': Comment on Gender Images and Myth in Advertising," in *Marketing Signs: New Directions in he Study of Signs for Sale*, ed. Jean Umiker-Sebeok, Berlin: Mouton de Gruyter, 521-531.

MacInnis, Deborah J. and Linda L. Price (1987), "The Role of Imagery in Information Processing: Review and Extensions," *Journal of Consumer Research*, 13 (4), 473-491.

McCracken, Grant (1987), "Advertising: Meaning or Information," in *Advances in Consumer Research*, Volume 14, eds. Melanie Wallendorf and Paul Anderson, Provo, UT: Association for Consumer Research, 121-124.

_____ (1986), "Culture and Consumption: A Theoretical Account of the Structure and Movement of the Cultural Meaning of Consumer Goods," *Journal of Consumer Research*, 13 (1), 71-84.

McGuire, William J. (1969), "The Nature of Attitudes and Attitude Change," in *Handbook of Social Psychology*, eds. G. Lindzey and E. Aronson, Reading, MA: Addison-Wesley.

Mick, David Glen (1988a), "Contributions to the Semiotics of Marketing and Consumer Behavior 1985-1988," in *The Semiotic Web: A Yearbook of Semiotics*, eds. Thomas A. Sebeok and Jean Umiker-Sebeok, Berlin: Mouton de Gruyter, 535,584.

_____ (1988b), "A Critical Review of the Comprehension Construct in Marketing Communications Research," Working Paper, Marketing Department, College of Business Administration, University of Florida.

_____ (1987), "Levels of Comprehension in Consumers' Processing of Print Advertising Language," Unpublished Ph.D. Dissertation, Indiana University.

_____ (1986), "Consumer Research and Semiotics: Exploring the Morphology of Signs, Symbols, and Significance," *Journal of Consumer Research*, 13 (2), 196-213.

Miyake, Naomi (1986), "Constructive Interaction and the Iterative Process of Understanding," *Cognitive Science*, 10, 151-177.

Morris, Louis A., David Brinberg, Ron Klimberg, Carole Rivera, and Lloyd G. Millstein (1986), "Miscomprehension Rates for Prescription Drug Advertisements," *Current Issues and Research in Advertising*, 9, 93-117.

Myers, Kathy (1983), "Understanding Advertisers," in *Language, Image, Media*, eds. Howard Davis and Paul Walton, Oxford: Basil Blackwell, 205-223.

Nöth, Winfried(1988), personal communication.

_____ (1987), "Advertising: The Frame Message," in *Marketing Signs: New Directions in the Study of Signs for Sale*, ed. Jean Umiker-Sebeok, Berlin: Mouton de Gruyter, 279-294.

Olson, Gary M., Susan A. Duffy, and Robert L. Mack (1984), "Thinking-Out-Loud as a Method for Studying Real-Time Comprehension Processes," in *New Methods in Reading Comprehension Research*, eds. David E. Kieras and Marcel A. Just, Hillsdale, NJ: Erlbaum, 253-286.

Pezdek, K. and G. W. Evans (1979), "Visual and Verbal Memory for Objects and their Spatial Locations," *Journal of Experimental Psychology: Human Learning and Memory*, 5, 360-373.

Raphael, Taffy E., Ann C. Myers, William C. Tirre, Mary Fritz, and Peter Freebody (1981), "The Effects of Some Known Sources of Reading Difficulty on Metacomprehension," *Journal of Reading Behavior*, 13, 325-334.

Richards, Jeff and Richard Zakia (1981), "Pictures: An Advertiser's Expressway through FTC Regulations," *Georgia Law Review*, 16 (1), 77-134.

Rossiter, John R. (1982, "Visual Imagery: Applications to Advertising," in *Advances in Consumer Research*, Vol. 9, ed. Andrew A. Mitchell, Ann Arbor, MI: Association for Consumer Research, 101-106.

_____ and Larry Percy (1983), "Visual Communication in Advertising," in *Information Processing in Advertising*, ed. Richard Jackson Harris, Hillsdale, NJ: Erlbaum, 83-125.

_____ and _____ (1980), "Attitude Change Through Visual Imagery in Advertising," *Journal of Advertising*, 9 (2), 10-16.

Rumelhart, David E. (1984), "Understanding Understanding," in *Understanding Reading Comprehension: Cognition, Language, and the Structure of Prose*, ed. J. Flood, Newark, DE: International Reading Association, 1-20.

Russo, J. Edward, Barbara L. Metcalf, and Debra L. Stephens (1981), "Identifying Misleading Advertising," *Journal of Consumer Research*, 8 (2), 119-131.

_____, Eric J. Johnson, and Debra L. Stephens (1986), "The Validity of Verbal Protocols," Working Paper, Marketing Department, Cornell University.

Schmidt, S. J. (1984), "The Fiction is that Reality Exists: A Constructivist Model of Reality, Fiction, and Literature," *Poetics Today*, 5 (2), 253-274.

Shavitt, Sharon and Timothy C. Brock (1986), "Self-Relevant Responses in Commercial Persuasion: Field and Experimental Teşts," in *Advertising and Consumer Psychology*, eds. Jerry C. Olson and Keith Sentis, New York: Praeger, 149-171.

Shepard, Roger N. (1978), "The Mental Image," *American Psychologist*, 33 (February), 125-137.

Sherry, John F., Jr. (1987), "Advertising as a Cultural System," in *Marketing Signs: New Directions in the Study of Signs for Sale*, ed. Jean Umiker-Sebeok, Berlin: Mouton de Gruyter, 441-461.

Shimp, Terence A. and Ivan L. Preston (1981), "Deceptive and Nondeceptive Consequences of Evaluative Advertising," *Journal of Marketing*, 45 (Winter), 22-32.

Watkins, Thomas (1984), "Misunderstanding Pictures in Print Ads," *Viewpoint*, Chicago: Ogilvy and Mather, Inc., Spring, 31-37.

White, Irving (1959), "The Functions of Advertising in Our Culture," *Journal of Marketing*, 24 (July), 8-14.

Zakia, Richard (1986), "Adverteasement," *Semiotica*, 59 (1/2), 1-11.

# Advertising Resonance: A Semiological Perspective
## Edward F. McQuarrie, Santa Clara University

A recent ad for J&B Scotch whiskey shows a slew of pebbles. The letters "J&B" are painted on each and the caption reads, "J&B on the rocks." An ad for Christian Brothers brandy has the caption "CB in orange," accompanied by a picture of the guitarist Chuck Berry dressed completely in orange. These ads are *resonant* by the definition of this essay. Resonance refers to an echoing or a doubleness within an advertisement. As such, it is an aspect of the formal structure of an ad. In semiological terms it can be classified as a rhetorical device (Durand 1987; Dyer 1982). Although the use of puns and double entendres in headlines is probably the most common instance of resonance (Grinnell 1987), other types of resonance can also be identified. The goal of this essay is to introduce and develop the concept of resonance with the aid of illustrations drawn from current magazine advertising.

It must be stated at the outset that resonance is a *special case*; most ads are *not* resonant by the definition above. At a guess, less than 10%, and perhaps less than 5% of magazine ads for consumer products make use of resonance. Perhaps more advertisers should adopt this strategy; certainly there is no a priori reason to believe that resonance is only appropriate for certain products or audiences. Nor is resonance so rare as to be a mere curiosity. Over the past two years, students of the author seeking to earn extra credit were able to gather over 200 instances of resonance in magazine advertisements. This judgement sample confirms that resonance does occur with some frequency, that it has been used by producers of a variety of products, and that it can be defined with sufficient specificity that novice judges can detect instances of it.

The primary focus of this essay is semiological rather than semiotic, in the usage of Holbrook (1987). Where a semiotic approach would seek to establish the effects of resonance on the viewer of an ad, the approach of semiology:

> "essentially involves *interpretation* or *hermeneutics* rather than statistics or experimentation. It draws upon the researcher's personal introspection and subjective judgement and finds its major supporting evidence in the body of the text itself" (Holbrook 1987, p. 102).

This essay concentrates on what can *said* by means of the device of resonance; the kinds of meaning that a viewer can derive from a resonant ad. However, semiotic concerns are touched upon in the discussion of future research directions. Prior to examining specific instances of resonance, an expanded definition will be offered, and a conceptual background established in terms of semiology.

## DEFINITION AND CONCEPTUAL BACKGROUND

Resonance occurs when there is a repetition of elements within an ad, and when this redundancy is such that an exchange, condensation or multiplication of meaning occurs. Simple repetition alone is not sufficient to create resonance. The elements must echo one another, that is, they must be arranged so as to modify the meaning that either would have alone. Any resonant ad involves a doubleness: one thing or class of thing has multiple meanings, or multiple elements are joined into a single meaning. Some kind of play or twist is necessary for resonance to occur. If the two elements simply sit side by side within the text of the ad, without acting upon one another, then the ad will not resonate.

Because resonance is an aspect of the formal structure of an advertisement, semiology is promising as a source of understanding. Both semiology and semiotics (related disciplines originating respectively in the work of the linguist de Saussure in Europe and the philosopher C.S. Peirce in America) are concerned with how meaning is conveyed through signs and symbols (Holbrook 1987; Mick 1986; Umiker-Sebeok 1987). As resonance is a semiological phenomenon of a specific kind, a brief explanation of certain semiological concepts will prepare the way for its interpretation in specific ads.

The basic concept in semiology is the *sign*, defined as a thing that refers to something other than itself (Fiske 1982). Any assemblage of signs, whether verbal or visual, is considered to be a *text*. It is helpful to consider a sign to be composed of *signifier* (the physical trace of the sign) and *signified* (the meanings associated with the signifier).

Semiological work with a *syntactic* focus concentrates on the relation between signifiers; work with a *semantic* focus concentrates on the nature of the signifieds which can be associated with a given signifier. There are three basic modes of association between signifier and signified: the *iconic*, the *indexical*, and the *symbolic*. An iconic sign resembles or is similar to its signifer; thus, a picture of a man in a suit carrying a *Wall Street Journal* might resemble a business man. An indexical sign has a factual or causal relation to its signified; thus, the picture of the *WSJ* might index investing, the financial markets, the management of money, and the like. A symbolic sign has a conventional or arbitrary relation to its signified; thus, in American society the *WSJ* could symbolize financial success and corporate status. Iconic signs operate as *metaphors*, while indexical signs operate as *metonyms* (in which the part stands for the whole).

Resonance is a syntactic relation with semantic consequences. The doubleness of signs in the text of the ad alters the nature of the signifieds associated with each and with the ad as a whole. As will be shown with examples, the use of resonance in ads allows a

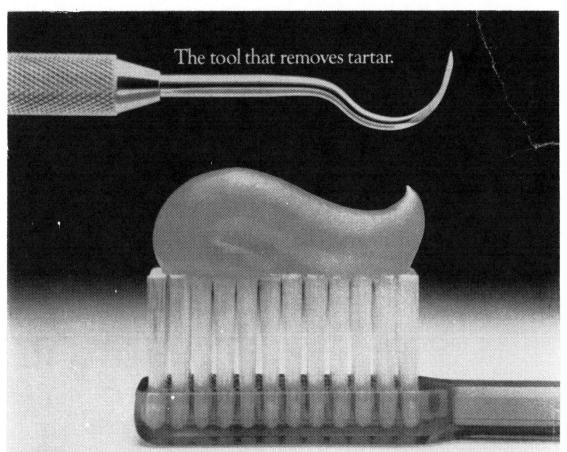

The tool that removes tartar.

The gel that helps keep it off.

# Introducing Tartar Control Crest in a New Fresh Mint Gel.

Tartar Control Crest Gel with fluoride helps prevent
ugly tartar buildup above the gum line between dental cleanings.

Crest has been shown to be an effective decay-preventive dentifrice that can be of significant value when used in a conscientiously applied program of oral hygiene and regular professional care. Council on Dental Therapeutics, American Dental Association. © P&G 1988.

kind of *figurative speech*. (Many other kinds of figurative speech are possible in ads without the use of resonance). Figurative speech used for persuasive effect is the subject matter of rhetoric, and a number of scholars have studied rhetoric in advertising, in particular the rhetoric of visual images (Barthes 1985; Dyer 1982). Durand (1987) has proposed an exhaustive scheme for classifying rhetorical figures in advertising. Within Durand's scheme resonance can be categorized as a false homology: either two different elements are made to have one meaning, or two meanings are condensed onto a single element.

As will be shown, the false homology on which resonance rests functions to open up the meaning of an advertisement. Resonance is a device for generating ambiguity and paradox. As figurative speech (Stern 1988), the use of resonance moves advertisements in the direction of poetry, rendering their meaning open rather than closed (cf. Noth 1987). In the analyses that follow, the connotative power of resonance will be stressed. Resonant ads may also be considered sympractic in Kloepfer's (1987) sense. As a rhetorical device, resonance is a means whereby the advertiser may communicate in a non-literal, tacit fashion that is suggestive and evocative. Resonance as a strategy is a far cry from Claude Hopkins' "salesmanship in print" or the "reason why" school; it has more in common with the impressionistic school of Theodore MacManus (Fox 1984).

As a semiological analysis of advertising texts, this essay has a number of predecessors. A brief discussion of Barthes (1985) and Williamson (1978) will set the stage for the interpretations that follow (see also Levy 1981; Leymore 1975; Liess, Kline and Jhally 1986; McLuhan 1951; Mick 1986; Umiker-Sebeok 1987; Vestergaard and Schroder 1985).

## Barthes

In the article "Rhetoric of the Image," written in 1964, Barthes (1985) analyzes at length a single magazine ad for a brand of pasta. This article is particularly useful in showing how elaborate and intensive can be the semiological analysis of a single ordinary ad. This essay follows Barthes in the explicit attention to image rather than language, to connotation rather than denotation in advertisement. In his analysis of the Panzani ad, Barthes points out that the syllables in the Panzani name will suggest an Italian origin to French ears. Furthermore, the pepper and the tomato shown in the ad, and the tricolor printing, will similarly suggest, in Barthes' phrase, "Italianicity." These connotations enhance the headline's literal statement of the product's Italian connection. Barthes goes on to point out that the opened string bag from which the vegetables spill suggests both a recent return from shopping, and a healthy image of a person who shops for fresh food. He notes further that the arrangement of the scene suggests a still life painting, thus incorporating by reference countless paintings of edibles. Drawing together these discontinuous signs, we may say that the advertisement connotes a product which is ethnic, perhaps exotic; fresh and wholesome; delectable in the timeless fashion of art.

Note that Barthes' semiological approach in this ad is primarily semantic, and that the emphasis is on the indexical and iconic representation of meaning. Barthes' approach is to apprehend various elements within the ad in terms of the figures of classical rhetoric. The layout in the Panzani ad *resembles* that of a still life painting (metaphor); the shopping bag spilled open connotes the shopping trip by representing one *piece* of that event (metonym or synecdoche). These are the primary routes whereby elements within ads acquire meaning: they either resemble or are associated with other objects, and acquire meaning thereby. Barthes' treatment differs sharply from the treatments of symbolism in advertisements commonly encountered in American textbooks on marketing, advertising and consumer behavior. These treatments tend to focus on the use of readily identifiable *conventional* signs (i.e., symbols as defined earlier). The Marlboro man is a good example. In these ads, cowboys and Western scenes serve as readily decoded symbols of a rugged masculinity. The tone and spirit of Barthes' interpretation of the Panzani ad is very different. It is more subtle and far-reaching.

Barthes frankly acknowledges the uncertain character of the meaning of images: "every image is polysemous; it implies, subjacent to its signifiers, a "floating chain" of signifieds of which the reader can select some and ignore the rest" (p. 28). This recalls the multivocal character of symbols discussed in Turner (1974). Barthes also states in uncompromising fashion that the creator of the image is no privileged authority as to the meaning of the image (p. 36); a position that also recalls anthropological work (Sherry 1987). Thus, the copy writer and art director who created the ad cannot necessarily tell us what it does and does not mean. The thrust of Barthes' analysis is to place advertisements alongside poetry, myth and dream, under the heading of image (p. 38). In summary, the approach taken by Barthes (1985) may be said to offer the reader of advertisements freedom of interpretation, a license to find meanings that are neither conventional nor patently obvious to all. This gift comes at a cost; there is no readily apparent means of verifying whether an analysis of connotation is correct or not (Liess, Kline and Jhally 1986).

## Williamson

In her book, *Decoding Advertisements*, Williamson (1978) analyzes in detail 116 magazine advertisements. In parallel to Freud's dream work, Williamson speaks of an "advertising-work." This term refers both to the system of signs whereby meaning is created, and more particularly to the idea that such systems contain a latent meaning that may be very different from the manifest meaning of the ad. An example will clarify this concept of latent meaning.

The first ad in Williamson (1978, pp. 18-19) is for Goodyear tires. The ad celebrates the braking power of the tires, showing a car stopped at the end of a jetty surrounded by water. The headline and body copy are in the finest tradition of the "reason why" school of advertising (Fox 1984). Stopping distance, durability and road-holding power are the gist of the linguistic text. The story communicated through the ads, that the driver has sped down the jetty and then hit the brakes in complete confidence, effectively dramatizes the selling point. All of this is manifest in the advertisement, and it easy to imagine any professor of marketing or advertising explicating these points of technique to a class of students.

Williamson begins her interpretation of the latent content of this ad by establishing an equation between the jetty and the tire. She justifies the equation in terms of the rounded end of the jetty and its suggestion of treads, and also the inclusion of the two tires hanging off the right side of the jetty. (These elements are resonant in the sense of this essay). Given this equation, or substitutability, between tire and jetty, the product is able to appropriate the qualities of the jetty: its sturdiness, its resistant qualities, its stopping power, its protection against water and chaos. And in fact, there is a substantive analogy between the functions of a sea jetty and an automobile tire which both permits and assists this substitution of one for the other. As a result, the message about the product is augmented; at some level the receiver takes away a stronger impression of the advantageous qualities of Goodyear 6800 Supersteels.

A key contribution of Williamson to the decoding of advertisements is precisely this emphasis on juxtaposition as a device where by images convey meaning.

> ... what seemed to be merely a part of the apparatus for conveying a message about braking speed, turns out to be a message in itself ... which involves a connection being made, a correlation between two objects (tire and jetty) not on a rational basis but by a leap made on the basis of appearance, juxtaposition and connotation. (p. 19).

She goes on to note that such meanings are created by the *formal structure* of the advertisement, rather than being spelled out linguistically. This is the syntactic focus spoken of earlier; a semantic approach to this ad might have lingered instead on the exact nature of that signified which a jetty signifier is suited to connote. Furthermore, because the connection is not explicitly stated, the viewer must draw it, and in so doing actively participate in construing the ad. Finally, the ad does not create the meanings associated with a sea jetty, but assumes the prior existence of a system of meaning in which jetties figure. The ad appropriates this system, and in so doing creates the jetty as a sign that carries certain meanings. When successful, this appropriation constitutes that sign as a carrier of certain values, i.e., as a currency. Once constituted as a currency, the jetty can exchange value with some other signifier, in this case the Goodyear tire.

These three ideas about reading advertisements—that juxtaposition and other types of formal structure communicate meaning, that a relatively active participation of the reader is required before such meanings can be realized, and that

signifiers connected by formal structure can exchange meanings—are all fundamental to the decoding of advertisements undertaken in this essay. These insights, in conjunction with Barthes' (1985) demonstration of how metaphor and metonym can serve to unlock the "floating chain of signifeds" associated with an ad, provide the basis for the interpretive techniques used to unravel the meaning of resonance in specific advertisements.

## A TAXONOMY OF RESONANCE WITH EXAMPLES

A review of ads thus far collected suggests that at least four types of resonance can be identified in magazine ads (Exhibit 1). These include resonance which is purely verbal, purely visual or which involves both verbal and visual elements; there are also instances of visual puns. Examples of each type will be briefly described, along with an indication of the meanings conveyed (cf. Pollay and Mainprize 1984).

*Visual* resonance occurs when two pictorial elements in the illustration echo one another's shape, contour or color. This is resonance among the signifiers, in which two elements are made to have a common meaning. The ad for Tartar Control Crest is a good example (Plate 1). Although the copy explicitly states the parallel in function between this toothpaste and that dentist's tool, the same statement is made again visually. The contour of the dollop of toothpaste echoes the shape of the dentist's pick. This visual echo may be more difficult to deny, and in any case augments or seconds the message in the literal text. On a more subtle level, the dentist's pick occupies the spot in the composition that would normally be filled by a tube of toothpaste.[1] This substitution in itself acts to equate the toothpaste and the tool. A second example is the ad for Aziza Mink Coat Mascara (plate 2). Here the visual resonance is more elaborate. The spikes of mink fur exactly echo the eyelashes of the model, establishing an equivalence between the characteristics of mink fur and any eyelash to which this mascara has been applied. Also, the triangle of face outlined by mink coat and mink hat echoes the shape of an eye photographed in profile. The implied statement is that this product will surround your eye with mink. Finally, the sharp spikes of fur, the triangle of the face, all echo the angles in the letters "A" and "Z" in the brand name. An exchange of meaning among Aziza, mink, and mascara is accomplished.

*Verbal* resonance occurs when the headline or body copy makes use of puns, word play or double entendre. Purely verbal resonance, with no assistance from an illustration, is not that common. Most often, as in the next category, a picture is required in order to convey the twist or second meaning. When verbal resonance alone is used, it typically occurs in the headline. Two examples from the food category are: "Berried Treasure" and "Fry first class." The first

---

[1]This interpretation suggested by John Sherry.

**PLATE 2**
Reproduced courtesy of Chesebrough-Pond's Inc., owner of the registered trademarks AZIZA and MINK COAT

headline, for Weight Watchers frozen desserts, functions to equate the sponsor's strawberry shortcake with treasure. The copy also contains the words "ruby," "crowning," "pearly," and "richly," along with two further mentions of "treasure." This is resonance among the signifieds: a condensation of the meanings of (rich) food and treasure is brought about. The effect is to communicate richness of taste in a manner difficult to deny. The second headline, for Idaho potatoes, functions to equate french fries made from Idaho potatoes with a higher level of quality. The copy also includes the statements, "the only way to fry," "the choice of frequent fryers," "first class serving ideas," and "help your products soar." A very humdrum product has been linked with the exhilaration of jet travel, and the status associated with flying first class.

Perhaps the most common type of resonance links *verbal and visual* elements to accomplish a twist or duality in meaning. An ad for Mink International shows a woman wearing a mink top and dark sunglasses, striding toward the viewer. An inset shows the same woman dressed less fashionably. The one word headline, "Minkover," effects a double pun: The model is wearing a mink pull*over*, and the inset of a "before" picture puns on the *make*over offered at cosmetic counters. Wearing mink provides a makeover, according to the ad; it will transform you. And indeed, the contrast between "before" and "after" is marvelous to behold; before, a bedraggled coed, hair untidily tied back, collar askew, hands held ready to be handcuffed, downbeat; after, a smiling, confident person, hair loose over the shoulders, striding forward, with eyes covered over and hands covered, upbeat. Before, the model is looked at, in Sartre's sense; after, she looks at you, become now an impenetrable observer. Before and after equates to under and over. The message generated by the resonance is that you should buy something mink and get on top of things; pull mink over you and cover whatever you may need to hide.

Another example of verbal—visual resonance is the ad for MasterCard®, in which the headline, "The world of golden possibilities," is echoed by a solid gold picture of the planet with continents embossed (Plate 3). The phrase "golden possibilities" suggests a future of hope and promise, and these feelings are transferred to the gold card by means of resonance. The gilded planet visually communicates that the gold card is accepted the world over. There is also the suggestion that with a gold Mastercard, you can buy anything in the world, perhaps the world itself. Anything is possible in this golden world.

The ad for Philip Kingsley styling spritz is somewhat more fantastic. A bottle of the product is shown with a lighted fuse along with the headline, "Blow up your hair." Multiple puns on the explosion theme continue throughout the copy. The literal function of the product—to add volume to limp hair— is dramatized by the second meaning anchored in the illustration: that your hair will be explosive, that you will sparkle. The resonance is completed by the faint "hair" of sparks thrown off from the fuse attached to the "head" of the bottle.

The ad for Finesse hair care products (plate 4) provides an example of resonance that directly incorporates the brand name (cf. Lutz and Lutz 1978). The product enjoys a name which has its own meaning in the language, a meaning which is quite appropriate to a hair care product. "Making Waves Takes Finesse;" you need this product to make hair this curly. Or, it takes a delicate skillful touch to make hair look this good. Or, only a person with finesse (read: knowledge of the correct hair product and its use) could manage blond curls this beautiful. Or, use of this product will enable you to cause a stir. This headline is a fine example of how a cascade of favorable meanings can be made to circulate within the text of an ad. The body copy continues in this vein with its statement that the product "lets you get hold of a splashier style." This both continues the watery theme, suggests making a splash, and reminds one of the movie Splash, in which Daryl Hannah, a beautiful blond woman with a head full of curls, starred as a mermaid. All favorable associations, and all cycling back to the product.

The ad for Gates ski gloves (plate 5) helps to make a point about the proper use of resonance. The picture shows a glove opened up, its fillings and materials exposed as if it were an animal on a dissection table. The headline reads, "No other glove company has the guts to run this ad." The pun comes across immediately: this glove contains filling materials and has internal structures that no other glove has. But the cliche meaning of "guts" continues to operate. The sponsor has courage; the other manufacturers do not. In this example, both meanings within the resonant ad are favorable; both enhance the sponsor. As a practical matter, this criterion may be the key to the successful commercial use of resonance: that the matrix of meanings generated by the resonant structure be largely or completely favorable. Compare an ad directed at restaurant owners that shows teacups full of tea with the headline, "Get your customers into a lot of hot water." The ad is resonant, but the double meaning does not enhance the product: why should a restaurant want to get its customers into trouble? When resonance does not serve to enhance the sponsor's product, it may be merely a trick used for shock value, of dubious merit.

In a *visual pun*, a picture is constructed that allows the viewer to read off a verbal message. The picture exists simultaneously as itself and as a verbal message, making it a pun. An example of a visual pun is the Travelers insurance ad (plate 6). A common office tape dispenser is shown loaded with red tape. "Red tape" is probably high on the list of the dissatisfiers that consumer associate with the insurance product category. The visual pun dramatizes the red tape concept in a way no mere words could do. It also facilitates the play on "stuck" in the headline: "you won't get stuck with this." The tape that is normally loaded into that dispenser is sticky; the visual pun communicates the sticky aspect of insurance paper work at a glance. The resonance is completed by the inclusion of the red umbrella at the bottom. The red tape and the red umbrella nicely

**EXHIBIT 1**
**TYPES OF RESONANCE IN MAGAZINE ADS**

| Type | Definition | Examples |
|------|------------|----------|
| 1. Visual | Repetition of shapes, colors and contours | Aziza Mink Mascara<br>-A model is photographed wearing mink coat and hat. Her eyelashes and the spikes of mink fur echo one another. |
| 2. Verbal | Headlines or body copy that make use of puns or word play | Weight Watchers<br>-"Berried treasure"<br><br>Idaho Potatoes<br>-"Fry first class" |
| 3. Verbal-Visual | Words in the headline or copy are echoed by elements in the illustration | Mink International<br>-A model in a mink pullover with the headline "minkover"<br><br>MasterCard Gold Card<br>-The planet in gold with the headline, "A world of golden possibilities"<br><br>Philip Kingsley Maximizer Styling Spritz<br>-The illustration shows a bottle of the product with a lighted fuse on top. The headline reads "Blow Up Your Hair," and the copy begins, "Explosive new volume for limp do-nothing hair..."<br><br>Finesse Hair Care<br>-A model with wavy hair and the headline, "Making waves takes Finesse"<br><br>Gates ski gloves<br>-A glove with insides cut open and the headline, "No other manufacturer has the guts to run this ad" |
| 4. Visual puns | An illustration visually depicts a common cliche' or recognizable phrase | The Travelers Universal Insurance<br>-A tape dispenser for use at an office desk is shown loaded with red tape. |

**PLATE 3**
Reproduced by Permission

**PLATE 4**
Reproduced by permission

summarize a duality at the heart of the insurance product. On the one hand, insurance is a *restriction*, a source of hassles, a quagmire of paper work (sticky tape); on the other, insurance is *protection*, shelter against the storm, a bulwark against loss (umbrella). The formal structure of the ad encompasses this duality.

A legitimate question is whether resonance is a novel strategy growing in favor, or whether it may enjoy a long history of occasional use. Puns in headlines probably go back a long ways (Grinnell 1987); but the deliberate use of verbal-visual resonance may be a relatively recent development. Some evidence relevant to this point comes from an examination of liquor advertisements. The collection of 200 ads gathered in 1986-87 contains over a dozen instances of resonant ads for liquor products (Exhibit 2). Several products, notably J&B whiskey, Christian Brothers brandy, Absolut vodka, Grand Marnier liqueur, and Johnnie Walker Red have based whole campaigns on series of resonant ads. Perhaps liquor advertising has always been this way; but it is notable that the advertising agencies for Christian Brothers and J&B whiskey got into a public spat over who deserved credit for "inventing" this new style of advertising (Alsop 1987). This suggests that the deliberate, systematic use of resonance may be a new style about to enjoy a vogue. This, in turn, may be a direct result of the diffusion into the advertising community of applied semiotics (Pendry and Holmes 1986; Umiker-Sebeok 1987).

To summarize, various types of resonance can be identified. All share a common characteristic: either two or more elements within the execution are related through resemblance, *or*, one element has two or more meanings. This doubleness is generative; it produces meanings that might not have been present if only one element had been included, or if the resemblance between the elements had been suppressed. Doubleness of this kind opens up the advertising text. The meaning of the ad is destabilized, rendered fluid. To show the extent of the meanings that can be generated through a resonant construction, two additional ads will be interpreted. The elaboration of meaning in these ads is so extensive as to suggest the term *complex resonance*.

## Glamour Magazine

An ad directed toward potential advertisers in Glamour magazine is headlined, "GLAMOUR ZIP." It shows a woman wearing an outfit unzipped at one shoulder. She holds a gloved hand so that it partly covers her face; this glove is also unzipped, and one eye peeks out between two fingers. The tag line reads "Glamour readers run up big department store tabs...." Ostensibly, the message is that readers of this magazine spend a great deal of money in department stores. At this level, the ad is an instance of "reason-why" advertising: buy space with us because our readers spend a lot of money on products like yours. The multilevel pun on "zip", however, opens up a more complex message.

Almost every meaning of the word "zip" functions in the service of the sponsor. First,

something about the type face in the headline suggests the Post Office's advertisements for the Zip code. The implication is that with Glamour magazine, you can reach readers where they live. Given the use of zip codes in marketing, there is a further implication of targeting; you can reach exactly your target market through buying space in Glamour. This is their true address, and you can best address your customers through this vehicle. The second pun on zip involves the two zippers shown in the ad. You can zip up your market with this vehicle, cover your most important prospects. You can unzip your target audience; advertising here will help you uncover what she really wants. She is open to you when she reads this magazine; you can unzip her, penetrate her indifference, get through to her. All of these plays on zipper are linked to the copy by the pun on "tabs." Zippers have tabs, and so do these readers have tabs, at department stores; you can pull these sales in your direction through advertising here; you can open up a market, close a sale. The third and fourth relevant meanings of "zip" are "fast" and "energetic." The female reader of Glamour is perhaps a little fast; she will respond readily to your entreaties if you advertise here. You can put some zip into your sales; these are energetic consumers.

On the purely visual level, there are a series of openings and revealings. One shoulder is laid bare by an unzipping, one wrist is similarly exposed. These two wedge-shaped openings echo a third: the space between two fingers from which the model peeks out at us. The theme throughout is seeing; you see a lot of her, as she will see a lot of you. Your ads will be seen in Glamour, you will get the exposure you seek; she will be exposed. What had been hidden will be revealed: your product, her preferences.

This ad indicates the wealth of meanings that can be invoked by the use of complex resonance. The meanings read from the formal structure of the ad are generated by the resonance among the elements. The uncertain meaning of "zip" in the title, in conjunction with the pictures of zippers, sets up a flow of meaning.

## Dean Markley Strings

In this ad for guitar strings, an old man's face is shown on top of a muscular young man's body, which strikes a performer's pose (plate 7). In conjunction with the headline, the message is straightforward: you are going to play guitar for a long time, until you're old; these guitar strings will go the distance with you.

The resonance begins with the picture of Jimmy *Dean*, over the mantel. Jimmy Dean is a symbol of youthful rebellion, and his signifieds are closely associated with the signifieds connected with "rock-and-roll." The pun on the brand name helps to associate this manufacturer with the spirit of rock and roll. Jimmy Dean died young, but the model in this ad has clearly lived a long time. A polarity is thus set in motion between youth and age, a polarity close to the heart of rock and roll. This polarity, figured most clearly in the body of the model, is echoed by the other furnishings in the room. The rocking chair by

## EXHIBIT 2

## A PARTIAL LIST OF RECENT LIQUOR ADVERTISEMENTS MAKING USE OF RESONANCE

| Brand | Verbal Component | Visual Component |
| --- | --- | --- |
| 1. Glenlivet Scotch | Just slightly out of reach | Bottle in tank sorrounded by piranhas |
| 2. Chivas Regal | When a silver lining isn't enough | Cloud outlines bottle |
| 3. Johnnie Walker Red | When it pours, Red stands out | People wearing red slickers sitting in the rain in an outdoor cafe |
| 4. J&B Scotch | J&B with a twist | Letter 'J' is twisted |
| 5. Absolut Vodka | Use of name as an adjective (e.g., "Absolut perfection") | Halo on top of bottle |
| 6. Vikin Fjord | Norwegians are perfectly clear about their vodka | Clear glass, clear water |
| 7. Finlandia | The Finnish Line | Line of Vodka bottles |
| 8. Gordon's Gin | England--known for its rock groups and its gin | Picture of Stonehenge |
| 9. Tanqueray Gin | Share the wreath | Bottle in shape of a wreath |
| 10. Christian Brothers | CB in orange | Chuck Berry dressed in orange |
| 11. E&J Brandy | I stand by my brandy | Person stands by large brandy bottle |
| 12. Bacardi Rum | Put your coke in the best of spirits | --------- |
| 13. Bailey's Original Irish Cream | Invite some friends over and make waves | Waves of liquid as glass is poured |
| 14. Mahola Mango Liqueur | The taste that will blow you away | Trees and liquid blown by wind |
| 15. Sambuca | Try a little wishful drinking | ---------- |
| 16. Grand Marnier Liqueur | Plays on grand (e.g., a grand setting) | Liqueur on a table cloth, floating free |

the fireplace, the tasselled ottoman, the pattern on the rug, the plate on the wall, the knick-knacks on the mantel, and the lamp are all of a style that we associate with the old and elderly. This is a grandparent's living room. The kinetic posture and bare muscled chest of the model are in marked contrast, a contrast that brings you back to the quintessential old man's face on the model, where the eyes of Jimmy Dean are locked, Jimmy Dean who died so young.

The resonance continues in the body copy: "Old rockers never die, they just lose the tension in their G string." An explicitly sexual element enters the text with this pun. An old guitar string is like a man who has lost his potency. Counting the headline and package there are altogether eight mentions of the word "long" in this ad. The words "strong" and "powerful" also characterize these strings. Is there something else which is long, strong and powerful? A theme of potency versus death and decline now matches the polarity between youth and age. Both these should resonate with the intended audience for this ad: people who play rock-and-roll music on guitar. The themes echo a tension that is central both to this style of music and to the young men who are enthusiastic about it.

It is appropriate for a manufacturer of guitar strings to attempt to create this rich tapestry of elaborations on potency, age and death. Few people care about guitar strings in themselves; it is guitars that are the focus of consumers' enthusiasm. Resonance functions here to enrich a mundane product. The strings are assimilated to matters much grander than themselves, and this serves the sponsor's purpose.

## IMPLICATIONS FOR FUTURE RESEARCH

This essay attempts only to identify and explicate the phenomenon of resonance. Future research could be conducted along either semiological or semiotic lines (Holbrook 1987). Each of these avenues will be discussed in turn.

### Semiological Research

Further research on the nature of the meanings generated by a resonant text could take several forms. The basic stance of this essay has been that resonance creates a more elaborate text, richer in meaning and more complex in implication. This thesis could be pursued much further. First, a way might be found to enumerate the meanings generated by various types of resonance, and to compare these to the volume of meanings generated by other kinds of rhetorical figures. Second, the rudimentary taxonomy presented here could be developed further, along the lines of Durand's (1987) rather complete schema for rhetorical figures in general. It may have occurred to the reader that in each of the ads analyzed, the operation of resonance was slightly different. A large collection of ads systematically analyzed might produce a more differentiated picture of how resonance operates to generate meaning. Third, investigations could be conducted into the kinds of meaning best conveyed through a resonant construction. This essay has

concentrated on resonance as a means of conveying *equivalence*, i.e., a claim that the sponsor's product is akin something else, resembles it or is intrinsically connected to it. Since a very common strategy is to promote a product through associating it with things that have value in their own right, this capacity of resonance is of wide import. Might resonance also be suited to the communication of other kinds of meaning? Only further semiological work with a broad array of resonant constructions can determine the answer.

An important problem that future semiological work will have to address is the *validity* of the kinds of interpretation of resonance offered in this essay. It is apparent that the interpretations constructed by a scholar in his study are unlikely to correspond in detail to the interpretations made by naive viewers of the ad. The assumption underlying this account, however, is that an ad that responds to the scholar's efforts is also one which will stimulate more interpretation, in total, among the mass audience. In other words, the claim is that the interpretations made by individual viewers-- those that notice the ad at all-- although fragmentary and incomplete in comparison with the scholar's exegesis, will as a total set be more elaborate than in the case of a non-resonant ad. Qualitative research among a sample of ordinary viewers could go a long way to reassure the skeptic that the intensive examination made by the scholar in fact corresponds to the meanings received by a general audience. Pendry and Holmes (1986) offer an example of such qualitative research. Since the fundamental source of validation for any semiological interpretation is the text itself (Holbrook 1987), convergent readings of a text by different readers may be as far as one can go toward satisfying more traditional social science concerns regarding validity.

### Semiotic Research

Like semiology, semiotics is devoted to the study of signs; unlike semiology, semiotics concerns itself with the effect of signs upon the readers of a text (Holbrook 1987). Thus a semiotic perspective on resonance would focus on what effect this kind of formal structure might have on the audience for an ad. The emphasis would lie more on whether resonance *works*, from the standpoint of the advertiser. Research would focus on the conditions under which a resonant construction will or will not succeed in producing a particular kind of effect upon viewers. A semiotic investigation would permit the finding that resonance has no unique or attractive communication effects, regardless of whether or not it is a distinct semiological phenomenon. In the author's opinion, resonance is no panacea, nor is there any reason to believe that resonance is an intrinsically superior execution from the standpoint of selling a product. Thus, the most recent edition of *Which Ad Pulled Best?* includes a number of resonant executions, few of which were notably successful by the criteria used (Burton and Purvis 1987).

Experimental semiotic research might take one of two avenues. The first would involve common sense perspectives tested through the usual apparatus

**PLATE 5**
Reproduced by Permission

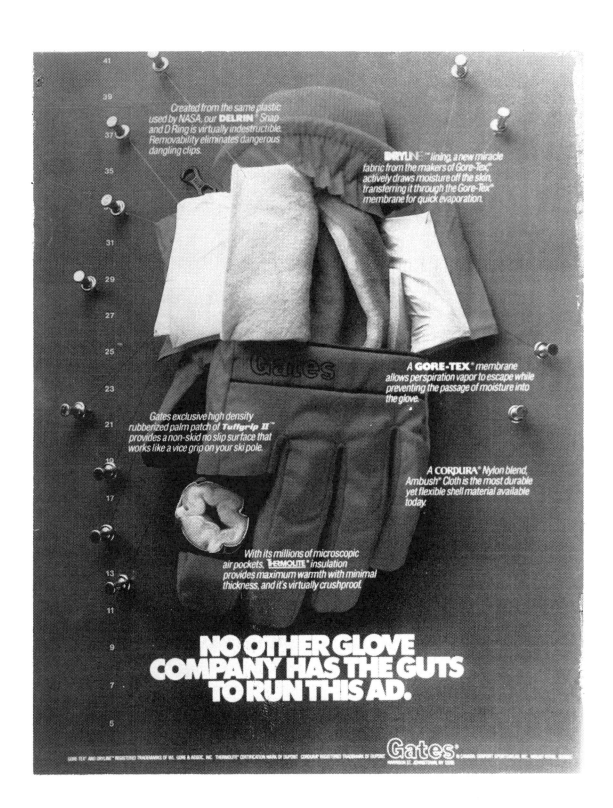

**PLATE 6**
Reproduced by Permission

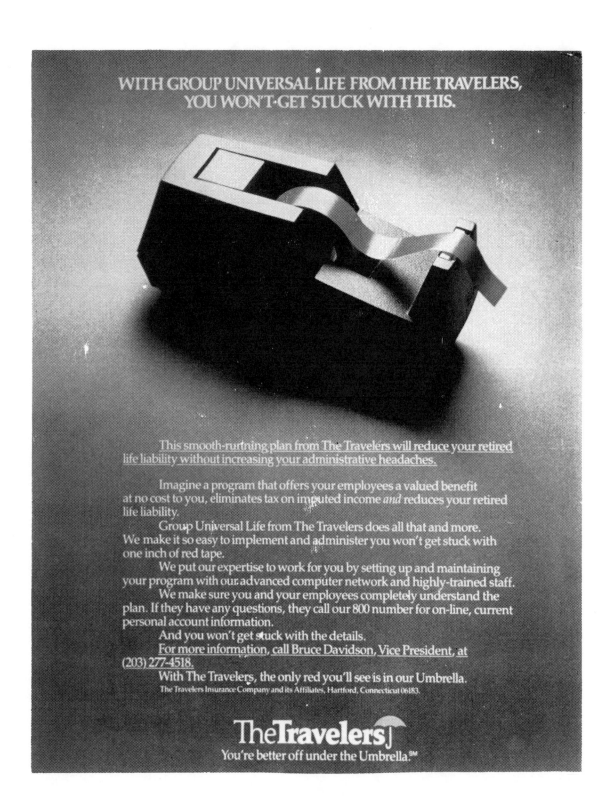

**PLATE 7**
Reproduced by Permission

of advertising research: measures of recall, persuasion, attitude-toward-the-ad, and the like. The second would link up with recent developments in cognitive psychology concerning non-verbal elements in advertising (Hecker and Stewart 1988). The first avenue will be discussed briefly, followed by a more detailed account of relevant work in cognitive psychology.

Common sense would suggest two likely effects for resonant executions. Because a resonant construction produces a more elaborate meaning structure, resonance might increase viewer *involvement* with the ad. With the availability of generally applicable measures of involvement (Zaichkowsky 1985), it ought to be possible to compare consumer response to a set of resonant ads against that to a control set of ordinary ads. A more behavioral measure of involvement-- time spent viewing-- could also be used. A precursor of such experiments would be Lutz and Lutz (1978), whose category of interactive imagery recalls resonance, and who were able to show superior memory for interactive executions involving the brand name. The key difficulty in such experiments will be the selection of a control group of ads similar to the resonant ads in all respects save the presence of resonance. While it may not be possible to meet this requirement of internal validity in the case of a collection of actual ads, there is also danger in assuming that the experimenter can concoct resonance for purposes of constructing a stimulus set. Non-professional and possibly uncreative instances of resonance manufactured for laboratory use may not adequately represent the phenomenon.

In addition to stimulating greater involvement in the advertisement, resonance might act more generally to influence attitude-toward-the-ad. The more complex structure and the use of figurative speech could cause viewers to like the resonant ads more, and this positive affect could generalize to the brand. Alternatively, puns may irritate a substantial fraction of the audience, causing a more negative attitude-toward-the-ad (Percy and Rossiter 1980). For some viewers, resonance may amount to no more than a joke that fails.

Resonance may also prove to be a particularly persuasive means of communicating equivalence between a product and some desirable quality. What makes resonance attractive as a device for conveying equivalence is its *non-literal* and *tacit* character. When a sponsor makes an explicit verbal claim that a product is like some other thing, the viewer can readily counter-argue. The explicit, verbal statement is an obvious influence attempt and it automatically alerts the viewer that resistance may be in order. With resonance, however, equivalence is connoted rather than denoted; the equation is not made straight out but simply implied. Because it not stated, refutation becomes more difficult. Research has shown that receiver counter-arguments are a key obstacle to persuasion (Wright 1974); hence, a tactic that forestalls counter-arguing may have much to recommend it.

Resonance that involves both verbal and visual elements may be related to cognitive psychological investigations on picture-word processing (Houston, Childers and Heckler 1987). Research in this tradition has suggested that the co-presence of verbal and visual representations of an object may facilitate memory for that object. Explanations for this effect vary. A depth of processing explanation would point to the greater number of elaborative operations performed by a viewer faced with related visual and verbal representations (Craik and Lockhart 1972). Alternatively, some theorists have argued that the brain uses dual coding, with separate systems for visual and verbal information (Paivio 1971). In that event, resonant ads would succeed not because of more elaborative processing by the receiver, but because they would leave a stronger memory trace through being coded twice. Edell (1988), in her review of non-verbal elements in advertising, draws on Bower's (1972) work on paired associates learning to categorize these explanations in terms of "strength of association" and "cue redundancy." Ads which stimulate elaborative operations strengthen the association between two stimuli, while brand names which are represented both visually and verbally benefit from cue redundancy.

An important point is that resonance is more amenable to an elaborative operations or strength of association explanation than to a dual coding or cue redundancy explanation. In fact, it is possible for dual coding to occur based on redundant verbal-visual cues without resonance being present. Consider an ad for Mink Difference hair products. "Mink" is present verbally, in the brand name, and visually, as a mink coat worn by a woman with beautiful hair; but this arrangement produces no resonance, no echo, no twist, no play on meanings. The mink coat, taken as a symbol of rich softness, may enhance the brand by its presence, and the visual image of mink may assist later retrieval of the brand name; but none of this involves resonance. Cue redundancy, then, is not a sufficient condition for resonance. The other two mink ads discussed earlier (Plates 2, 3) have redundant verbal-visual cues, but also have something more.

Pulling together these possible avenues for semiotic research suggests the following core proposition.

Proposition:     Elaboration in the stimulus invites elaboration as a response.

This suggests that cognitive responses of consumers ought to be a key dependent variable in experimental investigations of resonance. A resonant ad has a more elaborate text, and the most straightforward effect that can be imagined is a more elaborate response on the part of the viewer. This elaboration may have effects on memory, learning or persuasion, but should be evident in the cognitive responses made by consumers.

## CONCLUSION

The interpretations offered in this essay have been fairly elaborate, and undoubtedly strike some readers as far-fetched. At worst, what has happened is that I have appropriated individual advertisements for my own aesthetic consumption. After all, I have spent hours looking at certain of these ads, and have come back to them day after day. This is a treatment normally accorded only to works of art, myths, and other key components of culture. The actual experience of these ads by ordinary consumers is probably very different. The pages of a magazine are turned; a headline is read, an illustration glanced at; and then the page is turned again. Can there be a meaningful correspondence between the scholar's interpretation and that made by typical member of the viewing audience when their situations are so very different?

Painting the problem in these stark terms also points the way to a solution. From the standpoint of semiology, the ecological difference between the attentive scholar and the naive consumer is really irrelevant to whether the scholar's interpretation is useful or valuable. I grant the reader that no other viewer may ever have drawn the precise interpretation that I offer of certain ads. All that matters to me is that these interpretations be *possible*. It is the potential meaning of a resonant ad, and not its actual meaning to a concrete individual, that is of primary concern. I shall assume that the greater the ad's potential for meaning, the more likely it is that its realized meanings, as grasped by the collective audience for the ad, will be rich rather than thin, many rather than few. Any individual consumer will probably experience only a fraction of the potential meanings of the ad. But if the assumption be granted that greater potential equals greater realization of meaning in the collective audience, then the efforts of the scholar become a means of measuring this potential. Correspondence obtains not in terms of realized meanings, but in terms of meaningfulness.

In terms of practical implications, this essay may be read as encouragement to consider a resonant style. I would suggest that as the culture grows more saturated with promotional messages, and as consumers become increasingly inured against straightforward sales pitches, the subtlety and richness of a resonant style gain in appeal (Kloepfer 1987). As Fox (1984) argues, the "reason why" approach of Claude Hopkins has always been opposed by the softer, more allusive approach associated with Theodore MacManus. Resonance may simply be the latest version of this alternative style. From another perspective, Schudson (1984) describes consumer advertising in America as "capitalist realism," an art form which celebrates the principles and presumptions of our economic system and way of life. This essay can then be read as art appreciation for capitalist realism. As art appreciation, it may encourage creatives to go a little farther than they might otherwise have, and to seek even richer textures of meaning.

## REFERENCES

Alsop, Ronald (1987), "Advertisers Take a Dim View of Sincerest Form of Flattery," *Wall Street Journal*, September 24, 29.

Barthes, Roland (1985), "The Rhetoric of the Image," in *The Responsibility of Forms*, New York: Hill and Wang, 21-40.

Bower, Gordon (1972), Mental Imagery and Associative Learning," in *Cognition in Learning and Memory*, ed. Lee Gregg, New York: John Wiley.

Burton, Philip W. and Scott C. Purvis (1986), *Which Ad Pulled Best?*, 5th ed., Lincolnwood, IL: NTC Business Books.

Craik, Fergus I.M. and Robert S. Lockhart (1972), "Levels of Processing: A Framework for Memory Research," *Journal of Verbal Learning and Verbal Behavior*, 11 (December), 671-684.

Durand, Jacques (1987), "Rhetorical Figures in the Advertising Image," in *Marketing and Semiotics: New Directions in the Study of Signs for Sale*, ed. Jean Umiker-Sebeok, New York: Mouton de Gruyter, 295-318.

Dyer, Gillian (1982), *Advertising as Communication*, New York: Methuen

Edell, Julie A. (1988), "Nonverbal Effects in Ads: A Review and Synthesis," in *Nonverbal Communication in Advertising*, eds. Sidney Hecker and David W. Stewart, Lexington, MA: Lexington Books, 11-28.

Fiske, John (1982), *Introduction to Communication Studies*, New York: Methuen.

Fox, Stephen (1984), *The Mirror Makers: A History of American Advertising and Its Creators*, New York: William Morrow.

Grinnell, J.D. (1987), *National Register of Advertising Headlines & Slogans*, Westbury, NY: Asher-Gallant.

Hecker, Sidney and David W. Stewart (1988), *Nonverbal Communication in Advertising*, Lexington, MA: Lexington Books.

Holbrook Morris (1987), "The Study of Signs in Consumer Esthetics: An Egocentric Review" in *Marketing and Semiotics: New Directions in the Study of Signs for Sale*, ed. Jean Umiker-Sebeok, New York: Mouton de Gruyter, 73-122.

Houston, Michael J., Terry L. Childers and Susan E. Heckler (1987), "Picture-Word Consistency and the Elaborative Processing of Advertisements," *Journal of Marketing Research*, 24 (November), 359-369.

Kloepfer, Rolf (1987), "Sympraxis--Semiotics, Aesthetics, and Consumer Participation," in *Marketing and Semiotics: New Directions in the Study of Signs for Sale*, ed. Jean Umiker-Sebeok, New York: Mouton de Gruyter, 123-148.

Levy, Sidney J. (1981), "Interpreting Consumer Mythology: A Structural Approach to Consumer Behavior," *Journal of Marketing*, 45 (Summer), 49-61.

Leymore, Varda L. (1975), *Hidden Myth: Structure and Symbolism in Advertising*, New York: Basic Books.

Liess, William, Stephen Kline and Sut Jhally (1986) *Social Communication in Advertising: Persons, Products and Images of Well-Being*, Toronto: Methuen.

Lutz, Kathy A. And Richard J. Lutz (1977), "Effects of Interactive Imagery on Learning: Application to Advertising," *Journal of Applied Psychology*, 62 (August), 493-498.

McLuhan, Herbert Marshall (1951), *The Mechanical Bride: Folklore of Industrial Man*, New York: Vanguard Press.

Mick, David Glen (1986), "Consumer Research and Semiotics: Exploring the Morphology of Signs, Symbols and Significance," *Journal of Consumer Research*, 13 (September), 196-214.

Noth, Winfried (1987) "Advertising: The Frame Message," in *Marketing and Semiotics: New Directions in the Study of Signs for Sale*, ed. Jean Umiker-Sebeok, New York: Mouton de Gruyter, 279-294.

Paivio, Allan (1971), *Imagery and Verbal Processes*, New York: Holt, Rhinehart and Wilson.

Pendry, Colin and Margaret Holmes (1986), "Unusual Research for Unusual Advertising: Mixing Methods and Minds," in *Qualitative Methods of Research: A Matter of Interpretation*, Amsterdam: ESOMAR, 141-160.

Percy, Larry and John Rossiter (1980), *Advertising Strategy: A Communication Theory Approach*, New York: Praeger.

Pollay, Richard W. and Steve Mainprize (1984), "Headlining of Visuals in Print Advertising: A Typology of Tactical Techniques," paper presented at the American Academy of Advertising, Denver.

Schudson, Michael (1984), *Advertising: The Uneasy Persuasion*, New York: Basic Books.

Sherry, John (1987), "Advertising as a Cultural System," in *Marketing and Semiotics: New Directions in the Study of Signs for Sale*, ed. Jean Umiker-Sebeok, New York: Mouton de Gruyter, 441-461.

Stern, Barbara B (1988), "Figurative Language in Services Advertising: The Nature and Uses of Imagery," in *Advances in Consumer Research*, Vol. 15, ed. Michael J. Houston, Provo, UT. Association for Consumer Research 185-190.

Turner, Victor (1974), *Dramas, Fields and Metaphors*, Ithaca: Cornell University Press.

Umiker-Sebeok, Jean (1987) *Marketing and Semiotics: New Directions in the Study of Signs for Sale*, New York: Mouton de Gruyter.

Vestergaard, Torben and Kim Schroder (1985), *The Language of Advertising*, New York: Basil Blackwell.

Williamson, Judith (1978), *Decoding Advertisements: Ideology and Meaning in Advertising*, Boston: Marion Boyars.

Wright, Peter L. (1973), "The Cognitive Processes Mediating Acceptance of Advertising," *Journal of Marketing Research*, 10 (February), 53-62.

Zaichkowsky, Judith (1985), "Measuring the Involvement Construct," *Journal of Consumer Research*, 12 (December), 341-352.

# Materialism and the Modern U.S. Christmas

Russell W. Belk, University of Utah[1]

On December 24, 1951, in front of several hundred French children attending Sunday school, Santa Claus was hanged and burnt. The executioners were the priests of the Dijon Cathedral who condemned Santa as:

> a usurper and a heretic. He was accused of paganizing the festival of Christmas and installing himself like a cuckoo, taking up more and more room (Levi-Strauss 1963).

Pimlott (1962) calls the coexistence of the religious celebrations of the Christmas Nativity and the more Saturnalia-like secular celebrations of the same occasion, "the paradox of Christmas."

The present paper first presents a brief history of the modern Christmas and redefines the paradox of Christmas. It then explores the shifting ways that Americans look at Christmas, as evidenced by mass media treatments, considered both qualitatively and (for a subset of media treatments found in selected consumer magazines and in Christmas comic books over the past 40 years) quantitatively. These analyses suggest that there is little real threat to the sacred status of Christmas, primarily due to the increasing interpenetration of values celebrated by the Christian and commercial sponsors of Christmas.

## A BRIEF HISTORY OF THE U.S. CHRISTMAS AND ITS TWO MODERN DEITIES

### Origins

Although Christmas itself may be traced to a number of pagan winter festivals such as the Teutonic Yule and the Roman Saturnalia in pre-Christian Europe (Golby and Purdue 1986), neither these nor the various later European Christmas celebrations are sufficient to explain the modern American Christmas. This lack of continuity is partly due to one of the first backlashes against Christmas. This reaction arose among the religious immigrants to the American colonies. As Barnett (1954) notes, Puritan reaction against the "wanton Bacchanalian feast" of Christmas led these colonists to begin shunning the holiday as early as 1620. By 1659, the colony of Massachusetts had passed an ordinance to fine anyone caught observing Christmas by abstaining from labor, feasting, or other celebration.

It took another century before Christmas celebrations began to emerge in America among pockets of Dutch, English, and German immigrants, especially in New York and Pennsylvania (Golby and

Purdue 1986, McGinty 1979, Shoemaker 1959, Snyder 1985). And legal recognition of Christmas day by states and territories did not take place until the 19th century (1836-1890). Christmas celebrations are thought by some to have been dying out until a group of 19th century writers began to revive interest through sentimental Christmas tales tying the holiday to Victorian celebrations of home, family, and children (Golby and Purdue 1986). The most influential of these writers were Charles Dickens from England and Washington Irving from the U.S.. Dickens' (1843) *A Christmas Carol* was and remains the most influential of these tales. Barnett (1954) may overestimate Dickens' influence as almost single-handedly reviving Christmas, but his work clearly has had a dominant influence.

## Changes in the U.S. Christmas

Because Christmas in America reemerged as an amalgam of various European celebrations, it is appropriate to speak of the American Christmas celebration as unique. Present U.S. Christmas traditions and iconography include the German Christmas tree, the British Christmas card, and the Dutch Christmas cookie. While our modern Santa Claus draws on earlier European figures, he is a distinctly American creation (Belk 1987). Certain Christmas traditions such as Christmas dinner, charity to the poor, and role reversal and other social tension-reduction mechanisms have pre-Christian roots. However, most of our current Christmas celebration, including emphasis on family, card exchange, gift exchange, decorated Christmas trees, Christmas shopping, Santa Claus, Christmas carols, and Christmas cookies, and candy, either emerged or reemerged during the Victorian period (Snyder 1985, Golby and Purdue 1986).

While first generation European immigrants to America tended to preserve the celebrations of their home countries, adoption of U.S. Christmas traditions such as Santa Claus and exchanging gifts on December 25th rather than earlier or later in the month became a mark of acculturation in second and later generations (Sereno 1951, Shoemaker 1959). So strong were these symbols of Americanization that Santa and the Christmas tree were even adopted to some degree by second and third generation Jewish immigrants (Witt 1939, Matz 1961).

One inhibition to Christmas gift-giving in America, especially among English immigrants, was the prior tradition of giving only to servants and the poor during this season. As Snyder (1985) notes:

> In the antebellum South, as well as the North the association of Christmastime gifts with servants and slaves played a major role in holding back more widespread gift giving (Snyder 1985, p. 60).

[1]The author would like to thank reviewers Jeffrey F. Durgee, Grant McCracken, and Barbara B. Stern for their comments on an earlier version of this manuscript.

Snyder (1985) found that between 1820 and 1870 there was only a small amount of Philadelphia and New York newspaper advertising for Christmas presents, and these were most commonly presented as New Year's gifts or generic "holiday gifts". Based on his analysis of popular periodical editorial and advertising material, Waits (1978) finds that the period from 1880 to 1920 saw not only a great escalation in Christmas gift-giving, but a gradual shift from handmade gifts to manufactured gifts.

Several other phenomena in Victorian America supported this development of the commercial Christmas. One was the "Fancy Fairs" which were popular charity bazaars in which handmade Christmas gifts made primarily by women were sold (O'Neil 1981). Another was the development of opulent displays of Christmas merchandise by retail stores. In 1874 Macy's New York store presented a $10,000 tableau of imported dolls that started a tradition of Christmas window displays and gave birth to the occupation of window dressing (Snyder 1985). New York City Christmas shopping became a popular tradition, sanctioned by U.S. presidents and New York socialites. Just a year after Macy's first Christmas window display, the Christmas card was introduced from England and soon became a widely adopted part of U.S. Christmas tradition. While recent evidence suggests that religious themes are rare in contemporary Christmas cards (Hill 1969, Johnson 1971a, 1971b), Buday's (1954) history of the Christmas card and the sample of cards presented by Holder and Harding (1981) suggest that religious Christmas card motifs were always in a minority. Instead, popular themes were and remain home and family (especially nostalgic renderings of "old fashioned" homes and family life), Santa Claus, children, animals, and nature (especially snowy scenes).

The explosion of commercial Christmas in Victorian America was not without resistance and criticism. Editorials in *The Ladies' Home Journal* in 1890 complained that Christmas had become too commercial and was little more than a "festival of store-keepers" (O'Neil 1981). An early ethnography of department store toy departments in the weeks before Christmas found that clerks worked long days under trying conditions and that their Christmas commission-inspired eagerness irritated customers as well:

> As soon as the elevators emptied themselves on the floor, there was one mad rush of clerks with a quickly spoken, "What would you like madam?" or, "Something in toys, sir?" And the responses to these questions were indicative of the characters of the people making them. The majority were rude, some amused, and a few alarmed at the urgency of the clerks. One young boy, on being assailed by half a dozen at once, threw up his hands in horror, and said: "For God's sake, let me get out of here!" and fled down the stairs, not even waiting for the elevator (MacLean 1899, pp. 724-725).

Occasionally clergy railed against the commercialization of Christmas and demanded that Americans put the Christ back in Christmas (Barnett 1946, 1954). Such criticism was overcome by supporters of the popular Christmas in several ways. One was to invoke the metaphor of God's gift of Christ as suggesting that we too should give of ourselves for the sake of humanity. Of course when these gifts come not from personal service or personal hand-crafting but from the displays of department stores, the illusion that we are giving from ourselves becomes a bit harder to sustain. As Waits (1978) perceptively notes, the problem then becomes one of sacralizing the transfer of these objects from the profane world of commerce into the sacred sphere of Christmas. Sacred as used here does not necessarily have religious connotations. It means instead that which is regarded as significant, powerful, extraordinary, and self transcending (Belk, Wallendorf, and Sherry 1989). Waits (1978) finds that manufacturers and retailers help to sacralize manufactured commodities by designating certain items as "Christmas gifts" rather than mere merchandise. Appearance in special Christmas catalogs, Christmas displays, and in the co-presence of Christmas icons such as holly, wreathes, Santa Claus, and Christmas trees all aid in this de-commoditizing sacralizing process that Appadurai (1986) calls "singularization". Another Victorian invention that helps separate items from the world of commerce is gift wrapping (Snyder 1985). We remove all evidence of an item's commercial origin by removing the price tag, ceremonially wrapping it, creating mystery- a component of sacredness- (Belk, Wallendorf, and Sherry 1989). Based on his research on Christmas celebrations in Muncie, Caplow (1984) dubs this practice "The Wrapping Rule- Christmas gifts must be wrapped before they are presented." We then ritually exchange and unwrap these gifts in the presence of extended family in a ceremony that heightens the feeling that these are not merely utilitarian commodities but are instead "gifts of the self".

The popularity of "Christmas Clubs" since their 1910 origin is also testimony to the sacralization of purchased commercial gifts (Barnett 1954). Notably, these accounts are separated from regular savings accounts and they traditionally offer no interest (Waits 1978), although they may now offer token interest rates that are still below the market rates for other accounts. This helps to "launder" profane money and to reinforce the message that Christmas gift giving should be above considerations of mere investment and money. Separation of Christmas giving from the profane world of commerce would seem to be the most problematic when the gift is itself one of money. Indeed there are highly ambivalent attitudes toward money in our society (Belk and Wallendorf 1988). For instance, Webley, Lea, and Portalska (1983) found that holiday gifts of money to one's mother were widely seen as glaringly inappropriate. Although there is resistance to giving money to others as well, there are several ways in which even monetary gifts are sacralized. One is that almost all such gifts are from parents to children

(Caplow 1982, Caplow, et al. 1982) or from other higher status persons to lower status persons (Cheal 1986, Moschetti 1979). This helps to define such gifts as charity. In addition, when cash is given it is sometimes disguised in the form of a check or gift certificate, making it seem less monetary as with casino chips. When this is not the case, the gift is preferably removed from associations with the filthy lucre by being in uncirculated bills placed in special gift envelope wrapping (Snyder 1985).

A further way in which the commercial Christmas was sacralized and by which objections were overcome, involves organized religion acting as a friend rather than a foe. As Barnett (1954) documents, the relationship between religion and secular aspects of Christmas has been one of ambivalence during the past century. While there are occasional religious condemnations of the commercial aspects of Christmas, it is now more common for a priest or minister to implicitly or explicitly support the Christmas tree, Christmas gifts, Santa Claus, Christmas stockings, Christmas feasts and other aspects of the secular celebration. Barnett (1954) feels that this is an adaptive concession to inevitable forces, but this paper will later suggest other reasons for such a seemingly strange alliance.

## Santa Claus as Secular Christ Figure

The contemporary commercialized U.S. Christmas is symbolized and focused not on the Christ child, but on Santa Claus. Scholars generally agree that Santa Claus is uniquely American (Opie and Opie 1959, Wolf 1964, de Groot 1965, Hagstrom 1966, Oswalt 1970, Jones 1978, Carver 1982, Samuelson 1982, Golby and Purdue 1986, Belk 1987). Belk (1987) suggests that the major differences from earlier European figures are these:

1. Santa Claus lacks the religious associations of such figures as Santa Lucia, Saint Nicholas, Christkindlein, and the Three Kings.

2. Santa Claus lacks the riotous rebelliousness of figures such as Saturn and Knecht Ruprecht.

3. Santa Claus lacks the punitive nature of Sinterclaas (with his companion Black Peter), Ruprecht, Pelze-Nichol, and Saint Nicholas....

4. Despite his mythical nature, with his many appearances on corners, in stores and malls, and in homes, Santa Claus is a more tangible and real person than his predecessors and counterparts....As Caplow points out (Caplow, et al. 1982, p. 238; Caplow and Williamson 1980, pp. 224-225), Santa differs from the Easter Bunny by possessing a name, a known home and family, friends, great age, boundless generosity, and a gender.

5. Santa Claus is a bringer of numerous and substantial gifts, not merely the fruits, nuts, and simple homemade toys of the traditional European Christmas figures (Belk 1987, p. 87).

Shlien (1959) first suggested that the American Santa Claus is our most sacred folk hero after Christ, based on fulfilling most of Ragland's (1937) criteria (subsequently criticized) for heroism:

1. A distinguished or divine origin
2. Mysterious portents at birth
3. Perils menacing his infancy
4. Initiation or revelation
5. A quest
6. A magical contest
7. A trial or persecution
8. A last scene
9. A violent or mysterious death.

Hagstrom's (1966) scholarly parody also seriously suggests that Santa Claus is a sacred figure in a Durkheimian sense, citing as evidence Christmas rituals involving Santa and Shlien's (1959) finding that children were reluctant to eat cookie representations of Santa Claus.

Belk (1987) goes further in drawing parallels between the American Santa Claus and Christ:

The similarities of the secular Santa figure to the religious Christ figure include miracles (flying reindeer, traveling to all houses of the world in one night, and, reminiscent of the loaves and fishes miracle of Christ, Santa's bottomless bag of toys), elves as Apostles, reindeer as manger animals, letters to Santa as secular prayers pledging "good" behavior if they are granted, and offerings of cookies and milk as sacrifices placed upon a fireplace mantle altar. It is also possible to consider Santa's travels on Christmas Eve as parallel to Christ's journeys and secular Christmas carols about Santa as hymns. Just as Christ brought his gifts of love and salvation to earth and then ascended to heaven, Santa brings his gifts of toys and treats to houses and then ascends up the chimney. Furthermore, Santa is immortal, omniscient, knows how children behave, and holds them ultimately accountable for their actions by bestowing the rewards that he alone can offer. Belief in Santa constitutes faith....The title "Santa" also retains the ascription of sainthood. And somewhat more like contemporary images of God than Christ, Santa is portrayed as a wise and benevolent old man who sits on an ornate throne symbolizing his power and wisdom. He lives in the snow white purity of the North Pole, which has some parallels to heaven (Belk 1987, p. 90).

This is not to suggest that Santa Claus represents the same societal values as does Jesus Christ. In fact in many ways Santa may be seen a polar opposite to Christ:

In terms of appearance, Santa portrayals are old and corpulent while Christ portrayals are young and thin. Rather than humble white robes,

Santa dresses in rich reds and furs, and sometimes smokes a pipe. Santa is also more jolly and is often portrayed laughing his characteristic "ho, ho, ho." Christ lived in a land of warm deserts, while Santa lives in a cozy house nestled in the cold snow of the North Pole. Christ was single and Santa is married. And most importantly, the miracles of Christ provided health and necessities while the miracles of Santa Claus provide toys and luxuries. Indeed while Santa brings an abundance of good things, Christ often condemned these things and the wealth they represent (Belk 1987, p. 91).

Since the image of the contemporary American Santa Claus was heavily influenced by Clement Moore's (1822) poem, "A Visit From St. Nicholas" and Thomas Nast's illustrations in *Harper's Weekly* between 1863 and 1886, Belk (1987) turned to Nast's life and work to better understand the contradictions between portrayals of Santa and Christ. Based on Nast's avowed desire to make Santa's furs look like those of the Astors', the similarity of Nast's Santa figures to his characatures of nineteenth century plutocrats such as William "Boss" Tweed, and Nast's very similar depiction of a drunken Bacchus, Belk concludes that the American Santa Claus is the God of materialism and hedonism. Further evidence supporting this contention may be found in the highly materialistic content of children's letters to Santa Claus (Caron and Ward 1975, Richardson and Simpson 1982, Downs 1983, Bradbard 1985), the addressing of some of these letters to "Heaven" (Snyder 1985), the observation of children praying to Santa (Bock 1972, Waits 1978), the appropriation of Santa (but not Christ) in advertising and retail sales (Munsey 1972, Waits 1978, Watters 1978, Louis and Yazijian 1980), and in foreign opposition to (Pierce 1979) as well as support for Santa Claus as a symbol of American materialism (Plath 1963, Stenzel 1975, Yates 1985).

## A Reformulation of the Paradox of Christmas

Based on the preceding arguments, *both* Santa Claus and Jesus Christ are now sacred figures in the contemporary American Christmas. If Santa is now seldom seen as profaning Christmas in America, we must look elsewhere for that which opposes the sacredness of this dual deity Christmas. The most prominent text in which to search for an understanding of the modern American Christmas involves stories of neither Santa or Christ. It is instead the most often repeated and imitated secular Christmas story of all, Dickens' (1843) *A Christmas Carol* (Viola 1986). Bolton (1987) lists 357 scripts of this story for radio, stage (including mime and marionette versions), television, opera, and film (including animated cartoons), and this list is both incomplete and continually outdated as ever more versions of the popular story are produced. One writer in 1906 concluded "Dickens and Christmas are well-nigh synonymous words....Beyond question it was Charles Dickens who gave us Christmas as we understand it to-

day (Ley 1906)." Seventy years later opinion had not changed in the English-speaking world, as Hewet notes: "Dickens and Christmas...are so closely associated that one must make an effort to recall that he was hardly alone in the late-Georgian and early-Victorian England in hoping to revive the old Christmas ways (Hewet 1976)."

It does not exaggerate to suggest that *A Christmas Carol* has become sacred Christmas literature. As Bolton notes, " 'The Carol' quickly had become sacred fare suitable for matinees on Christmas (Bolton 1987, p. 234)". Although eight stage versions of *A Christmas Carol* opened in January and February of 1844, the play has achieved greater popularity in the second half of the twentieth century, partly because of Victorian reluctance to bring sacred works to the stage (Bolton, 1987). In 1909, a production of the play was criticized for rendering "a sacred subject" in "a style suited to the music hall" (Boulton 1987, p. 235).

The story in Dickens' famous tale of Scrooge, Christmas ghosts, and the Cratchits is notably non-religious and involves the following oppositions:

I.  Money, Self, and Others
    1.  Miserliness versus Generosity
    2.  Selfishness versus Brotherhood
    3.  Love of Money versus Love of People
    4.  Avarice versus Altruism
II.  Money and Spending
    1.  Saving versus Spending
    2.  Austerity versus Lavishness
    3.  Utilitarianism versus Hedonism
III.  Work, Home, and Family
    1.  Individual versus Family
    2.  Workplace versus Home
    3.  Work versus Leisure
IV.  Status Differentials
    1.  Age versus Youth
    2.  Rich versus Poor
V.  Emotions
    1.  Lack of Feelings versus Pity and Joy
    2.  Pragmatic Present versus Nostalgic Past and Hopeful Future

In each case the left side of the dialectic may be seen as profane and is represented by Ebenezer Scrooge in Dickens' tale. The right side is instead seen in the Cratchit family and represents an idealized vision of what is now regarded as sacred in Christmas. This may or may not be as Dickens would have wished it, but the author's intentions are no longer relevant to the impact of *A Christmas Carol*, except perhaps among literary critics.

In the present version of the paradox of Christmas, it is not the religious and secular Christmases that clash, but instead the sacred and profane values of the secular world. Walder observes that "Dickens wished to express his sense that there was a reality beyond the immediate and everyday, without implying a specific, dogmatic commitment (Walder 1981, p. 124)." The Profane here is the normal everyday state of the world and its power bases, while the sacred state of the world is exceptional and happens only once a year when we are all to be suffused with a Christmas spirit, which we avowedly regret cannot last throughout the year. In other words, the Christmas season represents sacred liminal time (Turner 1969) in which we transcend the concerns of the everyday world.

Notably, what is sacred in this equation is, as Boorstin (1973, p. 162) notes, "the National Festival of Consumption." It celebrates giving without consideration of the petty concerns of money and whether one can afford it (Yao 1981). This theme is paralleled in *A Christmas Carol* when the Cratchit family has a goose and plum pudding which they can ill-afford and when the quintessential miser Ebenezer Scrooge starts throwing his money around to all whom he encounters. Such acts help to define Christmas as sacred by being extraordinary and set apart from everyday life. It is the same spirit that Campbell (1987) finds characterizes contemporary consumer culture: the triumph of hedonism over utilitarianism.

At the same time, the values stressed in the Dickensian Christmas are not self-motivated. Love of humankind is stressed and inattention to fellow beings provokes guilt. The charity inspired makes Christmas the major fundraising period for many nonprofit organizations. In Dickensian spirit, it is the poor and orphans who are to be the major recipients of Christmas charity. They are symbolic of the sacred Christmas in two ways. First, they are the humble poor and second, they are children rather than adults. At the same time sympathy is additionally aroused because they are estranged from the family focus that is central to the modern Christmas. This precludes them from the warm hearth of home and the family Christmas meal that are also sacraments in Dickens' Christmas. Significantly, the family is a prominent Christian Christmas theme as well, with family sacralized in the manger depiction of the birth of Christ.

The contrasts of status in *A Christmas Carol* emphasize the extraordinary sacred nature of Christmastime as well. Unlike the rest of the year, the poor are attended by the rich and the young are attended by the old. Such status reversals are Christmas traditions that can be traced to pagan celebrations when master and servant roles were reversed and chaos overcame order as the Lords of Misrule reined. Although not a part of the American Christmas, the survival of Christmas cross-dressing (especially by males in female garb) that still exists in British culture to some degree, may also be traced to the Saturnalian reversal of traditional rules (Golby and Purdue 1986). As Barnett (1954) notes, part of the initial popularity of *A Christmas Carol* in both England and the U.S. was its ability to diffuse social tension between rich and poor. That the rich should serve the poor and the old the young at Christmas is also consistent with religious traditions and teachings, so that here too there is an overlap of values in religious and secular Christmases.

A final element in the Christmas legacy of *A Christmas Carol* is the Victorian sentimentalism that pervades the tale. Home is one important focus of this sentiment (Van de Wetering 1984). Scrooge mocks

the desire of his nephew and Bob Cratchit for home and family and offers that the poor and orphans can be housed in jails. Scrooge's cold heart is melted by scenes of his childhood and lost love. There is both a nostalgia for the past here and a longing for a mythical golden age of childhood (Belk 1988). Besides children and home, Victorian Christmas cards are crowded with animals and plants in another nostalgic focus on nature, pets, and such reminders of Spring as greenery and birds (e.g., Holder and Harding 1981). Nostalgic sentiment is also wrung out of the tale by Dickens in making Tiny Tim crippled. Walder (1981) suggests that this most emotional pivot of the *A Christmas Carol* may be related to the Biblical story of Lazarus. It is also an anticipated nostalgia that is evoked by Marley's reflections on his life and Scrooge's view of Tiny Tim's death and of his own life as prompted by the ghost of Christmas future. While ghosts and haunting are decidedly non-Christian, *A Christmas Carol's* nostalgic emphasis on reviewing how one has lived, as well as the Edenic longing for a simpler past echo prominent religious themes.

Thus, with the exception of its treatments of money and spending, the Christmas celebration popularized by Dicken's secular Christmas tale is quite complimentary to religious values. The paradox of Christmas may accordingly be seen to lie not in religious versus secular opposition, but in the sacred and profane oppositions emphasized in the secular world of *A Christmas Carol*. Rather than ask how the Nativity and Saturnalia-like celebration can coexist during Christmas or how Christ and Santa can both be a part of Christmas, we should focus on the paradox of the coexistence of a Cratchit-like Christmas in a presumably Scrooge-like world. If there is a threat to the modern Christmas it lies more in this sacred-profane battle than in the prior conceptualizations of the paradox of Christmas as lying in its religious versus non-religious aspects.

But even this oversimplifies the issues involved in how we view Christmas, because the sacred in Dickens' tale could eventually be desacralized and Christmas still survive as long as something else is sacralized to replace these values. For the time being however, there is no compelling sacred replacement. Therefore, the following analysis is confined to examining the preservation or erosion of the sacred "Cratchitness" of the Modern American Christmas. Because materialistic themes of money and spending are the least compatible with religious treatments, these themes will be the focus of particular attention in the analysis. If Christmas is indeed the national festival of consumption (Boorstin 1973), the manner in which the Cratchit-like values of spending, lavishness, and hedonism are preserved without invoking the Scrooge-like values of selfishness, love of money, and avarice, is of particular interest.

## CHRISTMAS IN THE MASS MEDIA

The present study involves a two part analysis of various media treatments of Christmas. The first is a qualitative analysis of a broad array of American media since 1940. The second part of the analysis involves a quantitative content analysis of Christmas advertising and editorial content in one "woman's magazine" and of comic book treatments of Christmas during the same period. The latter analysis will look at historical trends more carefully, while the qualitative analyses will focus more on the meaning of Christmas according to various types of mass media treatments. By combining these two portions of the analysis a more complete understanding of trends in the modern U.S. Christmas should arise. The focus on mass media treatments assumes that these treatments both influence and reflect American attitudes toward Christmas. By dramatizing and portraying idealized images of Christmas, these popular treatments may show more about how we would like to see Christmas than do individual celebrations of the holiday. These analyses also avoid the problems inherent in trying to measure attitudes and values directly.

## A Qualitative Assessment of Recent American Media Treatments of Christmas

*1. Film.* One testimony to the influence of Dicken's *A Christmas Carol*, as noted above, is the many film versions of the story that have been produced. Starting with a 1908 silent movie version in Great Britain and a 1910 Thomas Edison version in the United States, numerous films and animated cartoons have preserved and promoted this classic Christmas Story. Although there are some variations on the original story in these productions (e.g., in the movie *Scrooged*, Bill Murray's Scrooge is a ruthless network TV executive whose network features Christmas films like *The Santa Slayer* and Christmas specials featuring scantily clad women- Garcia 1988), they are close enough to the original story that they do not require additional discussion.

Since 1940, two of the most popular films about Christmas have been essentially the same film: *Holiday Inn* (Sandrich 1942) and *White Christmas* (Curtiz 1954). Both were musicals about a New England inn (featuring the Irving Berlin song *White Christmas*) and both starred Bing Crosby (with Fred Astaire in *Holiday Inn* and with Danny Kaye in *White Christmas*). Using *White Christmas* as an example of this genre, the thin plot begins in World War II Europe in a U.S. Army division where the old General (Dean Jagger) is about to be replaced by a tough younger General. When the in-coming General orders a halt to a Christmas entertainment the division is staging, Dean Jagger saves the production by assuring that the new General gets lost. Ex-soldiers Bing Crosby and Danny Kaye team up and become popular entertainers after the war. They next encounter the retired General as the failing owner of a New England Inn whose pre-Christmas business has been devastated by a lack of snow. They save the Inn by arranging a gala Christmas production there and inviting all of the members of the Army division that the General used to command. In the process, Danny Kaye arranges a marriage between confirmed bachelor Bing Crosby and fellow entertainer Rosemary Clooney. To end this perfect Christmas, the snow begins to fall.

Despite the lack of a conventional family unit, one dominant theme in this movie is family. The Army division that returns "home" to dinner at the nostalgic old Inn is a "quasi-family" (Foote and Cottrell 1950, Benney, Weiss, Meyersohn, and Riesman 1959). In addition to Bing Crosby's settling down to marry and raise a family (Rosemary Clooney will, of course, drop out of show business), the General also lives with a quasi-family consisting of his doting housekeeper and his daughter. That the formerly mighty general needs the help of his soldiers also reflects Christmas role reversal. The theme of money-be-damned gift giving is also in evidence in the film. Soldiers converge from all over the East to create a surprise gift of their presence and help for their General (father figure) in need, Crosby and Kaye's company performs without charge, and another ex-soldier in the division donates time in his television show to make the announcement that brings the old division together again. Finally, the entire nostalgic scene is sacralized by the "cleansing" and miraculous arrival of a snowfall on Christmas eve. As is true of nearly all of the popular Christmas films, there is no mention of the Nativity, Christ, or religion in the film, although Santa Claus is given some recognition.

Santa Claus is given much more explicit attention in the film *Miracle on 34th Street* (Davies 1947). The story begins when Kris Kringle is expelled from a nursing home for insisting that he is Santa Claus. Rather than follow the nursing home doctor's advice of committing himself to a mental institution, he goes to New York City where he fills in for a drunken Santa in the Macy's Thanksgiving Day Parade. He is so popular that he is hired as the store Santa for the Christmas season and begins to refer customers to arch-rival Gimbels' stores for gifts they can't find at Macy's. Because of the good publicity Macy's allows this, and other stores begin to respond in kind in order to reap similar benefits. Kris Kringle befriends Susan Walker, the young daughter of practical divorcee and Macy's publicity woman Doris Walker. He begins to awaken Susan's belief in Santa Claus and fairies, much to the delight of the impractical attorney Fred Walker who is in love with Doris.

After an examination by the store psychologist, Kris again gets in trouble because of his insistence that Santa is real. To save him from being committed to an institution, Fred arranges a sanity hearing for Kris. The judge finds not only that Kris is sane, but declares him to be Santa Claus after the U.S. Post Office delivers letters addressed to Santa (from Susan as well as letters from numerous other children) to Kris in court. Santa disappears over Christmas eve, the zoo finds their reindeer lathered up the next day, and Fred and Doris declare their love and plan to marry so that Susan can have a normal childhood.

*Miracle on 34th Street* develops several significant themes in the modern American Christmas. It provides miracles that prove Santa's existence to faithful children despite a doubting world of adults. Through the marriage of Fred and Doris it restores the sanctity of the family. And, as Barnett (1954) notes, it provides a rapprochement between the commercial world of shopping, competition, and department stores on one hand and the "Christmas spirit" of goodwill, generosity, altruism, and giving on the other. In fact, the story gains its dramatic impact through the triumph of the latter virtues in the improbable settings of the business world, psychiatry, and the courts. In addition, the story suggests another parallel to Biblical stories of Christ in the restoration of Santa's faith in humans through the faith of a few, in this case children (of God perhaps, but also of doubting parents).

One additional recent and popular film treatment of Santa is *Santa Claus the Movie* (Vinge 1985). This story provides a more complete legend of Santa Claus, with some parallels to the stories of Baum (1986). It begins in "the middle ages" when woodcutter Claus and his wife Anya, who love children but are childless, start out on their reindeer drawn sleigh to deliver the toys Claus has carved to his nephews for Christmas. On the way they encounter a terrible snow storm and fall asleep as the snow drifts around them. They awake at the North Pole in the care of the elf-like vendequm who "love children because they are small like them." These elves explain that they are now immortal and that Claus will now be called Santa Claus and fulfill the prophecy of "their venerable Ancient One" by delivering their gifts of the toys they make to all the children of the world.

All goes well until one overly eager elf, Patch (Dudley Moore) convinces Santa to use his modern automated assembly line in place of "making toys in the classic tradition of Santa Claus' own exquisite hand-crafted, hand-painted creations." Unknown to anyone until after Santa delivers the toys that year, they are all defective and serve to disillusion their child recipients. Santa is disgraced and Patch is so shamed that he goes to earth in an effort to redeem himself in Santa's eyes. There he meets a greedy toy manufacturer (John Lithgow) whose dolls have just been investigated by a Senate subcommittee because they have highly flammable clothes and are stuffed with nails and glass shards in an effort to cut costs and earn more profits, despite the danger to children. Knowing only that he is a big toy maker, Patch volunteers his services to design something that they can give to children next Christmas. Seeing this as a way to restore his company's reputation after the Senate hearings, Lithgow agrees and Patch uses some magic stardust he brought from the North Pole to make suckers that allow children to momentarily fly like Santa's reindeer. When the suckers are distributed (by Patch's high tech "Patchmobile") and prove highly popular, Lithgow talks Patch into making even more powerful magic candy canes that they can sell for hundreds of dollars for a March 25th celebration that he dubs "Christmas II".

In the mean time, Santa has befriended a poor orphan boy, Joe, and his rich girlfriend Cornelia, who turns out to be the ward of the greedy toy Czar played by Lithgow. When Joe gets ill on the streets, Cornelia secretly takes him into her house where he discovers Lithgow's plans. He and Cornelia warn Santa Claus who comes to earth to save Patch from the load of explosive candycanes he is carrying in the Patchmobile. The evil toy manufacturer is driven into exile by the police, Santa is vindicated in the eyes of children, Patch returns to the North Pole, and Santa

and Anya adopt Joe and Cornelia as the children they have always wanted but never had.

Besides providing a more complete and sacralizing legend of Santa Claus, Christ-like parallels can be seen in this Santa's resurrection, miracles, humanness, trials, caring, and ultimate triumph. Here it is children who lose faith and ultimately have it restored. Again the themes of the poor and orphans are used to produce sentiment and pity. In *Santa Claus The Movie* however, the themes of love of money versus love of people and avarice versus altruism are emphasized by pitting the selfless Santa against the greedy manufacturer. Not only is profit condemned more harshly than in *Miracle on 34th Street*, inhuman mechanical manufacturing is condemned in comparison to the more natural and human scale of Santa's hand-crafted toys.

The sacralization of Santa is carried even further in *One Magic Christmas* by Walt Disney Pictures (Barsos 1985). This film begins with a "Christmas angel," cast against type with Harry Dean Stanton, who is given the task of restoring the faith of a young mother who has lost "the Christmas spirit." She is the practical wife of an idealistic man who lost his job in June and dreams of opening a bike shop to sell the bikes that he now designs and builds in his basement. They have only $5000 left in the bank and when he wants to spend several hundred dollars on their children for the upcoming Christmas, she objects. Abby, the little girl in the family meets the Christmas angel as she goes to mail her letter to Santa. The angel asks her to give the letter to her mother to mail and the mother fails to do so, showing her lack of faith. She instead depresses her husband who goes for a walk around the block as she heads out on Christmas eve to work a double shift at the supermarket where she is a cashier.

The woman is later fired by her Scrooge-like boss and her husband is fatally wounded in a bank robbery attempt by a poor and desperate man who has been unable to sell his old car for $50 in order to afford Christmas presents for his son. In his escape attempt the man jumps in the father's car, drives off with Abby and her brother, is pursued by the police, and crashes off a bridge into the icy river. No one comes up, but the Christmas angel saves Abby and her brother who come home to learn that their father has died. With the help of the Christmas angel, Abby goes to the North Pole to visit Santa and implore him to bring her father back to life. Santa explains that he can't do that, but says that her mother can. He gives Abby a letter to Santa written by her mother when she was a little girl. When Abby returns and gives her mother the letter, her faith is restored and she goes out to mail Abby's letter to Santa. Just after she does so, she meets her husband who is returning from his walk around the block.

Having found the Christmas spirit and realized that it is not too late to change things, Abby's mother tells her boss she won't work on Christmas eve (and is not fired), buys a camp stove from the desperate poor man for $50, and tells her husband to take their last $5000 and open his bike shop. Her husband delivers a bike he made for "poor little Molly Monahan" who is quite grateful, he and a friend split the cost of renting a generator so they could light the town Christmas tree that the Town Council wouldn't pay to light, and Abby, her brother Cal, and her mother all see Santa from the attic of the grandparents' house on Christmas eve.

This highly sentimental story has carried the sacralization of Santa one step farther in providing him with the Christ-like power to raise the dead (there is a somewhat similar theme in the movie *Here Comes Santa Claus*- Giln 1984). Faith in Santa Claus, the angel (named Gideon), and the liminal non-linear time of the miracles in the film (Abby's travel to the North Pole, the father's resurrection, Santa's journey around the world) all reinforce this sacralization. At the same time, the Nativity, religion, and churches are absent in the film. This is clearly a secular sacredness. The non-utilitarian values of the idealistic and altruistic father win over the practical and unfeeling values initially held by the mother. The family, the poor, and children all triumph as well. And the mother's second chance after having seen the future echo Scrooge's reformation after his trip with the ghost of Christmas future.

One final genre of Christmas film that has emerged in the past several years should be recognized-the Christmas slasher film. This category is typified by *Silent Night Deadly Night* (Sellier 1984) and *Silent Night Deadly Night, Part II* (Sellier 1985). The first of these two films begins with mom, dad, their five-year old son, and an infant brother headed in the car to visit grandpa in a mental asylum on Christmas Eve day. The seemingly silent grandfather gets the five-year old aside and tells him that he had better run for his life when he sees Santa if he hasn't been good all year. The boy, little Billy, tells his parents that he is afraid of Santa Claus, but they try to reassure him. As they head home in the car, a man in a Santa Claus suit holds up a convenience store and shoots the clerk. As he counts the money he observes, "Thirty-one dollars! Merry fucking Christmas!" His car then breaks down and he flags down the family. Seeing Santa Claus they stop the car. The robber shoots and kills the father and rapes the mother before slashing her throat. Little Billy observes all of this from the bushes where he hides in terror, thinking that this must be his fault because he wasn't good enough.

We next see little Billy three years later in an orphanage run by nuns and a stern Mother Superior. There is some evidence that he is disturbed by Christmas when his Christmas drawings show a reindeer with its head cut off and Santa Claus with knives in his back. Nevertheless, the Mother Superior makes the reluctant child sit in Santa's lap, presumably traumatizing him further. Ten years later Billy gets a job at a toy store during the Christmas shopping season. He is forced to play the store Santa when the regular actor can't make it. In this role he tells children that they must be good or he'll have to punish them. At the store Christmas party he goes mad and begins a killing spree that brutally does away with seven people before he is shot by the police as he tries to axe-murder the Mother Superior in front of the Children at the orphanage. In *Silent Night Deadly*

*Night, Part II,* Billy's brother takes up where Billy left off and successfully kills the Mother Superior.

These films are a little different from *One Magic Christmas*. It is worth noting that they have been adamantly picketed when movie theatres have shown them. In fact the horror in the films achieves its impact by stark contrast to much that is sacred in Christmas. The Santa of goodwill, generosity, and love is turned into a vicious killer. Childlike credulity and faith is turned into terror. Religion is made an unwitting accomplice in bringing about this reversal. While role reversals are a part of Christmas, they involve gaiety rather than fear and never find Santa changing from good to evil. Similarly, while some authors have criticized the use of Santa Claus in coercing "good" behavior from children (Barnett 1954, Wolf 1964, Hagstrom 1966, Schwartz 1967), the American Santa merely threatens and never punishes or fails to reward (Belk 1987). It appears therefore that the slasher genre of Christmas film is more instructive in emphasizing what Christmas is not than what it is. At most, they represent a reaction against Christmas that so far has little public support. A more accepted ploy is to use the emotions of Christmas to make heinous crimes seem even more heinous, as in the remake of D.O.A. (Jankel and Morton 1988, McGuigan 1988). In this film the disruption of Christmas by murder is made even more impactful by having a toy Ferris wheel gift be the murder weapon and by having the dying wife fall against her husband so that they both crash into and topple the Christmas tree that has been the symbol of their happiness and family life. Similarly, in the movie *Less than Zero* (Ellis 1985, Kanierska 1987), expectations of a traditional Christmas with family are glaringly opposed by a Christmas featuring yuppie dance clubs, drug addiction, divorce, family rejection, homosexuality, and forced prostitution, all set against the sun, convertibles, and fake snow of Southern California.

*2. Television.* While a part of Christmas television fare consists of showing classic Christmas movies, there are several more unique aspects to Christmas on American television, including Christmas variety "specials," television commercials, made-for-television Christmas movies, animated cartoons, and Christmas episodes on regular television series. The first two of these television categories have recently been insightfully reviewed by Thompson (1988). His review finds that television Christmas specials usually represent a return to a home town (e.g., Ann Murray's Nova Scotia Christmas), ancestral roots (e.g., Johnny Cash's Christmas in Scotland), a symbolic home (e.g., Christmas in Washington- at the White House), a religious homeland (e.g., Perry Como's Christmas in the Holyland), or a symbolic family (e.g., the NBC Family Christmas). All involve a nostalgic view of family and home. In these shows there are four major ways, Thompson (1988) concludes, in which the Christian nature of Christmas is handled while trying to appeal to as broad an audience as possible. One is to ignore the problem and flaunt the religious aspects of Christmas (although this is an unusual strategy when even the title Christmas is often avoided by calling the shows "holiday specials"). A second strategy might be thought of as patronizing (e.g., inserting phrases such as "our Jewish friends") or granting religions equal time by recognizing Jewish and Muslim traditions as well as Christian ones. A third strategy is to couch Christian religious messages in ambiguous enough terms that they need not be identified as such (e.g., Ann Murray's "He Needed Me" song recast as ambiguously quasi-religious rather than romantic). A final strategy involves "paganizing" the presentation by concentrating on secular symbols such as Santa, Frosty, and Rudolf, instead of the religious Christ child.

Thompson's (1988) evaluation concludes that both the Christmas specials and the television commercials embedded in them invoke a common set of Christmas icons including children, orphanages, carols, gifts, wreaths, the hearth, trees, and Santas. They do this, he suggests, in order to create a buying mood by playing upon the audience's guilt. Several of the commercials by Hallmark and American Greeting Cards indeed seem similar to the Disney film *One Magic Christmas*, except that they culminate in an appeal to channel the emotions evoked into the purchase of Christmas cards. In both the television specials and commercials, "consecrating consumer culture" (Thompson 1988) seems an apt description of this effect.

Made-for-television movies also drip with nostalgia and themes of home and family. Prototypical examples of such movies are *The Homecoming- A Christmas Story* (Cook 1971- the pilot for *The Waltons* and adapted from Earl Hamner, Jr.'s novel, *Spencer's Mountain*), *The Gathering* (Kleiser 1977), and *A Christmas to Remember* (Englund 1978). Both *The Homecoming* and *A Christmas to Remember* celebrate the Dickensian pleasures of Christmas joy amid the poverty of rural Depression era America. *Home for the Holidays* (Moxey 1972) offers a bit of a twist because one of the four adult sisters who return to their father and his second wife at the farm where they grew up is a mysterious pitchfork-wielding homicidal maniac. By challenging the love and safety of the family and the joy and peace of Christmas, this television drama also acts to reinforce the sanctity of these values. And like Scrooge in *A Christmas Carol* the presence of a villain (or a disaster- e.g., *Christmas Miracle in Caulfield*, Taylor 1977) dramatizes the forces of good and evil in order to make the moral message clearer and stronger. Television movies have also helped to sacralize Santa as in the television remake of *Miracle on 34th Street* (Cook 1973) and in *The Christmas Star* (Shapiro 1986) in which a con man (Ed Asner) is transformed when children begin to believe that he is the real Santa.

The latter plot is echoed to some degree in one of the animated Christmas movies, *Ziggy's Gift* (Williams 1982). In this story the kind-hearted Ziggy inadvertently solicits money as a street corner Santa for a scam that keeps the money. The story shows that Christmas kindness extends to animals as well as people when Ziggy buys $175 worth of still living Christmas turkeys and releases them. He also rescues a stray dog and cat and uses his Santa outfit to cover a street person sleeping on the cold street. A policeman arrests both Ziggy and a pickpocket, thinking that they are both a part of the fraudulent Santa scam. But they stumble into a foster home full of orphans and wind up caroling and playing Santa for the orphans. Ziggy gives them a Christmas tree he had bought as well as the dog and cat that he rescued. The pickpocket's bag of loot magically changes into toys for the children. Seeing Ziggy's generosity, the policeman lets him go. Once again, belief in a sacred Santa (by the children) brings about love and generosity that provides hope for the hopeless, homeless, and poor.

The theme of Christmas love, Santa, and bringing Christmas to animals as well as humans is also evident in animated Christmas movies such as *Santa and the Three Bears* (Benedict 1969) and *The Bear Who Slept Through Christmas* (Sed-Bar and Depattie-Freldon 1983). The dog Snoopy also participates in Christmas in Charles Schultz' *A Charlie Brown Christmas* (Melandez 1965), except that here Snoopy joins most of the humans in this animated cartoon in exhibiting greed and excessive commercialism. Snoopy garishly decorates his dog house in order to win a light and display contest. Charlie Brown's sister Sally has a long list of gifts she desires but says that money (tens and twenties) is o.k. as well. And Lucy says she gets depressed at Christmas because she never gets what she wants (real estate). Only Linus, who reminds Charlie Brown of the religious origins of Christmas, and Charlie Brown, who buys a scrubby- looking small Christmas tree that others ridicule, exhibit the "true Christmas spirit". At the conclusion of the cartoon, the others get the spirit as well and show it by helping to decorate and invigorate the formerly lonesome and unimportant little tree. The Christmas miracles, role reversals, and triumph of brotherhood over selfishness are all here including some Christian religion in small doses.

More commonly, such religious messages are only evoked symbolically in a transformed way that aims at a broader audience than Christians seeking a Christmas focused on Christ. A prime example analyzed by Burns (1976) is the animated cartoon version of Theodor Seuss Geisel's *How the Grinch Stole Christmas*. The story, told in Seussian poetry by narrator Boris Karloff, involves an old hermit of the Who species who lives with his dog Max in a cave above the community of Whoville. Hating the joyous feasting and song of Christmas in the community below, he conspires to steal Christmas by dressing as Santa and removing the decorations, presents, and feast food from the homes of the Whos. Having done so, instead of the wailing he expects, he hears the same joyous singing down in Whoville. From this he learns that "Christmas does not come from a store," that "it must mean something more," and his heart "grows two sizes" as he comes to these realizations. Thus reformed, he returns the stolen symbols to the Whos and is seated at the head of the feast table and asked to carve the roast beast.

Burns (1976) observes that this tale successfully combines the story of Scrooge (as Grinch) and the legend of Santa Claus. It also contrasts the view that Christmas is material and comes from stores with the view that it is "something more". The something more is never explicitly defined as spiritual or Christian, but it retains the same characteristics of humanitarianism, fellowship, goodwill toward men, "the Christmas spirit," and brotherhood that are shared by both religious and secular celebrations of the modern Christmas. Burns (1976) also notes that Whoville is a world of innocent children and it is this world to which the Grinch ultimately succumbs, sealing the victory of young over old.

Regular television series sometimes do not have to prepare Christmas episodes because they are preempted by Christmas specials. In some cases they also choose to ignore the holiday. But in most instances of non-preempted shows, there is some incorporation of Christmas into the plots of one or two episodes. Conventions include visits to orphans (e.g., "Hill Street Blues"), non-family cast as one big happy family at Christmas (e.g., "Golden Girls"), magical cessation of wartime hostilities (e.g., "M.A.S.H."), problems in gift selection and gift-giving (e.g., "Moonlighting"), and family feasting (e.g., "Cosby Show"). While actors in these shows do not step far out of their characters in the series, there is in each case a recognition of Christmas as a special time, set apart form standard series fare.

Together with the showing of Christmas movies (both classics and made-for-TV varieties), Christmas advertising, Christmas specials, and animated cartoon Christmas shows, series deference to Christmas helps to make it virtually impossible that an American could watch network, local, or major cable television without becoming acutely aware of the Christmas season, now defined as occupying the high shopping season of Thanksgiving through Christmas day. In fact for some, these television celebrations of Christmas are no doubt a significant part of their Christmas celebrations. Television specials in particular draw large audiences (30+ shares are not unusual) and the familiar faces and performances of such actors as Andy Williams, John Denver, and Bing Crosby can perhaps be thought of as a quasi-family for more avid or isolated viewers.

*3. Magazines.* Since the demise of American popular weekly magazines like *Look, Life, Saturday Evening Post,* and *Colliers,* the American magazine market has fractionated into ever more special interest publications. In many of these, but not all, there is Christmas editorial material, Christmas cartoons, and Christmas advertising. Because of the enormity of this material, a full analysis of its Christmas content will have to await further work. However, the quantitative portion of this paper will systematically review Christmas editorial material and advertising in *Ladies' Home Journal.* Thanks to an analysis of Christmas issues of *Playboy* by Hall (1984) it is possible at present to make some observations about this surprising Christmas phenomena and to make a few other observations about Christmas magazines.

Hall (1984) notes what might seem a curious event at Christmas, the abnormally high sales of December and January Christmas issues of *Playboy* and *Penthouse* magazines. He interprets this phenomenon to the playful (a la Huizinga 1955) suspension of rules and convention that has characterized the holiday since Saturnalia celebrations and the Lords of Misrule. But another interpretation more in keeping with the Dickensian Christmas is that the values celebrated by *Playboy* are simply another manifestation of the same hedonistic values that characterize other aspects of the Christmas celebration, including overspending on gifts, over-indulging on Christmas foods and beverages, and enjoying the shower of material gifts that we feel too guilty to buy for ourselves (Marketing News, 1981).

The additional element of indulgence promoted in *Playboy* is sexual. Hall (1984) finds that this sexual license is most in evidence in the cartoons of the magazine. The majority of the Christmas issue cartoons have a Christmas or New Year focus and Hall detects three major themes. The first is the office party and typically involves a male boss who seduces a female employee, showing the transforming (i.e., magical) power of money and commoditizing sex. A second type of *Playboy* Christmas cartoon focuses on the "gift" of sexual intercourse by an attractive young woman who may be rewarding anyone from a doorman to a sugar daddy. This too commoditizes sex and removes it from the realm of family. The third type of Christmas cartoon found by Hall (1984) violates another sacred Christmas icon, Santa Claus. These cartoons typically portray him as a dirty old man or show him out of character by taking advantage of his special powers to gain entry to the normally closed home and family circle.

While Hall's (1984) interpretation of these cartoons as turning convention on its head has some appeal, the present interpretation is slightly different. Rather than going against the normal conceptualization of Christmas, such cartoons are merely emphasizing a different (sexual) set of self-indulgent rewards at Christmas. While the material rewards of gifts may appeal most to children, and the non-durable rewards of an abundant Christmas meal may appeal most to the poor, the set of rewards that *Playboy* suggests have the greatest appeal to men are those of sexual fantasy. All of these indulgences are manifestations of Campbell's (1987) contention that consumer culture emphasizes hedonism over utilitarianism.

On the other hand, the social rewards of family and of maintaining interpersonal ties have been suggested to appeal most to women (e.g., Caplow, Bahr, Hill, and Williamson 1982). If so, we should expect to find very different editorial material, cartoons, and advertising appeals in "women's" magazines. A test of this expectation must await further work, but it does appear likely that emphasis on food, decorating, and family tradition are more likely to appear in these magazines than in "men's" magazines.

The contribution of magazine advertising to the acceptance of consumer hedonism at Christmas is also illustrated in a specially prepared advertisement from a recent issue of *Harpers*. The Martin Agency was one of several advertising agencies asked to prepare an advertisement for one of the seven deadly sins. They drew avarice and prepared an ad showing Santa in a business suit reading children's letters to him at the North Pole. The headline says "The worlds foremost authority speaks out on the subject of greed." The body copy reads:

> Do you remember all of the things you told me you wanted as a child? Well, your list may have changed, but I'll bet it hasn't gotten any shorter. Perhaps you shouldn't be worried about that. Greed has always motivated men and women. It has motivated inventors to make better mousetraps, artists to create greater art and scientists to find cures for diseases and pathways to the moon. Just be sure to use your greed to good ends. Be greedy for knowledge. Be Greedy for the kind of success that helps you, your family and your friends. Be greedy for love. Just don't be greedy in ways that hurt others. Remember, I'll always be the first one to know if you've been bad or good. So be good for goodness sake.

Although we might expect that those lists that haven't gotten any shorter are for somewhat more material and less altruistic things than the rationalizing illustrations in the copy, the ad shows a very contemporary attempt to reduce guilt over the acquisitive greed that pervades the modern Christmas.

This is not to suggest that Santa can be used for any end. When the December 15, 1986 issue of *Maclean's* came out in Canada showing Santa on the cover with his coat off, displaying a camouflage t-shirt he wears underneath, and holding what appears to be a modern machine gun, there was an uproar throughout Canada. While the cover story pointed to the controversy involving war toys, readers complained that, in effect, the cover had gone too far and had profaned the sacred Santa figure. Indeed Christmas is to be a time of peace on earth, good will toward men and Christmas fact and legend discusses impromptu cease-fires and even exchanges of gifts between warring soldiers. The same sort of backlash that greeted the Christmas slasher movies warns that Santa is a major deity in the modern Christmas and that there is a core of Christmas values which cannot be subverted. Apparently materialism is one thing, but violence is quite another.

*4. Short Stories and Novels.* Perhaps because they can serve narrower and more diverse audiences, Christmas stories and books cover a broader range of types than the other media considered here. Three major types of stories can be recognized: traditional, cynical, and counter-stories (e.g., crime, horror, science fiction). The traditional category is aimed partly, but not wholly, at a child audience, while the latter categories seem to aim more at adults.

Traditional stories surely include those of Dickens (*A Christmas Carol* was only one of his annual tales) and O'Henry's "Gift of the Magi", as well as numerous stories that are variants of these tales. One of the things that makes these tales traditional is that they do not stray far from the Christmas values summarized in *A Christmas Carol*. They also tend to employ traditional Christmas symbols and describe warm scenes of family Christmas, joy, peace, generosity, snow, and nostalgia. They are often set in the past. In order to evoke more sentiment and emotion they also often involve the poor, the outcast, children, or Christmas tragedy. For example, although originating from a National Public Radio broadcast, "James Lundeen's Christmas" (Keillor 1983) tells the story of the Christmas past in small town Minnesota when James' father fell from a ladder in late November and returned to his family from the hospital just two days before Christmas. Mother has told James and his brother that Christmas will be sparse this year, but James keeps hoping for a Lionel train set and hopes that "some rich person" will read about their plight in the paper and get it for him. At the same time he has feared that his father may never come home and that he and his brother might then be adopted (but perhaps by a rich man with a train set in his basement). James is embarrassed and hides a shoe box at church with a slit for donations on top and "Lundeen Family Christmas" written on the side. They do have a small Christmas celebration and he gets boots and a knife, but realizes that his father's being home is the real present. He walks out across frozen Lake Woebegon and notes in looking back at his small house and the town that it looks like a big train set. He realizes that everything that Christmas is about "is contained in that house and its people."

Another example of a traditional story is Bess Aldrich's (1949) "Another Brought Gifts." In this story old Jed Miller is recalled. He was the small town Santa for years and gave children quarters telling them to live upright lives, do good in the world with the quarters, and bring happiness to other little children at Christmas when they got older. One Christmas he was old and sick in bed and almost didn't show up at the church play where he dispensed his quarters to the children. But he dragged himself out of bed and donned his Santa outfit one more time. When the church curtains caught fire after he had given out his money, he grabbed them and ran outside with them, saving the church full of people, but losing his life.

A final example of traditional Christmas stories is from a children's book, *Lucy's Christmas* (Molloy 1950). When the Maine house where Lucy lives with her parents and three siblings burns down, the family goes off to live in the woods where the father works as a logger in order to save money for a new house. In the fall they spend Sundays cutting Christmas trees and hauling them to the train depot where they are sent off to be sold. Lucy secretly puts a birch bark note in one of the trees explaining the family's situation, giving an address, and asking whoever finds it if they might send her brothers a Christmas present if they have something extra. The note falls off at the station, but the stationmaster finds it and rallies the town to build them a new house which is completed just in time to present to Lucy's family as a Christmas surprise, complete with a tree and presents.

These traditional stories with their clearly articulated values and Dickensian tone, can be contrasted to a more contemporary type of story showing at least some degree of cynicism toward Christmas. For instance, in John Updike's (1981) "Transaction," a man who is Christmas shopping while at an out-of-town conference, gets drunk and picks up a prostitute and buys a few hours of her time. After an awkward sexual encounter in his hotel room he awakes to find the condom he used and notes "...in the morning found it dry as a husk, where he had set it, on the bureau among the other Christmas presents." While there is greater pathos and sadness here than in the *Playboy* Christmas issues, the same hedonistic message underlies the cynicism.

Another cynical tale is Stephen Dixton's (1985), "A Christmas Story." The story presents a street person's view of spending Christmas hustling handouts. People give him money, but when he finishes collecting it on Christmas eve the flophouses are full and it is freezing out. He finds no one will let him stay in the basement or corridor of their house or apartment building and risks going down into the subway. There he is rolled for his $5 and some young punks try to set him on fire. The next day he goes back to begging and offering hollow reciprocal "merry Christmas" wishes to his donors. This story is perhaps a cynical version of "The Little Matchstick Girl." It lacks the uplifting ending of most traditional Christmas stories but carries a traditional Christmas message nevertheless: keep Christmas in the heart (i.e., sincerely care for other people) rather than just in the pocketbook.

A final example of a cynical Christmas tale is Helen Norris' (1985) "The Christmas Wife." It involves a man whose wife died several years ago, who decides that rather than spend the $600 it would take to fly to spend Christmas with his son in Los Angeles, he will hire a woman to be with him over the Christmas weekend. He hires a woman through a rundown agency and arranges for them to spend the weekend at a cabin he designed (he is a retired architect) as a summer home for a friend. He gives her some gifts he brought (a robe, a music box, and a figurine) and opens some gifts he had wrapped for himself in order not to embarrass her if she had not brought anything for him, although she did bring him a pound cake. She has a slight cold over the weekend, but they get along comfortably. While the weekend involves no sexual advances, he is attracted to her and asks if he may see her again. He can't because she is the wife of the owner of the rundown agency which provided her. The agency is desperate and the offer of $600 for the weekend is too good for them to pass up. While this story also has a cynical tone, it too emphasizes many of the traditional values of Christmas. Christmas is about family and this is not something that can be acquired as a commodity on the market. Nevertheless, the story involves such Christmas rituals and icons as gift-giving, the fire in the hearth, poverty, and a retreat to a simple life in the country.

If we are to find a complete renunciation of Dickensian Christmas values, perhaps it is in the third genre identified, the counter-stories of crime, horror and science fiction. Some sample titles here are *The Twelve Frights of Christmas* (Asimov, Waugh, and Greenberg 1986), *The Twelve Crimes of Christmas* (Waugh, Greenberg, and Asimov 1985), *A Carol in the Dark* (Jordan 1984), *The Twelve Deaths of Christmas* (Babson 1979), and *Murder for Christmas* (Godfrey 1982). In *A Carol in the Dark* (Jordan 1984) on the campus of Crosscreek University in a small South Dakota town a faculty member and later a student (at a faculty Christmas party) are mysteriously murdered shortly before Christmas. The murders coincide with a treasure hunt for a 40-year-old missing fortune. The plot leads to the Society of Perfect Strangers, a secret organization that only meets once a year for Christmas dinner in anonymous New York City, hunts treasures, and is composed of members who are supposed to know one another only by pseudonyms. The crime is solved (it was committed by the greedy head of the English Department) and the treasure found (in jewels hidden in the stained glass skylight of a Victorian house once owned by the an early founder of the town who died leaving hints that some of his fortune remained hidden). The hero also discovers a smaller crime of embezzlement by the treasurer of the Society of Perfect Strangers who promises to amend her ways.

The violence of the murders and the non-familial Christmas meetings of strangers seem superficially antithetical to Christmas here. Yet even in this tale traditional Christmas values are reinforced. It is nostalgically set in a small town with Victorian houses and links to prior history. The Society of Perfect Strangers' members are not really such strangers and act as a pseudo-family in their very familial Christmas feast to which they return (from all over the world) each year, just as true families are to do on Christmas. The faculty at the small college is also a pseudo-family and the town is small enough that they are in some senses a big happy family as well. (A similar pseudo-family is found in the boarding house residents of Babson's [1979] *Twelve Deaths of Christmas*.) Parties, meals, and acts of friendship also help the characters in the story, and the murders serve as shocking counter-points that emphasize the value of these rituals.

A second example in this counter-story genre is the science fiction tale "Planet of Fakers" by McIntosh (1986). An earth colony on a distant planet is not the only life on the planet as the colonists initially suppose. One day a man appears outside their protective dome and is invited in. He quickly learns their language and his lifeform begins to invade and take over the bodies of the colonists one at a time. They are killed when they are discovered, but this is difficult because anything that one of them knows instantly becomes knowledge of all of the others whom the life form has taken over. A group in the colony devotes its time to testing everyone in the community to detect the invaders. Because pencils were known only in the childhood of the colonists, giving each person an unsharpened pencil and asking what it is for works as a screening test for a while although since the wrong answers that result in the death of each invader detected are instantly known to the others, the test has a limited period of reliability. The squad charged with detecting the invaders is asked to come up with an infallible test so that they can return to earth in their space craft making sure that none of the invaders is aboard. They are able to do so by questioning each colonist about what used to happen on December 25th, what associations they have with red and white, what are pseudonyms for Santa Claus, and so on through the symbols of Christmas.

In this story it is especially significant that the colonists who have been unable to celebrate Christmas are saved by their knowledge of this nostalgic holiday. The test makes their survival dependent upon their intimate familiarity with the details of Christmas rituals on earth and the evil lifeforms are precluded from truly imitating humanity by their inability to learn these details of Christmas. Thus the return "home" of the space colonists is safeguarded by familiarity with the one set of symbols most clearly associated with home and family.

A final counter-story of Christmas is Robert Bloch's (1986), "The Night Before Christmas." Far from Clement Moore's poem, this story involves a wealthy man who commissions an artist to paint a portrait of his beautiful young wife, to be done in time for Christmas. The artist becomes sexually involved with his subject and the wealthy husband eventually learns of their affair. Just before Christmas when the portrait has been completed the artist comes to call and asks where his subject is. The patron responds that she is in the living room decorating the Christmas tree. In a sense this is true, for he has chopped up her body and hung her various body parts on the Christmas tree.

Although this macabre story certainly violates the peace and brotherhood theme of Christmas, in other ways it too supports traditional Christmas values. Gift-giving (including sexual favors), Christmas decoration, and penalty for violation of the sanctity of the family are all here. Similarly, the power of wealth is emphasized when the wealthy patron gets his final revenge. Here too, violation of the precepts of Christmas works to emphasize the strength of Christmas tradition rather than to undermine it.

*5. Comics and Comic Books.* Some of the most hedonistic, commercial, and anxious portrayals of Christmas appear in the syndicated cartoons carried by U.S. Newspapers. Some examples include:

A *New York Tribune* cartoon of 1946 shows a middle aged man telling a Santa sitting behind a sign reading "For Grown-ups only", "I wanna shiny New Eight Cylinder Convertible Coupe an' a Radio with Television reception an' a new garden tractor an' some rubber boots and' an out-board motor an'-[his wife interrupts] And I want an electric dishwasher and a new fur coat and...etc."

In a 1987 Bloom County strip in which a young girl sues Santa Claus for distributing war toys, the elf defending Santa tells the girl's attorney, "Please advise your client that unless she halts her spurious suit against my client, he'll have little recourse but to leave dead spiders in her stocking next year."

A 1985 The Family Circus cartoon (by Bill Keane) shows the four children playing with their toys in front of the Christmas tree and one announces "This is our best Christmas ever! Not a drop of clothes so far."

A 1986 Cathy comic strip (by Cathy Guisewite) has the following dialogue between Cathy and her friend Andrea-

A: Aren't you going to do all your Christmas shopping by catalogue this year Cathy?
C: No.
A: It's so Efficient!
C: Andrea, Don't you think you're missing the whole point?...the whole magical experience of going out shopping for your loved ones??!
A: Why? Because I can't touch the gifts I pick out for People?
C: You Can't try on any Clothes.

A 1986 B.C. comic strip (by Johnny Hart) shows Thor composing the following Christmas poem:
'Tis now the season of Good Cheer,
Of Snowflakes, Love, and Fun,
A Time when Distant Friends Draw Near
And Hearts Become as One.
A Time When Reason Conquers Fear,
And Noble Loving Deeds,
In Forms of Gifts Exchanged, 'Sincere'
...Fulfill Each Other's 'Greeds'.

Similarly, a 1985 Garfield cartoon (by Jim Davis) begins with Garfield's master saying "Merry Christmas Garfield! Open Your Presents, Buddy. What's the Holdup?" Garfield's thought bubbles read the response: "I'm just savoring the moment. This is my favorite morning of the whole year. All our differences are set aside and all the love we feel for one another is wrapped up in the gifts we have made with care. I love Christmas." He then leaps eagerly at the presents thinking "Enough of Sentiment. *Gimme!*"

A 1987 Dennis the Menace cartoon (by Hank Ketcham) shows Dennis asking his father, "Does the Christmas Spirit mean you've got the money to buy presents?"

A 1983 Miss Peach cartoon (by Mell Lazarus) shows the little Foster girl counselling a fellow student at the Kelly School Christmas Gifts Counselling Service:

FS: How does one go about getting Christmas gifts from people?
FG: By doing very nice things for them. In other words, obligate them shamelessly...

And a 1985 Bloom County cartoon (by Berke Breathed) shows the following Christmas morning dialogue between son and father:
S: A Record Player? [having just opened the gift]
F: Like it, son? It's State-of-the-art!
S: Actually, State-of-the-art would be compact audio discs...scratchless. Noiseless. Perfect sound reproduction.
F: Yeah? Well some of us subscribe to the theory that "obsolete" isn't always bad! So...You don't like your record player then?!
S: No, No! I lust for it. I'll just put it over here with my spiffy new slide rule.
F: Oo! You like that too, eh?

Perhaps because these cartoons must be so brief and their humor often confined to one-liners (the most vicious form of humor), they present the least flattering view of Christmas of any of the media reviewed here. The view they most commonly present is that of selfishness triumphing over brotherhood, thus emphasizing Scrooge-like values rather than Cratchit-like values. Nevertheless, the rituals of gift-giving, the sanctity of home and family, and the emphasis on hedonism and youth are all preserved. It is in fact the childlike flaw of greed that is perhaps most forgivable (especially among children and cartoon characters) at Christmas. It may also be noted that the Christmas of comics is almost entirely secular; religious themes are extremely rare. This is slightly less true of comic books, where stories have more room to unfold.

Because comic book Christmas stories are analyzed more completely in the quantitative section that follows, only an illustrative summary of some of these story lines will be given here. These examples will ignore the translations of familiar Christmas stories such as *A Christmas Carol*, "The Gift of the Magi," and *The Night Before Christmas* into comic book format.

"Donald Duck in A Christmas for Shacktown," (Walt Disney Productions 1951)- Donald Duck's nephews, Huey, Dewy, and Louie, plan to help Daisy Duck earn money for the poor children of Duckville's Shacktown. Uncle Scrooge McDuck (modeled on Dicken's Scrooge) pledges to match their contributions if they can earn $25. They do so, but Uncle Scrooge's money bin collapses into an underground cave due to its excessive weight. When the nephews find a way to retrieve the money, the grateful Uncle Scrooge gives them enough money to provide a really lavish Christmas for the kids of Shacktown. The money is used for toys for the children and is carried to Shacktown on a toy train that is

routed by crippled Joey's shack so that he too can share in the Christmas bounty.

"Betty and Veronica in Never Trust a Skinny Santa," (Archie Comic Publications, Inc. 1973)-Betty and Veronica rehabilitate a bum by fattening him up and getting him a job as a Santa at Veronica's uncle's department store. When the job ends at the end of the Christmas season, the rehabilitated man decides he wants to be a bum rather than trying to get another job. However, he can't do that because no one would give money to a fat bum. So he instead decides he will hang around (Veronica) Lodge's eating their food.

"The Land Behind the Sky-Holes," (May 1976)-Rudolf the Red-Nosed Reindeer finds a reverse land where Santa takes presents from children (by law) rather than giving them. Rudolf brings him to the real Santa Claus who sets him straight about Santa, Christmas, and giving.

"Frosty the Snowman and the Christmas Spirit," (Dell Publishing Company 1957)-Willy Penguin delivers Christmas trees in order to get a free one for his orphanage, but looses it in helping a little girl out of the water where the ice broke. She gives him and Frosty permission to take trees from the land of her selfish grandfather. The children at the orphanage sign cards thanking the grandfather who then reforms and invites them all for Christmas dinner.

"Santa's First Christmas Trip," (Dell Publishing Company 1941)- Santa was a clumsy woodsman and his brother Chris was the toy maker until an angel transforms Santa Claus so he can fix the toys that thieves had broken when he was taking them to children.

"Seasons Greetings," (Hall Syndicate, Inc. 1967)- Dennis the Menace, after asking Santa Claus for a bike, space helmet, tow truck, and sail boat, secretly uses his parents' credit card to shop for Christmas gifts for them. When he kiddingly says that he got them a diamond necklace and a solid gold fountain pen, they nearly faint.

"A Noggin at Mile End," (Warren Publishing Company 1977)- Santa's elf finds a poor deformed boy of 10 who is being kept as a sideshow freak with only a pair of pants to his name. He gives the boy a wish which he uses to turn himself into a handsome lad. The elf takes him to the North Pole to be a fellow elf and they run over his former greedy and selfish keeper with Santa's sleigh as they leave.

"Bugs Bunny," (Western Publishing and Lithography Company 1955)- Bugs Bunny works for Stingy Stengel's Department Store and when Stengel gets amnesia, Bugs convinces him he is Santa Claus. After Stengel gives the whole town presents and regains his memory, the town all loves him and he seems to enjoy it.

"Katy Keene's Christmas," (Lucas 1986)- Katy skates, skiis, parties, carols, shops, and gives out toys in a Santa outfit at an orphanage. She gets a modeling job for a charity fashion show and dates the owner. A rival hides her fashions, but gives them back after a ghost scares her into doing so. She tells Katy that she is good, kind, and has inner beauty.

"Oh What Fun to Laugh and Sing a Slaying Song Tonight!," (DC Comics, Inc. 1987)- An escaped convict shoots police and a Salvation Army Santa with whom he changes clothes. He runs to a blind girl's house who is waiting for Santa and robs the house. The real Santa arrives, restores the little girl's sight and runs over the convict with his sleigh.

As this set of examples suggests, the comic books about Christmas also seldom have a religious theme. They invoke secular Christmas legends of Rudolf the Red-nosed Reindeer, Frosty the Snowman, and Santa Claus to bring Christmas to children of all countries, to animals, and even to extra-terrestrials. Dorfman (1983) finds that de Brunhoff's Babar comic stories show Santa as a Western Imperialist. The comic books too give Santa Christ-like powers to heal and raise the dead, and also have a strong sense of justice and charity toward the poor and crippled. And they also show themes of hedonism, Christmas greed, and other Dickensian themes. Like the comic strips, they sometimes emphasize the dominance of Scrooge-like characteristics and sometimes emphasize Cratchit-like characteristics. A comparison of the relative frequencies of these themes is presented in the quantitative analysis of comic books.

6. *Other Media.* Other media will not be reviewed here, although they include Christmas plays, radio, music, Christmas cards, and other such art forms. These media are excluded primarily because they seem to offer less variation for the period since Barnett's (1954) Christmas work. Radio now serves primarily to broadcast music at Christmas, and the music has contributed few if any enduring additions to American Christmas music since the 1950s, despite many attempts to create new Christmas classics. Relatively few Christmas plays with new themes have not been presented in one of the other media reviewed above. And while Christmas cards might present a useful source of tracking changes in celebrations of Christmas, this too will have to await future analyses. While not mass media, Rook's (1985) archive of consumers' home movies and videos of Christmas is also worth further exploration. And another promising area for further exploration may be

Christmas home decoration with a spectrum ranging from the highly reserved decoration in Scarsdale, New York (Kirshenblatt-Gimblett 1983), to the co-ordinated decoration of homes on "Christmas Street" in Salt Lake City, Utah (Oxley, Haggard, Werner, and Altman 1986), and the Christmas decorating extremes of Rita (Pollay 1987) and Dolph (Kron 1983).

## A QUANTITATIVE ANALYSIS OF PRINT AD AND COMIC BOOK TREATMENTS OF CHRISTMAS

Two quantitative content analyses were conducted to examine potential changes in the frequency of materialistic Christmas themes over the past nearly 50 years. The first such analysis considered emphasis on Christmas and Santa Claus (argued above to be the secular god of materialism) in magazine advertising. Among American magazines the only one that has remained in the top ten in circulation since the 1940s is *Ladies' Home Journal* (See Belk and Pollay 1985). Therefore, ads of half a page or larger in the November and December issues of this magazine were chosen for investigation. The analysis of these ads was quite simple. They were coded for explicit mentions of Christmas (but not Thanksgiving or the ambiguous "holiday") or inclusions of Christmas iconography including wreaths, Christmas Trees, wrapped gifts, Santa Claus, and elves. The consideration of November issues was intended to detect any tendency over time to begin advertising earlier in an effort to stimulate earlier Christmas shopping. Every 5th year was sampled, with the total number of ads of a half page or larger ranging from 61 in December, 1982 to 169 in November, 1947.

Results were as follows in Table 1. Clearly there has not been a steady increase in Christmas emphasis in either November or December advertisements. Christmas emphasis peaked in the 1950s for both the November and December issues. The latest year's December advertisements show the highest frequency of Christmas ads since 1962, but there were still only about half as many Christmas ads (both absolute and relative) as were evident a decade earlier in 1952. Considering the percentage of the Christmas ads featuring Santa Claus, for the December issues Santa appeared in from 12.5% of the Christmas ads in 1972 to 37.5% of the Christmas ads in 1957, thus generally paralleling the results for the overall frequencies of Christmas ads over the period studied.

For the entire set of 853 December ads studied, 268 (31.4%) featured Christmas messages and 70 (8.2%) featured Santa Claus. A total of 3 ads featured any religious portrayal, and 2 of these ads were for bibles (the third was for encyclopedias and featured a photograph of a decorative three dimensional representation of 3 wise men). Taken as a whole and recognizing that it is more difficult and perhaps less useful for products that are unlikely to be used as gifts or as Christmas foods or beverages (e.g., soap, automobiles) to feature Christmas in their ads, these findings do suggest a strong emphasis on a material Christmas. However, there is no evidence to support a contention that we are increasingly commercializing

## TABLE 1

### PERCENTAGE OF ADS WITH A CHRISTMAS EMPHASIS

| YEAR | NOVEMBER ISSUE | DECEMBER ISSUE |
|------|----------------|----------------|
| 1942 | 1.0% | 19.8% |
| 1947 | 7.1 | 38.4 |
| 1952 | 9.8 | 50.6 |
| 1957 | 7.8 | 48.8 |
| 1962 | 7.1 | 29.1 |
| 1967 | 6.9 | 20.0 |
| 1972 | 7.3 | 16.5 |
| 1977 | 6.3 | 12.5 |
| 1982 | 2.7 | 19.7 |
| 1987 | 2.8 | 26.4 |

Christmas, at least not based on Christmas ads in *Ladies' Home Journal* since 1940.

Notably the percentage of December ads in *Ladies' Home Journal* featuring Christmas, is slightly *lower* than the percentage of articles featuring Christmas in these same issues (105 of 304 or 34.5%). This editorial content *does* suggest some tendency toward greater emphasis on Christmas with each of the four years considered in the 1970s and 1980s containing over 50% Christmas articles (whereas only 1962 did so in prior issues). Furthermore few of these Christmas articles (only 5.7%) were directly religious. The largest category of Christmas editorial material (36.1%) was fiction, with return to home, family, children, the past, and feasting the most common themes of this fiction. Christmas food was the next most popular focus in the Christmas articles (30.5%) followed by decorating (10.5%), gift-giving (8.6%), and fashions (7.6%). In each case, the focus was implicitly or explicitly on the family and on non-religious aspects of the Christmas celebration. Seldom is heard a discouraging word about Christmas in these pages and in the rare instances in which something negative is mentioned, it is apt to be consoling advice like: "Feel more frazzled than festive? Here is how to make the most of parties, keep peace in the family and give the best possible gifts" (December, 1987).

A check of the most recent Christmas issues of 12 other popular magazines suggests that it is the "home" magazines such as *Better Homes and Gardens*, *House Beautiful*, *McCall's*, *House and Garden*, and *Family Circle* that emphasize Christmas the most in editorial content, with an average of slightly over 50 percent of the editorial material featuring Christmas. Given the symbolic significance of home, family, and food in Christmas celebrations, this is understandable. It is also noteworthy that the major audience for each of these magazines is female. As Caplow (1982, 1984) found, it is women who do most of the gift selection, decorating, and food preparation for Christmas.

The comic books analyzed involved a set of 626 Christmas stories featured in Christmas issues of all popular comic book series since 1940. This included such diverse characters and series as Donald Duck, Bat Man, Betty and Veronica (Archie series), *Creepy*, Richie Rich, Rudolf the Red-Nosed Reindeer, Superman, Elvira, Frosty the Snowman, Bugs Bunny, Howard the Duck, *Santa Claus Funnies*, Dennis the Menace, Mickey Mouse, Fox and Crow, *A Christmas Treasury*, Alvin (The Chipmunks), *Christmas Parade*, Katy Keene, *Santa Claus Parade*, the Defenders, and *Xmas Comics*. Despite this diversity, none of these Christmas issues was published for the entire period studied (although Betty and Veronica Christmas specials have been published since the early 1950s and contributed approximately 45% of the stories analyzed and the Rudolf, Frosty, and Santa Claus series produced a large number of the 1950s stories analyzed).

Based on initial open-end coding of a sample of stories, 89 thematic categories were initially developed such as religion, generosity, charity, shopping, gluttony, drunkenness, seasonal decoration, peace, animosity, crowding, charity, depression, nostalgia/past times, and miserliness. A graduate student judge read and coded a sample of 100 stories for themes that were present and (in the case of multiple themes) for which, if any, theme was dominant (e.g. kindness triumphs over selfishness). The author coded these same stories and 94% agreement was obtained. This reliability was judged to be sufficiently high, so the author's coding was used for these and the remaining stories. Altogether 880 themes were coded for the 626 stories, or an average of 1.4 per story. After collapsing the themes coded into broader categories, the following overall results were obtained (Table 2).

It can be seen that overall, the sacred Christmas values of Cratchit-like themes dominate the profane Scrooge-like themes by almost 2 to 1. It can also be seen that the Christmas portrayed in Comic Books is a secular one, with only about 5 percent of the stories featuring religion (approximately the same percentage as was found in the editorial material of *Ladies' Home Journal*). In order to detect any apparent change in these tendencies over time, the 626 stories were

## TABLE 2

### THEMES IN OVERALL CHRISTMAS COMIC BOOK STORY SAMPLE

| THEMES | FREQUENCY (% OF 626 STORIES) |
|---|---|
| "Cratchit-Like Themes" | |
| Sacrifice/Generosity | 155 (24.8%) |
| Help/Altruism/Charity | 143 (22.8) |
| Tradition/Nostalgia/Homeade | 79 (12.6) |
| Goodwill/Hospitality/Love | 61 (9.8) |
| Faith/Magic/Christmas Spirit | 36 (5.7) |
| Religion | 33 (5.3) |
| Family/Children/Community/Feast | 28 (4.5) |
| Kindness/Good | 24 (3.8) |
| Thankfulness/Gratefulness | 17 (2.7) |
| TOTAL CRATCHIT-LIKE THEMES | 576 (92.0%) |
| | |
| "Scrooge-Like Themes" | |
| War/Crime/Belligerence | 95 (15.2%) |
| Commerce/Money/Competition/ Depression/Crowds/Profit | 64 (10.2) |
| Miserliness/Cynicism/Unfriendliness/ Ostentation/Anti-traditionalism | 55 (8.8) |
| Selfishness/Gluttony | 43 (6.9) |
| Materialism/Greed | 30 (4.8) |
| Ungratefulness | 17 (2.7) |
| TOTAL SCROOGE-LIKE THEMES | 304 (48.6%) |

classified according to whether they only emphasized sacred "Cratchit-like" Christmas values, only emphasized profane "Scrooge-like" Christmas values, or emphasized both. These results are shown by decade in Table 3.

With the exception of the 1940s when there were too few comic book Christmas stories for meaningful comparison, the relative frequencies of sacred and profane themes have remained quite stable over the remaining four decades. In no case does the frequency of only sacred ("Cratchit-like") themes drop below 50 percent and in no case does it exceed 60%. Whether or not this should be taken to imply a largely nostalgic (rather than cynical) image of Christmas, requires further discussion.

Consider three reasonably prototypical story lines that reflect the three categories above. A "Sacred Only ('Cratchit')" Christmas message is:

"The Greatest Christmas of All" (Warren Publishing Company 1977)- After giving out gifts from a bottomless sack, an old man freezes to death thinking about how the task literally fell to him when Santa's sack fell out of his sleigh on the very night his mother died of asthma while his drunken father laughed about it. Two boys find the bottomless sack now and they vow to continue the tradition of giving.

A "Profane Only ('Scrooge')" prototypical story is:

"Santa's Surprise" (Walt Disney Productions 1962)- The sons, daughters, nieces, and nephews of Mickey Mouse, Donald Duck, and the Big Bad Wolf all ask for small toys and Santa promises he will bring them. Seeing this, Uncle Scrooge dresses as a child and asks Santa for "Money, a factory, money, an airport, money, a plantation, money, stores, etc.".

And a story with both sacred and profane elements is:

"Betty and Veronica in Forgive and Forget" (Archie Comic Publications, Inc.)- Betty argues for the merits of giving and love at Christmas, while Veronica argues for the merits of getting and greed. Neither is convinced to change her mind.

While there are a few of the both sacred and profane stories in which the profane is merely played off against the sacred in order to dramatize the story (as with Scrooge versus the Cratchits in *A Christmas Carol*), in most of these stories the presence of both themes indicates an ambiguous message of what Christmas is about. In stories where the profane is dominant, the humor commonly derives from laughing at a side of Christmas and of ourselves that is socially unacceptable, but has a grain of truth to it. While we are ostensibly laughing at someone else, we may really be laughing at a side of ourselves that is

## TABLE 3

### DOMINANT COMIC BOOK CHRISTMAS STORY VALUE EMPHASIS

#### VALUE EMPHASIS

| DECADE | ONLY SACRED ("CRATCHIT") | BOTH | ONLY PROFANE ("SCROOGE") | TOTAL n |
|--------|--------------------------|------|--------------------------|---------|
| 1940s | 15 (88.2%) | 1 (5.9%) | 1 (5.9%) | 17 (100%) |
| 1950s | 115 (57.2) | 41 (20.4) | 45 (22.4) | 201 (100%) |
| 1960s | 46 (50.5) | 11 (12.1) | 34 (37.4) | 91 (100%) |
| 1970s | 103 (57.5) | 25 (14.0) | 51 (28.5) | 179 (100%) |
| 1980s | 81 (58.7) | 18 (13.0) | 39 (28.3) | 138 (100%) |
| TOTALS | 360 (57.5%) | 96 (15.3%) | 170 (27.2%) | 626 (100%) |

apparent enough to be recognized. Just as the stories combining sacred and profane treatments indicate our ambiguity about Christmas, the co-presence of stories where the sacred is dominant and where the profane is dominant suggests ambivalence as well.

### CONCLUSION

Most of the media treatments reviewed in this paper contribute to building and sustaining a mythology of Christmas as a time of love, family, generosity, charity, and other Cratchit-like values. However, the analysis of this myth also disclosed that while the modern American Christmas portrayed in the media is sacralized by these mythical themes and by its ritual consumption, it is also highly secular. If Christ is the hero of the traditional religious Christmas, Santa is the hero of the traditional secular Christmas. And Santa is a god of materialism and hedonism- of modern consumer culture. Still, most of the media seem comfortable with this modern Christmas and present it in a way that evokes almost exclusively warm and positive emotional reactions to their rendition of Christmas.

The two media in which our discomfort with this modern Christmas is most clearly presented are cartoons and comics. Perhaps this is because these media are least dependent on advertising revenues. Perhaps it is because they serve up their Christmases with a distracting humor. And perhaps, at least in the case of comic books, this is due to the fact that they are directed to children who are not yet called upon to buy, give, and retell the sustaining myths of Christmas. Whatever the explanation, it seems to have fallen to the simple and humorous cartoon format to tell us that there is something unsettling with the modern American Christmas. Perhaps we should take such cartoon messages seriously.

### REFERENCES

Aldrich, Bess S. (1949), "Another Brought Gifts," *Journey into Christmas and Other Stories*, New York: Appleton-Century Crofts, Lincoln, NE: University of Nebraska Press, 179-201.

Appadurai, Arjun (1986), ed., *The Social Life of Things: Commodities in Cultural Perspective*, Cambridge: Cambridge University Press.

Archie Comic Publications, Inc. (1973), "Betty and Veronica in Never Trust a Skinny Santa," *Archie Giant Series Magazine Presents Betty and Veronica Christmas Special*, 204, New York: Archie Comic Publications, Inc..

_____ (1979), "Betty and Veronica in Forgive and Forget," *Archies Giant Series Magazine*, 489 (December), New York: Close-up, Inc..

Asimov, Isaac, Charles G. Waugh, and Martin H. Greenberg, eds. (1986), *The Twelve Frights of Christmas*, New York: Avon Books.

Babson, Marian (1979), *The Twelve Deaths of Christmas*, New York: Dell Publishing.

Barnett, James H. (1946), "Christmas in American Culture," *Psychiatry*, 9, 51-65.

_____ (1954), *The American Christmas: A Study of National Culture*, New York: Macmillan.

Barsos, Philip (director, 1985), *One Magic Christmas*.

Baum, L. Frank (1986; original 1902), *The Life and Adventures of Santa Claus*, New York: Signet Classic.

Belk, Russell W. (1987), "A Child's Christmas in America: Santa Claus as Deity, Consumption as Religion," *Journal of American Culture*, Spring, 87-100.

_____ (1988), "Possessions and the Extended Self," *Journal of Consumer Research*, 15 (2), September, 139-168.

_____ and Richard W. Pollay (1985), "Images of Ourselves: The Good Life in Twentieth Century Advertising," *Journal of Consumer Research*, 11 (4), 887-897.

_____ and Melanie Wallendorf (1988), "Sacred and Profane Aspects of Money," paper presented at First International Sociology of Consumption Conference, Oslo, January.

_____, Melanie Wallendorf, and John Sherry, Jr. (1989), "The Sacred and the Profane in Consumer Behavior: Theodicy on the Odyssey," forthcoming, *Journal of Marketing Research*.

Benedict, Tony (director, 1969), *Santa and the Three Bears*.

Benney, Mark, Robert Weiss, Rolf Meyersohn, and David Riesman (1959), "Christmas in An Apartment Hotel," *American Journal of Sociology*, 65 (3), 233-240.

Bloch, Robert (1986, original 1980), "The Night Before Christmas," *The Twelve Frights of Christmas*, New York: Avon, 35-53.

Bock, E. Wilbur (1972), "The Transformation of Religious Symbols: A Case Study of St. Nicholas," *Social Compass*, 19, 537-548.

Bolton, H. Philip (1987), *Dickens Dramatized*, Boston: G. K. Hall.

Boorstin, Daniel (1973), *The Americans: The Democratic Experience*, New York: Random House.

Bradbard, Marilyn R. (1985), "Sex Differences in Adults' Gifts and Children's Toy Requests at Christmas," *Psychological Reports*, 56, 959-970.

Buday, George (1954), *The History of the Christmas Card*, London: Rockliff.

Burns, Thomas A. (1976), "Dr. Seuss' How the Grinch Stole Christmas: Its Recent Acceptance into the American Popular Christmas Tradition," *New York Folklore*, 2 (3 & 4), 191-204.

Campbell, Colin (1987), *The Romantic Ethic and The Spirit of Modern Consumerism*, Oxford: Basil Blackwell.

Caplow, Theodore (1982), "Christmas Gifts and Kin Networks," *American Sociological Review*, 47 (June), 383-392.

_____ (1984), "Rule Enforcement without Visible Means: Christmas Gift Giving in Middletown," *American Journal of Sociology*, 89 (6), 1306-1323.

_____, Howard M. Bahr, Bruce A. Chadwick, Reuben Hill, and Margaret H. Williamson (1982), *Middletown Families: Fifty Years of Change and Continuity*, Minneapolis: University of Minnesota Press.

_____ and Margaret H. Williamson (1980), "Decoding Middletown's Easter Bunny: A Study in American Iconography," *Semiotica*, 32 (3/4), 221-232.

Caron, Andre and Scott Ward (1975), "Gift Decisions by Kids and Parents," *Journal of Advertising Research*, 15, 15-20.

Carver, Sally S. (1982), "Santa Claus: A Man for All Seasons," *Hobbies*, 95 (December), 104-110+.

Cheal, David J. (1986), "The Social Dimensions of Gift Behaviour," *Journal of Social and Personal Relationships*, 3, 423-439.

Cook, Fielder (director, 1971), *The Homecoming-A Christmas Story*.

_____ (director, 1973), *Miracle on 34th Street*.

Curtiz, Michael (director, 1954), *White Christmas*.

Davies, Valentine (author; George Seaton, director, 1947), *Miracle on 34th Street*.

DC Comics, Inc. (1987), "Oh What Fun to Laugh and Sing a Slaying Song Tonight!," *Elvira's Haunted Holidays*, 1, New York: Elvira's House of Mystery Special.

Dell Publishing Company (1951), "Santa's First Christmas Trip," *Santa Claus Christmas Funnies* (Four Color 361), New York: Dell Publishing Company.

_____ (1957), "Frosty the Snowman and the Christmas Spirit," *Four Color*, 861, New York: Dell Publishing Company.

Dixton, Stephen (1985), "A Christmas Story," *An American Christmas: A Sampler of Contemporary Stories & Poems*, Jane B. Hill, ed., Atlanta: Peachtree Publishers, Ltd., 89-97.

Dorfman, Ariel (1983), *The Empire's Old Clothes: What the Lone Ranger, Babar, and Other Innocent Heroes do to Our Minds*, New York: Pantheon Books.

Downs, A. C. (1983), "Letters to Santa Claus: Elementary School-age Children's Sex-Typed Toy Preferences in a Natural Setting," *Sex Roles*, 9, 159-163.

Ellis, Bret E. (1985), *Less Than Zero*, New York: Simon and Schuster.

Englund, George (director, 1978), *A Christmas to Remember*.

Foote, Nelson and Leonard Cottrell, Jr. (1950), *Identity and Interpersonal Competence*, Chicago: University of Chicago Press.

Garcia, Guy D. (1988), "People," *Time*, 131 (13, March 28), 88.

Giln, Christian (director, 1984), *Here Comes Santa Claus*.

Godfrey, Thomas, ed. (1982), *Murder for Christmas*, New York: Mysterious Press.

Golby, J. M. and A. W. Purdue (1986), *The Making of the Modern Christmas*, Athens, GA: University of Georgia Press.

de Groot, Adriaan D. (1965), *Saint Nicholas: A Psychoanalytic Study of His History and Myth*, New York: Basic Books.

Hagstrom, Warren O. (1966), "What is the Meaning of Santa Claus?," *American Sociologist*, 1 (November), 248-252.

Hall, Dennis R. (1984), "The Venereal Confronts the Venerable: 'Playboy' on Christmas," *Journal of American Culture*, 7 (4), 63-68.

Hall Syndicate, Inc. (1967), "Season's Greetings," *Dennis the Menace Christmas Special*, Meriden, CT: Fawcett Publications, Inc..

Hewet, Edward W. (1976), "Christmas Spirits in Dickens," *Dickens Studies Newsletter*, 7 (4), December, 99-106.

Hill, C. R. (1969), "Christmas Card Selections as Unobtrusive Measures," *Journalism* Quarterly, 46, 511-514.

Holder, Judith and Alison Harding (1981), *Christmas Fare*, Secacus, NJ: Chartwell Books.

Huizinga, Johan (1955, original 1944), *Homo Ludens: A Study of the Play Element in Culture*, Boston: Beacon Press.

Jankel, Annabel and Rocky Morton (directors, 1988), *D.O.A.*.

Johnson, Sheila K. (1971a), "The Christmas Card Syndrome," *New York Times Magazine*, December 5, 38-29+.

_____ (1971b), "Sociology of Christmas Cards," *Trans-Action*, 8 (3), 27-29.

Jones, Charles W. (1978), *Saint Nicholas of Myra, Bari, and Manhattan: Biography of a Legend*, Chicago: University of Chicago Press.

Jordon, Cathleen (1984), *A Carol in the Dark*, New York: Dell Publishing.

Kanierska, Marek (director, 1987), *Less Than Zero*.

Keillor, Garrison (1983), "James Lundeen's Christmas," *News From Lake Woebegon*, St. Paul, MN: Minnesota Public Radio.

Kirshenblatt-Gimblett (1983), "The Future of Folklore Studies in America: The Urban Frontier," *Folklore Forum*, 16 (2), 175-234.

Kleiser, Randal (director, 1977), *The Gathering*.

Kron, Joan (1983), *Home-Psych: The Social Psychology of Home and Decoration*, New York: Clarkson N. Potter.

Levi-Strauss, Claude (1963), "Where Does Father Christmas Come From?," *New Society*, 63 (December 19), 6-8.

Ley, J. W. T. (1906), "The Apostle of Christmas," *The Dickensian*, 2 (12), December, 324-326.

Louis, J. C. and Harvey Z. Yazijian (1980), *The Cola Wars*, New York: Everest House.

Lucas, John (1986), "Katy Keene's Christmas," *Katy Keene*, 1 (February), Mamaronek, NY: Archie Enterprises.

McGinty, Brian (1979), "Santa Claus," *Early American Life*, 10 (6), 50-53+.

McGuigan, Cathleen (1988), "D.O.A., Shot by Shot," *Premiere*, 1 (9, May), 44-47.

McIntosh, J. T. (1986, original 1966), "Planet of Fakers," *The Twelve Frights of Christmas*, New York: Avon, 210-243.

MacLean, Annie M. (1899), "Two Weeks in Department Stores," *American Journal of Sociology*, 4 (6), 721-741.

Marketing News (1981), "Consumers' Need for Treats Means Marketing Opportunities," *Marketing News*, 8-9.

Matz, Milton (1961), "The Meaning of the Christmas Tree to the American Jew," *Jewish Journal of Sociology*, 3, 129-137.

May, Robert L. (1976), "The Land Behind the Sky-Holes," *Rudolf the Red-Nosed Reindeer*, New York: National Periodical Publications, Inc..

Melendez, Bill (director, 1965), *A Charlie Brown Christmas*.

Molloy, Anne (1950), *Lucy's Christmas*, Boston: Houghton Mifflin.

Moschetti, Gregory J. (1979), "The Christmas Potlatch: A Refinement on the Sociological Interpretation of Gift Exchange," *Sociological Focus*, 12 (January), 1-7.

Moxey, John L. (director, 1972), *Home for the Holidays*.

Munsey, Cecil (1972), *The Illustrated Guide to the Collectibles of Coca-Cola*, New York: Hawthorn Books.

Norris, Helen (1985), "The Christmas Wife," *The Christmas Wife*, Champaign, IL: University of Illinois Press, 251-276.

O'Neil, Sunny (1981), *The Gift of Christmas Past: A Return to Victorian Traditions*, Nashville, TN: American Association for State and Local History.

Opie, Iona and Peter Opie (1959), *The Lore and Language of School Children*, Oxford: Clarendon Press.

Oxley, Diana, Lois M. Haggard, Carol M. Werner, and Irwin Altman (1986), "Transactional Qualitites of Neighborhood Social Networks: A Case Study of Christmas Street," *Environment and Behavior*, 18, 640-677.

Pierce, Robert N. (1979), *Keeping the Flame: Media and Government in Latin America*, New York: Hasting House.

Pimlott, J. A. R. (1962), "...But Once a Year," *New Society*, 12 (December 19), 9-12.

Plath, David W. (1963), "The Japanese Popular Christmas: Coping with Modernity," *Journal of American Folklore*, 76 (302), 309-317.

Pollay, Richard W. (1987), "It's the Thought that Counts: A Case Study in Xmas Excesses," *Advances in Consumer Research*, Vol. 14, Melanie Wallendorf and Paul Anderson, eds., Provo: Association for Consumer Research, 140- 143.

Ragland, Fitz Roy (1937), *The Hero, a Study in Tradition*, Myth, and Drama, New York: Oxford University Press.

Richardson, John G. and Carl H. Simpson (1982), "Children, Gender, and Social Structure: An Analysis of the *Contents of Letters to Santa Claus*," Child Development, 53, 423-436.

Rook, Dennis (1985), "Consumers' Video Archives and Christmas Rituals," paper presented at 1985 Conference of the Association for Consumer Research, Las Vegas, October 19.

Samuelson, Sue (1982), *Christmas: An Annotated Bibliography*, New York: Garland Publishing Company.

Sandrich, Mark (director, 1942), *Holiday Inn*.

Schwartz, Barry (1967), "The Social Psychology of the Gift," *American Journal of Sociology*, 73 (1), 1-11.

Sed-Bar and Depattie-Freldon (Producers, 1983), *The Bear Who Slept Through Christmas*.

Sellier, Charles E., Jr. (director, 1984), *Silent Night Deadly Night*.

_____ (director, 1985), *Silent Night Deadly Night*, Part II.

Sereno, Renzo (1951), "Some Observations on the Santa Claus Custom," *Psychiatry*, 14, 387-398.

Shapiro, Alan (director, 1986), *The Christmas Star*.

Shlien, John (1959), "Santa Claus: The Myth in America," ETC.: *A Review of General Semantics*, 16 (4), 27-32.

Shoemaker, A. L. (1959), *Christmas in Pennsylvania: A Folk-Cultural Study*, Kutztown, PA: Pennsylvania Folklore Society.

Snyder, Phillip (1985), December 25th: *The Joys of Christmas Past*, New York: Dodd, Mead & Company.

Stenzel, Jim (1975), "Western Christmas-in a Japanese Sense," *Christian Century*, 92, 1183-1185.

Taylor, Jud (director, 1977), *Christmas Miracle in Caufield*.

Thompson, Robert J. (1988), "Christmas on Television: Consecrating Consumer Culture," paper presented at Popular Culture Association Annual Conference, New Orleans, March.

Turner, Victor (1969), *The Ritual Process*, Chicago: Aldine.

Updike, John (1981), "Transaction," Problems and Other Stories, New York: Fawcett Crest, 102-131.

Vinge, Joan D. (author; director Jeannot Szwarc, 1985), *Santa Claus The Movie*, New York: Berkley Books.

Viola, Tom (1986), "Dickens' Well-Seasoned Story," *The Guthrie Theater Program and Magazine*, December, 47-50.

Waits, William B., Jr. (1978), "The Many-Faced Custom: Christmas Gift-Giving in America, 1900-1940," unpublished doctoral dissertation, Rutgers University Department of History.

Walder, Dennis (1981), *Dickens and Religion*, London: Allen & Unwin.

Walt Disney Productions (1951), "Donald Duck in A Christmas for Shacktown," *Four Color*, 367, Poughkeepskie, NY: Western Publishing Company.

Walt Disney Productions (1962), "Santa's Surprise," *Christmas Parade*, 1, Poughkeepskie, NY: K. K. Publications.

Warren Publishing Company (1977), "A Noggin at Mile End," *Creepy*, 86 (February), New York: Warren Publishing Company.

_____ (1977), "The Greatest Christmas of All," *Creepy*, 86 (February), New York: Warren Publishing Company.

Watters, Pat (1978), *Coca-Cola: An Illustrated History*, Garden City, NY: Doubleday.

Waugh, Carol-Lynn, Martin H. Greenberg, and Isaac Asimov, eds. (1985), *The Twelve Crimes of Christmas*, New York: Avon.

Webley, Peter, S. E. Lea, and R. Portalska (1983), "The Unacceptability of Money as a Gift," *Journal of Economic Psychology*, 4, 223-238.

Western Publishing and Lithography Company (1955), "Bugs Bunny," *Bugs Bunny Christmas Funnies*, 4, New York: Dell Publishing Company.

Van de Wettering, Maxine (1984), "The Popular Concept of 'Home' in Nineteenth-Century America," *Journal of American Studies*, 18 (1), 5-28.

Williams, Richard (director, 1982), *Ziggy's Gift*.

Witt, Louise (1939), "The Jew Celebrates Christmas," *Christian Century*, 56, 1497-1499.

Wolf, Eric R. (1964), "Santa Claus: Notes on a Collective Representation," *Processes and Pattern in Culture: Essays in Honor of Julian H. Steward*, Robert A. Manners, ed., Chicago: Aldine, 147-155.

Yao, Margaret (1981), "Gift-Giving Spirit Haunts Some People Who Can't Afford It," *Wall Street Journal*, December 24, 1+.

Yates, Ronald E. (1985), "Japanese Merrily Leave the Christ Out of 'Kurisumasu'," *Chicago Tribune* (December 22), 1, 16.

# The Meaning of Christmas

Elizabeth C. Hirschman, Rutgers University
Priscilla A. LaBarbera, New York University[1]

## INTRODUCTION

Despite the fact that Christmas is the most important consumption festival in the United States, one which "mobilizes almost the entire population for several weeks...and takes precedence over ordinary forms of work and leisure (Caplow 1984, pp. 1306-1307)", it has received almost no attention in the consumer behavior literature, or, indeed, in the social sciences generally. As Caplow (1982, p. 383), author of two of the seven [2] social science investigations of Christmas we reviewed noted, "An ethnographer who discovered so important a ritual in some exotic culture might be tempted to make it the centerpiece of his cultural description; it is remarkable that social scientists have given so little attention to this conspicuous cluster of symbolic and practical acts."

The investigation of Christmas ties together several diverse strands of research inquiry within consumer research. One very conspicuous aspect of the Christmas festival is its emphasis upon *gift-giving* and *exchange processes* of interest both to consumer (cf, Belk 1979; Brinberg & Wood 1984; Sherry 1983) and marketing (cf, Bagozzi 1974; Hirschman 1987) researchers. Second, Christmas is a festival celebrating *sensory pleasure* -- the holiday foods and feasts, punch and eggnog, bright decorations, cheering music, and the scent of evergreens [3] (cf, Hirschman and Holbrook 1982; Holbrook and Hirschman 1982). Further, it is rich in both *consumption symbolism* and *mythology* (Rook 1986; Levy 1981); a time when many forms of sacred and secular iconography are blended together into a complex, evocative *social text* (cf, Mick 1986). Thus, by studying the meaning of Christmas, we may learn much not only about consumption, but about the overlap and interplay of many current consumption theories, as well.

### Christmas in Social Science Inquiry

The most thorough examination of the role of Christmas in American life was undertaken by Barnett (1954). By interpreting a diversified collection of documentary evidence, Barnett traced changes in the meaning of the American Christmas festival from early Colonial days to the middle of the Twentieth Century. In his view, Christmas had come to reflect many deep currents of the American value system and national character. Barnett concludes that the American Christmas had acquired a seasonal cult status involving participation by the majority of the population. There were formal religious aspects to this cult, but "Christmas is also nourished by the ties of family life, by affection for children, by a willingness to aid the needy, and even by the profit-seeking activities of modern business. The main rites of the cult are found in the midnight Mass of December 24th, the church service on Christmas Sunday, the family tree and dinner, Christmas shopping, gift giving, charity, Santa Claus' visit and the Christmas card custom... These activities are intended to banish anxiety, to enhance the present, and to secure the future (Barnett 1954, pp. 129- 130)."

Despite the thoroughness of Barnett's inquiry and the insights it provided on the ritual aspects of Christmas, three decades of rapid social change have now passed since Barnett's data were gathered. Six recent social science studies may provide more current insights on the meaning of Christmas and consumption.

The first of these, "The Christmas Potlatch..." (Moschetti 1979), examined the asymmetries of Christmas gift giving between different 'classes' of consumers, for instance, the marked tendency of parents to give greater quantities of gifts to their children, than vice versa. Moschetti extended the principle of asymmetry to "the broader community where adults donated money, toys, food and other gift items for distribution to abandoned children, children of the poor and the poor in general (Moschetti, 1979, p. 3)". He then developed propositions on the "differences in empowerment" available to various Christmas gift givers. Asymmetries in gift giving, he proposed, reflect differences in social power, with a greater quantity (and economic value) of gifts flowing from those with more social power to those with less social power. Moschetti's conjectures, though intriguing, were based primarily on speculation and ignored other plausible explanations for the asymmetries he observed, for example, altruism, symbolization of interpersonal bonding, and self-effacement, among others.

In contrast to the speculative nature of Moschetti's (1979) paper, are three articles by Caplow and his associate (Caplow 1982; Caplow 1984; Caplow and Williamson 1980) based upon ethnographic data gathered during the Middletown III

---

[1] The authors wish to thank Ronald Faber, Harold Kassarjian, Thomas O'Guinn, Clinton Sanders, and Barbara Stern for their constructive comments on an earlier version of this paper.

[2] Although several investigators have examined the iconography of Santa Claus (see Belk 1987 for a review), few have examined the festival of Christmas, *per se*.

[3] At least in northern climes.

Project.[4] The earliest (Caplow and Williamson 1980) deals with the contrasting iconographies of Christmas and Easter. As the authors note (p. 224), "Christmas and Easter are each double festivals having separate secular and religious iconographies and separate religious and secular modes of celebration." Caplow and Williamson also discerned several similarities in consumption practices between the two festivals, as well. Each is associated with a vacation from normal labor; each requires gift exchange activities and the exchange of cards, and each involves family reunions culminating in a celebratory family meal.

The Christmas festival is associated with a rich set of secular and sacred symbols: "Santa Claus, the Christmas tree, the holly wreath, mistletoe, and the poinsettia; snow and reindeer; hearths, chimneys and stockings; the yule log; egg nogs and hot toddies; ribbons and bows; tinsel and stars; roast turkey and roast goose; carols and caroling; the major color combination of red and green" compose the secular symbol set. The religious emblems of the festival include: "the manger with its surrounding animals, the star of Bethelem, the shepherds and their flocks, and the three kings bearing gifts (Caplow and Williamson 1980, pp. 224- 225)."

In a second paper based upon the Middletown III data, Caplow (1982) investigated the pattern of gift giving during the Christmas season. He observed that gift giving formed a significant part of the celebratory activity: the 110 respondents to a personal interview gave a total of 2,969 gifts and received 1,378 gifts, a mean of 27 gifts given and 13 received. Women were more likely than men to give ornaments, craft objects, food, plants and flowers. Men gave most of the appliances and sports equipment. Females were disproportionately active gift givers. Alone or jointly, they gave 84 percent of all the gifts and received only 61 percent. Caplow also found that "money gifts were common from employers to employees...Small money gifts are conventionally given at Christmas to newsboys, postmen, delivery men and other persons of relatively low status... (p. 386)", but no reverse instances were found, conforming to Moschetti's thesis of gift asymmetry and relative social empowerment.

Caplow concluded that the primary purpose of the Christmas festival, in general, and Christmas gift giving in particular was to reinforce social solidarity and kinship ties. The gifts given and received, the festivities shared, the meals taken together were a way of making tangible the "ties that bind" one generation to the next, sibling to sibling, and loved newcomers into the family group.

In his third paper on Christmas, Caplow (1984) described the social existence of several unwritten

rules concerning the proper celebration of the Christmas festival. He again emphasized the importance of this ritual code to signify the strength of interpersonal relationships and to communicate bonds of kinship. Across his sample, these rules were remarkably uniform and should be easily recognizable by the reader. For example, consider the *Tree Rule*: "Married couples with children of any age should put up Christmas trees in their homes. Unmarried persons with no living children should not put up trees (p. 1308)"; the *Gathering Rule*: "Christmas gifts should be distributed at gatherings where every person gives and receives gifts (p. 1312)" and the *Dinner Rule*: "Family gatherings at which gifts are distributed include a traditional Christmas dinner (p. 1312)" which includes "(1) turkey or ham, (2) dressing, (3) white potatoes, preferably mashed; (4) sweet potatoes in some form (5) cranberry sauce or salad, (6) green beans, baked beans or bean salad; and (7) pumpkin pie and other pies (p. 1313)." The widespread cultural acceptance of this unwritten code results in the homogeneous celebration of the Christmas festival and in commonalities of consumption patterns among those who participate.

A fifth inquiry into the meaning of Christmas was conducted by Belk (1987). Belk reviewed several articles published in the sociological, psychological, and anthropological literatures, as well as the popular press, dealing with the consumption ideology of Santa Claus and the Christmas festival. Belk's interpretation differs from those of Moschetti (1979) and Caplow (1980; 1982; 1984) in that he is particularly concerned with the materialistic and hedonistic aspects of the Christmas festival. For example, Belk suggests (p. 91) "...If Santa is a god, he is the god of materialism... Both Santa and attendant seasonal rituals (these include huge family feasts, office parties, New Year's Eve parties, and even the large circulation of Christmas issues of *Playboy* magazine) celebrate greed, gluttony, and hedonism... American society has reflected its deepest values onto Santa Claus." Following this same line of interpretation, Belk proposes that the well-known editorial by Francis Church (December 1897, *The New York Sun*) 'Yes Virginia, There is a Santa Claus' "argues for faith in material bounty and hedonistic joy (p. 93)."

Belk also views Santa Claus as a symbol of American attempts to promulgate commercialism and materialism across the world. "Unsatisfied with merely inculcating Santa's consumption values in children, it appears that Americans believe that the entire universe should adopt these values. For if others adopt these values, it seems to justify our own materialism (p. 96)." Belk concludes his interpretation by suggesting that "the modern Christmas ritual is more than the celebration of the family that Caplow suggests... It is also a celebration of consumption, materialism, and hedonism (p. 96)."

A final paper by Pollay (1986) uses a case history approach to illuminate the compulsive behavior that sometimes characterizes Christmas. Pollay details Rita G.'s custom of decorating her home from early October until January with an excessive

---

[4]Middletown III was an interdisciplinary project led by Theodore Caplow(University of Virginia) and funded by the National Science Foundation. Conducted during the late 1970's, it replicated the well-known Middletown I and II studies undertaken by Robert and Helen Lynd during the 1920's and 1930's.

display of Christmas decorations. Rita is described as "totally lucid, gregarious, responsive and occasionally philosophical (Pollay 1986, p. 140)." Yet her Christmas behavior is unusual in that she displays over 5,000 ornaments including wreaths, trees, and statues. These pieces are then filled-in with tinsel garlands, simulated snow, and ribbons. In addition to an abundance of Christmas tree lights around the home, there are music boxes playing seasonal tunes and some rooms are equipped with tapes playing seasonal music. Shower curtains, toilet seats, cookie jars, dishes, glassware, napkins, lighting and so on reflect the Christmas decor. In sum, Rita's large home is "decorated inside and out, from street to rooftop, from front to back halls, from floor to ceiling, and from pillar to post with every imaginable square inch filled with Christmas decorations, save for the necessary floor space and seating to permit some semblance of normal functioning (Pollay 1986, p. 140)."

Rita claims that her primary motivation for decorating is charity. Visitors are asked to deposit packaged food products to be distributed to the hungry. When a good deal of publicity was received in 1984, the 10,000 visitors produced 15,000 food items. A secondary motivation is the delighted reactions of the visitors. Rita takes pleasure in making children happy and "being part of making Christmas a magic period for people (Pollay 1986, p. 142)." She also exercises creativity in her decorating activity by trying to make each year's effort better, larger, and more successful. Pollay concludes that Rita's motivations "are not the vanity, social competitiveness or publicity seeking that might be assumed. Rather, her motivations are a complex of love of children, social identity, fulfillment of community expectations, desire to do good charitable work, pride of creativity and accomplishment of challenging goals (Pollay 1986, p. 142)."

To summarize, the research by Moschetti (1979), Caplow (Caplow 1982; 1984; Caplow and Williamson 1979), and Pollay (1986) suggests that Christmas gift giving is a means of symbolizing social ties and that the festival exhibits both sacred and secular dimensions of meaning. Belk (1987) adopts a more critical view of the Christmas festival, characterizing it as a largely secularized celebration of commercialism, materialism, and hedonism. Collectively, these prior works identify several common themes relevant to the Christmas festival: gift-giving, sociability and family togetherness, commercialism and materialism, hedonism and sensuality, and religious tradition and spirituality.

Except for Pollay's (1986) work, however, these studies relied on the interpretation of indirect forms of evidence or theorization to arrive at their conclusions. Moschetti and Belk, for example, relied upon existing social science paradigms or the re-interpretation of other's work to generate their propositions. Caplow conducted first-hand field investigations of the Christmas festival, but drew his interpretation from indirect indicators. For example, he inferred the meaning of Christmas gift giving by looking at the tangible flow of gifts, rather than by directly inquiring from respondents "*Why* are you doing this?" While Pollay examined the motivation behind excessive Christmas decorating, his inquiry was based on a single subject. Of course, there may be many instances in which directly questioning consumers about the purposes or meaning of their actions is inappropriate or likely to produce misleading responses. However, as ethnomethodologists point out (cf, Garfinkel 1967; Heritage 1984; Leiter 1980), there is also much to be learned by examining the meanings people construct to explain their behaviors or to describe personal events. The present study used such an approach to discover what meanings consumers ascribed to Christmas.

## WHAT DO CONSUMERS BELIEVE CHRISTMAS MEANS

Because prior investigations (Barnett 1953; Caplow and Williamson 1980) have suggested that Christmas has both sacred and secular meanings, we thought it appropriate to approach consumers who a priori might be expected to have a more sacred or secular orientation to life. Consumers who exhibited strong religious or commercial orientations (described below) were identified and asked to write an essay in response to the question: "What does Christmas mean to you?"[4] The individuals selected were drawn from four populations: (1) Evangelical Christians, (2) members of the Society of Friends ("Quakers"), (3) undergraduate business school students, and (4) candidates for the Master of Business Administration degree. The ideology of each group and the means used to obtain their cooperation in the research are described briefly below.

*Evangelical Christians.* Evangelical Christians are part of a conservative Protestant movement present in America since colonial times (LaBarbera 1987). In survey research Evangelicals have been defined as those Christians who have (1) had a *born again* experience, (2) believe in the inerrancy of the Bible, and (3) practice Christian evangelism (Gallup 1981). Evangelical Christians who participated in the present research were members of several congregations in New York. These congregations were contacted by one of the authors, who is an Evangelical. This author spoke to the congregations (usually at the close of Wednesday evening services) and distributed the essay questionnaires and self-addressed, stamped envelopes to those willing to participate in the study. A $2.00 donation to each church's charitable fund was promised, and paid, for each completed essay. A total of 60 essays was received.

*The Society of Friends ('Quakers').* Quakers historically were known for their extremely plain material lifestyles (e.g., black and gray apparel), as

---

[4]Some of the essay writers were Jewish. They were asked to write instead on the meaning of Hanukkah. Their responses are interpreted in the Appendix.

well as their commitment to human rights (Whalen 1984). During the meetings observed by the author, the Friends sat in silence on plain benches in an unadorned room. There was no pulpit, shrine, or minister as in other Protestant services. Instead, individual Friends spoke from their benches, if they were so moved. The essay questions and stamped, return envelopes were distributed at the close of each meeting. A total of 39 completed essays was returned. In lieu of direct monetary contributions to their congregations, which were declined, a donation was made to a local shelter for the homeless.

*Undergraduate Business School Students.* Consumers who would be expected to have a more secular orientation toward life are college students majoring in business administration. These persons have chosen to pursue instruction in finance, accounting, management, marketing, and similar activities central to the operation of the commercial sector. Essays were obtained from two sets of undergraduate business students at New York University. The first set was collected over a three week period from members of one of the author's classes. Students were assigned the essay as part of a take-home assignment in partial fulfillment of course requirements. Forty-two essays were collected in this manner. A second set of forty-nine essays was collected from students participating in the student subject pool of the undergraduate business school.

*Master of Business Administration Degree Candidates.* Persons pursuing the MBA degree typically may be expected to have a secular world view, in that they have chosen to seek extended instruction in the ideology of capitalist enterprise. Thirty MBA students, approximately half of whom were majoring in accounting and finance, the rest in management, marketing, economics, and business information systems at New York University, completed the essay. The essays were written out-of-class in partial fulfillment of course requirements.

## ANALYSIS

The several topics mentioned in the essays were organized by the two principal investigators into five primary categories, which largely reflected themes identified in earlier research: (1) Religion (Formal Sacredness), (2) Interpersonal Relationships (Communalism), (3) Secular Materialism, Cynicism, Commercialism, (4) Gift-giving (5) Sensuality and Hedonism. The contents of each of these categories is described below.

### Religion (Formal Sacredness)

An aspect of the Christmas festival downplayed in the accounts of both Caplow and Belk is its commemoration of a significant religious event, i.e., the birth of Jesus. To believers, this event and its commemoration have important theological meaning. Among our essayists, 55% of Evangelical Christians, 22% of Quakers, 17% of undergraduate business students, and 13% of MBA candidates included

religious themes in their essays.[5] Representative excerpts drawn from all four groups are given below:

"I do tend to attribute some religious aspects to it. I turn to feelings of a sense of holiness, a heightened belief in divinity or a higher force, in miracles, or perhaps ultimately in hope and the optimism of possibilities to be within the future...I seem to associate aspects of an infant with Christmas, personifying characteristics of innocence, renewal, and joy."

"There is also the religious aspect of Christmas. Even though I am not a real religious man, that is I don't go to church every Sunday, on Christmas Eve it is like I change personality. I feel closer to God, and usually I go to church. This may be the result of the atmosphere of love and serenity that the family experiences."

"It is the birthday of Jesus Christ...and the way in which we show our love for one another is through the presentation of gifts to the special people in our lives. It is also a time to reflect upon the love God has for us by giving us a precious gift -- his son, Jesus."

"I go to Mass on Christmas. It gives me a chance to thank God for all that I have. Sometimes I feel like a hypocrite because I don't go every week like I should."

"It is also a time to rethink the religious meaning of Christmas and how this affects my behavior towards others throughout the year. For example, it prompts me to try to be more charitable and consider those less fortunate than myself."

"...Christmas is a celebration of life, of the most perfect life ever conceived, and of the family, the most blessed family ever gathered. It is a time for all people, not only Christians, to reflect on what it means to be born, to be human, to be loved, to be touched, to be humble."

The expressions of religious sentiment above were drawn from essays from all four of the consumer groups we examined. They reflect a tendency across diverse groups of people to see in the Christmas religious festival a link to humanity, to God and to

---

[5]These proportions are provided as descriptive sample statistics only. Our intent was not to test whether one sampled group expressed a given theme more than another group, but rather to generate diversity by gathering responses from persons who had chosen different paths for their lives.

rebirth. These same themes were echoed in the essay descriptions of interpersonal relationships.

### Interpersonal Relationships (Communalism)

Expressions of the importance of interpersonal relationships at Christmastime were found across all four consumer groups: MBA candidates were highest at 43%, Quakers next at 38%, Evangelical Christians 25%, and undergraduate business students 20%. Excerpts reflecting the range of sentiments expressed are given below:

"To share in my husband's simple joy at it all."

"The true meaning of Christmas is the giving of love every day and the fact I can say that to those I am with on that day."

"Christmas has a very warm, sentimental family-oriented feel for me. I want the celebrating of the season (as opposed to just the *day*) to be very special and shared with relatives or close friends."

"Christmas is the season when we remember that Love is the greatest thing in the world... We make time to see friends and loved ones; to reaffirm the love we share with them, and to celebrate the holiday with them."

"The traditions which mean something are giving gifts, spending time with friends and family, and extending warm greetings to all I meet... Unselfish giving is a wonderful thing -- don't you wish it would last all year?"

"Our family gathers and reinforces its bonds."

"I hope that in the coming year the world will be a nicer place for my family and all families."

"Christmas is the time when everybody comes home."

"An excuse for people to get together and make each other happy."

"I love walking down the street and smiling at people I don't know and have them smile back simply because they feel Christmas inside."

"I like to believe that for one moment in time every being would share in a bond of peace and goodwill."

Clearly, these statements lend support to the Durkheimian notion that sacredness arises in part from the "miracle of sociability" (Durkheim ed. 1961); that interpersonal bonds can generate an aura of spirituality that binds mankind together. The Christmas festival appears to engender in many a sense of universal communality and genuine sentiment for others' welfare.

### Secular Materialism, Cynicism, Commercialism

In dialectic contrast to the expressions given above, there were also essay descriptions of Christmas filled with complaints of commercialism, frustration, loneliness and cynicism. To paraphrase Dickens: Christmas is the best of times; Christmas is the worst of times. Proportionately, these negative essay themes were cited by undergraduate business students in 28% of their essays, by MBA candidates in 20% of their essays, by Quakers in 13% of their essays and by Evangelical Christians in 12% of their essays. A representative sampling drawn from all four groups of consumers is given below:

"Looking around at today's commercialized Christmas...makes me sadder. It tells me that most people have missed out on the best part of Christmas."

"My daughter thinks Christmas is another day to receive gifts and cannot understand why, if it is Christ's birthday, everyone else is getting a gift."

"I must admit that I find the Christmas season to be too commercial and sometimes a burden of empty obligation."

"The tv programs concentrate mostly on Santa Claus, not on Christ."

"It is sad that so much regard is placed on [material] things instead of love and brotherhood. It is a sly idol that steals the true meaning of Christmas."

"I don't like the false thanks that often occurs."

"I have become increasingly tense over how much money we spend and over the requirement that I provide an enormous feast."

"I get up early and with cash and credit cards in hand go about the difficult and dirty task of spreading Christmas cheer."

"Fighting crowds of shoppers."

"The overall level of collective neuroses rises, as do guilt, false expectations, and disappointment."

"Aggressive advertising exploits the religious holiday."

"People become grumpy and tired and sick."

"Today it seems the importance of the present is its price."

"A season to worship credit cards."

"Christmas shopping is like going to war."

"Overworked, rude, hostile clerks."

"People who are alone and unhappy, feel isolated and abnormal."

"Depression is widespread."

It is ironic that the negative aspects of the Christmas festival, as described by those we queried, are virtually opposite to those viewed in a positive way by people from these same groups. Whereas in the two earlier categories, people described aspects of the Christmas festival that filled them with joy, united them into vital, loving kinship groups, engendered feelings of self-less giving and concern for the less fortunate, connected them to a Divine Presence, and evoked feelings of rebirth and eternity; this third set of comments provided accounts of Christmas that focused upon commercialization, selfishness, sadness, secularization, hypocrisy, pressure to perform undesirable rituals, stress, fatigue, disappointment, and depression.

One reviewer (C.S.) suggested that these negative affective aspects of Christmas may be due to the fact that Christmas is essentially a *gemeinschaft* festival embedded in a *gesellschaft* culture. The inevitable social stresses and emotional strains that result from trying to create a communal, spiritual atmosphere in a pluralistic, secularized society are focused and intensified during the Christmas season. At the same time that Christmas calls us home to family and friends, it tears us away from our many secular responsibilities and commitments. Christmas challenges us to create, during a relatively brief holiday, a reality that is fundamentally different from that which most of us construct during the rest of the year. As a result, many of us fail that challenge. Many consumers cannot create bonds of fellowship and communion, experience feelings of generosity and nurturance, and open-up their hearts, souls, and senses when these aspects of themselves have lain dormant for so long. Sadly, one of the least recognized, but most painfully experienced, costs of modern man's independence and individuality may be the existential angst and loneliness in which he has become suspended.

## Gift-Giving

The fourth category of themes dealt with a ritual activity central to the Christmas festival -- giftgiving. Proportionately these were distributed across the four groups of consumers we queried as follows: Quakers, 17%; undergraduate business students, 15% MBA candidates, 12%; and Evangelical Christians, 6%. The sacred/secular dialectic noted by Barnett (1954) and Caplow and Williamson (1980) was quite evident in people's attitudes toward both giving and receiving gifts. The following are representative pairs of oppositional statements excerpted from essays. For each pair, a statement expressing the sacred, interpersonal bonds associated with Christmas

giftgiving precedes one indicating more selfish, secular interests.

"To show people through presents that you care about them."

"I feel duty bound to buy, buy, buy."

"Christmas gives me a chance to give presents to those I enjoy."

"I look under the tree to see if there are any gifts with my name on them."

"It's giving someone the present they've been hoping for all year and holding the memory of their happiness."

"Christmas in the purely material sense has come to mean a real Catch-22: every year I attempt to outdo last year's performance by buying more lavish or original presents...while I try to lower my expectations for what I will receive in return."

"We give presents to each other to represent the gladness and celebration of Christ's birth."

"As I grew older Christmas became less and less a religious ceremony than a market for consumption..."

"As I wrap gifts I think of the person who's going to receive them and become filled with pleasure."

"I enjoy receiving gifts, but would be willing to forego that to be released of the burden and expense of buying gifts for others."

"I prefer a child's poem or picture, rather than a box from Macy's."

"For those I can't decide which present to get I give one of the following: cologne, perfume, Walkman, shaving cream, cigarette lighter, watch or sunglasses."

These statements illustrate the sacred and secular bipolar structure of Christmas gift giving. As Belk (1987) has argued, there is a materialistic, greedy, selfish side to gift giving during the Christmas festival and some of these statements support that view. Yet as Caplow (1982) has proposed, there is also evidence in these statements that gift giving can signify love and interpersonal bonding. The true meaning of the gifts given and received thus would appear to reside more in the spirit of the giver/receiver, than in the gift, itself.

## Sensuality and Hedonism

Many of the statements made regarding feasting and other holiday traditions such as caroling, stocking hanging and decorating the Christmas tree revealed yet another aspect of the festival -- the sensual and hedonic pleasures that are both revelled-in and regretted by consumers. The undergraduate business students expressed the largest proportion of these sentiments in their essays, 19%, followed by MBA candidates, 8%; Quakers, 8%, and Evangelical Christians, 1%. Some representative excerpts are given below:

> "Delicious pumpkin and mincemeat pies, colorful Christmas cookies, Jesus birthday cakes, hams and salads are proudly presented after hours of preparation."

> "Much delicious food that Mom prepares just for the occasion."

> "Hanging stockings, putting Rudolph on the lawn, and hanging mistletoe in the doorway."

> "The scent of spices."

> "Bright twinkling lights and festive decorations."

> "Children march on multi-colored snow from one house to the next singing Christmas carols and glancing up to the starlit sky to try to catch a glimpse of Santa and his reindeer."

> "A roaring fire."

> "It's smelling the Christmas tree."

> "Getting fat -- all the Christmas cookies, cakes, holiday dinners and parties -- I end up gaining at least 10 pounds."

The Christmas festival is a time of vivid and intense sensory stimulation: bright colors, spiced cooking aromas, 'spirited' drinks, blinking lights, happy music, bright fires, evergreen scents. The intensity of the sensory stimuli seems to correspond to the heightened sense of communal bonding, spiritual commitment and, perhaps, to our urge to acquire and give large quantities of tangible gifts. It *is* a festival of *excess*, and that excess includes positive as well as negative affective features. But it is perhaps more a function of how the individual chooses to participate in the excesses of the festival that determines whether the outcome is positive or negative. Some will use the heightened reality to create a spiritually uplifting, joyous time for themselves and their loved ones; others will over-indulge, become sensorially and materially bloated, and feel pangs of guilt, envy, and frustration. Each consumer creates from Christmas, what s/he is able.

### Integration of Sacred and Secular Themes

Finally, the four excerpts below exhibit the interweaving of sacred and secular themes and the generally positive affective tone that was typical of the majority of the essays.

An MBA candidate wrote:

> "At my house in Minneapolis, one knows that Christmas is near when my aunt and uncle arrive from Indiana. One of my fondest memories is playing Christmas carols on the piano or drinking eggnog while decorating the tree. Of course my brother and I always try to hide the paper chains that we made in kindergarten, but my mother insists on displaying them. On Christmas Eve, Grandma joins us for a typically Scandinavian meal: lutefish, krumkake, Yulekaka, Swedish meatballs, boiled potatoes, fruit soup, fruit cake, and rosettes abound. The smells of the house and the warmth of the fire are like no other atmosphere during the year. Then it's time to open gifts and realize that all of the pre-holiday hassles are worthwhile... Our relatives join us for a big turkey dinner and more togetherness in the evening."

The essay of an undergraduate business student stated:

> "Christmas time is the season of the year when family becomes the focus of all activities. The two weeks before Christmas Day are spent doing activities to prepare for a big family celebration on the 25th. Cooking and decorating the house are two of the main traditions we follow. We eat certain foods every year and decorate with ornaments that have been in our family for generations. Christmas time is also special because of the traditions that we have. For example, we always go to Mass on Christmas Eve and on Christmas morning we always drank champagne, even when we were little kids. I look forward to having all the relatives together to celebrate."

An essay from a Quaker read:

> "Christmas morning means opening stocking presents first, eating stollen bread and sausages, and waiting for all the older sisters and their respective beaus to arrive so we can open the good stuff. My mother is fanatical about Christmas and no details are spared. We always listen to traditional Christmas music and a family specialty, Dylan Thomas' *A Child's Christmas in Wales*."

Another undergraduate business student wrote:

> "On Christmas Eve great excitement is always felt through my whole house. Especially in the young twins; they cannot sleep for anticipation overtakes them... No one begins to open gifts until everyone is out of bed... The Christmas tree twinkles in the haze of dawn and gifts still wrapped beckon their new owners to come and peer underneath the colorful patterned paper. As always there is a china plate on the

tiny reading stand next to the fireplace. It is sprinkled with Christmas cookie crumbs and a glass that was filled with milk stands next to it empty. Two large footprints stamped in the ashes of the fireplace can always be found to add to the magical reality of Santa ascending up the chimney...The sharing of love, faith, and tradition with family and friends is what Christmas means to me. It is all very familiar and rarely varies from year to year. However, every year's celebration seems new to me and its love and magical makeup will always be deeply appreciated."

These texts evoke the multi-dimensional aspect of the Christmas festival and convey its diverse and sometimes contradictory symbolism. A theme common to all four is the centrality of family bonding; in one of its many essences, Christmas is a celebration and commemoration of *family life*. Its secular consumption aspects, such as feasting, decorating, and gift giving, all activate and require family interaction. Correspondingly, its religious iconography -- the nativity scene with the mother, father, and infant -- celebrates and commemorates the family. Thus, Christmas is, we propose, first and foremost a celebration of and by the family.

A second consistent theme is *consumption*. People enact the Christmas ritual by and through consuming. They give and receive presents, they make and eat special foods, they purchase and decorate a Christmas tree, they hang and fill stockings. Santa Claus, as Belk (1987) has insightfully pointed out, is undoubtedly the icon of the consuming aspect of Christmas. He comes and leaves presents and, in turn, he is given and consumes food (cookies and milk). Santa is both giver and consumer. Yet, unlike Belk, we do not find it appropriate to cast Santa in a negative light. He does, indeed, represent consumption, but consumption *may* be a means of making tangible the sacred interpersonal bonds that, by nature, are felt but not seen. We believe it is the attitude projected by the consumer that determines whether the nature of Christmas is sacred or secular, and not consumption, itself.

## THE MULTIDIMENSIONAL MEANING OF CHRISTMAS

More formally, the dimensions of meaning for Christmas we have discerned from this collection of essays may be depicted as shown in the Figure. The vertical axis we have labeled as a sacred/secular dimension. By *sacred* we refer to spiritual and emotional bonds that transcend the individual and connect him/her to a Deity or to mankind. Included in our conception of the sacred would be sentiments expressing familial and communal love, as well as formal religious beliefs. By *secular* we refer to aspects of the material world, especially those having to do with self- gratification, sensory pleasure, and commercialized activities. The horizontal axis represents a positive/negative affective dimension. Let us examine the contents of each quadrant.

### Quadrant I: Sacred-Positive

Quadrant I contains those elements of the essays which we interpreted as signifying positive sacredness. Two forms of sacredness are included in this quadrant: *formal religious sacredness* refers to those essay themes associated with Christian religious tradition, including acknowledgement of a unitary Diety and belief in the divine birth of Jesus. Essay themes of this genre were consistently positive in affective tone and cited such specifics as holiness, innocence, humility, thankfulness to a Diety, and the birth of Jesus.

Within our interpretive framework, *interpersonal relationships* are also viewed as sacred, in the sense implied by Durkheim (ed. 1961). Transcendant, spiritual bonds can connect the individual not only to a Diety, but also to family and friends, and even to a universal sense of belongingness to all humankind. The essay contents included under interpersonal relationships in this quadrant were those that reflected a positive emotional tone; specific essays cited sharing joy, giving love, extending oneself to others, and the sharing of peace and goodwill among all people. In our view, material expressions of these sentiments through gift-giving, charitable donations, and other tangible acts are not inconsistent with sacredness. If the gift represents love to the giver and the receiver, then it is sanctified.

### Quadrant II: Secular-Positive

The second quadrant contains essay elements which we viewed as representing the secular aspects of the Christmas festival having a positive emotional impact on consumers. There were two primary categories here. The *materialism* category refers to essay themes which described receiving presents, in a materialistic sense, as positive and enjoyable. Although this may be viewed by some readers as morally reprehensible, there are obviously those who enjoy getting many presents for Christmas because they enjoy having many *things*. Rather than condemning this form of material pleasure *a priori* (e.g., Belk 1987), it might be fruitful to examine this phenomenon with an open eye. It could be quite edifying to discover *why* some people enjoy getting and having many things.

Similarly, several essayists also associated *sensual/hedonic aspects* of the Christmas season with positive emotionality. Belk (1987) seems to view this part of the Christmas season as unsavory; whereas others (Hirschman and Holbrook 1982; Holbrook and Hirschman 1982) have applauded consumers' sensual and hedonic behaviors. Despite the differing normative perspectives of consumer researchers, some consumers do seem to enjoy Christmas for its heightened sensory experiences. These include such specifics as tasting traditional foods, smelling the scent of evergreens, seeing brightly colored lights, hearing carols, and feeling the warmth of a fire.

# FIGURE

## THE STRUCTURAL DIMENSIONS OF CHRISTMAS

SACRED

IV                                                          I

*Formal Religion:*                          *Formal Religion:*
  Taboo?                                       holiness, innocence,
                                               renewal, serenity, divinity,
                                               God's love, thankfulness,
                                               perfect life, Jesus' birth,
                                               humility toward God

*Interpersonal Relationships*               *Interpersonal Relationships:*
  burden of empty obligation,                  share joy, giving love,
  false emotion, loneliness,                   family and friends
  depression,                                  together, reaffirm bonds of
  resented family rites,                       love, extending self to
  guilt, competition, hostility,              others, home comings,
  rudeness                                     share peace and goodwill
                                               among all people

NEGATIVE <------------------------------------------------------------------------> POSITIVE
AFFECT                                                                        AFFECT

III                                                         II

*Materialism:*                              *Materialism:*
  commercialization,                           enjoy receiving many gifts
  Santa Claus promoted over
  Christ, materialism promoted over
  love and brotherhood,
  over-expenditure, aggressive advertising

*Sensory/Hedonic:*                          *Sensory/Hedonic:*
  physical and emotional exhaustion,           delicious food,
  over-indulgence in feasting                  brightly colored lights,
                                               caroling, scent of tree,
                                               drinking eggnog,
                                               decorating the house,
                                               drinking champagne

SECULAR

---

## Quadrant III:    Secular-Negative

Quadrant III contains those secular essay themes associated with negative emotionality. As in Quadrant II, the contents were interpreted as signifying materialism and sensory/hedonic experiences. Negative aspects of *materialism* derived from specific essays included the commercialization of Christmas, the deification of Santa Claus above Christ, excessive emphasis on having things versus loving relationships, and the pressure to overspend during the holiday season.

Aggressive advertising was viewed by some consumers as the origin of this undesirable over-emphasis on materialism.

The heightened *sensual/hedonic experiences* of the season -- which some revelled in -- were viewed by other consumers as leading to ennervation and self-destructive consumption behaviors such as gluttony. Both the consumer's willingness and ability to appropriately self-regulate sensual/hedonic stimulation may account for why some people looked forward to the heightened experiential aspects of the season, while others regretted and dreaded them.

### Quadrant IV:   Sacred-Negative

The final quadrant contained essay themes which had a negative affective tone and were sacred in signification.  In this quadrant we included essay contents which referred to the breakdown, dissolution or resentment of self-transcendant interpersonal relationships.  For some consumers, Christmas is an especially stressful and anxiety-ridden period, because they are unable to experience the sacred bonds of family and friendship that are so central to Christmas' meaning.  Feelings of emotional isolation, bitterness, personal mortality, and loneliness may become overwhelming to those who feel left out of the "family of mankind" sentiment generated by the season.  One empirical indicator of the damage wrought by the absence of interpersonal bonds is that suicides, acute psychotic episodes, and admissions to psychiatric clinics are all at high levels during the Christmas season. One intriguing absence in our essays was the lack of any negative comments concerning formal religion. In none of the essays did writers attribute hostile or angry emotional sentiments to theological elements of the Christmas season.  This was interesting, because certainly not all the essayists felt a strong religious commitment (some saying so explicitly), and several were willing to express disappointment and cynicism with other socially desirable aspects of the holiday, such as family relationships and gift-giving.

We believe that the marked absence of similar negative affect being directed toward religious ideology may be indicative of a cultural *taboo* against such emotional expression.  There may be a deeply embedded norm which permits consumers to express anger at their *own* family during Christmas, but which prohibits these sentiments from being directed at the sanctified Christmas family.  Since the existence of affective taboos is rarely reported in the social science literature on *modern* cultures (and none were cited in the studies reviewed for this paper), this might be a fruitful avenue for future interpretive inquiry.

## CONCLUDING   REMARKS

Christmas is the central festival of American culture, making manifest the norms and ideals that inform not only our consumption ideology, but also our societal character, as well.  Christmas is a study in contrasts, of many dialectics which we embrace as individuals and as a society.  It is both happy and sad, ingenuous and cynical, spiritual and crass, selfish and altruisitic, a celebration of God, a deification of Mammon.  Consumers make of Christmas what they can; what they will; what they wish.  The true meaning of Christmas lies within each of us; and for each of us, it is a unique truth.

## APPENDIX

### A  Brief  Excursus  on  Hanukkah

Hannukah, or the Festival of Lights, is a Jewish holiday commemorating a historic event in which the Temple at Jerusalem was re-dedicated after a fierce battle between the Hebrew Maccabees and the Syrians.  According to religious tradition, only one day's quantity of oil remained to relight the altar in the Temple, yet, miraculously, the oil burned for eight days.  As Jews have become more assimilated into mainstream (i.e., Protestant Christian) American culture, their celebration of Hanukkah -- which occurs for eight days in early-to-mid December -- has taken on many aspects of the Christian Christmas festival.  For example, in many Jewish households children now are given gifts by their parents on each of the eight nights of Hanukkah.  Further, the menorah (an eight-branched candelabrum used to signify the eight days of light) is now available in an electric version, which 'burns' Christmas tree lights, instead of the traditional candles.  Some Jewish households even incorporate a small evergreen tree (euphemistically referred to as a 'Hanukkah bush') into their celebration of this religious festival.

Within our sample were several MBA degree candidates and undergraduate business students of the Jewish faith.  Their essay assignment was to write about "What does Hanukkah mean to you?"  In keeping with the adaptation of Hanukkah to resemble Christmas in many of its ritual aspects (e.g., gift- giving, evergreen trees), their essays reflected a tendency to ascribe sacred and secular characteristics to this festival that reiterated those in the Christmas essays.  However, there were some instructive shadings of meaning, as well.

For example, consider some essay excerpts below on the *religious* aspects of the festival:

"Hanukkah in a religious sense means the remembrance and commemoration of good triumphing over evil, of the miracle of lights, and the assertion of freedom."

"Hanukkah is also a time for reflection about the history of my ancestors...Thinking about the story of the Maccabees as I light the menorah always makes me feel proud of the small group of Jews who won a war.  It also makes me think about hope and miracles."

"Jews have been through so much, [but] they've still managed to hold on to their religion.  I think of this during Hanukkah and hope that the religion will live on."

"Being proud of the fact that I am a Jew."

"It helps me remember who I am, the people I come from, and their past."

As these excerpts indicate, the religious aspects of Hanukkah (for these Jewish consumers) are centered much more around ethnic identity and heritage, than transcendant theological beliefs, as was the case for Christmas. In essence, the sacred, religious aspects of Hanukkah are closely akin to the sacred communal sentiment of interpersonal bonding -- except that here the bonding is to one's ancestors and their history. The Hanukkah festival and the Jewish people are viewed as one-and-the-same; to *celebrate* one is to *be* the other.

Despite this difference in the religious meaning ascribed to Hanukkah vis a vis Christmas, the Jewish essayists expressed sentiments about the *communal/interpersonal* aspects of Hanukkah that were analogous to those of their Christian counterparts.

"I tell my family I love them."

"Brings the family together, which adds to the fun and excitement of the 'giving' season."

"A happy time; a family time -- that about sums it up."

"A time to see faces that have been missed throughout the year."

Despite these positive, familial sentiments, these essayists also expressed the dialectic negative reaction to the *commercialism and materialism* of the season that characterized the Christmas essays.

"I basically think of Christmas and Hanukkah as a time for high prices, crowds, retail pressure, waste, and general fervor."

"Christmas/Hanukkah is a time for retailers to make more money...[It] has become representative of American commercialism..."

Some also expressed a negative response to the season that was not typical of their Christian counterparts. While some Christian consumers were disappointed and cynical over the superficiality and frustration of Christmas shopping and gift-giving, Jewish consumers sometimes experienced feelings of *alienation* and *isolation* due to their minority ethnic status.

"Christmas time brought with it feelings of coziness, frivolity and love...[which] made Hanukkah look rather shabby in comparison... A beautifully lit Christmas tree made the menorah appear quite drab..."

"I loved the Christmas season, but felt left out..."

"Hanukkah means days full of anticipation for the children, [but] also watching their difficulties in dealing with the hype of Christmas."

Although *gift-giving* is not as central to the celebration of Hanukkah as it is to Christmas, many Jewish essayists also cited this as an important aspect of the festival. As with Christians, Jews viewed gifts in both a secular and sacred sense:

"I remember awakening at dawn for eight straight days nearly bursting with anticipation. What would I get?!"

"We strive to show our warmth, caring and indebtedness to others by bringing gifts."

Finally, as with the Christian essayists, the Jewish writers also associated sensual and hedonic experiences with Hanukkah:

"Excellent food and great parties."

"Sleeping late."

"I can't get through the holidays without eating 3/4 of everything in sight."

"Eating latkes!"

Thus, like Christmas, Hanukkah has its own sensual pleasures and its own sources of hedonic guilt.

## REFERENCES

Bagozzi, Richard P. (1975), "Marketing as Exchange," *Journal of Marketing*, 39(October), 32-9.

Barnett, James H. (1954), *The American Christmas: A Study in National Culture*, Salem, New Hampshire: Ayer Company.

Belk, Russell W., (1987), "A Child's Christmas in America: Santa Claus as Deity, Consumption as Religion," *Journal of American Culture*, Spring.

_____ (1979), "Gift Giving Behavior," *Research in Marketing*, Vol. 2, J.N. Sheth, ed., Greenwich, CT: JAI Press, Inc., 95-126.

Brinberg, David and Ronald Wood (1983), "A Resource Exchange Theory Analysis of Consumer Behavior," *Journal of Consumer Research*, 10(December), 330-8.

Caplow, Theodore, (1982), "Christmas Gifts and Kin Networks," *American Sociological Review*, Vol 47, June, 383-392.

Caplow, Theodore and Margaret Holmes Williamson, (1980), "Decoding Middletown's Easter Bunny," *Semiotica*, 32, 314, 221-232.

Caplow, Theodore, (1984), "Rule Enforcement Without Visible Means: Christmas Gift Giving in Middletown," *American Journal of Sociology*, 1306-1323.

Durkheim, Emile, (1915,1961), *The Elementary Forms of Religious Life*, J.W. Swain transl., New York: Macmillan.

Gallup, George, Jr., (1981), "Defining the Devout: The Polls and Religious Belief," *Public Opinion Quarterly*, 4(April, May), 20.

Garfinkel, Harold (1967), *Studies in Ethnomethodology*, Englewood Cliff, N.J.: Prentice Hall.

Heritage, John, (1984), *Garfinkel and Ethnomethodology*, Cambridge: Polity Press.

Hirschman, Elizabeth C. (1987), "People as Products: Analysis of a Complex Marketing Exchange," *Journal of Marketing*, (January), Vol. 51, 98-108.

_____ and Morris B. Holbrook (1982), "Hedonic Consumption: Emerging Concepts, Methods and Propositions," *Journal of Marketing*, 46, (Summer), 92-101.

Holbrook, Morris B. and Elizabeth C. Hirschman (1982), "The Experiential Aspects of Consumer Behavior: Consumer Fantasies, Feelings, and Fun," *Journal of Consumer Research*, 9, (September), 132-140.

LaBarbera, Priscilla A., (1987), "Consumer Behavior and Born Again Christianity," *Research in Consumer Behavior*, Vol. II, J.N. Sheth and E.C. Hirschman, eds., JAI Press, Greenwich, CT., 193-222.

Leiter, Kenneth C., (1980), *A Primer on Ethnomethodology*, Oxford: Oxford University Press.

Levy, Sidney J. (1981), "Interpreting Consumer Mythology: A Structural Approach to Consumer Behavior," *Journal of Marketing*, 45(Summer), 49-61.

Mick, David Glen, (1986), "Consumer Research and Semiotics: Exploring the Morphology of Signs, Symbols and Significance," *Journal of Consumer Research*, 13(September), 196-213.

Moschetti, Gregory J., (1979), "The Christmas Potlatch: A Refinement on the Sociological Interpretation of Gift Exchange," *Sociological Focus*, Vol. 12, 1, January, 1-7.

Pollay, Richard W. (1986), "It's the Thought That Counts: A Case Study in Xmas Excesses," in *Advances in Consumer Research*, Vol. 14, eds. Melanie Wallendorf and Paul Anderson, Provo, UT: Association for Consumer Research, 140-143.

Rook, Dennis W. (1985), "The Ritual Dimension of Consumer Behavior," *Journal of Consumer Research*, 12, (December), 251-264.

Sherry, John F., Jr. (1983), "Gift Giving in Anthropological Perspective," *Journal of Consumer Research*, 10(September), 157-68.

Whalen, William J., (1984), *The Quakers*, Friends General Conference, 1520-B Race Street, Philadelphia, PA.

# Unpacking the Holiday Presence:
## A Comparative Ethnography of Two Gift Stores

John F. Sherry, Jr., Northwestern University
Mary Ann McGrath, Loyola University of Chicago[1]

## ABSTRACT

This paper describes an ethnographic study of two midwestern American gift stores. Using a processual model of gift giving, ethnographers employed participant observation and depth interviews in two separate retail contexts during the Christmas/Hanukkah season to create a thick description of elements of particular phases of the giving process. Summary ethnographies are presented in extended case study format as a baseline for comparing critical features of the phases, for deriving propositions about the contextual embeddedness of gift giving behaviors, and for interpreting the significance of retail environment on the social construction of the holidays. Implications of the study for infrastructural aspects of consumer behavior and marketing related to gift giving (such as female entrepreneurialism, organizational culture, etc.), are also explored. Directions for future research are outlined.

> Like so many Americans, she was trying to construct a life that made sense from things she found in gift shops. Kurt Vonnegut, *Slaughterhouse-Five or the Children's Crusade: A Duty Dance with Death* (1969)

## INTRODUCTION

While none of us may ever construct his or her reality in as disjointed or disfiguring a manner as does the mother of Billy Pilgrim, himself the protagonist of Vonnegut's black comedic novel, still we are profoundly affected by the gift giving relationships we forge over the lifecourse. Beyond the shallowness and desperation, implicit in the epigraph, of a search process merging bricolage and bric-a-brac, little of the sense-making apparatus and procedures of gift shopping in contemporary culture has been explored by writers or researchers. Since the probing of the semiotic significance of the gift itself has only recently been resumed (e.g., Cheal, 1987, Baudrillard 1981, Hyde 1979, MacCannell 1976), it is perhaps not too surprising that an institutional locus of meaning production and discovery--the retail gift shop--has been heretofore largely ignored. Consumer researchers of anthropological bent (Sherry 1983, McCracken 1988a) have called for the investigation of gift stores, while those espousing naturalistic inquiry methods have used such retail sites as a kind of comparative foil to less overtly commercial or profane consumption venues in the development of theoretic constructs (Belk, Wallendorf and Sherry 1989). The present chapter is devoted to creating an ethnographic baseline and a set of propositions by which a deeper understanding of the gift store as a complex institution may be derived.

The field study from which this ethnography emerges was framed in terms of a process model of gift giving proposed by Sherry (1983). This model describes the three stages of a transaction through which donor and recipient progress. All behavior antecedent to the actual gift exchange, most notably those conditions impinging upon search, occurs during the Gestation stage. The gift exchange itself, and its attendant ritual dynamics, occurs during the Prestation stage. The relationship between donor and recipient is realigned, and the course of future gift exchanges affected, during the Reformulation stage.

In elaborating this model, Sherry (1983) issued a detailed programmatic call for comprehensive, contextually sensitive research into gift giving behavior. In particular, he suggested that extended case study of the gift store, especially during ritually propitious seasons, would prove most valuable. Such study would assist in answering research questions associated with stages one and three of the processual model. The transformation of the purchased gift from conceptual to material realms, as well as from commodity to singular object, begins in this retail nexus. The investing of the object with "gift-ness," however shaped by advertising (Waits 1978), is catalyzed in the store. Meaning divestiture occurs here as well, when gifts are returned and exchanged. As a fieldsite, the gift store permits the researcher access to a range of gift giving behaviors, and facilitates efficient, holistic interpretation of a host of related issues. It is an opportune setting in which to begin tracking those "symbolic processes" Cheal (1986, 437) finds lacking in conventional studies of gift giving, and which are also underrepresented in conventional consumer research.

The following pages are devoted to several particular issues. First of all, the ethnographic methodology employed in the study is detailed, and the implications of such naturalistic inquiry for consumer research are reviewed. Secondly, two summary ethnographies of gift store activity are presented. These baseline thick descriptions are then compared and contrasted for the insight they provide into generalized and local understanding of consumer behaviors associated with gift stores. Thirdly, a short list of interpretive propositions is proposed, which reflects the researchers' understanding of their fieldsites. Finally, these propositions are offered as a springboard into further research.

---

[1]The authors would like to thank the following scholars for comments on earlier versions of this paper: Eric Arnould, Russel Belk, Rohit Deshpande, David Plath, Michael Solomon, and Melanie Wallendorf.

## METHODOLOGY

A recent spate of articles and presentations (for exemplars and extensive references, see Belk, Sherry and Wallendorf 1988; Belk, Wallendorf and Sherry 1989; Hirschman 1986; Hudson and Ozanne 1988; Sherry 1987a; Wallendorf and Arnould 1988) marks a reawakening of interest among consumer researchers in methods alternative to experiment and survey. The present chapter contributes to this re-emergence. The resurgence of qualitative research amounts to the dropping of the second shoe: the advocacy of a "broadened" conception of consumer behavior is now being accompanied by an advocacy of methods capable of accommodating this broadening. Thus, semiotic, humanistic, and naturalistic perspectives are being touted as correctives to a premature narrowing of focus, if not an absolute metatheoretical bias, within the discipline of consumer research. Without embroiling ourselves in the epistemological wrangle between so-called positivist and nonpositivist consumer researchers, nor embarking upon another tutorial exposition of alternative methods, we will lay out the tenets and limitations of the ethnographic approach we observed in our study.

Purposive or judgmental sampling governed site selection. Recognizing that among all consumer objects the "gift" is among the most likely to be imbued with a significant cultural biography (Kopytoff 1986), we selected retail outlets that specialized exclusively in merchandise positioned as gifts. That is, the principal function ascribed to objects in these stores by consumers and retailers alike is suitability as a gift (Thaler 1985). We found this emic ascription to be etically sound. The objects exist in a semiotic variant of a total institution (Baudrillard 1968; Goffman 1961), their intrinsic and extrinsic (or projected and projectible) meanings governed by the sociocommercial construction of "gift" as negotiated by retailer and consumer, and their cumulative impact creating a spatio-temporal dimension distinctly separate from the ordinary. As a promotional brochure from one of our shops suggests, these stores stock "everything you don't need, can't afford, but can't live without." In addition to this generic or hermetic judgment standard, issues of efficiency and comparability determined site selection. Thus we encountered informants whose primary situational objective was focused on issues related to gift giving, rather than on other buyer behaviors. Our observations and interviews occurred *in situ*, in a naturalistic context.

Each researcher selected one gift shop to investigate in detail. Because the study was explicitly exploratory, we sought to increase the quality and quantity of insight that might be brought to bear upon future comprehensive investigations, especially joint investigations of single sites, by immersing ourselves in separate fieldsites. Each of us discussed findings and conjectures on a regular basis throughout the study, and the direction of subsequent inquiry was shaped in part by these periodic discussions. This procedure has been termed "memoing" (Lincoln and Guba 1985, Strauss 1987). Our emergent design was guided solely by our shared assumption that significant activity occurred in gift stores, and that we could capture something of this significance in a thick description of our fieldsites.

Some elaboration on research bias will help clarify the design we employed in this study. As noted, we discovered no ethnographic precedent for our investigation. The nearest approximation unearthed, a curious hybrid of consumerist concern and muckraking exposé (Maclean 1899), was a covertly and unsystematically conducted participant observation study of selected activities in a number of Chicago department stores set during the Christmas season. As an early example of the kind of blitzkrieg ethnography (Sherry 1987b) that threatens sensitive interpretation of complex phenomena, despite the intriguing snippets of insight derived from transient field immersion, this sociological foray obliquely illustrated the potential contribution of a naturalistic inquiry of holiday retailing activity.

Given the impoverished but promising precedent for our study, and the fact that neither of us had conducted previous investigations that would plausibly allow us to construe our study as diagnostic research (Whyte 1978), we approached the problem from a virtual historical particularist perspective. Because the phenomena of interest were transient, and the duration of our field immersion was self-limiting, we focused principally on the creation of an ethnographic record that would enfranchise speculation within obvious limits of generalizability and permit the design of more sensitively targeted studies in the future.

With these modest aspirations and a chariness of affixing the label "ethnographic" to a single-season study, we settled on a pair of fieldsites. A conservative "one- researcher- one- site" principle was adopted for two reasons. Foremost among these was depth of understanding in the face of severe time constraints. By studying a single shop intensively, each of us was able to amass a far greater wealth of local detail to aid in the framing of a more comprehensive negotiated interpretation of gift store activity than would have been possible with a shared site design. In this sense, our exploratory study was incipiently confirmatory. The range of phenomena we hoped to describe was expected to overlap across stores, with outliers providing directions for additional research. A more pragmatic reason for single-site immersion had to do with the relative obtrusiveness of short-term ethnographic work. Our access to small, highly personalized and seasonally sensitive commercial sites depended in good measure upon our ability to interfere minimally with the round of life in the stores. The merit of a team approach (Belk, Sherry and Wallendorf 1988) is diminished to the degree that it impedes access to a site. Our consequent compromise was to transmute the notion of teamwork, triangulating our gender-mediated observations through routine, periodic discussions of our observations, interpretations and direction during passive and active stages of research, and negotiating the propositions with which we have concluded this chapter.

We selected our fieldsites to facilitate the kind of comparison that would allow the creation of an ethnographic record. That is, we used similarity as our principal criterion. Our stores carry comparable merchandise, and are operated as well as patronized by similar kinds of people. Owners, managers and clientele are drawn chiefly from the upper-middle class, with some spill-over from both lower upper and lower middle classes. Thus, we stress the exploratory nature of our study, and the clear limits to generalizability, and trust that future investigations of gift store activity which focus on outlets upscale or downscale with respect to our own will benefit from our description. Similarly, studies contrasting different kinds of outlets (family-owned and -operated vs. franchised, large vs. small, shops vs. mall stores, etc) are expected to benefit from this effort.

Seeking to exploit the liturgical calendar, we began the study early in December. Such timing allowed us access to shoppers during Hanukkah (beginning December 8 the year of this study) and Christmas gift giving seasons, as well as to the ambience of the commercial holidays. The study continued into the early weeks of January. Post-holiday investigation permitted researchers to include gift returns and exchanges, along with the purchase of self-gifts made possible through conversion of cash gifts and through sales, in their behavioral sampling frame. Each researcher spent between 12 to 24 hours per week, scattered across weekdays and weekends, days and evenings, at his or her respective site. In follow-up investigations, each researcher was able to attend a regional Gift Show at which store buyers routinely search, restock, trade information and observe trends. One of the researchers has continued to study her fieldsite longitudinally, and anticipates returning to the shop for her third season (McGrath 1988a).

Data were collected through participant observation, directive and non-directive interviewing, and to a limited degree by photography. Over time, researchers were given relatively unrestricted access to front and back regions (Goffman 1959) of their respective stores. As trust and rapport were established between ethnographers and informants, researchers' participation in the round of store life increased. Mere physical presence as an observer gradually gave way to active involvement of various kinds, as researchers became helpers during periods of peak activity. Depth interviews during periods of downtime, intercept interviews and periodic shopping with consumers, integrated throughout by observation *in situ*, made it possible for researchers to ask increasingly sensible questions about gift store activity as the study progressed. Data were recorded in field notes and journals. Member checking (Lincoln and Guba 1985) was observed to the extent that researchers solicited feedback on their observations from informants. Some key informants were provided with drafts of researchers' materials, and store owners were provided copies of the completed study as a condition of access and informed consent.

In the following sections, a summary ethnography of each of our field experiences is presented. We explore a number of settings, actors, events, processes and objects related to the processual model of gift giving. Pseudonyms are employed throughout these descriptions. The two gift shops are located in noncontiguous communities in the same greater metropolitan region of the midwestern United States. As a primarily descriptive exercise designed to generate insight into gift giving behavior, the limits to generalization of this study are clear. Further, the observations contained in the ethnographies are acutely time-bound, forged as they were during periods of peak activity.

## GIFT STORE I: THE MOUSE HOUSE

Tucked away near the corner of a festively lighted concourse of a very upscale suburban retail strip, nestled among restaurants, doctor's offices, specialty food stores, boutiques, spas and beauty parlors, is a quaint little gift shop called "The Mouse House." The shop takes its name from a once popular children's novel, and both the physical structure and ambience of its setting heighten the nostalgic story-book quality of the store. Every aspect of the Mouse House seems to invite the consumer's participation. The window display fronting the street is a traditional midwestern American Christmas scene, the flocked pane disclosing a beautifully decorated tree replete with ornamental angels and a host of assorted Christmas knickknacks. Upon opening the door, the consumer is met by the soft strains of seasonal carols and gently embraced by the pleasantly aromatic scent of a "Christmas brew" simmering in a kettle on the sill. An elderly golden labrador greets customers at the door, receiving frequent pats and comments from those entering the store, and jocular farewells from those leaving. An occasional customer is startled into laughter by the movement of a dog presumed to be stuffed.

### Ambience

This invited participation is enhanced as the customer moves further into the store. The modest size of the store (a roughly trapezoidal 450 square feet) is a structural asset. Rustic barrel tables and containers, nonlocking glass cabinets and shelving units of various construction crowd the aisles of the shops. Walls and ceiling beams hold merchandise. Hutches, chairs and couches are similarly laden with goods. Walkways are narrow, and the displays cornucopic, forcing browsers to slow their pace in order to avoid upsetting or overlooking items. Nowhere is there displayed a sign requesting browsers to refrain from handling the often fragile and costly items. In fact, such handling is expected and encouraged. Such design creates the impression that the store is on the verge of bursting with its contents, overflowing with treasures of every description. Thus displayed, the merchandise seems quite accessible and familiar.

This cornucopic effect is enhanced by the owner's practice of rearranging merchandise periodically, highlighting the formerly hidden and downplaying the familiar; the appearance of added abundance is achieved with no additional stock. Yet at no time does the store display appear chaotic or haphazard, despite the high traffic of the holidays. The owner's flair for interior design and appropriate groupings -- her sense for what McCracken (1988b) has called "Diderot unities," Cassirer (Fernandez 1986, 191) the "consanguinity of things" and Solomon and Assael (1987) "product constellations" -- acknowledged by clerks and customers alike, transforms the threat of clutter into a "Mouse House."[2] That is, one feels as if he or she has entered into a home, industriously over-furnished through the tirelessly acquisitive efforts of a tasteful hoarder.

## Merchandise

The Mouse House is stocked with a staggeringly eclectic variety of goods. In both emic and etic perspective, the objects range from kitsch to fine art, from dispensable to collectible. Prices themselves range from a few dollars to a few thousand dollars. A variety of crafts from local artisans graces the aisles and walls. Jewelry, statuary, tapestries, wall hangings and crystal are everywhere in evidence. Greeting cards, figurines, dolls, paintings and toys of various kinds abound. Seasonal and novelty items are popular. Nail sculptures share counterspace with crystal birdhouses. Mobiles and chimes, aquaria and stained lead glass, candles and photo albums, reindeer-visaged baseball caps and gag medicinal products (e.g., vasectomy pills) are all to be found in the shop. Marionettes, whiskey decanters, costly kaleidoscopes, music boxes, wrought iron strollers, brass rocking horses and ceramic sundials are also available. If there is a rationale or unifying theme to this assortment, it is the notion of "uniqueness." The owner admits to having a knack for identifying beautiful things, and uses scarcity as a standard in her aesthetic canon. Clerks and customers alike repeatedly affirm the perception of "uniqueness" that attaches to the Mouse House and its treasures. Even the gag items partake of this uniqueness. "Uniqueness" is employed by informants in several senses: items are literally one-of-a-kind; items are believed to be unavailable in any other accessible outlet, although duplicates exist in-store; items *in toto*, the assortment as collective offering, are believed to be unavailable elsewhere, as the synechdochic sacralization characterizing collections

(Belk et al 1988) would suggest. Most of the items have a biography with which the clerks are intimately familiar. Provenance, details on crafting and crafts people, acquisition history, pre- and post-purchase personal experience narratives attached to items, and a range of evaluations are just a few of the dimensions captured in many of these biographies.

## History

The Mouse House is a franchise operation that permits local owners a wide degree of latitude in personalizing the concept. Some owners are little more than passive operators who obtain all merchandising and operating ideas from the original "Main Mouse" and his network of owners; even buying may be completely delegated. Other owners are more entrepreneurial, and use the network for idea generation and information exchange, but prefer to personalize or localize their operation. Marilyn, the owner of our Mouse House fieldsite, is such an entrepreneur. She purchased a dying franchise, in which she was a clerk, five years ago as a "retirement" business. She relocated the shop, and has built it into a thriving concern. She avails herself of Mice "conventions" and "buying trips," but prefers to rely on her own sense of propriety. Frequently she commissions items from local artisans, and shops the U.S. coastal Gift Shows. She has established contacts in Europe as well. Success has forced her to move into her present retail location, double the size of her site just a year ago. Her personalization strategy has been effective. Customers have been overheard to speculate about the franchise-ability of the Mouse House. Others are surprised to learn that it is already franchised. Still others remark upon its "uniqueness" compared to its counterparts throughout the country. Marilyn does one third of her gross business and makes all of her profit during the Christmas season.[3] This December alone she has sold 83,000 dollars worth of merchandise, and taken back only 400 dollars worth of returns in January. She has finished 25% over her projection for the year.

## Choice Heuristic

Marilyn's business acumen and her selection standards reflect a tension between vocation and avocation. She is unable to articulate a choice heuristic with much precision. She enjoys "being around beautiful things" and claims a "knack" for buying them. Having always wanted to become an interior designer, she indulges this dream through the store, experimenting with color coordination, object groupings and the like. Relying on her own intuition and her husband's poor judgment ("If he likes it, I don't

---

[2] One informant, an art and set director, regularly "rents" props from the Mouse House (for 15-20% of cost--a transaction department stores won't consider but which in turn elevates their returns rate when purported "buyers" are finished using goods for a short duration) as backdrops or foregrounds for her work. "It would take me forever to set up a room if I used regular department stores. What they ["the Mice"] have on this one table here would be spread throughout an entire department in a regular store. I save all kinds of time here." Parenthetically she remarks, "Sometimes I go to the counter with $500.00 worth of stuff and whip out the old charge card. I love the look on the faces of the West Lake women shoppers when I do that!"

---

[3] That is, the store would not be profitable were it not for the increased sales during this season. Interestingly enough, one sixth of the gross business derives directly from the sales of miniature mouse collectibles. This line has been adopted as a special responsibility by one of the clerks, who maintains a detailed customer list.

buy it, if he doesn't, I do"), she searches the wares of artists and artisans, weighs the suggestions of Mouse House buying cliques, and attends several annual Gift Shows, until she discovers items she feels are "right" for her customers. This "rightness" is tied both to status, class and lifestyle dimensions of her client base, as well as to individual, idiosyncratic characteristics of particular customers. She is alive as well to trends, and believes the midwest is "at least two years behind the rest of the country." Thus, she will sometimes sacrifice her sense of propriety-- "I'm still buying mauve because the midwest doesn't know it's out" --but most often prefers to deliver coastal trends to an educable, impressionable clientele. She no longer carries "country" merchandise, despite her belief that the midwest doesn't know that "country is dead," because her particular customers are discriminating and *do* know that "country is dead." Marilyn is wary of trends, however, because they "die such horrible deaths." She avoids "popular" artists for similar reasons. She is as imprecise about the price-quality relationship as she is about her aesthetic canon, noting that "there is a *lot* of expensive 'tacky' stuff" in the marketplace competing for a buyer's consideration. Her own pricing policies are intuitive, with markups ranging as high as 400%. She has sold store fixtures to ardent customers, pricing the "goods" on the spot.

Marilyn attributes her success to intuition, enthusiasm and perseverance. The petite, middle-aged proprietor, dressed in as unfailingly stylish a manner as the giftware she has so carefully selected and arranged would demand, spends a good portion of her day in direct contact with her customers, many of whom specifically seek her out for conversation. She is clearly delighted with the work she has chosen, and with the skills she has developed on her own initiative. "I spent my whole life raising children," she observes. "I got my business training on the job." While these activities are bracketed as discontinuous events, with no overt or conscious relationship to each other, she appears to conduct her business operations much like a domestic economy. That such a gift business is peculiarly suited to a familial attitude is explored later in this chapter.

## Personnel

Marilyn staffs her shop with seven other full and part-time clerks, to whom she refers as "her girls" (and to the public as "the Mice"); her husband lends a periodic hand when his own work schedule permits. The Mice function largely as consultants to shoppers, dispensing advice when requested ("Will this tureen look good on an early American table?" "Is this good for a grandmother?"), but rarely initiate a sales interaction directly. "The ladies" (an emic term used by regular and occasional customers) are valued for their low-key, no-pressure approach and for their friendliness. Customers often compare shopping in the Mouse House to visiting friends at home. The shop is frequently likened to a living room. Such recontextualizing reflects the efficacy of sacralization (Belk, Wallendorf and Sherry 1989). The Mice are just as apt to be carpet sweeping or dusting around

shoppers as waiting on customers. Each of the Mice has a number of loyal customers for whom she pays special attention as new goods arrive in the store. This attention extends beyond mere in-store catering; a customer may be alerted to treasures before they are stocked, or items may be set aside and "reserved" for particular customers. None of the Mice works on a commission basis, and each professes to love her job. One of the Mice, Jane, observes tellingly,

> "If you want to know the truth, it's like a private club. Marilyn's gotten hold of seven women who love to open gifts! Marilyn's a great little shopper, and we love to see what she's bought. We don't make much. It's just a lot of fun for two or three months out of the year."

Each of the Mice emphasizes the thrill of opening new merchandise as it arrives. The UPS deliveryman is eagerly awaited. Marilyn reinforces these expectations, noting that she always shops (the major Gift Shows) with the "girls" in mind. This builds everyone's excitement and enthusiasm. She has recently purchased a 10,000 dollar music box, and secretly awaits its arrival, knowing how it will delight the Mice. She will subsidize the purchase through the sale of music box tapes, and not feel compelled to sell the music box itself. The box will add to the store's "fairy land" atmosphere, she rationalizes. It is as well a gift to herself. The Mice exhibit a custodial regard for most of the store's merchandise, and refer constantly to Marilyn's exquisite taste. They appear to experience vicariously a continuous gift exchange relationship with their employer.

## Seasonal Cycle

The holiday selling season at the Mouse House begins with a pre-Christmas Open House held in November, and concludes with a post-season clearance sale in early January. The Open House is Marilyn's way of allowing her 3000-customer direct mail prospect base the opportunity to enter what she calls her "inner sanctum," a privilege she believes these chosen few dearly love. Each of the Mice is able to identify a number of "big spenders" and "big givers" among the direct mail base. The former keep many of the purchased presents for themselves; the latter buy strictly to give to others. Marilyn advertises in local newspapers and this year took advantage of an opportune door prize she had won--free advertising time on a local cable station--to branch out into broadcast media. Clerks and customers alike identify word-of-mouth as the principal medium of persuasive communication. During peak season in December, the store is open days and some evenings, seven days a week. During this time there are distinct activity cycles that are distinguished by time and by patron gender. The heaviest traffic occurs in the late morning and early afternoon hours, when customer volume can shoot up from 0 to 50 in just a few minutes. Most of these shoppers are women. A milder burst of activity occurs in the evening hours, when male shoppers predominate. Weekend traffic is steady throughout the day, and dominated by couples. Length of stay ranges anywhere from two to 35 minutes, with repeat visits on the same or successive day a common occurrence. Traffic builds steadily until late Christmas eve, with males being the most frantic last-minute shoppers. As one Mouse accurately observes,

> "We get rid of all our dogs on Christmas eve. Men come in, and they're so desperate they'll buy anything. Tomorrow [a Saturday in late December] all the men will come in bringing their children to buy something for mother. They'll finally get around to it."

Few returns are processed after Christmas, and much seasonal merchandise is cleared in the January sale. The season concludes with a major rearranging of the stock and the decor, as the gift shop is prepared for the upcoming Valentine's Day holiday, and gradually readied for Easter.

## Range of Shopping Activity

Holiday shopping patterns exhibit an interesting mix of intention and caprice, hedonism and stress, gift selection and order-filling. A number of vignettes illustrates this range:

- Two middle-aged women move slowly down an aisle, handling many of the items and admiring their merits. The older of the two discovered the store "by accident" one day, having come in to browse while killing time before a doctor's appointment. She "fell in love with the place," and its "unique, expensive, good things," but was discouraged by the high prices. She had returned one day with her husband, who was captivated by a painting of a cheetah, to the point of fantasizing about how he might rearrange their living room to accommodate the painting. She began secretly to buy the painting on time, and plans to surprise her husband with the gift. Today she accompanies her sister, whom she brought along to share the "experience" of the store. Together, they search for gifts for their children, but the older sister buys several fragile collectibles for herself as well. The collectibles will be stored away until her children are grown and gone from home, and then properly displayed.

- A young woman searches the aisles for something "unique and unusual" for her child's teacher. She examines a clown figurine, thinking it appropriate for a teacher who is a weekend mime. "There are lots of teachers in my family, and they always complain about the crummy presents they receive. My children's teachers always tell me I give the best gifts."

- A middle-aged man enters the store with a shopping list in hand. He has come with a list of collectible figurines drawn up by his wife, essentially prepared to fill her order. But he has found a way to personalize his selection. His wife believes she will receive the figurines gradually over the years. He, however, sets about selecting over $500 worth of the tiny creatures, seeking to accelerate the pace of collection. Among the pieces selected is a mouse family with a male infant, which reminds the buyer of his new grandson. He refuses the wrapping service offered by the clerks, intending instead to allow his daughter to wrap the gifts in nondescript paper to conceal their nature and origin. "I'm the world's worst shopper," he states. "I hate it. I hate the crowds. I won't go to a department store and fight the parking. This store reflects a buyer with good taste. Merchandise is nicely displayed. I know my gift will be a good reflection on me."

- A young girl walks through the store with her mother, all the while pointing out "pretty" things, and seeks to elicit signs of approval and interest from her parent. "Shall I get *this* for you?" is a frequent question.

- A middle aged woman has come looking specifically for an owl statue like the kind her husband collects. During her search, she browses for additional items she might want. She decides upon a figurine of a bear playing with a turtle, feeling it well suited to her husband. She observes that, "this one [among several other variants] is *different* from all the other ones. I picked it even though it is more expensive. It's *doing* something!"

- A young woman selects a crystal bowl for its "pretty" and "unusual" qualities, intending to give it to a friend. She leaves with her purchase, but returns later in the day. On her second tour, she selects a birdhouse cleverly crafted with a golfing theme, for her sister's husband, who loves both golf and birds. Her selection is based upon her brother-in-law's annual complaint that grab-bag gifts are always sister-to-sister affairs. "Maybe now he'll be satisfied," she observes. She finishes her shopping by selecting a simple, inexpensive glass bowl for her mother-in-law.

- A young woman chooses a doll to present to her elderly mother, who is currently redecorating an apartment. The buyer has eyed the piece over the last few months, and feels it will be a nice departure from her traditional "bathrobes and perfumes" approach to Christmas giving. She likens her mother to the doll (in both appearance and presence), and thinks it will cheer the many elderly visitors her mother entertains.

- A young man carefully studies the shelves on his Christmas eve foray. He looks for gifts for more than half a dozen of his relatives. He does all his shopping on this particular day, claiming to do his "best under pressure." Having travelled all over town this morning, he intends to conclude his spree in the Mouse House. He has bought light fixtures for his father, and will install them as part of the gift. He has come to the Mouse House for "hanging stuff" for his mother, noting her great delight in wall hangings. Initially seeking stained glass, he was struck with the appropriateness of a set of wind chimes which caused him to think of his mother. He tailors his search to the personality of intended recipients: "It has to be something special that you pick out yourself; it has to suit that person just right. If they gave me a list, I wouldn't use it." This is the third consecutive year he's concluded a successful search at the Mouse House.

• Puzzling over a shelf of knickknacks, two teenage boys agonize over a selection for their mother. Spying a nearby display one exults, "Hey! This is the kind of shit she likes!"

• An elderly male carries an expensive ceramic Schnauzer to the register. The dog is the result of no specific search intention; the choice is dictated primarily by his wife's loyalty to the shop. He'd like a male version, but contents himself with the only available figure, which is female. "We travel too much," he reasons, "and can't have a real dog. I think she'll like this."

## Backstage Activity

While some of the Mice attend to consumers foraging through the aisles of the Mouse House, others of them disappear into the tiny working storeroom at the rear of the shop. Here, most often out of customers' sight and earshot, the Mice set about the activities of shipping and receiving, wrapping and repairing, and stocking and searching. In "the back," they are able to step outside of their Mouse personae, and to comment on the round of store life with little regard for decorum. Here they compare notes, trade gossip or rhetorical complaints, enjoy a brief coffee break, or slump against a convenient wall or shelf (which is often the sole respite from a long day spent entirely on their feet). Here is expressed elation or disbelief at the sale of a "dog," or disappointment at the sale of a favorite piece that has become a personal fixture or fantasy object. Expressed as well are observations of the boss' comportment: "Did you *hear* Marilyn bawl out that artist for flooding West Lake with his work? She's worried about his uniqueness!" Customers' behavior is similarly discussed: "Do you *believe* it? She didn't know the big "Miss Kitty" doll had parts [i.e., was anatomically correct] until she got it home and the kids found it in her closet! She was so embarrassed!" Or, "Some of them [women shoppers] know our stock even better than we do!" That activity in the back can become quite hectic is reflected in the triumphant declaration of Marilyn's husband, Joe, emerging wearily from a frenzied period of stock-pulling and wrapping: "Well, here it [a gift] is, Jane.

It's all wrapped, but I can't remember what it is!" On occasion, the back is invaded by customers, some of whom are store "friends," others of whom supervise the wrapping or customizing of their presents, and still others who use the phone and work table as a temporary command center, making frantic eleventh-hour consultations before committing to a purchase. In general, the order, candor, ambience and tempo of the storeroom and its activity contrasts noticeably with the fairyland of the store itself.

## Giving to Oneself

Because the Mouse House is located in an affluent suburban region known as the "West Lake," and because its merchandise is frequently so expensive (including such seasonal goods as a $1035 elfin statue and a $695 bust of Father Christmas), comments regarding "price-iness" are often elicited from consumers. Price is cited as a determinant of quality by some, and as a pretentious outrage by others. It is often linked to wistfully expressed desires, and figures into guilt-inducing or -relieving reactions exhibited by consumers. Observes one Mouse: "There's not a thing in the shop that anybody needs. The West Lake is the perfect place for that." Such exclusiveness is often referenced with regard to consumers' behaviors and fantasies involving the giving of gifts to self. Again, some verbatims are instructive:

• "I'd love to receive a gift from here, but would never buy anything here for myself. Buying here is a time investment. It shows that people *really* care if they take the time to shop here."

• "People send other people in here rather than buy for themselves all the time. It seems less frivolous. You feel guilty buying non-practical things for yourself. Or, you say that you're "*collecting*." That way, you're not *really* indulging yourself.

• "This [expensive piece of jewelry] is a present from me to me."

• A middle-aged woman selects two expensive kaleidoscopes and has them elegantly wrapped. "I'll give these to family members," she says, "and tell them, "*this* is what you are giving *me* this year."

• A middle-aged woman carries a large, talking "Gabby Gorilla" doll around with her during her lengthy search, speaking absent-mindedly to it all the while. She tells a clerk she is unsure to whom she will give the doll, but that someone will receive it as a gift. Concluding her search, and laying her selection at the counter she announces, "I've decided that nobody is worthy of this but me. I'm giving it to myself."

• "I wouldn't buy these things for myself--they're too extravagant and 'gifty,' if you know what I mean. I suppose if I *really* wanted to buy something for myself here I would, but.it's more things you'd just give to someone else as a gift."

- I wouldn't buy here for me, but I'd *love* to get. I've sent my husband here with 50/50 results. You don't really want to spend so much on yourself, but you don't mind so much when you give it away."

- "All I need to do is win the lottery. I can come back and buy what I want."

- Young woman, sweetly, to clerks: "Goodbye!" Same woman, sotto voce to husband: "Get me out of here before I go crazy and spend more!"

Thus it would seem that the gift store is more than just a treasure chest. It is also something of a Pandora's box. It can induce discomfort and distress, as well as delight. Desire is enkindled, yet often sublimated or canalized through the vehicle of the gift. Longing is fanned by prohibitive pricing and window shopping.

It is appropriate to conclude this ethnographic overview with an interpretation advanced by the gift store owner, and echoed by her "girls." Speaking of the gift business, she remarks, "People literally fall in love with it. With the piece and with the search." That passion motivates the search and figures largely in the bonding of the consumer with the purchased gift is confirmed by numerous informants. This love is clearly both erotic and agapic, a point to be considered later in the chapter.

## GIFT STORE II:  BAUBLES

Baubles is located in the downtown area of an older suburb of a major midwestern city. With a population of 75,000 this large, pre-Civil War city prides itself on its historic areas, preservation efforts, and century-old homes. It is nested among and affiliated with a neighborhood business cooperative, Poplar-Grove, named for the intersection around which the ten member stores are clustered. Most of the member stores are similar in size to the research site. The appearance of the downtown area, distinguished by restored paving-brick sidewalks, many deciduous trees substantial in size, and streetlights in a lantern design distinctive to the city, bespeaks wealth, and is an encapsulated reflection of one segment of the community. The surrounding member stores, specializing in gourmet bakery items, handmade jewelry, imported childrens' toys, fireplace equipment, women's clothing, and original artworks in paper, metal, and glass are relatively expensive small shops called boutiques which cater to an upper-middle class, urban and suburban clientele. Only one store in the Poplar-Grove area carries merchandise remotely similar to Baubles'. It is adjacent to the north, and is approximately three times as large as the focal store. Its one-of-a-kind ceramics, created by identified artisans, provides strong and direct competition to the merchandise in the focal store, but its reputation attracts customers interested in this type of merchandise into the general geographic area and into our focal store.

## Design and Decor

The specific store chosen for study may be classified as small by modern retailing standards, with 1,100 square feet of selling space and with an additional 500 square feet for receiving, administration and storage. Most of this storage space is below street level. The interior walls are white, but a variety of shapes and textures eliminate starkness. The store design, with some partial interior walls and half-walls, several built-in display areas with architecturally diverse shapes and angles, and the use of mirror accents, does not bespeak its rectangular shape. The south wall is almost entirely mirrored and visually widens the store. The window display is also a selling area, with carpeted steps for customer and staff access. Within the small retailing space, the owners and staff delineate areas of the store with names suggested by the design architect. The entrance and front window areas are designated "the canopy," as the ceiling is tented. Beyond the canopy on the left is the "crumbling Greek ruin," with half-walls and columns. Halfway between the front and rear of the store is the sales desk, cash register, and jewelry display case, beyond which is the area identified as "the Temple," characterized as High Renaissance and designed to camouflage an existing interior supporting post. The back right corner of the store is a large open area constructed of natural wood and called "the Frank Lloyd Wright" area. The back left is contemporary, with grid shelving that parallels a ceiling grid.

The merchandise is displayed on several pieces of furniture (a canvas chair and loveseat, a cushioned loveseat and chaise lounge with frames constructed of natural willow branches, some still sprouting leaves), a pine table, white formica tables and cubes, an antique hutch and a carved oak fireplace mantel. These display pieces vary greatly in size, shape and texture, and all are for sale. The furnishings convey an aura of hominess and hospitality, but due to the vast accumulation of merchandise which they hold, they cannot be used for repose. Store merchandise is also hung on the walls, or from cross pieces in the ceiling. Items hung from the ceiling by nylon filament appear to be floating in space.

## History

At the time of this study, Baubles is eight months old and the two owners of the store, Judith and Sarah, are involved in their first holiday selling season. They describe the opening of the store as a combination of hard work and lucky coincidences. Both had been thinking independently of opening a store when they were seated next to each other at a mutual friend's dinner party. (Now this friend, proud of their efforts and success, partially credits herself with the germination of Baubles, and visits the store frequently.) Neither owner had retailing experience; both are white, in their early forties, married to professionals, mothers of teenage children, and involved residents of the immediate community.

The gift store evolved from their original concept of a low-cost gourmet food store. The first several months of planning to open a store involved a process of interpersonal socialization and discernment. Together they visited several restaurants, sampled the food, and commented on the decor. They traveled together, shopped together, and read the same magazines. They discovered that they had similar tastes and that they both found shopping in small stores enjoyable and interesting. They moved away from the food concept, and "all-at-once the concept of the current store seemed right." They decided to open a small store with unusual, interesting merchandise.

> "It was a real seat-of-the-pants decision. We decided to put things in the store that we really liked, what we thought felt good. Amazingly, we've made very few errors in our inventory."

The name of the store was unanimously adopted as "right" when both women chanced upon it while simultaneously reading Victorian novels at the time of the store's inception. Two women who were hired as part-time employees one month prior to the opening of Baubles currently remain staff personnel.

## Owners

The two owners perceive themselves as having complementary, rather than identical, roles and personalities. "We are two very different people with the same tastes."

Sarah is very quiet, almost shy, and is a self-taught interior designer. She seldom talks with employees and customers, and is more socially reserved than her business partner. She continues to do some client decorating work for store customers, she undertakes all the major display changes, and she keeps the books. She is tall, slim and blond, always very fashionably, yet conservatively, dressed in solid brightly colored dresses or slacks and heeled pumps. Her perspective is visual and spatial. She attends to the physical appearance and arrangement of the store, and can locate a specific item in inventory with uncanny ease, indicating that she can "see" or envision the item in the storage area. Sarah is constantly rearranging items in the selling area, or getting items or permutations of items not currently on display from the storage area.

Judith, the other owner, is very outgoing, chatty and witty. She has dark, shoulder-length, permed hair and wears fashionable, but more outrageous, clothing than her partner. Before opening the store, she was the executive director of a community mental health association. She closely attends to costs, cashflow and profitability, as well as employee, customer, and vendor relations. When wrapping gifts, for example, she repeatedly stresses the importance of conserving boxes, colored tissue (and padding the item with less expensive white tissue) and ribbon. She admits that her knowledge of retailing has grown significantly in the eight months since the store has opened. This first Christmas/Hanukkah season precipitates some concern with regard to cashflow and inventory. She indicates that many vendors do not extend credit to

new businesses, but that their business has not been in a position to pay cash for all of their pre-holiday orders. She refuses to do business with vendors who will not extend credit, and many vendors relent to her demands. The owners complete the season without infusing additional cash into their business. To do this, Judith demonstrates her ability to get people to do what she wants them to do. An employee comments, "She can get people to do anything." Most of the ordering and delivering of the merchandise for holiday gift-giving is done in September and October, but the store does not have the revenue to pay for orders until November or December. Judith realizes after the first Christmas season that there is the possibility of needing an additional $15,000 to $25,000 of working capital for pre-holiday orders. The first holiday selling season is characterized as "very successful" in terms of profitability, although there exists no historical baseline against which to measure success. Since Hanukkah is early this year (December 8), "Baubles" does not experience a cash shortfall. They characterize themselves as "lucky" and realize that they may suffer cash shortfalls in subsequent years.

## Personnel

In addition to the owners, there are six female employees who work in the store. The remainder of the year there are three or four employees. All of the sales women work part-time, and thus have no fringe benefits, yet all evidence involvement in and commitment to the success of business. The commitment that the employees have to the success of this business is exemplified by Susan, who is a lifelong friend of Judith. She has worked in the store for three weeks before becoming an informant in this study, but her level of knowledge of procedures and merchandise and involvement in the store is substantial. She perpetually makes substantive display changes in the course of her time at work, apparently as a result of understanding the owners' strategy of constant change and as a way to keep herself amused and occupied. She characterizes herself as bright, very industrious, and creative.

The motivation for Susan's and other employees' work in the store is not financial need. While the owners and clients tend to be from the upper middle class, most employees are from the lower-middle class. Each engages in this employment as a type of "hobby" job. Each purchases significant amounts of store merchandise at a 20% discount, is paid $5.00 an hour, and receives no benefits. On two separate observation afternoons, employees ring up and pay for purchases that they have brought home as gifts for others the previous day they have worked at the store.

The employees appear to enjoy their jobs and their working environment. They exhibit interest in what is happening in each other's lives, and verbally acknowledge each other's arrivals and departures. They spend some idle time chatting, but are generally industrious, in both the presence and absence of customers. Without instruction, employees with free time begin inventorying merchandise, rearranging the placement of items, putting out new items for display, preparing boxes and wrapping materials to be used during busy times, and repairing damaged articles. On occasion, one employee does calligraphy to customize items.

The owners perceive that the employees have "fun" when the store is empty, and approve of this. There are candy and snacks available to employees at almost every observation. This first holiday rush is characterized as a team effort, with everyone working hard together. There is a general feeling of being short-handed. The emotional involvement of the owners and staff with each other and with the business is evident. Notes one informant:

"It was so crazy in here Saturday that when we finally closed, everybody hugged one another."

## The Importance of Place

The owners characterize "hot" and "cold" spots in the store; there are physical locations where placement of merchandise appears to accelerate or decrease in its selling rate when compared to an expected average. The "value" of a particular location within the site has been discovered by the owners though informal experimentation and intuitive correlation of sales to location. The researcher confirms that the areas around the Greek Ruin and the Renaissance temple appear to be a source of fewer sales, while merchandise near the store entrance, adjacent to the cash register and along the back wall appears to sell more quickly. The disparity is so great that the owners consider removing the Greek Ruin area, but hesitate due to the cost of such demolition. Resignedly, one owner sighs, "I can't sell a thing in there."

The owners and employees continually rearrange merchandise in the course of a selling day. The owners "totally take apart" the entire store every two weeks, moving the display pieces into different areas, and constructing new displays. This is motivated, so say the owners, in part to compensate for the unevenness in the attractiveness of selling areas. The owners say that customers report perceptions of a myriad of new merchandise following such rearrangements; an illusion of novelty is created by having the same items displayed in new locations and in the contexts of different adjoining items. Observations indicated that these arrangements were also made for the owners and sales staff, who become bored with their retail surroundings more frequently than do the customers.

One massive rearrangement takes place eight days before the store's first Christmas. The owners say they "could not stand the way things looked," describing the displays as "shopped out" and "not tight." They begin moving merchandise and display pieces at 4 p.m. on a Monday evening and finish, with a radically different appearance, around 10 p.m. the same evening. New items are in the "hot" and "cold" spots. One owner remarks that there is some new merchandise in the store, "but, in general, we fool them."

## Merchandise

The merchandise in the store may be characterized as eclectic. The owners strive to carry unique merchandise in a variety of textures, shapes, and colors, without a predominance of either country or modern styles. Many pieces are handmade, one-of-a-kind porcelains or handicrafts. Examples include baskets in unusual shapes woven from roots, handwoven woolen throws, woven wall hangings, masks, copper trays and cookie cutters in unusual shapes, glitzy art-deco jewelry, terra cotta framed mirrors, painted wooden bowls, poseable figures of human shapes constructed of wood, geese shaped from moss, and paper-mache human sculptures. Several items, such as paper mache sculptures and wall hangings, are on consignment from local artisans.

Generally the merchandise is colorful, aesthetically pleasing, and non-functional. One customer described it as "all the things you can live without, but don't want to." There are some towel and pot-racks, stools, bookmarks and scissors that are usable, but it is their form (animal shapes, abstract designs, unusual colors), not their function that makes them appropriate as merchandise in Baubles. For example, toilet plungers in the shape of flamingos and geese are stocked at a comparatively high price ($17 each), which reflects both the unique design and the inability of the consumer to find similar merchandise elsewhere. Such camp kitsch (Soskin and Ellison 1988) is discussed by Dorfles (1969), Greenberg (1957), McMullen (1968) and Schroeder (1977).

## Ambience

Judith characterizes the atmosphere of the store as "fragile, but deliberate." She is initially reluctant to allow the researcher to question customers because they might get "a strange or pushy view of the store." Appropriate customer interactions are carefully planned to reinforce the themes of "fun" and illusion. Each customer is usually greeted at the door by an owner or salesperson. The customer's need for assistance is assessed either by direct questioning or by implication. The customer who indicates a desire to browse is welcomed, and a salesperson stays at the side of the person, but in a quiet, low key manner. If the customer poses a specific gift-giving dilemma, the staff member suggests a gift item. In general, the function of the staff is to listen to and affirm the customer, and to provide background information about an object or an artisan. A staff member will often reinforce a choice with a comment like, "That's wonderful!" or "I love that!"

Lorraine, a clerk who was hired at the time of Baubles' opening, exhibits a way with customers that typifies the style of the store. She seldom leaves the customer's side once she starts to talk with a person about an item. Her voice can be quite loud, but with a customer she becomes very soft spoken. (Both owners independently comment to the researcher about the change in Lorraine's voice modulation since she began working at the store.) She assumes the role of communicating information to customers about artisans who crafted a piece, the geography of the area from which it has come, the materials from which it is created, how it works (if it works), and the uses to which the item might be put. She has the ability to establish a rapport with customers so as to learn the specifics of their gift-giving needs and to make appropriate gift suggestions. This first holiday season she proudly tells of spending two hours with a customer who eventually purchases $700 worth of merchandise.

The store is visually stimulating, but cassette and radio music is consciously used to manipulate the atmosphere. When the store is relatively busy, Judith tends to play a classical tape "to calm things down." Upbeat music is used to energize a quiet period and traditional Christmas songs (without lyrics) are interspersed. The atmosphere of the store is mentioned by some customers as a haven not only from the bitter-cold winter of the first Christmas season, but also from the frantic Christmas shopping found in many stores and mall settings. This atmosphere, calculated to be calming and visually pleasing, is perceived by some as a holiday gift to its customers or as a customer's gift to herself. Several shoppers make remarks about the atmosphere, reflecting the sacralizing and decommoditizing that takes place in the setting (Waits 1983; Kopytoff 1986).

> "Coming here is like coming to a gallery. It's not like coming to a store."

> "I hate to shop, but I like to come here. It's relaxing."

> "I love this store. I wish my home were like this."

> "In some small stores, it feels like the people are watching you, expecting you to take something; not like here."

## The Marketing Mix

Not explicitly mentioned by the owners, but implicit in the buying process, is a deemphasizing of the price component of the marketing mix. By focusing more attention on product uniqueness and on customer interactions, price becomes less of an issue. A week before Christmas many seasonal items are discounted. The owners claim that they do not believe in having sales or doing markdowns (although they have a storewide sale with all merchandise 30% off in mid-January) and want to avoid post-Christmas markdowns on seasonal items. "Having sales is not our policy." To mark items down they replace old price tags with new ones, adjusting prices downward with no tangible indication to customers. Some of the marked down items evidence price sensitivity. Notably, a hand-wrought tin house in which a candle is burned is priced at $37.50 until the week previous to Christmas. When the price is adjusted to $28, all five remaining in stock sell during a single afternoon, and are wrapped as gifts for their purchasers. "Around $30" is also mentioned by several customers as an appropriate price range for a specific gift choice, such as with a sister-in-law or a good friend. Christmas ornaments

are similarly reduced. Some large hand-carved wooden ornaments that are priced at $23 are later remarked at $19.50 but still do not sell.

Selling price and the cost of an item are of focal importance to the owners when making their product assortment decisions. Their rule of thumb in purchasing stock is not to buy anything that cannot be marked up at least 100%. "Buying smart" at the Gift Show is a two-step process. First an item is evaluated as to whether it can sell for twice its wholesale price by assessing its perceived value. The second step is an assessment of whether it "fits" or "belongs" in the store. Explanations of item choice were intuitive. "This feels right." "This belongs in the store." They articulate a fear of stocking too much "country" merchandise, a positioning strategy they seek to avoid.

## Shopping Behaviors

Judith notes a pattern in husband-wife buying behavior. Her observations confirm her theory that women generally do not feel they have the authority to purchase household acquisitions or gifts being given from the couple together. She says that women scout and browse during the week, and they often promise to "bring their husbands in on Saturday." She perceives that it is on the weekends, when the couple is together in the store, that purchasing takes place.

> "It's the craziest thing. The women will walk out of the store with a $200 piece of jewelry on an impulse for themselves, but they won't buy a ceramic for the dining room table at the same price without their husband's approval."

Several observations are made of a woman in her late twenties as she visits the store on three different occasions to examine a canvas covered loveseat and matching chair. She expresses the desire to order them, but she wants to have her husband come in for approval. On one occasion (a Saturday) she confides that he is home babysitting and baking Christmas cookies, "and you can't beat that." When he accompanies her on a subsequent Saturday, they agree on the design of the furniture, but they cannot settle on an appropriate color. They finally order the pieces in black on a subsequent visit.

The owners note a rhythm or cycle to the shopping day, which they feel is particularly evident on Saturdays. Mornings are slow, a time when they theorize people do their "necessary errands", and by the afternoon they are ready to do "this type" of shopping. "This type" appears to be gift and recreational shopping and browsing. By afternoon, as predicted, male customers begin to appear in the store, both alone and with female companions. The exception is the Saturday on which a televised professional football game disrupts predicted shopping patterns, presumably dissuading some male prospects from leaving their homes. Several female customers come in to buy and browse, many mentioning that they have left their children in the care of their televiewing husbands.

The lone male shopper becomes more prevalent as Christmas approaches. As predicted by the owners, the Saturday before Christmas, and Christmas eve itself, were frenetic shopping days for men. These male customers tend to make large and rapid purchases. One man drives from a suburb one hour distant to purchase a specific hand-sewn, beaded Venezuelan vest. Another male customer, entering the shop fifteen minutes before closing time, quickly chooses a bracelet and necklace for his wife. As these gifts are being wrapped, he purchases a second necklace, this one of beaded African design, which one of the sales people has been wearing. Such wearing of merchandise is a common display technique for jewelry in this store. Many of these men purchase a specific item as a gift for their wives, the choices apparently having been made in advance by the wives. The gift is not to be a surprise, but an orchestrated event, with the husband taking the role of purchasing agent. Notes one shopper,

"In my youth I used to try to be creative and buy things I liked. It was a disaster. Now I just ask for a list, and she's happy."

One man is disappointed to find that a specific ceramic clock for which he has come is not in stock. He peruses walls and shelves, hoping to find another appropriate item for his wife's gift, but laments, "You know how it is when you have your mind set on something." He finally orders the clock, which cannot be delivered for six weeks, and asks the clerk to wrap a store box into which he has placed a note explaining his inability to produce the clock for Christmas.

### Front- and Backstage

A dyadic separation exists between the store setting and its backstage or off-stage areas. (Goffman, 1959). Front stage, the selling area is orderly, spotlessly clean, polite, and customer- and service-oriented. Backstage is allowed to be disorderly and chaotic, with high cost-awareness, and a place where staff may speak off-the-record, eat, and smoke. Front stage sales clerks and owners are helpful, and reinforce a customer's purchase decision. When presented with an item a customer has chosen to buy, the clerk and often several others exclaim "that's wonderful" or "lovely". They take care with wrapping, and listen as the customer chats about the gift or its recipient. After the customer departs, backstage comments are made in the privacy:

"I didn't think we'd ever sell that!"

"That has been here since the store opened. I might get a bonus for selling it."

"That is one of the few things in this store that I personally cannot stand."

The owners and staff have defined and separated appropriate scripts for front stage and backstage. Judith relates the story of working with a married couple one Saturday. The wife has visited the store during the week and presents her husband with several gift alternatives. The husband methodically makes the gift and purchase choices. Judith reports being resentful of the husband's dominance and patronizing interaction with his wife. Her front stage comment to him is "You look like an organized person," to which he replied, "Yes, I am." She continues to work with them and stroke the gentleman's ego front stage, but comments backstage, "I hated him." By knowing and adhering to an appropriate on-stage script, Judith does not perceive the relationship as hypocritical or schizophrenic, but rather "the type of thing you must do in this business."

The cultural backgrounds of the store personnel contribute to the appropriateness of the stage metaphor. The staff is entirely Jewish with the exception of Sarah and one part-time staff member, and they are not personally involved in Christmas gift-exchanges. They have given gifts for Hanukkah early in December, and are uninvolved in the late December rush. They assume the role of actors, but not participants, in the buying process. Their lack of participation in the cultural holiday is in particular evidence in the display of seasonal items in the store. Christmas ornaments are piled in baskets, and there is no tree or wreath on which to hang them. There are several wooden peg decorations in stock which may be used to hang Christmas stockings in the absence of a fireplace mantel. These are lying about the store, rather than hung with sample stockings. The script for the celebration of the holiday is not clearly defined by those who observe, but do not participate in it. No informant reported being troubled by this dichotomy.

### SUMMARY COMPARISON

Overall, our gift shops exhibited significantly greater similarity than difference. Much of this parallelism may be attributable to the similarity of their neighborhoods and clientele. Both stores are haunts of upper-middle class shoppers, are the domain and creation of upper-middle class owners, and are staffed by upper-and lower-middle class employees. As such, these stores endeavor to attract and indulge the recreational gift shopper, someone who likes to shop and will "shop 'til she drops". Each store is positioned, either consciously or intuitively through the use of geography and image, as an up-scale institution.

Ironically, the stores are most similar in their deliberate positioning as "different". Each store is consciously constructed by its owner as a treasure hunt for her customers. "Discoveries" by shoppers are encouraged by the frequent rearranging of merchandise; ostensibly "new" items are foregrounded, while more familiar "other" merchandise arrangements are consigned to the background to function as context. The constant rearrangement of merchandise observed in both stores was at once a display strategy, a provision of challenge and suggestion to the problem-solving gift shopper, and a kaleidoscopic sensory experience.

Both stores maintain a semi-private backstage area where informal rules permit relaxed behavior; customers and researchers must gain the trust of store staff before being granted access to this area. It is in this region of each store that conversations involving gossip, teasing or suspicion may take place, where employees may reveal their "real" feelings about a customer or an object, and where disarray, dust, and disrepair are tolerated so as to be hidden from the front-stage area. The backstage area serves as a clubhouse of sorts for the staff members who vacillate between the role of observers of and participants in the gift buying experience of the customers.

A distinguishing characteristic of these stores is an imprecise articulation of corporate philosophy and creative concept. Rather, the emphasis is on constant attention to and preoccupation with details. One-of-a-kind items, not categories of merchandise, fill the store; their unifying theme, both from the etic and emic perspective, is the designation "gift". The perceived uniqueness of the merchandise and of the store aid in this specification, as does the constant activity of giving service. Altering displays, stocking, wrapping, dusting, returning phone calls, conversing with customers about personal lives as well as gift giving dilemmas, and managing relationships comprise the round of life in each store. Some of the principles advanced in quaint post-Depression era "how to" manuals on female entrepreneurship and the management of a female salesforce (e.g., Keir 1939, Peel, 1941/1953) have been reinvented or rediscovered by our owners. Intuition tempered by experience has produced common patterns, suggesting once again the singularity of the gift store as a retail enterprise.

The stores and their attendant activities are almost exclusively gender-specific activity areas. The conscious positioning and preoccupation with gifts is a culturally constructed female domain of responsibility (Caplow 1982; Cheal 1986, 1987). The perceived and elaborated importance of relationships, notably among staff and customers, and the feelings of comfort and pleasure associated with contextual, holistic (rather than linear and direct) shopping behavior we construe as feminine. Each store is a feminine domain, with the presence of males becoming more notable and desperate as the holiday approaches.

Considered as a product, the gift store experience is a complex and multi-leveled offering. The ambience of the store setting is a predominating marketing theme at both sites. The augmented product assortment (Kotler 1984, 473), a collection of offerings deemed suitable by both owners and customers as "gifts," includes the perceived "good taste" of the owner-buyer of each store, and it is this halo effect of the store's reputation that accompanies the gift object as it leaves the store. A second important part of the extended product offered by each store is the perceived pleasure found in the shopping experience, distinguished by customers from their experience in other stores. Customers are held in the embrace of the store setting which is perceived as a gift, and as a form of packaging which even configures merchandise obtainable in other retail settings as "unique." Immersion in the setting results in sensually experiencing (e.g., touching, smelling, etc.) objects

as a kind of foreplay culminating in the gift purchase. The packaging of this experience is a design feature we will consider in detail directly.

The connectedness between persons and objects and between persons, relationships and objects (Belk 1988) is highlighted in the observed consumer behavior of these gift shop settings. Gift choices by customers are often emotional and intuitive, with prospects--most notably females--often needing to "fall in love" with an object prior to purchase. This erotic love response to gift objects is distinct from the relational agapic love that exists between the giver and the receiver of the gift prior to the search. Customers construct or perceive a link between the object and its prospective recipient, quite frequently in-store. The object, which is "loved" by at least one of the exchange partners, will form a link between the two individuals. Following the process model proposed by Sherry (1983), the shopping behavior and gift choice which we observed in this study occurred during the Gestation phase of the gift-exchange process. This consumer behavior is a patterned repetition of the buyer behavior of the store owners who have already negotiated an earlier phase of Gestation (a meta-Gestation), during which they first registered a positive emotional response and an intuitive attraction toward an item before purchasing it as appropriate merchandise for their respective stores. The behavior of the store clerks is also mirrored later by consumers: the thrill of surprise upon initially seeing the merchandise, of touching it, and of choosing its context for display are commonly experienced.

Differences in the two stores are both mundane and dramatic. The Mouse House boasts a wider variety of merchandise and price ranges. Pricing merchandise deviates less from a standard formula based upon a constant multiple of cost at Baubles. The Mouse House has a longer history, and something of a heritage tied to its franchise roots. Because each store is a projection or institutional personification of its owner or owners (Belk 1988), the differences in the family life cycle and age of the owners are mirrored in differences in each store's staff, contents, and clientele. Marilyn, who is older and has grown children, tends to focus her life on the store, constructing a role for her husband's participation as well. Sarah and Judith shape the store within their larger lives, which include a shared preference for boutique shopping and the negotiating of the many roles involving their families and their community. These two women depend upon each other, rather than on spouses or children, and tend to hire friends (who tend in turn to resemble them in age and social standing) to support their efforts in the store.

One important contrast involves the ethno-religious differences of the owners and staff of the two stores. At the Mouse House both owner and staff fully participate in the Christmas convention as buyers and sellers, givers and receivers. For them, this becomes a working holiday season, and Marilyn and the Mice grapple with their personal gift-giving decisions while dealing with those of their customers. There is a holiday excitement in their decorating and planning both at home and in-store. Personnel juggle their work schedules to partake of personal celebratory events. At Baubles, the personal involvement level of the staff is lower, and the business mission-- profitability of a commercial enterprise engaged in its peak season--is less submerged. The Jewish owner and staff had participated in the Hanukkah celebration early in December, and while there was a mild personal involvement with a few traditional end-of-year gifts to be given (to secretaries, teachers, or service personnel), the principal concern was the staffing of the store at a level commensurate with the accelerated customer traffic. Decorations are nontraditional, nonreligious, and sometimes inappropriately displayed, due as much to miscomprehension and inexperience as to intentional ecumenicism or neutrality. We suspect that the owners of Baubles will become more commercially literate in liturgical codes as their familiarity with market segmentation grows (McGrath 1988a).

> Those classes [haves and have-nots] have been replaced by the Bored and the Entertained. The difference between them is the quality of shopping they are able to do. The bored buy cheap and boring things that look the same. The entertained buy expensive and unique-looking things.
> Andre Codrescu, *A Craving for Swan* (1986)

## SOME INTERPRETIVE PROPOSITIONS

Whether or not we accept Codrescu's (1986,98) acerbic assessment that in America shopping is life, the ritual dimension of gift selection appears undeniable. The totemic circuits (Plath 1987) of contemporary American culture through which such seasonal gifts as we have described must flow ensure that the significance of the search extends beyond immediate gift exchange relationships. These circuits--the semiotic channels that transmute artifacts to object codes--hallow search itself. Unlike Barth (1972), who feels that the key to the treasure *is* the treasure, we have construed the odyssey that is search as paramount: it is one manifestation of the magical search for authentic experience so critical to contemporary consumer culture (Stewart 1982). This extension applies as well to the investing of the gift with meaning. Gift giving is a striking illustration of the merger of symbolic and commercial economies. According to Baudrillard (1981, 64-65) the gift itself has neither use value nor exchange value. It does have symbolic exchange value, and paradoxically, is arbitrary and singular. For Baudrillard, the gift as "object" has little significance. Rather, the gift as "given" is supremely meaningful. Something of this semiotic import is evident in the imprecision and ineffability of our informants' choice heuristics. Further, Baudrillard regards the gift as ambivalent, a medium of relation and distance: love and aggression are embodied in the exchange. This ambivalence is apparent as well at the institutional level of the retail outlet. As part of the social expressions industry, the gift store embodies and engenders what Hochschild

(1983) has called the commercialization of feeling; it shapes and reflects the sacralization of consumption (Belk, Wallendorf and Sherry 1989). It remains for us to interpret the significance of this merger of symbol with commerce.

A number of themes emerges from a comparison of our baseline ethnographies. In recognition of the exploratory nature of our project, we present these themes in terms of five propositions deserving more systematic investigation. While these propositions are offered as an interpretive summary of our ethnographic work, they are intended as well to be guidelines for future research. The propositions apply to gift giving behaviors centered around gift stores, and are not alleged to have universal application.

### 1. Sense of Place is a Retail Strategy

In a recent set of essays bridging humanistic and social scientific traditions of inquiry, Hiss (1987a,b) has sensitively described the ways in which people experience places. In particular, he identifies simultaneous perception as a critical determinant of such experience. Simultaneous perception entails utter watchfulness, split-second reaction to innumerable variables, and a fluid body boundary (1987a, 53). This "evenhanded, instantaneous and outward-looking flow of attention" (1987a, 53) is displayed by many of our informants, and is elicited by the retail environment; the stores are designed to alter and disrupt mundane perceptions and assumptions by enriching stimulation. Mystery and legibility, as well as prospect and refuge (1987a, 63), characterize each of our gift stores. The built environment (Rappaport 1982) of the stores, from structural design and decor issues to object placement and rearrangement strategies, delivers a powerful message to all who enter. The experience of the store--its essentiality of place--is a gift, albeit at the level of compliance technique, from proprietor to prospect. The situation defined by the store is so persuasive that informants often feel constrained to purchase despite any particular initial intention. Notes one informant:

> "It's [the store] small, intimate, personal, friendly and nice. It [the merchandise] looks like it's all picked out special. It's such a contrast from other places I shop; the service is so great. I couldn't go back for *months* at least if I didn't buy something. It's like I'm insulting them [the staff] if I don't buy. Like they're saying, 'What's the matter? Didn't you like any of my stuff?' They appreciate you so much."

Just as in good poetry, where the "sound must be an echo to the sense," so also must the experience of the shop reinforce the spirit of the gift. This is the retail inscape. By creating such delightfully fantastic environments, the owners impart an added significance to the merchandise, which consumers then appropriate and intensify, as the purchased object completes its transformation to gift.

The overall importance of retail ambience to impression management, and in particular to shaping impressions of quality developed by consumers, is widely recognized (Mazursky and Jacoby 1985, Jacoby and Mazursky 1985). Marketers are routinely advised to construct appropriate social environments for their prospects (Darden and Schwinghammer 1985). Noting the paucity of research into such a managerially significant topic as ambience, Kotler (1974) coined the term "atmospherics" to describe the intentional design of buying environments to influence purchase behavior. While the architectural spirit of this concept is fundamental, both the term and its application can be broadened to include a more overarching set of consumption phenomena. For example, "atmospherics" denotes noise and interference, which, while arguably characteristic of buying environments, does not capture the calculated impression management Kotler has in mind. Secondly, the specific focus on purchase masks a more pervasive structuring of consumption itself. Finally, the reduction of atmospherics to just four sensory features--visual, aural, olfactory and tactile dimensions are noted by Kotler (1974)--blunts the exploration of simultaneous perception and synaesthesia which more accurately characterize ambience. Our study suggests that a more precise and higher order rendering of atmospherics is necessary.

In his eloquent appeal for enhanced topistic consciousness, Walter (1988) has observed that a true sense of place--the expressive intelligibility resulting from our ability to feel the essence of a place and grasp its meaning--has been diluted by systems of design and management that separate affect and cognition, and which fail to regard the imagination as an organ of perception. For Walter, place is a container of experience that has a specific way of being in the world (1988, 72; 117). His exhortation to rebel against the "keepers of the obvious world" who erect barriers "segregating features of experience" (1988, 3) has clearly moved both our gift store proprietors and most of their clientele. Noting that we have neither a theory that adequately comprehends the obvious world, nor a chorography that captures and harnesses the spirit of the place, Walter proposes the launching of a discipline he calls "pathetecture," which would explore the ways in which emotion is constructed through building (1988,9;119;143). Pathetecture would extend beyond mere architecture to encompass all structured human-object interactions. Recent explorations of "natural design" (Norman 1988), "sacred" dimensions of consumption (Belk, Wallendorf and Sherry 1989), corporate semiology (Gahmberg 1987), and cultural brandscapes (Sherry 1986) are just a few possible manifestations of a pathetectonic perspective. Such a perspective would enable consumer researchers to study the contextual essence, the literal grounding, of phenomena with unprecedented thoroughness. It would also permit marketing managers to approach "design" humanely, as a feature immanent in all elements of transaction. A gift store field site is a congenial natural laboratory within which to begin to elaborate pathetectural principles, given its privileged embeddedness in moral and political economies.

## 2. Gift Giving is the Work of Women

The ethnographic record suggests that women are the principal actors in gift exchange relationships. Hyde (1979, 108) remarks that in a "modern capitalist nation, to labor with gifts (and to treat them as gifts, rather than exploit them) remains a mark of the female gender." The etymology of the word gift shows the word itself to be a feminine noun, whose original meaning (Common Teutonic) is equivalent to "bride price" (the plural form equating to "wedding"); as a neutral noun (Old High German) it also denoted "poison," perhaps highlighting the ambivalent essence of the gift noted earlier. Bailey's (1971) work is instructive in regard to the latter rendering. Recent work by Cheal (1987), Garner and Wagner (1988) and McGrath (1988b) has demonstrated a strong gender linkage to gift giving. The ritual transactions necessary to the maintenance of the domestic economy in traditional American society are conducted principally by women. Gift giving is among the most important of these rituals, especially during the calendar period of the present study (Pollay 1986), and Cheal (1987, 151) construes the practice as the social reproduction of intimacy: the gendered nature of displaying love in American culture takes the form of "networks of love" (1987, 155) constructed in large part through gift exchange. That our gift stores are owned, operated and chiefly patronized by women, then is a significant cultural artifact. Of special import is the successful commercialization of this ritual responsibility. As meta-givers (i.e., those that sacralize the objects that will be resacralized as gifts) our shop owners establish the bounds of propriety for consumers selecting a gift. Coupling ritual expertise and responsibility with the rise in female entrepreneurialism, it may be safe to predict an increase in the number and success of gift stores opened by women in the near future. A more controversial prediction would posit that a gendered mediation between gift exchange and the market--between eros and logos in Hyde's (1979) scheme of things--might provide the model for a more personalized political economy and more humane workplace cultures.

Indications of just such a pacification or domestication of the workplace have arisen in the wake of the feminization of our society. If we accept Freud's (1961) assertion that work and love are life's principal motivations, their merger should be mutually enhancing and life-enriching. This merger is being catalyzed by the articulation of feminine with androcentric cultures so cogently described by Lenz and Myerhoff (1985). Adaptive characteristics attributed to women--a nurturing impulse, a need for relatedness born of a refined capacity for intimacy, a resistance to hierarchy and an affirmation of egalitarian relationships, a secular spirituality, a preference for negotiation and an antipathy to violence coupled with women's ancient repetitive devotion to process that orders the everyday life of a culture (Lenz and Myerhoff 1985, 4-9) are having an increasing impact on the contemporary workplace. A reintegration of domestic and political economies characteristic of preindustrial societies (where, significantly enough, gift economies figured prominently), and a blurring and diversification of the gender roles rigidified during industrialization are outcomes of feminization. A redefinition or repositioning of the concept of business "success" is another such outcome, which Lenz and Myerhoff (1985, 94) find especially characteristic of female entrepreneurs. This redefinition occurs in informal sector activities as well (Landman 1987).

Work by Wilkens (1987) confirms the link between entrepreneurship and the actualization of feminine values. Wilkens believes entrepreneurship to offer women escape from "the hall of mirrors" (i.e., the distorted image of femininity) created by androcentric work conventions: *working* in the business world may reinforce the negative messages that encourage women to emulate, ultimately imperfectly, imperfect masculine models, while *running* an independent enterprise subverts such reinforcing, and leads to self actualization (1987, 34). The shifting of feminine identities posited by Lenz and Myerhoff (1985) from the new feminine woman to the masculinized woman to the hybridized woman, in response to the pressures of contemporary culture change, is reflected in the range of workplace engagements, from the newly minted, corporate-bound MBAs to the bootstrapping entrepreneurs described in our study (see also Sherry 1988). While the giftware industry would seem to be a quite readily exploited niche by culturally "preadapted" female entrepreneurs, we suspect that the dynamics underlying gift economies are also strategically manipulated to great effect in other entrepreneurial ventures held in higher esteem by the culture at large.

A concluding comment on the darker side of female mediated gift exchange is warranted. As the epigraph from Codrescu would suggest, consumer behavior in contemporary culture is often trivialized in its very exaltation. Recreational shopping, itself potentially a symptom of alienation, has an unexamined half life. For some consumers, such shopping becomes ritualistic, and may potentiate the experience of transcendence (Belk, Wallendorf and Sherry 1989), or merely stave off the effects of withdrawal. The former transformation is at worst an occasion of false consciousness. The latter transformation is at best a compulsive disorder that threatens integration and autonomy. Like other disorders such as anorexia, bulimia, kleptomania, or agoraphobia, such ritualistic behavior is rarely examined by consumer researchers (see Faber and O'Guinn (1988) for a notable exception). During our study, we encountered a number of female consumers who were driven by the principle of "shop 'til you drop." Overconsumption can be emically justified if it results in gifts to self or others. Fieldwork with confirmed "shop-aholics" is urgently needed if such compulsions are to be adequately understood and addressed.

## 3. Eros and Agape Move the Gift

The gift store is a curiously commercial hybrid of collection and museum (Belk, Wallendorf and Sherry 1989). The superfluous stuff of consumer culture is fetishized within the shop (Debord 1983, 67). Employing the semiotic perspective latent in Baudrillard's (1968, 1981) work to insightfully revisionist ends, Sebeok (1987) expands the concept of fetishism beyond the realm of erotic aestheticism to consider a fetish as a supernormal sign. The ritualization by which an individual becomes imprinted by some object, and by which a cultural reproduces its critical structural categories is evident in our gift stores. Clifford (1988, 220) cites "collecting" and "display" as crucial processes of Western identity formation. To these we would add "consuming," to incorporate all experience of the object from acquisition through disposition. The objects our proprietors have collected and displayed are consumed by store personnel and clientele, by browsers as well as by purchasers. Meaning imputed to and through these objects by all of these stakeholders creates and reinforces a particular ideology. The objects our informants have chosen to "preserve, value and exchange" exist within an elaborate system of symbols (Clifford 1988, 221; Baudrillard 1968), which specifies that the stuff of "gifts" should be demonstrably "unique."

The abiding rightness of this stuff as affirmed by proprietor and prospect is its propriety as a gift. Recognition of this propriety is frequently couched in the idiom of "love culture" (Cheal 1987, 153-155). Not only are gifts sought for loved ones, whether kith or kin (the agapic motive), but the seeking itself has an amorous component (the erotic motive). Not only do our informants "love to shop" (or "hate to shop," despite or because of the holidays), but they also "fall in love" with the items they select. The bonding that occurs is not merely, or even chiefly, between gift exchange partners, but rather as well between consumer and object. The creative adaptation of Sternberg's (1986) triangular theory of love to consumer-object relations by Shimp and Madden (1988) hints at the significance of this bonding, but is a bit too timid and reductionist in nature to capture the phenomenon entirely. Fixed at the level of psychological process, and stunted by the omission of cathexis, hedonism and sacralization as dimensions of relationship management, this conceptual framework nonetheless draws attention to the impoverished technical vocabulary that characterizes much consumer research.

Drawing upon the work of G.H. Mead, Richardson (1987) has provided a useful ethnoarchaelogical account of the artifact as a "collapsed act." Richardson construes material cultural objects in part as symbols whose "meaning" emerges from whatever social interaction those objects help constitute. The sociality of the artifact has only recently begun to engage researchers, and the framing of questions has quickly outstripped any systematic search for answers. For Richardson (1987, 399), the artifact provides a preliminary definition of situation, and its evocative potential must be thoroughly probed if social reality is to be adequately interpreted. What is collapsed in the gifts singularized and circulated by our informants is multiplex: relationship management (Levitt 1983) between levels of self, producer and consumer, patron and client, donor and recipient. Fantastic and rational economies (Stewart 1982) are polarized and condensed in the gift.

The bonding that eros and agape facilitate between consumer and object requires much more empirical investigation before persuasive interpretations can be advanced. Neither the psychology nor philosophy of human-object relations (e.g., Csikszentmihalyi and Rochbert-Halton 1981; van Imwagen forthcoming), let alone the sociology of stuff (e.g., Appadurai 1986) has been sufficiently plumbed by consumer researchers interested in the experiential dimensions of consumption. Of signal importance to the development of such a subfield is the work of Elaine Scarry (1985). Speaking of our philosophical divestiture of objects, that discrediting of the significance of material objects with which we surround ourselves, Scarry advises us to trust our impulse to cling to objects. It is this clinging impulse that provides a clue to the true significance of objects, and which can impel a description of that significance; it can also alert us to the "revenge of things" (Artaud 1958) that is part of our consumer heritage. Of importance to the argument advanced in this chapter, Scarry undertakes an analysis of the interior structure of the artifact. Artifacts are a making sentient of the external world. An artifact is a "fulcrum or lever across which the force of creation moves back on to the human site and remakes the makers" (1985, 307). Thus, an artifact is a vehicle of projection and reciprocation. The "aliveness" of the artifact (that object-awareness is the implicit or covert norm, and object-unawareness the aberrant and unacceptable occurrence is brilliantly revealed and persuasively argued in her discussion of product liability litigation) and its constructive effect on consumers is effectively documented in her analysis. That gifts embody as well as facilitate bonding is stressed by our informants, and has been observed by other researchers in a variety of consumption settings (Belk, Wallendorf and Sherry 1989). If gifts are vehicles of behavior or embodied initiatives, and if they comprise a significant bulk of the stuff through which and in which selves are made (Arnheim 1987, Childe 1951), then much of their meaning resides in this communicative power; it resides as well in the stability and visibility of cultural categories that gifts make possible (Douglas and Isherwood 1979). Our study suggests that future consumer research might profitably concentrate upon the constituting role of objects, whether focused upon sociality (Appadurai 1986) or self (Belk 1988), and that gifts above all other consumer objects would be an expedient vehicle for such investigation.

## 4. Choice is Imprecise or Ineffable

The selection of a particular item is most often the culmination of a search that specifies the store as the questing ground but which envisions no specific grail. Informants know that if an appropriate gift exists, it must be concealed somewhere within the walls of our stores, and that it will reveal itself to them

if they root diligently enough through the aisles. "I'll know it when I see it," "It has to feel right," "This is just right for ___," and "I have to have this," are among the observations made by informants. A "knack," an "intuition," a "sense," and a "feeling" are the ultimate arbiters of propriety when it comes to identifying gifts. Few of our informants could articulate with much clarity the rationale for this propriety. This reinforces Hyde's (1979) conception of the gift as mystery, as well as the notion that many consumer goods exist largely as projectible fields that reflect the "blurry and fleeting images" consumers cast over them (Leiss, Kline and Jhally 1986, 242).

That gift giving behavior violates standard microeconomic principles (Thaler 1985) suggests that interpretation might better be served by exploring the ludic or hedonic dimensions of this activity. Search behavior described in our ethnographies appears to be driven in large measure by what Campbell (1987) has called "modern autonomous imaginative hedonism." In such search, "longing" and a "permanent unfocused dissatisfaction" work in tandem to shape behavior: "the desiring mode constitutes a state of enjoyable discomfort, and wanting rather than having is the main focus of pleasure-seeking" (Campbell 1987, 86-87). Our informants often report enjoying the treasure hunt and the fantasies engendered by the gift objects as much as the discovery of the appropriate gift itself. The "imaginative enjoyment of products" (Campbell 1987, 92) and the recreational shopping experience, are as much a part of the gift shop ethos as is the sheer availability of the gifts itself. Future research into hedonic motivation might well focus on such retail environments as appropriate fieldsites.

## 5. Process Model Guides Institutions

The comprehensive model of gift giving behavior proposed by Sherry (1983) to account for dyadic interaction or behavior exchange at the micro level can also be applied at an institutional level. That is, the model is useful in describing behavior that occurs within an institutional or organizational setting. For example, we have shown how owners effect the first transformation from object to gift, and how store clerks experience a vicarious gift exchange relationship with owners (as do consumers with the store itself). At an organizational level, Gestation occurs as owners search, Prestation occurs as store personnel display and sell merchandise, and Reformulation occurs as consumers increase or attenuate their loyalties to the shops. The model can be used to detail systematically within organizations the nature and frequency of gift giving behaviors so apparently essential to the commodification of ritual.

When applied to an institutional setting such as a retail outlet, the model foregrounds the kind of token gift exchange (Blehr 1974, Sherry 1983) that undershores more overtly celebrated giving. That is, informal infrastructural modes of exchange form an ongoing pattern that integrates social relationships and reinforces the formal structural ties individuals have to one another. This informal or undesignated gift giving, so routinized an interaction ritual that it is "remarkable to participants primarily in the breach"

(Sherry 1983, 162)--as in the seasonal lulls between peak activity periods in our stores, when deliverymen bring fewer packages and customer traffic slackens--contributes significantly to whatever organic solidarity an organization is able to evolve. The breadth and depth of such informal ritual activity within organizations, and the harnessing of this ritual to strategic vision, are topics worthy of much additional investigation.

## CONCLUSION

Using ethnographic method and extended case study approach, we have tried to plumb the significance of the gift shop in contemporary consumer culture. In the absence of comparable studies, this paper is presented as a baseline ethnographic record, clearly delineated and restricted in location, calendrical season, and social class. Despite these limitations, the complexity of the institution and the behaviors associated with it are replete with specifics that are well suited to such thick description. Through the comparison of two retail sites, we have generated several propositions that capture our present understanding of gift store activity. While the limits to generalizability are clear, we present our baseline ethnographies and interpretive frameworks as both a resource and challenge to future researchers to probe more widely and deeply into the institutional parameters of gift exchange.

## REFERENCES

Appadurai, Arjun (1986), *The Social Life of Things: Commodities in Cultural Perspective*, Cambridge: Cambridge University Press.

Arnheim, Rudolf (1987), "Art Among the Objects," *Critical Inqjuiry* 13 (Summer), 677-185.

Artaud, Antonin (1958), *The Theatre and Its Double*, New York: Grove.

Barth, John (1972), *Chimera*, New York: Fawcett Crest.

Baudrillard, Jean (1968), *Le Systeme des Objects*, Paris: Gallimard.

_____ (1981), *For a Critique of the Political Economy of the Sign,* St. Louis, MO: Telos Press.

Belk, Russell (1988), "Possessions and the Extended Self," *Journal of Consumer Research*, 15(2).

_____, John Sherry and Melanie Wallendorf (1988), "A Naturalistic Inquiry into Buyer and Seller Behavior at a Swap Meet," *Journal of Consumer Research* 14(4): 449-470.

_____, Melanie Wallendorf and John Sherry (1989), "The Sacred and Profane in Consumer Behavior: Theodicy on the Odyssey," forthcoming in *Journal of Consumer Research*.

_____, _____, _____, Morris Holbrook and Scott Roberts (1988), "Collectors and Collecting," *Advances in Consumer Research*, Vol 15, ed. Michael Houston, Provo, UT: Association for Consumer Research.

Blehr, Otto (1974), "Social Drinking in the Faroe Islands: The Ritual Aspects of Token Prestations," *Ethnos* 39(1), 53-62.

Campbell, Colin (1987), *The Romantic Ethic and the Spirit of Modern Consumerism*, New York: Basil Blackwell.

Caplow, T. (1982), "Christmas Gifts and Kin Networks," *American Sociological Review*, 48(6), 383-392.

_____ (1984), "Rule Enforcement Without Visible Means: Christmas Gift-Giving in Middletown," *American Journal of Sociology*, 89(5).

Campbell, Colin (1987), *The Romantic Ethic and the Spirit of Modern Consumerism*, New York: Basil Blackwell

Cheal, David (1986), "The Social Dimensions of Gift Behavior," *Journal of Social and Personal Relationsips*, 3:423-439.

_____ (1987), "'Showing Them You Love Them': Gift Giving and the Dialectic of Intimacy," *The Sociological Review* 35(1):151-169.

Childe, V. Gordon (1951), *Man Makes Himself*, New York: New American Library.

Clifford, James (1988), *The Predicament of Culture: Twentieth Century Ethnography, Literature, and Art*, Cambridge: Harvard University Press.

Csikszentmihalyi, Mihaly and Eugene Rochberg-Halton (1981), *The Meaning of Things: Domestic Symbols and the Self*, New York: Cambridge University Press.

Codrescu, Andre (1986), *A Craving for Swan*, Columbus, OH: Ohio State University Press.

Darden, William and JoAnn Schwinghammer (1985), "The Influence of Social Characteristics on Perceived Quality in Patronage Choice Behavior," in *Perceived Quality: How Consumers View Stores and Merchandise*, eds. Jacob Jacoby and Jerry Olson, Lexington, MA: Lexington Books, 161-172.

Debord, Guy (1983), *Society of the Spectacle*, Detroit: Black and Red.

Dorfles, Gillo, ed. (1967), *Kitsch: The World of Bad Taste*, New York: Universe.

Douglas, Mary and Baron Isherwood (1979), *The World of Goods*, New York: Norton.

Faber, Ronald and Thomas O'Guinn (1988), "Compulsive Consumption and Credit-Abuse," *Journal of Consumer Policy*, 11(1).

Fernandez, James (1986), *Persuasions and Performances: The Play of Tropes in Culture*, Bloomington, IN: Indiana Unviersity Press.

Freud, Sigmund [trans. James Strachey], (1962), *Civilization and Its Discontents*, New York: Norton.

Gahmberg, Henrik (1987), "Semiotic Tools for the Study of Organizations," in *The Semiotic Web*, eds. Thomas Sebeok and Jean Umiker-Sebeok, New York: Mouton de Gruyter, 389-403.

Garner, Thesia, and Janet Wagner (1988), "Gift Giving Behavior: An Economic Perspective," working paper, U.S. Department of Labor, Division of Price and Index Number Research.

Goffman, Erving (1961). *The Presentation of Self in Everyday Life*, New York: Doubleday.

Greenberg, Clement (1957), "Avant Garde and Kitsch," in *Mass Culture*, eds. Bernard Rosenberg and David White, 98-110.

Hirschman, Elizabeth (1986), "Humanistic Inquiry in Marketing Research: Philosophy, Method and Criteria," *Journal of Marketing Research* (August):237-249.

Hiss, Tony (1987a), "Experiencing Places--I," *The New Yorker*, June 22:45-68.

_____ (1987b), "Experiencing Places--II," *The New Yorker*, June 29:73-86.

Hochschild, Arlie (1983), *The Managed Heart: Commercialization of Human Feeling*, Berkeley, CA: University of California Press.

Hudson, Laurel and Julie Ozanne (1988), "Alternative Ways of Seeking Knowledge in Consumer Research," *Journal of Consumer Research* 14(4):508-521.

Hyde, Lewis (1979) *The Gift*, New York: Vintage.

van Imwagen, Peter (forthcoming) *Material Beings*, Ithaca: Cornell University Press.

Jacoby, Jacob and David Mazursky (1985), "The Impact of Linking Brand and Retailer Images on Perceptions of Quality," in *Perceived Quality: How Consumers View Stores and Merchandise*, eds. Jacob Jacoby and Jerry Olson, Lexington, MA: Lexington Books, 155-159.

Keir, Alissa (1939), *So You Want to Open a Shop*, New York: Whittlesey House.

Kopytoff, Igor (1986), "The Cultural Biography of Things: Commoditization as Process," in *The Social Life of Things*, ed. Arjun Appadurai, Cambridge: Cambridge University Press, 64-91.

Kotler, Philip (1974), "Atmospherics as a Marketing Tool," *Journal of Retailing* 49(4), 48-64.

_____ (1984), *Marketing Management: Analysis, Planning and Control*, fifth edition, Englewood Cliffs, NJ:Prentice-Hall.

Landman, Ruth (1987), "Washington's Yard Sales: Women's Work, But Not for Money," *City and Society* 1(1), 148-161.

Lenz, Elinor and Barbara Myerhoff (1985), *The Feminization of America: How Women's Values Are Changing Our Public and Private Lives*, Los Angeles: Jeremy Tarcher.

Leiss, William Stephan Kline and Sut Jhally (1986), *Social Communication in Advertising: Persons, Products, and Images of Well-Being*, New York: Methuen.

Levitt, Theodore (1983), "Relationship Managment," in *The Marketing Imagination*, ed. Theodore Levitt, New York: Free Press, 111-12;6.

Lincoln, Yvonna and Egon Guba (1985). *Naturalistic Inquiry*, Beverly Hills: Sage.

MacCannell, Dean (1976) *The Tourist: A New Theory of the Leisure Class*, New York: Schocker.

Maclean, Annie (1899), "Two Weeks in Department Stores," *American Journal of Sociology* 4(6), 721-741.

Mazursky, David and Jacob Jacoby (1985), "Forming Impressions of Merchandise and Service Quality," in *Perceived Quality: How Consumers View Stores and Merchandise*, eds. Jacob Jacoby and Jerry Olson, Lexington, MA: Lexington Books, 139-153.

McCracken, Grant (1988a), "Matching Material Cultures: Person-Object Relations Inside and Outside the Ethnographic Museum," forthcoming in *Advances in Nonprofit Marketing*, ed. Russell Belk, Greenwich, CT: JAI Press.

_____ (1988), *Culture and Consumption*, Bloomington, IN: Indiana University Press.

McGrath, Mary Ann (1988a), "A Natural History of Gift Giving: The Perspective from a Gift Store," working paper, Loyola University.

_____ (1988b), "Gift Giving and Receiving: Implications and Limitations of the Exchange Perspective in Consumer Behavior," working paper, Loyola University.

McMullen, Roy (1968), *Art, Affluence and Alienation: The Fine Arts Today*, New York: Mentou.

Norman, Donald (1988), *The Psychology of Everyday Things*, New York: Basic Books.

Peel, Arthur (1941/1953) *How to Run a Gift Shop*, Boston: Charles T. Branford.

Pollay, Richard (1986), "It's the Thought that Counts: A Case Study in Xmas Excesses," *Advances in Consumer Research*, Vol. 14, eds. Melanie Wallendorf and Paul Anderson, Provo, UT: Association for Consumer Research, 140-143.

Plath, David (1987), "Gifts of Discovery," *Liberal Education* 73(4):12-16.

Richardson, Miles (1987), "A Social (Ideational-Behavioral) Interpretation of Material Culture and Its Application to Archaeology", in *Mirror and Metaphor*, ed. Donald Ingersoll and Gordon Bronitsky, Lanham, MD: University Press of America, 381-403.

Rosenberg, Bernard and David M. White, eds. (1957), *Mass Culture: The Popular Arts in America*. Glencoe, IL: Free Press.

Schroeder, Fred (1977), *Outlaw Aesthetics*, Bowling Green, OH: Bowling Green University Popular Press.

Sebeok, Thomas (1987), "Fetishism," working paper, Research Center for Language and Semiotic Studies, Indiana University.

Sherry, John F., Jr. (1983). "Gift-Giving in Anthropological Perspective." *Journal of Consumer Research* 10(2):157-168.

_____ (1986), "Cereal Monogamy: Brand Loyalty as Secular Ritual in Consumer Culture," paper presented at the Annual Conference of the Association of Consumer Research, Toronto, October.

_____ (1987a), "Heresy and the Useful Miracle: Rethinking Anthropology's Contributions to Marketing," in *Research in Marketing*, Vol. 9, ed. Jagdish Sheth, Greenwich, CT: JAI Press, 285-306.

_____ (1987b), "Keeping the Monkeys Away From the Typewriters: An Anthropologist's View of the Consumer Behavor Odyssey," in *Advances in Consumer Research*, Vol 14, eds. Melanie Wallendorf and Paul Anderson, Provo, UT: Association for Consumer Research, 370-373.

_____ (1988) "A Sociocultural Analysis of the Flea Market," Working Paper, Northwestern University.

Shimp, Terence and Thomas Madden (1988), "Consumer-Object Relations: A conceptual Framework Based Analogously on Sternberg's Triangular Theory of Love," *Advances in Consumer Research*, Vol. 15, ed. Michael Houston, Provo, UT, Association for Consumer Research, 163-168.

Solomon, Michael and Henry Assael (1987), "The Forest or the Trees? A Gestalt Approach to Symbolic Consumption," in *Marketing and Semiotics: New Directions in the Study of Signs for Sale*, ed. Jean Umiker-Sebeok, Berlin, Mouton de, Gruyter, 189-217.

Soskin, David and Nick Ellison (1988), *The Tacky Book*, Los Angeles, CA: Price Stern.

Sternberg, Robert (1986, "A Triangular Theory of Love," *Psychological Review*, 93(2), 119-135.

Stewart, Susan (1982), *On Longing*, Baltimore: Johns Hopkins University Press.

Strauss, Anselm (1987), *Qualitative Analysis for Social Scientists*, NY: Cambridge University Press.

Thaler, Richard (1985), "Mental Accounting and Consumer Choice," *Marketing Science* 4(3):199-214.

Vonnegut, Kurt (1969), *Slaughterhouse-Five or the Children's Crusade: A Duty Dance with Death*, NY: Dell.

Waits, William (1978), *The Many-Faced Custom: Christmas Gift-Giving in America*, unpublished PhD. dissertation, Rutgers University.

Wallendorf, Melanie and Eric Arnould (1988), "'My Favorite Things:' A Cross-Cultural Inquiry into Object Attachment, Possessiveness, and Social Linkage," *Journal of Consumer Research* 14(4), 531-547.

Walter, Eugene (1988), *Placeways: A Theory of the Human Environment*, Chapel hill, NC: University of North Carolina Press.

Whyte, William F. (1978), "Organizational Behavior Research -- Where Do We Go From Here?" in *Applied Anthropology in America*, eds. Elizabeth Eddy and William Partridge, New York: Columbia University Press, 129-143.

Wilkens, Joanne (1988), *Her Own Business: Success Secrets of Entrepreneurial Women*, New York: McGraw-Hill.

# "Homeyness"
# A Cultural Account of One Constellation of Consumer Goods and Meanings
## Grant McCracken, University of Guelph[1]

## ABSTRACT

This paper offers a cultural account of the constellation of consumer goods and meanings in North America called "homeyness." It reports ethnographic data collected in and on the modern North American home. The paper considers the physical, symbolic and pragmatic properties of homeyness, and attempts to show its cultural character and consequences.

## INTRODUCTION

This paper offers a cultural account of the constellation of consumer goods and meanings called "homeyness" in modern North America. It draws on anthropological theory, ethnographic research, and a wide range of social scientific scholarship to consider the cultural characteristics and consequences of this neglected cultural phenomenon. The account is divided into four parts. The first reviews the scholarly precedents and objectives of the paper. The second treats the physical properties of homeyness, as these were described by respondents in a recent ethnographic research project. The third treats the symbolic properties of homeyness: its cultural meanings and logic. The fourth and final part of the paper treats the pragmatic properties of homeyness: the uses to which it is put by contemporary North Americans and its larger structural consequences.

The research reported in this paper was conducted in an urban area of southern Ontario in the summers of 1985 and 1986. Forty individuals were interviewed. The interview for each respondent took 6 hours in total. Interviewers were conducted in the respondent's home, almost always in the living room. All respondents lived in free-standing houses. The 40 respondents were divided into two equal categories by distinctions of status (blue collar vs. managerial). The following characteristics were common for all: race (Caucasian), religion (Protestant), ethnicity (British), time in Canada (at least third generation) and marital status (married). Men and women were almost equally represented.

Research was conducted using ethnographic methods and a four-step method of qualitative inquiry described in McCracken (1988d). The study was designed to investigate the cultural logic, the underlying beliefs and assumptions, of one aspect of consumption behavior in modern North American life. It was also to show how the cultural meanings contained in homeyness are put to work in the "projects" of individual North Americans as they construct notions of self and world (McCracken 1986b). In sum, this paper is designed to show what homeyness means, how it means, and with what cultural consequences it means.

## SCHOLARLY CONTEXT

The present study has its foundations in several of the social sciences. It is designed to address a range of research topics. I review these fields and topics here.

Anthropologists have been as prepared as anyone to speculate on their own society, but they have been fastidiously unwilling to examine the ethnographic details of mainstream North American life (Gulick 1973; Varenne 1986). The study of homeyness takes anthropology into the domestic heart of North American society. It seeks to demonstrate that the theoretical issues that concern the field can be investigated just as readily in the petrie dish of modern life as they can in more conventional field sites. More particularly, it seeks to show that the issue of cultural "construction" may be investigated in modern North America (Bruner 1984: 2-3). As this paper will try to show, homeyness is one of the chief instruments by which some North Americans construct several of their most important concepts of self and family.

The study also is designed to draw from and contribute to the renaissance that is now taking place in the study of material culture both in anthropology and american studies (Appadurai 1986; Bronner 1983; Cordwell and Schwarz 1979; Glassie 1973; Kavanaugh 1978, Lechtman and Merrill 1977; Neich 1982; Prown 1980, 1982; Quimby 1978; Rathje 1978; Reynolds and Stott 1987; Richardson 1974; Schlereth 1982; Wolf 1970). This growing body of work has sought to deepen our understanding of the ways in which material culture makes culture material. The present paper is designed to show the "homeyness" of some North American homes puts certain symbolic and pragmatic properties at the disposal of the family, and so resident in the material culture of the home, homeyness helps to realize certain definitions of sociality and rootedness that are otherwise inaccessible. I hope to encourage the contention, implied by Prown, that there are some things about social life that can only be captured through the study of material culture (1982: 3).

The paper is also designed to draw on and contribute to the field of history, especially as this field devotes itself to the origins and development of the consumer society (Braudel 1973; Campbell 1983, 1987; Fox and Lears 1983; Harris 1978, 1981; Horowitz 1985; Lears 1981; McKendrick, Brewer, and Plumb 1982; Miller 1981; Mukerji 1983; Pope 1983; Shi 1985; Williams 1982) in general, and the relationship between material culture and the development of the North American home and family (Clark 1976, 1986; Doucet

---

[1]The author wishes to thank the Social Sciences and Humanities Research Council of Canada for funding the research reported in this paper. Thanks are also due to the following individuals for their comments on earlier versions of the paper: Russel Belk, K.O.L. Burridge, Susan McKinnon, Mary Ellen Roach Higgins, Floyd Rudman, Melanie Wallendorf, and Linda Wood. Katherine Burke is especially thanked for her willingness to serve as an expert informant.

*Interpretive Consumer Research © 1989*
*Association for Consumer Research*

and Weaver 1985; Gordon and McArthur 1985; Handlin 1979; Holdsworth 1977; Leach 1984; Marchand 1985). The present study examines the cultural logic that has allowed domestic environments to serve as sites of individuality, sanctuaries against work, centers of spirituality, and staging grounds for that intensely important bundle of activities, values, and undertakings in Western societies called "domesticity." As Clark has noted, the North American home is a place charged with "symbolic and moral meaning" (1986: 238). The present study is designed to demonstrate that much of this meaning is caught up in and depends upon the homeyness constellation of consumer goods.

This paper is also designed to contribute to and draw from the fields of environmental studies, architecture and geography (Agrest and Gandelsonas 1977; Altman, Rapoport, and Wohlwill 1980; Carswell and Saile 1987; Carlisle 1982; Duncan 1981; Krampen 1979; Rapoport 1982; Saile 1984; Tuan 1982), and their study of household design and furnishing (Forty 1986; Kine 1986; Korosec-Serfaty 1976; Kron 1983, Jackson 1976; Lawrence 1981, 1982, 1984; Pratt 1981), and "home" (Altman and Werner 1985; Giuliani, Bonnes and Werner 1987; Hayden 1981; Seamon 1979; Tognoli 1987; Wright 1980, 1981). The present paper provides an ethnographic account of the "centering" and "place attachment" characteristics of the home environment, topics that have drawn some interest in the field but relatively little research (Tognoli 1987: 658).

This study is also concerned to contribute to and draw from the sociological study of material possessions. Sociologists have examined the emotional and structural significance of special possessions (Csikszentmihalyi and Rochberg-Halton 1981), the status significance of material goods (Blumberg 1974; Davis 1956, 1958; Felson 1976; Laumann and House 1970; Rainwater 1966), the larger consumer system and its creation of cultural meanings (Gottdiener 1985; Hirsch 1972), patterns of preference (Gans 1974), the use of objects as role models (Rochberg-Halton 1984), the commodification of the body (O'Neill 1978), and the sociology of collecting (Danet 1986), to name a few of the relevant studies that touch on home life and consumption.

Interestingly, however, the sociologists who have considered homeyness have come away perplexed. In his study of the homes of post-war Detroit, Felson could find no ready explanation for what he called the "Bric-A-Brac factor" (1976: 414). Candidly, he admits to aspects of the home "beyond the reach of this writer's sociological imagination" (1976: 414). Laumann and House in their study of living room furnishings suffered a similar difficulty, and acknowledge "distinctions beyond the untutored grasp of our interviewers" (1970: 338). I would contend that much of the sociological significance of consumption behavior must evade our grasp if we insist on investigating this behavior outside of its ethnographic context. The object of the present study is to use the holistic perspective provided by such a context. It seeks to comprehend homeyness clearly by capturing it whole.

The field of consumer research is now host to a range of scholarship that bears on the present study. The field has been called upon to consider the materialism of

North America (Belk 1985), the use of ethnographic methods (Belk 1987; Deshpande 1983; Hirschman 1985; Hirschman and Holbrook 1986; Holbrook 1987; Wallendorf 1987), the political implications of consumption patterns (Caplovitz 1967; Firat 1986), the development of consumer pathologies (Faber, O'Guinn and Krych 1987; Gronmo 1984, 1986), patterns of product symbolism (Hirschman 1981; Holbrook and Hirschman 1982; Holman 1980; Levy 1978, 1981; McCracken 1988a; Mick 1986, 1988), the institutional implications of consumption (Mayer 1978; Nicosia and Mayer 1976), the effect of consumption patterns on family interaction (Olson 1985), the nature of 'favorite object' attachment (Wallendorf and Arnould 1988), consumption rituals (Bloch 1982; Rook 1985), and consumption folklore (Sherry 1984). The present study is designed to pursue these several objectives in the finely detailed context of the ethnographic context of the North American home. It is hoped that, in this way, it will contribute to the study of "macro consumer behavior" (Belk 1987: 2).

## HOMEYNESS: PHYSICAL PROPERTIES

According to the Oxford English Dictionary, "homey" is an adjective that refers to things "resembling or suggestive of home; home-like, having the feeling of home, homish." According to the OED, it first appeared in written English almost exactly a century ago, in 1885. But the term "homey" is regarded as a vulgar term, unfit for polite discourse. Commentators on the family, the home, and domestic affairs in this century have eschewed it, preferring the daintier "home-like" (Anonymous 1968; Boschetti 1968; Brenan 1939; Morton 1936; Robinson 1941).

If the term has been avoided by social commentators, it has been embraced with enthusiasm by North Americans. Respondents in the research conducted for this study applied the adjective "homey" to a range of domestic phenomena in modern North America. They considered it a property of many aspects of the home, including its colors, materials, furniture, decorative objects, arrangement, interior design, and exterior characteristics. As these respondents tell it, the creation of homeyness is one of the most pressing objectives of their domestic circumstances and family lives. By their account, homeyness is an "effect" keenly to be sought for virtually every aspect of the home, from its exterior surfaces to the smallest details of the mantle piece. Let us the physical properties identified as homey.

"Homey" colors are the "warm" colors: orange, gold, green, brown. The preferred materials for interior walls are wood, stone, and brick. The only acceptable material for furniture construction is wood. Fabrics for furniture are relatively unfinished natural fibres. Fabric patterns are florals (especially chintz) or conversationals. Furniture styles are traditional, home-made, hand crafted, colonial or antique. One respondent, for instance, looked forward to replacing an arborite kitchen table with a round pine table and six cane-back chairs.

Objects are homey when they have a personal significance for the owner (e.g., gifts, crafts, trophies, mementoes, family heirlooms). A home-made ashtray assembled from shells collected on a summer holiday by the children served one family as a reminder of an important time and place in the history of the family, and was therefore considered especially homey. Objects can also be homey when they are informal or playful in character (e.g., the novelty ashtray, a pillow in shape of football, a pillow with verse in needle point). Plants and flowers are objects that contribute to the homeyness of a room. Some objects are homey because they support or contain decorative objects (e.g., wooden hutches and "what-nots"). Decorative objects such as glass or china objects of a very particular character can be homey, but interestingly this class of objects is, on the whole, dangerous to the homey effect (as we shall see below). Objects that mark the season (e.g., corn in autumn, holly for Christmas) are homey. Pictures of relatives, pets, and possessions are also homey. Paintings of certain kinds can have a homey character, especially sentimental treatments of landscapes or seascapes. Books in quantity can "furnish" a room and give it a homey character.

Arrangements are homey when they combine diverse styles of furnishing in a single room. They are also homey when they establish patterns of asymmetrical balance, and when they pair and center heterogeneous objects. Homeyness can also be achieved by the judicious combination of particular colors, fabrics, and pieces of furniture. For many people, the important principle of arrangement is redundancy, and they bring many homey things together into a single arrangement. For others, homey objects are best used sparingly and in isolation.

Homey interior details include bay windows, breakfast nooks, wainscotting, wood beam ceilings, kitchens, dens, "snug" rooms, low ceilings, and fireplaces. Exterior characteristics include a low slung "bungalow" roof, well enclosed and well treed backyards, paned and mullioned windows, shutters, porches, lawn ornaments, ivy covered walls, plants and shrubs close to and encompassing the house, mock Tudor timbering, brass lanterns and other lamps, an asymmetrical front, and a small front door.

Respondents used a very particular set of adjectives to describe "homeyness." A favorite characterization of the homey place was to say that it looked "as though someone lived there." The terms "informal," "comfortable," "cozy," "relaxed," "secure," "unique," "old," "rich," "warm," "humble," "welcoming," "accommodating," "lived in," "country kitchenish" were all used as glosses. The terms "private," "nice and bright," were also used, though less frequently. Respondents said homeyness is a feature of the home that is immediately and intuitively obvious. As one respondent put it, "I can go into a hundred homes and I can tell in a second whether it's homey or it isn't, just by the feel of it...".

This indeterminacy is apparently characteristic of homeyness. As the historian Handlin notes, "Authors like Catherine Sedgwick [b. 1789] and John Howard Payne [b. 1791] never specified the particular characteristics of an ideal home but claimed only that the quality they admired was a feeling, a spirit, or an atmosphere that was indefinable and indescribable." (1979:15). As we shall note below, homeyness is no simple sum of material parts, but an intangible, illusive quality that can be difficult to define or to achieve.

But if respondents sometimes found themselves unable to capture what homeyness is, they rarely suffered any difficulty in saying what it is not. The enemies of homeyness, that is to say, were easily characterized. One respondent described an ornately formal living room as "cluttered up with a whole lot of fancy stuff" and therefore unhomey. The terms used to characterize unhomey homes were "pretentious," "formal," "stark," "elegant," "cold," "daunting," "sterile," "show piece," "reserved," "controlled," "decorated," "modern," and even "Scandinavian."

## HOMEYNESS: SYMBOLIC PROPERTIES

The term "symbolic property," refers to the meaning and the logic that gives a physical property its cultural significance. In the case of homeyness, more particularly, "symbolic property" refers to the kinds of meanings that inhere in homey phenomena, the assumptions on which these meanings rest, and the strategies by which these meanings are actuated.

Homeyness as a cultural property is intensely prescriptive and intensely elusive meaning. It represents a domestic condition that is highly valued by North American culture bearers but not easily achieved by them. The difficulty is that there are many forces that work against the realization of homeyness. Sometimes the notion, like any ideal moral condition, is simply more than North Americans can sustain. It is better than their best efforts. Sometimes it is contradicted by other cultural principles that work to shape the family and the home. Sometimes it is, due to an evanescent character, difficult to capture, to make actual, to realize. While North Americans know homeyness when they see it, they do not always have a clear idea of how it is accomplished. Furthermore, there is no simple formula for the creation of homeyness. Like all really important cultural achievements, homeyness is most compelling when it somehow transcends itself, when it is greater than the sum of its mechanically prescribed parts.

These several factors and the difficulty they present in realizing homeyness in the world have a profound effect on its character. They cause it to assume a deeply processual nature. "Homeyness" as a cultural phenomena is of necessity constantly under construction by those who would make it present in their lives. It is constantly in need of refreshment and recreation if it is to survive and succeed in the world. In order to capture the cultural character of a phenomenon with these characteristics, it is necessary to go beyond its meaning and its grammar, and to capture the logic and the strategies, the symbolic properties, by which it operates.

For the purposes of exposition, I have distinguished eight symbolic properties of homeyness. I review these properties below, characterizing how each is intended to act upon the individual, and the culture logic by which it does so. I examine, in turn, the diminutive, the variable, the embracing, the engaging, the memorial, the authentic, the informal, and, finally, the situating properties of homeyness. These properties are rehearsed here in order of their primacy. Each property helps to support every subsequent one. Each property helps to extend every previous one. The following eight properties have a "telescoped" relationship to one another.

## The Diminutive Property

Homeyness has a diminutive aspect. As we have seen, ceilings are low, doors and windows are small, space is divided and filled, lines are broken and repeated, and shapes little and sometimes organic. Homeyness cannot survive the bleak expanse of an off-white wall. It cannot tolerate sparse furnishings, clean, uncluttered lines, or "elegance" of any kind.

This property of homeyness helps to give the domestic environment manageable proportions. As Levi-Strauss suggests in *The Savage Mind*, that which is "quantitatively diminished ... seems to us qualitatively simplified" (1966: 23). The diminutive aspect of homeyness has a simplifying power; it makes an environment more graspable, conceivable, thinkable. It gives an environment the "human scale" that has preoccupied post-modern architecture. It stands in opposition to the monumental and brutalist aspects of modern built form, and represents habitable space that is "manageable" both as a place to use and as a place to grasp. In the language of anthropology (cf. Levi-Strauss 1963; Tambiah 1969), the diminutive property helps to make these places "good" to think because it makes them "easy" to think.

## The Variable Property

Homeyness has a variable aspect. It appears deliberately to eschew uniformity and consistency. This property is most clearly illustrated by the preference respondents showed for local houses made of "rubble-stone" rather than cut stone. Rubble stone is highly variable in shape and size, and must be piled "higgledy-piggledy," whereas cut stone, being consistent in size and shape, is laid in uniform rows. Confronted with this concise choice between the variable and the uniform, respondents declared their preference for the variable. In their view, variable "rubble-stone" made a home more homey.

This variable property of homeyness is also evidenced by the preferred patterns of fabric, furniture arrangement, exterior design, and what-not collections, in all of which variability is highly prized. It is this property of homeyness that explains its hostility to classical patterns and definitions of order. Homeyness is seen to be inconsistent with symmetry, balance, and visibly premeditated order.

This property of homeyness is calculated to make homey environments appear more particular and therefore more "real" than nonhomey environments. The logic of this association is this: variability makes things appear more contingent, contingency makes things appear more individual and authentic. Homey phenomenon is supposed to be relatively haphazard, highly contingent, phenomenon, the particular outcome of particular intentions, desires and events. It is not supposed to be the work of premeditation, routinized process (e.g., mass manufacture), or anonymous calculation. This makes the homeyness ideology vulnerable to several ironies and contradictions. For instance, the very woodwork and "ginger bread" that

gives certain surfaces the appearance of contingency (and homeyness) exists only because of the invention of new sawing technologies, and the mass manufacture this made possible. Just why this property of homeyness should succeed in making homey environments appear more "real" is not entirely clear. But it is worth noting that Miller (1972:364) has observed a very similar pattern for the theater. Miller notes that stage performances have greater veracity when they contain "contentless" or contingent signals.

## The Embracing Property

Homeyness has an embracing aspect. This is partly a function of the smallness and variableness of homey space. But is also the result of the way in which the homey environment is filled, organized, and contained. For the surfaces of the homey environment exhibit a pattern of descending enclosure. Each surface is enclosed by a greater surface and in turn encloses a lesser one. This hierarchical chain of enclosure creates the embrace of the homey environment.

The first act of encompassment begins with the neighborhood and yard. Some neighborhood, especially for instance the cul-de-sac, have a strongly encompassing character (Brown and Werner 1985). The presence of trees on public streets and fences, shrubbery, and ornaments in private yards also contribute to a sense of enclosed space.

For some homes the first enclosing surface is the ivy (Hedera Helix var. 'Hibernica,' `Angularis,' or `Dentata Variegata,') that climbs and encompasses the exterior wall of the house. This has the effect of embedding the exterior of the house in a still greater exterior, adding a layer to the encompassing folds of the house, and obscuring the hard and man-made surfaces of the house in a surface that is not only organic but also evocative of benign pastoral images and cloistered institutional ones.

The next potentially embracing surface of the home is the roof line. When a home has an overhanging "hipped" roof, it is seen to be embraced by it and made more homey. This roof line appears in several architectural styles common to 19th and 20th century North America (e.g., mock Tudor cottage, pitched Gothic house, California bungalow, and some of the domestic architecture of Frank Lloyd Wright). A variation of this encompassing effect is repeated in the canvas awnings that are sometimes placed over windows. These awnings serve in a sense to "roof" the window and give the house a homey appearance by adding to its embracing surfaces.

The next potentially homey surface of the house is the external wall. Respondents argued that this surface was especially homey when it consists in small and variable units (the diminutive and variable properties at work in a larger one). The wall of a mock Tudor home therefore qualifies, as does brick, stone, and any wooden surface with Gothic or "ginger bread" ornament. Massive walls with unbroken spaces and lines were seen to be incapable of the homey embrace and one respondent was moved to compare these external walls to those of a prison compound, the least homey of environments.

Another interior surface is the books that sometimes line the walls of a den, study or library. Here we see the creation of another layer, interior instead of exterior, man-made instead of natural. This layer, like the one before it, helps, in a visual sense, to buttress the outside and fortify the inside. But additional symbolic resources are deployed. This layer of books is the real and potential source of the layers of knowledge and understanding with which the individual mediates his or her relationship to the world and constructs the self, a point to which we shall return below. It is therefore the source of additional encompassing materials. But just as important, a wall of books represents ports to an extraordinary intellectual and imaginative geography in which the individual is free to "lose" or "find" (and so construct) the self. Books supply encompassed material as well.

The other furnishings of the wall of the homey environment help to extend its embrace. The sheer abundance of pictures and hangings for the wall create another layer, this one of objects of the family's own manufacture. These pictures record the family's past and present (e.g., wedding and graduation pictures), its internal and external relationships (e.g., mothers' day cards, team photographs, club plaques), and its accomplishments (e.g., diplomas, bowling trophies, stuffed fish). They represent a layer the family has made of itself for itself.

The "memory wall," as we may call it here, appears to have a special relationship to the family. The family, in modern North America, is a highly performative cultural entity. It must make itself a family out of its activities and connections, out of its enacted roles and performed relationships. The "memory wall" appears to capture both aspects of this constructed family's "encompassed/encompassing" logic. As an encompassing surface, the wall of family memorabilia stands for the family as corporation, the larger, containing, institution the family has made for itself through its shared activities, accomplishments and interconnections. As an encompassed surface, the memory wall stands for the smaller, contained, individualized diversity that exists within the family. Using yet another "part-whole" logic, the wall repeats this rendering of the family. The entire body of wall ornaments stands for the corporation, subsuming individual pieces within a larger whole. But every particular piece in the collection stands as an individualized part, representing the personal experiences and achievements of an individual.

The furnishings of the room help to complete the process of encompassment. They make up the last ring of material intimacy in the home. One group of these furnishings encircle the wall and a second set create small pools at the center of the room. Chairs and sofas drawn into a circle, focused on an imaginary center point, are the final surround in this material world. When this circle is occupied, a final human surround is accomplished. The final piece of the encompassing process can be the odor of cooking food that surrounds the individual as he or she enters the home (Howe 1987).

In sum, the embracing aspect of homeyness demonstrates a descending pattern of enclosure. The structure of the neighborhood, the foliage of the street and yard, the ivy of the exterior wall, the overhanging roof, the exterior wall, the books of the interior wall, the memory wall, the furnishings of the room, the

constructed family, and the constructed self, all work by graduated stages to create the sense of enclosure. Each ring of intimacy encloses the next, so that the center of a room has a deeply embedded quality. The occupant of such a space is removed and protected from the outside world by an intricate series of baffles and mediators.

The process of enclosure has, from a logical point of view, an active quality that aids in its representation. Each layer of intimacy (except the first and last) is both encompassed and encompassing. Outer layers enclose inner layers which in turn enclose still more inner layers. This logical relationship of encompassing and encompassment, arrayed as it is in a hierarchical series, gives the notion of enclosure a repetitive and a shifting quality. The acts of encompassing and encompassment are repeated again and again in the household. Furthermore, what is enclosed at one moment is enclosing in another. These two qualities makes the embracing property of homeyness conceptually lively; more active than passive in character, more visible and plain.

But the process of enclosure also has a dynamic quality from an historical point of view. All of the elements of the encompassing hierarchy require time to be established. The ivy takes time to grow, the books take time to collect, the memory wall takes time to create, the furniture time to buy and arrange, the family time to construct, the self time to assemble. There is a strong developmental aspect to the embracing property. It takes time to accomplish; the layers go on bit by bit. This too helps to emphasize the embracing process.

The process of enclosure even has a dynamic quality from a social point of view. It is created by diverse agents, including the forces of a domesticated nature (e.g., the ivy), an anonymous market place (e.g., the house), a personalized literary community (e.g., books chosen by the family), by a family (e.g., the memory wall), and by an individual (e.g., hobby products). The embracing quality of the homey space is a collective accomplishment to which diverse parties contribute. This diversity of contribution gives it a quality of contingency that it could not have were it the work of a single individual or group engaged in a single project.

All of these layers for these several reasons help to give homey space an encompassing character, and to iterate and reiterate the room's containing quality. The occupant of such a space is held, almost cosseted, by its contents. This aspect of the homey principle gives it the ability to make the individual feel secure and protected from external threat. In this capacity, the homey space has the same symbolic and psychological value as a parental embrace. It offers security from real but especially from imagined dangers. The psychological satisfactions to be drawn from this protection is, respondents claim, quite considerable. That it is, in the colloquial sense of the term, merely "symbolic" protection, does not appear to make it any less comforting, important, or desirable.

The encompassing powers of the homey environment are sometimes felt most acutely and consciously by those who wish least to feel their effect. Children who have recently moved away from home, sometimes complain, on their return, of the "stifling" and "infantilizing" quality of the home and its ability to reduce them to old patterns of dependency. This is homeyness at work.

But if respondents understand the encompassing quality of homey phenomena in these psychological terms, as an embrace, the ethnographic observer may give another, somewhat more structural, account. The embracing property of homeyness appears to take some of its emotional power from its special relationship to the constructed character of the family and individual. For the family and the individual cannot fashion the embracing aspect of homeyness without fashioning the self and family. Cultivating a homey environment, and especially constructing the memory wall, contribute willy nilly to the construction of the self and the family. Some of the intense satisfaction attached to homeyness, some of its resemblance to the parental embrace, stems perhaps from this special relationship to the processes by which the self and family take shape.

## The Engaging Property

Homeyness has an engaging aspect. It appears deliberately designed to engage the observer. This process begins with the "welcoming" objective of homey phenomena. There is no ethnographic study that enables us to understand how, in this culture, it is possible to speak sensibly of a holly wreath, for example, as "welcoming." But respondents found this an unexceptional, indeed necessary adjective for a range of decorative materials. They were able to suggest (but more frequently merely to imply) that the wreath has something in its character that extends an invitation for interaction, promises a warm reception, represents a certain emotional tone for the interior within. Homey objects, respondents say, are supposed to "draw" the observer in.

Like the embracing property, this engaging property of homeyness has a graduated character. Engagement in homeyness works by stages, becoming more intense as the individual is more deeply insinuated into the homey environment. The holiday wreath on the front door attempts a relatively public and general species of engagement. As the individual moves into the home, he or she encounters increasingly specific and personal gestures. The arrangement of the house, of a room, of the furniture of a room, of the large decorative details in the room, of the small decorative "touches" (as they are called), all of these can be charged with homeyness, and each draws the individual still further into engagement.

The engaging strategy extends to and governs even the demeanor of individuals within the homey space. By convention, the occupants of a homey space are supposed to be "open" to new arrivals, and prepared to "greet" them with generosity and warmth. This notion of "openness" is an important one for respondents, and their insistence on it points to the existence of the engaging strategy as well as the encompassing strategy. Openness is meant to be played out not just in the material culture of the homey environment but even in the behavior of its occupants. The occupant of the homey space, when part of a group, is supposed to greet a visitor by breaking the circle and rising to meet the visitor. The body is itself "opened,"

as the occupant turns to face the visitor and extends an open hand in greeting. It is most important that the face be, in a sense, "open," tilted back slightly with mouth and eyes opened with surprise, pleasure and "recognition." The orientation of the entire room, both its animate and inanimate objects, opens in greeting (and then, when the visitor has been made part of the group, closes again so that they too are encompassed).

The process continues with the arrangement of chairs in a manner that invites interaction, the presence of playful, amusing objects that demand a reaction, and the existence of objects such as magazines, knitting, and even games or puzzles. The homey room may also contain home-made furniture, wall hangings, and art objects, all of which seem designed to occasion conversation and the opportunity for engagement. All of these things invite the occupant to become a participant, if only as the close observer of a lively environment (cf. the Victorian precedent discussed by Clark 1986: 117-120). They also invite several occupants to become conversational partners whose interaction with the room prompts interaction with one another and vice versa.

Previous properties have already succeeded in containing and embracing the occupant. This one now demands a more active, autonomous, and self directed kind of relationship. Homeyness has moved from a passive involvement to active involvement, the great *sine qua non* of all projects that seek engagement. With engagement, the homey environment has found a powerful way to strengthen its relationship with the occupant.

## The Mnemonic Property

Homeyness has an mnemonic aspect. The most striking objects here are the house itself, replete with family association and history, trophies, gifts from children or friends, photographs of the family, tourist mementoes, hand crafted pieces of furniture and decorative objects. All of these carry an unmistakable historical character. Indeed they have been called the family archives (McCracken 1987). The mnemonic significance of objects is so strong that it can override aesthetic and other "decorator" considerations. One respondent found herself caught between aesthetic and mnemonic considerations and referred to a picture,

> "[that] I really don't like but someone who I really care a lot about gave it to us as a wedding present. I put it up because I like this woman [but] I have it on this backside of the wall so you can't really see it as you come in."

These objects are intended to recall the presence of family and friendship relationships, personal achievements, family events, ritual passages, and community associations. Some respondents spoke of these objects not just as a record of their past but even as a kind of proof and enactment of it. In the language of semiotics, these memorial objects "index" the presence of certain aspects of personal and family life even as they play these aspects out in the manner of a performative (Pierce 1932).

This aspect of homeyness has the effect of deeply personalizing the present circumstances. The place that is containing, embracing, and engaging, is now very strongly particularized and localized in time. It is made a place in time. This temporal "emplacement," as we might call it, of the homey environment is accomplished by the expressing, indexing and performance of the family's historical meanings and recollections. The individual is now much more vividly "somewhere" than before because the environment is much more vividly "sometime" than before. The engaging aspect of homeyness helps to substantialize the environment in which the individual finds him or her self.

### The Authentic Property

Homeyness has an authentic aspect. Respondents spoke of homey spaces and things as being somehow more "real" and somehow more "natural" than certain alternatives styles of furnishing. They spoke of homey things and space as being strongly opposite in character to things that were "contrived," "artificial," and "forced." In their view, inauthentic styles were the product of modern aesthetic, interior designers, show pieces homes, and high status individuals.

All of the aforementioned cultural properties help homey spaces and things assume this authentic character. The small, variable, intimate, engaging, and mnemonic aspects of homey phenomenon all contribute here. But the key to this aspect of homeyness is its intensely personal nature. Homey things and spaces, as we have seen, reflect the particular details of personal lives. Homey things and spaces help distinguish the home from the homes around it, and its occupants from other people. It emphasizes the individuality of the individual and the family in a society that insists with special intensity on this discrimination even as it inevitably engages in patterns of materialism that threaten to obscure it. As Forty suggests, "...in contemporary Western society, home life is the only effective signifier of personal authenticity" (1986: 152).

Homeyness succeeds in this because it is seen to be untouched by the calculations of the market place, the doctrines of politics or religion, the falsehoods of the status system, the impersonations of the fashion world, the contentions of the advertising enterprise, or any of the other meanings that are served up by the meaning manufacturers of a mass society. Homeyness is the record of a life, a particular life, lived without ulterior motive, creating its own meaning for its own purposes.

The authentic aspect of homeyness helps then to complete the process of emplacement by giving it a spatial dimension. Through the creation of a slew of entirely personal details, it creates a highly centered sense of place. Indeed it is this aspect of homeyness that helps to create the impression that, in the valued phrase with which respondents characterized the highest accomplishment of the homeyness enterprise, "someone lives here."

### The Informal Property

Homeyness has an informal aspect. Each of the physical properties identified above can be located on a formality continuum and in every case the homey choice falls at the informal end. Homey colors are the most "warm" and "friendly." The materials are relatively unfinished, almost deliberately unfine. The furniture positively embraces a rustic, relatively crude appearance. Decorative objects are often inexpensive. They are valuable not for their formal beauty or skillful execution but for their humor or sentimentality. Arrangements avoid classical symmetries or modern spareness, and a relative clutter is enjoined. Interior and exterior details of the house design are deliberately rustic, rural, cottage-like, and unprepossessing. Indeed the homey look appears deliberately to eschew any stylistic characteristic that is associated with the formal, the ceremonial, the distant, the disengaged, or the decorous. It appears constantly to work to suggest a certain humility and accessibility. As one respondent put it, "my house says, `look at me, I'm really beautiful but I'm not pretentious, I'm humble.'"

Homey homes and rooms appear deliberately to seek to "lower the tone" of human interaction. As the same respondent explained, "here [in the homeyest part of the house] you could throw things around and I wouldn't worry about breaking anything. Like you could put glasses on this furniture and I wouldn't care and you can just, you know, really be comfortable and not worry about things." She opposed homey places to places "that make you want to be more careful." In short, homey places are supposed to reassure the occupant that no special formality of dress, posture, demeanor, or conversation is required of them. From the respondent's point of view, one of the great objectives of homeyness is that it "puts people at their ease."

Another respondent reacted to a picture of a grand living room with almost violent dislike for its formal tone. He explained that in a visit to one of the residences of Queen Elizabeth II he had found evidence of homeyness. He was especially impressed with "the rooms that they [the Royal family] lived in where the TV set was and you could tell they sat around and had a few drinks before dinner and watched the news or whatever and it looked like it was lived in and yet by God it is the home of the queen and far more homey than that thing [i.e., the room pictured in the stimulus photograph]. That looks like one of the state rooms that they put up to hold a state banquet." According to this impassioned account, even the most formal of social creatures, a royal family, avoids the tyranny of formal surroundings.

The homeyness strategy appears to diminish the formality of the room in order to diminish the formality of the interaction that takes place within it. It is not clear how this transformation is accomplished but it is perhaps the case that the homey environment presents a face that is deliberately without defenses or pretenses in order to reassure the occupant that he or she may forgo defenses and pretenses of their own. Homeyness serves as a vital cue to the rules that govern a particular domestic universe. It says, in effect, "you may 'be yourself' without risk of embarrassment or ridicule." It appears designed to ease participation, to reassure the individual that the involvement is, from an impression management point of view, almost entirely riskless.

## The Situating Property

Homeyness has a situating aspect. The occupant of homey space is not just contained, embraced, engaged, reminded, emplaced, and reassured, he or she is also deliberately situated within it. In this final stage of the homeyness enterprise, the occupant of homey space becomes, in effect, part of the arrangement. This aspect of homeyness is accomplished by all of the aspects that have gone before, especially the smallness, intimacy, embracing, engaging, mnemonic, emplacing, authenticating character of the phenomenon. Once all of these properties have worked their dramatic effect upon the occupant, the occupant is situated within the homey field as an integral part of it. In this final stage the individual ceases to be an observer, ceases to be a participant, and becomes finally simply a part of the surrounding homey environment.

As we have noted, the largest objective of the symbolic properties of homey objects and their arrangement is involvement. This process is advanced and completed when the occupant is drawn into the configuration of objects and their meanings in such a way that he or she is, in a sense, claimed by it. Homey objects and their arrangement seek to make the individual a homologue of the environment, an intergral part of the whole. Successfully situated in homey space, the occupant of homey space becomes a homey creature. He or she appears to take on the properties of the surrounding space and objects. A kind of meaning transfer has been achieved.

This is homeyness in its most powerfully transformative, performative mode. It is homeyness as an active agent of culture working to metamorphose the individual. In a sense, the material culture circle is completed. For homeyness represents an ideology with which individual invests material culture with very particular culture meanings. Once in place, however, these meanings then turn back upon the individual in such a way that he or she is claimed by them. Individuals create homey material culture, and, eventually, homey material culture returns the favor.

## Symbolic Properties In Sum

These are the chief (but not the only) elements in the cultural enterprise homeyness represents. Individually and in combination, these eight symbolic properties of homeyness work to create the involvement of the occupant of a domestic environment and finally to claim them in a thoroughgoing sense. Homeyness seeks to make the occupant fully occupying of homey space and so to claim his or her full attention and affect. The diminutive property makes the homey environment thinkable, the variable property makes it real, the embracing property makes it cossetting, the engaging property makes it involving, the mnemonic property makes it emplacing in time, the authentic property makes it emplacing in space, the informal property makes it reassuring and riskless, and the situating property makes it fully capturing. The cumulative affect of these persuasive properties can be very powerful. It can situate individuals in the world as few other cultural devices can. Homeyness is for many people the adhesive that attaches them to self, family, time and place.

# HOMEYNESS: PRAGMATIC PROPERTIES

The term "pragmatic properties" refers to the objectives of a cultural phenomenon, the work it is capable of accomplishing in the social world. The distinction intended here between symbolic and pragmatic properties treats symbolic properties as the internal objectives of a cultural phenomenon such as homeyness and the pragmatic properties as its external objectives. In the case of homeyness, more particularly, "pragmatic properties" refers to the ends to which homeyness is put as individuals work to construct certain kinds of meaning in their lives (Bahktin 1981: 270; Bruner and Plattner 1984; Mertz and Parmentier 1985; Shweder and LeVine 1984; Silverstein 1976: 18; Singer 1984; and Tambiah 1977). There are indeed many pragmatic properties of homeyness, many ways in which it is pressed into service in the creation of the social self and world. Only four of these are discussed here. These include the use of homeyness as an enabling context, as a status corrector, as a market place corrector, and as a modernity corrector.

## Homeyness as An Enabling Context

The first pragmatic property of meaning is its use as an "enabling" context. Here homeyness has as its objective the creation of a meaningful context within which other meanings become possible. It deploys its various symbolic properties to enable the creation of these meanings. It is a necessary condition of these meanings.

Cultural phenomena are now widely understood to have a performative or processual character (Austin 1965; Sapir 1931; Tambiah 1977). The assumption here is that these phenomena must be continually performed, enacted or (re)produced in social life in order to have a clear, credible and fully "actual" existence for the individual and the collectivity. As Bruner puts this, "self and society [can] not be taken as given, as fully formed, fixed, and timeless, as either integrated selves or functionally consistent structure. Rather, self and society are always in production, in process..." (1984: 2-3). There are many species of symbolic activity that serve to produce the self and society. They include language, the drama of everyday life, ritual and ceremony, art, narrative traditions in the form of stories, proverbs, and myths, and all of the categories of material culture (built form and its furnishings not least among them). All of these activities rehearse the self and society in a manner that makes them more transparent to reality, actual, and obvious.

My contention here is that homeyness has a very particular role to play in the domestic version of the production process. Its larger purpose here is to create the stage on which all of the various domestic enactments of self and family can be undertaken. These enactments cannot be successful (or, in Austin's phrase, "felicitous") unless homeyness has endowed the house with its particular symbolic properties and powers of engagement.

Homeyness serves as an enabling context in three ways. First, it "drenches" the home environment with properties (smallness, realness, particularlity, risklessness, etc.) that help the individual successfully to enact their conception of the family and the roles they play within it. Families who live in environments without homey meaning can no more enact their notions of what a family is than a theater company can perform Gilbert and Sullivan's Pirates of Penzance without the aid of costumes and scenery. They do not have access to the vital companion meanings that are necessary to give their performances credibility and power. For instance, the family deprived of its homey breakfast nook is deprived of a vital prop for a ritual activity important to creation of family solidarity (Saile 1985). The family deprived of the "memory wall" loses a key dramatization of its collective past and individual achievement (cf. Boschetti 1984). Fathers and mothers deprived of their dramatic props lose badges of office, symbols of power, assurances of solicitude, to name just a few. A family deprived of all homey meanings must encounter insuperable difficulties in the process by which the family is created and sustained.

But if homeyness is profitably compared to the stage and sets of a performance, it may also be compared to the "prompter" who gives a performance direction and continuity. In this second capacity, homeyness creates an environment dense with symbolism from which the actors of the family take their cue. To take one example, the cossetting character of a homey environment helps to remind a family of one of the values by which its relationships are supposed to be oriented. To take another, heirlooms can evoke one of several notions of family continuity and the individual's responsibility thereto (e.g., McCracken 1988b) while craft and handiwork can stand for the preferred modes of family participation and contribution (e.g., McCracken 1987). The homey environment helps continually to prompt the actors in the home, reminding them of the roles and larger objectives of family life. Without these cues and prompts the family is bereft not just of the stage and scenery of their performance, but of the instruction and reminder that gives it consistency and continuity. It is, incidentally, precisely this cuing ability of homeyness that can help the home imprison the individual in sex-role stereotypes.

Third, the homeyness enterprise of engagement works upon each individual to bind them to the family and to ensure his or her participation there in good times and bad. In this capacity, homeyness exercises its gravitational powers to sustain the commitment and conviction of family members. It helps ensure participation that the dramatic company will continue to attend and continue to perform with enthusiasm.

It is noted above that homeyness has its own strongly processual character, and it is appropriate here to observe how this compares to the processual character of the family itself. Both homeyness and the family are constantly under construction through the scripted and innovative efforts of the members of the family. But one takes precedence over the other. Homeyness must be created before the self and the family can be created. And it must be continually created in order for the self and the family to be created. In other words, it is only if and as homeyness is fully realized that the performative efforts particular to the family can be undertaken felicitously. As more than one respondent put it, "you just can't have a family without a home."

From a general theoretical point of view, this is a phenomenon of some interest. Increasingly, attention is being given to the context-dependent nature of meaning (e.g., Mertz 1985:4; Silverstein 1976). In this case, the context is not the surrounding linguistic material nor the other elements of a ritual but the carefully manipulated material environment, an inanimate world. Homeyness gives us an opportunity to see how the context provided by material culture can be used to create, and manipulate meaning. It shows us an enabling context that consists not in words, or actions, but in things.

For the theoretical perspective more particular to material culture studies in anthropology and American studies, this pragmatic aspect of homeyness is also of interest. For here is an instance of material culture on which other kinds of culture, especially in its performative and processual mode, especially depend. We have witnessed material culture simply reflecting cultural categories and principles (Adams 1973, McCracken 1982), we have seen it serving as performatives (Kavanaugh 1978) and as operators (McCracken 1985), but we have yet to see it, as we do here, serving in something like a meta-performative role. This is a neglected species of material culture to which we may wish to be more sensitive.

From the point of view of the study of the ethnography of North America, the "culture and built form" perspective within environmental studies and consumption behavior, this aspect of homeyness is also of some interest. This understanding encourages attention to the pragmatic as well the more traditional cultural properties of the home. The study of homeyness encourages us to reflect with new energy on how people are the users of the meaning with which their homes are endowed. It encourages us to see how the meaning in the built environment is put to work. The study of homeyness allows us to glimpse people making contexts that then make them.

## Homeyness as a Status Corrector

The second pragmatic property of homeyness may be called the "status corrector" use. As the social sciences have noted since the work of Veblen (1912) and Simmel (1904), much of the person-object relations of modern North Americans are devoted to the creation and communication of status messages. It is less well noted that this symbolic strategy has, of necessity, given rise to countervailing strategies. Homeyness is one of these. Homeyness allows the individual to defend against status strategies. It allows for the containment, management and repudiation of these strategies. Homeyness performs this work in two quite different ways for two quite different social groups.

High standing groups have a decidedly ambivalent attitude about homeyness (Seeley, Sims and Loosley 1956: 52). As a prevailing tone for home furnishings, it is careful avoided. My expert respondent on this and other issues, an interior decorator, remarked that the adjective "homey" is never used by her clients to describe their wants and needs. This was echoed by the ethnographic data collected for the project. Respondent testimony reveals that homeyness is regarded as having the power to "ruin" the beauty, formality, and calculated charm of an interior, and to embarrass, perhaps even disqualify, the high standing individual. This potent and dangerous power is rewarded with the contempt of high-standing individuals who mock homeyness as overstated, sentimental, and "noisy."

It is entirely possible that homeyness is something that upwardly mobile families must dispense with as they begin their upward climb. Observing the value of homeyness in the construction of the family and the self, it is worth wondering here just what the consequences of the repudiation of homeyness might be. My expert respondent offered the astute suggestion that the current popularity of the color "peach" stems from the fact that it resembles (without reproducing) the warm homey colors that families must relinquish as they move up. This is one way of "smuggling" homeyness into new material circumstances.

The highstanding do nevertheless depend on homeyness to relieve certain of the burdens created by their status strategies. The chief of these burdens is the difficulty that some individuals experience living in environments that are fully dedicated to status symbolism. Interiors that are "perfect" from a status point of view are sometimes also perfectly uninhabitable. The Crestwood Height dwellers of 1940's Toronto claimed that they found their club more homey and inhabitable than their homes. They preferred to stay at the club for fear of "marring the theatrical arrangements prescribed [for their home] by the decorator" (Seeley, Sims and Loosley 1956: 53).

For these individuals carefully controlled access to homeyness is exceedingly valuable. The Crestwood Height dwellers chose the safe keeping of a distant club, but one respondent in the research project choose instead to "permit" a number of homey objects in his home. These included a piece of tourist art, two reminders of his summer cottage, and a den. Unlike the rest of the home, where "everyone has to be on their best behavior," the den and the homey pieces were seen to be engaging, informal, playful and relaxed, and a valued refuge from the exacting demands of the family's status strategy.

Highstanding individuals use homey objects both as a status strategy and a status corrector. In the first capacity, homey, attention-getting objects are placed in the living room to provoke the curiosity of the guest and to give the host the occasion to tell a self aggrandizing story about his or her recent trip to a "fascinating little country in Asia." In the second, homey objects are used deliberately to "lower the tone" of an otherwise daunting room, and put the guest at his or her ease. Hosts often use these objects as conversational opportunities to tell stories against themselves.

Homeyness has a very different pragmatic significance of homeyness for middle standing groups. Research results suggests that these groups embrace homeyness without ambivalence. For these groups homeyness is an unalloyed good, difficult to achieve, challenging to sustain, but always and unambiguously desirable. For this group the accomplishment of homeyness is one of the great objectives of family life.

Certainly, it is embraced in this manner in part because of its first pragmatic property. Middle standing families like homeyness because it is the necessary condition of their successful enactment of their concept of the family. But it is also true that homeyness serves this group as a status corrector. Respondents suggested that homeyness was their bulwark against status competition. They described their homey environments as safe domains impervious to the demands (and the taunts) of the status system. Without homeyness, it appears, they would be the helpless captives of this system, constantly prone to "buying up" in a ceaseless battle for prestige (McCracken 1988c). A homey environment turns the occupant's attention away from this battle, and provides satisfactions and solidarities against which the battle dwindles into unimportance. For many of the middle class respondents, homeyness is home-made meaning, whereas all of the meanings of the status game are market-made meanings. By using homeyness as their bulwark against the status system, individuals protect themselves from the intrusions and demands of the designer, the marketer, and the showy neighbor, some of whom, respondents said, create homes of beauty but precious little joy.

The social sciences have for too long imagined that status meaning is the chief meaning carried by the material culture of a consumer society. They have also just as glibly supposed that when consumer goods carry status significance, they do so in a simple positive manner. It is time to see that goods carry many meanings additional to those of status, and that some of these meanings are very deliberately at odds with the status system and the objectives of conspicuous consumption.

It is worth emphasizing here that homeyness has a kind of multivocality, assuming one meaning for those of high standing and another for those of middle standing. The variability of the meaning of cultural phenomena in complex societies is a topic of some special interest for the semiotic and symbolic anthropologist (Berstein 1974; McCracken and Roth 1986; Schatzman and Strauss 1955). The study of homeyness suggests that this diversity of meaning is present in the very construction of the domestic world and that it may be driven in part by diverse status strategies.

## Homeyness as a Market Place Corrector

Respondents suggested that the homeyness aesthetic was especially useful as a means of stripping their possessions of their commercially assigned meanings. Consumer goods enter the home complete with class, gender, role, and age meanings, as these have been transferred out of the global cultural structure of North American society into the material culture of the market place (McCracken 1986). Some of these meanings are welcome ones for the consumer and the family, but others bear little relationship to the present constellation that organizes these lives, and still others come bearing profoundly disruptive potential. The efforts a family must make to create a homey environment help to strip and transform these meanings. The coffee table that leaves the store teeming with the market meanings (i.e., status symbolism, fashion currency, and pretensions to elegance) fast becomes a somewhat plainer, more companionable piece in the company of homey objects and homey creatures. Homeyness is so powerful in this respect it can even transform goods that are charged with a bogus "homeyness" (e.g., those with a false wood-grain finish) into genuinely companionable objects.

The best illustration of this function of homeyness is brought out by the dislike of interior designers that was voiced by several respondents. These designers stand accused of introducing into the home, whole assemblages of consumer goods that remain impervious to the meaning manipulation efforts of the home owner. Designers are seen to prevent the creation of a homey environment and to leave the individual defenseless against the alienating power of the unreconstituted commercial goods.

This aspect of homeyness is of special theoretical interest because the social sciences have on the whole been inclined to accept the popular view that North Americans are necessarily the passive recipients of commercial manipulated meanings. There is reason to think, on the contrary, that North Americans are for some purposes entirely capable of judiciously selecting and manipulating the meanings of the market place. Far from being the vulnerable playthings of the forces of marketing, they are possessed of their own culturally constituted powers of discrimination. The study of homeyness helps us to see one of the mainstays of this culturally endowed (and endowing) ability. More research is needed here to tell us which social groups have these powers of discrimination, and whether their distribution varies with class, age, and sex.

### Homeyness as a Modernity Corrector

The fourth pragmatic property of homeyness is its ability to contend with modernity. Respondents indicated that they regard modern styles of house design and furniture as unattractive, inhospitable, and severe. The unkindest thing one respondent could say about interior furnishings was to call them "Scandinavian." Respondents complained that modern design made the home cold and unforgiving. This position is nowhere better illustrated than in the comments that appear in Creighton and Ford's *Contemporary Houses Evaluated by Their Owners* (1961). This wonderful ethnographic document shows some 36 houses designed after the modern style, and provides the comments of their occupants. In the words of one family, "The major lack that we have begun to feel...is some place to retreat to from the very openness that we like so much. We need a small cozy, den-like room to sit in sometimes as a change of pace" (1961: 219). In the words of another, "We like the open planning, but there are times when human beings have a need to feel closed in and comfortable. At such times we use the library" (1961: 195).

Modern homes with the undifferentiated, multifunctional, open-plan spaces, long lines and smooth unbroken surfaces, and lack of ornament, violate many of the tenets of homeyness. They especially contradict the intentions of the diminutive, the variable, and the embracing aspects of homeyness. But the modern aesthetic also contradicts the mnemonic, authentic, informal and situating properties of homeyness. Indeed so thoroughgoing is the opposition between homeyness and the modern aesthetic the latter appears almost to have been created in contradistinction to the former.

The discomfort of North Americans notwithstanding, the modern style has prevailed as the motif of exterior and interior design and it will be some time before post-modern developments loosen its grip on the domestic home. In the interim, homeyness has served as a kind of corrector here. It has allowed families to give more habitable meanings to environments that are otherwise potentially forbidding and even "Scandinavian."

In sum, homeyness is put to many purposes in the social world of contemporary North Americans. It is used to establish an enabling context for the family's construction of itself. It is also used as a status corrector, serving high standing groups in one way and middle standing ones in quite another. It serves as a market place corrector and an instrument with which individuals can strip incoming consumer goods of their commercially assigned meanings and give them a set of entirely different ones. Finally, homeyness serves as a modernity corrector, giving respite from the difficulties and aesthetic alienation that is induced by the modern style of home design and decoration. This is a limited inventory of the functions of homeyness, but it is enough perhaps to reveal the depth and extent of its usefulness in this modern developed society.

### CONCLUSION

From a general perspective, homeyness appears to play a curious and vital part in the larger cultural system of modern North America. I have tried to argue that there is a continuity between the properties of the family and the properties of its material circumstances. Both the family and the home are supposed to be diminutive, contingent, embracing, engaging, backward looking, authentic, informal and situating. This continuity is not the simple shadow of cultural ideas on the surfaces of the "real" world. As I have tried to argue above, when individuals and families undertake the creation of homeyness, they are engaged, willy nilly, in the creation of the family and the self. The symbolic properties of the family, in other words, follow from the creation of the symbolic properties of the homey home. Homeyness, as a set of interior design ideas, is also a set of cultural specifications for the creation of a social group and a cultural domain. Homeyness supplies the template for the construction of an environment and a family together.

But we may go further. The construction of homeyness also aids in the construction of a system of relations in which the home is situated. For homeyness supplies some of the meaningful co-ordinates according to which the family and the home are to be discriminated from other domains, especially those of work and public life. When the home and family are given homey symbolic properties, when they are made diminutive, contingent, embracing, engaging, backward looking, authentic, informal and situating, they are made to exist in contradistinction to other meanings and domains contained within the North American cultural system. They come to exist in opposition to meanings and domains that are deliberately comprehensive, systematic, rational, instrumental, individualistic, disengaged, forward looking, contrived, and formal. To this extent, the ideology of homeyness enters into the processes by which we fashion the distinction between "private" and "public" domains, and "personal" and "anonymous" ones. It helps us to construct and mark the distinctions between the affective and the instrumental, the natural and the artificial, and the authentic and the contrived. In short, homeyness is intimately caught up in and an organizer of some of the symbolic properties by which certain of the most crucial cultural categories and distinctions are known in modern North America. Homeyness helps fashion the architecture of the home, the family, and the culture all at once.

But if we shift from a collective to an individual point of view, it is possible to observe homeyness in a still more dynamic performative mode. The pragmatic properties of homeyness give the individual a means by which to fashion their relationship with the larger institutions of modern society. It lets them reckon with the intrusion of alien meanings from the market place, the distracting competitive impulses of a mobile society, and the unwelcome aesthetics of changing fashions. Homeyness helps the individual to mediate his or her relationship with the larger world, refusing some of its influences, and transforming still others. It plays its role here by empowering the individual to select and refuse the cultural meanings, to be a discriminating consumer in the culture of the consumer society. The process also happens in tandem. It is in creating the homey home that the individual fashions his or her relationship with the outside world. Here, too, homeyness creates the template for the architecture of both material and social circumstances, this time from the individual's point of view.

This paper offers an account of the physical, symbolic and pragmatic properties of homeyness. It has attempted to show why this neglected and perplexing cultural phenomenon should prove so preoccupying for the North American householder. The anatomy of homeyness offered here identifies eight symbolic properties by which homeyness pursues its conspiracy to capture the thought and affect of the individual, and four pragmatic properties according to which homeyness is pressed into service in the accomplishment of vital social and cultural work. Several of the social sciences have been evoked in this analysis and it is hoped that the paper will reciprocate these contributions and stimulate further interdisciplinary exchange.

## REFERENCES

Adams, Marie Jeanne (1973), "Structural Aspects of a Village Art," *American Anthropologist*, 75 (February), 265-279.

Agrest, Diana and Mario Gandelsonas (1977), "Semiotics and the Limits of Architecture," in *A Perfusion of Signs*, ed. Thomas Sebeok, Bloomington: Indiana University Press: 90-120.

Anonymous (1968), *Choosing accessories for the home*, Michigan State University Cooperation Extension Service Bulletin E-635.

Altman, Irwin, Amos Rapoport, Joachim F. Wohlwill, eds. (1980), *Environment and Culture*, New York: Plenum Press.

_____ and Carol M. Werner, eds. (1985), *Home Environments*, New York: Plenum Press.

Ames, Kenneth L., (1982) "Meaning in Artifacts: Hall Furnishings in *Victorian America*, ed. Thomas J. Schlereth, Nashville, Tennessee: The American Association for State and Local History, 206-221.

Appaduari, Arjun ed. (1986), *The Social Life of Things: Commodities in Cultural Perspective*, Cambridge: Cambridge University Press.

Austin, J. L. (1965), *How to Do Things With Words*, New York: Oxford University Press.

Bakhtin, Mikhail M. (1981), *The Dialogic Imagination: Four essays by Mikhail M. Bakhtin*, ed. Michael Holquist, trans, Caryl Emerson and Michael Holquist, Austin: University of Texas Press.

Belk, Russel W. (1984), "Manifesto for a Consumer Behavior of Consumer Behavior," in *1984 AMA Winter Educators' Conference: Scientific Method in Marketing*, eds. Paul F. Anderson and Michael J. Ryan, Chicago: American Marketing Association, 163-167.

_____ (1985), "Materialism: Trait Aspects of Living in the Material World," *Journal of Consumer Behavior*, 12 (3 December), 265-280.

_____ (1987), "The Role of the Odyssey in Consumer Behavior and in Consumer Research," in *Advances in Consumer Research*, Vol. 14, eds. M. Wallendorf and P. Anderson, Provo, UT: Association for Consumer Research, 357-361.

Bloch, Peter H. (1982), "Involvement Beyond the Purchase Process: Conceptual Issues and Emperical Investigation," in *Advances in Consumer Research*, Vol. 9, ed. Andrew Mitchell, Ann Arbor, MI: Association for Consumer Research, 413-417.

Blumberg, Paul (1974), "The Decline and Fall of the Status Symbol: Some Thoughts on Status in a Post-Industrial Society," *Social Problems*, 21 (4 April), 480-498.

Boschetti, Margaret (1968), *Color Harmony for Interiors*, Michigan State University Cooperative Extension Service Bulletin 637.

Braudel, Fernand (1973), *Capitalism and Material Life 1400-1800*, trans. Miriam Kocham, London: Weidenfeld and Nicolson.

Brenan, Charlotte W. (1939). *The Arrangement of Home Furnishings for Comfort, Convenience, and Beauty*, Cornell Bulletin for Homemakers Bulletin 388.

Bronner, Simon J. (1983), "'Visible Proofs': Material Culture Study in American Folkloristics," *American Quarterly*, 35 (3), 316-338.

Bruner, Edward M. (1984), "Introduction: The Opening Up of Anthropology," in *Text, Play and Story: The Construction and Reconstruction of Self and Society*, eds. Edward Bruner and Stuart Plattner, Washington: American Ethnological Society, 1-16.

Caplovitz, David (1967), *The Poor Pay More*, New York: Free Press.

Campbell, Colin (1983), "Romanticism and the Consumer Ethic: Intimations of a Weber-Style Thesis," *Sociological Analysis*, 44 (4), 279-295.

_____ (1987), *The Romantic Ethic and the Spirit of Modern Consumerism*, Oxford: Basil Blackwell.

Carlisle, Susan G. (1982), "French Homes and French Character," *Landscape*, 26 (3), 13-23.

Carswell, J. William and David G. Saile, eds. (1987) *Purposes in Built Form and Culture Research.* Proceedings of the 1986 conference on Built Form and Culture Research, November 5-8, 1986, University of Kansas.

Clark, Clifford E., Jr. (1976), "Domestic Architecture as an Index to Social History: The Romantic Revival and the Cult of Domesticity in America, 1840-1870," *Journal of Interdiciplinary History*, 7 (1 Summer), 33-56.

_____ (1986), *The American Family Home, 1800-1960*, Chapel Hill: University of North Carolina Press.

Cohen, Lizabeth A. (1982), "Embellishing a Life of Labour: An Interpretation of the Material Culture of American Working-Class Homes, 1885-1915," in *Material Culture Studies in America*, ed. Thomas J. Schlereth, Nashville, Tennessee: The American Association for State and Local History, 289-305.

Cohn, Jan (1979), *The Palace or the Poorhouse: The American House as Cultural Symbol*, East Lansing: Michigan State University Press.

Cordwell, Justine and Ronald A. Schwarz eds., (1979), *Fabrics of Culture*, Hague: Mouton.

Creighton, Thomas H. and Katherine M. Ford (1961), *Contemporary Houses Evaluated By Their Owners*, New York: Reinhold Publishing Corporation.

Csikszentmihalyi, Mihaly and Eugene Rochberg-Halton (1981), *The Meaning of Things: Domestic Symbols and the Self*, New York: Cambridge University Press.

Danet, Brenda (1986), "Books, Butterflies, Botticellis: A Sociological Analysis of the "Madness" of Collecting" paper given at the 6th International Conference of Culture and Communication, Temple University, Philadelphia, October 9, 1986.

Davis, James A. (1956), "Status Symbols and the Measurement of Status Perception," *Sociometry*, 19 (3 September), 154-165.

_____ (1958), "Cultural Factors in the Perception of Status Symbols," *The Midwest Sociologist*, 21 (1 December), 1-11.

Deshpande, Rohit (1983), "Paradigms Lost: On theory and Method in Research in Marketing." *Journal of Marketing*, 47 (Fall), 101-110.

Doucet, Michael J. and John C. Weaver (1985), "Material Culture and the North American House: The Era of the Common Man, 1870-1920," *The Journal of American History*, 72 3 (December), 560-587.

Douglas, Mary and Baron Isherwood (1978), *The World of Goods: Towards an Anthropology of Consumption*, New York: W. W. Norton and Co.

Duncan, James S. ed. (1981), *Housing and Identity: Cross-Cultural Perspectives*, London: Croom Helm.

Felson, Marcus (1976), "The Differentiation of Material Life Styles: 1925 to 1966," *Social Indicators Research*, 3, 397-421.

Firat, A. Fuat (1986) "A Macro Theory in Marketing: The Social Construction of Consumption Patterns," in *Philosophical and Radical Thought in Marketing*, eds. Richard P. Bagozzi, Nikhilesh Dholakia, and A. Fuat Firat, forthcoming.

Forty, Adrian (1986), *Objects of Desire: Design and Society from Wedgwood to IBM*, New York: Pantheon Books.

Friedman, Monroe (1985), "The Changing Language of a Consumer Society: Brand Name Usage in Popular American Novels in the Postwar Era," *Journal of Consumer Research*, 11 (4 March), 927-938.

Fox, Richard Wightman and T. J. Jackson Lears, eds. (1983), *The Cutlure of Consumption: Critical Essays in American History, 1880-1980*, New York: Pantheon Books.

Gans, Herbert J. (1974), *Popular Culture and High Culture: An Analysis and Evaluation of Taste*, New York: Basic Books.

Giuliani, Maria Vittoria, Mirilia Bonnes and Carol M. Werner, eds. (1987), *Home Interiors: A European Perspective*, special issue of Environment and Behavior, 19 (2 March), 146-259.

Glassie, Henry (1973), "Structure and Function, Folklore and the Artifact," *Semiotica*, 7 (4), 313-351.

Gordon, Jean and Jan McArthur (1985), "American Women and Domestic Consumption, 1800-1920: Four Interpretive Themes," *Journal of American Culture*, 8 (3), 35-46.

Gottdiener, M. (1985), "Hegemony and Mass Culture: A Semiotic Approach," *American Journal of Sociology*, 90 (5), 979-1001.

Greenhouse, Carol J. (1985), "Anthropology at Home: Whose Home?" *Human Organization*, 44 (3 Fall), 261-264.

Gronmo, Sigmund (1984), "Compensatory Consumer Behavior: Theoretical Perspectives, Emperical Examples and Methodological Challenges," *1984 AMA Winter Educators' Conference: Scientific Method in Marketing*, eds. Paul F. Anderson and Michael J. Ryan, Chicago: American Marketing Association, 184-188.

_____ (1986), "Compensatory Consumer Behavior: Elements of A Critical Sociology of Consumption," Working Paper, Norwegian Fund for Market and Distribution Research, Oslo, Norway.

Gulick, John (1973), "Urban Anthropology," in *Handbook in Social and Cultural Anthropology*, ed. J. Honigmann, Chicago: Rand McNally, 979-1029.

Handlin, David P. (1979), *The American Home: Architecture and Society, 1815-1915*, Boston: Little, Brown, and Co.

Harris, Neil (1978), "Museums, Merchandizing, and Popular Taste: The Struggle for Influence," in *Material Culture and the Study of American Life*, ed. Ian M. G. Quimby, New York: W. W. Norton and Company.

_____ (1981), "The Drama of Consumer Desire." in *Yankee Enterprise: The Rise of the American System of Manufacturers*, eds. Otto Mayr and Robert C. Post, Washington: Smithsonian Institution Press, 189-216.

Hayden, Dolores (1981), *The Grand Domestic Revolution: A History of Feminist Designs for American Homes, Neighborhoods and Cities*, Cambridge: M.I.T. Press.

Hirsch, Paul M. (1972), "Processing Fads and Fashions: An Organization-Set Analysis of Cultural Industry Systems," *American Journal of Sociology*, 77 (4 January), 639-659.

Hirschman, Albert O. (1982), *Shifting Involvements*, Princeton, NJ: Princeton University Press.

Hirschman, Elizabeth C. (1981), "Comprehending Symbolic Consumption," in *Symbolic Consumer Behavior*, eds. Elizabeth Hirschman and Morris B. Holbrook, Ann Arbor: Association for Consumer Research, 4-6.

_____ (1985), "Scientific Style and the Conduct of Consumer Research," *Journal of Consumer Research*, 12 (2 September), 225-239.

_____ and Morris B. Holbrook (1986), "Expanding the Ontology and Methodology of Research on the Consumption Experience," in *Perspectives on Methodology in Consumer Research*, eds. D. Brinberg and R. J. Lutz, New York: Springer-Verlag, 213-251.

Holbrook, Morris B. (1987), "From the Log of a Consumer Researcher," in *Advances in Consumer Research*, eds. M. Wallendorf and P. Anderson, Provo, UT: Association for Consumer Research, 365-369.

_____ (1987) "What is Consumer Research?" *Journal of Consumer Research*, 14 (1 June), 128-132.

_____ and Elizabeth C. Hirschman (1982), "The Experiential Aspects of Consumption: Consumer Fantasies, Feelings, and Fun," *Journal of Consumer Research*, 9 (2 September), 132-140.

Holdsworth, Deryck W. (1977), "House and Home in Vancouver: Images of West Coast Urbanism, 1886-1929," in *The Canadian City: Essays in Urban History*, eds. Gilbert A. Stelter, Alan F. J. Artibise, Toronto: McClelland and Stewart.

Holman, Rebecca (1980), "Product Use as Communication: A Fresh Appraisal of a Venerable Topic," in *Review of Marketing*, eds. Ben M. Enis and Kenneth J. Roering, Chicago: American Marketing Association, 250-272.

Horowitz, Daniel (1985), *The Morality of Spending: Attitudes Toward the Consumer Society In America, 1875-1940*, Baltimore: Johns Hopkins University Press.

Jackson, J. B. (1976), "The Domestication of the Garage," *Landscape*, 20 (2 Winter), 11-19.

Joseph, Nathan (1986), *Uniform and Nonuniform: Communication through Clothing*, Westport, CT: Greenwood Press.

Kavanaugh, James V. (1978), "The Artifact in American Culture," in *Material Culture and the Study of American Life*, ed. Ian M. G. Quimby, New York: W. W. Norton, 65-74.

Korosec-Serfaty, P., ed. (1976), *Appropriation of Space*, Proceedings of the Third International Architectural Psychology Conference at the Louis Pasteur University, Strasbourg, June 21-25, 1976.

Krampen, Martin (1979), "Survey of Current Work on the Semiology of Objects," in *Semiotic Landscape: Proceedings of the First Congress of the International Association for Semiotic Studies*, eds. Seymour Chatman et al., The Hague: Mouton, 158-168.

Kron, Joan (1983), *Home-Psych: The Social Psychology of Home and Decoration*, New York: Clarkson N. Potter, Inc.

Laumann, Edward O. and James S. House (1970), "Living Room Styles and Social Attributes: The Patterning of Material Artifacts in a Modern Urban Community," *Sociology and Social Research*, 54 (3 April), 321-342.

Lawrence, Roderick J. (1981), "The Social Classification of Domestic Space: A Cross-Cultural Case Study," *Anthropos*, 76, 649-664.

_____ (1982), "Domestic Space and Society: A Cross-Cultural Study," Comparative Studies in Society and History, 24 (1), 104-130.

_____ (1984), "Transition Spaces and Dwelling Design," *Journal of Architectural and Planning Research*, 1, 261-271.

Leach, William R. (1984), "Transformations in a Culture of Consumption: Women and Department Stores, 1890-1925," *The Journal of American History*, 71 (September), 319- 342.

Lears, T. J. Jackson (1981), *No Place of Grace: Antimodernism and the Transformation of American Culture 1880-1920*, New York: Pantheon.

Lechtman, Heather and Robert S. Merrill, eds. (1977), *Material Culture: Styles, Organization, and Dynamics of Technology*, St. Paul: West Publishing Co.

Levi-Strauss, Claude (1963) *Totemism*, trans. Rodney Needham, Boston: Beacon Press.

_____ (1966), *The Savage Mind*, Chicago: University of Chicago Press.

Levy, Sidney J. (1978), "Hunger and Work in a Civilized Tribe," *American Behavioral Scientist*, 21 (4 March/April), 557-570.

_____ (1981), "Interpreting Consumer Mythology: A Structural Approach to Consumer Behavior," *Journal of Marketing*, 45 (Summer), 49-61.

Marchand, Roland (1985), *Advertising the American Dream: Making Way for Modernity, 1920-1940*, Berkely: University of California Press.

Marcus, George E. (1985), "Spending: the Hunts, silver, and dynastic families in America," *Archives Europeennes de Sociologie*, 26 (2), 224-259.

Mayer, Robert (1978), "Exploring Sociological Theories By Studying Consumers," *American Behavioral Scientist*, 21 (March/April), 600-613.

McCracken, Grant (1982), "Rank and Two Aspects of Dress in Elizabethean England," *Culture*, 2 (2), 53-62.

_____ (1985), "Dress Colour at the Court of Elizabeth I: An Essay in Historical Anthropology," *Canadian Review of Sociology and Anthropology*, 22 (4 November), 515-533.

_____ (1986a), "Culture and Consumption: A Theoretical Accounts of the Structure and Movement of the Cultural Meaning of Consumer Goods," *Journal of Consumer Research*, 13 (1 June), 71-84.

_____ (1986b), "Advertising: Meaning or Information?" in *Advances in Consumer Research*, Vol. 14, eds. Paul Anderson and Melanie Wallendorf, Provo, Utah: Association for Consumer Research, 121-124.

_____ (1987), "Culture and Consumption Among the Elderly: Research Objectives for the Study of Person-Object Relations in An Aging Population," *Ageing and Society*, 7 (2 June), 203-224.

_____ (1988a), *Culture and Consumption: New Approaches to the Symbolic Character of Consumer Goods and Activities*, Bloomington: Indiana University Press.

_____ (1988b), "Lois Roget: Curatorial Consumer in a Modern Society," in *Culture and Consumption: New Approaches to the Symbolic Character of Consumer Goods and Activities*, Bloomington: Indiana University Press, 44-53.

_____ (1988c), "Diderot Unities and the Diderot Effect" in *Culture and Consumption: New Approaches to the Symbolic Character of Consumer Goods and Activities*, Bloomington: Indiana University Press, 118-129.

_____ (1988d), *The Long Interview: A four-step method of qualitative inquiry*, Newbury Park: Sage Publishers.

_____ and Victor J. Roth (1985), "Does Clothing Have a Code?: Empirical Findings and Theoretical Implications in the Study of Clothing as a Means of Communication," University of Guelph, Department of Consumer Studies, Working Paper 86-101.

McKendrick, Neil, John Brewer, and J. H. Plumb (1982), *The Birth of a Consumer Society: The Commercialization of Eighteenth-Century England*, Bloomington: Indiana University Press.

Mertz, Elizabeth (1985), "Beyond Symbolic Anthropology: Introducing Semiotic Mediation," in *Semiotic Mediation: Sociocultural and Psychological Perspectives*, eds., E. Mertz and R. J. Parmentier, Orlando: Academic Press, 1-19.

Mertz, Elizabeth and Richard J. Parmentier, eds. (1985), *Semiotic Mediation: Sociocultural and Psychological Perspectives*, Orlando: Academic Press.

Messerschmidt, Donald A., ed. (1981), *Anthropologist at Home in North America*, New York: Cambridge University Press.

Mick, David Glen (1986), "Consumer Research and Semiotics: Exploring the Morphology of Signs, Symbols and Significance," *Journal of Consumer Research*, 13 (2 September), 196-213.

_____ (1988), in press, "Contributions to the Semiotics of Marketing and Consumer Behavior," in *The Semiotic Web: A Yearbook of Semiotics*, eds. Thomas A Sebeok and Jean Umiker-Sebeok, Berlin, Mouton.

Miller, Jonathan (1972), "Plays and Players," in *Nonverbal Communication*, ed. R. A. Hinde, Cambridge: Cambridge University Press.

Miller, Michael B. (1981), *The Bon Marche: Bougeois Culture and the Department Store, 1869-1920*, Princeton: Princeton University Press.

Morton, Edith F. (1936), *The Attractive Home*, Pennsylvania State College Division of Agricultural Extension Circular 177.

Mukerji, Chandra (1983), *From Graven Images: Patterns of Modern Materialism*, New York: Colubia University Press.

Neich, Roger (1982), "A Semiological Analysis of Self-Decoration in Mount Hagen, New Guinea," in *The Logic of Culture*, ed. Ino Rossi, South Hadley, Mass.: J. F. Bergin, 214-231.

Nicosia, Francesco M. and Robert N. Mayer (1976), "Toward a Sociology of Consumption," *Journal of Consumer Research*, 3 (2 September), 65-75.

Olson, Clark D. (1985), "Materialism in the Home: The Impact of Artifacts on Dyadic Communication," in *Advances in Consumer Research*, Vol. 12, eds. Elizabeth C. Hirschaman and Morris B. Holbrook, Provo, UT: Association for Consumer Research, 388-393.

O'Neill, John (1978), "The Productive Body: An Essay on the Work of Consumption," *Queen's Quarterly*, 85 (2 Summer), 221-230.

Peirce, Charles S. (1932), *Collected Papers of Charles Sanders Peirce*, Vol. 2, eds. Charles Hartshorne and Paul Weiss, 3 vols. Cambridge: Harvard University Press.

Pollay, Richard (1986), "The Distorted Mirror: Reflections on the Unintended Consequences of Advertising," *Journal of Marketing*, 50 (2 April), 18-36.

Pope, Daniel (1983), *The Making of Modern Advertising*, New York: Basic Books.

Pratt, Gerry (1981),."The House as an Expression of Social Worlds," in *Housing and Identity: Cross-Cultural Perspectives*, ed. James S. Duncan, London: Croom Helm, 135-180.

Prown, Jules D. (1980), "Style as Evidence," *Winterthur Portfolio*, 15 (3 Autumn), 197-210.

_____ (1982), "Mind in Matter: An Introduction to Material Culture Theory and Method," *Winterthur Portfolio*, 17 (1 Spring), 1-19.

Quimby, Ian, ed. (1978), *Material Culture and the Study of Material Life*, New York, W. W. Norton and Co.

Rainwater, Lee (1966), "Fear and the House-As-Haven in the Lower Class," *Journal of the American Institute of Planners*, XXXII (1 February), 23-31.

Rapoport, Amos (1982) *The Meaning of the Built Environment*, Beverly Hills: Sage Publications.

Rathje, William (1978), "Archeological Ethnography," in *Explorations in Ethnoarchaeology*, ed. Richard A. Gould, Albuquerque: University of New Mexico Press of America.

Richardson, Miles (1974), "Images, Objects and the Human Story," in *The Human Mirror: Material and Spatial Images of Man*, ed. Miles Richardson, Baton Rouge: Louisiana State University Press, 3-14.

Robinson, Charlotte Brenan (1941), *The Arrangement of Home Furnishings*, Cornell Bulletin for Homemakers Bulletin 463.

Rook, Dennis W. (1985), "The Ritual Dimension of Consumer Behavior," *Journal of Consumer Research*, 12 (3 December), 251-264.

Rudmin, Floyd (1986), "Psychology of Ownership, Possession and Property: A Selected Bibliography Since 1890," *Psychological Reports*, 58, 859-869.

Sapir, Edward (1931), "Communication," *Encyclopedia of the Social Sciences*, first edition, 78-80.

Sahlins, Marshall D. (1976), *Culture and Practical Reason*, Chicago: University of Chicago Press

Saile, David G. ed. (1984), *Architecture in Cultural Change: Essays in Built Form and Culture Research Conference*, October 18-20, 1984, University of Kansas.

Seamon, David (1979), *A Geography of the Lifeworld*, London: Croom Helm.

Seeley, John R., R. Alexander Sim and E. W. Loosley (1956), *Crestwood Heights: A Study of the Culture of Suburban Life*, Toronto: University of Toronto Press.

Schlereth, Thomas J. (1982), "Material Culture Studies in America, 1876-1976," in *Material Culture Studies in America*, ed. Thomas J. Schlereth, Nashville, Tennessee: The American Association for State and Local History, 1-75.

Sherry, John F. (1984), "Some Implications for Consumer Oral Tradition for Reactive Marketing," *Advances in Consumer Research*, ed. Thomas C. Kinnear, Provo, UT: Association for Consumer Research, 741-747.

Schatzman, Leonard and Anselm Strauss (1955), "Social Class and Modes of Communication," *The American Journal of Sociology*, LX (4), 329-338.

Schneider, David M. (1968), *American Kinship: A Cultural Account*, Englewood Cliffs: Prentice Hall.

Shi, David E. (1985), *The Simple Life: Plain Living and High Thinking in American Culture*, New York: Oxford University Press.

Shweder, Richard A. and Robert A. LeVine, eds. (1984), *Culture Theory: Essays on Mind, Self and Emotion*, Cambridge: Cambridge University Press, 11-55.

Silverstein, Michael (1976), "Shifters, Linguistic Categories, and Cultural Description," in *Meaning in Anthropology*, eds. Keith H. Basso and Henry A. Selby, Albuquerque: University of New Mexico Press, 11-55.

Simmel, G. (1904), "Fashion," *International Quarterly*, 10, 130-155.

Singer, Milton B. (1984), *Man's Glassy Essence: Explorations in Semiotic Anthropology*, Bloomington: Indiana University Press.

Tambiah, Stanley J. (1969), "Animals are good to thing and good to prohibit," *Ethnology*, 8 (4 October), 424-459.

_____ (1977), "The Cosmological and Performative Significance of a Thai Cult of Healing Through Mediation," *Culture, Medicine, and Psychiatry*, 1, 97-132.

Tognoli, Jerome (1987), "Residential Environments," in *Handbook of Environmental Psychology*, eds. I. Altman and D. Stokols, New York: J. Wiley and Sons, 655-690.

Tuan, Yi-Fu (1982), *Segmented Worlds and Self*, Minneapolis: University of Minnesota Press.

Veblen, Thorstein (1912), *The Theory of the Leisure Class*, New York: Macmillan.

Varenne, Herve (1977), *Americans Together*, New York: Teachers College Press.

_____ (1986), "Doing the Anthropology of America," in *Symbolizing America*, ed. Herve Varenne, Lincoln: University of Nebraska Press, 34-45.

Wallendorf, Melanie (1987), "On the Road Again: The Nature of Qualitative Research on the Consumer Behavior Odyssey," in *Advances in Consumer Research*, Vol. 14, eds. M. Wallendorf and P. Anderson, Provo, UT: Association for Consumer Research, 374-375.

_____ and Eric J. Arnould (1988), "'My Favorite Things': A Cross-Cultural Inquiry into Object Attachment, Possessiveness, and Social Linkage," *Journal of Consumer Research*, 14 (March 4), 531-547.

Williams, Rosalind H. (1982), *Dream Worlds: Mass Consumption in Late Nineteenth Century France*, Berkely: University of California Press.

Williamson, Judith (1978), *Decoding Advertising*, New York: Marion Boyars.

Wolf, Arthur P. (1970), "Chinese Kinship and Mourning Dress," in *Family and Kinship in Chinese Society*, ed. Maurice Freedman, Stanford, CA.: Stanford University Press, 189-207.

Wright, Gwendolyn (1980), *Moralism and the Model Home: Domestic Architecture and Cultural Conflict in Chicago*, 1873-1913, Chicago: University of Chicago Press.

_____ (1981), *Building the Dream: A Social History of Housing in America*, New York: Pantheon.

# Critiques

Critiques of the interpretive papers in this volume were invited from outspoken empiricists. Their views are presented in the following section.

# Naturalistic, Humanistic, and Interpretive Inquiry: Challenges and Ultimate Potential

Shelby D. Hunt, Texas Tech University[1]

## ABSTRACT

Many researchers are now both advocating and adopting naturalistic, humanistic, and interpretive inquiry methods. The purpose of this paper is to provide a constructive and critical commentary on this developing trend in consumer research. This paper proposes that in order for naturalistic, humanistic, and interpretive methods to reach their ultimate potential, they must respond to (at least) four separate challenges. Although these challenges reveal that I find *some* of the positions (apparently) advocated by naturalistic, humanistic, and interpretive researchers to be problematical, this does not mean that I do not admire and respect their efforts. Rather, I agree with Laudan when he states that in academia "healthy disagreement (unlike imitation) is the deepest sign of admiration" (1977, p. ix).

## CHALLENGES AND ULTIMATE POTENTIAL

In recent years several researchers have been adopting naturalistic, humanistic, and interpretive inquiry methods for studying both marketing and consumer research phenomena. The volume in which this paper is published represents a natural outgrowth of interest in these procedures and the purpose of this paper is to provide a constructive critique of them. Several factors severely delimit both the breadth and depth of the critique, including page limitations and (more importantly) the diversity and heterogeneity of the papers in the volume and the naturalistic, humanistic and interpretive methods.

At the outset, I should admit my own positive bias towards the humanities and their function in both academe and society. I strongly believe that naturalistic, humanistic and interpretive inquiry can play a positive role in developing both marketing and consumer research. At the same time, we must recognize that naturalistic, humanistic and interpretive research efforts are in their early, formative stages in marketing and consumer research. Therefore, the extent to which these methods can develop their ultimate potential depends in part on the paths taken by their "early adopters." This commentary is offered in the constructive spirit of one colleague's suggestions as to which "paths" advocates of these methods might take in order to maximize the likelihood that the potential will be fulfilled.

[1]The author wishes to thank Professors Roy Howell, James B. Wilcox and Robert W. Wilkes of Texas Tech University and Professor Harvey Siegel of the University of Miami Philosophy Department for their helpful comments on an earlier draft of this paper.

I suggest that the ultimate fulfillment of the potential of these methods depends in part on how advocates of naturalistic, humanistic and interpretive inquiry respond to four challenges. Each challenge poses its own set of problems, but each appears to be amenable to resolution.

## CHARACTERIZATIONS, MISCHARACTERIZATIONS AND CARICATURIZATIONS

Many of the discussions involving naturalistic, humanistic and interpretive inquiry (hereafter referred to as "N-H-I" methods) seem to start off with a ritualized bashing of those scholars who hold contemporary views as to the nature of science and scientific inquiry. These scholars are labeled "positivists" and their views are contrasted with the enlightened views of N-H-I. Unfortunately, instead of *characterizing* the view of contemporary social science, the ritualized bashing degenerates into blatant *mischaracterizing* or (worse) *caricaturizing*.

The paper by Ozanne and Hudson typifies the procedure of both mischaracterizing and caricaturizing contemporary social science (hereafter referred to as C-S-S). First, consider that they label C-S-S as "positivist." Now, the term positivism was coined in the 19th century by the French philosopher Saint-Simon, one of the founders of a movement known as social positivism, which had as its central objective the promotion of a more just society through the application of the knowledge generated by science and the scientific method. August Comte, Saint-Simon's colleague, articulated and developed the movement's "positive philosophy of science," which has been claimed by Laudan to be "the most important single development in the last century" as to theories of the scientific method (1968, p.29). Later in the 19th century, the physicist Ernst Mach continued the development of positivist philosophy and strongly influenced Einstein in the development of relativity theory (Holton 1970). The positivist movement culminated with the logical positivists of the Vienna Circle in the 1920's. However, a key premise of logical positivism, the verifiability principle, was demonstrated to be untenable in the early 1930's. Thereafter, the Vienna Circle was disbanded (under pressure and persecution from the Nazi's), and logical positivism, formally speaking, ceased to be. Many of the logical positivists continued to work in the general area of empiricist philosophy and some became associated with the research program (in Lakatosian terms) now called logical empiricism.

Although many philosophers of science characterize their philosophy as being *empiricist*, I know of no contemporary philosopher of science who characterizes his/her work as "positivist." For example, Laudan calls his perspective "historical empiricism" (1979, p. 46). Furthermore, although many *practitioners* of C-S-S call their work "empirical," none characterize its nature as "positivistic." In fact, most philosophers of science and practitioners of C-S-S would object strongly to being labeled "positivist." Then why do Ozanne and Hudson (as well as many others in these debates) choose to identify practitioners of C-S-S with a label that not only mischaracterizes their views, (associating them with such discredited beliefs as for example, the verifiability principle) but one which practitioners find objectionable? The answer lies in applying some concepts of the illuminating paper by Stern in this volume. In particular, Stern points out that words have both a denotative and a connotative meaning. Although "positivist" *denotes* a set of views (including the discredited verifiability principle) held by an identifiable set of people at a particular period of time, over the last several decades the term (rightly or wrongly) has taken on a highly pejorative *connotation*. Thus, by adopting a pejorative, rather than neutral, label for C-S-S, Ozanne and Hudson bring negative connotations into the debate.

Phillips (1987) has chronicled the ongoing diatribe being conducted by a host of writers (including, he notes, Lincoln and Guba) against contemporary social science. In a section entitled "Rampant Anti-Positivism," he concludes:

> [T]here have been many exaggerated claims about the evils of positivism, and about the beneficial effects of its demise.... First, many factual errors are made when researchers refer to positivism. Indeed, without suggesting that those who make the errors are dishonest, it seems as if the word "positivism" arouses such negative feelings that it is often used in a blanket way to condemn any position at all that the writer in question disagrees with, irrespective of how positivistic that position really is (1987, p. 94).

Note that Ozanne and Hudson use "interpretive" to identify naturalistic, humanistic and interpretive inquiry. Although "interpretive" may not accurately denote all the characteristics of N-H-I inquiry (as Professor Belk has commented to me), it to my knowledge has no pejorative connotation. Furthermore, it at least is a label chosen by practitioners and advocates of N-H-I, themselves, and not "pinned" on them by advocates of C-S-S.

As a straightforward example of caricature, consider Ozanne and Hudson's claim that a fundamental premise of practitioners of C-S-S is that an "immutable social reality" (p. 2) exists, a "single unchanging reality" (p. 2). "Immutable" is a very strong word implying that social reality is *totally* unchanging. Can anyone seriously claim that practitioners of C-S-S believe that social reality (for example, the relationships among attitudes, intentions, and behaviors of consumers) is totally unchanging? Is this not a *caricature* of C-S-S? As another caricature example, Ozanne and Hudson paint C-S-S researchers as believing that human behavior is "entirely deterministic" (p. 7) rather than "entirely voluntaristic" and propose their own "middle ground position," since "humans seem to indicate some evidence of choosing freely and some evidence of being influenced by internal/external forces" (p. 7). Their discovery of the "middle ground" will hardly seem revelatory to practitioners of C-S-S who have long considered most human behavior to be indeterministic, to be explored through "tendency laws" (Hunt 1983, p. 200) and the like. Is there a better word than *caricature* to describe Ozanne and Hudson's assertions?

Although I have restricted my examples to those in this volume from Ozanne and Hudson, similar rhetorical devices seem all too commonplace throughout the literature. Most importantly, mischaracterizing through pejorative labeling and using caricatures both demean and damage the cause of those who advocate N-H-I. Such devices are normally adopted only by those whose positions are weak or unsound and, therefore, are surely unnecessary for advocates of N-H-I.

The preceding paragraphs point out the first challenge for advocates of N-H-I is to raise the level of the debate by avoiding pejorative labeling and the caricaturizing of the views of their colleagues in C-S-S. The use of these rhetorical devices may serve well when "preaching to the committed." However, such techniques are unlikely to gain "converts."

## DEMONSTRATE THE VALUE OF YOUR PRODUCT

The objective of all research is to produce *knowledge*, or (more epistemologically modest) knowledge-claims. Every university discipline has an extant body of knowledge and all scholarly journals associated with academic disciplines evaluate manuscripts according to whether each submitted manuscript contributes to, or extends, the extant body of knowledge as judged by a jury of one's peers. Essentially, the process of evaluating manuscripts for a scholarly journal involves answering three questions: 1) What is the nature of the purported contribution to knowledge of the manuscript? 2) What is the extent of the purported contribution to knowledge? 3) Is the purported contribution to knowledge *genuine*?

The first evaluative question categorizes the purported contribution. Does the manuscript fall within the domain of the journal? For example, is the manuscript truly in the area of consumer behavior, or is it marketing management, or is it personnel management, and so forth. The second question, identifying the *extent* of the purported contribution, is actually a composite of three sub-questions. First, to what extent is the purported contribution new? That is, has the contribution been previously reported in the literature? The second aspect of the extent criterion is, roughly speaking, a quantitative dimension. In the judgment of the reviewers is the contribution "large enough" to warrant publishing in the journal. Alternatively, is the contribution-to-page-length ratio large enough? The third aspect of the extent question has to do with the value of the contribution. Will the manuscript be valuable in encouraging further research? Does the manuscript have value for decision-makers? Does the manuscript have value for government policy? In addition to the nature of the contribution and the extent of the contribution, the manuscript review process evaluates the *genuineness* of the contribution. How do we know that the knowledge-claims in the manuscript are true, or trustworthy, or verified, or confirmed, or (in philosophy of science terms) have "high epistemic warrant"?

It seems to me that the product, or output, or knowledge-claims, of interpretive inquiry faces serious and significant (but not insuperable) difficulties with all three of the major criteria that scholarly journals impose on manuscripts. Consider the major knowledge-claim extensively discussed in the Holbrook, Bell and Grayson paper (originally developed in Holbrook and Grayson (1986)). As I understand their work, the major knowledge-claim resulting from their interpretive inquiry is that "consumption symbolism contributes to the development of character in a work of art" (p. 36). This knowledge-claim of interpretive inquiry provides an excellent illustration, since it has already been published in the *Journal of Consumer Research* and, therefore, has survived the peer-review process. (Presumably, the results of many interpretive studies, just like the results of many studies conducted using the methods of C-S-S, would not pass the peer-review process of major journals, such as *JCR*).

How might reviewers have applied the first criterion to the Holbrook-Grayson contribution? The reviewers would obviously have to ask themselves whether the contribution was more about "consumption symbolism" (and therefore appropriate for *JCR*) or whether the contribution was more in the area of "art" (and therefore more appropriate for another journal)? My experience has been that most journals receive many manuscripts where, in the judgment of the reviewers, the nature of the contribution is outside the domain of the journal. Second, how would the *extent* criterion be applied to the Holbrook-Grayson contribution? I suspect that some reviewers might contend that, since works of art mirror society, and since it is "well known" (from the hundreds of life-style and psychographic studies) that many people significantly express their personalities through consumption symbols, that the Holbrook-Grayson contribution may not represent a "new" addition to the body of knowledge. Further, I suspect that some reviewers might contend that, even if the contribution is "new," it is not "large enough" for a journal such as *JCR*. Finally, with respect to *extent*, what is the value of the contribution? Will it encourage further research? If so, of what kind? Does the contribution have value to any of *JCR*'s publics in addition to researchers? (Although *JCR* does not purport to be a "managerial" journal, it does purport to be relevant to public policy and other societal issues).

With respect to the third criterion, is the Holbrook-Grayson purported contribution *genuine*? To what extent is it true that "consumption symbolism contributes to the development of character in a work of art"? (For those who consider the word "true" to be naive, naughty or nefarious, they may substitute surrogates, such as warranted, justified, credible, or trustworthy. Notably Holbrook, Bell and Grayson do not avoid the word "truth", since they claim "the humanities in general and artworks in particular contain truths that escape procedures of the hypothetico-deductive method" (p. 39)). The reviewers will ask whether the Holbrook-Grayson knowledge-claim is in some meaningful sense *genuine*. After all, Holbrook and Grayson do not simply claim that it is *possible* to interpret consumption symbolism as contributing to the development of character. Rather, they claim that "consumption symbolism *contributes* to the development of character." This implies the necessity of demonstrating that the Holbrook-Grayson interpretation satisfies appropriate criteria for good, well-conducted, truly justificatory, interpretive research; and not bad, poorly conducted, nonjustificatory, interpretive research.

It is clear that the Holbrook-Grayson contribution satisfied the reviewers of *JCR* on all three criteria discussed in the preceding paragraphs. Nevertheless, I am sure the authors of that paper would be the first to admit that much needs to be done to smooth the way for publishing (and thus disseminating) the work of future research efforts. Therefore, interpretive researchers must consciously address the second challenge: clearly demonstrating that the nature of their purported contributions to knowledge reside within the domains of their chosen publishing outlets, showing that the *extent* of their contributions (i.e. their newness, significance and value) and justifying that their contributions are *genuine*. In this regard the paper by Wallendorf and Belk in this volume is exemplary. Contrary to the oft-cited claim that there are no universal standards or values (across different approaches or paradigms or "disciplinary matrixes"), they note that "trustworthiness" is to them considered "to be a scientific universal," although "the particular way that trustworthiness is evaluated will vary considerably depending on the research program and the philosophy within which the research operates" (p. 69). Their paper builds upon the criteria for evaluating humanistic inquiry developed by Hirschman (1986) and clearly demonstrates that there are both good procedures to adopt in actually conducting naturalistic inquiry and that these procedures can be used as evaluative criteria for assessing the justificatory warrant of the knowledge-claims generated by such research.

With respect to demonstrating the value of interpretive inquiry, it seems strange that advocates of N-H-I are characterizing their inquiry in such a manner as to render it fundamentally irrelevant to public policy and other significant social concerns. Ozanne and Hudson claim that "while interpretivists may identify patterns of behavior, they believe that the world is so complex and dynamic that causal relationships cannot be identified" (p. 2). Similarly, Hirschman, claims that "phenomenal aspects cannot be segregated into causes and effects" (1986, p.239).

As an implication of claiming that interpretive inquiry cannot yield causal knowledge, consider the issue of the impact of television advertising on children. This is currently a significant social issue about which there are direct public policy implications. It would seem that interpretive inquiry might have a role to play in identifying how children interpret the messages or "texts" received from the television screen. Further, such interpretive inquiry might yield knowledge, or at least some tentative hypotheses, about how children's interpretations of television advertising are formed (a causal imputation). Such interpretive inquiry might then give guidance to public policy in this important area. But, public policy decisions in this kind of area *inherently* involve causal imputations. That is, if television advertising has no *effect* on children's beliefs, attitudes, or values, then any government regulation would be unnecessary or ineffective. If television *does* have a (deleterious) effect on children, what kind of government regulation would negate or overcome the effect? *In fact, most government regulation necessarily implies that a particular law or regulation will bring about, or "cause," some desirable consequence.* Therefore, I question why advocates of N-H-I choose to define and circumscribe their inquiry to be irrelevant to public policy. Curiously, there is no reason for them to do so, except perhaps as a reaction (over-reaction?) to the strong emphasis on causal processes in C-S-S and the reliance (over-reliance?) on the views of those such as Lincoln and Guba (1985). Finally, it should be noted, substituting Hudson and Ozanne's "mutual, simultaneous shaping" (1988, p. 512) for "cause" does not save N-H-I from irrelevancy. To suggest that a child and a television set are engaged in "mutual simultaneous shaping" strains credulity beyond all reasonable limits. (Consider for starters the implications of the word *simultaneous* on the child/television set example).

## INTERPRETIVISM AND RELATIVISM

Both the Anderson paper and the Peter and Olson contribution present spirited defenses of the appropriateness of relativism for consumer research. Both position their papers as a reply to Calder and Tybout (1987), who adopt a sophisticated falsificationist perspective for analyzing various kinds of knowledge-claims. Much of the content of the Anderson, Peter and Olson papers contains rather standard arguments against falsificationism as a demarcation criterion to separate science from nonscience. In this section I shall not analyze their attack on falsificationism. Rather, I shall focus on the more fundamental issue of demarcation in general.

Consistent with his previously stated positions (1983, 1986) Anderson claims that "we currently have *no* universally applicable criterion by which we can demarcate scientific knowledge from any other kind of knowledge" (p. 10). He cites Laudan (1980) as a reference and notes that "unfortunately this

is often thought to imply that all knowledge-claims are on an equal epistemic footing" (p. 10), referring to Hunt (1984). He claims that "very little follows from the fact that philosophers have been unable to come up with a *universal* demarcation criterion" (p. 10), and speaks again in favor of what he calls "science$_2$--the definition of science by societal consensus" (p. 10). Is it the case that nothing of great importance follows from the demarcation issue? Stated more succinctly, is it the case that "societal consensus" alone constitutes the reason why there are astronomy departments in universities but not astrology departments, that there are medical science departments but not palmistry departments? I and many others believe that it is not just "societal consensus," but rather that *the societal consensus is backed by very good reasons,* as can be illustrated by analyzing what may be called the "nature of science argument."

The "nature of science argument" according to a fundamental premise (noted hereafter as "R1") of the relativist point of view, as stated by Anderson and detailed in Hunt (1984), may be concisely summarized as follows:

R1. *There are no fundamental differences separating the sciences and the nonsciences.* ("The search for [demarcation] criteria that separate science from nonscience"...has been "signally unsuccessful" (Anderson 1983, p. 18). Since there are no objective criteria separating science from nonscience, "science is whatever society chooses to call science" (Anderson 1983, p. 26)).

R2. *The knowledge-claims of the nonsciences have as much epistemological warrant as the sciences.* (That is, we have no good reason to believe and act on the knowledge-claims of the sciences in preference to the nonsciences. Statement R2 is *logically implied* by R1 because, if we had good reasons to believe and act on the knowledge-claims of the sciences, such reasons would constitute "fundamental differences" that could be used to separate science from nonscience).

R3. Therefore, statement R2 implies that if a palmist should diagnose a person as *not* having bone cancer (an example of a nonscience knowledge-claim), such a diagnosis would have equal warrant as the diagnosis of a medical doctor that the person *did* have bone cancer (an example of a science knowledge-claim).

A reconstruction of the "nature of science argument" according to modern empiricism (as detailed in Hunt (1984) and drawing upon works such as Hempel (1969), Radner and Radner (1982), Rudner (1966) and Siegel (1986)) would be:

E1. *There are fundamental differences separating the sciences and nonsciences.* (Sciences differ from nonsciences in their method of verifying knowledge-claims).

*E2. The knowledge-claims of sciences have greater epistemological warrant than the knowledge-claims of the nonsciences.* (Since the knowledge-claims of the sciences are intersubjectively certifiable through open empirical testing, people have good reasons for accepting such claims and acting upon them in preference to the knowledge-claims of nonsciences).

E3. Therefore, E2 implies that if a palmist should diagnose a person as *not* having bone cancer and a medical doctor should diagnose that same person as *having* bone cancer, the person has good reasons for believing the diagnosis of the medical doctor and acting accordingly. (Palmistry has not adopted the verification system of open empirical testing and, therefore, is not a science).

Anderson reviewed the narrative versions of the preceding nature of science arguments and lamented that empiricists often cast "proffered alternatives" as "relativistic flights of fancy that lead to epistemological anarchy and the abandonment of rationality and objectivity" (Anderson 1986, p. 156). He did not deny that the empiricist version accurately reflected the views of modern empiricism. Nor did he do a detailed analysis of the relativist version, pointing out logical flaws or empirical inadequacies. Rather, he dismissed the argument as a "straw man." To avoid the impression of possibly mischaracterizing Anderson's reasons for dismissing the argument, he is quoted at length:

> The type of relativism attacked by Hunt (1984) has *never* been advocated by any of the participants in the current debate. The object of Hunt's critique is a straw man known as judgmental (Knorr-Certina and Mulkay 1983) or "nihilistic" relativism. In this view, all knowledge claims are equally valid and there is no basis on which to make judgments among the various contenders. *(Indeed, a careful reading of even the most radical of contemporary relativists will reveal that this does not even approximate their views, e.g.,* Collins 1975, 1981; Feyerabend 1975, 1978a) (page 156 emphasis added).

Is it true that the above argument (indicating that the relativism advocated by Anderson and others inexorably leads one to be indifferent between the claims of palmistry and medical science) is a "straw man?" Is it truly the case that "a careful reading of *even the most radical* of contemporary relativists will reveal that this does not even *approximate* their views?"

## Is the Nature of Science Argument a Strawman?

Since Anderson uses Feyerabend as an example of a contemporary relativist who would not subscribe

to the so-called "nihilistic" relativism presented in the preceding argument, we shall examine Feyerabend's views on the subject. Feyerabend is one of the most prominent and widely cited supporters of a relativist view of science (Suppe 1977). Indeed, all of the relativist writers in consumer research draw heavily from his works for intellectual sustenance, reference him liberally, and even refer to him as a relativist "hero" (Olson 1987). In addition to many articles extolling the virtues of relativism, Feyerabend has published several books on the subject, including: *Against Method* (1975) and *Science In A Free Society* (1978b). In the 1978 book he extends and further clarifies the positions taken in the 1975 book. (All references to Feyerabend in the following sections refer to his 1978 work). Further, he addresses and answers many criticisms of his work from other philosophers of science. He is quoted here at length (again, to avoid the charge of mischaracterization) concerning his answer to a critique by a philosopher named Tibbets:

> [Tibbets] also asks: 'If he had a child diagnosed with Leukemia would he look to his witchdoctor friends or to the Sloan Kettering Institute?' I can assure him that I would look to my 'witchdoctor friends' to use his somewhat imprecise terminology *and so would many other people in California* whose experience with scientific medicine has been anything but encouraging. The fact that scientific medicine is the only existing form of medicine in many places does not mean that it is the best and the fact that alternative forms of medicine succeed where scientific medicine has to resort to surgery shows that it has serious lacunae: numerous women, reluctant to have their breasts amputated as their doctors advised them, went to acupuncturists, faithhealers, herbalists and got cured. Parents of small children with allegedly incurable diseases, leukemia among them, did not give up, they consulted 'witchdoctors' and their children got cured. How do I know? Because I advised some of these men and women and I followed the fate of others (pp. 205-206, emphasis in original).

Recall that Anderson dismissed the "nature of science argument" on the basis that "a careful reading of even the most radical of contemporary relativists will reveal that this does not even approximate their views" (1986, p. 156). The above quote clearly shows that, to the contrary, any careful observer of relativists' writings knows that the relativist "nature of science argument" very closely reflects the logical implications of their views!

How do relativists (such as Feyerabend) reach such extreme positions that even their followers (such as Anderson) dismiss relativist views as "nihilistic" nonsense? The answer lies precisely in Feyerabend's fundamental beliefs about the existence of many, equally viable, "ways of knowing" that he calls research "traditions". These fundamental beliefs are very similar, if not precisely the same, as those (supposedly) now championed by relativist consumer researchers.

## Feyerabend on "Ways of Knowing"

Central to the relativist philosophy of Feyerabend is the construct of a knowledge-creating "tradition." Feyerabend notes that science is but one of many such traditions, each constituting a "way to know." What are these other traditions? Throughout his 1978 book he discusses and defends mysticism (p. 31), magic (p. 74), astrology (p. 74), rain dances (p. 78), religion (p. 78), "mythical world views" (p. 78), tribal medicine (p. 96), parapsychology (p. 103), all non-Western belief traditions (p. 102), and witchcraft (p. 191). Each "way of knowing" is equal, since "traditions are neither good nor bad, they simply are" (p. 27). (This is similar to Science2 in Anderson's terms).

Feyerabend notes that in the 17th, 18th, and 19th centuries the scientific tradition was but one of the many competing ideologies and was in fact a "liberating force" because it "restricted the influence of other ideologies and thus gave the individual room for thought" (p. 75). However, he believes science today does not have a liberating effect since it has turned into a "dogmatic religion." He believes "the very same enterprise that once gave man the ideas and the strength to free himself from the fears and prejudices of a tyrannical religion now turns him into a slave of its interests" (p. 75).

How did the consensus emerge that the knowledge claims of science were preferred by society over the knowledge claims of competing traditions? Is it not because society rationally and reasonably determined that scientific knowledge-claims had more epistemological warrant, were more likely to be true? (Science1 in Anderson's terms). Emphatically not, asserts Feyerabend:

> It reigns supreme because some past successes have led to institutional measures (education; role of experts; role of power groups such as the AMA) that prevent a comeback of the rivals. Briefly, but not incorrectly: Today science prevails not because of its comparative merits, but because the show has been rigged in its favor (p. 102).

Specifically, for Feyerabend how did these other traditions lose out? "These myths, these religions, these procedures have disappeared or deteriorated not because science was better, but because *the apostles of science were the more determined conquerors*, because they *materially suppressed* the bearers of alternative cultures" (p. 102, emphasis in original).

How was the material suppression of rival traditions and the triumph of the "apostles of science" accomplished? The suppression of rival traditions was accomplished, he contends, through the actions of scientists, both individually and through their collective associations, aided and abetted by such diverse groups as "liberal intellectuals, white missionaries, adventurers, and anthropologists" (p. 77).

As examples of suppressive tactics, Feyerabend notes that anthropologists "collected and systematized" knowledge about non-Western traditions and developed "interpretations" that "were simply a consequence of "popular antimetaphysical tendencies combined with a firm belief in the excellence first, of Christianity, and then of science" (p. 77). Liberal intellectuals aided the suppression by first "loudly and persistently" proclaiming that they defend freedom of thought, while at the same time not recognizing that this freedom of thought only "is granted to those who have already accepted part of the rationalist (i.e. scientific) ideology" (p. 76). Feyerabend, himself, even contributed to the suppression while teaching at the University of California at Berkeley: "My function was to carry out the educational policies of the State of California, which means I had to teach people what a small group of white intellectuals had decided was knowledge" (p. 118).

Feyerabend concludes that "the prevalence of science is a threat to democracy" (p. 76) and proposes his solution to the problem of science in society. He addresses this issue by first proposing the following rhetorical questions (concerning Science1 and Science2):

> But -- so the impatient believer in rationalism and science is liable to exclaim -- is this procedure not justified? Is there not a tremendous difference between science on the one side, religion, magic, myth on the other? Is this difference not so large and so obvious that it is unnecessary to point it out and silly to deny it? (p. 78)

Feyerabend answers his rhetorical questions concerning the differences between science1 and science2 thusly: "Rationalists and scientists cannot rationally (scientifically) argue for the unique position of their favorite ideology" (p. 79). Therefore, he proposes, in order to have a free society "is it not rather the case that traditions [mysticism, magic, astrology, rain dances, religion, mythical world views, tribal medicine, parapsychology, all non-Western belief traditions and witchcraft] that give substance to the lives of people must be given equal rights and *equal access to key positions in society* no matter what other traditions think about them? (p. 79, emphasis added).

The preceding discussion of Feyerabend's relativist views on research traditions in society clearly shows how he arrives at conclusions so extreme as to be labelled "nihilistic" and "a straw man" by Anderson. One might suppose that Feyerabend is simply engaging in academic gamesmanship or sophistry and that he did not intend for readers to take his views seriously. Brodbeck notes that relativists believe "science is in effect a game" (1982, p. 3), which is consistent with Anderson's view that "the important question we must ask is how can I convince my colleagues in the scientific community that my theory is correct?" (1982, p. 15). As Krausz and Meiland (1982, p. 6) have pointed out, the sophists in ancient Greece were among the first relativists in western intellectual history. From whom we get the term "sophistry," these philosophers delighted in weaving incredibly convoluted arguments that *they* knew to be false, but that the *less sophisticated* would (or could) not know.

Clearly, however, Feyerabend is no sophist! The preceding discussion demonstrates that he recognizes how extreme are his premises concerning the nature of the scientific "tradition" (the knowledge-claims of the sciences are no better than the knowledge-claims of the nonsciences) and is willing to accept their logical consequences (palmistry and medical science should have "equal rights" and "equal access to key positions"), no matter how extreme those consequences may appear to others. Most importantly, he not only intellectually accepts these extreme consequences, but (unlike a sophist) he also acts upon them (referring now to the first long quote of Feyerabend in this paper where he indicates he has both used and referred others to "witchdoctor friends").

Unfortunately, many relativists are not as consistent as Feyerabend. The issue was *never* (as Anderson and others have stated it) whether relativists embraced "nihilistic" conclusions (like R3), but whether relativist beliefs (like R1) *implied* nihilism. Relativist advocates wish to emphatically proclaim Feyerabend's extreme premises concerning the nature of science, yet unlike him, they wish to deny (indeed, pejoratively dismiss) the logical consequences of those premises. For the purposes of present discussion, let us label this position as "weak-form" relativism (consistent with Anderson's "weak-form incommensurability" (1986, p. 164)) and in order for its advocates to avoid the charges of nihilism, sophistry, and/or the pain of logical inconsistency, let us explore how they might defend such a position.

## Weak-form Relativism

Anderson, and presumably (but not necessarily) other consumer behavior relativists, do not share the extreme conclusions on the nature of science held by writers such as Feyerabend (such as statement R3). Yet, they wish to embrace Feyerabend-like premises on science (such as statement R1). Is it possible, therefore, to salvage the weak-form relativism championed by them? A satisfactory answer to this question lies not in them simply *denying* that they agree with the extreme conclusions of the relativist argument on the nature of science (that the diagnoses of palmists should be given equal epistemological status to the diagnoses of medical science). To do so is much like killing the messenger who brings bad news. Rather, since the conclusions of any argument are entailed in its premises, advocates of weak-form relativism must re-examine their premises in order to salvage their position, for extreme premises yield extreme conclusions.

Modifying statement R1 to make it less extreme might be a useful starting place for weak-form relativists. Such a modification might be as follows:

R1a. Although in most cases it is impossible to find fundamental differences separating what

society chooses to call "science" from "nonscience," there are isolated instances (like medical science versus palmistry) where such differences are obvious.

Weak-form relativists would then have to identify and state the characteristics that so "obviously" differentiate science from nonscience in each such "isolated instance." Further, they would have to show how these differentiating characteristics lack commonality (each obvious instance is totally idiosyncratic) and defend this lack of commonality as a reasonable position. *Or* they would have to identify the *common* differentiating characteristics across the "isolated instances" and defend how these commonalities differ in some significant fashion from what practicing scientists (and those philosophers of science who live in the supposed "fairy tale" world of modern empiricism) call the *scientific method* of verification through open empirical testing. Otherwise, weak-form relativists would be forced to *deny* one of their most cherished precepts: that science does not differ from nonscience through its method of verification of knowledge-claims.

Clearly, the preceding procedure for salvaging weak-form relativism would seem to be an extraordinarily difficult task at best, or devastating to the relativist agenda at worst. Therefore, modifying statement R2 as a possibility to salvage weak-form relativism should be examined.

Statement R2 of the relativist argument indicates that the knowledge-claims of the nonsciences have as much epistemological warrant as the knowledge-claims of sciences. Anderson has already made a useful start in the direction of modifying R2 when he noted that "society bestows a high epistemological status on science because it believes that science generally functions in the best interests of society as a whole" (Anderson 1983, p. 26). Advocates of weak-form relativism could modify their position on R2 by *agreeing* with society:

R2a. Society does bestow and *ought to bestow* a higher epistemological status on the knowledge-claims of the sciences than on knowledge-claims of the nonsciences.

Justifying statement R2a would pose a significant challenge for relativists. Although society may bestow a privileged epistemological position on science capriciously and arbitrarily (as Feyerabend states and Anderson implies in his science2: "science is whatever society chooses to call a science"), weak-form relativists, as professed scholars of science, would have to explain exactly *why* society ought to bestow a superior position on the knowledge-claims of science. Precisely *why* is it reasonable to believe that science, in preference to nonscience, functions "in the best interests of society as a whole?" This would seem to necessarily imply that weak-form relativists would have to claim that the procedures that science uses to justify its knowledge-claims are somehow *better*. That is, its "way of knowing" or "tradition" is *superior*. But if the verification procedures for scientific knowledge-claims are better than the procedures used by nonsciences, then, on pain of continuing inconsistency, weak-form relativists would have to again give up their belief that there are no fundamental differences separating the sciences from the nonsciences. And therein lies the rub. In order to "save" relativism, the weak-form relativists have to destroy it.

Contrary to the verdict of Anderson (relying on Laudan's views), many philosophers of science continue to believe that there are fundamental differences separating science from the nonscience, which provide good reasons for societal consensus (Grove 1985). For example, a recent article in the *Philosophy of Science* by Siegel reviewed the debate and notes that "Laudan's rejection of a unique SM [Scientific Method] depends on a failure to distinguish between general principles of appraisal and specific instantiations of such principles" [or "techniques"] (1985, p. 528). He goes on to note that the methodological criteria of science that collectively constitute the scientific method can best be expressed as a "commitment to evidence," as exemplified by "a concern for explanatory adequacy, however that adequacy is conceived; and insistence on testing, however testing is thought to be best done; and a commitment to inductive support, however inductive inference is thought to be best made" (p. 528). Thus, "science's commitment to evidence, by way of SM, is what justifies its claim to respect -- science is to be taken seriously precisely because of its commitment to evidence" (p. 530). However, the preceding conclusions by Siegel about scientific method do not imply that he claims that science is the *only* domain in which the epistemic worthiness of beliefs, hypotheses, or claims may be putatively established on the basis of evidence. Rather, "SM extends far beyond the realm of science proper. But this is only to say that SM can be utilized widely. It is still properly labeled *scientific* method" (p. 530).

One of the problems with the entire demarcation issue in science is the word "demarcation," itself. This unfortunate choice of words (by Popper) tends to suggest (connote) that an *unequivocal* judgment can be made in all cases using a single, simple criterion (like "falsifiability"). Borderline cases, such as parapsychology, are then brought forth by relativists such as Anderson as examples that purportedly demonstrate the science/nonscience distinction to be just a societal convention rather than a societal consensus based on good reasons. The fallacy of such a ploy is evident as pointed out by Grove (1985). *Most, if not all, genuine and useful categorizational schemata have borderline cases.* Should biology dispense with the male/female distinction because some entities share characteristics of both sexes? Should consumer research dispense with consumer goods/industrial goods because some goods at some times can be either? Should advocates of N-H-I dispense with the trustworthy research/nontrustworthy research distinction just because the truth-content of its knowledge-claims cannot be known with certainty? How about

rational/irrational? Objective/subjective? Or, I suggest, truth/falsity?

Should interpretivist consumer research adopt relativism as Anderson, Peter and Olson propose? The preceding analysis should (at the very least) sound a cautionary note: *any philosophy* whose underlying premises lead to conclusions so extreme that they are dismissed as "nihilistic" nonsense *by the philosophy's own advocates* must be considered highly suspect, if not intellectually impoverished. Such a philosophy would seem to poorly serve the needs of researchers of any kind. Nevertheless, Hudson and Ozanne imply that consumer research should strongly consider relativism since it is "based on the premise that every approach to consumer research may have something to offer" (1988, p. 520). Hudson and Ozanne (mistakenly, as Muncy and Fisk (1987), Vallicella (1984), Margolis (1983), and Hacking (1982) point out) equate the premises of relativism with diversity, tolerance and pluralism. But relativism, as Feyerabend has so forcefully argued, implies epistemological anarchy, not a tolerant epistemological pluralism. And just as ethical relativism does not imply the tolerance of ethical diversity (Harrison 1982), and just as political anarchy does not imply a tolerant, pluralistic democracy, epistemological anarchy does not imply a tolerant, pluralistic science.

So, the third challenge for N-H-I inquiry is to advocate a tolerant pluralism, without relativism. The reasons for this challenge will become even clearer after we discuss incommensurability.

## INTERPRETIVISM AND INCOMMENSURABILITY

Ozanne and Hudson evaluate the procedures for producing knowledge-claims in interpretivism and C-S-S, concluding that "the knowledge outputs of these two approaches are incommensurable" (in abstract). The notion that paradigms are incommensurable was first introduced by Kuhn in his influential 1962 book, *The Structure of Scientific Revolutions* and was strongly argued by Feyerabend in his early work. It is most curious that Ozanne and Hudson would claim that interpretivism and C-S-S are incommensurable, since now even Feyerabend concedes that "incommensurability as understood by me is a rare event," and that "incommensurability is a difficulty for philosophers, not for scientists" (1987b, p. 81).

Of the many new concepts that Kuhn introduced to the analysis of science in his 1962 work, incommensurability has been one of the most controversial and extensively discussed. Kuhn's original argument provided that in "normal" science (e.g. the paradigm of Ptolomy) all the members of a scientific community implicitly accept a common paradigm, which contains 1) a content (concepts, laws, theories, etc.), and "exemplars" (standard examples of problems that the content of the paradigm solves), 2) a methodology (the procedures by which further knowledge within the paradigm is to be generated) and, 3) an epistemology (a set of criteria by which the knowledge generated within the paradigm is to be evaluated). Kuhn claimed that a new rival paradigm (e.g. Copernicus) emerges in "revolutionary" science only when the existing paradigm is faced with "anomalies." This rival or competing paradigm is considered *incommensurable* with the previous dominant paradigm.

Kuhn's claim of incommensurability rests upon Gestalt psychology and the work of Hanson (1958) and Wittgenstein (1953). Arguing by analogy, Kuhn compares the views of the advocates of the rival paradigms as being similar to the familiar "duck/rabbit" illustration in Gestalt psychology textbooks. (In this classic example of Gestalt, subjects are shown an ambiguous drawing in which some people "see" a duck, others "see" a rabbit, and some people can "switch" back and forth, "seeing" either). Kuhn proposes that there are no paradigm-neutral criteria for adjudicating the conflict between the dominant paradigm and its rival. Rather, when the "revolutionary" paradigm is successful, the former adherents to the dominant paradigm undergo a "Gestalt switch" (from "duck" to "rabbit"), or a "conversion" process.

Exactly what does incommensurability mean? After Kuhn's 1962 work, various writers began pinning him down as to precisely how he proposed incommensurability should be interpreted. Space limitations prevent a detailed description of all the interpretations and their resultant analyses. Rather, we here shall only mention some of the most prominent interpretations and point the reader toward the literature that evaluates them.

One of the earliest interpretations was the *meaning/variance* view that scientific terms change meaning from paradigm to paradigm. This view was critiqued by Shapere (1964 and 1966), Scheffler (1967, chapter 3) and Kordig (1971, chapters 2 and 3). A second analysis, the *radical translation* interpretation, suggests that in some meaningful way the actual terms involved in one paradigm cannot be translated into the language of its rivals. This interpretation was suggested by Kuhn, himself, in his *postscript* to the 1970 edition of *Structure* (pp. 200-204). The radical translation view has been analyzed by Kitcher (1978), Moberg (1979) and Levin (1979) (the radical translation view is also critiqued in my own 1983, pp. 368-372). A third interpretation of incommensurability has been the *incomparability* view that rival paradigms simply cannot be meaningfully compared. This interpretation was critiqued by Scheffler, Shapere and Kordig in the references previously cited and also by Laudan (1976) and Putnam (1981).

Although, as previously mentioned, the details of the analyses cited in the preceding paragraph cannot be extensively developed here, some flavor of the arguments can certainly be presented. For example, consider the *incomparability* interpretation. Most assuredly, incommensurability *cannot* imply incomparability, for to recognize that the "revolutionary" paradigm is incommensurable with the rival "dominant" paradigm (as Siegel (1980, p. 366) has noted) is at the very least to imply that the paradigms can be *compared*. How would one even know that the paradigms are *rival* if they could not be

compared in some meaningful way? Similarly, the *radical translation* thesis is fundamentally flawed. As Putnam points out, to contend that the language of one paradigm cannot be translated into the terms of another paradigm "and then to go on and describe [both paradigms] *at length* [in the same language] is totally incoherent" (p. 114). Finally, the *meaning-variance* thesis (that some concepts or terms that are used in the revolutionary paradigm have a meaning that is different from how the concepts or terms are used in the dominant paradigm) may present difficulties in communicating, but surely does not imply *incommensurability* in any meaningful sense. Again, how can the two paradigms be genuinely *rival* paradigms if they are "talking" about different phenomena? Roughly speaking, it's like "Aha! Here we have been arguing and all the time you were discussing apples and I was discussing oranges!"

The many detailed analyses of the concept of incommensurability over the last several decades have led most philosophers of science to agree with the summary evaluation most recently put forward by Hintikka: "The frequent arguments that strive to use the absolute or relative incommensurability of scientific theories as a reason for thinking that they are inaccessible to purely scientific (rational) comparisons are simply fallacious" (1988, p. 38). Ironically, advocates of the *meaning-variance* interpretation of incommensurability have demonstrated the cogency of the logical positivist view about the purpose of the philosophy of science. The logical positivists held that philosophers could and should clarify the language of science and, therefore, increase the ability of various scientists to talk with each other when working in different (in today's vernacular) "paradigms."

Much more interesting for our purposes here than the fact that incommensurability has been discredited in the philosophy of science, is the reaction of Kuhn himself to critiques of incommensurability. Kuhn has been very sensitive to the complex issues raised by these critiques and has attempted to modify his position accordingly. In his 1970 revision of *Structure* he claimed that his critics had completely misinterpreted his views on incommensurability when they claimed that "the proponents of incommensurable theories cannot communicate with each other at all; as a result, in a debate over theory-choice there can be no recourse to *good* reasons; instead theory must be chosen for reasons that are ultimately personal and subjective; some sort of mystical apperception is responsible for the decision actually reached" (pp. 198-199, emphasis in original). That is, Kuhn now wishes to deny the previous rhetoric about "conversions" and "Gestalt-shifts." Rather, he now emphasizes the reliance on "good reasons." Moreover, the reader should note that Kuhn does not just say "reasons," but "good" reasons, which would seem to necessarily imply that there are some paradigm-neutral standards that can be used to assess the adequacy of rival paradigms. However, Kuhn has not simply stopped with advocating *good reasons*. In his 1976 work he has again attempted to further clarify his concept of incommensurability and now seems to be construing incommensurability as analogous to the concept of a mathematical algorithm:

> Most readers of my text have supposed that when I spoke of theories as incommensurable, I meant that they could not be compared. But "incommensurability" is a term borrowed from mathematics, and it there has no such implication. The hypotenuse of an isosceles right triangle is incommensurable with its side, but the two can be compared to any required degree of precision. What is lacking is not comparability but a unit of length in terms of which both can be measured directly and exactly (pp. 190-1).

Why has Kuhn been so anxious to modify and thereby retreat from his earlier, highly provocative, "Gestalt-shift" position? It is precisely because Kuhn has recognized that his earlier position implied relativism and irrationality:

> My critics respond to my views...with charges of irrationality, relativism, and the defense of mob rule. These are all labels which I categorically reject (1970a, p. 234).

But, why should one of the most eminent historians of science of this century wish to "categorically reject" the charge of relativism? Is not relativism roughly analogous to *diversity* and *pluralism*, as Ozanne, Hudson, Peter and Olson suggest? Isn't it *obviously* the case that "the way in which social and consumer behavior research is actually practiced is best construed from a critical relativist perspective" (Anderson 1986, p. 167)? No. As Barnes and Bloor (themselves strong advocates of relativism) point out: "In the academic world, relativism is everywhere abominated" (1982, p. 21). Generally speaking, most philosophers of science go to great lengths to avoid having their views associated with "abominated" relativism because they recognize the extreme conclusions that stem from relativistic doctrine. Capsulized in very succinct form, the argument that motivated Kuhn to retreat from incommensurability goes as follows:

1. It is difficult, if not impossible, to accept *incommensurability* (in any nontrivial, interesting, or meaningful sense) without accepting *relativism.*

2. It is difficult, if not impossible, to accept *relativism* (in any nontrivial, interesting, or meaningful sense) without accepting *irrationalism.*

3. It is difficult, if not impossible, to accept *irrationalism* (in any nontrivial, interesting, or meaningful sense) without denying that it is possible to have *knowledge* about the world.

4. It is difficult, if not impossible, to deny that we can have *knowledge* (in any nontrivial, interesting, or meaningful sense) about the world without denying that there has been scientific *progress*.

5. It is difficult, if not impossible, to deny that there has been scientific *progress* (in any nontrivial, interesting, or meaningful sense) without denying that we *know* more about the world now than we did before the rise of modern science in the 17th century.

Stove (1982) reviews the works of those he calls the "modern irrationalists," including Kuhn and Feyerabend, and states his own version of the conclusion of the preceding argument:

> Much more is known now than was known 50 years ago, and much more was known then than in 1580. So there has been a great accumulation or growth of knowledge in the last four hundred years. This is an extremely well-known fact, which I will refer to as (A). ...So a writer whose position inclined him to deny (A), or even made him reluctant to admit it, would almost inevitably seem, to the philosophers who read him, to be maintaining something extremely implausible. ...Everyone would admit that if there has *ever* been a growth of knowledge, it has been in the last four hundred years, so anyone reluctant to admit (A) must, if he is consistent, be reluctant to admit that there has ever been a growth of knowledge at all. But if a philosopher of science takes a position which obliges him, on pain of inconsistency, to be reluctant to admit *this*, then his position can be rightly described as irrationalism...(pp. 3 and 4).

The extreme nature of the conclusion of the preceding argument shows why Kuhn has been so anxious to demonstrate that one can accept *incommensurability* without accepting *relativism* and *irrationalism*. (Kuhn's philosophy, to his chagrin, is now used as a standard example of irrationalism in such reference works as the *Dictionary of the History of Science* (1981, p. 360)). Further, it explains why those, like Anderson (1986 and 1988), who willingly accept relativism take such great pains to attempt to show that "their version" of relativism is neither self-refuting, nor irrationalistic. It also shows clearly the consistency of Feyerabend when he denies that the knowledge generated from science differs in any meaningful or genuine way from magic, astrology, rain dances, religion, mythical world views and witchcraft (as previously discussed in this paper). Indeed, as Siegel has noted, except for logically consistent relativists such as Feyerabend, by the time that others get through qualifying and modifying concepts such as incommensurability and relativism, often labels such as "critical pluralism" more appropriately characterize what is left (1988, p. 132).

## Is Interpretivism Incommensurable?

We are now in a position to better assess the claim by Ozanne and Hudson that "the knowledge outputs of these two approaches [N-H-I and C-S-S] are incommensurable" (in abstract). The evidence for their conclusion comes from their examination of Bower's [C-S-S] approach to studying emotion defined as "a physiological, internal state"... stored in memory in an associative network," and comparing it with Denzin's "interpretivist approach," where "emotions are defined as self-feelings; they are feelings of and for one's self (p. 4)". Thus, the claim of incommensurability is based on the assertion (which for the present purposes we shall assume to be true) that "it was clear that what was perceived to be the phenomenon of emotion changed when investigated" (p. 6) by the two researchers. Ozanne and Hudson then buttress their incommensurability claim by citing Shapiro (1973), who attempted to integrate "the data of a more interpretive methodology and the data of a more positivist methodology," and concluded that her problems "were the result of her measuring different things" (p. 6).

It is clear that Ozanne and Hudson are using the meaning-variance interpretation of incommensurability, as previously discussed. That is, although Bower and Denzin were using the same term (emotion), they were not referring to, or measuring, the same phenomenon. This is another "apples vs. oranges" example. Is this a nontrivial, interesting, or meaningful kind of incommensurability? Obviously, the (presumed) fact the Bower and Denzin mean very different things when using the same term poses significant problems for them in communicating with each other. But, in what meaningful way does this imply that "the knowledge outputs of these two approaches are incommensurable"?

As previously noted, the concept of incommensurability comes from such classic examples of Kuhn as the rival knowledge-claims of Ptolemy and Copernicus. One paradigm claimed that the Sun revolved around the Earth and its rival claimed that the Earth revolved around the Sun. Clearly, these are two *rival*, or competing, claims. The problems between Ptolemy and Copernicus were not, simply, a result of them using common terms (e.g. "Earth," "Sun" and "revolve") in different ways. In Ozanne and Hudson's example, however, the two researchers are using the same concept (i.e., "emotion") to mean very different things! Therefore, the knowledge-claims of Bower and Denzin, although *different*, cannot be considered to be "rival," or "competing" and are *not incommensurable* in any meaningful epistemic sense. (This is not to say that the research *programs* could not, or do not compete for resources or the interest of other researchers. But, although there have been numerous interpretations of the concept of incommensurability, to my knowledge no one has ever seriously advanced a "resources" interpretation).

It may be possible that contemporary social science and naturalistic, humanistic and interpretive inquiry are incommensurable in some nontrivial, interesting and meaningful way. However, the work of Ozanne and Hudson provides no justification for the claim. Contrary to Ozanne and Hudson, the paper by Holbrook, Bell and Grayson in this very volume tacitly acknowledges *commensurability* when they develop an experimental test of the Holbrook-Grayson hypothesis using C-S-S methods. Although Holbrook, Bell and Grayson claim that the humanities contain "truths that escape procedures of the hypothetico-deductive method," (p. 40) such a claim does not imply incommensurability, (nor, it should be observed, do they claim it does).

The preceding analysis implies a fourth challenge: practitioners and advocates of N-H-I, instead of retreating into purposely encapsulated, purportedly incommensurate, semantical cocoons, should make strong and continuing efforts to clarify the meanings of their major concepts, especially when such concepts are shared with C-S-S and are used differently. Only through such a careful process can it be shown where the knowledge outputs are genuinely competitive, or rival, with those of C-S-S. There is no reason to *assume* in advance that in the event of genuinely *rival* knowledge-claims between C-S-S and N-H-I such claims will be incommensurable. Most certainly, incommensurability would seem to be a curious and counter-productive goal for practitioners and advocates of N-I-H to pursue.

## CONCLUSION

The purpose of this paper has been to present a constructive, yet critical commentary on the emerging areas of naturalistic, humanistic, and interpretive inquiry. I remain as firmly convinced as ever that N-H-I inquiry has significant potential for advancing knowledge in both the marketing and consumer research areas. Even though the challenges facing N-H-I inquiry are significant, they are not insuperable. Certainly, the N-H-I agenda is not furthered when the views of their colleagues who conduct C-S-S are presented in caricature form. It is difficult to keep discussions of the differences between C-S-S and N-H-I on a cognitive level when caricatures such as "single immutable reality" and "entirely deterministic" are employed. Just as obviously, practitioners and advocates of C-S-S should likewise avoid such caricatures. One useful step in this direction is for both sides, especially when each is being critical of the other, to use direct quotations in their critiques, rather than simple, paraphrased references. For example, why reference Lincoln and Guba (strong critics of C-S-S) when one purports to portray or characterize the beliefs of C-S-S? Why not quote, or cite, a practitioner or advocate of C-S-S?

A second challenge for N-H-I is to clearly demonstrate the value of its knowledge-claims and the truth-content (or validity or trustworthiness, or warrant or credibility) of same. This can only be done, as I've indicated, by developing appropriate criteria for evaluating the knowledge-claims of N-H-I. Further, although "knowledge for knowledge's sake" is indeed a characteristic of science, no commentator on science to my knowledge claims that *irrelevancy* of knowledge-claims is, or ought to be, a goal of science. By defining the nature of N-H-I inquiry to *preclude* the possibility of identifying causes and effects before such inquiry even begins, advocates of N-H-I (unnecessarily) make such inquiry irrelevant to major problems in society.

A third challenge facing N-H-I inquiry is to be pluralistic, without being relativistic. Although, as it has been shown, one can be both relativistic and pluralistic at the same time, relativism neither implies pluralism, nor does pluralism imply relativism. If advocates of N-H-I embrace relativism because they (mistakenly) believe that it implies (or is implied by) pluralism, they will either spend much valuable time (as do most relativists) defending that *their*, highly modified version of relativism does not imply irrationalism or they will have to accept (as does Feyerabend) "nihilistic" nonsense.

A final challenge for N-H-I is to defend the proposition that the knowledge outputs of its inquiry are different in some meaningful sense from the knowledge outputs of C-S-S without advocating that such knowledge outputs are incommensurable with C-S-S. Simply put, the fact that knowledge-claims are *different*, whether by nature of subject-matter or means of production or verification, does not imply that they are *incommensurate*. Incommensurability is a very strong concept and its value and meaning are debased when it is used as a synonym for "different." Again, if advocates of N-H-I truly wish to characterize their method of inquiry as producing incommensurate knowledge outputs, much time will be wasted in defending the position that *their* incommensurable knowledge outputs do not imply relativism and irrationalism. It would be most curious and unfortunate if advocates of N-H-I were to adopt incommensurability at the same time that the originator of the concept (Kuhn) is retreating from it and when one of the concept's most radical defenders (Feyerabend) is conceding that incommensurability is a "rare event" and "is a difficulty for philosophers, not for scientists" (1987b, p. 81).

Thirty years from now, how will scholars evaluate the history of naturalistic, humanistic and interpretative inquiry in marketing and consumer research? Will it be viewed as a significant addition to other methods in the quest for scientific progress? Or, will it be viewed as a "blip" in the scientific enterprise, much like the motivation research flap in the 1950's? The nature of the historical verdict on naturalistic, humanistic and interpretivist inquiry will be determined in large measure by how its practitioners and advocates respond to challenges such as those detailed in this paper. Until such time, interpretive inquiry is much more like a promissory note than a certified check.

# REFERENCES

Anderson, Paul F. (1982), comments in "Current Issues in the Philosophy of Science: Implications for Marketing Theory -- A Panel Discussion," ed., J. Paul Peter, in *Marketing Theory: Philosophy of Science Perspectives*, eds., Ronald F. Bush and Shelby D. Hunt, Chicago, IL: American Marketing Association, 11-16.

_____ (1983), "Marketing, Scientific Progress, and Scientific Methodology," *Journal of Marketing*, 47 (Fall), 18-31.

_____ (1986), "On Method of Consumer Research: A Critical Relativist Perspective," *Journal of Consumer Research*, 13 (September), 155-173.

_____ (1988), "Relative to What - That is the Question: A Reply to Siegel," *Journal of Consumer Research*, Vol. 15, No. 1 (June), 133-137.

_____ (1989), "On Relativism and Interpretativism - With a Prolegomenon to the "Why" Question," in *Interpretive Consumer Research*, ed., Elizabeth Hirschman, Berkeley, CA: University of California Press, Ltd, forthcoming.

Barnes, Barry and David Bloor (1982), "Relativism, Rationalism, and the Sociology of Knowledge," in *Rationality and Relativism*, eds., Martin Hollis and Steven Lukes, Cambridge, MA: The MIT Press, 21-47.

Brodbeck, May (1982), "Recent Developments in the Philosophy of Science," in *Marketing Theory: Philosophy of Science Perspectives*, eds., Ronald F. Bush and Shelby D. Hunt, Chicago, IL: American Marketing Association, 1-6.

Calder, Bobby J. and Alice M. Tybout (1987), "What Consumer Research Is...," *Journal of Consumer Research*, 14 (June), 136-140.

Collins, H.M. (1975), "The Seven Sees: A Study in the Sociology of a Phenomenon, or the Replication of Experiments in Physics," *Sociology*, 9, 205-224.

_____ (1981), "Son of the Seven Sees: The Social Destruction of a Physical Phenomena," *Social Studies of Science*, 11, 33-62.

*Dictionary of the History of Science*, (1981), eds., Bynum, W.F., E.J. Browne, and Roy Porter, Princeton, NJ: Princeton University Press.

Feyerabend, Paul (1975), *Against Method*, Thetford, U.K.: Lowe and Brydone.

_____ (1978a), From Incompetent Professionalism to Professionalized Incompetence - The Rise of a Breed of Intellectuals," *Philosophy of the Social Sciences*, 8 (March), 37-53.

_____ (1978b), *Science in a Free Society*, London, U.K.: Verso.

_____ (1987a), *Farewell to Reason*, London, U.K.: Verso.

_____ (1987b), "Putnam on Incommensurability," British Journal of the Philosophy of Science, 38, 75-92.

Grove, J.W. (1985), "Rationality at Risk: Science against Pseudoscience," *Minerva*, III (Summer), 216-40.

Hacking, Ian (1982), "Language, Truth, and Reason," in *Rationality and Relativism*, eds., Martin Hollis and Stephen Lukes, Cambridge, MA: The MIT Press, 48-66.

Hanson, N.R. (1958), "The Logic of Discovery," *Journal of Philosophy*, 55, 1073-1089.

Harrison, Geoffrey (1982), "Relativism and Tolerance," in *Relativism: Cognitive and Moral*, eds. Michael Krausz and Jack W. Meiland, Notre Dame, IN: University of Notre Dame Press.

Hempel, Carl G. (1969), "Logical Positivism and the Social Sciences," in *The Legacy of Logical Positivism*, eds., Peter Achinstein and Stephen F. Borker, Baltimore, MD: John Hopkins Press, 163-194.

Hintikka, Jaakko (1988), "Two Dogmas of Methodology," *Philosophy of Science*, 55, 25-38.

Hirschman, Elizabeth C. (1986), "Humanistic Inquiry in Marketing Research: Philosophy, Method, and Criteria," *Journal of Marketing Research*, 23 (August), 237-249.

Holbrook, Morris B. and Mark W. Grayson (1986),, "The Semiology of Cinematic Consumption: Symbolic Consumer Behavior in *Out of Africa*," *Journal of Consumer Research*, 13 (December), 374-381.

_____, Stephen Bell, and Mark W. Grayson, (1989), "The Role of the Humanities in Consumer Research: Close Encounters and Coastal Disturbances," in *Interpretive Consumer Research*, ed., Elizabeth Hirschman, Berkeley, CA: University of California Press, Ltd., forthcoming.

Holton, G. (1970), "Mach, Einstein and the Search for Reality," in *Ernst Mach, Physicist and Philosopher*, eds., R.S. Cohen and R.J. Seeger, Dordrecht: Reidel Publishing.

Hudson, Laurel Anderson and Julie L. Ozanne (1988), "Alternative Ways of Seeking Knowledge in Consumer Research," *Journal of Consumer Research*, 14 (March), 508-521.

Hunt, Shelby D. (1983), *Marketing Theory: The Philosophy of Marketing Science*, Homewood, IL: Irwin.

_____ (1984), "Should Marketing Adopt Relativism?" in *Scientific Method in Marketing*, eds., Paul F. Anderson and Michael J. Ryan, Chicago: American Marketing Association, 30-34.

Kitcher, P. (1978), "Theories, Theorists, and Theoretical Changes," *Philosophical Review*, 87, 519-47.

Knorr-Cetina, Karen D. and Michael Mulkey (1983), "Introduction: Emerging Principles in Social Studies of Science," in *Science Observed*, London: Sage Publications.

Kordig, C.R. (1970), "Feyerabend and Radical Meaning Variance," *Nous*, 9, 399-404.

Krausz, Michael and Jack W. Meiland (1982), *Relativism: Cognitive and Moral*, Notre Dame, IN: University of Notre Dame Press.

Kuhn, Thomas S. (1962), *The Structure of Scientific Revolutions*, Chicago, IL: University of Chicago Press.

_____ (1970), *The Structure of Scientific Revolutions*, Enlarged ed., Chicago, IL: University of Chicago Press.

_____ (1970a), "Reflections On My Critics," in *Criticism and the Growth of Knowledge*, eds., Imre Lakatos and Alan Musgrave, Cambridge, U.K.: Cambridge University Press, 231-278.

_____ (1976), "Theory-Change as Structure-Change: Comments on the Sneed Formalism," *Erkenntnis*, 10, 179-99.

Laudan, Larry (1968), "Theories of Scientific Method From Plato to Mach: A Bibliographical Review," in *History of Science*, Vol. 7, eds., A.C. Crombie and M.A. Hoskin, Cambridge, MA: W. Heffer and Sons Ltd, 1-63.

_____ (1976), "Two Dogmas of Methodology," *Philosophy of Science*, 55, 25-38.

_____ (1977), *Progress and Its Problems*, Berkeley, CA: University of California Press, Ltd.

_____ (1979), "Historical Methodologies: An Overview and Manifesto," in *Current Research in Philosophy of Science*, eds., Peter D. Asquith and Henry E. Kyburg, Jr., East Lansing, MI: Philosophy of Science Association, 55-83.

_____ (1980), "Views of Progress: Separating the Pilgrims From the Rakes," *Philosophy of the Social Sciences*, 10, 273-286.

Levin, M. E. (1979), "On Theory Change and meaning Change" *Philosophy of Science*, 46, 407-24.

Lincoln, Yvonna S. and Egon G. Guba (1985), *Naturalistic Inquiry*, Beverly Hills, CA: Sage Publications.

Margolis, Joseph (1983), "The Nature and Strategies of Relativism," *Mind*, Vol.42, 548-567.

Moberg, D.W. (1979), "Are There Rival, Incommensurable Theories?" *Philosophy of Science*, 46, 244-62.

Muncy, James A. and Raymond P. Fisk (1987), "Cognitive Relativism and the Practice of Marketing Science," *Journal of Marketing*, 51 (January), 20-33.

Olson, Jerry C. (1987), "The Construction of Scientific Meaning," presented at the 1987 *Winter Marketing Educators' Conference*, Chicago, IL: American Marketing Association.

Ozanne, Julie L. and Laurel Anderson Hudson (1989), "Exploring Diversity in Consumer Research," in *Interpretive Consumer Research*, ed., Elizabeth Hirschman, Berkeley, CA: University of California Press, Ltd., forthcoming.

Peter, J. Paul and Jerry C. Olson (1989), "The Relativist/Constructionist Perspective on Scientific Knowledge and Consumer Research," in *Interpretive Consumer Research*, ed., Elizabeth Hirschman, Berkeley, CA: University of California Press, Ltd., forthcoming.

Phillips, O.C. (1987), *Philosophy, Science and Social Inquiry*, Oxford, U.K.: Pergamon Press.

Putnam, Hilary (1981), *Reason, Truth and History*, Cambridge, U.K.: University of Cambridge Press.

Radner, Daisie and Michael Radner (1982), *Science and Unreason*, Belmont, CA: Wadsworth Publishing Co.

Rudner, Richard S. (1966), *Philosophy of Social Science*, Englewood Cliffs, NJ: Prentice-Hall.

Scheffler, I. (1967), *Science and Subjectivity*, Indianapolis, IN: Bobbs Merrill.

Shapere, D. (1964), "The Structure of Scientific Revolutions," *Philosophical Review*, 73, 383-394.

_____ (1966), "Meaning and Scientific Change," in *Mind and Cosmos: Explorations in the Philosophy of Science*, ed., R. Colodny, Pittsburgh, PA: University of Pittsburgh Press, 41-85.

Shapiro, Edna (1973), "Educational Evaluation: Rethinking the Criteria of Competence," *School Review*, (November), 523-549.

Siegel, Harvey (1980), "Objectivity, Rationality, Incommensurability, and More," *British Journal of the Philosophy of Science*, 31, 359-384.

_____ (1985), "What is the Question Concerning the Rationality of Science?" *Philosophy of Science*, Vol. 52, No. 4 (December), 517-537.

_____ (1986), "Relativism, Truth, and Incoherence," *Synthese*, 68 (August), 225-259.

_____ (1988), "Relativism for Consumer Research? (Comment on Anderson)," *Journal of Consumer Research*, Vol. 15, No. 1 (June), 129-132.

Stern, Barbara B. (1989), "Literary Explications: A methodology for Consumer Research," in *Interpretive Consumer Research*, ed., Elizabeth Hirschman, Berkeley, CA: University of California Press, Ltd., forthcoming.

Stove, David (1982), *Popper and After*, Elmsford, NY: Pergamon Press, Inc.

Suppe, Frederick (1977), *The Structure of Scientific Theories*, 2nd ed., Urbana, IL: University of Illinois Press.

Vallicella, William F. (1984), "Relativism, Truth, and the Symmetry Thesis," *The Monist*, Vol. 67, No. 3 (July), 452-467.

Wallendorf, Melanie and Russell W. Belk (1989), "Assessing Trustworthiness in Naturalistic Consumer Research," in *Interpretive Consumer Research*, ed., Elizabeth Hirschman, Berkeley, CA: University of California Press, Ltd., forthcoming.

Wittgenstein, Ludwig (1953), *Philosophical Investigations*, Oxford, U.K.: Basil Blackwell.

# Interpretive, Qualitative, and Traditional Scientific Empirical Consumer Behavior Research

Bobby J. Calder, Northwestern University
Alice M. Tybout, Northwestern University

There can be little doubt that, at this stage in the development of consumer research, methodological pluralism is desirable. Although, we believe, that traditional scientific empirical research on consumer behavior has made progress, it would clearly be difficult to argue that it has enjoyed sufficient success to preempt other approaches. Our premise at the outset of this analysis is that other approaches should be explored and methodological pluralism encouraged.

To embrace methodological pluralism ought not to imply, however, that all approaches to consumer research should be treated similarly. We contend in fact that methodological pluralism can only work *if* the differences between different kinds of studies are recognized and the strengths and weaknesses of each approach are assessed in terms of these differences. The alternative is not pluralism but methodological babble.

We have proposed a framework (Calder and Tybout, 1987) for grouping different approaches so that their unique strengths and weaknesses can be discussed relative to the nature of a particular approach. In the present analysis we will elaborate on this framework and then use it to comment on three important issues we see arising from the present volume. We will not attempt a micro-level critique of individual studies, believing that this is premature given the acknowledged preliminary nature of much of the work. It is not premature, however, to focus on the broader methodological issues raised by studies using new approaches.

## THE CALDER-TYBOUT FRAMEWORK

Researchers have used a variety of labels in introducing new approaches to consumer research: interpretive, naturalistic, qualitative, humanistic, and the like. The Calder-Tybout (1987) framework seeks to reduce these to three broad classes of research: interpretive, qualitative, and scientific.[1] This is not to say that other labels do not carry important distinctions. Our contention is only that (a) these three classes have integrity at a general level and (b) are sufficient for making some important methodological points.

Each approach is best characterized in terms of the type of knowledge it seeks to produce. The goal of the interpretive approach is an understanding of

---

[1] For the purposes of this chapter, we will be referring to the three types of knowledge and their respective implied methodologies as general "approaches." In an effort to make the labels for the approaches intuitively meaningful, we use the descriptors interpretative, qualitative (rather than everyday) and scientific. For a more detailed discussion of the types of knowledge and their implied methodologies the interested reader is referred to Calder and Tybout (1987).

behavior in terms of a particular system of ideas and from the frame of reference of these ideas. Data are made meaningful by virtue of the application of these ideas, and this gives rise to "interpretation" as the most general label for this exercise. Interpretations are proposed and evaluated among a community of scholars sharing the particular system of ideas. We have argued that this methodological process seems consistent with a philosophy of critical relativism, although problematic issues arise in this regard (Hunt, this volume).

The goal of the qualitative approach is an understanding of behavior in terms of how consumers themselves interpret and give meaning to their own behavior. Data are considered to be self-reflexive. They supply their own meaning. Researchers attempt to articulate how consumers explicitly or implicitly view themselves on the assumption that these views will shape subsequent behavior. The appropriate methodology is thus to come into sufficient contact with the consumer's world to experience it as the consumer does (Calder, 1977). The appropriate philosophy is the common sense world of everyday ideas.

The qualitative approach can obviously be viewed as a version of the interpretive in which behavior is being interpreted from the standpoint of the ideas of consumers. We believe, however, that separating the two is useful. Applying a system of ideas that consumers may never even have heard of versus discovering the ideas that consumers use are very different enterprises.

The goal of the scientific approach is to understand behavior in terms theories that have been subjected to rigorous empirical testing. Although theories provide interpretation, the key point is that theories are capable of and have been subjected to empirical testing. Interpretation is a matter of theory application and is derivative of empirical theory testing (see Calder, Phillips, and Tybout, 1981).

We have argued that the methodology of rigorous empirical testing is best guided by a particular version of sophisticated falsificationism (Calder and Tybout, 1987). Theories should not be regarded as proven or true. They have scientific status because of and subject to attempts to refute them. The practical process of attempting to refute theories is of course itself fallible. Researchers can be mistaken about data. Nonetheless, the guiding objective is to test theory against data.

The main question that arises from the Calder-Tybout framework is whether, even at this level of generality, the three approaches can be differentiated. Anderson (1983, 1986, and this volume), for instance, contends that the scientific approach cannot be distinguished from other approaches. He argues that philosophers of science continue to debate the demarcation of science form non-science and that the falsificationist view is not universally accepted. In particular, falsificationists have not dealt at an operational level with the problem of fallible data. Because there is not agreement, and everyone recognizes that data may in practice be fallible, it is argued that no demarcation of science is possible.

Our position is that the fact that demarcation is in practice fuzzy does not mean that demarcation is in principle useless. Our use of falsificationism has always been as a guiding objective that characterizes the nature of the scientific effort. Perhaps communication is best served by illustrating the spirit in which we distinguish scientific from other approaches. A recent comment by Stephen Hawking, arguably one of our greatest scientists, captures this spirit well.

Any physical theory is always provisional, in the sense that it is only a hypothesis: you can never prove it. No matter how many times the results of experiments agree with some theory, you can never be sure that the next time the result will not contradict the theory. On the other hand, you can disprove a theory by finding even a single observation that disagrees with the predictions of the theory. As philosopher of science Karl Popper has emphasized, a good theory is characterized by the fact that it makes a number of predictions that could in principle be disproved or falsified by observation. Each time new experiments are observed to agree with the predictions the theory survives, and our confidence in it is increased; but if ever a new observation is found to disagree, we have to abandon or modify the theory. At least that is what is supposed to happen, but you can always question the competence of the person who carried out the observation. (Hawking, 1988, p. 16)

The boundary between science and other approaches in our framework is meant to reflect the spirit of Hawking's comments. As a matter of normative principle, the scientific approach is fundamentally oriented to challenging theories with data. Use of the word "scientific" of course can connote many other things. Not the least of these is that the scientific approach is necessarily superior to other approaches. Although there is nothing in our use that implies this, it may be useful to soften the label by referring as we do here to traditional scientific empirical (TSE) studies of consumer behavior. In any event, we again assert that we do not intend to preclude other approaches by demarcating the scientific.

Likewise, we would resist the use of terms such as post-positivist to characterize other approaches. Such labels imply the demise of traditional scientific empirical studies. Methodological pluralism is again best served by not defining any approach as precluding another approach. Moreover, as Calder and Tybout (1987) point out, the term positivist is used much too loosely to be descriptive of any approach. Further, as Hunt (this volume) notes the historical meaning of the label "positivist" is incompatible with the TSE studies to which it is often applied.

The other boundaries in the Calder-Tybout framework are also intended to provide normative guidance. Calder (1977) has discussed the demarcation of the qualitative approach from the scientific. In practice it may be very difficult to say whether a specific study is scientific or qualitative. And the tendency to dress up any piece of research in the cloak and trappings associated with scientific theory is hardly helpful. In principle, however, the research goals are very different.

The Calder-Tybout framework can be used to analyze three important issues that cut across the present volume. The first is the contention that critical relativism, a view that we have argued might serve as a methodological base for the interpretive approach, should instead be adopted as a more general philosophy and a challange to our framework. This claim is related to the view already discussed that the scientific approach cannot be distinguished from other approaches. The specific issue to be addressed in more detail is the critical relativists' attack on traditional scientific empirical studies. We will argue strongly for the central role the TSE approach gives to challenging theory with data. The second issue concerns the need to draw stronger conclusions from qualitative research and while doing so to avoid going beyond consumers' perspectives to another system of interpretation. And the third issue concerns the tendency to stretch the interpretive and qualitative approaches beyond research and into expressiveness.

## THE CRITICAL RELATIVISTS' ATTACK ON TSE RESEARCH AND OUR FRAMEWORK

Before turning to issues that more directly relate to the general purpose of this volume, we focus upon the two chapters, one by Anderson and one by Peter and Olson, that have as their primary objective discrediting our distinction between the scientific and interpretivist approaches. Although we recognize that the detailed rebuttal we present may be of only limited interest to a general audience, the strongly worded and largely unsupported conclusions advanced by these critics leave us little choice but to devote a portion of this chapter to answering their charges.

### Scientific Knowledge and the Demarcation Issue

As mentioned in the introduction, demarcating science from non-science has come under attack. Here we address some of the more specific concerns raised. Anderson's objection to demarcation stems from the observation that philosophers of science cannot agree on a basis for creating such mutually exclusive categories. He worries that our criteria of confronting a theory with data that *could* reveal its weakness, and accepting as scientific those theories that succeed in providing a better account for the data than available rivals, would require that we consider parapsychology "science". Hunt (this volume) provides an excellent and detailed response to Anderson's anti-demarcation argument, so we will only reiterate his observation that *"Most, if not all, genuine and useful categorization schemata have borderline cases* (Hunt this volume, p. 192)," and add parenthetically that if a theory that some might label as parapsychological does survive rigorous testing procedures, and credible rival explanations for the phenomena it explains cannot be generated, then perhaps this *particular* theory (not any or all parapsychological accounts) warrants the label science.

By contrast, Peter and Olson evidence concern not for what our demarcation would *include* in the domain of scientific knowledge but rather for what it might *exclude*. Specifically, they contend that invoking a falsification criterion for scientific knowledge would lead to excluding from the domain of science the work of Newton and Einstein, general models of consumer behavior such as the Howard and Sheth Model, and mathematical models of consumer behavior. These inferences do not follow logically from the position we advance and suggest that Peter and Olson are confusing researcher's personal motivations and behavior with the status of the knowledge they create. It is well documented that individuals, both in their role as researchers and as everyday consumers, evidence a tendency to seek confirmation for their views rather than refutation. However, scientific status should not, and typically is not, accorded to claims unsupported by data that *could* contradict them. That is, researchers rarely, if ever, succeed in gaining acceptance for their theories on the basis of data they alone collect in a confirmatory fashion. Typically they must account for the data of others and phenomena observed in the world at large. Theories such as those of Newton and Einstein gain acceptance for precisely the reason that they explained phenomena for which previously there was no good account, and it is in this sense that they survived "falsifications", or perhaps a more accurately, survived attempts to reveal their weaknesses. Thus, in our view the motives of the theory creator or champion are not per se pivotal in judging the theory, though they *could* render certain rival explanations more plausible thereby calling the theory into question. The *theories* advanced by Newton and Einstein met our criteria for scientific knowledge at a point in time -- they accounted for phenomena better than their available rivals. Whether they continue to be accorded scientific status depends on their ability to account for new data that become available. Notice that because we see no inherent superiority of post hoc over a priori explanations of phenomena, data already available at the time a theory is developed afford valid tests of its adequacy. (See Sternthal, Tybout and Calder 1987 for more on the post hoc versus a priori distinction.)

However, Peter and Olson are correct in inferring that *some* general models of consumer behavior and *some* mathematical models may not meet our criteria for scientific knowledge. Each model requires its own assessment. "Box and arrow" or flow chart models may be valuable frameworks for integrating scientific knowledge without necessarily themselves being scientific. They may be more usefully viewed as systems of hypothesized relationships, some of which may be neither well-specified nor tested empirically. On the other hand, one can also imagine a general model of consumer behavior that *is* itself scientific because it is grounded in empirical tests of all the relationships hypothesized. This would not require that all relationships be tested simultaneously, rather multiple experiments, each exploring a subset of the hypothesized relationships might serve as evidence for

the model. Likewise, mathematical models may or may not be scientific depending upon how they are constructed and whether they are superior to available alternatives. Certainly some modeling efforts, such as applications of LIRSEL, have the potential to yield knowledge we would consider scientific.

The more general concern that Peter and Olson appear to have is that, under our framework, all of consumer research would not automatically be considered scientific. We wonder why such a notion is so troubling? As we consistently have argued, interpretive and everyday/qualitative knowledge are not inherently more or less valuable than scientific knowledge. The three types of knowledge merely are generated with different goals in mind and therefore should be judged according to different criteria. Holbrook and O'Shaughnessey (1988) express what may be motivating Peter and Olson's concern--the fear that knowledge not falling under the heading of "science" be viewed as unpublishable in the leading journals in the field. We would hope that such a concern is unwarranted. After all there are many prestigious journals that make no claim of presenting scientific knowledge in fields such as the humanities. However, whether or not different types of knowledge should be represented in a single journal such as the *Journal of Consumer Research* or whether multiple outlets would be more appropriate is not for us to say. It is an issue that deserves discussion among journal editors and their editorial boards. What should be clear, however, is that little is solved by arguing that *all* types of knowledge are scientific. The need for demarcation, problematic as it may be in classifying some specific cases, seems clear. Indeed, it is interesting to observe that the criticism of demarcation in this volume focuses on our distinction between scientific and interpretive knowledge, suggesting tacit acceptance of the demarcation between scientific and everyday knowledge. Of course, logically, one cannot reject the possibility of demarcation and exclude *any* knowledge from the domain of science.

## Normative Criteria and the Sociology of Science

The issue of demarcation is related to a second criticism, which centers on whether our version of sophisticated methodological falsification (SMF) either *should be* or *is* the methodology of scientific knowledge. Because it would be naive for us to argue that *all* knowledge generation would be well served by SMF, this discussion presupposes the possibility of demarcation and the goal of creating scientific progress.

Anderson contends that sophisticated falsificationism fails to offer an accurate account of the history of science and it also does not provide (nor was intended by Lakatos to provide) normative criteria for conducting research. Peter and Olson echo these sentiments and raise specific normative questions they believe falsificationism leaves un-answered. Several points need to be made in responding to these charges. First, although the history and sociology of science is a fascinating topic to discuss, it was not the topic of the Calder and Tybout (1987) paper. Thus, the observation that individual researchers don't necessarily behave like "good falsificationists" is simply an acknowledgement of the sociological forces at work and is not itself damaging to the normative contention that the SMF methodology is the one most likely to serve the goals of science. Moreover, our version of falsificationism is actually more consistent with the general evolution of *theories* (though not necessarily the behavior of individual scientists) in fields such a physics than Anderson and Peter and Olson suggest (see Hawking, 1988).

Second, we are less concerned with Lakatos's intentions for sophisticated methodological falsificationism than we are with how some of the general notions of falsification *could* be coupled with comparative theory testing to provide some general normative guidance. This is not to deny the value of SMF in providing meaningful reconstructions of historical events so that progress many be assessed or observed, nor is it intended to suggest that a series of very specific rules for *conducting* (as opposed to judging) research will be possible.

More generally, while we make reference to the historical roots and evolution of falsificationism by citing Popper and Lakatos respectively, it should be apparent that the intent was not to adopt the views of either of these philosophers wholesale - instead we build upon them in developing our own position. Ironically, in arguing that we are "instrumentalists," Anderson both notes that Popper was a "strident anti-instrumentalist" and in the same sentence mockingly characterizes Popper as our "hero". This effort to pigeonhole us and our views via "guilt by association" with Popper, "positivism" and now, "interpretivism", not only is riddled with the sort of inconsistencies Anderson himself notes, it also does little to encourage a meaningful dialogue. We do not assume that Anderson finds heros in and shares all the views of scholars such as Laudan, Feyerabend and Wittgenstein. His efforts to criticize our position would be better directed at the *content* of the arguments *we* present than at applying ill-fitting pejorative labels and reacting to the larger body work authored by philosophers we reference only in passing.

It is our position that a falsificationist orientation (in the very simple sense of continuing to subject theories to tests in which they *could* fail or have their weaknesses revealed) coupled with a commitment to selecting theories comparatively (i.e., preferring ones that provide the most complete yet parsimonious account of available data) can and should be the general methodology for generating scientific knowledge. Note that these principles do not assume that theories can be demonstrated to be either true or even unequivocally false, nor is there any inductive implication that the greater the number of tests a theory has survived the "better" it is. Moreover, the interpretation of data will change as theories evolve and it is conceivable that a theory might reasonably be discarded and later resurrected (perhaps in some revised form) when additional data for which it can account become available. All we suggest is that a process of ongoing testing, and a preference at any point in time for theories that provide a better explanation than their rivals offers the *possibility* of scientific progress. This is the best we can hope for.

With this broad statement of our position on the methodology for creating scientific knowledge in mind, we now turn to the practical issues raised by Peter and Olson. They question the adequacy of our view in providing normative criteria asking "How many attempts to refute a theory must be made to conclude that the theory is falsified? In comparative 'tests' of alternative theories, how much better must the empirical results be before a winner is identified? Who decides what constitutes a valid falsification test? What is to be concluded when some comparative results support one theory and some support the other? (this volume, p. 25)"

We offer several responses to these questions. First, no matter what the criterion, judgment will always play a role in choosing among theories. But, if individuals share the overall goal of progress in understanding/accounting for phenomena, then many disputes can be resolved and general guidelines are possible. As suggested in outlining our broad view, the number of theory tests *per se* says nothing about whether or not a theory should be abandoned. Further, theories typically are and should be abandoned on a comparative basis -- it is appropriate to abandon one theory when there is a superior alternative. Thus, theories may continue to be used even though some of their weaknesses have been exposed if no rival presents itself. In comparing theories that compete, we argue that the one that parsimoniously accounts for the greater number of phenomena (and not studies or data per se) should be preferred. No doubt there will be many instances in which no theory is clearly superior, and these are areas in which any verdict must await further research. For example, if two theories explain the same number of only partially overlapping phenomena, the limitations of both theories would be apparent and, ideally, further research would seek a broader theory than could encompass the phenomena explained by both of the previous theories. (An example of such a situation is reported in Tybout, Sternthal and Calder 1983.) As to who decides what constitutes a valid falsification test, from a normative perspective this should be other researchers who, irrespective of their own research program, share an overriding commitment to scientific progress as measured by explaining an ever increasing set of phenomena. Practically, judgment occurs via the review process, and sociological agendas, of course, may dominate this normative criterion.

In sum, we argue scientific knowledge is best served by continuously testing theories and comparatively selecting the ones that can best account for a set of phenomena at a point in time. There cannot and should not be hard and fast rules such as five tests are better than four, or tests that following traditional experimental procedures (i.e., random assignment to treatments, manipulation checks, process measures) are *inherently* superior to ones that do not observe these conventions. The adequacy of a test can only be known post hoc -- good tests are ones that render rival explanations for the data implausible. Strategies such as increasing the number of tests and employing traditional experimental procedures only have value to the extent they serve this goal, not the reverse. (See Sternthal et al. 1987 for more on this topic.)

## Falsificationism is Passe´

Finally, critics of our position are fond of characterizing falsificationism as so outre that only a backwards country bumpkin would mention this "f-word" in the same breath with current philosophy of science (Anderson this volume; Holbrook and O'Shaunghnessy 1988; Peter and Olson this volume). They assert that even the "advanced" physical sciences have abandoned falsificationism.

We suspect that much of this response stems from equating falsificationism with Popper's original formulation and has little to do with the brand of falsificationism we advocate. Perhaps the term "falsificationism" carries so much excess baggage it would facilitate future communication to think of our view at a more operational level as the "empirical-comparative" approach. In any case, our views appear quite compatible with the positions of many leading scientists (e.g., Hawking 1988). Even Holbrook and O'Shaunghnessy (1988) see sufficient merit in a falsification orientation to claim that it is an integral part of the interpretivists' Hermeneutic Circle!

## Critical Relativism is Descriptive Rather than Normative Methodology

Anderson chastises us for not heeding his contention that critical relativism is first and foremost a descriptive methodology and does not constitute a set of normative guidelines. Therefore, he reasons, it is inappropriate for us to argue that "interpretive knowledge implies critical relativistic methodology."

We acknowledge that Anderson has indeed stated that critical relativism is a descriptive enterprise. However, as noted by Siegel (1988), Anderson's efforts to disavow any normative claims for critical relativism are undermined by the very label *critical* relativism (an oxymoron?), his argument that critical relativists are somehow more "hard-headed" than positivists in judging knowledge products, and his on-going promise to "cash-out" the implications of critical relativism at the "workbench level." This cannot be a purely descriptive enterprise.

Further, our original framework sought to pair knowledge types with very general methodological approaches and not vice versa. Thus, aspects of Anderson's critical relativism that *are* descriptive may contribute to understanding of research as practiced under any approach. But normative features, such as the notion that knowledge outputs should be judged on a variety of non-empirical as well as empirical bases and the contention that multiple accounts for a phenomenon should be viewed relativistically rather than competitively, seem to reflect a methodological orientation compatible with the goals of interpretative knowledge as we have defined it. Of course, critical relativism does not outline specific steps for conducting a piece of research any more than does our falsificationist approach. What is lacking in critical relativism as a normative methodology at this point is that, although it specifies a range of considerations in judging knowledge products (e.g., a program's methodological, ontological, metaphysical and axiological commitments), and it tells us what *not* to do (e.g., don't judge on strictly empirical bases or

comparatively), it stops short of telling us how to recognize a "good" interpretive knowledge product.

## Critical Relativism and Data

Both Anderson and Peter and Olson complain that we accuse critical relativists of avoiding data when in reality they (critical relativists), "...recognize that empirical results can play an important role in generating social consensus about theories," but are "...much less impressed with empirical data and its role in science than are Calder and Tybout (Peter and Olson, this volume p.26)." Our point was not that critical relativists would refuse to consider data. Rather we were arguing that the possibility of appealing to *non-empirical* factors in evaluating theories is more an illusion than a reality. How might one argue the merits of a methodology, ontology, axiology etc., if not by appealing to some form of data or empirical observation? We did not intend to suggest that critical relativists ignore data -- just the opposite. We suggest that they are no better or worse than empiricists in their reliance on data. The primary difference lies in whether the data under consideration are limited to controlled studies or give greater emphasis to observations of naturally occurring events.

Unfortunately, as part of their case for the superiority of the critical relativists' approach over traditional empirical science, Peter and Olson call into question the validity of experimental data; stating, "...we know that well-trained researchers can construct empirical data and results to support or refute almost any theory without violating 'accepted standards' of research in the field (p.26)." As active empirical researchers ourselves, we can only imagine that such a statement was intended to be more provocative than literal. How could they *know* such a thing? Have they as researchers found desired results so easy to produce as to make them this cynical? Could their subjects be that much more cooperative and the reviewers of their papers that much more naive than the ones we encounter? Why are journal rejection rates so high? Is it because most researchers are poorly trained in the art of producing desired results or is it that reviewers are as cynical as Peter and Olson and reject research conforming to 'accepted standards' unless it also fits their personal/political sensitivities? And if empirical tests are flawed, does it follow that instead of attempting to improve them we should place greater reliance on more subjective means of choosing among theories? We can only hope that the Peter and Olson view of empirical work is not widely shared. It certainly does not fit our personal experience nor our view of the field.

## Anderson's Illustrative Critique of Tybout, Sternthal and Calder (1983)

Finally, Anderson argues against traditional empirical science and for the broader range of research methods embraced under critical relativism on the grounds that the knowledge products of traditional empirical science have been, in the eyes of many, disappointing. To this end he focuses on a article in which Tybout et al. (1983) report four experiments examining an availability-valence explanation for multiple request techniques (i.e., foot-in-the-door and door-in-the-face). To borrow a phase from Anderson's chapter, "space limitations" do not a permit a detailed point by point response. However, we will react to several of the broad themes raised.

First, the study is presented as both an example of positivist research and psychological instrumentalism. As alluded to earlier, there would seem to be a fundamental contradiction in these labels in view of positivism's association with the verifiability principle and instrumentalist's reliance on constructs lacking any real world referent. We would prefer not to use either label and consider ourselves simply to conduct TSE studies.

Second, Anderson charges that we have "altered" Tversky and Kahneman's (1973) availability hypothesis. We can only agree and suggest that such action is necessary and desirable in the process of broadening the scope of a theory. Tversky and Kahneman focused on judgments of the frequency of event occurrence. The availability or ease with which information related to events could be retrieved was sufficient to make predictions in this context. By contrast, we examined compliance behaviors. Here, predictions required anticipating both the availability information *and* the valence or favorableness of that information. Thus, part of our intended contribution was extending the basic availability notion of Tversky and Kahneman. It is difficult to see why that should be criticized per se.

Third, because the constructs we discuss are availability of information in memory and judgment, Anderson draws upon a recent review of the memory-judgment literature by Hastie and Park (1986) in an effort to demonstrate that there may be multiple explanations for our findings. Specifically, he suggests that it is unclear whether on-line or memory based processing is responsible for the results we predict and observe. The general spirit of this effort is one we wholeheartedly endorse. Progress is best made by generating and ruling out alternative explanations and it is always desirable to push extant theorizing toward more precise predictions regarding the underlying process.

However, several caveats are relevant to Anderson's particular, and in context, peculiar, efforts along these lines. First, any viable rival explanation must account for at least as much data as the advocated theory. Anderson only alludes to an explanation for outcomes in one of the four experiments we report and offers no interpretation for the larger multiple request literature that we review and explain. Because the multiple request outcomes our theorizing accounts for span ones involving delay (and thus are more prone to memory-based judgment) and ones involving contiguous requests (which although favoring on-line availability effects would still require accessing long-term memory to assign a favorable or unfavorable valence to the available behavior), rival explanations based on the memory based versus on-line judgments are not highly plausible. But, had Anderson been able to generate a viable rival explanation for our results we would view it as signaling a direction for future research and progress, both of which would be welcome. We fully expect that our explanation will be modified/extended (as we did with

Tversky and Kahneman's hypothesis) or discarded as new theorizing and data become available.

More generally, after labeling us as "instrumentalists," Anderson charges that "instrumentalists' lack of concern for the details of process, their excessive emphasis on prediction, and their casual attitude toward the *meaning* (emphasis original) of the key concepts mentioned in their theories has led 'positivistis' and interpretivists alike to turn away from this approach" (p. 16). Although we may share with instrumentalists the view that theoretical constructs are unobservable, if Anderson has accurately depicted the instrumentalists' position on the importance of the meaning of constructs (and we suspect he has not), then it is most certainly not *our* view. The very essence of our position on theory testing is one of ruling out rival explanations, in other words, triangulating operationalizations to arrive at a single plausible interpretation for the constructs underlying a phenomenon. It is difficult to imagine how this can be construed as a "casual" attitude toward the meaning of key constructs. Moreover, we know of no alternative to examining the correspondence between data and theory as a basis for ruling out rival explanations. To suggest that theoretical constructs and processes can be directly observed, as Anderson seems to imply when espousing the virtues of ethnomethological approaches (p. 21), is to dispute the basic notion that theories are abstract and therefore generalizable. Could this be his intention?

Finally, Anderson speculates about how an ethnomethodologist might view the multiple request situation. He summarizes this discussion with the following observation; "...it is the different (metaphysical) conceptions of man that lay at the heart of the distinctions between ethnomethodology and psychological instrumentalism. For the latter, man is often a judgmental dope whose verbal and motor behavior result from the operation of an autonomous central nervous system. On the other hand, while ethnomethodologists see man performing his mundane everyday activities in a largely unreflective fashion, there is always the possibility of choice (p.21). " Stated more graphically, the psychological instrumentalist bears more than a passing resemblance to the manipulative mad scientist of horror film fame and the ethnomethologist is someone you wouldn't mind having as a next door neighbor. Anderson concludes by suggesting that, as consumer researchers, we might do well to select our approach on the basis of which model (psychological instrumentalism or ethnomethodology) we would like to have applied to ourselves.

In contrast to Anderson's focus on the differences between his view of psychological instrumentalism and ethnomethology (which undeniably exist), we are impressed with what these approaches have in common. For example, Anderson's ethnomethodological interpretations of compliance with multiple request strategies were remarkably similar to the self-perception and bargaining-concession explanations offered in the psychology literature. (And it should be recalled that these explanations were by themselves inadequate to account for the total pattern of findings in the literature, thus motivating the Tybout et al. 1983 research.) Further, the contention that the basic premises of cognitive psychology necessarily cast subjects in the pejoratively-termed role of "judgmental dopes" is downright silly. The observation that many cognitive responses are so well learned as to require no conscious attention (i.e., they are "automatic") is better viewed as evidence of an adaptive human organism or a "judicious processing." Moreover, psychologists devote considerable attention to exploring the conditions under which automatic processing will be interrupted and conscious attention devoted to choosing among alternative courses of action. Thus, cognitive psychologists address the very same issues that Anderson attributes to ethnomethologists and it would seem that they are if anything more concerned with probing the underlying process. Finally, we can not hope to progress in our scientific understanding of the world if we choose explanations on the basis of the extent to which they flatter our self-images or conform to our intuitions.

Despite the foregoing disagreements with Anderson's comments on Tybout et al. (1983) in particular and cognitive psychology in general, we end our response on a note of harmony. We share with Anderson a desire to push extant theories toward greater specificity and clarity and we applaud his effort to do so by attempting to develop rival explanations for a phenomenon. We hope this type of dialogue will continue but suggest it would be better served by avoiding pejorative characterizations of alternative approaches.

In sum, the foregoing discussion reveals that Anderson's and Peter and Olson's criticisms largely reflect misrepresentations and misunderstandings of our views and as such cannot support their conclusion that they discredit our framework. With this established, we now turn to some of the implications of our framework for the qualitative and interpretive approaches.

Before continuing, it should be noted that although the title of this book suggests the focus is on the interpretative approach, several of the chapters report research that, within our framework, seem more reflective of the qualitative approach. To clarify this distinction we now turn to a discussion of the nature of qualitative research.

## DRAWING CONCLUSIONS FROM QUALITATIVE RESEARCH

The TSE approach rejects the relativist's critique and assigns a central role to challenging theory with data and little importance to the source of theory. The qualitative approach is exactly opposite in this respect. It seeks to capture the explicit or implicit theories (ideas) a group of consumers have about their own consumption behavior. It takes these theories at face value and adopts the attitude that consumers have, that these theories are naturally right (see Calder, 1977).

Even if one could show that consumers' theories might be wrong from a scientific or interpretive point of view, this would miss the point of the qualitative approach. The goal is to represent how the world is seen by the consumer. The researcher may or may not accomplish this goal. But, if the goal is met, there is no question of challenging the theory.

It is in this vein that several of the widely cited dictates of Lincoln and Guba (1985, p. 37) make imminent sense:

• Realities are multiple, constructed, and holistic.

• Knower and known are interactive, inseparable

• Only time- and context bound working hypotheses (ideographic statements) are possible.

These reflect the very nature of qualitative research. (But note that this hardly implies that the contrary assumptions made by the TSE approach are invalid.)

As already noted, the qualitative approach eventually comes down to the dictum that what people think to be true will ultimately affect their behavior. This may not actually be the best explanation. Perhaps a TSE or interpretive approach can do better in a given area. But it certainly is an important explanation of consumer behavior to consider and this is affirmed by the extensive use of focus groups and other qualitative methods in marketing practice.

Let us return to the point alluded to above that any particular qualitative account can be wrong. Not, as noted, in a scientific sense, but simply in terms of errors in the way the qualitative account is constructed. In a recent article in the anthropological literature, Heider (1988) points out a number of potential errors that can be made, such as looking at different subcultures or the same cultures at different times or the different orientations among ethnographers. And in the present volume Wallendorf and Belk make a number of recommendations aimed at guarding against such errors. Prolonged engagement, rapport with consumers, triangulation across researchers, researcher self-analysis all are held up as desirable safeguards.

Such safeguards are clearly reasonable. In looking at recent qualitative studies as represented by this volume, however, we are struck by a different, though related issue. Yes, it is important that qualitative studies develop better safeguards against error. It is equally important, however, that *qualitative studies develop conclusions strong enough to be checked for error.* Heider (1988, p. 75) provides a good example. Ethnographers who spend longer time in the field are apparently more likely to find that deaths are attributed to witchcraft. One can immediately begin to consider whether time in the field is a source of error in the conclusion of some researchers that witchcraft attributions are not made in a culture. Our point is that this depends on the researcher having in fact drawn a conclusion for or against witchcraft attribution. As Heider puts it, the presence or absence of witchcraft is "a truly determinable fact" (p. 75). We need such determinable conclusions in consumer research in order to begin to assess the possibility of error.

A qualitative analysis by Sherry and McGrath in the present volume provides a case in point. They provide a thick ethnographic description of two gift stores. The possibility or error is amply acknowledged: the study is said to "enfranchise speculation within obvious limits" (p. 149). But what of the conclusion?

The two strongest and clearest conclusions (or "propositions deserving more systematic investigation," p. 161) drawn by Sherry and McGrath are that a sense of place is important for the retail stores and that gift giving is the work of women. On the one hand these conclusions do fit the ethnographic description. On the other hand, they fit so loosely and generally that it is difficult to see how the ethnography has contributed to a richer understanding of how the consumer perceives the retail place and takes it into account or how women see their role in shopping. As specific as the authors get is the conclusion that some female consumers are "driven by the principle of shop 'til you drop.' What this means qualitatively from the view of the consumer, however, is not developed as a conclusion of the research.

Another case of extensive description but weak conclusions is Hirschman and LaBarbera's (this volume) analysis of the meaning of Christmas. The conclusion is that Christmas is multidimensional in meaning: "both happy and sad, ingenious and cynical, spiritual and crass, selfish and altruistic..." (p. 145). Again, the conclusions do not seem to capture and communicate what the idea of Christmas is to a group of consumers from their perspective.

Our point is that the richness of the qualitative approach is not being reflected in the conclusions of the research. It is true that if the conclusions are weak or general enough they are not likely to be wrong. But with stronger, more definitive conclusions we could begin to explore whether they are right or wrong.

Our suspicion is that part of the reluctance to draw strong conclusions in qualitative studies of consumer behavior stems from a misconception perpetuated by Lincoln and Guba (1985, p. 37). Two more of their dictates are:

- All entities are in a state of mutual simultaneous shaping, so that it is impossible to distinguish causes form effects.

- Inquiry is value bound.

If taken literally the first of these points would seem to almost prohibit conclusions from qualitative research. Nothing can be linked to or used to explain anything else. Yet the whole point of qualitative research is to show how the ideas of consumers shape their thinking and behavior. Thick descriptions that capture consumer experience are necessary, indeed, at the heart of qualitative methodology. How else, to experience the consumer's world?

But description per se is not enough. The researcher has to draw conclusions that reveal chains of logic and point up perceptions that shape behavior. There is nothing in this that denies the nature of qualitative research.

A final point regarding the conclusions of qualitative research. We detect a tendency to substitute interpretation and even value judgments for true qualitative conclusions. For instance, in the Sherry and McGrath conclusion regarding "shop 'til you drop" the authors go on to label these women as "shopaholics" and call for an understanding of their "compulsions."

Now it is very doubtful that women see themselves in this light; or at least we see nothing in the thick description to suggest this. It may well be that from some other, interpretive perspective the notion of compulsion is appropriate. This is not, however, faithful to the qualitative approach.

We can of course anticipate a response that it is not possible in practice to avoid interpretation in providing an ethnographic description. We acknowledge that in a sense this may be true. But it is still useful to attempt in principle to minimize non-consumer interpretations in qualitative accounts.

At the very least it seems to us inconsistent to in fact purposely exceed the limits of thick description in order to draw conclusions. Again the Sherry and McGrath analysis provides a good illustration of our point. In discussing their sense of place conclusion, the authors go on to note that this may seem to be only the store "atmosphere" effect that has been widely discussed in the marketing literature. They claim however that their study suggests a more "higher order rendering of atmospherics" (p. 162). Yet to develop this they go to a discussion of "pathetecture" rooted in an interpretive literature far removed from the world of the consumer.

It may well be impossible not to have some interpretation creep into qualitative accounts. Clearly it is possible to avoid deliberately mixing the two in such a way as to confuse the ways conclusions are being reached.

Moreover, it is certainly possible to avoid going all the way to pure value judgments in order to reach qualitative conclusions, even though Lincoln and Guba may seem to justify this. In this volume Belk uses content analysis of cartoons to identify the role of materialism in the modern Christmas. As with the Sherry and McGrath article, the description is interesting. But the conclusions are especially puzzling:

..it seems to have fallen on the simple and humorous cartoon format to tell us that there is something unsettling with the modern American Christmas. Perhaps we should take such cartoon messages seriously. (Belk, p. 132)

Unsettling to whom?

## RESEARCH OR EXPRESSIVENESS?

New approaches to consumer research offer the real possibility of bringing fresh creativity to the field. However, we worry that this creativity may be masked by expressions of personal sentiment. Even worse, such expressions may actually masquerade as research creativity.

This expressiveness seems to range from the relatively innocuous to the somewhat bizarre. Two instances found in the present volume are illustrative. Consider first Hirschman and La Barbera's analysis of the meaning of Christmas. We have already contended that their conclusions fail to do justice to their qualitative approach. It must be added that they go beyond these conclusions to express an appreciation of Christmas as an individual, personal experience.

Consumers make of Christmas what they can;
what they will; what they wish. The true meaning
of Christmas lies within each of us; and for each
of us, it is a unique truth. (p. 145)

What this truth is and how its explication can contribute
to an understanding of consumer behavior is only further
obscured by this sort of poetic statement. What we have
is an expression of personal sentiment. There is no
creative insight or even inspiration that can be of use in
the research process. There is a danger of style before
substance.

The Holbrook, Bell and Grayson's paper in this
volume expressly argues for a broader view of
interpretation, one that incorporates artistic expression
at its roots. Thus the authors present not only literary
criticism but a personal experiment in "irony" as well.
They describe a study that was first submitted to the
*Journal of Consumer Research* and reviewed by one of us
(BJC). The study is a personality impression formation
study in which subjects make inferences based on a short
story that describes consumption behavior. The study is
motivated as an empirical attempt to test Holbrook and
Grayson's (1987) interpretive work.

This study was rejected by the journal. Although
not presuming to speak for the editor, it seems clear to us
that most TSE researchers would regard this study as
making a very limited contribution. It's main weakness
is that the theory being tested is very limited. That
subjects do form impressions from consumption
information has long since been established. The
impression formation literature has become quite large,
with a number of theoretical issues emerging that require
empirical testing. The Holbrook et al. study fails to
make contact with any of these issues. The study would
perhaps have made a contribution fifteen years or more
ago.

Holbrook, Bell, and Grayson contend that they
are submitting their interpretive ideas to empirical
testing as suggested by Calder and Tybout (1987). They
fail to realize, however, that their theory (that people
infer personality from behavior) carries over nothing
from their interpretive work. It is hardly an example of
inspiration. And, as we have said, the study does not
even attempt to connect with existing theory. The mere
fact that the study uses a simulated short story has no
bearing on the rigor of the theory test. No theoretical
variable is operationalized through the story.

The authors wish to argue though that *either* their
study supports their interpretive work (and since the
study carries almost nothing over from this work it is
unclear how this could be the case) *or* (and they prefer
this) that the study is:

... a piece of sustained irony that casts self-
critical doubt on the use of falsificationist
procedures to clarify the meanings of artworks
and that thereby reaffirms the potential validity
of interpretivism (p. 39).

The logic appears to be as follows: because the theory in
this study is sterile, it follows that TSE theory is always
inferior to interpretive work--"we freely acknowledge the

inevitable limitations and weaknesses in the empirical
enterprise" (p. 40). Obviously, the logic here is
tortured. Moreover, it fails to take into account that it
was Holbrook et al. who set up the theory test that
"proves" the inferiority of the TSE approach to their
interpretive work.

Beyond the inadequacy of the Holbrook et al.
logic, there is something more troubling. It is the idea
that one's personal intentions in submitting a paper
somehow matter and that reviewers are somehow
obligated to read between the lines to detect larger
meanings (e.g., any intended irony). It seems to us that
this turns the entire research enterprise into an exercise
in expression.

## CONCLUSIONS

We have not attempted a micro-level review of
individual research programs since there seems to be a
consensus that emerging approaches in consumer
research are not as yet well enough developed to warrant
this and might even be hampered by it. Instead we have
focused on three, more macro impediments to the
developments of new approaches as reflected in this
volume and recent published articles.

We hope that, taken in conjunction with Hunt's
critique, our comments help to expose the vacuousness
of the critical relativists' attack on traditional scientific
empirical research. This research does not reduce to be
the same as any other research approach. It is a specific
approach that must be debated on its own terms as we
have tried to do (see Sternthal et al. 1987). Misguided
attempts to undermine the special concerns of this
approach can only endanger true methodological
pluralism.

We also hope to have made it clear that
methodological pluralism is a goal that both TSE
researchers and qualitative and interpretive researchers
can support. At this point we need to focus on
impediments to the development of qualitative and
interpretive approaches. This can only be done through
constructive criticism. In this spirit we call for an effort
to reach stronger, more truly qualitative conclusions in
qualitative research. It is our belief that questions of
methodological error can be more readily addressed if
this is done.

Finally, we applaud creativity in interpretive
work and research efforts, in general. However, we
caution that creativity is not synonomous with self-
expression. What is needed is creativity in advancing
the research process, and thus our understanding of
world, from each of the three perspectives.

## REFERENCES

Anderson, Paul F. (1983), "Marketing, Science Progress
and Scientific Method," *Journal of Marketing*, 47,
18-31.
Anderson, Paul F. (1986), "On Method in Consumer
Research: A Critical Relativist Perspective," *Journal
of Consumer Research*, 13, 155-173.
Calder, Bobby J. (1977), "Focus Groups and the Nature
of Qualitative Marketing Research." *Journal of
Consumer Research*, 14, 353-364.

Calder, Bobby J., Lynn W. Phillips and Alice M. Tybout (1981), "Designing Research for Applications," *Journal of Consumer Research*, 8, 197-207.

Calder, Bobby J. and Alice M. Tybout (1987), "What Consumer Research Is...," *Journal of Consumer Research*, 14, 136-140.

Hastie, Reid and Bernadette Park (1986), "The Relationship Between Memory and Judgement Depends on Whether the Judgement Task is Memory-Based or On-Line," *Psychological Review*, 93, 258-268.

Hawking, Stephen (1988), *A Brief History of Time: From the Big Bang to Black Holes*, Bantam Books: NY.

Heider, Karl G. (1988), "The Rashomon Effect: When Ethnographers Disagree," *American Anthropologist*, 90, 73-81.

Lincoln, Yvonna S. & Egon G. Guba (1985), *Naturalistic Inquiry*, Beverly Hills: Sage.

Holbrook, Morris B. and Mark W. Grayson (1986), "The Semiology of Cinematic Consumption: Symbolic Behavior in *Out of Africa*," *Journal of Consumer Research*, 13, 374-381.

Holbrook, Morris B. and John O'Shaughnessy (1988), "On the Scientific Status of Consumer Research and the Need for an Interpretive Approach to Studying Consumption Behavior," *Journal of Consumer Research*, initial draft of paper that is forthcoming December.

Seigel, Harvey (1988), "Relativism for Consumer Research? (Comments on Anderson)," *Journal of Consumer Research*, 15, 129-132.

Sternthal, Brian, Alice M. Tybout and Bobby J. Calder (1987), "Confirmatory versus Comparative Approaches to Judging Theory Tests," *Journal of Consumer Research*, 14, 114-125.

Tversky, Amos and Daniel Kahneman (1973), "Availability: A Heuristic for Judging Frequency and Probability," *Cognitive Psychology*, 5, 207-232.

Tybout, Alice M., Brian Sternthal and Bobby J. Calder (1983), "Information Availability as a Determinant of Multiple Request Effectiveness," *Journal of Marketing Research*, 20, 280-290.

## AFTER WORD

Both Shelby Hunt and Bobby Calder and Alice Tybout initiate their commentaries on the papers in this volume on notes of reconciliation and pluralism, and for that I am quite happy and grateful. I do not know Bobby Calder well, but I do know Shelby and Alice and I like them, so I have always felt personally uncomfortable with professional disagreements that I or my interpretivist-minded friends may have with them. This is especially true when theoretical debates have occasionally escalated into nastiness and purposeful distortions of one another's positions by both parties. Shelby, I believe, has sincerely and graciously extended his hand to us and I believe it is appropriate for us all to begin to heal the rift.

(I even have a wild fantasy that at some upcoming ACR or AMA conference I will take all of the authors in this book out for beers. We will all get wildly drunk, dive into the swimming pool, and emerge cleansed of our past grudges. Since, as Russ Belk can attest, I have a way of translating my fantasies into actions, all the above-mentioned combatants had better be ready. The next time they see me coming I will have beer money in my hands).

I have nothing else major to say regarding Shelby's paper. It is interesting, well-written, and thought-provoking and the few nits I might pick I will talk over with him directly.

Discussing the Calder and Tybout paper is more difficult, primarily because they define interpretivism more narrowly than do many (most) interpretivists. I think Russ Belk, Melanie Wallendorf, John Sherry, and Grant McCracken, for example, would likely all consider their research (as represented in this volume) to be interpretive (in the Calder & Tybout sense), in that it does represent a personal or interpersonal *construction* of the meaning(s) of the social texts they studied. However, they would label their work also as ethnographic (or `qualitative' in the Calder & Tybout sense), in that they, at least in part, have also attempted to *reconstruct* the meanings of the original authors of these texts -- i.e., how the consumers they studied construed the meaning of their lives, their homes, or their possessions. Alice and Bobby, for reasons I must be too feeble-minded to grasp, segregate these two types of interpretation into "interpretive" and "qualitative". This, to me, is an artificial and arbitrary distinction that won't work within the current consumer research context, because virtually all interpretive works in consumer behavior (including those in the present volume) are a *blending* of the author's pre-existing mental texts and those which s/he is interpreting. To try to segregate the two "origins" of the resulting interpretive product is like trying to pull apart the various metals that compose an alloy.

I believe also that most interpretivists would disagree with Calder and Tybout's assertion that some data "are self-reflexive. They supply their own meaning. Researchers attempt to articulate how consumers . . . view themselves . . . (p. 197)." By the very act of "articulating" how consumers view themselves, the researcher must interject something of the self, i.e., his/her own text.

Bobby and Alice then go into a detailed discussion of their differences with Paul Anderson, J. Paul Peter and Jerry Olson. Because I am not intellectually prepared to shed any additional light on the merits of this debate, I will refrain from comment.

The points Calder and Tybout raise about interpretive inquiries not boiling down into succinct statements of conclusion require addressing, however. First, I apologize if the concluding comments made in my paper with Priscilla La Barbera did not seem to follow directly from the earlier descriptive analysis. When I wrote them, I *thought* they did, but if they did not communicate well or accurately, then I should have done a better job. However, one difficulty faced by all interpretivists (which is perhaps overcome better by some than by others) is to summarize the diverse, multi-vocal images contained in a text in a few concise phrases or sentences. This is because the text doesn't mean just:                ; it means:

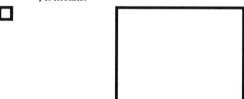

to use a geometric metaphor. The information contained in the big box cannot be squashed down into the little box without oversimplification and distortion. If you want to know what the conclusions are, you have to read the big box -- the whole interpretation.

Finally, I had to chuckle at Calder and Tybout's disavowal of the Sherry and McGrath terms "shop 'til you drop" and "shopaholic". These are social concepts about which Alice and I share deep personal knowledge, both of us serving as the discipline's primary archetypes (interpretive-jargon) or concrete operationalizations (empiricist-jargon) of the terms. I will never forget the time Alice and I both showed up late for a Marketing Thought Task Force meeting in Chicago. Alice had been slowed down by her discovery and purchase of a new suit at Saks. I was late because I had changed my plane tickets to have a few extra hours to "explore" Water Tower Place Shopping Center, before heading home. The moral of this is: Researchers, whether empiricist or interpretivist, are people, too. Let's all try to interject a little more *humane-ness* as well as humanism, in our professional thoughts and actions. It couldn't hurt!